Essential
Psychopathology
Casebook

A Norton Professional Book

Essential Psychopathology Casebook

MARK D. KILGUS, M.D., Ph.D.

WILLIAM S. REA, M.D.

Editors

W. W. Norton & Company

New York • London

For information about permission to reproduce selections from this book, write to
Permissions, W. W. Norton & Company, Inc., 500 Fifth Avenue, New York, NY 10110

For information about special discounts for bulk purchases, please contact W. W. Norton
Special Sales at specialsales@wwnorton.com or 800-233-4830

Manufacturing by Courier Kendallville
Production manager: Leeann Graham

Library of Congress Cataloging-in-Publication Data

Essential psychopathology casebook / Mark D. Kilgus and William S. Rea, editors. — First edition.
      pages   cm
   "A Norton professional book."
   Includes bibliographical references and index.
   ISBN 978-0-393-70822-6 (pbk.)
   1. Psychology, Pathological.   2. Mental illness—Diagnosis.   I. Kilgus, Mark D., editor of
compilation.   II. Rea, William S., Jr., editor of compilation.
   RC454.E785   2014
   616.89--dc23   2013049992

ISBN: 978-0-393-70822-6 (pbk.)

W. W. Norton & Company, Inc., 500 Fifth Avenue, New York, N.Y. 10110
www.wwnorton.com
W. W. Norton & Company Ltd., Castle House, 75/76 Wells Street, London W1T 3QT

1 2 3 4 5 6 7 8 9 0

To the suffering and their clinicians
who together seek understanding and share hope.

Contents

PART II: MOOD PATHOLOGY

PART III: ANXIETY PATHOLOGY

PART IV: BLENDED PSYCHOPATHOLOGY

PART V: PERVASIVE PSYCHOPATHOLOGY

Acknowledgments

WE ACKNOWLEDGE THE faculty in the Department of Psychiatry and Behavioral Medicine at Virginia Tech Carilion School of Medicine who have contributed the clinical material and decision-making for this casebook. These gifted clinicians aspire to be effective teachers and to integrate research into practice. They have chosen to serve in an academic department with all of its incumbent responsibilities. We offer the department's mission to underscore the challenges and commend the efforts of these dedicated faculty members.

The mission of the Virginia Tech Carilion Psychiatry education programs is to train excellent clinicians who:

- Comprehensively evaluate, understand, and treat psychiatric disorders using a biopsychosocial and spiritual model
- Teach enthusiastically and model life-long learning
- Integrate research and discovery within clinical practice
- Pursue self-appraisal, individual development, interprofessionalism, and leadership.

Major recognition and thanks to our publisher, Deborah Malmud, Director of Norton Professional Books, for encouraging our work and deftly facilitating the entire process.

MARK D. KILGUS, M.D., PH.D.
Professor and Chair

WILLIAM S. REA, M.D.
Associate Professor and Vice Chair

Essential
Psychopathology
Casebook

CHAPTER **1**

Introduction: Clinical Decision Making

Mark D. Kilgus, M.D., Ph.D. and William S. Rea, M.D.

A PERSON LEARNING a new set of skills starts by learning a set of rules. Learning mental health treatment is no different. A novice clinician learns certain criteria for diagnosis of a condition, examines the individual to be diagnosed, and compares that individual's attributes to the criteria. Because the criteria have been empirically tested, retested, and confirmed, this process leads the trainee to making reliable diagnoses. Similarly when in learning therapy, the trainee assimilates rule-based criteria and applies them to an individual patient or client.

Master clinicians do not seem to follow a rigid rule book. An expert practitioner will develop hypotheses about the causes of a person's condition within minutes of sitting down together and without asking all the questions that permit the rules to be tested. Questions are asked to confirm or refute a diagnostic impression, rather than laboriously sorting through a rule-based algorithm. Watching a master clinician at work brings to mind qualities of fluidity, confidence, and deftness to which trainees aspire. Senior clinicians work by means of pattern recognition rather than rule-based decision making.

How does that process of growth from rule-based to pattern-based clinical work occur? What can be done to facilitate the growth? That is the purpose of casebooks, including this one. However, one cannot learn diagnosis and formulation without logging many hours with real patients. By spending time with patients, clinical acumen grows and the clinician gradually achieves mastery.

An aspiring painter learns, among other skills, how to duplicate or describe a color she observes. All colors can be made with mixtures of blue, red, and yellow pigments. Some are lighter or darker, duller or brighter, or warmer or cooler. All are made of the same three pigments in different proportions. A master painter seems able to effortlessly mix exact and subtle colors, using the same three pigments that a beginning painter struggles to combine. Our text opens a window into the minds of senior clinicians who are like those experienced painters. By observing the decision-making processes of these clinicians, the trainee begins to discern the primary aspects of psychopathology. Just as a painting is produced with three primary colors, so psychopathology is the manifestation of three primary aspects (mood, anxiety, and thought). A painting rarely is composed of a single primary color; likewise, psychopathology is typically a mixture of disruptions in mood, anxiety, and thought. In other words, pure anxiety disorders, pure mood disorders, or pure thought disorders are rare. Contemporary master painter Susan Sarback (2007) in her book *Capturing Radiant Light and Color in Oils and Soft Pastels* notes that the same color appears different to the viewer depending on the colors adjacent to it. For example, blue next to orange appears more vivid than blue next to green. Similarly, as an example in psychopathology, panic presents differently in a rigidly organized obsessive person than it does in a disorganized schizophrenic individual.

When researchers design studies of psychopathology they attempt to simplify the picture to develop clear rules. Rather than dealing with the myriad combinations of anxiety, thought, and mood disruption in their enormous complexity and subtlety, researchers simplify and look at disruption in a single sphere (for example, mood). It is the equivalent of learning to paint with only blue at first. Clinicians know that people who have only disruption of mood and no distortions of thought or anxiety are as rare as paintings that use only shades of blue. A common frustration for new mental health practitioners is the realization that very few of the people they encounter fit neatly into such pure diagnostic categories. From studies of these subjects with rare presentations, researchers make generalizations about the more common mixed psychopathology. These generalizations may or may not be valid when applied to psychiatric illness with co-occurring mood, anxiety, or thought issues. Consequently, the evidence to inform practice may be a misrepresentation and only partially accurate or completely misleading.

Just as each painting in the world is unique but at the same time a combination of three primary colors, so is each person uniquely presenting with mental health problems. Paintings have a spectrum of almost infinite, subtle differences and possibilities with the mixture of colors in varying amounts. Furthermore, if we consider other characteristics of pigment (light/dark, bright/dull, warm/cool) the variability expands even more. With psychopathology the severity of the presentation as well as prognosis and amenability to treatment depends on the person's internal resources to address the illness and associated problems. As with the lightness or darkness of a painting, the value or weight of the psychopathology will be influenced either positively or negatively by such factors as the person's intelligence, insight, motivation, locus of control, and will. These are often referred to as resiliency factors.

Just as a painting represents a moment in time, the clinical assessment of a patient represents the disorder at the specific time of presentation. But illnesses progress and change in how they look over time. Sometimes the psychiatric illness is colored vividly and unmistakably recognized; at other points in time the colors are more muted and the psychopathology more subtle (less diagnostic certainty). If psychiatric symptoms remain vivid over time, their chronic presence becomes incorporated into the person's personality and interferes with normal and adaptive human development. These individuals develop a pervasive and usually maladaptive pattern of interacting with others that is almost immutable—a personality disorder. For example, a person with prominent symptoms of anxiety may experience distress when meeting new people and over time may develop an introverted or avoidant personality. Another person with similar symptoms may self-medicate with alcohol and eventually find himself struggling with a substance use disorder.

The clinical cases in this book are about real people suffering from psychopathology. Reviewing these cases will assist inexperienced clinicians with recognizing real clinical conditions, not ones fabricated to teach a classification system or describe a pure form of psychopathology. The cases are presented by sequentially addressing the questions listed below which represent the usual progression of an experienced clinician's decision making. This casebook is intended as a clinical companion resource for *Essential Psychopathology and Its Treatment*, 3rd ed. (Maxmen, Ward, and Kilgus, 2009). The cases in this book are roughly grouped into sections based on some of the core disturbances in the case. The first grouping includes disorders of thinking, such as cognitive disorders and psychoses. The second grouping is characterized by disorders of mood, and the third by disorders of anxiety. The fourth group comprises a mixture of mood, anxiety, and thought symptoms that may have originated from a dysregulation in one of the primary groups and progressed to involve the others. These disorders may be complicated by substance use which frequently begins as an attempt to self-medicate. The last group consists of persistent disorders that tend to be lifelong and resistant to change. Any given case can involve alterations in thought, mood, and anxiety, and reasonable people may disagree as to which section it should belong.

The cases in this book were written by experienced clinicians based on real individuals (anonymized). Just as some painters have a style that is hyperrealistic and detailed and others paint more impressionistically, there is variability among the presentation styles within these cases. The length of the case often correlates with the complexity of the disorder and the clinical uncertainty related to insufficient evidence. There is no particular order in which the cases should be read, just as there is no particular requirement to start with examination of a particular painting and then progress to another in a museum. Some cases are very detailed; others are more like sketches. The important lessons to be learned have to do with observing the decision-making process of experienced clinicians. To clarify these processes, the chapters are organized consistently throughout the book according to the format that follows.

1. Is there a recognizable pattern in the *clinical presentation*? One might think of this as the information that creates a global impression. The details of the clinical presentation determine the overall distinctive feature or most prominent symptom cluster. We consider the present illness, history, and mental status of the patient. See Table 1.1 for an outline of the mental status exam.

A caveat in the description of clinical presentation is that some aspects of the presentation may be difficult to capture on paper; for example, suppose a clinician asks an individual, "Are you thinking of killing yourself?" Two different

Table 1.1. Mental Status Examination (MSE)

A. Behavior (general description) (behaving)
    1. Appearance
    2. Activity (including impulse control, psychomotor activity)
    3. Attitude (relating to the examiner, eye contact)
    4. Articulation (speech)
B. Sensorium (basic cognition, awareness) (sensing)
    1. Consciousness
    2. Orientation (person, place, time, situation)
    3. Memory (registration, immediate, recent, remote)
    4. Attention/Concentration
C. Emotion (feeling)
    1. Affect (type and lability)
    2. Mood (including suicidal/homicidal ideation, plan, or intent)
    3. Congruency (appropriateness to expressed thought content and/or mood)
D. Thought (thinking)
    1. Thought process/form
        a. Word usage/language
        b. Stream of thought (production and quantity of thoughts)
        c. Continuity (association of thoughts)
    2. Thought content
        a. Relationship to reality (delusions)
        b. Concept formation (abstractability)
    3. Intelligence and information
        a. Simple calculation
        b. Fund of knowledge (current events, geography)
    4. Insight and judgment
E. Perception (perceiving)
    1. Hallucinations
    2. Illusions
    3. Depersonalization/derealization

patients may each reply, "No." However, one of them may respond promptly, with good eye contact, and spontaneously adding all the reasons she has to live. The other may answer "No" only after a significant pause, with poor eye contact, in a monotone, with no further words. Clearly in such a situation the nonverbal communication is at least as important as the verbal.

2. What is the *functional impairment*, significant distress, or interference with normal development? Without functional impairment the clinical presentation would typically not meet the threshold for classification as a disorder. In other words, signs and symptoms of psychopathology are present but do not warrant a diagnosis or treatment. (Is this a disorder versus just a symptom?) On the other hand, there may be functional impairment without meeting all of the criteria for a full-blown disorder. In such cases, the diagnosis may not be exactly specified and yet requires clinical attention and treatment.

All of us have had the experience of feeling some emotional distress. We might get a traffic ticket, fail to get a promotion at work, be anxious about an upcoming test, or have trouble concentrating when we are sleep-deprived. In none of these circumstances is there sufficient pervasive distress or impairment in our daily functioning to consider seeking mental health treatment. To warrant consideration for treatment, the person must suffer either significant distress or functional impairment. The impairment for adults can be in areas of vocational or social functioning. For children and adolescents, impairment can be not only in educational (the equivalent of vocational) and social functioning but also in ways that interfere with fundamental developmental steps. For example, a pervasive school phobia, if untreated, can lead to arrested development as an adolescent avoids the necessary exploration and formation of healthy peer group relationships that are necessary to establish a stable and well-formed identity.

3. What are the primary colors you would choose to paint this clinical picture? Is the painting mostly blue, red, or yellow? Whatever the predominant color, how do the other primary pigments contribute to the effect of the painting? How might the observers be able to communicate about a recognized pattern? Over many years, mental health professionals have collected information establishing the reliability and validity of diagnoses. Diagnoses are critical for two primary reasons: first, an accurate diagnosis conveys some expectations about how the disorder will progress, what complications it may cause, and the eventual outcome. Second, a diagnosis should point us toward relatively effective treatment. The *Diagnostic and Statistical Manual* (DSM) of the American Psychiatric Association collates these criteria and is periodically revised. The newest iteration, DSM-5, was published in May 2013. The *DSM diagnosis* (according to the latest version) is referenced frequently for diagnostic criteria in each of the cases, but most of the evidence to guide clinical practice is based on studies using the nosology of previous versions. Fortunately the vast majority of diagnoses are similar in the new DSM. The conceptual changes include:

- Moving toward an etiologically based classification versus clinical consensus and organizing disorders according to a developmental perspective. This is based on evidence from cognitive, behavioral, and neurological science.
- Boundaries between disorders over the life course are more fluid and on a spectrum with dimensional measures that cross traditional diagnostic boundaries.
- Less emphasis on reliability while stressing the validity of the diagnostic categories (the degree to which diagnostic criteria reflect the comprehensive understanding and manifestation of an underlying psychopathological disorder).
- Removal of the multiaxial format so that all diagnoses are listed together including the former Axis IV stressors as *V*, *Z*, or *T* codes.

Major diagnostic changes in DSM-5 include:

- Autistic disorder, Asperger's disorder, and Pervasive Developmental disorder are consolidated into a single diagnosis called Autistic Spectrum Disorder.
- Substance Dependence and Abuse are eliminated in favor of the overarching diagnostic category called Substance Use Disorder, with severity depending on how many of the 11 symptom criteria are present.

- The mood disorder classifications are streamlined.
- Neurocognitive disorders are specified according to subtypes based on the latest findings establishing etiologies. Major Neurocognitive Disorder with a broad range of possible etiologies replaces the diagnostic category of Dementia.
- For Personality disorders, the current 10 disorders remain but there is an alternate hybrid model of classification that includes both dimensional and categorical approaches in five broad areas versus the previous three clusters.
- Anxiety disorders are now separated into four groups determined by whether the anxiety is fear-based, obsessive-compulsive, trauma-related, or dissociative.
- Specific changes in diagnostic categories are highlighted in the cases that follow.

According to the DSM-5,

a mental disorder is a syndrome characterized by clinically significant disturbance in an individual's cognition, emotion regulation, or behavior that reflects a dysfunction in the psychological, biological, or developmental processes underlying mental functioning. Mental disorders are usually associated with significant distress or disability in social, occupational, or other important activities. An expectable or culturally approved response to a common stressor or loss, such as the death of a loved one, is not a mental disorder. Socially deviant behavior (e.g., political, religious, or sexual) and conflicts that are primarily between the individual and society are not mental disorders unless the deviance or conflict results from a dysfunction in the individual.

There are 157 separate disorders in DSM-5, which represent a decrease of 15 from the 172 separate disorders in DSM-IV. Development of the DSM-5 classification was guided by the emerging scientific evidence for lifting artificial boundaries between some disorders and pulling together a spectrum of previously separate disorders. This approach is in contrast to former editions that emphasized "splitting" disorders into multiple separate conditions. So 50 disorders were integrated into 22 new spectrums or combined disorders for a net decrease of 28 disorders. To this were added 13 new diagnoses. Approaches to validating diagnostic criteria for discrete categorical mental disorders include antecedent evidence (similar genetic markers, family traits, temperament, and environmental exposure), concurrent evidence (similar neural substrates, biomarkers, emotional and cognitive processing, and symptom similarity), and predictive evidence (similar clinical course and treatment response). Until incontrovertible etiological or pathophysiological mechanisms are identified to fully validate specific disorders or disorder spectrums, the most important standard for the DSM-5 criteria will be their clinical utility. The diagnosis of a mental disorder should assist clinicians in determining prognosis, treatment plans, and potential outcomes for their patients.

It is important to realize that there may be enormous differences between two people with the same DSM diagnosis. During one of his productive periods,

Pablo Picasso painted several "blue" paintings. A half-century earlier, Claude Monet had painted views of the Seine River that were predominantly blue. Although both groups of paintings were blue, no one could confuse works of these two painters. Other than DSM diagnosis, factors that can influence the outcome of treatment include the resources available to the afflicted individual. Does the person have strong motivation or will to change his life? "Will" represents the patient's internal resources (the wherewithal) to effect clinical improvement. How do various DSM disorders compromise will or the sense of control a person has over his or her life? Similarly, social and spiritual resources can markedly affect the outcome of a person's psychopathology. .

4. *Epidemiology* is critical in recognizing patterns of mental disorder. A particularly aggressive form of lung cancer called oat cell carcinoma is highly associated with depression. In fact, depression can be the presenting symptom of this cancer. However, it would be foolish to assume that every person who presented with depressive symptoms was likely to have oat cell carcinoma. When you hear hoof beats your first thought should be "horses," not "zebras." (However, if your "horse" has stripes, you should reconsider!) If someone is experiencing a different reality (and you have no more information available), the odds are much greater that the delusions are associated with a mood disorder rather than with schizophrenia. We know from epidemiology that mood disorders with psychotic features are much more common than pure thought disorders. As more clinical information is brought to light, the odds may change considerably as one observes the "stripes" of schizophrenia. Additionally, with modern survey techniques, we are finding that mental disorders in some cases are more prevalent than we had previously thought.

5. What is the *differential diagnosis*? It is important to consider not only the common cause of the clinical presentation but also other possible causes. For example, a young man presents depressed, using drugs. Several weeks after he is detoxified, he is still depressed. Was his depression due to drugs or not? Other times the clinician may miss an underlying color in the clinical picture, such as delusional thinking or traumatic anxiety. If not best explained by a single disorder (diagnostic parsimony), what comorbid disorders may account for parts of the clinical picture? What special assessment is indicated to resolve diagnostic uncertainty?

6. In terms of what we know about the most probable disorder, are the conditions usually associated with *etiology and pathogenesis* present? A common example of this is the diagnosis of post-traumatic stress disorder (PTSD). One of the criteria is for the individual to have suffered a very significant trauma, often a life-threatening one, that precipitated the disorder. If there was no significant trauma, it is difficult to justify a diagnosis of PTSD. What are the predisposing, precipitating, provoking (exacerbating), and perpetuating factors for this clinical picture? A case formulation attempts to understand why a person presents in exactly this way, in this setting, at this time, rather than earlier, later, elsewhere, or differently.

7. What is the *natural course without treatment*? This is important information

in regard to informed consent. For a person to give consent to treatment, he or she must know the risk of not getting treatment. If a person has a phobia of flying but intends to never travel by plane, treatment becomes less of an issue than for a flight attendant experiencing the same symptoms. So as in other medical conditions, diagnosis of a mental disorder is not always equivalent to an absolute need for treatment.

It seems fairly intuitive that a disorder beginning early in childhood that continues untreated for decades will have more of a life impact and a worse course than a similar disorder presenting at a more advanced stage. For each individual there are certain critical tasks that must be achieved at various ages—for example, establishing an identity separate from one's family, making one's mark in the world, and forming peer relationships. From a developmental perspective, the clinician addresses how the disorder may present at different stages of development.

Each of us has traits that are fairly invariant throughout our lives. We may be more extroverted or introverted or have a sunnier or gloomier disposition. We also have states that we go through that vary more frequently. We might be more anxious or sad at various times of our lives without this being a character trait. Over time untreated state disorders (like anxiety, thought, or mood disorders) condition behavior and cause the individual to make choices or engage in relationships that become gradually more rigid. These untreated state disorders become trait (personality) disorders.

Some disorders in their natural course give rise to increased risk for other disorders. For example, untreated mania carries a higher risk of associated substance abuse. Certain subtypes have different prognoses with different complications and secondary disorders.

8. What are the *evidence-based biopsychosociospiritual treatment options*? Like diagnostic research, treatment research attempts to simplify the patient population studied. It is not uncommon, for example, in schizophrenia research to exclude schizophrenics with active substance abuse problems. Although this does lead to "cleaner" research, we know that at least 50% of schizophrenics have alcohol or drug problems. Therefore the "evidence-based" research does not really reflect the patient population seen in clinical practice, and the treatment may not be effective. So it is important to determine what evidence is available, how reliable it is, and how well it applies to the person you are treating. How does one choose among evidence-based options? Are there well-established therapeutic principles to follow? Another factor in weighing treatment options has to be the cost to the individual and society. Daily individual therapy may be a proven option with excellent outcomes that is simply not available to a person who lives in a remote rural area without that resource.

9. What is the *clinical course with management and treatment*? Most mental health problems arise from multiple life factors that have been present for some time before the person presents for treatment. The duration of disorder prior to treatment, as well as the individual's level of functioning prior to onset of the disorder, can strongly influence outcomes. In the following chapters, it is not

uncommon to find that multiple modalities of treatment can help. It is important to describe the factors that led the clinician to recommend a particular treatment over others. An algorithm that is frequently used is symbolized by the mnemonic STEPS: safety, tolerability, effectiveness, price, and simplicity. Despite evidence for efficacy, if the treatment is not practical, the chance for adherence is slim and its effect negligible. So evidence-based (efficacious) treatment is not the same as effective treatment.

10. Are there any *systems-based practice issues* that influence the provision of optimal mental health care? The systems issues include clinical service delivery, the costs and funding of services, the organization of mental health services, and philosophies of care. For example, within the same country or region there can be enormous geographic disparities in the availability of health care. Even in health care systems in which treatment is rendered with no or minimal cost (for example, the Veterans Affairs system in the United States) the distance the person lives from the medical center may condition whether he or she can access the care.

Does the case involve any *legal, ethical, or cultural challenges*? The clinician faces ethical conflicts daily and with most cases. What laws relate to this clinical presentation? How is cultural sensitivity necessary for the clinician in this case? What sort of boundary issues arise?

The *history, terms, and resources* sections of each chapter provide interesting historical perspective, define some of the terms critical to understanding the disorder, and identify helpful websites, practice parameters, and seminal journal articles for reference. In addition to scholarly papers consulted in writing about the diagnosis and treatment of the clinical cases, it is sometimes useful to reference depictions of the disorder in popular culture. For some of the cases, a character from a movie or a book may offer a reasonable illustration of real psychopathology. However, most mental health professionals have had the experience of wincing while watching a big-screen interpretation of a psychiatric disorder.

REFERENCES

American Psychiatric Association. *Diagnostic and Statistical Manual of Mental Disorders* (5th ed.). Arlington, VA: American Psychiatric Association, 2013.

Maxmen J, Ward N, Kilgus M. *Essential Psychopathology and Its Treatment* (3rd ed.). New York: W. W. Norton & Company, 2009.

Sarback S. *Capturing Radiant Light and Color in Oils and Soft Pastels*. Cincinnati: North Light, 2007.

PART I

Thought Pathology

CHAPTER 2

Waning Cognition in the Elderly

Kye Y. Kim, M.D.

CLINICAL PRESENTATION

Chief complaint: "I don't know why I am here. She says I am forgetful."

History of present illness: Jim is a 67-year-old retired schoolteacher, who presents to the Memory Disorders Clinic with his wife. He began noticing himself becoming forgetful approximately two years ago, but he did not pay much attention to it and ascribed it to his retirement. He thought that since he retired he was probably not using his brain as vigorously as he used to. Also, his wife, Janice, thought nothing of the change, blaming it on his old age. Jim states that initially, the change was insignificant. He would forget the grocery items that he was supposed to get or misplace his keys. However, he was able to recall or find them eventually. This change was basically an annoyance to him, but he was able to manage it. Over the past year, things got steadily worse. At one point, his wife found that he missed a car payment and paid an electricity bill twice. It was markedly unusual for him. Janice started paying more attention to his "absent-mindedness." Recently, she was very alarmed that he couldn't find his way home from the mall, where he regularly took morning walks. He called her from his cell phone and said frantically, "Honey, I have no idea where I am right now."

Lately, Janice notices him to be rather socially awkward at church with the other parishioners. He gradually stops addressing them by their names. During casual conversations, he often looks puzzled and seems to experience difficulty comprehending conversations or finding words. When she asks about it, he becomes very upset and attempts to minimize his difficulty. Additionally, when he misplaces his tools in the garage and can't find them, he becomes suspicious and thinks that the neighbors' kids might have stolen them. His wife also notes him spending a lot of time meticulously securing all the doors and windows in the evening. He is lately unwilling to go out shopping and spends more time watching TV in the family room. He has quit reading his favorite magazine, and they are simply piled up, unopened, on the tea table.

He rarely lets Janice know how he feels. She doesn't think he is sad, but he doesn't seem to be interested in anything. He no longer becomes excited even when his favorite football team scores a touchdown. However, he gets easily irritated when asked to do his daily routines, such as shaving or taking showers. It is a significant change, because he was always meticulous about his appearance. One Sunday morning when they were getting ready for church, Janice observed that his pants were unzipped and had a wet spot. The most difficult challenge that she faces at this point is that he still wants to drive. He gets furious when asked not to drive. He manages to drive to places nearby with her tactful cuing. Still, she is very uneasy about him driving, even with her in the car.

Janice now has to make sure that he takes his medications for hypertension, diabetes, and arthritis. She fills his weekly pillbox every Sunday evening. Without her monitoring, he completely forgets to take his pills. He is able to swallow them without much trouble. He is still able to boil water in the microwave oven to make his instant coffee. Janice is uncomfortable about him using a stove, even though it is electric. One morning, she found the burners on with an empty water pot. He often finds himself standing in front of the refrigerator staring at it, wondering why he is there.

Jim maintains a fair appetite. He is no longer picky about what he eats and doesn't seem to care. Janice feels that Jim doesn't enjoy eating. Every action he makes appears to be very mechanical. His once favorite restaurants are not appealing to him anymore. Janice feels very sad about what has happened to him and her marriage. Both eagerly waited for their retirement. They loved their teaching jobs, but they thought it was time to enjoy the rest of their lives. They planned to visit their children's families in California and Colorado and take several cruises to a few exotic places. Lately, Janice finds herself in a low mood, but is still able to push herself to do "the job" every day. She used to enjoy her church activities such as Women's Ministry, fund-raising auctions, and cookie sales. Lately, however, her social life is very limited by her home situation. She enjoys phone calls from her children and church friends, but she senses something is missing in her life. She was a lifetime avid book reader, but no longer enjoys reading books. She finds herself constantly preoccupied with Jim's condition and their undefined future. She senses slight irritations when their son, Jamie, attempts to offer unsolicited advice on the phone. She thinks to herself, "He never stops." She loves her daughter's listening ears. Cindy calls every Wednesday evening from California without fail and Janice eagerly awaits her phone call.

A week ago, there was a crisis. Jim managed to unlock one of the side doors and get out of house while Janice was clearing the table after dinner. She couldn't find him in the front or back yard and frantically drove around the neighborhood for almost an hour. Eventually, she found him standing outside a nearby convenience store. Jim looked scared and was trembling. He mumbled to her, "They are here again. We have to get out of here, otherwise we will all be killed." She was so mad at him initially, but found herself crying when she saw his scared and vacant gaze. He had no idea what he did to her that dark evening.

Janice wonders what would happen to them if she were unable to care for him at home. She wishes that her children were living nearby. She doesn't expect them to help her in any way, but would like to talk to them in person when she has to make some serious decisions. "What if both of us move to an assisted living facility?" she asks herself.

Psychiatric history: Jim had no psychiatric issues up until a bout of depressive symptoms in his mid-forties. He associated it with his midlife crisis, because he could not find a specific trigger for the depression. He did not see a mental health professional, but his primary care physician prescribed nortriptyline. He was on it for approximately six months and was able to overcome his mood symptoms without much difficulty. He still remembers that the medication made him thirsty all the time.

In his college days, he experimented with marijuana transiently, but he never indulged in illicit substances. He smoked heavily, up to two packs a day, during his tour in Vietnam, however; he was able to quit smoking completely in his mid-thirties. He considers himself a social drinker. Jim never abused any type of over-the-counter drugs, and he takes a multi-vitamin tablet faithfully every day.

Other medical history: He had a tonsillectomy when he was a child. Jim had two episodes of dizzy spells with confusion in his mid-fifties. His primary care physician thought that he had a transient ischemic attack (TIA). He has chronic medical conditions: hypertension, diabetes, and arthritis of both knees. He presently takes metoprolol with hydrochlorothiazide, glyburide, and celecoxib.

Other history (developmental, educational, occupational, family and social, legal): Jim was born in a small town in Pennsylvania. His childhood was uneventful until his father, a factory worker, was killed in a motor accident when Jim was 11 years old. His mother was a housewife, but she had to take on some odd jobs at times to raise five children. Jim is the third child with two older sisters and two younger brothers. His father was a hard worker and was very strict with his children. He never smoked or drank, which Jim always thought was rather different from his friends' dads. He never missed church on Sundays and expected his children to be clean and dressed up in their Sunday best.

Things became tough after he passed away, but his mother somehow managed through this period. His older sisters had to get jobs when they were old enough. Jim was a good student throughout his junior high and high school years. He had a few friends and spent much of his leisure time reading books on world history. He was a frequent visitor to the city library. He joined the track team when he was a sophomore in high school. He was a good runner and once won a county-wide school championship.

Soon after he was done with high school, Jim was drafted into the U.S. Army and took his first tour in Vietnam. He was assigned to an artillery battalion near the Mekong River. He still recalls multiple attacks made by the Viet Cong guerrillas on rainy nights with explosions, screaming, and confusion. Janice says he rarely talks about it. He came home after the war ended and entered college on the GI Bill. He graduated with a degree in history and found a teaching job in a high school not too far away from his hometown. Here he met Janice, a teacher at the same school, After two years of courting, they married.

Jim enjoyed his teaching job. He always thought he made a living doing what he loved to do. Janice always thought that he was a good husband and a good father to their two kids. Jim wasn't too crazy about social activities; he would rather stay home, read books, and maintain the house and lawn. He had two or three fellow teachers with whom he associated at lunch and other school events. For some reason, he attended church only sporadically, even though he was a regular attendee throughout his high school days.

Janice has no doubt that they have had a solid marriage, and their two children are now married with their own kids. Jamie is a computer engineer who is happily married and has two little boys. Cindy is a registered nurse who married her high school sweetheart and has a daughter. Cindy often tells them to move to Colorado when they retire. Jim and Janice wish that they could see their grandkids more often. They truly enjoy watching them grow through interactive video using Skype. They often talked about taking trips to see their children and spending some time with their families when they retired. Throughout Jim's life, he never had any significant difficulty with the law other than a few parking tickets. They both tried hard to save money, so they might have enough to comfortably retire. Both believe they are financially stable for their middle-class lifestyle.

Mental status examination: The patient is a 67-year-old male who appears to be his stated age. He is casually dressed in a striped dress shirt and a sport coat with khaki pants. There is no psychomotor agitation or retardation. He looks slightly nervous and puzzled. The patient keeps looking at his wife, who is sitting nearby. He shows no bizarre behavior, but occasionally grimaces unhappily. His speech is sparse and nonspontaneous, and his answers are a nonelaborative "yes" or "no." He has no dysarthria. He is fully alert, but is disoriented to time. His remote memory is felt to be normal, but his recent memory is significantly impaired. Although his attention is fair, the patient is unable to recall even single items after five minutes. His affect is blunted but felt to be appropriate and he describes his mood as "okay". He denies suicidal or homicidal ideations. His verbal production has definitely decreased, but he has no flight of ideas or loosening of association. At one point, he is tangential in speech but seemingly unaware of it. He is unable to properly interpret two common proverbs. His ability to do simple calculations is impaired even with much cuing. He doesn't know the name of the capital city of France. The patient is unaware of his condition. His social judgment is felt to be grossly impaired based on his wife's account. He simply stares at the interviewer when asked what he would do if he saw an addressed envelope that was stamped and sealed on the street. He denies delusions or hallucinations, but his wife's report suggests that he can be paranoid in thinking. As for the results of cognitive screening tests, he scored a 20 on the Mini-Mental State Exam (MMSE). Additionally, he scored 6 on the 10-point scoring system on the Clock Drawing Test (CDT).

IMPAIRMENT IN FUNCTIONING

Jim's functional impairment is substantial at this point. First, there is a significant concern about his safety in relation to his tendency to wander off and leave the stove on. Another challenge is his insistence on driving. All of these have major potential for unsafe situations. This impairment implicates significant changes that his wife has to make to his home environment before an accident happens. Aphasia is another challenge for his wife. His declining ability to converse will continue to lessen Jim's social activity. She may have to help him with this potentially sensitive deficit. Also, his deteriorating activities of daily living (ADL) ability will provide an additional challenge for her. His inability to dress properly and take care of his toileting has already begun. There will be more ensuing impairments as Jim's condition progresses.

DSM DIAGNOSIS

Jim's clinical picture primarily lies in his impairment in memory, although he presents with other associated symptoms. The previous edition of DSM classified dementia syndromes within the category of Delirium, Dementia, and Amnestic and Other Cognitive Disorders. His symptomatology and relevant background information rule out delirium, amnestic disorder, and other cognitive disorders. In DSM-5 Major or Minor Neurocognitive Disorder replaces the diagnosis of dementia with subtypes based on a broad range of etiological factors according to the latest findings. In addition to interference with independence in everyday activities, Neurocognitive Disorder due to Alzheimer's Disease is diagnosed when there is strong evidence for a progressive decline in memory and learning, with no other neurodegenerative disease or condition explaining the cognitive deterioration and impairment. It should be noted that decline from a previous level of performance in memory and learning is accompanied by decline in at least one or more cognitive domain (complex attention, executive function, language, perceptual-motor or social cognition). When the cognitive deficits occur exclusively during fluctuations of attention, the patient may have a delirium due to the physiological consequence of another medical condition, substance intoxication, or substance withdrawal.

Jim's clinician used two screening tests, the MMSE and the CDT, to measure his cognitive functioning. The commonly accepted cut-off MMSE score for dementia has been less than 24/30. Considering his educational background, his cut-off would have been 27/30 according to the age-correlated scoring system. As for the CDT, its scoring system is rather complex; but one with a score of 6/10 or lower identifies 78% of Alzheimer's disease (AD) patients. Nonetheless, his scores from these tests suggest that his cognitive functions are impaired and he meets the diagnostic criteria for dementia.

Jim's vital signs were essentially within normal limits. His review of systems was noticeable for slight swelling and tenderness in both knees, slightly diminished vibration sense in both lower extremities. He showed no primitive reflexes. His review of systems revealed chronic knee pain and a vague right-sided dull headache. His routine dementia medical work-up was noncontributory and a brain MRI without contrast revealed age-appropriate brain atrophy with mild periventricular white matter lesions. The initial working diagnosis is a dementia of Alzheimer's type (Major Neurocognitive Disorder due to Alzheimer's Disease according to DSM-5) along with hypertension, type II diabetes, and osteoarthritis of both knees.

EPIDEMIOLOGY

Today, it is estimated that as many as 5.2 million Americans have AD. By 2050, up to 16 million will have the disease as the incidence of AD rises commensurate with the aging population. Of adults over 65 years, one in eight has AD, and nearly half of people aged 85 and older have the disease. AD is the sixth leading cause of death in the United States and the fifth leading cause of death for those aged 65 and older. It is also noted that about half a million Americans younger than age 65 have some form of dementia including AD.

DIFFERENTIAL DIAGNOSIS

Dementia is a descriptive term for a collection of symptoms related to cognitive decline that can be caused by a number of medical conditions that affect the brain. It is not caused simply by normal age-associated changes. There are more than 100 different medical conditions that are known to be associated with dementia. Some of them can be reversible. To rule out any reversible medical condition, the American Academy of Neurology has recommended a complete blood count, electrolytes, serum glucose, blood urea nitrogen, calcium, thyroid function tests, and a vitamin B_{12} level as part of medical work-up for patients with memory complaints. Clinicians should remain flexible in terms of ordering other lab studies depending on the patient's clinical presentation. Either head CT or brain MRI should be considered for all patients with dementia symptoms. AD is the most common irreversible cause of dementing conditions. Some of the important dementing conditions that may be included in differential diagnosis of AD are vascular dementia, Lewy body dementia, frontotemporal dementia, normal pressure hydrocephalus, dementia associated with Parkinson's disease, delirium, and pseudodementia.

Vascular dementia accounts for up to 20% of all dementias. A single strategic infarct, multiple infarcts, or white matter disease may all cause a dementing condition. Cardiovascular accidents yield a ninefold increased risk of dementia. Typically, vascular dementia shows a stepwise progression of cognitive deficits along with other motor and sensory deficits. This condition is often associated with vascular disease, vasculitis, or atrial fibrillation.

Individuals with Lewy body dementia often fall with clinical features of Parkinsonism. Also, they are noted for fluctuation of cognition and recurrent and well-formed visual hallucinations. Lewy body dementia is more often recognized and it is up to 25% of dementia cases. Patients with this condition tend to be sensitive to adverse effects of antipsychotic agents.

Frontotemporal dementias often present with gradual changes in behavior and personality such as depression, delusions, anxiety, and impulsivity. As a result, persons with this type of dementia are not uncommonly diagnosed as having a psychiatric disorder. Also, impairment in language is prominent. Family history of early onset dementia is often present. Structural imaging or functional imaging studies can be useful in differentiating this condition from AD.

Individuals with normal pressure hydrocephalus often present with memory difficulty and poor concentration. Also, they may have gait disturbance and urinary incontinence in addition to dementing symptoms.

Parkinson's disease is a progressive neurodegenerative disorder that is associated with dementia in up to 70% of cases. Dementing symptoms often occur later in the disease course.

Patients with delirium may mimic the symptoms in dementia. Delirium is the most common psychiatric condition caused by medical illness. It is clinically manifested by acute change in attention and arousal, memory, and other cognitive functions. Delirium is a brain failure in a global sense. Generally, older adults are at higher risk. Delirium may lead to irreversible damage and cause dementia.

Pseudodementia refers to a dementia of depression. In older adults, cognitive impairment caused by depression is not uncommonly misdiagnosed as a dementia. Patients with this condition often have prior history of depression. There is usually a stressor that might have triggered this change. Cognitive symptoms may differ from those associated with AD. Individuals with pseudodementia may show psychomotor retardation, more variability in memory function, and more errors of omission. They may deny feeling depressed, but they may suffer from neurovegetative signs of depression.

ETIOLOGY AND PATHOGENESIS

Family history of dementia is a significant risk factor for AD. Especially, early onset AD is genetically complex. About 5% of AD patients develop this condition before age 60. Early onset AD is associated with mutations on a gene locus on chromosome 21, encoding for amyloid precursor protein; mutation on gene loci on chromosome 14 and 1; and presenilin 1 and presenilin 2, respectively. The pattern of autosomal-dominance transmission is often involved in early onset AD. The role of genetic risk factors in late-onset AD is less clear; however, first-degree relatives of an individual with AD are three or four times more likely to develop this disease over a lifetime compared with someone who has no affected family members. Additional vulnerability genes have been identified. Among them, ApoE4 allele, is known to be a risk factor for late-onset AD. Nearly 100%

of persons with Down's syndrome develop the neuropathologic changes of AD after the fourth decade of life. Nongenetic risk factors associated with AD are advanced age, gender, low education, head injury, cardiovascular conditions, aluminum, and other toxic agents. It is noticed that some psychiatric conditions are associated with AD as risk factors. They are depression, personality changes, and post-traumatic stress disorder. Of additional interest, obesity and diabetes have been implicated as a risk factor.

There are multiple histopathologic changes in the AD brain. Macroscopically, the AD brain is significant loss of neurons and shrinkage of large cortical neurons, which results in widened sulci with narrowed convolutions and enlarged ventricles. The unique neuropathologic changes include the accumulation of senile plaques and neurofibrillary tangles; although this may occur with age and other diseases, the extent of damage and accumulation is much more significant in AD. Senile plaques build up between synapses and contain deposits of a protein fragment known as beta-amyloid. Beta-amyloid appears to be the primary component of senile plaques in the AD brain. It is the product of cleavage of the amyloid precursor protein (APP), a transmembrane protein of unclear function. APP is cleaved at specific locations by three secretase (alpha, beta, and gamma secretases). Neurofibrillary tangles are intraneuronal cytoplasmic inclusions in AD brain and are hyperphosphorylated fibers of another protein called tau. Tau is a normal axonal protein with important functions in the microtubules. Neurofibrillary tangles are most closely correlated with the progression and extent of severity of AD. These senile plaques and neurofibrillary tangles form in a predictable fashion with AD—beginning in the entorhinal cortex and the nucleus basalis and then become much more diffuse. Most experts believe that these accumulations block communication between neurons and disrupt vital activities that neurons need to survive. Other pathophysiologic changes with AD are the gradual decline of acetylcholine and inflammation. Death of cholinergic neurons in the nucleus basalis causes a significant reduction in levels of acetylcholine. Acetylcholine is an important neurotransmitter of the learning and memory function. There is much scientific debate on the primary or initial pathologic process leading to the cascade of events causing ongoing degradation of the brain in AD.

Although Jim's family history of AD is not clear—since his father died at a young age and there is no information on Jim's grandparents—his past history of having suffered from a bout of depression and possibly from post-traumatic stress disorder brings up an interesting point. Those two conditions are currently considered independent risk factors for AD. In addition to the aforementioned neurobiological changes that may occur in Jim's brain, his gradual awareness of cognitive decline may activate his defense mechanisms that characterize his personality style. His rigid style may cause him to experience more difficulties with progressive cognitive deficits. Those difficulties are manifested by the changes in his mood, anxiety, and irritability. He appears to be coping with those by becoming more withdrawn and regressed. Additionally, even minor changes in his environment may provoke and precipitate neuropsychiatric symptoms in him, which would put his wife in challenging situations. As his cognitive impairment worsens, Jim may become less adaptable to his milieu and respond with various types of neurospychiatric symptoms that clinicians commonly treat in older adults with AD.

NATURAL COURSE WITHOUT TREATMENT

The clinical course of AD varies among individual patients. However, most undergo rather distinctive stages of the illness (mild, moderate, and severe). The duration of each stage varies from one patient to another. Each stage also brings unique challenges to individuals with AD, their caregivers, and clinicians. The total duration of AD is 9 to 12 years on average from symptom onset to death. The average length of time from symptom onset until diagnosis is approximately two to three years. Also, the average duration of time from diagnosis to long-term care facility placement is roughly three to six years. Predictors of more rapid institutionalization include extrapyramidal signs, the presence of psychotic symptoms, young age at onset, and current cognitive dysfunction.

In patients whose initial MMSE scores ranged from 10 to 26, the average rate of decline per year is about 3 points, but the variability is considerable. Parkinsonian signs, hallucinations, and delusions have shown to be associated with a more rapid decline. Mortality in AD averages less than 10% annually. Medical survival for persons with AD is about three to six years. Causes of death in AD include pneumonia, sepsis, and other common causes of mortality in the elderly, such as cardiovascular disease and stroke.

EVIDENCE-BASED TREATMENT OPTIONS

The treatment of AD patients uses a combination of pharmacotherapy and psychosocial interventions. Primary pharmacotherapy for AD includes the acetylcholinesterase inhibitors (AchEIs) and glutaminergic antagonists. No supplements, vitamins, or herbal remedies have demonstrated any significant effect currently. Nonsteroidal anti-inflammatory drugs (NSAIDs) were initially one of the promising agents, but they have not been shown to alter the course of the illness or reduce the rate of cognitive decline. Other medications are used to treat the neuropsychiatric symptoms of AD, such as depression, delusions, hallucinations. Psychosocial interventions include educational programs for caregivers and other involved family members, facilitation of access to community services, review of safety issues, and review of legal and financial issues. Both medical and psychosocial interventions should be initiated simultaneously to effectively assist the patients and their families.

The numbers of potential pharmacotherapeutic agents for AD continue to grow, but only the agents that may delay progression of the disease are available now. Presently, there are three FDA-approved AchEIs available in the market. Donepezil, rivastigmine, and galantamine have been shown to have cognitive and other clinical benefits in mild to moderate AD patients. The first AchEI, tacrine, is approved by the FDA and currently rarely used due to significant liver toxicity. Donepezil has recently been approved for severe AD. Although the pharmacological premises for those agents are derived from the cholinergic hypothesis, it should be noted that rivastigmine dually inhibits acetylcholinesterase and butyrylcholinesterase. Also, galantamine acts as an AchEI and a nicotinic agonist. However, it is not yet clear that their extra mode of action benefits declining cognitive function of AD patients. Memantine is another antidementia agent that indicated for use in patients with moderate to severe AD. It antagonizes glutamate-gated N-methyl-D-aspartate (NMDA) receptor channels. The NMDA receptor is known to play an important role in learning and memory. Additionally, high levels of glutamate result in excitotoxicity, which causes neuronal apoptosis.

Evidence for the benefits of AchEIs in the treatment of AD has been subject to extensive review. Though almost all studies have demonstrated a reduced rate of cognitive decline or even some improvement in cognitive function, effect sizes have been consistently small, averaging an approximate three-point difference in the Alzheimer's Disease Assessment Scale-Cognitive (ADAS-COG) after three to six months of treatment. It has been argued that this difference does not translate into a clinically meaningful outcome. A separate analysis using a minimum four-point difference found that only 10% more patients responded to an AchEI than placebo. There have been multiple studies to review the research methodology, cost-effectiveness, and noncognitive measures of improvement in relation to AchEIs. In addition to pharmacotherapy for cognitive symptoms of AD patients, pharmacotherapy for neuropsychiatric symptoms and psychosocial interventions are essential in treating AD patients. They are discussed in detail in the following section.

CLINICAL COURSE WITH MANAGEMENT AND TREATMENT

The general treatment strategy is to initiate a trial of AchEI when the diagnosis of AD is established. Start the patient at the lowest dose, to be taken with meals to avoid gastrointestinal side effects. Increase the dose until reaching recommended dose every four to six weeks. When the patient is on a stable dose, the same cognitive test, such as the MMSE, should be repeated every three to six months. At each visit, patients should be checked for side effects. Among many known side effects of AchEIs, gastrointestinal side effects, such as nausea, diarrheas, and anorexia, have been the most frequent use-limiting adverse events. The gastrointestinal side effects appear to be dose-dependent. In terms of drug interactions, the use of AchEIs in patients with high-dose NSAIDs or warfarin may carry a slightly greater risk because of concern over the possibility of gastro-intestinal bleeding. If the patient continues to worsen, change to a different AchEI. Memantine is approved by the FDA for moderate to severe AD; in practice, it is often used as an adjunctive treatment with AChEIs. It is renally excreted, so the clinicians may take caution with patients with kidney diseases. When used in combination with donepezil, the response seems superior than when used alone. There is no consensus on when to discontinue antidementia agents, but one strategy is it should be continued until patients reach the stage of severe dementia or when accelerated decline would have no further effect on quality of life.

Managing neuropsychiatric symptoms in AD can be a significant challenge to caregivers, families, and clinicians. They include mood symptoms, delusions, hallucinations, verbal and physical aggression, inappropriate sexual behavior, apathy, disrupted sleep pattern, and so on. More than 90% of patients will exhibit at least one neuropsychiatric symptom at some point during their illness. The most frequently reported symptoms include apathy, agitation, and depression. The presence of these symptoms have been associated with accelerated morbidity and increased mortality in addition to earlier institutionalization. They have also been associated with increased caregiver stress and care cost.

Successful management strategies of neuropsychiatric symptoms in AD often must be individualized for each patient and may require a combination approach of pharmacotherapy and nonpharmacotherapy. Nonpharmacotherapy may be initiated first or along with pharmacotherapy depending on the severity or circumstance of the symptom. As for nonpharmacotherapy, a broad range of approaches have been investigated, including sensory enhancement and relaxation techniques, increased social contact, behavior therapy, caregiver education, structured activities, pain management, pet therapy, and therapeutic garden. Although most studies on nonpharmacological approaches report some improvement, many are neither rigorously blinded nor well controlled.

Several classes of medication have been shown to be effective in ameliorating neuropsychiatric symptoms in dementia, including AchEIs, antidepressants, antipsychotics, and mood stabilizers. The selection of the appropriate pharmacological treatment should be individualized depending on the specific symptoms presented by the patient. Careful consideration should be given that the fact that many older adults are already taking multiple medications for other medical conditions. The use of AchEIs has demonstrated modest reduction in the overall frequency and severity of neuropsychiatric symptoms with the most robust improvement in apathy and hallucinations. Memantine also showed modest efficacy in behavioral symptoms when used alone or in conjunction with donepezil. Selective serotonin inhibitors such as citalopram and sertraline are effective primarily for depressive symptoms. Mood stabilizers such as valproic acid and carbamazepine may be helpful to stabilize agitation, but their utility is limited by potential drug interactions and a relatively high incidence of adverse effects. Both antipsychotic agents, typical and atypical, have proven to be effective in modestly reducing a wide range of neuropsychiatric symptoms. A recent Cochrane review suggested that risperidone and olanzapine can be effective in reducing aggression, and risperidone in treating psychosis. This was supported by CATIE-AD trial with superiority of both agents evident over both quetiapine and placebo. However, the use of atypical antipsychotics in dementia carries a black box warning from the FDA in association with a 65% increase in all-cause mortality with risperidone in particular associated with a three-time increased mortality. Considering all available evidences, a sensible management strategy would suggest an initial focus on optimizing environmental and psychosocial interventions. If these fail, then the use of pharmacological approach may be used with ongoing periodic review.

Psychosocial interventions are essential in treating AD patients. The intervention should begin with educating the patient and the family in a supportive and caring way. Ensure patient safety including driving, wandering behavior, and fire hazard. This may have to include modifying the home environment, installment of dead-bolt locks, and removal of clutter on the floor. Patient and family may address legal issues (such as wills, health care proxy, durable power of attorney) early. Appoint someone to assist with financial management, such as bill paying. Also, be sure to continue health maintenance. When appropriate, address the possibility of various community services or long-term care placement. Consider an adult day care program, respite care, home health aides, and soon. Be aware that almost 75% of AD patients eventually require a long-term care facility. This process brings various challenges to the patients and their families in terms of emotional and financial tolls. One more important issue is caring for the caregivers. Over 50% of caregivers develop clinical depression and other psychiatric conditions. They need to be referred to support groups or other sources of information and coping skills.

At Jim's initial evaluation, he was already considered to be in the moderate stage based on the comprehensive evaluation that looked at his cognitive function and ADL ability. Also, screening tools such as the MMSE and CDT supported the determination. With his consent, Jim was initially placed on donepezil 5 mg daily and then it was increased to 10 mg daily after four weeks. He did not experience any particular side effects other than initially having loose stool for a week or so. His physician chose this agent because Jim has no significant gastrointestinal problems and the medicine had simple titrations and once-a-day dosing. Also, he was not taking warfarin or high-dose NSAIDs. His doctor decided not to prescribe a psychotropic agent for his occasional verbal outbursts since he generally responded to Janice's diversion and she didn't feel threatened or unsafe. Janice prepares Jim's pillbox every Sunday and always keeps it on the kitchen table. She also writes notes as reminders for him and places them on the refrigerator door. Jim has responded well to the treatment in all aspects considering that his condition was to be progressive in its course. At his three-month follow-up visits with a geriatric psychiatrist, he has maintained his initial MMSE and CDT scores. Janice attends a caregiver support group sponsored by the Alzheimer's Association's local chapter. At the suggestion of the support group, Jim has begun to go to a nearby adult day care center. Although he was reluctant to leave home, he has gradually become used to it and seems to enjoy a variety of activities and programs offered there. He attends three times a week and spends six hours each time. This greatly helps Janice in that she is relieved from daily caring for him and has time to attend to her own needs.

SYSTEMS-BASED PRACTICE ISSUES

Dementia is frequently under-recognized and under-diagnosed by physicians and other health professionals. One study discovered that physicians fail to recognize cognitive impairment in 40% of their cognitively impaired patients. In another study by, only 19% of primary care patients who were found to have dementia by an expert panel of investigators had documentation of dementia in their medical record. A meta-analysis of the literature revealed that 50–66% of dementia cases in primary care samples across multiple studies had not received a dementia diagnosis. One of the barriers to dementia diagnosis is that a positive screening test alone is not sufficient for making an accurate diagnosis. Some researchers emphasize the importance of proceeding through the "standard of care diagnostic procedures for dementia diagnosis," rather than simply diagnosing AD based solely on the results of a dementia screening test. However, older adults frequently refuse further diagnostic assessment for dementia after receiving positive results on dementia screening tests, and many are unwilling to undergo routine screening for memory problems.

This brief overview of some of the challenges related to dementia screening in primary care demonstrates the complicated, multifaceted nature of this issue. Multiple medical comorbid conditions further complicate the role of primary care physicians in the care of patients with dementia. Primary care patients with dementia have 2.4 chronic conditions on average and receive 5.1 medications. Alarmingly, 50% of dementia patients were found to be exposed to at least one anticholinergic medication, despite their already existing cholinergic deficit. Such exposure to anticholinergic medications puts patients with dementia at a higher risk for anticholinergic adverse effects (e.g., delirium, falls, increased cognitive deficits). Also complicating the care of patients with dementia in primary care are their decreased ability to recall recent symptoms and language deficits that impair the ability to report symptoms or drug side effects.

It has been well documented that cognitive impairment is associated with increased use of health services; that is, patients with cognitive impairment were more likely to be hospitalized and visit the emergency department. They were also found to be less likely to visit ambulatory clinics. By contrast, health service use rates decreased when a geriatric psychiatrist was involved in patient care. Specifically, institutionalization rates were significantly lower in patients receiving care from a geriatric psychiatrist (4.6%) compared to those who were being seen only by their primary care physicians (30%). On a related note, one study found that family doctors wanted more education on AD. Also, these physicians expressed concerns regarding limited access to consultation with specialists (neurology, geriatrics). In addition, the study revealed that physicians were "generally unaware" of community resources available for patients and caregivers; unfortunately, they indicated that they were not interested in learning more about such community resources.

Despite multiple suggested models of dementia care, there has been a lack of consensus in terms of how to best provide comprehensive care to AD patients during the course of illness trajectory. Of interest, a collaborative dementia care model has been developed, based on biopsychosocial interventions, improved quality of care, quality of life, and the behavioral and psychological symptoms of dementia. for both the patient and the caregiver. This model includes a care manager to coordinate care, standardized protocols for care delivery and ongoing follow-up, and access to information technology to help support care management. However, implementing this innovative care delivery model requires significant clinical practice redesign.

In Jim's case, his primary care physician practices in a multispecialty clinic setting where he had relatively easy access to a geriatric psychiatrist. He and Janice were referred to a local caregiver support group and day care center by a social worker at the clinic. Also, their church's senior group lay leader, Bob, pays special attention to them. He calls them on a weekly basis and provide spiritual support. He and other members make home visits periodically. When Jim is at the center, Janice tries to find the time to attend her book club meeting and enjoys this carefree social gathering. She now feels that she is able to cope with this unexpected circumstance through these arrangements and information acquired from various professionals involved in his care. She is clearly aware of Jim's prognosis, possible behavioral symptoms, and perhaps eventual long-term care placement. Thinking of all these makes her sad, but she doesn't feel alone against this challenge because her children are only a phone call away.

LEGAL, ETHICAL, AND CULTURAL CHALLENGES

Driving performance is expected to decline as AD patients progress. Revocation of driving privileges in patients with AD is one of the most challenging issues for clinicians and caregivers. Despite the controversies, the bottom line should be the patient's and others' safety. The American Academy of Neurology has issued guidelines that state patients with dementia severity of Clinical Dementia Rating (CDR) = 1 or greater pose a significant safety risk and should be carefully evaluated. There is no consensus on best methods for assessing driving safety, but road testing is known to be the most accurate. Use of a driving simulator can be useful. However, clinicians who lack the resources may have to rely on their clinical judgment.

Patient and family may address legal issues (such as wills, health care proxy, and durable power of attorney) early. As the patient's condition worsens, it may become necessary to appoint someone to assist with financial management, such as bill paying. Patients may be unwilling to give up on their financial responsibilities. Generally, clinicians' cautious but frank discussion with the patient can be helpful. There can be contention among family members regarding financial decisions over the patient's asset. It is very important that the clinicians should keep a neutral stance by strictly focusing on clinical matters. Individual caregivers struggle not only with their own emotional needs but also with the dynamics of a family and social system. The power balance in the family shifts when the family elder gets sick; the shifting of various roles and related decision-making power can entail significant discomfort or conflict. Depending on their roles in the family and relationship to the ill parent, siblings may differ in their approaches to caregiving involvement and decisions for a parent. Also, to what extent the family caregiver(s) should step in and suggest or insist on alternative living arrangements, oversight of the checking account, supervision of medications, or taking away car keys are heart-wrenching decisions. This dilemma represents a conflict between the ethical principles of autonomy and beneficence. One of the foundations of American culture is respect for the individual's self-determination. However, it should be noted that cultural factors are extremely important in approaches to decision making. Individual autonomy is not the primary value in many cultural groups, and respect for the individual—both before and after incapacity associated with dementia—entails considering decisions from the perspective of the needs of the family and community.

Jim fought Janice all the way not to give up his car keys even after several incidents of getting lost. However, when he drove into another car in the parking lot of a shopping plaza, Janice felt very unsafe about him driving even when she was with him in the car. At a follow-up visit with his geriatric psychiatrist, he was advised to quit driving when Janice informed the doctor of this incident. The doctor also noted Jim's poor performance in the CDT. The psychiatrist notified the Department of Motor Vehicles of his opinion on Jim's driving. As a result, Jim reluctantly handed over his car keys to Janice. That was perhaps the saddest day for Jim in his entire life.

Fortunately, Jim has not shown many neuropsychiatric symptoms other than his initial catastrophic responses in the beginning stage and occasional outbursts with Janice over some perceived demands. Janice is well informed of the behavioral changes associated with his condition. She has become much conscious of their safety and knows that she should immediately call 911, the Adult Protective Agency, her children, or her neighbors if she senses any type of unsafe situation.

Both were referred to an attorney who specializes in legal and financial issues related to seniors. When they had a consultation meeting with the lawyer, both Jamie and Cindy were able to participate via teleconference call. The attorney addressed legal and financial management issues. The legal issues such as advance directives, wills, and durable power of attorney had been completed when Jim was well since he always wanted to be well prepared for any situation. Janice and her children feel comfortable about the arrangement that they made with the attorney.

TERMS

Agnosia: inability to identify faces, colors, or objects despite normal perceptual processes.

Aphasia: loss or impairment of language function.

Delirium: fluctuating disturbance of consciousness (reduced ability to focus, sustain, or shift attention), cognition (memory, orientation, or language deficit), thought process and content (tangentiality, incoherence, paranoid and other delusions), perception (illusions, hallucinations), affect (dysphoria, emotional lability, or anxiety), and behavior (agitation, lethargy) due to direct physiological consequences of a general medical condition, medication side effects, or substance intoxication or withdrawal which develops over a short period of time (usually hours to days). Also referred to as an "acute confusional state" or "acute brain syndrome."

Delusions: false belief incongruent with the patient's cultural and educational background.

Executive function: the process of bringing together and coordinating information for a purpose, such as decision making; includes skills such as mental flexibility and response inhibition.

Hallucinations: altered perceptual state (auditory, visual, tactile, olfactory) with no external stimuli.

REFERENCES AND RESOURCES

American Psychiatric Association. Practice guidelines for the treatment of patients with Alzheimer's disease and other dementias of late life. *Journal of American Psychiatric Association* 1997;154(5):1–39 (supplement).

Cotterell D, Brown M. Evidence-based pharmacotherapy of Alzheimer's disease. In: Stein DJ, Lerer B, Stahl SM (Eds.), *Essential evidence-based psychopharmacology* (2nd ed.). Cambridge: Cambridge University Press, 2012.

Cummings JL. Alzheimer's disease. *N Engl J Med* 2004;351(1):56–67.

Folstein MF, Folstein SE, McHugh PR. "Mini-mental state," A practical method for grading the cognitive state of patients for clinicians. *J Psychiatr Res* 1975;12(3):189–98.

Karel MJ, Moye J. The ethics of dementia caregiving. In: LoboPrabhu SM, Molinari VA, Lomax JW (Eds.), *Supporting the caregiver in dementia: a guide for health care professionals*. Baltimore, MD: Johns Hopkins University Press, 2006.

Matthews BR, Miller BL. Alzheimer's disease. In: Miller BL, Boeve BF (Eds.), *The behavioral neurology of dementia*. Cambridge: Cambridge University Press, 2009.

Querfurth HW, LaFerla FM. Mechanism of disease: Alzheimer's disease. *N Engl J Med* 2010;362(1):329–44.

Sakauye K. Differential diagnosis and treatment. In: *Geriatric psychiatry basics*. New York: W. W. Norton & Company, 2008.

Schneider LS, Tariot PN, Dagerman KS, et al. Effectiveness of atypical antipsychotic drugs in patients with Alzheimer's disease. *N Engl J Med* 2006;355(15):1525–38.

Alzheimer's Association home page, http://www.alz.org.

Away from Her (2007): Julie Christie was Oscar-nominated for Best Actress for her portrayal of Fiona, a woman with Alzheimer's who voluntarily enters a long-term care facility to avoid being a burden on Grant (Gordon Pinsent), her husband of 50 years. After a 30-day separation (recommended by the facility), Grant visits Fiona and finds that her memory of him has deteriorated and she's developed a close friendship with another man in the facility. Grant must draw on the pure love and respect he has for Fiona to choose what will ensure his wife's happiness in the face of the disease. Christie won a Golden Globe Award for Best Actress in a Motion Picture (Drama) for her performance.

The Notebook (2004): A romantic drama film based on a novel by Nicholas Sparks. The film stars Ryan Gosling and Rachel McAdams as a young couple who fall in love in the 1940s. Their story is narrated from the present day by Duke, an elderly man (James Garner) telling the tale to a nursing home resident, Allie. As he finishes the story, Allie briefly becomes lucid and remembers that the tale is the story of how she and Duke met.

Chapter 3

New-Onset Psychosis in the Elderly

Saira Arif, M.D.

CLINICAL PRESENTATION

Chief complaint: "I hear voices."

History of present illness: Betty is an 85-year-old married, Caucasian female with no previous history of psychiatric illness, brought to the outpatient psychiatry clinic by her husband on account of having auditory hallucinations and delusions. She is sitting quietly in a chair. Her husband reports that for the past two months Betty has been suspicious of him. She believes that he is not loyal to her and is involved with another woman. She argues with him and follows him secretly, wherever he goes. She told him that she hears a female voice in the house and it must be the woman with whom she suspects he is involved. She has become increasingly upset and agitated over the past two months and argues with her husband frequently. He tried to explain to her that this is not true and that he is not having an affair, but she is adamant that he is hiding his affair from her.

Betty started hearing voices approximately two months ago. At times she hears noises, and sometimes she hears the voice of one or more persons. She at first believed that her husband brought a woman into the house. She later started believing that the woman and other people are now living in her house. She hears voices of multiple people, using foul language. Sometimes she hears them singing. The voices do not talk to her and are not commanding, and she mostly hears them when her husband is not around. These voices wake her up early in the morning. Overall the voices have progressively gotten worse, affecting her relationship with her husband and causing significant stress in her life. She has been having frequent arguments with her husband. For the past month she has started seeing people in her house. She has seen a woman in the house multiple times, and believes that her husband has brought her into the house. She has anxiety and stress related to the current symptoms, otherwise she does not have depressed mood and has no problems with appetite and energy. She has disturbed sleep as voices wake her up early in the morning. She does not enjoy activities as much as she used to, due to the voices as well as due to the fact that she believes her husband is unfaithful. She does not have any suspicion about anyone other than her husband. She never had symptoms consistent with mania or hypomania. She does have problems with her memory and has been forgetful for few months, does not remember recent events, and has problems coming up with words. Otherwise, her overall functioning is not impaired.

Betty's husband provided a history consistent with the foregoing and reports that her current symptoms started approximately two months ago. Symptoms stay the same and do not seem to fluctuate over the course of a day. She was seen by her primary care clinician for these psychotic symptoms. Her husband brought the records from her family physician, including labs and imaging reports. Routine laboratory tests including urinalysis, CBC, CMP, B$_{12}$, TSH, and RPR were all unremarkable. A CT scan of the head showed mild cortical brain atrophy, mild cerebral ventricular enlargement, and mild periventricular white matter changes. Betty's son called the clinic to provide additional information. He states he is concerned about his mother's current symptoms because he has noticed that she has been increasingly forgetful over the past year. Although mild problems with memory started more than a year ago, it became more noticeable and worsened in past year. She often has difficulty remembering recent information. She asks the same questions repeatedly about recent events and gets upset when someone points it out. She exhibits problems with finding words and remembering names on introduction to new people. She misplaces things and loses them often. There have been few instances when she had left the stove on. She has been unable to cook as effectively as before and has been having problems with managing her finances. She does not drive and has never driven in the past.

Past psychiatric history: Betty has no previous psychiatric history. She has never been diagnosed with any psychiatric illness and has never been on any psychotropic medication. She never had any episodes of depression or mania or psychotic symptoms in past and has never been hospitalized to any psychiatric unit.

Past medical history: Betty has hypertension, hyperlipidemia, and gastroesophageal reflux disease. No history of stroke or transient ischemic attack (TIA), no history of cardiac disease reported. No history of head trauma or seizure disorder. Her current medications include atorvastatin, amlodipine, and omeprazole.

Family history: There is no history of any psychiatric illness in Betty's family, including major depression, bipolar disorder, or schizophrenia. Her mother died in a nursing home at the age of 90 years and had problems with memory in later years of her life. Betty's father died at the age of 70 years from heart disease.

Social history: Betty was born and raised in Traverse City, Michigan. She was the only child of her parents and had a very good childhood. She was a good student and finished high school. After graduation she got married to her high school boyfriend. She has been married to him for 63 years. She lives with her husband, who is now 87 years old. She still remembers the beautiful days when she was dating him, and she remembers the first gift he gave to her. She has one son who lives close to her house. He is supportive and sees her often. She worked in the past as a cook in a restaurant before her son was born. She has not worked in over 50 years and has been a homemaker. Her husband reports that she has managed the finances and has helped him keeping books all her life, until a few months ago when she had started having difficulties with it. She loves reading books and follows current affairs and news. She has always been well informed about current affairs, but for the past several months she did not seem to remember daily events and forgets them often. She used to cook gourmet dishes and is known for making delicious food but has not been able to do so for some time.

Substance abuse history: There is no history of tobacco smoking, alcohol, or recreational drug abuse.

Mental status examination: Betty is an elderly white female with average build, well dressed and well groomed. She walked into the room with slow gait. No psychomotor abnormalities are noticed. Impulse control is intact. She is cooperative and has fair eye contact. Her speech is spontaneous, soft, and fluent with average rate and rhythm. She is alert and oriented to time, place, person, and situation. Registration is mildly impaired. Immediate and recent memory are impaired. Remote memory is intact. Overall she is able to provide information during the interview, but does exhibit some deficits in memory of personal history. Concentration is impaired. Her affect is mood congruent, mildly anxious, and restricted. She describes her mood as "fair." There are no suicidal or homicidal ideations, intent, or plan. Language overall is average except difficulty finding the right word at times. Thought process is linear and goal directed, with normal association. Thought content is positive for delusions. She is able to abstract proverbs. She has some difficulty doing simple calculation. Intelligence is average. She is able to name the current president of United States, but is unable to name three presidents prior to the current one. Insight is limited. Judgment is intact. She has had auditory hallucinations on and off, but are not present at the time of interview. There are no current visual hallucinations. No illusions, depersonalization, or derealization present.

Neurological exam: Glabellar and palmo-mental reflexes are positive. No focal neurological deficits present. No other positive finding on neurological examination.

Mini-Mental State Exam (MMSE): 23/30.

IMPAIRMENT IN FUNCTIONING

Betty has memory impairment for approximately one year with progressive decline in functioning, which is a required criteria for the diagnosis of Dementia of Alzheimer's Type. Emergence of psychotic symptoms superimposed on her cognitive deficits have further deteriorated her illness, causing significant stress in her life with marital problems. Overall cognitive decline has caused impairment in functioning as well as safety concerns, prompting an assessment of her ability to live independently. She is unable to do tasks as effectively as she used to. Her symptoms have been affecting her relationships and social life. Decline in overall functioning is most often recognized by the family. With progressive decline and worsening in cognitive abilities, more functional impairment results with reduced independence in daily activities. Presence of psychotic symptoms has been found to be associated with more rapid cognitive decline. Emergence of psychotic symptoms hence warrants prompt treatment and consideration of biopsychosocial aspects of treatment intervention.

DSM DIAGNOSIS

Betty presents with complaints of hallucinations and delusions, causing significant distress in her life along with marital problems. Delirium, Schizophrenia, Other Specified Schizophrenia Spectrum, Other Psychotic Disorder, and Mood Disorder with psychotic symptoms were considered. After the important piece of additional information provided by her son, Other Specified Psychotic Disorder due to Alzheimer's Disease, with hallucinations and delusions, was suspected. This also underscores the importance of acquiring collateral information in geriatric patients.

The criteria for psychosis of Alzheimer's disease (AD) requires the presence of AD, psychotic symptoms (which were not present before the diagnosis of AD), a duration of psychotic symptoms for one month or longer, and impairment in functioning caused by the psychotic symptoms. Exclusion criteria involves exclusion of other psychiatric illnesses that can cause psychotic symptoms (schizophrenia, mood disorder with psychotic symptoms, psychotic symptoms of delirium, psychotic symptoms due to general medical condition, or medication-induced psychosis).

In DSM-5, Major or Minor Neurocognitive Disorder replaces the diagnosis of Dementia with subtypes based on a broad range of etiological factors according to the latest findings. In addition to interference with independence in everyday activities, Neurocognitive Disorder due to AD is diagnosed when there is strong evidence for a progressive decline in memory and learning, with no other neurodegenerative disease or condition explaining the cognitive deterioration and impairment. It should be noted that decline from a previous level of performance must occur or more than one cognitive domain (complex attention, executive function, learning and memory, language, perceptual-motor, or social cognition). When the cognitive deficits occur exclusively during fluctuations of attention, the patient may have a delirium due to the physiological consequence of another medical condition, substance intoxication, or substance withdrawal.

Betty presented with symptoms that meet the DSM criteria for Dementia (Neurocognitive Disorder) and also the criteria for Other Specified Psychotic

Disorder due to AD. Her cognitive deficits include impaired ability to learn new information (manifested by problems with remembering recent events and information, increased forgetfulness, problems with remembering names) and impairment in executive functioning (inability to manage finances or inability to cook effectively, both of which require planning, organizing, and sequencing). Impaired ability to learn new information is typically the initial symptom of AD. Impairment in remote memory appears in later stages of AD and is intact in this case, as Betty is able to recall important and detailed information from her past. The presence of impairment in both memory and executive functioning, satisfies the DSM criteria for a Major Neurocognitive Disorder of the Alzheimer's Type. There is impairment in overall functioning, which represents a decline from her previous level of functioning (she has not been able to do tasks as effectively as before). Her symptoms started gradually and progressively worsened over one year before the psychotic symptoms emerged, with no previous history of psychiatric illness. Psychotic symptoms appeared several months after the cognitive impairment was first noticed. They are present for more than a month and have caused functional impairment.

EPIDEMIOLOGY

In the review of studies on epidemiology of and risk factors for psychosis of Alzheimer's disease, Ropacki and Jeste (2005) found the median prevalence of psychotic symptoms (delusions or hallucinations) in patients with AD was 41.1%, the median prevalence of delusions was 36%, and the median prevalence of hallucinations was 18%. Delusions of theft found to be most common type of delusions reported. Visual hallucinations reported to be more common than auditory hallucinations. Both delusions and hallucinations found to be present in 7.8–20.8% of subjects. Higher prevalence of psychotic symptoms were found to be present in inpatient settings compared to outpatient. In 85-year-old individuals with AD, the prevalence rates of psychotic symptoms have been found to be 36%. Cumulative incidence of hallucinations and delusions in patients with probable AD was 20.1% at one year, 36.1% at two years, 49.5% at three years, and 51.3% at four years. Late onset of schizophrenia (after age 40) is overrepresented by married females.

DIFFERENTIAL DIAGNOSIS

Psychosis in late life is common and affects patients and their caregivers. There are multiple etiologies of late-life psychosis. When an elderly patient comes with psychosis, medical illnesses and medication-induced symptoms must be ruled out first. Betty came with the presenting complaints of only the psychotic symptoms, so medical illnesses and medication-induced symptoms should be ruled out first. She was seen earlier by her primary care clinician and medical causes of current symptoms were eliminated. She does have hypertension, hyperlipidemia, and gastroesophageal reflux disease. All her labs were within acceptable limits of normal.

The common causes of new onset psychosis in later life are:

1. Delirium caused by medications or certain medical conditions, as well as alcohol and or substance use or withdrawal.
2. Dementia (major neurocognitive disorder)-related psychosis.
3. Primary psychiatric disorders, including affective disorders with psychotic symptoms, late-life schizophrenia (including late-onset and early onset schizophrenia), and delusional disorder.

The most common type of psychosis in the elderly related to underlying medical and neurological conditions is psychosis due to dementia. Dementia is reported to be a greatest risk factor for development of psychosis in the elderly, due to the presence of dementia itself as well as increased risk of delirium in dementia patients.

Delirium

Delirium is characterized by changes in consciousness with attention deficits, changes in cognition and perceptual disturbances (not better accounted for by dementia), acute onset, and fluctuation of symptoms over the course of the day. Delirium is one of the diagnoses considered with new-onset psychosis in elderly. Dementia patients have increased susceptibility for delirium, so it is important to find out if the psychotic symptoms are due to delirium, dementia, or both. Careful history about the presence of symptoms before the acute change and the subsequent course of illness help in resolving this question.

The first step in the evaluation and treatment of a patient with late-life psychosis is to rule out delirium and its causes. Once delirium is ruled out, the next step is to find out if the psychotic symptoms are due to dementia or other psychiatric illnesses. An important distinguishing feature of delirium is the alteration/fluctuation in the level of consciousness. Dementia patients do not have this characteristic feature. Memory impairment is present in both dementia and delirium, but the patient with dementia is usually alert. Psychotic symptoms of delirium are present in the context of alteration in consciousness and fluctuating course, which makes it distinguishable from other psychotic illnesses in elderly. Presence of underlying acute general medical conditions favors the diagnosis of delirium. Common causes of delirium in elderly are medication-induced side effects, infections, metabolic abnormalities, cardiovascular diseases, central nervous system disorders, substance intoxication and withdrawal, and so on. Cognitive impairment and older age are important risk factors (among several others) for delirium.

Betty has gradual onset and progressive decline in cognitive function. Alteration in level of consciousness is not present, and the course is not fluctuating.

Absence of acute medical condition as well as negative workup for delirium are two points against the diagnosis of a delirium.

Dementia-Related Psychosis

Psychotic symptoms in patients with dementia are commonly in the form of delusions and hallucinations. Delusions are the most common psychotic symptoms in patients with AD and are usually nonbizarre, simple, and paranoid. The most common delusion is delusion of theft. Other delusions include delusions of partner/spouse being unfaithful, or a delusion that a caregiver will abandon the patient, specific persons spying on patient, or someone impersonating the spouse or significant other, have also been observed in patient with AD. Complex, elaborate delusions as seen in schizophrenia are not usually seen in AD. Hallucinations are second common psychotic symptoms. Visual hallucinations are more common than the auditory hallucinations. As the cognitive impairment progresses, the patient's ability to explain and verbalize psychotic symptoms declines. In those cases the patient's behavior explain the presence of psychosis. Patients with dementia are susceptible to delirium. Medical causes and medication-induced psychosis need to be ruled out first in an evaluation of new-onset psychosis in an elderly patient. Collateral history from family helps in generating the differential diagnosis. Presence of cognitive impairment before the onset of psychotic symptoms helps differentiate dementia-related psychosis from primary psychotic illnesses, in which history of psychotic symptoms precedes the development of cognitive impairments.

Once delirium and other medical causes of psychosis are ruled out and dementia with psychotic symptoms is suspected, evaluation and investigations should be done to find out the type of dementia. Different types of major cognitive disorder (dementias) should be ruled out to make the diagnosis of Alzheimer's dementia. Most of the dementias are progressive and irreversible, but some are reversible, including normal pressure hydrocephalus and vitamin deficiencies including B_{12} and thiamine. Workup to rule out reversible causes of dementia should be done first in an elderly patient with psychosis.

Dementia of the Alzheimer's type (DAT) is the most common type of dementia. Five percent of population at age between 65 to 74 years is affected by AD. Prevalence doubles every 5 years after the age of 65 years. Approximately 50% of individuals older than 85 years have DAT. Age and family history are the main risk factors, as well as history of head trauma and Down's syndrome. The initial symptom is short-term memory loss, which progresses gradually to more cognitive decline and functional impairment. Personality changes with impaired judgment occurs in later stages. Betty's age, family history, as well as presence of memory impairment typical of AD, impairment in executive functioning, gradual onset and progressive decline all favor the diagnosis of AD. Her intact remote memory, MMSE score of 23, and current level of functioning all suggest the diagnosis of early stage AD.

Vascular dementia is characterized by a stepladder pattern of cognitive decline with the presence of focal neurological deficits. Stroke increases the risk of dementia. Risk factors for stroke and heart disease, including diabetes, hypertension, and hypercholesterolemia, are also the risk factors for small vessel vascular dementia. It is also common that both conditions, small vessel disease vascular dementia and AD, occur together. When this happens, small vessel disease pathology adds to that of AD pathology. It is important to recognize this possibility, and its effect on the treatment and prognosis.

Betty has associated risk factors for stroke, including hypertension and hyperlipidemia. CT scan of the head shows mild periventricular white matter changes, which reflects small vessel disease. Although her overall pattern of memory impairment and cognitive decline (gradual onset and progressive course, absence of the focal neurological deficits, and absence of the history of stroke or TIA) favors the diagnosis of AD, she also has risk factors for small vessel disease vascular dementia and stroke, including hypertension and hyperlipidemia. As mentioned, these factors further contribute to the cognitive impairment and pathology of AD.

Lewy body dementia is dementia with one or more of the following: visual hallucinations, parkinsonism, and fluctuation in alertness or attention. Lewy body dementia is characterized by the presence of well-formed visual hallucinations, often early in the illness. Symptom progression is faster than in AD but with an insidious onset and gradual progression. Typically dementia precedes the motor deficits. There is an extreme adverse sensitivity to antipsychotic medications. Betty has gradual progressive cognitive decline with appearance of auditory hallucinations and delusions. Vivid visual hallucinations as well as fluctuation in alertness or attention are absent.

Frontotemporal dementias, including Pick's disease, usually presents with changes in personality (disinhibition, impulsivity) and social behavior disturbances, followed by cognitive impairment. Language impairment can also occur. Betty has impaired recent memory, which appeared first, with gradual progressive cognitive decline, and absence of personality changes. These findings are against the diagnosis of frontotemporal dementias.

Normal pressure hydrocephalus is characterized by cognitive impairment, gait disturbances, and urinary incontinence. It is associated with ventriculomegaly with or without cortical atrophy. Betty does not have these symptoms.

Thiamine deficiency, B_{12} deficiency may also result in dementia. These causes are ruled out because the labs are unremarkable and patient does not have symptoms consistent with thiamine or B_{12} deficiency.

Psychotic Disorders

Onset of psychotic symptoms in late life may result from psychotic illnesses including schizophrenia, delusional disorder, or affective disorder (bipolar or depressive disorders) with psychotic symptoms.

Late-onset schizophrenia: In a patient with new-onset psychotic symptoms in later life, diagnosis of late-onset schizophrenia should be considered. Careful history and collateral information are important and helpful in evaluation and diagnosis. For the diagnosis of late-onset schizophrenia, all criteria for the diagnosis of schizophrenia should be met; in addition, the age at the onset of symptoms has to be 40 years or more. No prodromal symptoms of schizophrenia should be present before 40 years of age. Delusions and hallucinations are the common symptoms in patients with late-onset schizophrenia. In late-onset schizophrenia, paranoid schizophrenia is more likely than in early onset schizophrenia. Flat affect and formal thought disorder are present but are less prominent than in younger patients with schizophrenia. Pointers against the possibility of this diagnosis in Betty include presence of cognitive impairment and decline before psychotic symptoms emerged, absence of negative symptoms, and presence of overall ability to maintain relationships.

Early onset schizophrenia: Criteria should be met for schizophrenia before 40 years of age. Cognitive impairment is present in early onset schizophrenia but has overall stable pattern. Features against this diagnosis in Betty's case are absence of psychotic symptoms prior to the age of 40 and absence of prodromal symptoms, negative symptoms, and previous history of psychiatric illness or treatment. Progressive cognitive decline, memory impairment with deficits in short-term memory, and rapid forgetfulness started before psychotic symptoms emerged, and are all in favor for AD with psychotic symptoms.

Delusional disorder: Delusions in dementia resemble delusional disorder. Presence of cognitive impairment before the onset of delusions favors the diagnosis of psychosis of AD.

Psychosis secondary to substance abuse and dependence: Betty has no history of substance abuse and dependence.

Mood disorders with psychotic symptoms: Betty has never had depressive, manic, or hypomanic episodes. No previous history of affective disorders reported. Absence of mood symptoms, presence of memory problems at the onset, gradual and progressive cognitive decline, decline in overall functioning, and emergence of psychotic symptoms in context of cognitive decline favors the diagnosis of psychosis of AD.

Betty presented with complaints of psychotic symptoms only. As mentioned, new-onset psychosis in elderly patients could be due to variety of reasons, and each needs to be ruled out carefully to construct the appropriate treatment plan. She was seen by her family physician, and acute medical conditions, as well as medication-induced symptoms, were ruled out. Delirium is ruled out because the workup for delirium is negative, there is no alteration in level of consciousness, and the course is not fluctuating. Cognitive impairment preceded the psychotic symptoms, with gradual onset and progressive decline in cognitive function, which favors the diagnosis of dementia-related psychosis. Exclusion and consideration of specific features and characteristics in this case will help ruling out different types of dementias. Her age, family history, as well as presence of memory impairment typical of AD (impairment in executive functioning, gradual onset, and progressive decline), all favor the diagnosis of AD. Her overall pattern of memory impairment and cognitive decline (gradual onset and progressive course, absence of the focal neurological deficits, and absence of the history of stroke or TIA) all help in ruling out vascular dementia, but she has associated risk factors for stroke, including hypertension and hyperlipidemia, with CT scan findings suggestive of small vessel disease, which further contributes to the cognitive impairment and pathology of AD. Impaired recent memory, which appeared first, with gradual progressive cognitive decline, and absence of personality change rules out Frontotemporal dementias. Absence of gait disturbances, urinary incontinence, ventriculomegaly with or without cortical atrophy, normal B_{12} and thiamine level rules out normal pressure hydrocephalus, dementia due to thiamine deficiency, and B_{12} deficiency are ruled out, as the labs are unremarkable and patient does not have symptoms consistent with thiamine or B_{12} deficiency. Presence of cognitive impairment and decline before psychotic symptoms emerged, absence of negative symptoms, presence of overall ability to maintain relationships, absence of psychotic symptoms prior to the age of 40, no previous history of psychiatric illness or treatment, and no history of substance abuse and dependence rule out late-onset or early onset schizophrenia, mood disorders with psychotic symptoms, and psychosis secondary to substance abuse and dependence. Presence of memory problems at the onset, gradual and progressive cognitive decline, decline in overall functioning, and emergence of psychotic symptoms in context of cognitive decline favors the diagnosis of psychosis of AD.

ETIOLOGY AND PATHOGENESIS

Some of the risk factors for AD include increasing age, family history, and genetic factors. Increasing age is the greatest risk factor for late-onset AD. Five percent of the population between the ages of 65 and 74 is affected by AD, and the prevalence increases to >40% in persons age 85 years or older. Family history is a significant risk factor, especially history of AD in first-degree relatives. Genetic factors include four chromosomal abnormalities that are prominent: mutations on gene locus on chromosome 21 encoding for amyloid precursor protein, on chromosome 1 encoding for presenilin 2, and on chromosome 14 encoding for presenilin 1 are associated with early onset AD. Presence of APOE-e4 allele on chromosome 19 is a risk factor for late-onset AD.

Other possible risk factors for AD are female gender, low educational achievement, head injury, ethnicity (African American), and disorders causing cardiovascular damage including diabetes, hypertension, coronary artery disease, hyperlipidemia, smoking, and atrial fibrillation. Heavy alcohol abuse; exposure to heavy metals like aluminum, copper, and zinc; and vitamin B_6, B_{12}, and folate deficiencies (which may increase homocysteine level) are other possible risk factors of AD. Increase homocysteine level can cause damage to arteries and increase the risk of coronary artery disease and stroke. Homocysteine level was found to be high in patients with AD, according to some studies.

Several studies have been done to examine the risk factors and associations of psychosis in AD. Different variables were examined, including ethnicity, age, age at onset, sex, family history, and genetic factors. Association between psychosis of AD and different variables is not clear. African American ethnicity has been found to be associated with increased risk of psychosis of AD, whereas family history of dementia, older age, and female gender have weak associations with increased risk of psychosis of AD. Older age, duration of AD, and later age of onset of AD have less consistent association with psychosis of AD. Fifty percent of late-onset AD patients develop psychosis, which is associated with more rapid cognitive decline. Newer studies and data suggest possible genetic basis of psychosis in AD and is thought to represent a distinct phenotype.

Psychosis of AD has been reported to be associated with increased incidence of extrapyramidal syndrome (EPS), cognitive decline, frontotemporal dysfunction, and auditory and visual deficits. Increased densities of senile plaques, neurofibrillary tangles, and paired helical filament–tau protein in specific cortical areas reported to be present in patients with psychosis of AD.

Etiology of neuropsychiatric symptoms of dementias is still not clear. Studies have found an association between neuropsychiatric symptoms in AD and dysfunction in specific cerebral areas, altered neurotransmitters level, and severity and extent of neurodegenerative changes. Some of the neurotransmitter dysfunctions that have been found to be associated with psychotic symptoms in AD are increased subcortical norepinephrine levels and decreased cortical and subcortical serotonin levels.

Some of the risk factors that might be involved in the etiology of Betty's illness include old age, probable family history of late-onset dementia, cardiovascular risk factors (including hypertension, hyperlipidemia), female sex, years of education, and late-onset AD.

Betty's memory problems noticed around the age of 83. As mentioned, the prevalence of AD increases with age. Her mother had probable dementia, reportedly had memory problems, and died in a nursing home. Late-onset AD has a genetic factor involving mutation of APOE-e4 allele on chromosome 19. Other possible risk factors that might be involved in her case are history of hypertension and hyperlipidemia.

Her symptoms of psychosis improved somewhat after addition of cholinesterase inhibitors, suggesting possibility of cholinesterase deficiency as a cause of her psychotic symptoms. Some studies suggest an association between acetylcholine deficiency and the neuropsychiatric symptoms of dementia, based on the effectiveness of acetylcholinesterase inhibitors in the management of neuropsychiatric symptoms of dementia.

NATURAL COURSE WITHOUT TREATMENT

In the early stages of AD, psychotic symptoms and behavioral disturbances, particularly agitation, are more likely to develop. Behavioral disturbance is more likely to persist. As the disease progresses and severity of illness increases, psychotic symptoms decrease. This is likely a result of severe cognitive decline and resultant inability of patients to communicate their psychotic symptoms in the later stages of illness. Psychosis in dementia has major clinical and psychosocial consequences. AD with psychosis is associated with greater and more rapid cognitive decline compared to AD without psychosis. Psychosis in dementia is related to greater caregiver distress and poor quality of life. It is also noted to be related to greater prevalence of extrapyramidal signs, decreased physical health, and increased mortality. Psychosis of dementia has been reported to be linked with aggression, agitation, and anxiety. It predicts functional decline and subsequent institutionalization, as behavioral disturbances and agitation often result in institutionalization. As the presence of psychosis in dementia is an important factor predicting the course of the disease and its sequelae, early detection and management are crucial.

EVIDENCED-BASED TREATMENT OPTIONS

Management of the neuropsychiatric symptoms of dementia involves both pharmacological and nonpharmacological interventions. Nonpharmacological treatment approach includes identification and modification of factors exacerbating the symptoms, safety measures, maintaining routine and modification of behavior, and use of sensory intervention, caregiver/family education, and support to help cope with the affected family member. Supportive therapy and behavioral management of the patient can also be effective in various stages of AD. Management should begin with evaluation of medical and environmental causes of behavior. Use of nonpharmacological interventions as a first-line treatment or as an adjunct to pharmacological intervention depends on the nature and severity of symptoms. Studies done to assess the effectiveness of nonpharmacological interventions have shown inconsistent or limited quality patient-oriented evidence. Larger, well-designed, controlled trials are needed to assess the effectiveness of nonpharmacological intervention in the management of neuropsychiatric symptoms of dementia.

Neuropsychiatric symptoms of dementia are common and can result in significant stress and problems for patients as well as their caregivers. Various pharmacological agents are used to treat neuropsychiatric symptoms of dementia with a growing evidence base of double-blind, placebo-controlled, randomized controlled trials or meta-analyses. The atypical antipsychotic agents, olanzapine and risperidone, have the best evidence for efficacy. These two agents were found to have modest but statistically significant efficacy, with less adverse effects at lower doses. Use of cholinesterase inhibitors have also shown small but statistically significant efficacy. Use of these agents has shown a delay in time to institutionalization, which could be a result of improved behavior or preservation of functioning. These modest responses are significant in lowering the burden of care or stress for patients and their caregivers and in improving quality of life.

Conventional antipsychotics have been used for psychosis in dementia, but their use is limited since the atypical antipsychotics were introduced. Conventional antipsychotics are effective for the management of psychosis in dementia, but their side effects profile limit their use in patients with dementia. They have significant risk of side effects including EPS and tardive dyskinesia. Risk of EPS with neuroleptic medications is higher in elderly patients compared to younger patients. Other side effects that are of concern in elderly population include cardiovascular and anticholinergic effects. Randomized controlled trials of these agents found small efficacy, common adverse effects, and no difference among specific agents.

Atypical antipsychotic medications have emerged as promising agents for the treatment of psychosis and severe agitation in patients with dementia, although data are still limited. Although these agents generally have better tolerability in elderly patients, the recommended dose range is lower and titration should be gradual in older patients compared with younger patients. Placebo-controlled trials of risperidone and olanzapine have shown improvement in psychosis or severe agitation in dementia patients. Effective doses are reported to be 1–2 mg of risperidone (2 mg dose associated with more risk of EPS) and 5 mg olanzapine.

Atypical antipsychotics use is complicated by their side effects profile and a black-box warning from the FDA (increased mortality risk in elderly dementia patients on conventional or atypical antipsychotics; most deaths reported due to cardiovascular or infectious events). Frequent side effects of atypical antipsychotics are sedation (especially with clozapine, quetiapine, and olanzapine), orthostatic hypotension, and EPS at higher dosage (especially with risperidone). Risk of tardive dyskinesia is lower with atypical antipsychotics than with typical antipsychotics. Other notable side effects of atypical antipsychotic medications are metabolic syndrome, anticholinergic symptoms, and prolongation of the QT interval. Due to their side effect profile, use of atypical antipsychotics should be judicious with close monitoring.

Effectiveness of cholinergic agents (donepezil, rivastigmine, galantamine) in the treatment of psychosis and behavioral disturbances in patients with AD has been a focus of research. Use of donepezil has been shown to improve behavioral disturbances in patients with AD. Use of other agents (rivastigmine, galantamine) for behavioral disturbances and psychosis in AD has shown promising results in initial studies. Other medications including antidepressants, mood stabilizers, and pain management have their place in addressing neuropsychiatric symptoms of dementia.

CLINICAL COURSE WITH MANAGEMENT AND TREATMENT

The first step in the management of an elderly patient with new-onset psychosis is the workup to rule out delirium. Detailed and careful history is important in determining the chronology of symptoms, presence of acute medical problems, exclusion of infectious or metabolic etiology, exclusion of potentially offending prescription medications, and substance intoxication or withdrawal. Laboratory tests including CBC, CMP, and thyroid functions are preliminary to rule out causes of delirium. Once delirium is excluded, the next step is to determine if the psychotic symptoms originated from dementia or from another psychiatric disorder. Again, a detailed and careful history as well as collateral information is important in differentiating psychosis of dementia and other psychiatric illnesses. Neuropsychological testing for detailed and complete evaluation of cognitive function would help in establishing the diagnosis of dementia and also in delineating the specific cognitive deficits, which will help in managing and treating the patient. Once the diagnosis of dementia is made, workup to determine the type of dementia and to differentiate between certain types of dementias should be done.

Patients with newly diagnosed dementia with psychotic symptoms should be evaluated for appropriate pharmacological treatment. There are two major classes of pharmacological treatment of AD. First is the treatment of cognitive and global symptoms, and second is the treatment for behavioral and psychotic symptoms. Appropriate management and pharmacological intervention can delay institutionalization, reduce excessive morbidity, and reduce stress and burden for the patient and caregivers. Goals of treatment vary with disease stage. In early stages the goal is to improve cognition and slow progression of disease. In the middle stages preservation of function, that is, activities of daily living (ADLs), maintaining safety, and delaying institutionalization, is the goal. In later stages, emphasis moves toward management of difficult behaviors through pharmacological interventions as well as with manipulation of physical and social environment.

Acetylcholinesterase inhibitors and NMDA receptor antagonists are the only FDA-approved treatments for AD. The cholinesterase inhibitors have been approved for the mild to moderate AD. Clinical trials of acetylcholinesterase inhibitors including patients with mild to moderate AD have shown significantly less deterioration statistically, but clinically marginal benefits with respect to cognition, daily function, and behavior. Memantine is an NMDA receptor antagonist that is approved for moderate to severe dementia to preserve functioning and delay institutionalization.

The second major form of treatment for behavioral and psychotic symptoms of AD is the use of antipsychotic medications, which, as a general rule, should only be used if the symptoms are troubling and burdensome for caregivers or causing distress or danger for the patient. As mentioned, atypical antipsychotic medications have been reported to be effective in treating these symptoms.

Nonpharmacological treatment of behavioral disturbances in AD: In addition to the pharmacological treatment, the importance of nonpharmacological treatment interventions should be recognized in the management of behavioral disturbances in AD. Caregivers of the dementia patient should be educated about the disease and should be routinely screened for fatigue and depression. Caregivers should be informed of the availability of resources, such as adult day care centers, respite care, and home health services, and should be encouraged to make use of these resources when needed. Day care centers for patient with AD offer structured activities for patients and a respite for the caregiver. Occupational therapy as well as social work referrals should be considered timely.

Another important area in the management of dementia patients is to ensure safety of the patient and others. Modifications in the house is often needed to maximize the safety, for example, unplugging dangerous appliances, good lighting, locks on ovens and cabinets, and removing knives and guns from home. Measures to avoid wandering behaviors, including patient ID bracelets, complex door locks, or alarm system installation, might be needed. Home health, day care, assisted living facility, and nursing homes are the options available for dementia patients depending on the stage of dementia and the patient's need. Providing information regarding available resources for dementia patients and caregivers, including Alzheimer's Association and support groups.

Music, pet therapy, and touch are a few examples of sensory interventions that may be effective for dementia patients, depending on the severity and stage of illness. Relaxation techniques and structured activities might also help in management of neuropsychiatric symptoms of dementia.

Education and support of the caregiver of patient with dementia is very important. Caregivers should be educated about the disease process—its symptoms, course, and prognosis—helping them have realistic expectations regarding the patient's abilities and functioning and helping them understand the patient's new limitations. It is also important to help them understand the unintentional nature of symptoms, to educate them about simple approaches to deal with problem behaviors with the goal to create a stress-free environment and less confusion for the patient. Reassuring a caregiver is sometimes the only intervention needed. Give them information regarding available resources for dementia patients and caregivers, including the Alzheimer's Association and support groups.

Betty was diagnosed with psychosis of AD and her dementia was in mild to moderate range based on the evaluation of her cognitive functioning and with the help of screening tool such as MMSE. The clinician discussed the diagnosis with Betty and her husband and recommended treatment. Acetylcholinesterase inhibitors were offered, but Betty refused to consent. To address immediate concerns, due to current psychotic symptoms and stress resulting from those symptoms, she was started on olanzapine 2.5 mg qhs, with her consent. It was chosen because it is more sedating and has less risk of EPS as compared to risperidone. She tolerated the medication; her paranoia and agitation got better, but her hallucinations did not completely go away. Her insight was somewhat improved. Olanzapine was increased to 5 mg qhs. She later agreed to try acetylcholinesterase, and donepezil was started at 5 mg qday for four weeks and then increased to 10 mg qday. She reported significant improvement in her hallucinations after the initiation of the two medications. Nonpharmacological interventions were made, including education of her husband and her son about her diagnosis, its symptoms, course, and prognosis, helped them have realistic expectations regarding her abilities and functioning, understanding her new limitations and the unintentional nature of her symptoms. They were offered simple approaches to deal with problem behaviors and reduce her stress and confusion. For example, questions that required her to remember something should be avoided, because it may cause her stress by making her aware of her memory deficits. The clinician discussed the measures that needed to be done to maximize her safety and that of others, including unplugging dangerous appliances, locks on ovens and cabinets, and removing knives and guns from home. Home health, day care, and assisted living facility options were discussed as well as information regarding available resources (including the Alzheimer's Association and support groups). Betty and her husband later moved to an assisted living facility for safety considerations and for assistance in day-to-day living. At next follow-up appointment, Betty reported no psychotic symptoms. Her MMSE was stable.

SYSTEM-BASED PRACTICE ISSUES

Dementia is an important cause of excess medical care use and costs and represent a significant burden to individuals and society. Timely diagnosis and use of appropriate interventions are important. It is a shared responsibility between a primary care and a specialist. There should be appropriate and timely use of screening tools for cognitive impairment as well as use of appropriate treatment in all clinical settings. Primary care physicians have important role in managing patients with dementia. Dementia is underdiagnosed and undertreated in elderly primary care patients. Recognition and diagnosis of dementia in primary care clinics is problematic, and probably the result of various factors including case complexity (patients with multiple comorbidities and on multiple medications), time constraints, and reimbursement problems. Also, limited access to consultation and specialists, lack of education on AD, and lack of awareness regarding community resources are some of the other problems identified.

Medical care use cost as well as institutionalization rates are reported to be decreased if a geriatric psychiatrist is involved in the care of a dementia patient. It is important to use dementia treatment appropriately to improve quality of life for dementia patients and their caregivers as well as for managing the excess costs of AD. Cognitive function tests suitable for primary care clinics should be used.

LEGAL, ETHICAL, AND CULTURAL CHALLENGES

Two main ethical/legal issues in Betty's care are:

1. Informing the patient about the diagnosis of AD, and
2. Decisional capacity/informed consent for the trial of antidementia medications and antipsychotic medications.

Because there are effective medications for dementia available, importance of early diagnosis and informing patients and families about the diagnosis has increased. Early diagnosis helps patients prepare wills and advance directives, including durable power of attorney, and make informed decisions about medications. Thus it is important to inform and educate the patient about the diagnosis when AD is suspected. Elements of informed consent include explaining the diagnosis and nature of the illness, nature of the proposed treatment and its purpose, risks and benefits, available alternative treatments with their risks and benefits, and outcome if no treatment is done. *Decisional capacity* and *decisional competency* refers to the ability of an individual to make specific decisions at a particular moment. *Competency* is a legal term. Incompetency is determined by a judge, whereas *capacity* is a clinical determination. Decisional capacity has four major elements: ability to understand, reason, appreciate, and express a choice.

Evidence from the clinical and neuropsychological evaluations demonstrated that Betty was capable of making informed decisions at her current stage of AD. Risks, benefits, and alternatives to treatment were discussed as well as the black box warning of increase mortality with use of atypical antipsychotics in patients with dementia. She agreed to a trial of olanzapine for psychotic symptoms and donepezil for memory problems. It is important to reevaluate her capacity to make informed decisions periodically and reeducate her about the medication side effects, risks, benefits, and alternatives at follow-up visits.

Patients should be encouraged to appoint a surrogate decision maker before incapacity. Two types of advance directives can be taken before incapacity, including instructional directives (such as living wills, and orders such as do not resuscitate or do not intubate) and proxy directives, including durable power of attorney and health care agents for health care. After incapacity, state law and regulations explain who can make decisions for the incapacitated person. Family and close friends most commonly provide surrogate decision making. When these are not available, a court-appointed guardian should be considered.

The nature and course of Betty's illness was explained to her and to her husband. She was encouraged to appoint a surrogate decision maker, durable power of attorney, or make a living will. It was recommended to her that she appoint someone to manage her account, pay bills, and manage her finances. Another legal consideration would be the evaluation of driving privileges and safety risk. In this case it was not needed because Betty does not drive. Her husband and son were involved in the discussion of the foregoing recommendations and were supportive.

TERMS

Aphasia: loss of the ability to communicate verbally or using written words.
Delirium: fluctuating disturbance of consciousness (reduced ability to focus, sustain, or shift attention), cognition (memory, orientation, or language deficit), thought process and content (tangentiality, incoherence, paranoid and other

delusions), perception (illusions, hallucinations), affect (dysphoria, emotional lability, or anxiety), and behavior (agitation, lethargy) due to direct physiological consequences of a general medical condition, medication side effects, or substance intoxication or withdrawal which develops over a short period of time (usually hours to days). Also referred to as an "acute confusional state" or "acute brain syndrome."

Executive function: The cognitive process that regulates an individual's ability to organize thoughts and activities, prioritize tasks, manage time efficiently, and make decisions.

Hallucinations: Altered perceptual state, without an external stimulus.

Paranoia: Suspicion and exaggerated distrust of people or their actions without evidence or justification.

REFERENCES AND RESOURCES

Folstein MF, Folstein SE, McHugh PR. "Mini-mental state," A practical method for grading the cognitive state of patients for clinicians. *J Psychiatr Res* 1975;12(3):189–98.

Iglewicz A, Meeks TW, Jeste DV. New wine in old bottle: late-life psychosis. *Psychiatr Clin North Am* 2011 Jun;34(2):295–318. Review.

Ostling S, Gustafson D, Blennow K, Börjesson-Hanson A, Waern M. Psychotic symptoms in a population-based sample of 85-year-old individuals with dementia. *J Geriatr Psychiatry Neurol* 2011 Mar;24(1):3–8; Abstract.

Paulsen JS, Salmon DP, Thal LJ, et al. Incidence of and risk factors for hallucinations and delusions in patients with probable AD. *Neurology* 2000 May 23;54(10):1965–71. Abstract.

Ropacki SA, Jeste DV. Epidemiology of and risk factors for psychosis of Alzheimer's disease: A review of 55 studies published from 1990 to 2003. *Am J Psych* 2005 Nov; 162(11):2022–30. Review.

Sadavoy J, Jarvik LF, Grossberg GT, Meyers BS. (Eds.). *Comprehensive textbook of geriatric psychiatry* (3rd ed). New York: W. W. Norton & Company, 2004.

Alzheimer's Association home page, www.alz.org.

Two Hollywood movies that may illustrate dementia include *Away from Her* and *The Notebook*.

CHAPTER 4

Delirium

Nina Khachiyants, M.D.

CLINICAL PRESENTATION

Chief complaint: "They took my food from me."

History of present illness: Earl is an 83-year-old Caucasian divorced man who was brought to an emergency department from an assisted living facility (ALF) for evaluation of confusion and unusual behavior.

According to the ALF staff, for the last two days Earl has become agitated, combative with peers and staff during care, and was yelling at and trying to hit his roommate for no reason. In addition, he accused one of the nurses of stealing food from him. He was crying and sobbing on several occasions and was not able to explain the reason for his tears. He complained of seeing green lizards and yellow frogs on the wall last night. He was unable to sleep well during the night and was drowsy during the day. His appetite was poor, and he refused to drink liquids for the last two days. He has had several episodes of urinary incontinence and more frequent trips to the bathroom for urination for the past several days, which never happened before. On several occasions he complained of pain during and after urination. According to ALF staff reports, Earl was constipated for the last four days, which was resolved only partially with stool softeners.

Per ALF staff report, Earl demonstrated significant changes in his functioning for the past several days, and on several occasions he was not able to participate in group activities due to lack of attention, focusing, and concentration and difficulties in following commands. He was not able to perform simple hygienic procedures or dress himself appropriately in the morning. Over the past week, Earl demonstrated some fluctuations in his level of consciousness: during the morning and early afternoon he was more alert, talkative, and able to recognize peers and staff members. However, in the late afternoon, evening, and at night he was more confused, disoriented, and agitated, with some irritability and crying spells.

While in the emergency department, he was not able to maintain attention during conversation with the examining physician and frequently fell asleep during the interview. He was easily arousable, but needed to be redirected multiple times.

His daughter reported that this gentleman had suffered from dementia for the past few years, with gradual memory loss, difficulties remembering recent events, and occasionally misplacing things. His current medications are tramadol for chronic back pain on as-needed basis, diphenhydramine for insomnia, and donepezil for declining cognition. Per ALF staff report, his current symptoms showed a significant change from his usual presentation.

Until several days ago, Earl had not demonstrated agitation, combativeness, emotional instability, or verbally threatening behavior since admission to the facility. His daughter described him as a very gentle, kind, and nice person, who does not have any history of psychiatric illnesses or history of substance abuse/ dependence in the past.

Physical examination at the emergency department was positive for low-grade fever (100 °F orally), pulse 98 beats per minute, blood pressure 99/60, and mild tenderness at the costovertebral angle on the left side.

According to previous medical records and Earl's daughter, he had no prior history of mental illnesses until the onset of the dementia. His daughter described him as a very strong and stable person who was trying to be independent and take care of himself throughout all his life until age 78, when he had his first visit to clinician to address gradual memory loss. Earl was evaluated by geriatric clinician and was diagnosed with initial stage of dementia of Alzheimer's type, with late onset. Mini-Mental State Examination (MMSE) score at that time was 22/30, and he was started on donepezil 10 mg by mouth at bed time to slow down cognitive decline; later memantine 10 mg by mouth once a day was added to his treatment regimen as he demonstrated progressive memory loss. His last appointment with the clinician was six months ago, and at that time MMSE score demonstrated decline to 18/30, and the dose of memantine was increased to the maximum dose of 10 mg by mouth twice a day. During his last visit to the clinician, Earl did not show any anxiety, mood, psychotic symptoms, or behavioral disturbance.

Medical history: Earl has chronic back pain due to degenerative disk disease of the spine, for which he was taking tramadol as needed; this was the only medication that was able to control his chronic pain effectively. Also, he has had chronic insomnia, which was treated by diphenhydramine as needed. His medical history was negative for hypertension, other cardiovascular diseases, diabetes, or any other medical conditions.

Substance abuse history: Earl's daughter denied that her father had ever abused alcohol or any illegal substances. He is a former cigarette smoker and quit smoking completely more than 30 years ago.

Family psychiatric history: His daughter reported no known family history of mental illnesses in her father's family.

Other history (social, educational, occupational): Earl was born and raised in Richmond, Virginia. He had one older sister who died of stroke several years ago. Earl was married once for 37 years, but currently has been divorced for more than 10 years. His ex-wife does not participate in his care. His daughter lives in the same town and regularly visits her father at the ALF. Currently she serves as Earl's power of attorney (POA).

Earl graduated from the University of Virginia and worked as an architect for a local industrial builder company.

He retired at age 74 and continued to lead an active lifestyle, swimming, fishing, participating actively in his church activities, and visiting his daughter's family and his two grandchildren. Over the next several years he demonstrated gradual decline in his mental and social functioning and needed increasing supervision from his daughter. At age 80 he was placed in the ALF due to the need for assistance with activities of daily living.

MENTAL STATUS EXAM

Behavior: 83-year-old Caucasian male, mildly underweight, with short gray hair. He was dressed in casual clothes with fair grooming and hygiene. He was not cooperative, with poor eye contact, and demonstrated moderate psychomotor agitation with restlessness and frequent changes in body positions. There were no abnormal movements, tremor, or muscle rigidity. His gait was without gross abnormalities, with normal steps, and well balanced.

Speech was spontaneous, fluent, well articulated, and meaningless, with decreased volume but increased rate and latency.

Sensorium: Earl was awake, but with fluctuating level of consciousness, disoriented to time and place, but oriented to person. During the interview, he demonstrated several episodes of falling asleep, but was easily arousable. He was not aware of being in a hospital. He was easily distracted, was not able to focus and concentrate. Cognition was impaired. His short-term and long-term memory were impaired; he was not able to register or to retained information.

Emotions: Affect was anxious, labile, with several crying spells, and mood congruent. Earl was not able to describe his mood, but stated, "I am afraid." He denied suicidal or homicidal ideations, plan, or intent; however, reliability of this statement was poor.

Thought process: thought process was mostly disorganized, at times circumstantial, with inappropriate use of words, and occasional thought blocking during the interview.

Thought content: Earl was delusional about staff members stealing food from him. He was lacking abstract thinking. Complete thought content evaluation was impossible due to confusion and disorientation.

Intelligence and information, including fund of knowledge and ability to calculate was impossible to evaluate due to confusion and disorientation.

Insight and judgment were impaired.

Perception: he seemed to responding to internal visual stimuli by tracking and picking up some imaginary objects in the air and on his clothes.

Earl looked very distressed, given his presentation and behavior. However, he was not able to elaborate on his feelings or reasons for distress.

MMSE including memory evaluation (registration, immediate, recent, and remote) was impossible to conduct due to his confusion and disorientation. At times, he was not able to recognize his daughter and ALF staff member.

IMPAIRMENT IN FUNCTIONING

Although Earl already had some problems with his memory, his functioning significantly deteriorated in the past few days. The ALF staff reports that he was not able to communicate his needs and interact with peers and staff members appropriately, was easily distracted, and was not able to participate in group activities due to inability to sustain or shift attention. He has difficulties with focusing and concentration. His short-term and long-term memory are impaired as well. Also, Earl has difficulties with following commands. He is increasingly not able to perform simple hygienic procedures or dress himself appropriately. The clinical picture described here reflects functional impairment in several domains.

DSM DIAGNOSIS

The emergency department clinician who evaluated Earl suspected that he may be exhibiting clinical signs of Delirium due to general medical condition. The clinical presentation included several core features of the diagnosis, including: disturbance of consciousness with reduced awareness, concentration, and the ability to focus; a change in cognition with disorientation, language disturbances, and perceptual disturbances (e.g., hallucinations); development of above-mentioned disturbances over a short period of time with fluctuations of consciousness during the course of the day.

Earl seemed to meet these criteria; however, to meet the full criteria for delirium, the patient must have evidence from the history, physical examination, or laboratory findings that the disturbance is caused by the direct physiological consequences of a general medical condition. He demonstrated clinical signs and symptoms that were suggestive of urinary tract infection and needed confirmation by laboratory tests for the same.

One of the difficulties with diagnosing delirium is that the clinician is often without the benefit of much verbal input from the individual. In this case, Earl clearly suffers from a delirium due to a general medical condition. This delirium is superimposed on a dementia of the Alzheimer's type. However, it is not clear whether the delirium is solely due to a urinary tract infection or to multiple factors, including side effects from medication and possible chronic pain.

Among Earl's internal resources that might affect improvement in his condition are adherence to treatment, good support from his daughter, adequate premorbid functioning with good social and interpersonal skills before delirium development, and no history of other psychotic disorders, except for dementia. Although Earl did have dementia prior to onset of delirium, he was relatively well compensated in the structured setting of the adult living facility.

In DSM-5, the diagnostic criteria for neurocognitive disorders has been significantly restructured, but the criteria for delirium due to a general medical condition is unchanged. DSM-5 recognizes the dual dimensions of neurocognitive disorders: that neurocognitive decline may be due to specific, well-documented etiologies (Lewy body dementia, vascular dementia, etc.) but that in many cases the particular individual's dementia has multiple causes. It also recognizes the spectrum of the severity of these disorders.

EPIDEMIOLOGY

Delirium is a fairly common and serious condition among the medically ill elderly population: the point prevalence of delirium is 1.1% for people 55 years old and older. Medically ill, hospitalized persons exhibit delirium in 10–30% of cases. Elderly persons who are recovering from hip fracture surgery are found to have delirium in 40–50% of cases. Some studies demonstrate that persons recovering from cardiotomy develop delirium in more than 90% of cases. Terminally ill persons exhibit delirium in 80% of cases. Ten to fifteen percent of elderly persons present with delirium on admission to the hospital, and 30–40% of hospitalized persons older than age 65 demonstrate at least one episode of delirium. Sixty percent of nursing home residents at age 75 and older suffer from repeated episodes of delirium. The three-month mortality rate of elderly persons who developed delirium is approximately 23–30%, and the one-year mortality for the same patient population is close to 50%. The mortality rate of elderly persons with an episode of delirium during hospitalization is 20–70%. In addition to causing significant distress to persons, families, caregivers, and other medical personnel, the presence of delirium in medically ill persons has been associated with increased morbidity and mortality, prolonged hospital stay, increased cost of care, increased hospital-acquired complications, poor functional and cognitive recovery, decreased quality of life, and increased placement in nursing homes and other specialized supervised long-term care facilities.

DIFFERENTIAL DIAGNOSIS

It is important to differentiate delirium from other conditions because delirium may be life-threatening and should be approached as a medical emergency.

Consider the following conditions to differentiate from delirium:

1. Dementia: a gradually progressing course, lack of fluctuation in and out of a confusional state (except for Lewy body dementia). Patients with dementia are usually alert, with much less major attention deficit and less sleep disturbance. Differentiation is less straightforward as dementia progresses and alertness and attention are impaired.

Although Earl has had symptoms of dementia for the past five years, he developed acute changes in his mental status, significant attention deficit, emotional instability, and behavioral disruptions within several days. All those changes indicated an obvious shift from his baseline state and favors much more toward delirium, which was superimposed on preexisting dementia.

2. Depression: in addition to depressed mood, decreased energy level, poor sleep, changes in appetite, feelings of hopelessness, helplessness, psychomotor retardation, and other symptoms, persons with depression may present with a reduced level of alertness, emotional lability, and appearing withdrawn, but without acute symptom onset, fluctuating level of consciousness, significant attention deficit, or perceptual disturbances in the form of visual hallucinations. Also, depression can be distinguished from delirium on the basis of an EEG (lack of diffuse slowing of background activity).

Although Earl demonstrated emotional lability with episodes of crying and sobbing, the full clinical picture of this patient did not match description of depression.

3. Schizophrenia/psychosis: hallucinations and delusions are better organized and more constant than in delirium; usually no changes in level of consciousness or orientation. Also, hallucinations in schizophrenia in vast majority of cases are auditory. The visual hallucinations are more characteristic in cases of delirium, which indicate some organic/medical causes of this particular perceptual disturbance. Schizophrenia, however, usually begins in adolescence or young adulthood.

Although Earl demonstrated some disorganized behavior (combativeness, yelling, pacing, and agitation) as well as paranoid delusions of one of the nurses stealing food from him, the full clinical picture did not match description of schizophrenia/psychosis. Onset of schizophrenia at age of 83 would be highly unusual.

4. Factitious disorder: characterized by intentional production or feigning of physical or psychological signs or symptoms with motivation to assume sick role. In clinical practice a clinician can reveal factitious nature of symptoms by greater inconsistencies on mental status examination, which is not the case with Earl. In rare cases factitious disorder can be distinguished from delirium on the basis of an EEG (lack of diffuse slowing of background activity). The clinical picture of Earl did not match descriptions of factitious disorder.

A useful clinical rule of thumb is that any sudden changes in consciousness, cognition, or behavior in an elderly person should be considered to be delirium until proven otherwise, and any possible etiology should be investigated promptly and thoroughly.

Delirium is frequently underdiagnosed in elderly demented persons, in part because people with dementia may already have communication difficulties. Clinicians should have a high level of suspicion for delirium whenever there are acute changes in a person's behavior or mental status. In most elderly persons, delirium is a multifactorial event. Various precipitants do not alone cause delirium but interact with other underlying risk factors. Elderly people who are suffering from acute or chronic medical conditions and who are cognitively impaired or under psychological stressors are therefore particularly prone to delirium.

Clinical manifestations of delirium include altered (decreased) level of consciousness; diminished ability to focus, sustain, or shift attention; cognitive impairment; disorientation in time and place; relatively rapid onset (hours to days); relatively brief duration (days to weeks); and fluctuations in intensity of the symptoms during the day.

Other associated symptoms are as follows: thought process disorganization, perceptual disturbances (illusions, hallucinations), psychomotor retardation or hyperactivity, sleep-wake cycle disruption, emotional lability, behavioral disturbances (agitation, disorganization), autonomic hyperactivity, myoclonus, and dysarthria.

Clinical evaluation of every person with suspected delirium includes vital sign monitoring (temperature, pulse, respiration rate, oxygen saturation, blood pressure including orthostatic); frequent mental status examinations (arousal, attention, orientation) to monitor fluctuations in attention and arousal; neurological examination (evidence of head trauma, nuchal rigidity, papilloedema, reflexes, motor or sensory deficit, focal neurological signs, seizures); assessment of possible cardiovascular compromise (arrhythmia, murmurs, cardiomegaly); evaluation of respiratory tract (excursion, auscultation, cough); examination of abdomen (liver enlargement, bladder/urinary retention, palpable fecal impaction); assessment of skin (lesions, signs of dehydration, inflammation).

Comprehensive diagnostic studies should be done promptly and include the following laboratory tests: full blood examination (CBC, creatinine, electrolytes, glucose, calcium, liver function tests), urinalysis, MSU (if urinalysis abnormal), PT, PTT (if indicated), urine toxicology screen, chest x-ray, cardiac enzymes, ECG, blood, sputum, urine cultures and sensitivity (if fever present, cough and/or abnormal chest radiograph, urinary urgency/abnormal urinalysis), arterial blood gases (if shortness of breath, cough present, and/or abnormal chest radiograph), thyroid function tests, B_{12} and folate serum levels, VDRL, HIV test, CT brain scan (if history of falls, patient/client on anticoagulant therapy, or focal neurological signs present), lumbar puncture (if headache or fever and meningeal symptoms are present), EEG (may assist in determining etiology: epileptic or nonepileptic seizure activity; distinguish depression, psychosis, or mania from delirium).

Characteristic EEG findings in delirium include diffuse slowing of background activity; delirium due to alcohol or sedative-hypnotic withdrawal is manifested on EEG by low-voltage fast activity.

Scales and Tests to Assess Patients with Delirium

1. The Mini Mental State Exam MMSE is a screening instrument for brief assessment of cognitive functioning in adults, which includes evaluation of individual's orientation to time and place, recall ability, short memory, and arithmetic ability. The 11-item MMSE can be scored immediately after administration with a maximum of 30 (no impairment). The cut-off point to indicate cognitive impairment is generally between points 23 and 25. The MMSE has been used extensively in assessment of persons with delirium. The use of serial MMSEs reflects acute changes in cognition in older hospitalized adults and is helpful in the diagnosis and monitoring of the recovery from delirium. Specific items of the MMSE are helpful in screening for delirium, and they include the question about the current year and date, the backward spelling task, and copying a design.

2. The Mini-Cog is a screening instrument for cognitive impairment and is recommended for use in all elderly persons admitted to the hospital. This instrument requires minimal training of the examiner, needs minimal equipment (paper and pencil or pen), and takes approximately three to five minutes to administer. Persons are asked to listen carefully, remember, and repeat three unrelated words the tester provides. Next, the person is asked to draw the face of a clock on a blank sheet of paper or on a sheet that has the clock circle already drawn. The person is asked to write the numbers on the clock and draw the hands of the clock to indicate a specific time. The person is asked to repeat the three words. Each correctly recalled word is equal to 1 point; an abnormal clock is 0 points and a normal clock is 2 points. Possible scores range from 0–5, with 0–2 suggesting high and 3–5 indicating low likelihood of cognitive impairment. The Mini-Cog predicts delirium in older adults, and patients with abnormal results are five times more likely to develop delirium compared to those with normal scores.

3. Delirium Rating Scale (DRS) is a 10-point observer-rated scale that evaluates various symptoms of delirium. DRS scoring is based on interview, clinical evaluation, nursing report, family report, and laboratory testing. The total score represents a sum of each item. The total score range is from 0 to 32. A cut-off score of 10 or greater has been proposed as indicating delirium. The higher score indicates greater severity of the delirium. As delirium improves, or resolves, an improvement in DRS score is expected.

4. The Delirium Index (DI) is intended as a measure of the severity of delirium based on observation from a nonpsychiatrist clinician, without additional information from family members, nursing staff, or medical charts. The DI includes seven domains: disorders of attention, thought, consciousness, orientation, memory, perception, and psychomotor activity. Each domain is scored from 0 (absent) to 3 (present and severe). The total score ranges from 0 to 21 and a higher score indicates greater severity.

The immediate concern for Earl is the acute change in his mental status, as well as emotional and behavioral changes, which all present an obvious deterioration from his baseline state. All possible reasons for acute mental status changes should be explored as soon as possible to prevent severe medical and psychiatric complications or even death.

Medical work-up revealed that Earl has a urinary tract infection (UTI) and constipation with the absence of bowel movement for the past four days. On interview the patient denied having any pain or burning sensation while passing urine. Also, he denied having abdominal pain or discomfort. His vital signs check revealed moderate tachycardia, with pulse 90 beats per minute, and his blood pressure was in a low range, fluctuating from 105/60 to 96/54. However, thorough observation of the patient revealed that he has had more frequent trips to the bathroom for the past few days, and his appetite is poor for the past week. His CBC showed moderate leukocytosis with WBC count 9.4, and his urinalysis was remarkable for WBC esterase 3+. Microscopic analysis revealed more than 30 WBC and 15 RBC, with presence of bacteria.

Earl scored 19 out of 32 on the DRS, which was highly indicative of delirium.

Most probably, Earl developed delirium due to multiple etiologies including UTI, chronic constipation, dehydration, and anticholinergic (diphenhydramine) and opioid-like analgesic medication (tramadol) side effects.

A person with delirium should be closely observed and monitored for safety because he is at high risk for falls with physical injuries and aggressive or threatening behavior toward himself and others due to acute mental status changes.

In Earl's case, the treatment of his general medical conditions (UTI, constipation, dehydration, and medication side effects) will probably improve or even resolve symptoms of delirium with return to baseline for his condition.

ETIOLOGY AND PATHOGENESIS

Elderly persons have increased risk for developing delirium, probably due to age-related changes in stress-regulating neurotransmitter and intracellular signal transduction systems of the brain. Severe medical conditions and other physiologic insults may impair blood-brain barrier permeability. For example, the "sick euthyroid syndrome" is a condition of dysregulation of thyrotropic feedback control where levels of T3 and/or T4 are at unusual levels, but the thyroid does not appear to be dysfunctional. This condition is often seen in starvation, critical illnesses, or patients in intensive care units, and increased activity of the hypothalamic-pituitary-adrenal axis plays an important role in development of delirium in geriatric persons.

There are several theories to explain the pathogenesis of delirium. Based on the neurotransmitter hypothesis, various neurotransmitter systems are involved in this condition through decreased oxidative metabolism in the brain, which causes acute cerebral dysfunction. Clinical manifestations of delirium may be related to excessive release of dopamine, norepinephrine, and glutamate, decreased cholinergic function, and dysregulation in gamma-aminobutyric acid and serotonergic activity. Other neurotransmitters, including histamine, somatostatin, and endorphins, are also involved in development of delirium.

Glucocorticoid hormones play an important role in mobilization of energy substrates for coping with stress. However, prolonged and excessive secretion of cortisol and other glucocorticoid hormones may have deleterious effects on memory and mood. Some studies demonstrated correlation between basal cortisol level and severity of delirium. Several reports describe cases of delirium in hypercortisolism associated with surgery, Cushing's syndrome, and dementia.

According to the inflammatory theory, the development of delirium may be explained by increased cerebral secretion of cytokines, which play an influential role in activity of different neurotransmitters. This increase might represent a reaction to various physical stresses.

There are multiple etiological factors for delirium, which may include:

1. Intracranial: epilepsy, head trauma, meningitis, encephalitis, neoplasm, cerebrovascular disorders.
2. Extracranial:
   a. Endocrine: hypoglycemia, hyperglycemia, pituitary, pancreatic, adrenal, parathyroid, thyroid hypofunction or hyperfunction.
   b. Pulmonary: hypoxia, pneumonia.
   c. Cardiovascular: hypotension, hypertension, cardiac failure, arrhythmias.
   d. Liver: hepatic encephalopathy.
   e. Kidney: uremic encephalopathy, urinary retention, or urinary tract infection.
   f. Vitamin deficiency: thiamine, nicotinic acid, B_{12}, folate.
   g. Dehydration: inadequate fluid intake, diuretic use, sweating.
   h. Major electrolyte disturbances of any cause.
   i. Systemic infections, intoxications, fever, sepsis.
   j. Constipation or fecal impaction.
   k. Pain, thirst, and hunger.
   l. Alcohol withdrawal/intoxication syndrome.
   m. Sensory impairments.
   n. Polypharmacy (and drug interactions), including over-the-counter medications.
   o. Drug reaction or intoxication: anticholinergic agents, sedative-hypnotic, alcohol, benzodiazepines, opioids, anticonvulsants, antihypertensive agents, antiparkinsonian agents, antipsychotic drugs, cardiac glycosides, cimetidine, ranitidine, clonidine, insulin, disulfiram, steroids, phenytoin, salicylates, and phencyclidine.

Major risk factors for delirium include advancing age, preexisting cognitive impairment/dementia, prior episodes of delirium, catatonia, life-threatening medical condition, hyponatremia, hypernatremia, visual impairment, hearing impairment and other sensory deprivation, use of indwelling catheter, use of physical restraints, use of multiple medications, return from hospitalization, surgical interventions, depression, and psychosis.

Risk factors for developing postsurgical delirium include general anesthesia, exposure to meperidine, exposure to benzodiazepines (benzodiazepines with longer half-life are more strongly associated with delirium than are short-acting preparations), previous history of delirium, alcohol-related medical problems, preoperative use of narcotic analgesics, and admission to neurosurgery. In elderly hospitalized patients, the risk of delirium decreased significantly after day 9. In elderly post–hip surgery patients, most cases of delirium occurred during post-operative days 2–5.

NATURAL COURSE WITHOUT TREATMENT

The onset of delirium is usually acute; however, it is not uncommon for some persons to demonstrate some subtle prodromal symptoms, including anxiety, restlessness, poor sleep, changes in appetite, or unreasonable fears several days before the full picture of delirium develops. In most circumstances, the duration of delirium is about one week, but symptoms of delirium usually correlate in length with the causally related medical condition. After prompt identification and treatment of the medical condition, which leads to removal of causative factors, the major symptoms of delirium usually resolve within three to seven days; however, some residual symptoms may continue for several weeks. In some cases, delirium persists for months and may be associated with permanent deterioration in cognitive function. There is a positive correlation between the age of the person and the duration of delirium symptoms.

Recent studies do not demonstrate that cognitively normal patients who suffer an episode of delirium have increased risk of dementia in the following years. However, in many cases delirium may unmask previously existing but well-compensated early dementia with mild brain dysfunction.

There are three major delirium subtypes:

- Hyperactive (agitated, hyperalert); recognized more often.
- Hypoactive (lethargic, hypoalert); underrecognized, especially in people over age 65.
- Mixed (includes alternating features of both).

The most common findings on mental status examination in persons with delirium are fluctuating level of consciousness (the literature describes the sensorium of persons with delirium as "waxing and waning"), confusion, disorientation, psychomotor activation (restlessness, agitation, combativeness) or psychomotor retardation, picking at clothes or sheets, falling asleep during the interview, mumbling or shouting speech, incoherent, illogical or disorganized thought process, paranoid or other delusional thoughts, perceptual abnormalities (illusions, visual, auditory, tactile, gustatory, olfactory hallucinations), irritability, anxiety, depression, euphoria, and sundowning in elderly demented persons, which is characterized by cognitive, behavioral, and emotional disturbances occurring in the late afternoon, evening, or at night.

Delirium is usually a reversible condition if early detection, reduction of risk factors, and proper management of underlying causative medical illness are provided to the person. Fast improvement or resolution of symptoms of delirium makes the prognosis of this acute medical condition more favorable. Unfortunately a state of delirium is not always reversible. One study presented that once delirium occurs, only about 4% of persons demonstrate full resolution of symptoms before discharge from the hospital, and it was not until six months after hospital discharge that an additional 40% of persons demonstrated full resolution of symptoms.

Undetected and untreated delirium is a deleterious, life-threatening condition that can have devastating consequences in the elderly persons with high rates of morbidity and mortality. Available evidence indicates that early detection, reduction of risk factors, and better management of this condition can decrease its morbidity rates.

EVIDENCE-BASED TREATMENT OPTIONS

Evidence-based practice guidelines include nonpharmacologic and pharmacologic treatments for the prevention and management of delirium. Elderly adults at high risk for delirium require interventions that eliminate or lessen the effects of potential risk factors.

Given the complexities of delirium syndrome, the multileveled approach in treatment of each person with delirium should be implemented.

According to the American Psychiatric Association Practice Guidelines for the treatment of delirium, after diagnosis and assessment of clinical status of the patient, a clinician should follow several principles of psychiatric and environmental management.

Psychiatric management: coordinate with other clinicians, including general medical and specialty clinicians; identify etiological factors and correct them; initiate acute interventions, including urgent symptomatic therapeutic interventions, increased observation and monitoring of the patient's general medical condition, vital signs, fluid intake and output, and oxygenation level; provide necessary disorder-specific treatments for reversible causes of delirium, for example, hypoglycemia, hypoxia or anoxia, hyperthermia, severe hypertension, alcohol or sedative withdrawal, Wernicke's encephalopathy, or anticholinergic delirium; monitor and ensure safety to prevent harm to self and others with least restrictive and effective measures; assess and monitor psychiatric status and adjust treatment strategies accordingly; establish and maintain alliances with delirious person and family; educate patient's family, nursing staff, and other medical clinicians regarding the illness; and provide postdelirium management to prevent recurrences.

Environmental and supportive management: environmental interventions to reduce factors that may exacerbate delirium, including changing lighting to cue day and night; reducing environmental overstimulation and understimulation; correcting visual and auditory impairments by eyeglasses or hearing aid, and have more familiar people and familiar objects available for the patient; structure and support the person by reorienting him or her to person, place, time, and circumstances, and reassuring the patient about the common but usually temporary and reversible nature of the condition; support and education for patient's families and friends about common but usually temporary and at least partly reversible nature of delirium; encourage patient's families and friends to reassure and reorient the patient by increasing staff time with the patient and by bringing in familiar objects to the patient.

Specific somatic interventions:

1. High-potency antipsychotic medications, such as haloperidol, are the treatment of choice for delirium. When using haloperidol to treat delirium, monitor ECG. If QTc intervals are greater than 450 msec, the clinician should consider a cardiology consult and medication discontinuation.
2. Newer antipsychotic medications, such as risperidone, olanzapine, and quetiapine have been used to treat delirium. However, randomized, double-blind, placebo-controlled trials for these medications in patients with delirium are not yet available.

Other somatic treatments for underlying medical condition:

1. Oxygen for hypoxia.
2. Fluids for dehydration.
3. Rapid cooling for hyperthermia.
4. Antihypertensive medications for hypertension.
5. Benzodiazepines and thiamine for alcohol withdrawal.
6. Thiamine for Wernicke's encephalopathy.
7. Thiamine followed by 5 ml of 50% glucose for hypoglycemia.
8. Cholinergic medications, such as physostigmine or donepezil for anticholinergic delirium.

Evidence grading for guidelines and recommendation in management of delirium:

A1. Evidence from well-designed meta-analysis or well-done systematic review with results that consistently support a specific action (e.g., assessment, intervention, or treatment): none.
A2. Evidence from one or more randomized controlled trials with consistent results: intervention strategies aimed at prevention for elderly persons at high risk is the most effective approach; prevention, early detection, and treatment of major postoperative complications; appropriate environmental stimuli and treatment of agitated delirium; promotion of nutrition; elimination of unnecessary medications/medication management; discontinuation of urinary catheter; early mobilization; appropriate use of glasses and hearing aids.

B1. Evidence from a high-quality evidence-based practice guideline: studies suggest that primary prevention of delirium is probably the most effective strategy for reducing the overall incidence of delirium of hospitalized medical/surgical patients. Postoperative patients who receive gabapentin for managing pain experience less delirium.

B2. Evidence from one or more quasi-experimental studies with consistent results: clinicians' implementation or adherence to multicomponent intervention strategies is essential to improve patient outcomes; for nurses and clinicians to appropriately intervene and treat delirium, education is an essential system-level intervention necessary to improve patient outcomes; guidance for nursing staff for providing care; a scheduled pain protocol; ambulation, whenever possible; staff education on delirium; clinician education on delirium, including identification of assessment, risk, and underlying causes of delirium; guidance for staff nurses regarding care; electrolyte balance; orientation to current reality, including modifications to the environment such as clocks and calendars; consistent caregivers; sleep promotion; educational intervention for nurses and physicians for increasing awareness and knowledge of delirium alone leads to improvement in outcomes; reorientation procedure such as calendars in the room, orientation techniques incorporated into routine care, provision of information of patient progress; prophylactic use of haloperidol has some effect on the duration and severity of delirium in postoperative patients who are at intermediate or high risk of developing delirium.

C1. Evidence from observational studies with consistent results (e.g., correlational, descriptive studies): guidelines without support systems (e.g., education and resources for implementation) fail to improve the process and outcomes of care in elderly persons at risk for the development of delirium; recommendation for referral to liaison psychiatry for further evaluation; multicomponent guideline including person assessment, the identification of risk factors and implementation of prevention and management strategies for delirium; atypical antipsychotic medications reduce the severity of delirium in elderly and/or postoperative persons.

C2. Inconsistent evidence from observational studies or controlled trials: music as a therapy using CD players.

D. Evidence from expert opinion, multiple case reports, or national consensus reports: family interaction with person focusing on use of eye contact, frequent touch, and verbal orientation to time, person, and place.

CLINICAL COURSE WITH MANAGEMENT AND TREATMENT

Treatment of delirium should be started by promptly identifying the possible cause. It is very important to address the potential cause and any precipitating factors for delirium in each person.

First, start with nonpharmacological interventions: provide psychological, physical, sensory, and environmental support; one-to-one nursing observation for safety reasons (if agitated or restless). Also, allow family members or regular sitter to stay with the patient. Provide frequent assurance and reorientation to person, place, and time (familiar pictures, calendars, clocks); keep lights on, avoid eye patches. Use relaxation strategies to reduce anxiety and assist with sleep.

Pharmacological intervention should include the treatment of the underlying medical condition.

Thorough review of the person's list of medications should be performed with possible discontinuation of medications that might significantly contribute to development and continuation of delirium. The most notorious medications that might cause delirium are anticholinergic agents, sedative-hypnotics, alcohol, benzodiazepines, opioids, anticonvulsants, and antihypertensive medications.

Use of benzodiazepines for agitation in delirium is not recommended in the vast majority of cases. It is mainly justified in combination with antipsychotic medications, or in cases of delirium caused by seizures or withdrawal from alcohol or sedative-hypnotics. High risk of sedation, worsening of cognition, and/or "paradoxical agitation" after benzodiazepine administration in elderly persons should be seriously considered.

Several important steps have been advised to prevent delirium in hospitalized elderly persons. These steps are as follows: avoid changes in person's surroundings; provide appropriate lighting; reorient person; facilitate visitation from family and friends; address dehydration and constipation; address hypoxia; actively evaluate for infection with subsequent treatment; avoid unnecessary catheterization (the presence of bladder catheter is a known risk factor for delirium); address immobility/encourage person to walk; assess for pain; review the list of medications; address poor nutrition; address sensory impairment; promote good sleep.

In Earl's case, the immediate treatment of UTI with antibiotic medications would be warranted. The choice of medication might be empirical with subsequent adjustment according to the results of culture and sensitivity.

Constipation should be treated with diet modification, laxatives, stool softeners, or enema. Tramadol (an opioid-like analgesic) should be tapered, and diphenhydramine (anticholinergic properties) should be discontinued due to propensity of both medications to induce or maintain delirium, as well as contribute to constipation.

If Earl is determined to be dehydrated, his fluid balance should be restored with IV fluids if needed. Frequent reevaluation of vital signs will be necessary to monitor Earl's medical condition.

To maintain Earl's safety, he should be hospitalized on a medical unit and closely observed for possible agitation, aggression, or threatening behavior. Also, he should be evaluated for fall risk with attempts to reduce possible risk factors, if possible.

Always evaluate elderly persons with delirium for imminent dangerousness to self or others. The person's agitation or physically aggressive/threatening behavior might be approached with behavioral modification first. Ensure the safety of the person and others.

Antipsychotic medications (haloperidol, risperidone, olanzapine, and quetiapine) which may be used for treatment of behavioral and severe emotional disturbances (severe anxiety, hallucinations, fear, delusions) when these symptoms cannot be controlled by nonpharmacological methods, and if they are causing significant distress to the persons or placing them or others at risk.

The long-term issues involve treatment of chronic medical conditions, abnormal behavior, mood disturbances, anxiety, as well as appropriate placement to address the patient's medical, personal, psychological, and social needs.

SYSTEMS-BASED PRACTICE ISSUES

Delirium primarily has a multifactorial etiology where the presence of predisposing factors and interaction with precipitating factors increases an elderly person's vulnerability to the development of delirium. The multifactorial nature of delirium has led to studies of hospitalized persons focusing on multiple interventions aimed at reducing and/or eliminating factors that can be changed.

Several process indicators have been suggested to achieve the most favorable outcome in persons with delirium. The Delirium Knowledge Assessment Test was proposed to assess knowledge that health care workers have regarding delirium. Assessing knowledge allows for better staff education about screening and assessment for delirium, which is very important for prevention and management of delirium.

Outcome indicators are those that might demonstrate improvement in cases of consistent use of the guidelines. Following major outcome measures to monitor in persons with delirium, they are as follows: incidence of delirium in elderly persons during hospitalization; presence of delirium at hospital discharge; use of physical or chemical restraints during hospitalization; and person safety incidents during episodes of delirium.

According to several studies, 32–60% of delirium cases were unrecognized by clinicians caring for elderly persons. The major barriers to recognition of delirium in medically ill persons are as follows: lack of awareness, misdiagnoses (hypoactive form of delirium, which is more common than hyperactive form, is frequently confused for depression, dementia, or senescence in hospitalized patients), and the fast pace and focus on technologies in hospital care (limited lime spent on patient observation, administration of cognitive assessment tests, and gathering history from family members regarding patient's cognitive changes).

There are several obstacles that make it difficult to manage aggressive behavior and frequent falls in delirious residents at Assisted Living Facilities (ALF) or nursing homes: lack of staff; lack of time; frequent staff shifts; many residents requiring assistance; highly stimulated environment; unrecognized pain, hunger, or other unmet needs; alienation from family; social isolation; decreased quality of care; and polypharmacy with increased risk of medication side effects.

Another major system issue is that the behavioral disturbance and diminished ability to communicate may obscure the underlying medical problems causing the delirium. Emergency personnel may triage the delirious person toward a psychiatric unit when he or she is better served on a medical unit where aggressive treatment may be needed.

LEGAL, ETHICAL, AND CULTURAL CHALLENGES

Establishing rapport with the patient who presents with symptoms of delirium and the patient's family is a very important first step. First, greet the person warmly by name, and then introduce yourself. If possible, shake hands with the patient. In case of the first contact with the person, explain your role and involvement in the patient's care. For a delirious person who has problems with attention, you might repeat this part of the introduction several times to improve rapport and communication. Show genuine interest in the person and willingness to help. When family members are in the room, be sure to acknowledge and greet each one of them, asking about each person's name and relationship to the patient. If the person is capable of comprehending, let him or her decide if family members should be present during your interview to respect their confidentiality. Always be attuned to the person's needs by helping him or her find a comfortable place. You have to attend to physical discomfort, pain, or anxiety at the beginning of the interaction with the elderly person to encourage the patient's trust and develop good rapport.

Consider differences in cultural background and preferences about interpersonal space. Make a good eye contact with your patient. Lighting also makes a difference, especially for delirious persons, because inadequate lighting may enhance their confusion and psychotic symptoms, including visual/auditory hallucinations, or paranoid thinking.

Spend some time on small talk to put the patient at ease. Give the patient and family your undivided attention.

In elderly persons with delirium, always discuss availability of family members to serve as authorized representatives or guardians, should the patient lack capacity for medical decisions, release of information, or advance directives.

Educate the family about the patient's condition, treatment plan, prognosis, possible course of the illness and future placement options. Involve the patient's family in informed decisions about treatment options, consent for the treatment, importance of release of information for communication with other medical providers, and surrogate decision making, if the patient lacks capacity for these decisions. Ask family members for willingness and suitability to serve as the patient's power of attorney or guardian.

Consent for release of information and treatment should be obtained from the patient's authorized representative or guardian as soon as possible, should he/she be found to have lack of capacity for informed treatment consent and release of information.

Earl was evaluated by his attending physician. Assessment of his capacity to give informed consent for treatment, release of information, and advance directives revealed that he lacks capacity to make rational decisions about his treatment due to inability to comprehend information provided and make reasonable choices. However, Earl needs immediate treatment for dehydration, UTI, and constipation, which are major contributing factors in delirium development in his case.

If the person lacks capacity to consent for treatment, you should define a substitute decision maker for him or her. An authorized representative (AR)/power of attorney (POA), or guardian will have to decide about treatment options for the particular person. Always obtain informed consent for treatment from person's AR/POA/guardian before treatment initiation! In majority of cases, close family members will be eligible to serve as the person's surrogate decision makers, who are to act in the best interests of the person in making decisions about treatment options.

Elements of informed consent for treatment are as follows:

1. Comprehensive information about medical condition, possible course of illness and prognosis, as well as treatment options, pros and cons of various treatment options, is provided by clinician to patient and/or person's family.
2. Assessment of decision-making capacity.
3. Decisions are made by person voluntarily.

The person should be informed about the nature and purpose of the evaluation. Make certain the person has an adequate opportunity to learn about his or her medical or psychiatric situation and options for the treatment.

To make decisions about treatment, the person has to demonstrate decision-making capacity, which includes:

1. Ability to comprehend information provided.
2. Communicate choices and preferences.
3. Appreciate significance of decisions about treatment.
4. Ability to reason.

Capacity to give consent for release of information includes the person's agreement to disclose information related to his or her diagnosis, treatment, prognosis, and discharge options to doctors, relatives, or other third parties. The person supposes to comprehend the purpose, possible benefits, and potential disadvantages of release of information.

Capacity to appoint surrogate decision maker/POA and make advance directives includes the person's ability to understand basic functions and responsibilities of surrogate decision maker/POA to make informed decisions about treatment options and extent in case if person lacks capacity for the same.

TERMS

Delirium: fluctuating disturbance of consciousness (reduced ability to focus, sustain, or shift attention), cognition (memory, orientation, or language deficit), thought process and content (tangentiality, incoherence, paranoid and other delusions), perception (illusions, hallucinations), affect (dysphoria, emotional lability, or anxiety), and behavior (agitation, lethargy) due to direct physiological consequences of a general medical condition, medication side effects, or substance intoxication or withdrawal which develops over a short period of time (usually hours to days). Also referred to as an "acute confusional state" or "acute brain syndrome."

REFERENCES AND RESOURCES

Cole MG, McCusker J. Improving the outcomes of delirium in older hospital inpatients. *Int Psychoger* 2009;21(4):613–15.

Fick DM, Agostini JV, Inouye SK. Delirium superimposed on dementia: a systematic review. *J Am Geriatr Soc* 2002;50:1723–32.

Kamholz B. Update on delirium: diagnosis, management, and pathophysiology. *Psych Ann* 2010;40(1):52–62.

Mittal V, Muralee S, Williamson D, McEnerney N, Thomas J, Cash M, ampi RR. Review: delirium in the elderly: a comprehensive review. *Am J Alz Dis* 2011;26(2):97–109.

Quick reference to the American Psychiatric Association practice guidelines for the treatment of psychiatric disorders, Compendium 2006. Arlington, VA: APA, 2006, 19–30.

Sadavoy J, Jarvik LF, Grossberg GT, Meyers BS. *Comprehensive Textbook of Geriatric Psychiatry* (3rd ed.). New York: W. W. Norton & Company, 2005, 525–44.

Aurora Borealis (2003). A romantic drama film directed by James C.E. Burke and starring Joshua Jackson, Donald Sutherland, Juliette Lewis, and Louise Fletcher. One of the main character, Ron (Donald Sutherland) claims that he has seen the Northern Lights (a.k.a. aurora borealis) from a balcony. Ron is fast deteriorating with Alzheimer's disease.

CHAPTER 5

First Psychotic Break

Yad Jabbarpour, M.D.

CLINICAL PRESENTATION

Chief complaint: "The dean wanted me to come here." . . . "There's the buzzing of everything, stars, quarks. The particles buzz. They're connected. (*long pause*) I really don't like to talk about it." . . . "Kali is killing me."

History of present illness: Samantha is a 21-year-old junior at a local university who presents with no previous formal psychiatric history. She is referred by the dean's office due to her professors' reports of worsening grades and her odd and withdrawn behavior in class. Samantha worries that "something is going on."

Samantha had been doing academically well through her sophomore year, achieving a GPA of 3.6 and had chosen to major in physics. During the first two years of college, she had been active with her interests in martial arts, especially jujitsu, and swimming. Although she does not describe herself as "social," she says she likes hanging out with her peers. The level of her friendships involves the following: she describes having a "friend" in physics with whom she has spoken about string theory and a person in her martial arts class with whom she walked to the local coffee shop after class a few times. Others describe her as "quiet" and "hard to figure out."

She describes problems beginning this past summer. She had decided to spend her summer break at home and initially had a job at a summer martial arts camp for kids. Her previous hometown jujitsu instructor had gotten her the job. However, with "the stress of all those yelling kids," she had to quit her employment. She says she became "nervous" in having to provide the instruction; especially with a large number of children.

After leaving the job, she spent most of her time at home. At her parents' house, she moved from her old bedroom into a basement room. She says the change gave her more privacy and a place to clear her mind. She adds that her little sister often had "loud music playing . . . or the radio," and that she wanted it "quieter." She spent time "daydreaming a lot and thinking." She became interested in Eastern religions, particularly Hinduism. She left the house rarely, usually for late-night walks. Her parents complained about her sleep routine with not awakening until 2 pm after staying up through much of the night. Her thoughts became focused on "an interconnectedness" between not only quantum mechanics and general relativity but also a "meta-inter-intra-connectedness to the Hindu gods and perhaps all religions." She wrote in her online journals about how "bosons and fermions and everything could be the bridges" to Hindu deities and other things beyond this dimension via "Kalions that destroy the barriers we see." She searched for mathematical physics formulas to support a "meta-string-uni-theory." She began to believe that physics formulas had some additional meaning that would allow a connection with the spiritual realm.

She remembers being cautious about telling her experiences to her parents. She feels disconnected from them and adds, "I sometimes wondered if they were not my *faux parenti*. You never know." She recalls her parents this past summer "nagging" her about fixing her hair and taking showers. Her mother had convinced her to go to the beauty salon the week prior to college starting back for the autumn semester. Samantha hated the shampoo, cut, and styling; not liking being touched physically; that the experience felt "just way too much . . . I had to walk out."

Upon returning to college, she was assigned a new roommate. They rarely spoke and only saw each other every two or three days. Samantha slept often on the sofa in the physics department library. She started the semester "okay" but said she had difficulty paying attention. She would find herself drifting into thoughts of her "meta-string-uni-theory" and began to experience a sense of her own connectedness with this universe yet a disconnection from classes, her professors, her family, and even her jujitsu. She adds that she feels as if she has been extricated from that reality, a reality "that felt it was that of another person on another planet . . . like Thomas Anderson, 'Neo,' in *The Matrix*."

Her preoccupation with the universal theory began to fill much of her thoughts and her writing. She began to journal profusely during the past five weeks on her pursuit of the theory. She shows some of her work on her computer tablet and shares some of her journaling (on paper). The initial journal entries from the summer are somewhat comprehensible. However, the entries that she shares from the past two weeks are rambling and not coherent with run-on, incomplete sentences and nearly illegible notes and formulas scribbled on the sides and other spaces of the papers.

Over the same time period of the past few weeks, her sleep became more erratic. She intermittently missed classes, as well as jujitsu, and she stopped swimming. Professors began noticing a change from a student who used to be "a little eccentric and shy but really smart" to "disheveled and odd." One faculty member even commented that when he saw her enter the classroom tardy to sit in the back of the room, "I thought she was a homeless lady." She had also become more withdrawn, intensely preoccupied, and ever more nervous. Although she spoke minimally to others, when she did converse, Samantha tended to overelaborate and was difficult to understand due to her speech being so jumbled.

She confides experiencing "signals" coming from the radio, which first started from her sister's music in the summer. She first thought these experiences were part of "the interconnectedness" until they began to bother her more. Samantha thought that one of the questions on an exam, which she was able to answer, was a direct result of having thought of that topic the evening before. These experiences trouble her.

The dean became involved because of faculty concerns about Samantha's odd behavior, decreasing academic efforts and falling grades.

She thought about seeking treatment but held off because she did not want to be seen as "one of those" who came to the college counseling center. She confided that she was also worried that she would be diagnosed with "schizophrenia." She worries that she will "end up like Aunt Beth," her mother's sister. Because of her perceived, family shame about Aunt Beth, Samantha shares her ambivalence about the clinician contacting her parents and sharing information about the diagnosis. Samantha recalls how Aunt Beth would go weeks and months worried that her phone was being tapped and that the walls were bugged. Samantha remembers when she was about eight years old and visited her Aunt Beth's home to find that the drywall had been sledgehammered. She recalls the mixed, stale smell in the room of construction, mildew, and urine. She describes the image of the gray-white gypsum plaster on the floor, an artifact of her aunt's search for the CIA's monitoring, and the pile of dirty dishes in the living room and kitchen. Aunt Beth had committed suicide two years later. As a teenager, Samantha wondered if she could get the illness but given her strengths and good grades believed she could "head it off." She had written a report on schizophrenia during her sophomore year in high school. She shares that some of her present journaling and sketching is her "mirror analyzing" to gain data to figure out whether she has schizophrenia.

She pulled out two sketches: One drawing she did late this summer (Figure 5.1), which she describes in the following manner: "She's stuck. Cornered and bound to the chair. In a room like in Sartre's *No Exit*. She's barbed-wire-bound to Second French Empire furniture. No way out. (*pause*) My parents kept on nagging."

The clinician asks, "I don't know a great deal about *No Exit*. Please tell me more about the play."

Samantha responds, "There are these three souls who are damned to Hell. Their torture for all eternity is to be stuck together. One room. They hate each other. (*pause*) There's no exit. (*pause*) It's like schizophrenia. Except with schizophrenia you're not bound to two people you hate. You're bound to yourself being schiz."

Her second sketch (Figure 5.2) was drawn about a week ago, late at night in some notes. She had cut out the image and placed it in her journal.

When asked her thoughts on the sketch, she responded, "Don't know. A witch or something, I guess. Harry Potter riddled and horcrux'ed. Trying to fly. There's a dark cloud. He can't get out. No parents to save him. (*pause*) They're fakes behind the *Mirror of Erised*. . . . There's a window. I don't know why he doesn't see it."

Figure 5.1 "She's stuck . . ."

Samantha has made attempts to self-diagnose her experiences. Using the Internet, she says she has reviewed her symptoms and wonders if she has "Asperger's, depression, or even OCD." She keeps coming back to schizophrenia but does not want the diagnosis: "I don't want to be a schizophrenic like Aunt Beth." In Samantha's explanation she approaches the analysis of her experiences with the scientific objectivity of a physicist, but would then be ripped out of the cool distance of the scientist into the utter fear that she has schizophrenia; that she was losing her mind; she was losing her entire self, disintegrating into a buzzing, resonance with the particles of the universe; to be reconstructed into the homeless lady with the shopping carts, the college student everyone fears, or Aunt Beth.

There is no history of alcohol or drug abuse. She has had beer a few times in her life. She smoked a joint at a physics party last spring, but it made her feel "weird." When asked to elaborate, she says she became "disconjoined from myself" and "scared." Looking back she wonders if that started her problems. She adds that she feels guilty for having smoked the marijuana.

Samantha discusses her distress with these experiences. Schoolwork has become overwhelming in several areas for her: concentrating, organizing, paying attention, wondering about things, getting sidetracked, overwhelmed by her

Figure 5.2 "A witch or something . . ."

thoughts about cosmology or about a preoccupation with Hinduism. She finds herself forgetting how to spell specific words; getting stuck on the spelling of *of*, explaining that "sometimes it just doesn't look right."

She worried over the past several weeks but denies feeling sad or depressed. Although she has experienced a diminished interest in her academics and jujitsu, this change she attributes to her shift in interest to her theories. She denies recurrent thoughts of death and does not acknowledge feeling worthless. Samantha denies symptoms of mania with no grandiosity, no inflated esteem, no decreased need for sleep, and no excessive involvement in pleasurable activities—for example, no buying sprees, no sexual indiscretions or foolish college endeavors. There is no pattern of obsessions otherwise or compulsions.

Psychiatric history: Samantha denies any history of seeing a mental health clinician. In the fifth grade, the public school recommended psychological evaluation due to her constricted emotions, paralysis at times in group learning, and her intense preoccupation with Harry Potter. Consideration for an individualized education program (IEP) was made. However, her parents elected to remove Samantha from the school. Later, in a private middle school, she would go the school counselor's office during lunch period about once a month. She said the counselor was nice, and the office gave her a quiet place to be if the library was locked. The counselor had an open-door policy but did not formally engage in meetings because neither Samantha nor her teachers voiced any concerns.

Family psychiatric history: Samantha's mother experienced several months of postpartum depression with her first two pregnancies but got through the experience with herbal medication and meditation. Her mother's younger sister, Aunt Beth, was diagnosed with schizophrenia at the age of 23 and died by suicide in her early forties. There was a maternal great-aunt who had been hospitalized with "a nervous breakdown" early in her life. The family did not know the specifics about that history because she had moved to a distant state and was estranged from the family.

There is otherwise no history of bipolar disorder, anxiety disorders, obsessive compulsive disorder (OCD), autism, Asperger's, other mental illnesses, or suicide within the family.

Medical history: Samantha has no medical issues. She had a tonsillectomy and adenoidectomy at eight years of age with no complications. Her last normal menstrual period was two weeks ago. She has not been sexually active and views herself as heterosexual. She denies a history of head injuries, seizures, having allergies, or taking any medications. She has never been hospitalized. She is a nonsmoker although she smoked a cigarette once when she was 13 "to see what it was like."

Developmental: Samantha is the youngest child from her biological parents with two older siblings: a brother, who is the eldest, and her sister, the middle child. The pregnancy was unplanned and described as normal except for her mother experiencing some hyperemesis gravidarum (morning sickness) during the first trimester and flu-like symptoms during her second trimester. Her father wanted a third child; however, her mother had mixed feelings about "bringing another child into the world." Her mother confided to the interviewing clinician that during the worse period of the morning sickness, she had fantasies of terminating the pregnancy. There was otherwise no exposure to toxins, alcohol, substances, or illnesses. Samantha reached her developmental milestones on time during her infancy and toddler years in regard to motor, physical, language, and cognitive development. Her social and emotional development was notable for not having many friends and seeming to be overly focused in her school-age years on science fiction and fantasy books. Her mother described Samantha's childhood temperament as "slow to warm up" and "withdrawn at times." Samantha described her childhood as "fine" and denied any history of neglect, abuse, or other trauma. Her physical development was within normal limits, reaching milestones on time.

Educational/occupational: Samantha has a high school education in which she performed academically well in a private school, graduating with honors. She was in a Montessori school during her preschool years through kindergarten and had five years in public school. During her first five years of elementary school, she was picked on and made fun of by peers for being "a nerd," which was attributed to her having "a different way of acting" and her preoccupation with Harry Potter. After two tries in private schools where she "didn't fit in," her parents found a small, private school known to be more adaptive to Samantha's learning style and manner of relating—a school also with peers who were more accepting of her differences. She took the SAT, scoring well with a perfect score in math. She was accepted to most colleges to which she applied and chose her university because of the reputation of the sciences. Although she thought about majoring in mathematics, she had some struggles from her perspective with linear algebra. She still received an A–. She chose physics as her major with hopes of continuing into graduate school and perhaps getting a job in the same city as her brother. She confides the she worries she will not be able to continue college or that she will be kicked out.

Family/social: Samantha's mother is an accountant and described as somewhat eccentric. She has been a vegan for three decades and enjoys science fiction and fantasy reading. Her father is a high school chemistry and physics teacher and enjoys listening to classical music. He also speaks French fluently and intermittently teaches French because the school lacks a teacher. Samantha does not recall her parents socializing much and claims they do not have many close confidants. Samantha's older brother is an engineer who lives with his wife approximately 30 minutes from the college. She speaks of fond childhood memories, playing Frisbee, running around the neighborhood, and playing computer games until late in the night with him. They text each other nearly every day. She had an "okay" childhood relationship with her sister, who is presently living at home with her parents after spending a year traveling out West after college. Her sister presently works in a coffee shop in her hometown.

Samantha has never had a boyfriend, although she says in high school she had a crush on a peer. The crush lasted the last three years of her time at high school. She only spoke to the boy a few times and was paralyzed by anxiety to talk with him.

She found interest in the martial arts in her late elementary school years and continued in jujitsu into her sophomore college year. She felt empowered and balanced by the practice. She swam on a swim team in middle school, but asked her parents if she could stop swimming on the team after several years because the meets were too loud. Up until this semester, she still found solace in swimming early in the morning when there were few people at the pool.

The influence of Aunt Beth's illness and death on the family story is notable. Beth had been hospitalized throughout much of her adult life, including three long hospitalizations in a state psychiatric facility. Although she had been a "prodigal child" and accepted to an Ivy League school, she dropped out of college in her first year. She maintained odd jobs, including janitorial work, but in time required supplemental government income to get by. In the last five years of her life, she was "always delusional" and also viewed as being depressed. She had been kicked out of her apartment, lost jobs, stopped her treatment, "hooked up with the wrong men," became homeless, and began drinking. After two unsuccessful suicide attempts, she died by hanging a day after her birthday. The family had mixed feelings of sadness, frustration, and anger toward Aunt Beth, in addition to feelings of guilt and helplessness for not being able to support her enough. Samantha's mother secretly wondered if she could have prevented the suicide "if only . . ." However, openly the family focuses frustration with Aunt Beth's last case manager and psychiatrist "for not doing enough." The family story entails themes of general distrust and devaluation of psychiatrists and medication.

The family is nondenominational. Samantha's father had been raised Catholic. Samantha would go to mass and service during holidays with her father when she was school age.

Legal: There is no legal history. Samantha says she was stopped once by the police in her hometown this summer when she was walking late at night and stopped a couple of times by campus security—once she had to show her college ID. She became fearful when they drove the car slowly beside her before asking if she was okay. She adds, "I guess they were just doing their job. I didn't like it." She neither has access to a weapon nor is interested in obtaining one.

Mental status exam: Samantha is a petite, thin, Caucasian female, wearing dirt-stained black jeans and a deep blue, cotton hooded sweatshirt over which she has a black winter coat. The sweatshirt hood is pulled over her head, and strands of unkempt brown hair are exposed. There does not appear to be significant psychomotor agitation although she fidgeted during the first third of the interview. There is no evidence for abnormal movements with no tremors, dyskinesias, or tics. She relates to the interviewer with ambivalence, seeming to want to answer questions fully, yet being cautious of what she shares and initially hesitant of even being in the office. Her eye contact is minimal, offering a few, rare glances followed by general gaze aversion. Her speech is idiosyncratic with a strained, soft voice; no phonic tics. The fluency and rhythm are normal; neither being slurred, pressured, unclear, aphasic, nor with disarticulation. She is fully alert. Consciousness is neither clouded, reduced, nor hyperaroused. She is oriented to time, place, self, and situation. Her immediate, recent, and remote memory are intact. She is able to spell "house" forward and backward with no errors although she paused during the exercise. Her affect is fundamentally blunted and flat at times, yet with a range into detached with periods of nervousness and caution. There are a few times when she smiles and then averts gaze. These events are not associated with any topic of the conversation or other environmental stimuli that would be mood congruent with humor. She describes her mood as "edgy like a sandpaper-corner Kali." She denies homicidal ideation and suicidal ideation. However, when asked if she has thoughts that life is worth living, she responds that her life might not have meaning if she has schizophrenia like her aunt.

Language choice is idiosyncratic with a poverty of content of thought; she speaks at great length yet in a vague and digressive manner that lacks content richness. She expressed rare neologisms—for example, describing a feeling in the past as being "disconjoined" and her parents as "faux parenti." Her thought processes are illogical and incoherent at times. She demonstrates some blocking when discussing the primary content of her thinking regarding her "uni-theory." She can be more coherent and fluid with her answers when asked direct, close-ended questions. She expressed intermittent loose associations, which were more pronounced during subject matter that was less reality-based. She has a convicted belief in her uni-theory for which she has made an extensive effort to prove. The thoughts entail religious themes. These beliefs are not reflective of cultural norms. She also has a marked tendency toward misidentification of her parents as impostors and a sense of disconnection with reality. Although she mentioned her similar experiences of the protagonist, Neo, from the science fiction film, *The Matrix*, in terms of depersonalization and disconnection from reality, it does not appear as if she is experiencing delusions of control, which she denies. She also denies delusions of persecution, jealousy, grandiosity, and erotomania. Ideas of reference are evidenced by her signals from the radio and the significance she inferred from the questions on an exam being a direct result of her prior thoughts. Concept formulation tends to be overly abstract. In responding to similarities—"How are the following items similar? A chair and a table"—she said, "furniture of four-legged stature connected by floor and air and person sitting at it and all." When asked for a possible interpretation of the proverb "two heads are better than one," she answered, "sometimes not . . . it would be confusing with there being so much information, neurons criss-crossing with quantum modulation into de Broglie waves. . . . Well, maybe better than one. It can't always be done alone." She is able to perform serial 7's with only rare blocking. Her intelligence is likely above average, including vocabulary and a good fund of knowledge with an awareness of science, campus events, and international topics. Her insight varies between wondering if she has a mental illness, including her distress about her symptoms, and a fixed focus on believing that her thoughts and experiences are real. Judgment is fair. Although she denies visual, olfactory, and tactile hallucinations, she refuses to discuss whether she is experiencing auditory hallucinations; yet she describes later that "the buzzing" involves hearing from outside her head, "almost like too many people talking." Thought content support ideas of reference from radios and other music devices. She discusses the experiences of depersonalization and derealization with her classes, peers, and family in comparison with "this other world" of understanding the universe. She reveals a belief that her parents might be impostors. Themes from a sketch (Figure 5.2) support such.

IMPAIRMENT IN FUNCTIONING

An important area of assessment for psychiatric disorders is assessment of impairment of functioning. Overdiagnosis can occur in situations of formulating a person's characteristics into a formal psychiatric diagnosis where there is no disorder, where no impairment or risk of impairment of functioning exists. Does a student's eccentricity forebode prodromal schizophrenia, or is this unconventional behavior a developmental expression of herself? For Samantha, impairment of functioning has begun and is at risk for further worsening. She has experienced a steady deterioration in her well-being across several domains, including educational functioning; her interpersonal relationships with family, peers, and professors; and influence on her maturation as a young adult and her own goals.

Developmental functioning is at risk. As young adults, persons continue to develop across several domains. Her academic advancements will influence her occupational functioning in the upcoming years, which will dovetail into social development and sense of self. A person's relationship and social skills learning continues through young adulthood. One can use Erik Erikson's Psychosocial Stages of Development as a paradigm to formulate a young adult's struggle of "intimacy versus isolation." Young adults develop skills for intimacy and loving relationships with others during this time. If barriers exist for this developmental trajectory, one can fail to gain these skills and experience loneliness and isolation. Being affected by a severe mental illness at this stage can theoretically affect further development in middle adulthood with "generativity versus stagnation," during which a person's sense of self can be stressed by struggles with relationships, occupational functioning, and a sense of accomplishment and usefulness in the world. Did Aunt Beth in her latter years experience the developmental tragedy of loneliness, isolation, and stagnation? How may Samantha's recovery be different?

Emotional regulation also continues to be developed and can be affected. These domains are all areas for secondary prevention of sequelae of schizophrenia and areas to strengthen; they can also be areas of resiliency for her recovery.

Samantha's impairment in functioning is substantial, dating back to her school-age years and worsening over the past few months and weeks. This young woman changed schools several times until finding the academic setting that was the best fit for her. She had difficulties with social interactions, and most recently a decrease in her academic function has been noted by her professors, engaging the dean's office at her college. She presently has a break in reality and requires assessment of safety issues. Her external supports are further affected by her delusional system as exemplified by a belief that her parents are impostors. The meaning of schizophrenia to Samantha and her family and the effect of Aunt Beth's illness and suicide will be important. This theme will likely have an effect on engagement in treatment, choice of treatment, trust of clinicians, and hope for recovery. On the other hand, she has several resiliency factors, which can be a foundation for her recovery. Her intelligence is likely above average. She seems to have an observing ego, the ability for insight and self-monitoring, self-direction, and determination. Her academic drive and interests in jujitsu and swimming can be strengths and evidence for her ability to sublimate. The family likely also has resiliency, given their functioning and caring.

Samantha's case highlights the importance of distinguishing distress from impairment. It is apparent to all who know her well—faculty, fellow students, and family—that Samantha's psychiatric symptoms grossly interfere with her ability to function in multiple roles in her life. Even for people who come into brief social contact with her, it is apparent after a few minutes that something is not quite right in her functioning. Her disorganization, intensity, and preoccupation with global concerns are all matters that Samantha makes no effort to conceal. She has little or no insight. Contrast this situation with the case in which the person is profoundly depressed, is aware of it, and is struggling to overcome the impediment to performance that the illness brings.

A person like Samantha may believe that she is functioning quite well. She may believe that others simply do not understand the compelling importance of the issues with which she is preoccupied.

In many ways it is this lack of insight that can be most crippling in individuals with psychosis. It frustrates them that others cannot grasp the importance of their concerns. The lack of insight impairs compliance with continued treatment and often leads to relapse.

DSM DIAGNOSIS

The clinician who interviewed Samantha is formulating the case in a biopsychosocialspiritual manner.

What biological factors might be predisposing, precipitating, and provoking the symptom complex that Samantha is experiencing? The genetic load includes a maternal aunt with schizophrenia and a suicide. Maternal postpartum depression is also a risk factor. One can only hypothesize the mental illness and genetic risk of such from the maternal great-aunt. Influenza during the pregnancy and possible nutrition are areas of possible influence. Although doubtful after one joint, drug use can provoke and even cause psychotic symptoms. An organic etiology should always be considered as a rule out in first-episode psychoses; however, there does not appear to be an obvious general medical condition causing her symptoms.

What are the psychosocial issues at play, influencing Samantha as a person, her presenting symptoms, and her family system? Not only is the genetic load of mental illnesses a weight of concern, so is the psychodynamic and family load of the meaning of Aunt Beth's illness and suicide. How might the family narrative of Aunt Beth influence the treatment? Other psychosocial dynamics might affect treatment: for example, the clinician hypothesizes that the mixed feelings her mother had during the pregnancy and consideration for abortion might have an unconscious influence on her connection with her daughter. How can the influence of Samantha's misidentification delusions involving her parents be mitigated so as to maximize the support that her parents may provide?

Resiliency factors also exist. These psychological strengths will be outlined in other sections of this chapter; they are strengths that could help this young adult through the critical period of first-episode psychosis and into a recovery that is meaningful to her.

Samantha appears to be seeking a spiritual understanding for her world, albeit presently through a delusional system. Spiritual focus and existential issues might be important to her as she moves into a maintenance phase of the illness.

For Samantha the differential diagnoses under DSM-5 are many, including Schizophreniform Disorder, Schizophrenia, Cannabis-Induced Psychotic Disorder, Psychotic Disorder Due to a General Medical Condition, and Schizotypal Personality Disorder. A Brief Psychotic Disorder is not likely due to the duration of symptoms. A provisional specifier is a consideration because of the uncertainty of actual recovery from the disturbance. If criteria for either schizophreniform disorder or attenuated psychosis syndrome are met but the person progresses over time with expression of symptoms, then the diagnosis would likely shift to schizophrenia. For Samantha, there does not appear to be a marked stressor coincidental with the onset of the symptoms. The duration of her primary symptoms had been just over six months. One could consider that going to college, changes in developmental role at that time, and the transitions between home and the academic community to be possible predisposing stressors. The clinician's working DSM diagnosis is schizophrenia, first episode, currently acute, with a provisional diagnosis of a premorbid and possible co-occurring schizotypal personality disorder. In DSM-5, the diagnostic criteria for schizophrenia are largely unchanged from the previous edition.

Overlap and comorbidity exists between the diagnoses of schizotypal personality disorder and schizophrenia. Premorbid onset of schizotypal personality disorder can be viewed as a correlated disorder, perhaps a slightly different phenotypic expression of the same underlying disease, or perhaps a component of the prodrome. Demonstration of a pervasive pattern of deficits, socially and interpersonally, occurs with the person having reduced capacity or discomfort with close relationships. Perceptual or cognitive distortions can occur with ideas of reference, magical thinking, body illusions, and beliefs that are eccentric and not consistent with subcultural norms. The person's affect may be blunted or inappropriate, as well as their manner of relating and appearance being viewed as peculiar. With a lack of close friends, relationships are isolated to first-degree relatives. Excessive social anxiety might occur—even with persons with whom familiarity exists. Paranoid fears and suspiciousness may infiltrate those relationships.

EPIDEMIOLOGY

Each year approximately 1 in 10,000 adults develops schizophrenia. The lifetime prevalence among adults occurs within the range of 0.5% to 1.5%. World Health Organization studies and other epidemiologic analyses assess that these rates are relatively stable across countries and cultures. In addition, rates have also been stable over the past half century of the studies. The age of onset is usually between the late teens to mid-thirties. Prodromal symptoms might start early and show themselves in childhood. High genetic load increases risk, especially in first-degree relatives.

DIFFERENTIAL DIAGNOSIS

A clinician must initially focus on answering several key questions to confirm or invalidate a hypothesis of the diagnosis of schizophrenia: are these phenomena psychotic or nonpsychotic? Are they an expression of a norm within a culture? Are the symptoms being driven by an underlying mood or anxiety disorder? Is this case an adult expression of a childhood-onset developmental disorder? Is there an organic etiology to the symptoms? What is the influence of substance use on precipitating or provoking the symptoms? Do psychotic defense mechanisms explain the presentation in a setting of a personality disorder? What are my own countertransference reactions to the person in front of me that might sway the diagnostic formulation?

The foundation for assessment is a comprehensive clinical evaluation, including all components of the history and a thorough mental status examination. Obtaining information from multiple sources is indispensable for providing insight to the person being served. Sources of information may include previous treating clinicians, records, other colleagues in the medical field, family members, teachers, and persons in the legal system. Confidentiality is important to respect, and releases of information are necessary. However, in an emergency confidentiality may be breached; in fact, obtaining input from these sources in an emergency may be compulsory even if the person with schizophrenia refuses release.

Medical assessment can be an essential step in the workup of a person for prodromal or first-episode schizophrenia, including a thorough medical history and physical. To rule out an organic cause, laboratory testing might be indicated. Brain imaging studies are a consideration if the medical evaluation shows evidence of an organic etiology.

Psychological testing may be a complementary tool to help evaluate the differential diagnosis or elaborate on the extent of the symptoms. Neuropsychological testing can aid in the assessment of functioning and especially cognitive impairments and strengths, which in turn can be used to guide rehabilitative efforts and qualify the person for supportive services. The Minnesota Multiphasic Personality Inventory might be an instrument to help elicit personality structure and overlying psychopathology. A Brief Psychotic Rating Scale can help as an outcome measure for positive symptoms of schizophrenia while the Positive and Negative Syndrome Scale can help for the same outcome monitoring but in both positive and negative symptom domains. The Yale-Brown Obsessive Compulsive Scale can help qualify and quantify obsessive-compulsive features if they exist in the presentation and if one is considering the diagnosis of obsessive compulsive disorder (OCD). Projective testing is not used often, yet can help elicit the depth and breadth of pathology, including thought content, emotional themes, and object relations in some circumstances. Projective testing is provided via consultation with psychology colleagues and may make use of Rorschach (ink blot) testing or thematic apperception tests.

Occupational therapy consultation can sometimes be helpful—for example, with formal independent living assessment—to evaluate a person's functional strengths and areas for potential rehabilitation.

ETIOLOGY AND PATHOGENESIS

Although the etiology for schizophrenia is not known, the causes are most likely multifactorial. Genetic loading increases predisposition for schizotypal traits, prodromal symptoms, and schizophrenia. First-degree biological relatives of persons with schizophrenia have an increased risk for developing the illness that is approximately 10 times greater than the general population. Twin studies support a higher concordance rate of 25% to 50% among monozygotic twins. However, the genetic heritability is complex and does not follow simple Mendelian inheritance. The twin study concordance rates show that genetics alone does not explain the etiology.

Environmental factors also increase risk and include complications during pregnancy and delivery, as well as abnormal fetal development and poor maternal nutrition. With most of the studies being retrospective, it is difficult to elicit causality. The association of maternal influenza during the pregnancy and the child's later schizophrenia has been difficult to assess fully; however, it does appear that first-trimester maternal exposure to influenza is a risk factor. The role of stress and substance in regard to inducing the onset of the illness or being a risk factor for relapse is also an area of focus.

Schizophrenia affects multiple neural pathways. Dopaminergic systems are involved and have been a foundation for medication research. The first antipsychotic medications and their efficacy and the psychotic-inducing effects of amphetamines provided the foundation for the "dopamine hypothesis" in the etiology of schizophrenia. However, the illness appears to be much more complex, involving multiple neurotransmitter systems and the gradual changes in the brain's neuroanatomy. Other monoamines are affected. Serotonin, glutamate, gamma-aminobutyric acid, and N-methyl-D-dspartate systems are implicated.

Neuropathology in schizophrenia is evidenced by decreased cortical volume, increased sizes of lateral and third ventricles, disproportionate loss of volume from the temporal lobe and hippocampus, and decreased thalamic volume. Microscopic changes also occur and range from smaller cortical and hippocampal neurons to disarray of hippocampal neurons and neuron loss. Such anatomic pathology coupled with the deterioration of cognitive function supports schizophrenia being viewed by some as not only a neurodevelopmental disorder but also a cognitive disorder with similarities to a dementing process. This formulation resonates with Emil Kraepelin's historic terminology of schizophrenia as dementia praecox.

NATURAL COURSE WITHOUT TREATMENT

Schizophrenia is diagnosed most often between the late teens and mid-thirties. Prodromal symptoms may start earlier and perhaps show themselves early in a person's childhood. Although not all persons who have a prodromal phenotype progress into a formal psychotic disorder, the symptoms can be associated with decreased function and increasing disability over time.

Over the past two decades interest in prodromal symptoms has grown to better elicit the criteria for the clinical high-risk state for psychoses. A recent meta-analysis of 23 studies of high risk people revealed that approximately 25% of those assessed as high risk develop a psychotic disorder over the follow-up time, which was on average a little over two years. Of those who developed a psychotic disorder, nearly three-fourths developed schizophrenia and about 10% developed psychoses associated with a mood disorder.

The clinical course of schizophrenia can vary based on the person's resiliency, supports, onset history, genetic load, comorbidity, and other factors. In general the median age of onset for schizophrenia is earlier for men, starting in the late teens to mid-twenties, and slightly later for women, on average not until the late twenties. Illness progression may be insidious with a lengthy and complex prodromal phase or abrupt with rapid onset of psychoses. Some longitudinal studies do exist and support that the course and outcome can be variable. Some persons can experience a recovery manifest by no interepisode, residual symptoms, whereas others experience a course of chronic symptoms, decreasing function, and high comorbidity for whom recovery is more of a challenge. Full lifetime remission does not appear to be common for this disorder. Poor prognostic indicators include insidious onset with a long prodromal phase, early onset, male sex, cognitive impairment, poor insight, anosognosia, high comorbidity, and prominent negative symptoms. A significant proportion of people with schizophrenia experience primary or persistent negative symptoms, which are robustly associated with low function and poor outcomes.

On the other hand, persons with acute and later age of onset, brief duration of the active phase, less cognitive impairment, good premorbid function, associated mood disturbance, absence of anosognosia, and more resiliency factors tend to display a better outcome. Women tend to do better than men. Early treatment and treatment adherence, perhaps with both medications and psychosocial treatments, might provide for a better prognosis. For some, the lifetime course may be manifest by a plateauing of symptoms, relapses, and functioning, whereas for others the course may be more challenging and treacherous. Persons with schizophrenia have high rates of comorbid alcohol and substance use disorders, nearly five times greater than the general population. Suicide rates are also significantly higher for persons with schizophrenia. Risk factors for clinicians to consider when assessing suicide risk in persons with schizophrenia include a history of suicide attempts, paranoid or undifferentiated symptom predominance, comorbid depressive states, command hallucinations (especially those to kill oneself), severe agitation and panic, comorbid substance use, being less than 40 years old, and having more than a high school education. A clinician can formulate the last two risk factors as being potential loss issues given that a person with schizophrenia early in life and with upper-level education might experience a greater sense of loss if there is a deterioration in function, drop in socioeconomic level, and a sense of their and their family's hopes and dreams not being realized. Especially in these situations, the hope of recovery and the need for support can be vital.

The link between violence and mental disorders has received increased attention over recent years, including the focus for college settings. The predictors of violence in this population tend to be associated with a history of violence, comorbid substance use, younger age, male sex, juvenile detention, and perception of hidden threats or delusions of control. Aggression ideation, threat, intent, and means, including access to weapons, should be assessed. For persons who are treated and have no comorbid substance abuse and no history of violence, the chance of violence over three years is the same as that for any other person in the general population. Of note, negative symptoms of schizophrenia might be a risk reduction factor. Although media attention has tended to focus on the risk of persons with schizophrenia victimizing others, a greater proportion of the victimization is toward persons with severe mental illnesses. Twenty-five percent of the people in the United States living with mental illness suffer a violent crime—for example, rape/sexual assault, robbery, assault, murder—in comparison with 3% of the general population.

What happens when persons with first- or early episode schizophrenia stop their medication? One study of successfully treated persons at eight months of treatment compared two randomized situations: continuation of medication versus discontinuation of medication. Persons randomized to the continuation group had a significant less likelihood of relapse than the discontinuation group: 21% versus 43%. In fact, for the persons who had medications stopped, only 20% were relapse-free for a median period of 15 months. Another study of medication withdrawal showed the following: 96% of persons experienced an exacerbation of psychotic symptoms or a relapse. Among individuals experiencing an exacerbation or relapse, eight months was the median time to relapse.

EVIDENCE-BASED TREATMENT OPTIONS

Evidence-based and promising best practices exist for schizophrenia, including first-episode psychoses. In regard to prodromal syndromes for schizophrenia, a foundation of evidence is being published to help guide the clinical assessment, outline the diagnostic criteria, and offer treatment options for those who do not meet the criteria for schizophrenia but who are at risk. A recent randomized controlled trial of interventions for young people at ultra-high risk of psychosis evaluated the effectiveness of various interventions: cognitive therapy plus low-dose risperidone, cognitive therapy alone, or supportive therapy plus placebo. This 12-month outcome study concluded that first-line antipsychotic medication is not advised as an initial approach and that initially providing supportive therapy is the present recommendation. Future studies will help elicit the best models of selective prevention for attenuated psychosis syndrome.

For working with a person with first-episode psychoses, the first step for a clinician is to assess safety. Safety risk assessment focuses include suicide risk assessment, aggression risk assessment, and evaluation of the person's ability to maintain adequate activities and function of daily living in a safe environment. Commitment criteria vary by state but usually address the following questions: is the person at immediate risk to harm self or others due to a mental illness? Is there a substantial likelihood that due to a mental illness the person will suffer serious harm due to lack of capacity to provide for his basic human needs—that is, is gravely disabled? A person with first-episode and especially multi-episode schizophrenia can be challenged by meeting their basic needs like food, clothing, and shelter. Homelessness is a very real danger for persons with schizophrenia and increases a person's risk for victimization. Provision of supportive housing can be a best practice to improve outcomes. The safety assessment will help answer the question, does this person require emergent psychiatric hospitalization, a crisis bed, or increased supports and good outpatient follow-up in the community? One would need to assess the appropriate setting for treatment in the least restrictive setting based on the safety assessment.

The clinician will need to coordinate ruling out a medical etiology for the symptoms of first-episode psychoses. A medical history, a thorough physical exam, including a comprehensive neurologic component, and judicious use of laboratory and clinically indicated radiologic studies can be helpful. In addition, assessment for substance use is standard of practice. Substance use can be a cause of the psychoses, can be a trigger for the expression of the illness in at risk persons, and can be a co-occurring problem—all of which may require treatment.

The therapeutic relationship is the foundation for all treatments. Engagement begins at first contact. A balanced, empathetic and professional approach is important. A clinician's style of being overly sympathetic or warm may push a person away from treatment, whereas being overly quiet and wary with a cold questioning style may trigger increased paranoia. Engagement can be even more challenging if the clinician is worrying about his or her own safety.

Assessing and respecting the wishes of the person served is key but not always easy. Clinicians are often trained to treat. However, persons with schizophrenia are frequently not ready to be treated. The Prochaska and DiClemente Stages of Change Model can be helpful in this setting. The person presenting for the first time with symptoms of schizophrenia might be in a precontemplative stage of change and does not intend to be diagnosed or treated. Anosognosia with poor insight may be an exacerbating factor that keeps the person from considering that there is a problem. Some patients presenting might be at a contemplative stage of change in which they are ambivalent: ambivalent about telling the clinician about the delusions and voices, ambivalent about engaging family, ambivalent about the diagnosis, ambivalent about treatment, and even ambivalent about the clinician. Motivational interviewing techniques and motivational enhancement can be helpful in working with the person as he or she transitions into preparation for treatment and the components of a treatment plan. Stigma for the person with symptoms and for the family has also been shown to be a significant barrier between untreated illness and a person's recovery.

A recovery-based approach is built on the ethical principle of autonomy. The foundation for treatment is the person's goals on which the clinician and the person with the illness build a treatment plan. The fundamental elements of a recovery-based program includes a self-direction, person-centered, and strength-based approach, with an understanding that the path is holistic, nonlinear, and peer-supported for which individuals have personal empowerment and responsibility.

Medication is an evidence-based, key component of treatment of the acute phase and maintenance phase of the illness. The level of evidence is high with many well-controlled studies. A shared decision-making approach with psychoeducation is a promising practice to engage the patient with his or her wishes for pharmacologic treatments. Informed consent for treatment is fundamental. Antipsychotic medications are the treatment of choice for acute positive symptoms. For first-episode schizophrenia, antipsychotic medications other than clozapine and olanzapine are recommended. Antipsychotic dosing tends to be lower than for persons with chronic schizophrenia experiencing relapses. Early treatment has been shown to be associated with better symptom reduction. There does not appear to be significant differences between first general antipsychotics and second generation with the choice being based on individual preference, side effect profile, relevant medical history, and risk. Therapeutic dosing and a course of treatment for four to six weeks is important. One cannot determine that a person has failed a trial with inadequate dose and of short duration—for example, only two weeks—unless an adverse drug reaction stops the trial. Monitoring for side effects and complications focus on several areas—for example, movement disorders (extrapyramidal/Parkinsonian side effects, acute dystonias/dyskinesias, tardive dyskinesia, neuroleptic malignant syndrome [NMS]) and metabolic syndrome (weight gain, body mass index, fasting blood sugars, lipid profile). For some antipsychotics special monitoring may be required—for example, cardiac monitoring with EKG. Although clozapine is an evidence-based treatment for strong consideration for treatment-resistant schizophrenia (especially for those who present with persistent symptoms of hostility, high risk for suicide, and in situations with a history of NMS), persistent dystonias or tardive dyskinesia—given the adverse side effect profile—clozapine should not be considered until a person has failed at least two good trials on other antipsychotics. Although antipsychotic medications are indicated for the treatment of positive symptoms, the level of current evidence is insufficient to support pharmacologic treatments for negative or cognitive symptoms.

Agitation can be debilitating for persons in an acute phase of the illness. Acute agitation can also be associated increased risk for aggression and self-harm. Several double-blind, randomly controlled studies support the effectiveness of oral or intramuscular antipsychotic medications alone or in combination with a rapid-acting benzodiazepine (e.g., lorazepam) for acute agitation. Although there is no current evidence to support the recommendation for the use of benzodiazepines for treating the symptoms of anxiety, depression, or hostility in people with schizophrenia, clinical practice supports its use. Formal research in this area would be helpful.

In the maintenance phase, antipsychotic medication dosing may be decreased to a lower, therapeutic range. The clinician's and the person's monitoring for relapse symptoms is important. Medication adherence can also be a significant problem. The CATIE Study and others have shown the reality that many persons with schizophrenia have difficulty remaining on their antipsychotic medication. In addition, maintaining medication treatment over months and even years can be a struggle—especially if insight is poor and the person is experiencing dry mouth, constipation, sluggish thinking, weight gain, or sexual dysfunction. Although these medications have benefit, they can also have challenging side effects for people. Long-acting forms of medication—haloperidol decanoate, prolixin decanoate, risperidone or paliperidone long-acting—can help with medication adherence. Psychoeducation alone usually does not improve medication adherence. Best practice strategies that help people with schizophrenia with medication adherence include the following: daily dosing of medications instead of three-times-a-day regimens, providing concrete instructions, helping the person navigate calling the doctor and pharmacist should they run out of medications, shared decision making, adjusting medication dosing and complementing treatment with cognitive behavioral therapy (CBT), medication reminder systems, self-monitoring tools, cues, and reinforcements. Problems with adherence will recur. Booster sessions may be needed to reinforce and consolidate a person's successes with treatment acceptance.

Comorbidity problems—depression, agitation, substance use, nicotine dependence, metabolic syndrome, medical problems, homelessness, suicidality—can seriously affect people with schizophrenia over their lifetimes with worsened disability, morbidity, and mortality.

Persons with schizophrenia experience high comorbidity with alcohol and substance use disorders. In turn, these disorders further increase risk of disability. Three decades of research informs the best practice of screening, assessing, and treating co-occurring alcohol and substance use disorder. The opportunity for secondary prevention exists for the at-risk population of persons with first- or early episode schizophrenia who do not carry the comorbid diagnosis. Key components of an evidence-informed treatment include the following: motivational enhancement to help persons through the stages of change; CBT interventions that help with treatment engagement, coping skills training, and relapse prevention. A system of care that is evidence-based includes Assertive Community Treatment (ACT).

Persons with schizophrenia have a high rate of nicotine dependence, as well as the medical morbidity and mortality associated with tobacco use. For short-term abstinence, best practices include offering buproprion sustained release with or without nicotine replacement. Although the current evidence base does not exist for tobacco cessation education and support groups, consensus supports its consideration.

Obesity and associated metabolic syndrome has a higher risk ratio with persons with schizophrenia. Many of the medications prescribed are associated with weight gain and metabolic syndrome. Metabolic syndrome is a grouping of risk factors, which includes increased waist circumference, elevated triglyceride level, low HDL cholesterol, hypertension, and high fasting blood sugar. People with even a subset of these conditions meeting the criteria for metabolic syndrome have been show to have an increased risk for coronary artery disease, type II diabetes, and stroke. If weight gain or metabolic syndrome are considered an adverse drug event, changes in the medication regimen and alternative pharmacologic treatments should be offered for consideration. Evidence-based psychosocial weight loss interventions also exist and should be of at least three months in duration. Even modest weight loss has been associated with benefits in cardiovascular function with behavioral and/or education programs. Evidence-based weight management interventions for persons with schizophrenia tend to include psychoeducation with a focus on nutritional counseling, caloric expenditure monitoring, and portion control. Other psychosocial interventions involve motivational enhancement, self-management, goal setting, regular weigh-ins, self-monitoring of daily food and activities, and dietary and physical exercise modifications.

Persons with schizophrenia or prodromal schizophrenia may have skills deficits due to their underlying disorder or the effect of their symptoms on their development as a person. Improving social skills and even maintaining activities of daily living can have meaning to a person. Clinicians can offer various techniques of instruction, modeling, corrective feedback, rehearsal, and ongoing social reinforcement to help a person gain, practice, and maintain skills. Gains can occur in social skills, activities of daily living, work setting interpersonal skills, and even drug refusal skills. Although substantial evidence supports that persons with schizophrenia who lack these everyday skills can gain them and that community function improves, the evidence base ranges from weak to mixed to support the generalization of benefits to relapse prevention and decrease of general psychopathology.

Addressing interpersonal problems can be important to support a person's recovery. Focuses might include concretely helping a person with relationship skills. Role-playing can help a person gain and practice communication skills to negotiate a phone call, asking someone on a date, or asking a professor or a boss for an extension on a project. Symptom intrusion can affect relationships and function. Skills building and CBT can target this problem.

Family involvement and family intervention is a best practice important to offer. Schizophrenia not only affects the identified patient but touches all persons in the family system. Persons with schizophrenia often not only have contact with their family members but rely on them for support and love. Family members can be challenged with the role changes and in coping with a loved one with an illness that can affect safety. Families may also need to manage their hopes and dreams for the person. Family interventions have been shown to improve the person's functioning, decrease relapse rates, and decrease family burden. Key components of family intervention include illness education, crisis intervention planning, and support and training strategies for coping with the effect of the illness and its sequelae. Evidence-based family interventions are often at least nine months in duration and occur within highly structured programs. From the evidence base, brief interventions and superficial involvement does not appear to have much effect on outcomes.

Cognitive behaviorally oriented psychotherapy is a best practice treatment to offer to persons with schizophrenia to help with a range of challenges from medication adherence to negative symptoms to relapse prevention. Persons with schizophrenia can have residual symptoms that affect their functioning even with optimal pharmacologic treatment. In addition, a person might decide to work with the psychiatrist for lower doses of medication and coping with the interepisode symptoms via alternative, adjunct treatments. CBT can help a person cope with a range of problem areas associated with schizophrenia: positive symptoms, cognitive problems, negative symptoms, interpersonal problems, treatment adherence, mindfulness, relapse prevention, and maintaining treatment gains. For example, CBT can help target cognitive problems associated with formal thought disorders: pseudo-philosophical thinking in which a person discusses esoteric religions, science fiction, or the vital importance of mathematical formulas and pi, can affect a person's ability to interact with others. Sometimes these thoughts can fulfill a person's existential need to find meaning in life, which is especially developmentally poignant for young adults. Therapists can help the person develop methods to address these issues and find other areas to find meaning. Wooliness of thoughts, talking past the point, loosening of associations, and tangential thoughts with schizophrenia can affect a person's flow of thought. CBT can help the person learn techniques to improve communication skills, identify the links between ideas, and help the person self-identify and monitor automatic thoughts or obsessive images that precede problematic thinking or even thought blocking. Several controlled studies, including a meta-analysis, have established the benefit of CBT to reduce positive symptoms, including delusions and hallucinations, as well as negative symptoms, social functioning, and overall symptom load. However, a few other studies have not confirmed such benefits, including a paucity of research in the area of CBT for first-episode psychoses. Although cognitive remediation, which focuses on improving attention, reasoning, and memory, is offered at times for persons with schizophrenia, current rigorous clinical trials do not exist for this psychosocial intervention.

Work is part of a complete and meaningful life. Schizophrenia can steal a person's ability to have a livelihood. Supported employment is an evidence-based psychosocial intervention that can help a person with schizophrenia who wants employment. Randomly controlled studies have consistently demonstrated the effectiveness of supported employment to improve competitive employment with higher wages earned and hours worked in comparison with traditional vocational services. For many, however, supported employment is not an option due to the lack of funding for this evidence-based treatment. Studies have supported efficacy in various cultures and different countries. Key components of effective supported employment include community-based, competitive jobs; rapid job search instead of prolonged pre-employment preparation; ongoing vocational support; and the integration of mental health services with employment. The person's choice in job opportunities is respected. Although the outcomes of long-term job retention and financial self-sufficiency do not have a strong evidence base, supported employment can improve function, self-esteem, and decrease hospitalization rates.

Fidelity of psychosocial treatments with the evidence-based models is crucial for success. Mental health systems, however, are sometimes balancing the need to adapt programs to their settings, the cultures of persons they serve, and funding issues. However, outcomes can be affected by not maintaining fidelity with evidence-based models.

Involvement of "consumers" in the development, delivery, and provision of mental health services is becoming more common in practice. Peer support and peer-delivered services are a pillar of a recovery-oriented mental health system. Peer support specialists can have a key role in a person's treatment team. A peer who has experienced a mental illness can support a person with schizophrenia in the process of recovery in a way that a clinician or even a family member cannot. They can also help the person cope with the illness, manage the everyday struggles, bolster hope, and help the person navigate a complicated mental health system. Wellness recovery action plans are an example of a CBT-informed approach to use peers and others in a supportive manner to help the person develop their own plan for recovery and crisis prevention. However, current literature is lacking to support peer interventions as an evidence-based strategy.

Support groups, including the National Alliance on Mental Illness and Mental Health America, can provide support for persons with schizophrenia and their family members. Such groups provide a voice of advocacy and education. In addition, the groups can provide a sense of connection with others as persons progress in their recovery. Meetings and conferences are a format in which psychoeducation occurs and evidence-based practices are shared by experts in the field.

CLINICAL COURSE WITH MANAGEMENT AND TREATMENT

In the situation for Samantha, two initial focuses come to mind: (1) How does the clinician engage Samantha with the goal of building a therapeutic relationship? (2) How does the clinician assess safety? There does not appear to be an

FIRST PSYCHOTIC BREAK

immediate safety issue in regard to her risk of harm to herself or others in the near future. However, she has several risk factors for suicide, including agitation, poor sleep, perceived risk of loss, the meaning of schizophrenia, perceived loss of supports with the potential Capgras-like delusion that her parents are impostors, and the family history of suicide of her Aunt Beth. The setting of treatment will be informed by the safety assessment. If she is assessed as being at higher risk for harm to herself or others, inpatient treatment or perhaps a crisis bed might be of help. Universities sometimes have beds available if hospitalization is not required. Given that she does not have support in the college community, one might consider this option of treatment in her hometown setting with the support of her parents. A medical withdrawal from the semester is considered, weighing the risks and benefits. However, she chooses to remain at the college setting for a few days in the college infirmary. She was evaluated by a physician, and there was no evidence for a medical etiology for her symptoms. Lab testing and physical examination were all normal.

What is the clinician's role with the college? In this case, the dean was not concerned about a threat to the campus and did not want an official report. If this was the case, the limits of confidentiality and the role of the clinician would need to be defined—for example, the role of the clinician as consultant to the dean versus treating clinician—and would need to be communicated to Samantha.

Initially Samantha is hesitant to allow contact with her parents. However, with an explanation that she could control the limits of confidentiality in a non-emergency and revoke the release at any time, she agreed to allow communication with her parents as long as the "diagnosis of schizophrenia" was not released to them. She also provides releases of information to contact her childhood pediatrician, professors, the dean's office, and her brother and his wife. A phone call is made with her parents. They provide history over the phone and decide to make the 11-hour trip to the college the next day. The brother also visits.

Samantha has capacity to make decisions regarding release of information and informed consent for treatment. She is initially hesitant about a medication, becoming overly focused on the diagnosis. Samantha wants to know "100%" what the diagnosis is. The clinician does not provide an "absolute, 100%" diagnosis but does review the working diagnosis.

With informed consent for treatment, she begins medication treatment. An antipsychotic medication, risperidone, is started at a dose of 2 mg at night. Risperidone is chosen because of its lack of side effects at doses lower than 6 mg a day. She does not want an overly sedating medication and is worried about metabolic syndrome. She is also aware that it is available by long-acting injection, which might be less stigmatizing when she returns to a dormitory.

Her first night she experiences sleep problems; trazodone 25 mg at night is prescribed, which helps her partially. Trazodone is an antidepressant, which at low doses is a useful agent to help with sleep without risk of addiction. Another 25 mg is provided. The total of 50 mg trazodone helps her sleep a total of five hours that night. The clinician meets with her the next morning, listening to her experiences. After the first night Samantha expresses a fear of her situation and an overwhelming sense of panic. She asks for something to help. Relaxation techniques are tried, but she becomes even more disorganized. A 1 mg dose of lorazepam is offered and helps quell her severe agitation and sense of panic. She naps for a few hours and awakens, more able to discuss her wishes to return home. A medical leave of absence is offered for consideration. Samantha wants the leave. With release, contact is made with the dean's office to coordinate the leave. The parents arrive. A family meeting occurs. A crisis and support plan is developed to help support them through the transition of the next several days. Follow-up plans are made in her hometown with a clinician for the day after their day of travel. Hand-off communication occurs from the clinician.

After eight weeks the clinician receives a phone call from Samantha and her parents, asking for a follow-up appointment. Samantha and the family have made plans for her to move back to the area to live with her brother and her sister-in-law. Her medication had been increased to 6 mg a day. She has experienced a significant decrease in positive symptoms of schizophrenia, which she rates presently as a 1/10 in comparison with a 10/10 when she was first seen. She complains about being most debilitated by feeling her mind being extremely slowed and problematic daytime somnolence. The clinician focuses on reconnecting and supporting the therapeutic relationship and uses motivational enhancement techniques. Hearing Samantha's concerns about side effects, the clinician works with her: risperidone is changed to nighttime dosing.

Over the weeks of treatment and ongoing assessment, the clinician and Samantha work together. Initially the clinician assesses her as in a precontemplative stage with continued ambivalence about the diagnosis and treatment. Shared decision making helps analyze the benefits and risks of various treatments. She pieces apart the issues associated with Aunt Beth's life in comparison with the choices she wants to make for her own future. Further involvement of her brother occurs. Although she remains hesitant about involvement of her parents, the clinician maintains contact with them. Family-based services are provided.

Samantha and the clinician develop a relapse plan and monitor the risk factors for relapse. They are able to decrease the dose of risperidone to 4 mg at night. She communicates her wish to return to college at the beginning of the next academic year. The clinician, Samantha, and the family work toward this goal and begin a proposal, which includes communication with the dean's office. They, too, are supportive of the plan and ask to be kept involved in Samantha's timeline and return.

Treatment focuses also include skills building with a goal toward return to college and the ability to socialize and interact with others. Samantha excels at the CBT homework and finds her ability to analyze a strength not only for skills building and journal homework but also for mindfulness.

By the summer, Samantha has obtained a job at a local café. She finds her best niche as a barista. She will restart school with plans to take a half-load academically. She has reconnected with jujitsu and its provision of empowerment and balance for her. She also started swimming again. She swims in the early mornings at an outdoor pool, noting the rhythm between the sounds above water and the silence underneath the surface.

SYSTEMS-BASED PRACTICE ISSUES

Treatment for schizophrenia will often entail a system-based approach with an interdisciplinary team of clinicians, which also includes the person with schizophrenia and may also involve family members, medical colleagues, peer-support specialists, academic professionals and even the legal system. The system, a complex network of public, private, academic, and volunteer organizations, has been identified as being fragmented and underfunded over the decades. These barriers and gaps in care make provision and navigation of services challenging for both clinicians and persons with schizophrenia. Teamwork, flexibility, creativity, and communication are crucial elements to support high-quality and safe services. Community mental health systems are the backbone for the provision of systems of care for persons with schizophrenia.

For children, adolescents, and young adults with first-episode psychoses, involvement of the educational system is an important dimension for a person's treatment plan. The clinician may liaise with the school system as an advocate for the student to help in provision of education services, including the development of an individualized education plan. In higher education settings, professors and deans may be involved in supporting assessment and treatment. Students are often self-referrals to treatment. If a college deans refers a student for mental health services, it is typically without requiring an "official report." In high-risk circumstances, more detailed information may be requested. Following the shooting tragedy at Virginia Tech in April 2007, there is now better collaboration between different campus agencies; as well as the emergence of Threat Assessment Teams on many campuses. Students may sometimes be escorted by academic staff to a college mental clinic for same-day triage appointments or urgent mental health consultations if there are acute mental health concerns. Sometimes, a dean's office requires documentation confirming that the student has a psychiatric disorder and is being seen at the counseling service on an ongoing basis as a condition for academic allowances, medical withdrawals, or academic enrollment.

High-risk and high-profile students on campuses are often discussed at a multidisciplinary conference attended by deans, academic staff, campus police, case managers, and representatives from a university counseling service. The office of the dean of students has the authority to mandate treatment for seriously disturbed students and can suspend students who refuse voluntary treatment. In crisis situations, confidentiality can be breached. Otherwise, the deans request that students sign a release of information form to permit the exchange of information with treatment providers.

ACT is a system-based service of care with a long history of evidence support-ing its efficacy. Although ACT programs would be less of a consideration for per-sons with first-episode psychoses, ACT should be offered to persons with high rates of psychiatric hospitalization and homelessness.

Assisted outpatient treatment (AOT), also known as involuntary outpatient commitment or mandatory outpatient treatment, is allowed by law in many states and supported somewhat by state funding. This system approach has been best studied in New York under "Kendra's Law" and has been shown to improve treatment adherence, decrease hospitalization rates, decrease homelessness, decrease victimization, reduce caregiver stress, and reduce violence, arrests and incarcerations. Arguments against AOT include the loss of self-choice in the community and that the benefits are related less to the commitment and more to the provision of adequate funding for services.

Pilot projects and initial studies are presently showing medical homes and behavioral health homes as an approach to serve persons with complex system needs.

LEGAL, ETHICAL, AND CULTURAL CHALLENGES

The clinician may have to contend with various legal issues when working with a person with schizophrenia: confidentiality, assessment for capacity, pursuit of a surrogate decision maker, informed consent, advance directives, commitment, forced medications, restraint use, Tarasoff duty to warn, and other forensic issues associated with the increased risk, especially if untreated, of violence, ille-gal acts, and being victimized.

Before starting treatment, one needs to assess the person's capacity to make informed consent decisions, as well as the person's capacity to make decisions related to release of information. After receiving psychoeducation and having a dialogue with the clinician, does the person with schizophrenia understand the risk and benefits of the proposed treatment, including alternatives and no treat-ment? If not, then a surrogate decision maker needs to be designated. Parental consent is applicable to children and also when serving an adolescent. Informed assent can be a helpful method to operationalize shared decision making when working with a teenager and even an older child. For adults advance directives are a legal tool for persons to make treatment decisions and potentially assign a decision maker ahead of time should they lose capacity to make decisions in the future. Advance directives have utility in the field of mental health, including for persons with schizophrenia.

Sometimes clinicians and persons with schizophrenia are faced with the diffi-cult situation of decision making associated with commitment. A person may not want psychiatric hospitalization. However, due to immediate safety issues as a result of a mental illness of high risk of harm to self or others or being gravely disabled, the courts may commit a person to a psychiatric bed. In many states the courts also have the ability to commit the person to outpatient services and rule on judicial authorization for treatment. On an inpatient basis, immediate safety issues of violence and self-destructive behavior may require forced treatment. If all less restrictive alternatives have been considered and immediate safety issues of violence toward others or self exists, restraint use or seclusion might be indicated as a last resort.

Persons with schizophrenia are at increased risk for interface with the legal system. Correlated with the deinstitutionalization movement and the historic resource-deficient community mental health system, there has been an increasing transinstitutionalization of persons with schizophrenia into jails and prisons. The largest institution serving the mentally ill is the Los Angeles County Jail. Crisis Intervention Team (CIT) programs teach police officers and other first responders techniques to help de-escalate and triage persons with mental illnesses and developmental disabilities. The CIT model has been reported to prevent deterioration into further legal problems and divert persons from the legal system into mental health services. Mental health courts have also been shown to serve the same function of diversion.

Clinicians may be working directly in jail and prison settings, including first diagnosis for persons with early onset schizophrenia. Other forensic issues include formal forensic evaluations of the person with restoration for capacity to stand trial, capacity to stand trial forensic evaluations, mental status at the time of offense evaluations, and the treatment and forensic evaluations associated with persons adjudicated not guilty by reason of insanity. Some persons with schizophrenia may only display illegal behavior, but some may have co-occurring antisocial behavior. Schizophrenia is not protective for psychopathy. Legal consequences such as the consideration of prosecution should still be considered for illegal activity.

Clinicians may be faced with duty to warn laws and responsibilities. The 1974 and 1976 court decisions associated with *Tarasoff v. Regents of the University of California* held that mental health professionals have a duty to protect individuals who are being threatened with bodily harm by a patient. Confidentiality may need to be breached in these situations.

In the big picture, persons with schizophrenia are much more likely to be victims of crime than to commit violent crimes. Clinicians may be involved in assessing these risk areas and mitigating them with skills building, supportive housing, and homeless intervention programs.

Many of the legal challenges—confidentiality, informed consent, commitment, forced treatment, duty to warn—have ethical underpinnings. The decisions of the clinician, family members, and court are often structured around balancing the ethical principles of beneficence of treatment, nonmaleficence of doing no harm, social justice for the public, respect of the person's autonomy to make decisions, and release of information. When is it not appropriate to hospitalize a person with schizophrenia beyond their will? When can confidentiality be compromised and when not? Even if a clinician believes that a treatment is necessary, when is it just for him or her to respect a person's choice to refuse all medications offered? When is a clinician obligated to compromise the clinician–patient relationship and forced with a duty to warn a potential victim?

Clinicians may also struggle with ethical issues in various roles. Most often the clinician has a single role of serving the patient. However, clinicians might also be in a role as consultant, primarily serving the person or organization asking a question: the courts may be asking for a forensic evaluation in which the clinician is not in a clinician–patient role but in service to the courts and the legal system. The clinician may also be serving a school system or university setting, being asked to provide an assessment to an organization's administration. In situations like these, it is ethically important for the clinician to define clearly their role and describe the limits of confidentiality and any potential dual interest.

Ethical issues also exist at the level of diagnostic formulation. What is the risk of harm with the clinician diagnosing schizophrenia given the diagnosis's stigma and prognosis? Furthermore, what are the risks and benefits in diagnosing and treating an attenuated psychosis syndrome? Ethical arguments support the beneficence of early treatment and prevention. Far too often persons with first-break psychotic symptoms go without treatment, enduring long periods of delayed treatment and misdiagnosis. This lost time from treatment has been associated with increased disability. However, others have debated the need "to do no harm," given that psychotic disorders such as schizophrenia are chronic illnesses. There are risks of stigmatizing, treating people who would not have otherwise progressed into schizophrenia, and exposing them to side effects of medications. Nonindicated treatment may affect a child's, teen's or young adult's development, including sense of self and identity and relationships. What is the effect of labeling? What is the effect on school function and occupational function? Could future insurability even be compromised and denied? Ethical argument has also occurred regarding the ethics of diagnostic inclusion of a schizophrenia prodrome into DSM-5.

Although epidemiological studies show that rates of schizophrenia are relatively stable across cultures and countries, it is important for the clinician to be sensitive to cultural and socioeconomic issues in both the assessment and treatment phases. Cultural norms and subculture norms need to be respected and taken into account. This sensitivity is applicable, for example, when assessing delusions. Is sorcery and witchcraft a norm for this traditional culture or abnormal in content or intensity for the belief system of the person's culture? A person's affect that appears blunted or even flat with associated gaze aversion may be a norm for the culture and should be formulated appropriately not as psychopathology from the mental status examination. Some evidence exists that clinicians have a risk of overdiagnosing schizophrenia when working with some ethnic groups in comparison with other racial cohorts. The phenotypic expression of schizophrenia might also vary across countries. For example, persons with schizophrenia in developing nations tend to experience more acute courses and a better outcome than persons in industrialized countries where paranoid subtypes are more often diagnosed. Co-occurring catatonia tends to be diagnosed more in non-Western nations than in the United States.

TERMS

Delusions: fixed, false beliefs, which may be nonbizarre or bizarre. Delusions may take various themes, including paranoia, grandiosity, persecutory, erotomanic, religious, or somatic. Delusions may be complex and may include delusions of misidentification—for example, Capgras delusions, which entail a false belief that close acquaintances, usually family members, have been replaced by impostors. The phenomenon was described in a 1923 paper, by two French physicians, Joseph Capgras (for whom the syndrome is named) and Jean Reboul-Lachaux. Capgras syndrome has a co-occurrence incidence as high as 15% in adult inpatients diagnosed with schizophrenia.

Hallucinations: perception of a sensory process that is experienced as "real" yet in a setting of no external source for the perception. The hallucination may occur in various sensory areas, including auditory, visual, olfactory, and tactile. If hallucinations are experience schizophrenia, they tend to be auditory and less visual. Olfactory hallucinations may be associated with temporal lobe seizures; tactile hallucinations with withdrawal (e.g., the formications of alcohol withdrawal).

Ideas of reference: belief or perception that an external phenomena refers directly to them with perhaps some special personal significance—for example, the belief that a talk-show host is speaking directly to them.

Negative symptoms: negative refers to the absence of characteristics. These symptoms can have significant effect on function and are challenging to treat. The symptoms refer to a person's loss of interest and amotivation, lack of expression of emotion (the blunted or flat affect of "blank looks"), neglect of personal hygiene, social withdrawal, and reduced ability to engage with the environment around them. About 25% of persons with schizophrenia experience the deficit syndrome.

Neologism: newly created word or combination term, which may not be readily understood by others but may be inferred.

Positive symptoms: positive refers to the presence of psychotic characteristics, generally viewed as hallucinations, delusions, disorganized speech, and bizarre or disorganized behavior.

Prodrome: a set of early symptoms and signs that might be a manifestation of an impending disease. The recognition of prodromal schizophrenia has been recognized for over a century as noted by the Swiss psychiatrist Eugen Bleuler, who was an early contributor to the world's understanding of schizophrenia. Several constructs exist for the prodrome of schizophrenia, including prodromal risk syndrome, psychosis risk syndrome, at-risk mental state, clinical high risk, putative prodrome, ultra-high-risk, and basic symptoms approach. Studies on schizophrenia's prodrome have led to the proposed and accepted new diagnosis of Attenuated Psychosis Syndrome for DSM-5. The objectives for the new diagnostic category were to help guide early identification of at risk persons, support treatment, and guide research. However, the proposal has also generated clinical and ethical debate.

Recovery: while recovery in the medical field is viewed by a return to a person's premorbid state of health or a restoration and return to a baseline of health from sickness, recovery in the field of mental health has become a paradigm of service over the past decade. SAMHSA (the Substance Abuse and Mental Health Services Administration) defines recovery as "a process of change through which individuals improve their health and wellness, live a self-directed life, and strive to reach their full potential."

Thought disorder: thinking so disorganized with looseness of associations, circumstantial or tangential thinking, thought blocking, neologisms, and word salad that there is significant dysfunction in the processing involved in thinking and in expression of one's thoughts.

REFERENCES AND RESOURCES

American Academy of Child and Adolescent Psychiatry (AACAP), Practice parameter for the assessment and treatment of children and adolescents with schizophrenia, *J Am Ac Child Adol Psych* 2001;40:7(Supplement), http://www.aacap.org/galleries/Practice Parameters/JAACAP%20Schizophrenia%202001.pdf.

American Psychiatric Association (APA) Practice Guideline, Treatment of patients with schizophrenia, April 2004, http://psychiatryonline.org/guidelines.aspx.

Aviv R. Which way madness lies. Can psychosis be prevented? *Harper's Magazine* 2010 Dec;35–46.

Buchanan RW, Kreyenbuhl J, Kelly DL, et al. The 2009 schizophrenia PORT psychopharmacological treatment recommendations and summary statements. *Schiz Bull* 2010 Jan;36(1):71–93, http://schizophreniabulletin.oxfordjournals.org/content/36/1/71.full.pdf+html.

Buckley PF, Miller BJ. (Eds). Schizophrenia. *Focus: J Lifelong Learn Psych* 2012 Spring;10(2).

Dixon LB, Dickerson F, Bellack AS, et al. The 2009 schizophrenia PORT psychosocial treatment recommendations and summary statements. *Schiz Bull* 2010 Jan;36(1):48–70, http://schizophreniabulletin.oxfordjournals.org/content/36/1/48.full.pdf+html.

Jones PB, Barnes TR, Davies L, et al. Randomized controlled trial of the effect on quality of life of second- vs. first-generation antipsychotic drugs in schizophrenia: Cost Utility of the Latest Antipsychotic Drugs in Schizophrenia Study (CUtLASS). *Arch Gen Psych* 2006;63:1079–87.

Lieberman JA, Stroup TS, McEvoy JP, et al. Effectiveness of antipsychotic drugs in patients with chronic schizophrenia. *N Eng J Med* 2005;353:1209–23.

National Alliance on Mental Illness, What is schizophrenia?, http://www.nami.org/Template.cfm?Section=schizophrenia9.

National Institute of Mental Health, Schizophrenia, http://www.nimh.nih.gov/health/topics/schizophrenia/index.shtml.

Saks ER. *The Center Cannot Hold: My Journey through Madness*. New York: Hyperion, 2007. Autobiography of a gifted woman with schizophrenia: she battles with the illness into a recovery distinguished by academic honors at Vanderbilt, Oxford, and Yale

Law School and becoming a professor at the University of Southern California Gould School of Law.

Substance Abuse and Mental Health Services Administration, Recovery support, http://www.samhsa.gov/recovery/.

A Beautiful Mind (2001). A biographical film based on the life of John Nash, a Nobel laureate in Economics, and his first break of psychoses during his early years at Princeton. The Oscar-winning film was inspired by a bestselling, Pulitzer Prize–nominated book of the same name by Sylvia Nasar.

π (*Pi*) (1998). An award-winning psychological thriller about a fragile, paranoid mathematician who believes that everything in nature can be understood through numbers and obsessively searches for a specially significant 216-digit number.

Canvas (2006) film written and directed by Joseph Greco about his personal experience growing up in a family with a schizophrenic mother who suffers primarily from auditory hallucinations.

CHAPTER **6**

Thought Disorder with Negative Symptoms

Jay Thornton, M.D.

CLINICAL PRESENTATION

Chief complaint: "I don't like this medication [risperidone] because of the way it makes me feel and I don't really want to take it anymore"

History of present illness: Joseph, a 20-year-old male, presents along with his mother for an initial follow-up visit after a two-week hospitalization due to a psychotic decompensation. One year ago he was admitted to a psychiatric hospital near his college after he was found by worried friends in a field standing naked waiting for a visit from the Antereans, aliens from a galaxy far away. Always an avid science fiction buff, he had become more and more obsessed with the subject, sending long letters to numerous individuals at the college and public officials regarding the imminent and severe repercussions, including loss of life on a massive scale, if the aliens were not greeted properly. He had become more reclusive, failing classes, not eating or taking care of himself. On campus he became periodically agitated screaming "can't you hear them?," claiming he was getting special messages from the aliens. When police had come to the field he became agitated and combative and had to be subdued, resulting in injury to one of the officers. Assault and battery charges were filed but were later dismissed. He had been started on haloperidol, improved over a period of a couple weeks, and discharged returning home to his parents. At this first hospitalization a medical evaluation occurred (CT scan, extensive blood work, and neurological consult), which were negative. Joseph and his family sought care with a private psychiatrist, but things did not go well. The patient took medications sporadically, isolated himself in his room, and did not pay attention to his grooming/hygiene. His room was kept in squalor with the patient daring his patients to come in. He eventually ran away from home and was found in a neighboring town, wandering the streets and mumbling, and was picked up at a local business on trespassing charges. Soon he was transferred to a local hospital where he became agitated, yelling about ominous happenings if the aliens were not stopped according to the signals he was getting. At the hospital he was started on risperidone at the insistence of his parents to try something new; he seemed to improve over a period of a few weeks and was discharged to his follow-up appointment today. Today Joseph says he doesn't like the risperidone as he paces, feels emotionless and restless, and his muscles ache. At least "I don't walk like a robot like I did on the Haldol." He states the hospitalizations were due to "things getting blown out of proportion." He denies auditory and visual hallucinations, is no longer getting signals from the aliens but is still interested in the Antereans, and believes others are oblivious of the potential dangers. He does not feel a compulsion to warn others, however. His mother says he has been taking his medications, largely out of fearfulness of upcoming court proceedings regarding the legal charges. Otherwise he is clear that he would no longer take the medication due to its side effects. He is largely holed up in his room, which is in total disarray. He seemingly does nothing during the day and has no interest in returning to college. His mother is perplexed about her son's apparent change in personality, desires, goals, and dreams. She proudly notes his older brother is a lawyer and older sister excels in her own graphic design business.

Past psychiatric history: Prior to one year ago there was no psychiatric history. One year ago the patient was hospitalized with a diagnosis of brief reactive psychosis and discharged on haloperidol. Wanting the best follow-up for their son, he was taken to one of the better known private psychiatrists in town who continued the haloperidol. The dose had been reduced to accommodate the patient's complaint of side effects. As noted, he stopped the medication, psychiatrically decompensated, and was rehospitalized. He was started on risperidone and remains on that currently along with benzatropine to be used as needed for muscle stiffness/spasms.

Family psychiatric history: Maternal grandmother, who is now deceased, was described as odd and suspicious, taking "nerve" medications of some kind. Otherwise there is no history of mental illness in family. Paternal grandfather had an alcohol problem but is currently not using alcohol.

Other medical history: No acute or chronic medical problems are noted and the only medications currently taken are risperidone and benzatropine. He had his tonsils removed as a child.

Other history (developmental, educational/occupational, family/social, and legal): Patient met all of his developmental milestones. There was no physical/sexual/verbal abuse growing up in the family. He has an older brother and older sister, both of whom excelled in school. Patient was an average student, not failing any grades and completing high school. He was not entirely a "loner" but gravitated to a few other "geeky" friends also interested in science and science fiction. Role-playing games seemed to absorb a lot of his time rather than any sports or school club activities. He enrolled in a nearby college with the ultimate goal of becoming an engineer. He had to drop out due to the onset of the psychotic symptoms. Currently, he stays to himself, does not have any friends to speak of, and spends most of his time on the computer playing various games. He has assault and battery charges that were dismissed, but he now faces trespassing charges, which are pending.

He never indulged in alcohol use to any great degree, but did frequently use marijuana in the past. At one point he was using the marijuana daily and admitted to his parents he had several "near misses" where he almost got caught by legal authorities. His parents initially blamed his lackluster school performance on the marijuana use. He has not used any drugs since the onset of his illness. He did begin smoking cigarettes at about a pack a day after his psychotic break, much to his parents' dismay. He becomes very irritated if he doesn't have access to cigarettes when he wants them.

Mental status exam: Twenty-year-old white male appears younger than his stated age and is somewhat disheveled with unkempt hair in casual clothes. He fidgets and occasionally gets up, paces, and sits down. He is mildly hostile/angry and negativistic. He has a normal tone and flow of speech. He is alert and oriented to person, place, time, and situation. Remote/recent/immediate past recall are intact. He is able to do serial 7's correctly. He uses scientific terms sometimes in an unusual manner. Otherwise he does not volunteer information readily. Mood is mildly angry at times with blunted affect. He denies any suicidal ideation/plan/intent.

Brief responses seem to be organized but paranoid ideas are inserted at times. He is fairly concrete, interpreting proverbs literally. He is aware of current events but gives them "global conspiracy" meanings at times, reading special meanings into some everyday event. He denies hearing voices and seeing things.

IMPAIRMENT IN FUNCTIONING

Patient has impairment in reality testing and communication as well as major impairment in work, school, family relations, judgment, and thinking.

Once again, we see in Joseph's case that there are two synergistic reasons for his impairment. First, his positive and negative symptoms greatly interfere with his ability to lead a normal life. Second, the intensity of his beliefs combined with his lack of insight make it very difficult for him to have a true therapeutic alliance with family and clinicians.

Joseph's side effects from medication are real and distressing for him. Should the clinician insist that Joseph continue on these medications, without attempting to ameliorate the side effects, the therapeutic relationship between them would be damaged.

DSM DIAGNOSIS

Joseph satisfies the DSM criteria for diagnosis of schizophrenia, episodic with residual and prominent negative symptoms. He also shows evidence of nicotine dependence (like many individuals with schizophrenia) as well as cannabis abuse. Because of the short history of schizophrenia, it is difficult to determine whether he might also satisfy a diagnosis of schizotypal personality traits premorbidly. In

DSM-5, the diagnostic criteria for schizophrenia are largely unchanged from previous editions.

This patient presents with a one-year history of hallucinations, paranoid delusions, affective blunting, apathy (seemingly not caring), avolition (lack of drive or goal-directed behavior), decreased interest in social activities and relationships, and increased isolation. He has maintained a preoccupation with an organized delusion (i.e., the Antereans). He does not have and has not had disorganized speech or behavior or catatonic symptoms. Affect has some blunting, but is not flat. He has progressed beyond the time-specified psychoses of Brief Reactive Psychosis (one month) and Schizophreniform Disorder (six months). He has bizarre delusions and prominent negative symptoms and thus does not have Delusional Disorder. An extensive medical workup occurred on his first presentation, which was negative, ruling out medical etiologies. Toxicology screens eliminated a substance use connection. Since one year has elapsed, a longitudinal course specifier can be used of episodic with prominent negative symptoms. When treated the hallucinations dissipate and the delusions, never entirely gone, submerge into the background and he does not act on them. One could argue his course is continuous with waxing and waning symptoms and with partial response to medications. The negative symptoms and noncompliance in this case would not be in dispute. Additional diagnoses of cannabis abuse and nicotine dependence can be given. The cannabis abuse is in sustained remission due to no use in a year, but the nicotine dependence is continuous.

EPIDEMIOLOGY

Lifetime prevalence rate of schizophrenia across countries and cultures is 1%. The incidence is higher among persons born in urban areas of industrialized countries. It is equally prevalent in men and women. Peak age onset is 10–25 years for men and 25–35 years for women. It is estimated that 80% of individuals with schizophrenia smoke cigarettes and that 50% or more have a substance use disorder.

In many ways the "positive" symptoms of schizophrenia like hallucinations or delusions are more easily treated than the "negative" symptoms like apathy, decreased insight, or decreased social awareness. Although the positive symptoms are more easily observed, the negative symptoms have a huge long-term impact on the course of illness. People suffering from schizophrenia have a worse prognosis if negative symptoms are a prominent part of their illness.

DIFFERENTIAL DIAGNOSIS

First and foremost, any initial presentation of psychosis needs a thorough workup to rule out medical etiologies. A variety of neurological, endocrine, metabolic conditions, and substance use disorders need to be considered and ruled out. Once this is accomplished the appropriate psychotic disorder diagnosis needs to be made. Differentiation between Schizophrenia, Major Depression with psychotic features, Bipolar Disorder (manic or depressed with psychotic features), Delusional Disorder, and the Cluster A Personality Disorders (Schizoid, Schizotypal, and Paranoid types) are important to determine an effective treatment plan.

For the purposes of this case study, it will be assumed the diagnosis of schizophrenia has been accurately made. The differential diagnosis in this case is whether the negative symptoms observed are part of the schizophrenia illness itself, or whether secondary depression or the medications are adding to the picture. Assessment tools include the Brief Psychiatric Rating Scale, Positive and Negative Symptom Scale, and Scale for the Assessment of Negative Symptoms. Typically, the negative symptoms can be ascribed to the schizophrenia itself if there is no mood component. Individuals with pure schizophrenia usually describe having flat moods or "no feelings." Antipsychotic medications can cause or exacerbate this feature. It is not entirely uncommon for patients to become depressed, describing a depressed mood and/or sadness related to the multiple losses incurred in most cases (less independence and multiple new barriers to achieving life goals and dreams that existed prior to the onset of the illness). In the current case study, the negative symptoms, some of which appeared to an attenuated degree prodromally, appear to be a part of the schizophrenia illness itself. Although not readily apparent, a depressive component does not appear to be present.

Additionally, what are the identified causes of the patient noncompliance (as this determination will help craft a more effective treatment approach)? Poor compliance with medications may be related to factors from the patient (comorbid drug abuse, housing instability, attitudes toward illness), the illness (psychotic symptoms, lack of insight), the medication (akathisia or motor restlessness, stiff or painful muscles, emotional blunting, sedation), the environment (support system, level of service treatment by the provider), or the medical team itself (such as in a poor doctor–patient relationship). Each of these problems requires a different focus, and it is not uncommon for treatment plans to focus on multiple factors at once. In our current case a lack of insight appears to play a large role, along with some medication side effects, negative symptoms of the illness, and a limited support system.

ETIOLOGY AND PATHOGENESIS

There is a definite genetic component with an approximately 50% concordance rate in monozygotic twins. Biochemically the dopamine hypothesis indicates too much dopaminergic activity in the mesocortical and mesolimbic tracts in the brain. The "positive" symptoms of schizophrenia (hallucinations, delusions, thought/speech disorganization) are thought to occur from an excess of dopaminergic activity in the brain. However the "negative" symptoms (affective flattening, alogia, avolition) are thought to be caused by low dopaminergic activity in the prefrontal cortex. Another theory puts forth serotonergic activity as an additional etiology as well as loss of gamma aminobutyric acid neurons (which exert an inhibitory effect on dopamine). The hypoglutaminergic hypothesis is based on the effects of phencyclidine and ketamine, which bind to a site within the NMDA receptor channel and block cation flow through the channel. This produces behavioral effects including positive and negative and cognitive impairments. Reduced volumes of cortical gray matter and enlarged lateral and third ventricles in the brain on CT scan are consistent findings. One theory regarding negative symptoms such as anhedonia (decreased ability to experience pleasure) is due to degeneration in the norepinephrine reward neural system. Evidence suggests that adolescents with a family history of schizophrenia or a "psychosis-prone" or paranoid personality are more likely to become psychotic if they smoke cannabis than are adolescents without these features. Although overall risk for people developing schizophrenia is small, a vulnerable minority using marijuana during adolescence increases the risk of developing schizophrenia.

NATURAL COURSE WITHOUT TREATMENT

The course of schizophrenia is variable, with some individuals having exacerbations and remissions and others remaining chronically ill. Complete remission with return to full premorbid functioning is rare. For those that remain chronically ill, some remain stable and some have a deteriorating course. Several studies have shown that over the 5–10-year period after the first hospitalization for schizophrenia, only 10–20% of patients can be described as having a good outcome. Twenty to thirty percent of all schizophrenic patients lead somewhat normal lives, 20–30% continue with moderate symptoms, and 40–60% remain significantly impaired their entire lives. According to the DSM there are a number of factors related to a better prognosis: good premorbid adjustment, acute onset, later age at onset, absence of poor insight, being female, precipitating events, associated mood disturbance, treatment with antipsychotic medications soon after onset, consistent medication compliance, brief duration of active phase, good interepisode functioning, minimal residual symptoms, absence of structural brain abnormalities, normal neurological functioning, a family history of mood disorder, and no family history of schizophrenia. Patients with repeated bouts of psychotic decompensation, mostly due to poor medication compliance, tend to take longer to respond at each treatment episode and may have increasingly suboptimal improvements on subsequent medication trials. Negative symptoms may be prominent early on and serve as prodromal features. Positive symptoms then appear but are more responsive to treatment. Negative symptoms tend to persist interepisode and may steadily worsen over the course of the illness.

EVIDENCE-BASED TREATMENT OPTIONS

Schizophrenia is a complex, devastating illness that on many occasions seems to rob individuals of their lives at a most important time when they are beginning to establish themselves as autonomous individuals. Negative symptoms produce the most disability over the long haul in treatment-compliant patients. Add to this the fact that many of the medications used for treatment can produce side effects similar to the negative symptoms, and a real dilemma ensues. In the 2009 Schizophrenia PORT (Patient Outcomes Treatment Team) study, there was insufficient evidence to recommend any specific pharmacologic treatments for negative symptoms. In this same study there was not sufficient evidence to conclude that long-acting injectables (LAI) antipsychotics prevented relapse any better than oral agents. Despite this, in clinical practice most have found that the second-generation "atypical antipsychotics" (SGAs) tend to produce more improvement in negative symptoms in individual patients (they have activity at dopaminergic and serotonergic receptor sites). All of the antipsychotics seem to treat the positive symptoms, but results vary greatly from patient to patient for each agent. In patients willing to take a LAIs, the relapse rate seems to be reduced for those with good response to the agent. PORT does indicate that clozapine and olanzapine should not be first-line treatments for the first psychotic break and that clozapine should be used after failure of two other antipsychotic trials. The NIMH CATIE study found a high discontinuation rate and no advantage of SGAs over perphenazine (proxy for first generation antipsychotics or FGAs). With the lack of clear direction and conflicting study results . . . what to do? The bottom line is that antipsychotic medication selection should be individualized based on preference of patient and treatment provider (arrived at collaboratively if possible), prior treatment response, side effect experience, adherence history, relevant medical history and risk factors, and long-term treatment planning.

The process of selecting, changing, and dosing antipsychotic medications dictates listening to the patient and considering their concerns, no matter how bizarre you think they are. Showing concern and that you have heard the patient projects empathy and begins the process of developing rapport. Problem solving with the patient who is on board with the solution goes a long way in encouraging compliance. Because schizophrenia is a complex disease with complicated treatment, having other mental health professionals assisting in the patient care is essential (case managers, nurses, therapists, vocational specialists, substance abuse treatment specialists). It is incumbent on all parties to stay in communication and produce a coordinated treatment plan which needs to be dynamic with changes dependent on the clinical picture. Program of Assertive Community Treatment (PACT) teams are an evidence-based treatment option and is an intensive coordinated approach involving multiple disciplines. Although expensive programs to maintain due to the low patient-to-staff ratios, the cost effectiveness has been demonstrated in numerous studies in terms of decrease in frequency of hospital readmits and reduced length of stay in the hospital. Involvement of the patient's families, friends, and significant others are key.

When this process fails, there is a subset of patients who will respond to court-ordered outpatient treatment if available in your jurisdiction and assuming it is a workable system. In this case study, threat of repercussions from the legal system has induced at least short-term improved compliance.

Extrapyramidal symptoms (muscle spasms, motor restlessness) are very uncomfortable symptoms and may lead to noncompliance. They are fairly easily treated with anticholinergic agents such as benzatropine or trihexyphenidyl and the dose adjusted properly. Addition or adjustment of these agents and using the lowest effective dose of the antipsychotic should limit the uncomfortable symptoms to some degree. Discussing the connection between taking the medication and staying out of the hospital in several ways may help mitigate the limited insight. There is an unfortunate choice between more chance of tardive dyskinesia, a permanent muscle movement disorder with the FGA and developing metabolic syndrome (hyperlipidemia, diabetes) with the SGAs. The SGAs are generally better tolerated, but this is patient-specific. The patient should be involved with which set of possible side effects they are willing to chance and live with. As noted previously, SGAs have a better reputation at improving negative symptoms. Alternatively, selective serotonin reuptake inhibitors, mirtazepine, and selective monoamine oxidase B inhibitors have appeared promising at helping negative symptoms. Stimulant medications are not routinely used due to possible exacerbation of positive psychotic symptoms from an increase in dopaminergic activity.

Regarding compliance, several things could be done. The patient should be referred to a community mental health center to obtain much-needed services, such as case management and therapeutic activities. Medication visits alone are not generally sufficient for treating a patient with this severe level of pathology. Negative symptoms and compliance can be improved by developing positive relationships with other mental health professionals and peers (club houses, groups). CBT and supportive therapies appear to be most effective among the psychotherapies. The family can be supported by education regarding the illness and their role in the patient's recovery. Family can be referred to the National Alliance for the Mentally Ill (NAMI) for support. The patient's parents and other family members should be dissuaded from comparing the patient to excelling siblings and the patient's premorbid level of functioning. "High expressed emotion families" that are more critical of the patient, expressing little warmth and more hostility and dissatisfaction, result in higher relapse rates in patients. If the patient does not like taking pills every day or is forgetful or inconsistent, then offering an LAI form of the oral agent (if available) can be helpful. In this case study, risperidone is available in an LAI form (an every-two-weeks injection). If the patient is compliant with the injections, this will enable a steadier blood level of the agent, increasing the chances that positive symptoms will not return that could lead to another decompensation and hospitalization. It can be presented as a treatment modality that removes the burden of remembering to take an oral regimen on a daily basis. PACT teams and other intensive outpatient treatment can monitor the patient daily if needed to ensure the oral form is ingested. For patients adept at "cheeking," or holding the pill in their mouth until the supervising treatment team member leaves the vicinity, orally dissolvable or liquid forms (if available) may be helpful. In this case, risperidone does come in an orally dissolvable form that instantly dissolves in the mouth, preventing cheeking behaviors.

CLINICAL COURSE WITH MANAGEMENT AND TREATMENT

In the case study, Joseph exhibits some akathisia (motor restlessness/pacing) and has a vague complaint that he doesn't like the way the medication makes him feel. Nailing down the vague complaint may take time and more often than not means the patient is missing the positive aspects of the psychotic experience (i.e., the excitement surrounding communicating with extraterrestrials). Because this patient remains symptomatic to some degree, reduction in dose would not seem feasible. The akathisia and muscle aches can be more readily addressed. The benztropine currently used is not effective, so changing to another agent such as trihexyphenidyl could address both issues. Adding a beta blocker such as propranolol or a benzodiazepine such as clonazepam could further address akathisia, which often proves difficult to treat. Longer term, moving to a different antipsychotic agent could be considered. Because this patient demonstrates a respect for the legal system, outpatient court-ordered/-mandated treatment could be considered once his legal issues are resolved and if compliance remains an issue. In the meantime, attempts at engagement in treatment should be continued with efforts from a multidisciplinary team including case management and a therapist adept in one of the evidence-based therapies for individuals with schizophrenia. Discussions should include smoking cessation with use of nicotine replacement or bupropion treatment. The patient should be referred to an appropriate psychosocial treatment modality and the family referred to NAMI.

Summary of important points:

1. Treat the acute positive symptoms first because this will improve patient adherence to other aspects of treatment.
2. SGAs are generally better tolerated than FGAs, but selection of the most effective agent for the patient's positive symptoms is most crucial.
3. Empathetically listen to patient observation and complaints about the medication and try, if at all possible, to select an agent mutually agreed on by patient and treatment provider.
4. Take side effects seriously and treat them aggressively to remove one other barrier to patient compliance.
5. Refer patient to a community mental health center or similar facility to provide a more comprehensive array of services in conjunction with medication management.
6. For patients with repeated episodes of decompensation due to noncompliance, among other factors, a multidisciplinary intensive treatment program such as PACT is often helpful.

7. Discourage use of any substances such as alcohol or illegal drugs and refer to an appropriate evidence-based psychosocial treatment venue if necessary.

8. Encourage smoking cessation, for health reasons and to improve antipsychotic effectiveness. Bupropion sustained-release 150 mg bid is a recommended medication treatment from the PORT study.

9. Get patient's support system (family, friends, significant other, etc.) on board and involved with the treatment program and provide education about the illness and the various treatment benefits and limitations. NAMI is a good resource for this purpose.

10. When all else fails, court-ordered outpatient treatment can be considered for selected patients in jurisdictions where it is available.

SYSTEMS-BASED PRACTICE ISSUES

Community mental health centers (CMHCs) were established under the CMHC Act in 1963 under President John F. Kennedy to treat the mentally ill in their communities. The defined population is generally the chronically and severely mentally ill, including patients with schizophrenia and other psychotic disorders. Throughout the 20th century and into the 2000s, the rise of managed care, dramatically escalating health care costs, and diminishing government budgets, among other factors, have worked to limit resources for treatment of the severely mentally ill. Despite this, the CMHC system remains intact in every state, though varying greatly from state to state. A wide range of services are still generally available and perfectly suited for the patient with schizophrenia, including case management, medication management, individual and group therapies, occupational therapy, social programs (such as club houses), and substance abuse treatments. Most centers employ an escalation of level of services from routine for stable patients to more intensive services, including hospital diversionary programs for those patients decompensating or becoming more symptomatic. The previously mentioned PACT teams are available around the country (though space for new patients is severely limited). Based on public health principles, most community mental health activities and programs are aimed at tertiary prevention, which focuses on reducing the prevalence of residual disabilities in the population. The largest majority of these programs treat the negative symptoms of schizophrenia and compliance issues.

LEGAL, ETHICAL, AND CULTURAL CHALLENGES

Immediate treatment for patients who have been noncompliant and become symptomatic to the point of potential harm to self or others (and in most states inability to care for self) can be taken to a hospital against their will using temporary detainment procedures that vary markedly from state to state. For patients with repeated noncompliance, decompensations, and hospitalizations, mandated court-ordered outpatient treatment is available in many states. However, the processes and utility of this option vary widely. For individuals who get caught up in the legal system while symptomatic, some states have established a "therapeutic docket" within the traditional court system or separate mental health courts. These processes are only effective if the patient is willing to "play ball," so to speak, and follow the rules (participate in treatment and court appearances) due to fearfulness regarding the legal consequences.

Ethical issues abound in this area and often create complicated dilemmas, sometimes with no clear answers and no obvious path to a good outcome. Individual rights must be balanced against potential harm to the patient and/or others. Although some situations are black and white, many are gray, requiring the clinician's best judgment. It is then imperative to obtain as much information as possible, not just from the patient, but from family, significant others, and other caregivers to make the best possible decision. This may require the serious act of breach of patient confidentiality when the patient is not cooperative and potentially dangerous to himself or others.

Psychiatric advance directives are available to patients in some states and are similar to medical advance directives. These legal instruments help engage the patient in their own treatment and are intended to increase medical professionals' adherence to the wishes of the patient during times when their decision-making capacity and communication may be compromised, such as in a florid psychotic episode.

Cultural issues may become front and center, as what is considered "out of touch with reality" in one culture may be considered "the norm" in another. A trusted interpreter is essential to make sure communication is accurate for gathering information and imparting explanations and instructions to the patient. Most interpreters and family members can be helpful in understanding cultural differences and nuances. For example, observation of delusional thinking (false beliefs) cannot be accurately made unless the evaluator can assess the validity of the beliefs, and this can be culturally specific.

TERMS

Acceptance and commitment therapy: a variation of CBT that strives to modify the individual's relationship to his or her thinking more broadly than in CBT. The patient is encouraged to note psychotic symptoms and negative thoughts "mindfully." Experiential exercises such as meditation are used. Goal setting and coping strategies are made use of.

CATIE study: the NIMH Clinical Antipsychotic Trials of Intervention Effectiveness (CATIE) study designed in 1999–2000 with first results available five years ago.

Cognitive behavioral therapy (CBT): an evidence-based psychotherapeutic approach addressing distorted cognitive thought processes to change dysfunctional emotions and maladaptive behaviors through a goal-oriented, systematic approach.

Compliance therapy: a relatively short intervention that is applied during the acute illness phase focused on medication adherence, with the goal of increasing adherence. Motivational interviewing is used extensively. The therapy occurs in phases initially reviewing illness history, exploring ambivalence toward treatment, and then using medication as a strategy to enhance quality of life.

CONSIST: the Cognitive and Negative Symptoms in Schizophrenia Trial (CONSIST) in regard to the efficacy of glutaminergic agents for negative symptoms and cognitive impairments.

Decompensation: in the context of this case, a worsening of psychiatric symptoms (usually meaning more prominent positive symptoms) leading to a deterioration in daily functioning of the individual. For individuals with schizophrenia living with prominent negative symptoms, it can mean a deterioration from a previously observed higher baseline of functioning.

Extrapyramidal symptoms: side effects of antipsychotic medications (greater in FGAs than in SGAs) consisting of muscle movements. These movements range from motor restlessness (akathisia) to muscle spasms/dystonic reactions (oculogyric crisis or inability to move eyes; torticollis or twisted neck) to pseudoparkinsonism (tremor, hypokinesia, rigidity).

First-generation antipsychotics (FGAs): older neuroleptic or typical medications to treat psychotic symptoms. First developed in the 1950s, the medications range from the less potent and more cholinergic chlorpromazine to the more potent (and more likely to cause extrapyramidal side effects) medications such as haloperidol. Other agents include mesoridazine, thioridazine, fluphenazine, perphenazine, trifluoperazine, pimozide, thiothixene, molindone, and loxapine.

NAMI: National Alliance for the Mentally Ill, the nation's largest grassroots mental health organization dedicated to building better lives for the millions of Americans affected by mental illness. NAMI advocates for access to services, treatment, supports, and research and is "steadfast in its commitment to raise awareness and build a community for hope for all of those in need." This is an excellent resource for patients and for friends and family of those with mental illness.

Negative symptoms: for schizophrenia, alogia (poverty of speech), affective blunting (lack of emotional expression), avolition (inability to initiate activities), anhedonia (loss of enjoyment in favored activities), attentional impairment (inability to concentrate). Negative symptoms may be primary and associated with the positive symptoms of the illness or secondarily associated with extrapyramidal symptoms, depression, and/or environmental deprivation. Negative symptoms remain the main barrier to a better quality of life for individuals living with schizophrenia.

Personal therapy: a long-term endeavor performed in stages tailored to the degree of recovery from the acute psychotic episode. A major goal is to develop an understanding of the patient's mood states, especially negative affects and a more adaptive response to emotional stresses. The therapy includes formal illness educational workshops and traditional social skills training. Techniques of modeling, practice feedback, and homework assignments are used.

PORT: the Schizophrenia Patient Outcomes Treatment Team project is an effort to provide evidence-based pharmacologic and psychosocial treatment recommendations for the treatment of schizophrenia. It consists of periodic extensive reviews of the relevant research literature in schizophrenia treatment. The first such review was in 1998 and the last update was in 2009.

Positive symptoms: in schizophrenia, hallucinations (abnormality of perception), delusions (false beliefs), disorganized speech and thought, agitated motor control, and disorganized behavior.

Second-generation antipsychotics (SGAs): atypical agents, include agents such as risperidone, olanzapine, and clozapine that have less propensity to induce muscle movement disorders but more of a propensity to cause hyperlipidemia and blood sugar dysregulation. Other agents include paliperidone, quetiapine, ziprasidone, aripiprazole, asenapine, iloperidone, and lurasidone.

Supportive therapy: therapy focused on the "here and now," defining reality more clearly with practical problem solving. Strategies include providing reassurance, offering explanations, and giving guidance and suggestions.

REFERENCES AND RESOURCES

Buchanan RW, et al. The 2009 Schizophrenia PORT psychopharmacological treatment recommendations and summary statements. *Schiz Bull* 2010;36:71–93.

Dickerson FB, Lehman AF. Evidence-based psychotherapy for schizophrenia 2011 update. *J Nerv Mental Dis* 2011;199:520–26.

Hales RE, et al. Public psychiatry and prevention. *American Psychiatric Press Textbook of Psychiatry* (3rd ed.). Arlington, VA: APA Press, 1999. Chapter 42, 1535–54.

Knoedler WH. The continuous treatment model: role of the psychiatrist. *Psych Ann* 1989 Jan;19(1):35–40.

Lieberman JA, Stroup TS. The NIMH-CATIE Schizophrenia study: what did we learn? *Am J Psych* 2011;168:770–75.

Stein LI, Test MA. Alternative to mental hospital treatment: I. Conceptual model, treatment program, and clinical evaluation. *Arch Gen Psych* 1980 April;37:392–412. Evidence basis for development of Training in Community Living (TCL) programs, which are the basis of PACT programs.

Tandon R, Jibson MD. Negative symptoms of schizophrenia: how to treat them most effectively. *J Family Prac* 2002 Sept;1/8 99.

Tattan TMG, Creed FH. Negative symptoms of schizophrenia and compliance with medications. *Schiz Bull* 2001;27(1):149–55.

A Beautiful Mind (2001). A Hollywood film depicting both the negative and positive symptoms of schizophrenia from the point of view of the patient, as well as the possible perils and benefits of treatment. Starring Russell Crowe.

Canvas (2006). Drama film about a family dealing with a schizophrenic mother. This movie depicts auditory hallucinations.

A comprehensive website for general information regarding schizophrenia is www .schizophrenia.com. Also see www.nimh.nih.gov.

The APA Practice Guideline on Schizophrenia (2004) and the APA Practice Guideline Watch (2009) are not entirely up to date.

CHAPTER 7

Insanity

Karl Northwall, M.D.

CLINICAL PRESENTATION

Chief complaint: "Satan's trying to get me to sin."

History of present illness: Mike is a 23-year-old unmarried male who has been transferred from the local jail to the state hospital for his fifth hospitalization on an emergency court order for treatment and restoration of capacity. "Restoration of capacity" is a legal term referring to the fact that, because of his psychiatric symptoms, he cannot significantly cooperate with or contribute to his legal defense against criminal charges. The judge in this case decided that treatment of his psychiatric illness would likely result in an improvement in his ability to contribute to his own defense.

Mike had been discharged from the state hospital 10 months ago with a diagnosis of chronic paranoid schizophrenia and cannabis abuse and had been noncompliant with treatment. He had been discharged to a local assisted living facility and was following up outpatient psychiatrically with the local community mental health center. His discharge medication was a depot risperidone 37.5 mg that he received intramuscularly every two weeks. He refused all referrals to substance abuse programs. At his first outpatient visit, he told the psychiatrist that he would not take his risperidone injections. The psychiatrist negotiated with him, and finally got him to agree to take aripiprazole 20 mg orally every day. The assisted living facility supervised him taking this medication. Several months ago he started refusing to take it. He started leaving the facility for extended periods of time each day with "friends" and would return looking "glassy-eyed" and "stoned." Staff observed him talking to himself when there was no one around. When asked about this, he said that he was "rebuking Satan." He accused staff and peers of stealing his possessions and began getting into verbal altercations. Later these possessions were found in his room. He started refusing to bathe or change his clothes. He became religiously preoccupied, and began going to local church offices to talk to ministers about his sins; he requested holy water to sprinkle around his bed to keep the "Catholic catechisms" from getting into his soul at night. He spent hours doing individual "Bible study." He claimed that Satan wanted to "mark him with the beast of the east and play ball." He accused a male staff member of attempting to rape him and called the local police to complain of this. They found his complaint to be unfounded. He went to a local church office and became enraged at the secretary, saying she was staring at him and wanted to have sex with him. He grabbed the computer she was using, threw it on the floor, and threatened to "slap the evil out of her." She called 911, the police came, and he assaulted them and had to be subdued with pepper spray. During the altercation with them he bit one of them, drawing blood. He was charged with assault on a police officer, malicious wounding, and destruction of property and was taken to jail. He was seen by the psychiatrist providing services to the jail, who recommended that he continue on aripiprazole, but he refused to take it. He refused to bathe or change clothes. He talked to himself and laughed for no reason. He defecated on the floor, broke a sprinkler head, drank water from the toilet, and accused the staff of poisoning him. At times he said that his peers were staring at him and wanted to have sex with him, and he got into physical altercations with other inmates, getting a number of disciplinary write-ups and finally being placed in isolation. He was found to have tied strings and placed rubber bands around his scrotum at times. While in isolation, staff observed him shouting, "No!" and then hitting himself in the face. A consultation by the forensic psychiatrist serving the jail found him to be not competent to stand trial, and at the psychiatrist's request the judge entered an order transferring him to the state hospital for emergency treatment and restoration of competency to stand trial.

Past psychiatric history: Mike's first psychiatric hospitalization was at the age of 18 when he decompensated during his first semester of college. At that time he had also been using cannabis. His family had taken him to their family physician, who referred them to a clinician at the community mental health center, who arranged hospitalization at a private psychiatric hospital.

At that time he was hearing the voice of Satan, who was telling him to have sex with men and women, which he felt offended God. At that time he was found to have procured elastic bands that were used for nonsurgical castration of sheep. He felt that his prior sexual promiscuity had offended God and was going to remove the offending body part. He had a workup for an organic cause of psychosis and had a CT of the head without contrast and an EEG, both of which were normal. He did not respond to treatment with ziprasidone in a dose up to 60 mg bid there, and after two weeks was subsequently transferred to the state hospital for further treatment. There he was treated with risperidone at a final dose of 4 mg at bedtime to which he responded after a month. He did have a dystonic reaction, which responded to treatment with benztropin and was continued on 1 mg twice daily. His hallucinations and delusions gradually subsided, but he continued to have amotivation, anhedonia, and asociality. He was discharged to his family and lived with them. He did not improve enough to return to college, but he did start work cleaning some houses for his father's real estate business. After a year of treatment, he and his family requested that risperidone be stopped, as they felt that it was sedating him, slowing his thinking down, and causing weight gain of 30 pounds. The psychiatrist agreed to this, discussing with them the warning signs of a recurrence of illness.

Within several months he had a recurrence, with auditory hallucinations and recurrence of his delusions—including that he had again offended God. He was rehospitalized at a private psychiatric hospital, risperidone was restarted, and his symptoms again abated. He again lived with his family, but did not return to his previous level of functioning and started using cannabis. He became accusatory toward his parents, feeling that they were trying to poison him, and was rehospitalized just three months after his previous release. This time he refused to take medication, did not improve, and was transferred to the state hospital. He was found not to have capacity to consent to treatment; his mother was appointed his authorized representative and consented to treatment, including treatment over objection. This time he was placed on haloperidol, which was given intramuscularly if he refused oral administration. He finally started taking it by mouth and was able to be discharged three months after admission. He again started smoking marijuana, quit taking his medication, and relapsed. He became accusatory of his parents, and this time held his mother hostage with a butcher knife, refusing to let her leave the kitchen until she signed a "confession" that she was poisoning him. She called 911 when he let her go; he was picked up by the police, taken to the emergency room, and this time sent directly to the state hospital. He again refused medications, was found not to have capacity to consent, and this time his father was appointed his authorized representative. He was placed on risperidone, which it was felt he had responded better to (and again was given intramuscular haloperidol if he refused oral medication), and it was decided to give depot medication to help ensure compliance on discharge. His mother was now quite afraid of him, and his parents did not wish him to return home to them. An apartment was found for him, and a trial of letting him live independently was made. He again ceased his medication, began smoking cannabis, relapsed, and was rehospitalized with a similar course. This time, seeing as how he was not successful in living independently and his family did not want him back home, placement was found in an assisted living facility, where he was prior to this current hospitalization.

Family psychiatric history: Paternal grandfather had a "nervous breakdown" in his twenties and wound up being hospitalized repeatedly psychiatrically. His wife divorced him several years later, and his father was essentially raised in a single-parent family. The family has lost touch with him. From the description, it appears that he had a schizophrenic illness. A maternal uncle has an alcohol and drug problem, abusing cannabis and methamphetamines.

Other medical history: He had an umbilical hernia repair as an infant. Had asthma as a child but "grew out of it." He fractured his left ulna in a school accident, which healed without sequelae.

Other history (developmental, educational/occupational, family/social/educational, legal): His mother was extremely ill with the flu during the pregnancy. Labor and delivery were normal. He met developmental milestones on schedule. He was an extroverted child, and played well with others. There is no history of getting into fights. He is the oldest of three children. There is no history of physical or sexual abuse. He did well scholastically and participated in athletics. There were no behavioral problems. He is from a middle-class family. They lived in a small community of about 12,000. Both parents are college educated. His parents drank socially. Father owns a real estate business and mother is a nurse. They are Methodist and attended church regularly. The family was close and got along well. He was popular in high school, and started dating in 10th grade. He was more interested in football and girls than academics, but did well enough to be accepted in college. There is some history of drinking beer in high school with the other "jocks." His parents grounded him several times for coming home drunk after parties. They tended to feel that "boys will be boys" and did not regard this as a serious problem.

The expectation in his family was that everyone goes to college, so he did, even though he had no particular major in mind. He had decided to live on campus at a major university about 30 miles from home and came home on weekends sometimes. He tried out for the football team, but it was soon obvious that he was not serious about this. He enrolled in "general studies." He had a roommate who smoked cannabis, and soon he started using it also. In high school he had used alcohol some, but denied any other drugs. At first he came home on weekends, but soon started staying at school and partying on the weekends. He had many "girlfriends" and was very sexually active with them. He started skipping classes. He started mentioning to others that God was talking to him, and at times he also had demons and Satan talking to him. He started to become preoccupied with his "sins," in particular his sexual promiscuity. He began neglecting his hygiene and didn't shave or change his clothes. He quit socializing, withdrew from his friends, and became preoccupied with the Old Testament and the book of Revelations in the Bible. He began to be suspicious that the food in the cafeteria was being poisoned and would only eat canned foods that he opened himself. His roommate became worried about him and contacted his family. His family had noticed that his phone calls home had become brief and infrequent. He complained that someone was listening in on his calls and that his phone was being tapped. His calls finally ceased altogether. His family called his faculty adviser, who said that he had not seen him in several weeks and that he had quit going to classes. They went to his dorm room, and found him in filthy conditions, sitting on the floor clutching his Bible, looking wild-eyed and tired. He had no legal history at that point. They persuaded him to come home with them, and called their family doctor, who referred them to the mental health center.

Mental status exam: Twenty-three-year-old male appearing his stated age who is unkempt, unshaven, has long hair, and is dressed in an orange jail jumpsuit. The right side of his face is bruised and swollen. He is overweight. He appears tense, is very watchful of the interviewer, and has an intense stare. He is superficially cooperative, but is irritable at times. He has poverty of speech, but normal volume. He wants to know if the interview is being recorded. He often inquires into the purpose of specific questions. Staff has observed him shouting "*No!*" several times and then striking himself forcefully in the head with his right hand. He is alert and oriented to person, place, time, and situation. Immediate, recent, and remote memory are intact. He does serial 7's slowly and without errors, but questions why this is being asked of him. He is circumstantial in his speech and at times has loose associations. Affect is blunted and very limited in range, but is angry at times. He says his mood is good. He denies plans of wanting to harm himself or others. He says he is a victim of a conspiracy, which started when his parents were poisoning him at home, and continued with the assisted living facility and jail trying to poison his food. He volunteers that poison gas was also being pumped into his jail cell through the heating system. He says that Satan is telling him to sin and have sex with men and women, and when he prays to God to resist this and rebukes Satan, Satan takes possession of his right hand and hits him. He claims that cannabis is a "Sacramento Californication ritual for water and mind purification." He can do simple calculations, and fund of information appears appropriate to his age and education, although he is reluctant to answer questions. He admits to hearing the voices of God and of Satan. He also at times is getting "messages from Satan" which tells him things like "you're a faggot, go ahead and screw men." At other times Satan has told him of others in jail, "hit him, or *I'll* screw you." God at times tells him that he needs to "purify himself." He also hears voices of males and females that he doesn't know which are inside of his head and tell him that he is being poisoned. He feels "electric shocks" to his brain when he is "thinking incorrect thoughts." He will not answer questions about whether he has thoughts of needing to castrate himself. He says, "God is wrathful, and Satan is powerful, and they will explode on the just and unjust alike."

IMPAIRMENT IN FUNCTIONING

The positive symptoms of schizophrenia (exaggerations or distortions of normal mental functions) are much easier to see and are what usually lead to hospitalization, but the negative symptoms are much more chronically disabling. Negative symptoms include restriction in the range and intensity of emotional expression, in the fluency and productivity of thought and speech, in initiation of goal-directed activity; inability to experience pleasure; impaired social relationships; and impaired ability to pay attention and decreased working memory. Positive symptoms generally respond better to treatment. Profound impairment socially, occupationally, and educationally is not uncommon. Individuals with schizophrenia seldom marry. Schizophrenia is the fourth leading cause of disability in individuals 18–44 years old in developed countries.

Mike's case presents an intriguing and difficult ethical dilemma. In our society we generally have the right to choose or refuse treatment for an illness. In situations where the symptoms of the illness either lead to danger for the individual or for others (that is, suicidality or homicidality) there are legal remedies under civil commitment laws to protect the person by confinement and, under judicial authorization laws, to administer medication against the person's will to restore the normal state of mind.

In Mike's case he was already confined in jail. However, he has a right to exert an active defense against the criminal charges facing him. The symptoms of his psychiatric illness markedly limited his capacity to defend himself in a court of law and for this reason the judge ordered involuntary treatment for restoration of capacity. In effect, the judge has determined that Mike's right to an affirmative criminal defense outweighs his right to refuse treatment.

DSM DIAGNOSIS

Mike is a young man who started having psychotic symptoms (including delusions and hallucinations), failure to achieve educational goals, disorganized speech (looseness of associations), and disorganized behavior at about the same time that he started abusing cannabis. A diagnostic consideration at that time would have included substance-induced psychotic disorder. His symptoms did start with the use of that substance, and if indeed caused by that would be expected to persist as long as the abuse continued. This diagnosis is only made when the symptoms cannot be better accounted for by another mental disorder. The persistence of symptoms longer than a month after cessation of the substance abuse would militate against that diagnosis. He subsequently had a recurrence of his illness when there was no evidence of substance abuse, although subsequent episodes occurred concurrent with cannabis abuse. He has never presented with a delirium. He has psychotic symptoms of hallucinations, formal thought disorder, and disorganized behavior, so he does not have a diagnosis of a delusional disorder. He has had negative symptoms of his illness between episodes of positive symptoms, such as failure to achieve academically and lack of volition. The duration of his illness has been greater than six months, so he does not have a diagnosis of a brief psychotic disorder or a schizophreniform disorder. His lack of insight into his illness and the necessity for treatment, called anosognosia, is very characteristic of schizophrenia. It is associated with higher relapse rates, increased number of involuntary hospitalizations, and a poorer prognosis. Insight into the illness and compliance with treatment is associated with better outcomes. The individual wants you to work with him on the assumption that what he believes and is experiencing is real, and it may be quite difficult to form a therapeutic alliance.

In this case the primary disturbance of the individual is in his thinking, rather than mood or anxiety. He is hypervigilant and overinterprets internal stimuli.

The diagnostic criteria for schizophrenia in DSM-5 are largely unchanged from the previous edition.

EPIDEMIOLOGY

Schizophrenia is found in all cultures. The prevalence is estimated to be 0.8% to 1%. The incidence is about 0.3% to 0.6% annually. The modal age on onset is

18–25 years old in men and 25–35 years old in women. It is diagnosed a little more frequently in men than women.

Because of both positive and negative symptoms, schizophrenics are more likely to run afoul of the law. Most offenses for which they are charged are relatively minor including trespassing, vagrancy, or being drunk in a public place. However, schizophrenics have been found to be as much as four times more likely than people in the general population to commit violent crime. Most commonly these crimes are committed while the persons are psychotic and would not have acted this way if not psychotic.

Involuntary commitment to the hospital and treatment are far more common in schizophrenia than in other psychiatric illnesses. As many as 90% of individuals with schizophrenia do not realize that they have an illness and do not want treatment. Commitment laws generally state that (1) the individual must have a mental illness (generally this excludes personality disorders and traumatic brain injury) and (2) must be dangerous to themselves/others or be unable to care for their basic needs. How imminent such danger must be varies from state to state. Noncompliance to medication is a common cause of relapse and rehospitalization. Mandatory outpatient treatment is a way to reduce rehospitalization rates and increase quality of life for patients. Because commitment criteria also relate to dangerousness, this also is a way to manage that aspect. Such laws are highly variable from state to state. Issues that such laws have to address include forced medication by injection and enforcement for noncompliance.

DIFFERENTIAL DIAGNOSIS

A wide variety of medical disorders can cause psychosis. Examples of these are Cushing's syndrome, Huntington's disease, substance intoxications, brain tumors, adverse drug effects and delirium. Hallucinations involving smell or taste should raise suspicions of a brain tumor or temporal lobe epilepsy. The duration of the symptoms determines the diagnosis of brief psychotic disorder or schizophreniform disorder. A delusional disorder would have only a nonbizarre delusion and would not have hallucinations, disorganization, or negative symptoms. A schizoaffective disorder would have to have a major depressive episode, manic episode, or mixed episode concurrent with schizophrenic symptoms at some time during an uninterrupted period of the illness. A substance-induced psychotic disorder or delirium would require that the psychotic symptoms be initiated and maintained by the substance. A mood disorder with psychotic symptoms would require that the psychotic symptoms be exhibited only during the mood disorder. A pervasive developmental disorder would have a very early onset and would have the absence of prominent delusions or hallucinations. Schizoid, paranoid, or schizotypal personality disorders would not have the severe psychotic symptoms of schizophrenia. In this individual, a comorbid disorder would be cannabis abuse.

ETIOLOGY AND PATHOGENESIS

Risk factors include living in an urban area, immigration, and late winter/early spring time of birth (which may reflect exposure to a virus in utero). It is diagnosed 1.4 times more frequently in men than women. There does appear to be a substantial genetic component. The risk in a first-degree relative is about 12%, in a dizygotic twin 16%, and a monozygotic twin 50%. A polygenic signal has been observed in genome-wide association studies, which could be partly related to genetic effects on negative and disorganized symptoms. Some of the first genes that have been robustly implicated in schizophrenia are NRXN1, DLG2, and ZNF804a. A rare deletion on chromosome 22 has been linked to a 10-fold increase in the risk of schizophrenia. There appears to be some overlap in the genetics of bipolar disorder and schizophrenia. Individuals who develop schizophrenia may show IQ deficits as early as age three. One major theory holds that connectivity between parts of the brain is impaired. There is a massive pruning of neuronal connections and consolidation of neural pathways that occurs in adolescence, with myelination of some major pathways not occurring until the late twenties. A cognitive dysmetria has been postulated with a disturbance in the pontine-cerebellar-thalamic-frontal feedback loop. Brain scans can show volume loss in dorsolateral prefrontal cortex, medial temporal lobe, the thalamus, and superior temporal gyrus, among other areas, with time. A subgroup may have enlarged lateral and third ventricles. A consistent loss in brain tissue is shown in most studies. Developmental abnormalities shown in some patients include midline abnormalities and abnormalities in neuronal migration.

The onset of schizophrenia is felt to be years before the onset of symptoms. DSM-5 initially proposed the inclusion of an attenuated psychosis syndrome, but this wound up in the "needs more review" category. It would certainly be desirable to detect this disorder as early as possible to try to prevent it. The advantage of diagnosing it would be that there then could be trials regarding to how to best treat this condition and prevent schizophrenia. The false positive rate was quite high in preliminary studies, leading to concerns that there would be pressures to treat this prodromal illness with antipsychotics, needlessly exposing many individuals to the potentially severe side effects of these medications. Predicting factors include cognitive deficits, social isolation, school failure, substance abuse and positive family history, and soft neurological signs.

The most prominent biochemical theory for schizophrenia is the dopamine hypothesis. The hypothesis is that an overstimulation of dopamine causes psychotic symptoms. Medications that block dopamine show efficacy in reducing positive symptoms. Medications that increase dopamine, such as amphetamines, cocaine, bromocriptine, and L-dopa, can trigger psychotic symptoms. Negative symptoms, however may be associated with a deficiency of dopamine in the prefrontal cortex. At usual doses, all antipsychotics may worsen negative symptoms by blocking dopamine in this area. Newer antipsychotics, which affect 5HT2 receptors, also suggest a role for serotonin in the pathophysiology. Newer theories postulate that glutamate and GABA may also be involved. It is unlikely that schizophrenia is a single-neurotransmitter disease.

Psychosocially, "high expressed emotion," which is critical and unsupportive, significantly adversely affects the course of schizophrenia.

Cannabis use disorders in particular have been implicated in the pathogenesis of schizophrenia. There appears to be a 40% increase in risk of developing psychosis in those who abuse cannabis. However, cannabis use may be an effect and not a cause of schizophrenia. The individual may be smoking to relieve anxiety and agitation from hallucinations or delusions. Also, marijuana is sometimes laced with hallucinogens.

NATURAL COURSE WITHOUT TREATMENT

The symptoms of schizophrenia may be placed in three main categories: positive, negative, and cognitive. Positive symptoms are an exaggeration of a normal brain function. Hallucinations are sensory experiences with no basis in reality that are felt to be real. The most common type of hallucination in schizophrenia is auditory (present in 70–80% of patients) followed by visual. Voices that command a person to perform an action are of particular concern, since they may be acted on. Olfactory and gustatory hallucinations are rare and should trigger concerns about temporal lobe epilepsy or brain tumor. Delusions are fixed, false ideas that are not amenable to reason. They need to be considered in the context of a person's educational and cultural background. Delusions may include grandiose, paranoid, jealous, nihilistic, or religious themes. Schneiderian first rank symptoms, although not included in the DSM, are not uncommon. These include feeling that one's thoughts are being broadcast out loud, thoughts are being inserted into one's mind, or thoughts are being withdrawn from one's mind. They can also include experiences that your body is being controlled by some outside force. Defects in cognition lead to thought disorder, which presents as illogical, disorganized speech. The associations between ideas may be loose, making it hard to follow the patient's conversation. There may be outright incoherence, circumstantiality, tangentiality, or poverty of content. Rhyming (as in this case) or punning may occur. Behavior may be disorganized, and appearance may be bizarre. Negative symptoms are an absence of mental functions that are normally present. There may be no motivation (avolition), lack of willpower (abulia), lack of socializing (asocial), and lack of pleasure (anhedonia). Lack of insight into the fact one has an illness (anosognosia) is extremely common and makes adherence to treatment a challenge.

There is considerable heterogeneity as to onset, course, and outcome. The course is more benign in nonurban settings. Women tend to have better outcomes than men do. Good outcomes are associated with acute onset, later age at onset, good premorbid functioning, normal neurological functioning, high intelligence, and negative family history. Emil Kraepelin's original diagnostic category of dementia praecox emphasized a progressive downhill course. The first several years tend to be characterized by positive symptoms and frequent hospitalizations, later having more negative symptoms. About 22% of patients will have one episode with no impairment. About 35% will have several episodes with minimal impairment between episodes or residually. The remainder will have episodes with no return to normality. The recovery movement has challenged the traditional bleak view of outcomes for schizophrenia. Cynthia Harding defines recovery as reconstituted social and work behaviors with no need for meds, no symptoms, and no need for compensation. Significant recovery is defined as success in all but one of these areas. Her study of 269 chronic, back-ward patients released to a very active biopsychosocial rehab program showed that 20 to 25 years later half to a third showed considerable improvement or recovery. Better prognosis is associated with acceptance that one has schizophrenia, having hope, and regarding oneself as a person—not an illness.

Depression is a common complication, with about half of patients having symptoms at some point during their illness, and a suicide rate of about 10%, with half of these occurring within six months of a discharge. Many times depressive symptoms will follow an episode of acute illness.

The general population has about a 4% incidence of cannabis use or dependence, whereas individuals with schizophrenia have about a 25% incidence. Cannabis use has also been associated with a poorer clinical course. The abuse of alcohol and cocaine is also significantly more frequent in schizophrenic patients.

Homelessness is a problem in people with schizophrenia, particularly since the radical down-sizing of the state hospitals, which was not accompanied by a shift in finances to the outpatient sector. Individuals with schizophrenia, generally not realizing that they have an illness, often do not use resources that are available. About 30% of the homeless nationwide have a mental illness.

Individuals who have a mental illness are no more likely than anyone else to be violent and, indeed, are much more likely to be victims of violence than average. Nonetheless, there is a subpopulation who are more violent than average, and females with schizophrenia have an incidence of violence similar to males, unlike the general population. Comorbidity with substance abuse seems to account for a large part of this.

EVIDENCE-BASED TREATMENT OPTIONS

There is no treatment at this time that will cure this illness. The object is to minimize symptoms, treat comorbid disorders, decrease relapses, and improve quality of life. Support of families, including referring them to National Alliance for the Mentally Ill (NAMI) is valuable.

Antipsychotic medication is the mainstay of treatment for acute illness and prevention of relapse. Long-term outcome is improved when treatment of acute episodes is initiated rapidly. All present antipsychotic medications block D2 receptors. The newer atypical antipsychotics also affect 5HT receptors and were initially touted as treating negative symptoms also, but turned out to be not very effective for this. Other receptors that may be blocked to varying degrees include noradrenergic, cholinergic, and histaminic. The extent to which these are blocked determines other side effects. The choice of a medication will be determined by the clinician's preference, the patient's history of response to previous treatments, and the side effect profile. Response to medication is very individual, and several trials may be necessary to find one that works best. Control of hallucinations and delusions usually takes several weeks. Generally the high-potency antipsychotics are more likely to cause extrapyramidal side effects and the low potency ones to cause sedation. Acute side effects can include dystonic reactions, sedation, blood pressure drops, and anticholinergic effects. Anticholinergic side effects tend to correlate inversely with parkinsonian side effects. Long-term side effects include tardive dyskinesia (more common with typical antipsychotics) and metabolic syndrome (more common with atypical antipsychotics). These long-term side effects can be severe, so it is imperative to have informed consent when prescribing these medications. There is no known treatment for tardive dyskinesia. Risk of developing it is related to total lifetime dose of antipsychotic medication, so it is necessary to strive for the lowest effective dose. It is generally mild but can be severe and grotesque in 3–5% of patients. It was observed in patients with schizophrenia prior to the discovery of antipsychotic drugs. There are clinical scales such as the Abnormal Involuntary Movement Scale, which can be used to monitor for the emergence and severity of this syndrome. Discontinuation of the medication may lead to remission of the tardive dyskinesia, but can also lead to relapse of the illness. Patients at risk for metabolic syndrome should be monitored for weight, lipid profile, blood pressure, and glucose. Diet and exercise can be useful, although difficult to get patients to do. Parkinsonian side effects are related to the degree of total dopaminergic blockade, 80% blockade being associated with parkinsonism, whereas only 60% blockade is necessary for antipsychotic effect, so it may be possible to decrease the dose some and obtain relief without decreasing therapeutic effect. Dosage should be individualized. Blood levels of medication are generally only useful for detecting problems with compliance or determining if someone is a slow or rapid metabolizer of medication. If medication is initiated in an inpatient setting, it is necessary to consider the patient's outpatient habits in determining the dose. For example, olanzapine levels may be decreased by as much as 40% in the presence of cigarette smoking, so if a patient is not smoking as an inpatient, he could be a compliant outpatient but still decrease his effective dose and then relapse. Noncompliance with medication is frequently a problem. In the landmark CATIE study, 74% of patients discontinued their antipsychotic medication before 18 months. Depot forms of haloperidol, fluphenazine, risperidone, olanzapine, and paliperidone are available. Use of these depot medications is associated with a significantly lower risk of rehospitalization.

Failure of two other antipsychotics should lead to consideration of clozapine. About half of patients who show no improvement on other antipsychotics will show improvement on clozapine, sometimes dramatically. Clozapine has also been shown to unequivocally improve negative symptoms in some patients and does not cause tardive dyskinesia. Studies have showed that the suicide rate in patients on clozapine is far lower than for other antipsychotics. A blood level of clozapine plus its chief metabolite, norclozapine (which is psychoactive) above 450 ng/ml correlates with clinical effect. Clozapine is more difficult to use than the other antipsychotics, having five black box warnings, including a risk of agranulocytosis necessitating frequent monitoring. The "best of the rest" of the antipsychotics, from phase 2 of the CATIE study, is olanzapine—which has a very substantial risk of metabolic syndrome.

Psychosocial treatment is usually not possible during the initial part of an acute episode. Acute psychosis impairs attention and concentration, reality testing, and can be overwhelming with psychotic sensory input. Initial contacts should be brief and supportive in nature. Direct confrontation of delusions should be avoided. External stimuli should be minimized. A therapeutic alliance can be useful in obtaining compliance. The family should be contacted and involved if at all possible. It is extremely important to educate them and gain their support. Referral to groups such as NAMI can put them in contact with others who have undergone this experience and can guide them. Any guilt they have about having "caused" this illness should be defused and the disease should be demystified. Families who have a high expressed emotion style can be educated in ways to reduce this. The 2009 PORT study has a number of evidence based recommendations for psychosocial treatments. The evidence for these treatment is moderate to strong. ACT (Assertive Community Treatment) should be provided for those at risk of relapse or who have recent homelessness. Anyone who has a goal of employment should be offered supported employment. Individuals who have deficits in interpersonal and activities of daily living skills should have training. Persons with persistent psychotic symptoms should be offered CBT to reduce psychotic symptoms. Token economies for long-term inpatient or residential programs can improve personal hygiene and interpersonal interactions. Those who have families involved can benefit from family interventions, including illness education, crisis intervention, emotional support, and training in how to cope with illness symptoms and related problems. Those with comorbid substance use disorders can benefit from specific treatments for those problems. Their recommendations also included a specific recommendation for weight management. Cognitive remediation, addressing specific cognitive defects in memory, reasoning, and attention, is a treatment that may be useful that is currently undergoing further study.

CLINICAL COURSE WITH MANAGEMENT AND TREATMENT

Treatment may be divided into three phases: acute, transitional, and chronic. Acute care deals with episodes of acute psychosis, when positive symptoms are florid. Danger to self and others is an immediate focus of treatment. Antipsychotic medication is started—which may take several weeks to take effect. If necessary for agitation, an antipsychotic with sedating side effects or a benzodiazepine can be used. Benzodiazepines can also be useful in patients who present with catatonic symptoms. If a patient is assaultive and unable to control themselves, physical restraints may be necessary. Orthostatic blood pressures and sedation must be monitored to prevent falls. Positive symptoms can be ameliorated to some extent—more so than negative ones. Decreasing the length of time someone is acutely psychotic improves the prognosis.

Transition from inpatient care must be planned carefully, as this is a period of time when the risk of relapse and the risk of suicide is high. Day treatment programs may be useful, providing structured activities and monitoring medication compliance. Education of the patient and family about early signs of relapse should be done.

Chronic care should include maintenance antipsychotic medication. Duration of antipsychotic therapy should be at least a year after the first episode, and indefinitely for those who have had multiple episodes or two episodes in five years. As in other chronic diseases, it is often difficult to get someone to take medication when they are not symptomatic. The burden of side effects and the lack of insight most persons with this illness have contribute to many insisting that they be taken off medication. Education of the patient and family about the early signs of relapse and ongoing outpatient visits to monitor for relapse are critical if a trial off medication is decided on. The development of tardive dyskinesia and/or metabolic syndrome can make it more difficult to convince someone to remain on medication.

With optimal medication and psychosocial treatments, most patients can lead a satisfying life and participate in society.

In Mike's case, once his current legal difficulties are resolved, the courts might choose to impose a mandatory outpatient treatment order. Such an order would require Mike to attend therapy and take medication, most likely in an intramuscular depot form. The treating clinicians, most commonly at a public community mental health center, would be required to report to the judge any noncompliance on Mike's part. Such noncompliance could result in the judge issuing an order to the police to detain Mike. Such mandatory outpatient treatment orders are periodically reviewed by the courts to assure that, when they are no longer necessary, they may be stopped.

SYSTEMS-BASED PRACTICE ISSUES

Mental health services are chronically underfunded, and although there are evidence-based practices, practically it is often difficult to get these services. There has been a transinstitutionalization of patients with schizophrenia from the old state hospitals to the jails and prisons. It has been estimated that one in five persons in jail or prison is seriously mentally ill, far outnumbering the number in psychiatric hospitals. There is a shortage of psychiatrists, and psychiatric residency programs have not filled in years. More than 50% of active psychiatrists are over 55 years old. While there has been a lot of research and advances in knowledge, the translation of this to improved clinical practice has been less than hoped.

LEGAL, ETHICAL, AND CULTURAL CHALLENGES

Refusal of medication is not uncommon. Assessment of capacity to consent to or refuse treatment is an essential part of the initial evaluation. Capacity is task-specific. An individual may have capacity to give releases of information, but not consent to treatment, for example. Antipsychotic medications can have serious side effects, and informed consent should be obtained before long-term prescribing of them. To give consent to treatment, an individual should be able to describe the diagnosis, the proposed treatment, the benefits and risks of treatment, the risks of no treatment, and be able to consider this information rationally. Seeing as how most individuals with schizophrenia do not realize they have an illness, having capacity to consent to treatment is the exception rather than the rule. Someone who has the patient's best interests at heart will make decisions considering the individual's values, has capacity, and fits the state's definition of a person who can make decisions for another person can be authorized to make decisions for the individual. If not such person is available, than a hearing may be held and a judge may authorize specific treatments. In criminal cases, the judge ordering the patient to the hospital can also order treatment, although they don't always do so.

Competency to stand trial is based on an individual's ability to understand their charges, the legal process, and their ability to comport their behavior appropriately in a courtroom. It is not dependent on any specific psychiatric diagnosis. A person may be psychotic and yet be competent to stand trial. Competency to stand trial can actually be taught in some cases. Education can be provided as to what the charges are, what pleas of innocent/guilty/no contest mean, what penalties can be imposed, and the roles of their attorney, prosecuting attorney, judge, and jury. The level of understanding and decision-making ability necessary to be competent to stand trial will depend on the complexity of the case and the potential seriousness of the outcome. A capital murder trial would require far more of an individual than a petty larceny trial. Psychosis, mania, depression, or other psychiatric conditions may make an individual not competent to stand trial. Successful treatment of those conditions may restore competence. It's important to realize that an individual cannot be required to take medications in jail without a judge's order. If ongoing medication will be necessary for an individual to stay competent, that needs to be stated in the report to the judge.

Insanity is a legal concept, not a medical one. There is no specific psychiatric diagnosis that would render one "insane." Most states allow a plea of "not guilty by reason of insanity." The idea is that someone who was not in control of his actions should not be held morally culpable for them. Intoxication, unless given the substance involuntarily, does not qualify as a reason. The exact definition as to what constitutes insanity varies from state to state. All require that the individual have a "mental disease or defect." The federal standard requires also that "[the defendant] was unable to appreciate the nature and quality or the wrongfulness of his acts" at the time of the offense. Generally, this can be broken down to two factors. First, can the individual understand right from wrong? This may be an issue with psychosis or dementia. Second, did the individual have an "irresistible impulse" such that if an officer was at their elbow, they still would have acted the same? This can be an issue with mania. This defense is raised in about 1% of felony cases and is successful about 25% of the time. A person can be locked up far longer if found "not guilty by reason of insanity" than if found guilty. The standard for release is that the person is no longer a danger to society, not that he or she served the sentence.

HISTORY

There are three German health professionals who are important in the evolution of the diagnosis of schizophrenia. Emil Kraepelin, regarded by some as the founder of modern scientific psychiatry, in the early 1900s based his definition on the study of the course of individual case histories. He identified "dementia praecox," which was characterized by a phenomenology of delusions, hallucinations, motor symptoms, emotional blunting, avolition, and social isolation. In particular, he regarded the typical course and prognosis as a key feature of the illness. He felt that the illness was characterized by an inexorable deteriorating course. He felt that a common pattern of symptoms was important in diagnosis. In 1911 Eugen Bleuler introduced the term *schizophrenia* to replace dementia praecox. He felt the central characteristic was the splitting of psychic functions, and that cross-sectional symptoms were more important then the course and prognosis. He felt that it was not always incurable. He is famous for the "4 A's" of schizophrenia: affect (inappropriate of flattened), autism (preoccupation with internal stimuli), ambivalence, and association (loose associations). Kurt Schneider espoused certain symptoms as typical of schizophrenia, including thought insertion, thought withdrawal, thought broadcasting, and delusions of control. He also further commented on the phenomenology of auditory hallucinations.

REFERENCES AND RESOURCES

American Psychiatric Association, Practice Guidelines for the Treatment of Psychiatric Disorders Compendium 2006. Arlington, VA: APA, 2006.

Courtenay MH, et al. The Vermont longitudinal study of persons with severe mental illness, I: Methodology, study sample and overall status 32 years later. *Am J Psych* 1987;144(6):718–26.

Lieberman JA, et al. Clinical Antipsychotic Trials of Intervention Effectiveness (CATIE) investigators: Effectiveness of antipsychotic drugs in patients with chronic schizophrenia. *N Engl J Med* 2005;353:1209–23.

The National Alliance on Mental Illness is an excellent resource for information, support, education, and education on schizophrenia. Their website is www.nami.org.

The website www.schizophrenia.com has a lot of information and links to other websites.

The website http://psychiatryonline.org has access to books and journal articles.

The Hollywood film *A Beautiful Mind*, shows the life of Nobel laureate John Nash, a brilliant mathematician at Princeton. His hallucinations are portrayed as visual instead of auditory in the film, given the difficulties portraying auditory hallucinations. He had severe paranoia and delusions about working in cryptography for the U.S. government. He underwent insulin shock therapy as well as taking antipsychotic medication, which he later said he only took when under duress. He recovered gradually with the passage of time. The devastation to his life, as well as the burden on his family and friends, is empathetically portrayed. This film was honored by NAMI for the year's Most Outstanding Contribution to Public Understanding of Mental Illness in 2002.

CHAPTER **8**

Delusions

Sachinder Vasudeva, M.D., M.S.

CLINICAL PRESENTATION

Chief complaint: "My wife is cheating on me."

History of present illness: Jeff is a 44-year-old white male with no previous psychiatric history, referred to a therapy clinic by his pastor. He is accompanied by his wife of 22 years, Jill. He is seen first, and then with his permission, they are seen together.

Over the past couple of years, Jeff has been accusing his wife of infidelity. There were no precipitating events, but about two to three years ago, he started suspecting that "something was going on." He started asking Jill where she had been, whom she met, and "if there was anything else" she wanted to tell him. At first, she thought it was "cute" that after 22 years of being married, he was starting to get a little jealous, but when this persisted over a few weeks, and it became clear that he was not joking, she started to get annoyed. Her efforts to convince him that "nothing was going on" were met by accusations that she was not being totally honest with him. Over the next few weeks, he started to examine their credit card bills more closely for "evidence" that she was seeing someone else. She caught him a few times checking her cell phone when he thought she would not notice. Gradually, things got to the point where he tried to follow her to work twice.

She talked to his brother and his wife, who lived in the same town. His brother acknowledged that Jeff had brought up this issue to him a couple of times and that he did not know what to do. He and Jeff had always been quite close and he was not aware of Jeff using drugs. When Jill suggested seeking therapy, Jeff was at first upset, saying, "First you break our marriage vows and now you're trying to say I'm crazy," but he agreed to talk to their pastor, who also happened to be a friend of Jeff's parents. The pastor met with them individually and together and suggested seeing a therapist.

But for the pastor's suggestion, Jeff does not think that he would have seen a counselor. He offers that if his wife were suffering from something "such as a compulsive sexual behavior," he would be happy to see someone with her to get her the help she needed. Jeff's understanding of the visit is that the meeting was "to see if she had a problem, and for me to see how I can deal with it, although I think I'm doing just as fine as I can, under the circumstances."

Jeff denies any history of mood problems. He does acknowledge that more recently, he has been "somewhat depressed" about his marriage. He feels "down on and off," but he has not experienced any disabling depression. He reports sleeping well for the most part, still enjoys spending time with his children, and has continued with his woodworking projects. He does not feel fatigued or easily tired. He is able to concentrate on his work as a manager at a factory that makes door and window parts. He has not noticed any appetite or weight fluctuations. He weighs 204 pounds, "up from 176," when he graduated from college. He has tried to be involved in regular exercise but has been unable to because of poor stamina due to his allergies; he does walk the dog since their son left for college about a year ago. He denies any thoughts of wanting to hurt himself.

He denies any episodes of excessive elevation of his mood and does not endorse other symptoms of hypomania or mania. He denies that he has excessive worries or that he experiences anxiety attacks. He denied symptoms suggestive of obsessive compulsive disorder, though he acknowledges that lately he has been somewhat preoccupied with his marital issues.

He denies any auditory or visual hallucinations. On being asked about olfactory and tactile hallucinations, he hesitatingly admits that on occasion, recently, during intimacy with his wife, he thought he "smelled another man's odor on her." He has never smelled "rotten eggs" or anything offensive at such times. He is not sure why that odor is there only occasionally, but thinks it may be "because she had been with him recently."

When asked about his marital "issue," he acknowledges that he loves his wife and would not want them to separate. He says, "I know for a fact that she continues to cheat on me." When asked how he knows this, he replied, "You just know when something like this happens, and the smell of another man on her is further proof, not that you need any." He is not willing to concede that his wife may be loyal to him.

He laughs when asked if someone like the aliens or some other mystical powers may be influencing his thoughts or controlling his wife's actions.

He does not know whom she is seeing, or if there is one man or woman, or more than one person whom she may be sleeping with. He was "raised a Christian" and knows that "people may give in to temptation, but that does not mean that our marriage has to end." He would like her to be faithful to him, "and when that happens, I'll just know in my heart, there's nothing she has to do to prove to me that she is faithful again."

He has never physically threatened his wife and does not think he would hurt her. If he came face to face with her "beau," he thinks he would be upset, but does not think he would do anything to physically hurt him or her. He does not own a gun.

Jeff denies recent or current drug use. He smoked marijuana a few times in college. He may have a beer or two at social gatherings or a couple of beers while watching a game, but he denies any other drug consumption. He denied any past problems related to drug or alcohol use. He does not use tobacco.

Medical history: Jeff reports no chronic medical problems, other than seasonal allergies in the spring, during which he takes over-the-counter medication. He has occasional shoulder pain "if I've done heavy lifting," for which he takes ibuprofen for a couple of days. He has no history of seizures. He had a tonsillectomy as a child and wisdom teeth extractions when he was in college.

Family history: Jeff is not aware of any psychiatric history including mood or anxiety problems, paranoia, or drug or alcohol abuse. His maternal grandmother is in a nursing home for dementia, and his maternal grandfather has diabetes.

Social history: Jeff was born and raised by his parents. He was the youngest of three siblings. He has an older brother, who lives in the same town, and older sister who lives in the adjoining state. He does not recall being told that he was "slow or late" in doing things. He denies any physical, sexual, or emotional abuse as a child, although he and his siblings were occasionally spanked, but that was "very rare and never excessive." He reports doing well in school academically with a B average and was active socially. He was a "history major with a minor in accounting" in college. He dated a few girls in high school and college, and met Jill in their junior year of college; they married soon after graduation. The marriage has been mostly happy, "without any major issues, until recently." They have a 20-year-old son who recently started college.

His wife works in a bank. His parents and brother's family live close by. Besides his family, he has a few close friends. He lists his faith, family, and friends as his main sources of support. Finances are "okay, a bit strained by trying to keep our son's student loans low." He denies legal problems or major stress at work.

History from other sources: Jeff and his wife were referred by their pastor, who sent a note with the wife stating that, from knowing the family for a few years and from talking to Jill, their family, and some friends, there was nothing to indicate that she had been unfaithful.

When Jill is seen, with permission from Jeff, she is easily tearful and reiterates that she has been faithful all through her marriage. She is unable to understand "what has caused him to start suspecting me after all these years of being married? He just won't believe me." She confirms that she did not feel unsafe in her husband's presence. She has never known him to be a violent person. She is somewhat embarrassed to discuss that Jeff could "smell a man's odor" on her. He had accused her of that in the past, and she had tried to explain to him that she had not been with anyone else. She confirms the rest of the history he had narrated.

Mental status exam: Jeff is a 44-year-old Caucasian male, appropriately groomed, who is cooperative with the interview process. No abnormal movements, tremors, or tics were noted. He was alert; oriented to time, place, person; and was able to attend to the conversation. His speech was clear and fluent and of normal volume and tone. He describes his mood as "who would be happy if his wife was seeing someone else?," and his affect is broad ranged and congruent with his mood. His thought process is goal-directed, without any evidence of tangentiality or derailment. He is not seen to be responding to any internal stimuli. He holds the unshakeable belief of his spouse's infidelity. He appears to have at least average intelligence, and is able to perform serial 7 subtraction from 100 without any problems. He is also able to recall three words given to him after a few minutes. His judgment does not appear to be impaired, but he is seen to lack insight.

IMPAIRMENT IN FUNCTIONING

Delusional disorder is peculiar because the person's overall functioning is not as impaired as one would expect with such disturbance in reality testing. Jeff can generally continue to function, at least to some degree, in areas of his life which do not involve the delusion. He might be able to work, indulge in hobbies, and socialize with acquaintances, as long as the topic of Jill and his concerns about her fidelity do not arise. Over time the relative impact of the delusion on Jeff's life will spread. As he becomes more obsessed with the delusion, it will become harder for him to avoid raising the topic in situations where it would not normally occur.

Delusional disorder often is present for a very long time before treatment is sought. As a result the impairment tends to be much longer and more refractory to treatment than it would be if the problem were addressed early.

DSM DIAGNOSIS

Delusional disorder is a psychosis characterized by an isolated fixed and false belief in the absence of other psychotic symptoms (although there may be transient tactile or olfactory hallucinations in keeping with the delusion). Delusional disorder cannot be diagnosed if the individual meets the criteria for schizophrenia. Symptoms must be present to a significant degree for at least a month.

Safety issues are especially important to consider in terms of any thoughts of wanting to hurt self or others.

The DSM-5 recognizes five specific types of delusional disorders but there are others that may not fit any of these categories. These non-mutually exclusive categories are listed in order of their frequency (highest to lowest):

1. Persecutory delusions that the patient is being purposefully maltreated in some way.
2. Somatic delusions that the patient has a physical deformity or condition.
3. Grandiose delusions of being especially talented, wealthy, powerful, or influential.
4. Jealous delusions that the patient's partner is unfaithful
5. Erotomantic delusions that someone is in love with the patient.

6. Mixed type: delusions combining elements from more than one of the above types.
7. Unspecified type.

EPIDEMIOLOGY

Delusional disorder is not a very common diagnosis, with an estimated prevalence of 0.03%. With a mean age of onset of 40 years, it is slightly more common in women than in men. It seems to occur at a slightly higher rate in people who have sensory impairment, social isolation, history of recent immigration, or a family history of delusional disorder. It does not occur at a higher rate in family members of people who have schizophrenia.

Relatively few people (10–20%) who are diagnosed with delusional disorder are later diagnosed as having schizophrenia or a primary mood disorder. Hence it is not considered to be a precursor for schizophrenia or mood disorders.

DIFFERENTIAL DIAGNOSES

The DSM classifies delusional disorder among psychotic disorders. A delusion is defined as a "false, unshakeable belief." It may be described as "bizarre" if it is not a plausible event. For example, if Jeff believed that aliens were abducting his wife every so often, the delusion would have been considered bizarre. In this case his fixed, false belief in his wife's infidelity is a plausible delusion, as it is certainly possible that his wife is seeing someone else. Several differential diagnoses need to be kept in mind.

1. Schizophrenia: the most common of all psychotic disorders, usually has an earlier age of onset and is accompanied by other psychotic symptoms, such as hallucinations and/or disorganized behavior or speech. There is also gradual cognitive decline in schizophrenia (hence its old name, dementia praecox). Persecutory delusions are often seen in schizophrenia.
2. Depression: although Jeff acknowledged being "somewhat down," he did not appear to meet criteria for a major depressive episode or dysthymic disorder. From the history, it appears that the depression did *not* precede his delusional belief. One may propose "adjustment disorder with depressed mood," as a diagnosis, but the depressive symptoms were by no means disabling for Jeff.
3. Bipolar disorder: may also include psychotic symptoms either when the patient is depressed or when he or she is manic. The psychotic symptoms are also episodic and usually congruent with the mood state. There is also history to support the onset of mood problems prior to psychosis. This would be especially important to rule out in someone who has erotomanic or grandiose delusions.

4. Cognitive disorders such as dementia or delirium: dementia is a disorder associated with gradual loss of memory and executive functioning, usually seen in the elderly. Delirium is a psychiatric complication of a medical/metabolic problem, especially in the elderly; this may include psychotic symptoms, but these are accompanied by an alteration of sensorium and also by an inability to pay attention or concentrate.

5. Drug-induced psychosis: several drugs such as cocaine, PCP, methamphetamine, and so-called bath salts can make people psychotic. Typically people display psychotic symptoms while still intoxicated with these drugs. Typically, such states of drug intoxication are also associated with agitation and hallucinations rather than an isolated delusion.

6. Personality disorder: paranoid personality disorder is characterized by a pervasive and usually lifelong distrust of people, rather than a break from reality in an isolated situation. It would be especially important to rule this out in someone with persecutory delusions.

7. Other medical/metabolic conditions that may rarely cause psychosis such as temporal lobe seizures, cranial tumors, and thyroid and other endocrine abnormalities. This may be an especially important differential to consider in someone with a somatic delusion (such as one of parasitosis or the belief that one is infested with some kind of parasites).

8. Other conditions: body dysmorphic disorder, a somatoform disorder, may mimic somatic type of delusional disorder.

NATURAL COURSE WITHOUT TREATMENT

Delusional disorder rarely remits on its own, usually becoming more entrenched and unchallengeable over time. It causes enormous disruption in relationships—even with those who do not bear the brunt of the delusion. For example, it may be difficult to maintain a relationship with someone who is extremely obsessed with the injustices perpetuated by the telephone company.

Favorable prognostic factors include a sudden onset with an identifiable stressor, female gender, a shorter duration of illness, good premorbid social/occupational adjustment, and an onset before age 30. Persecutory, erotomanic, and somatic delusions are believed to have a more favorable prognosis than other types. Overall, at long-term follow-up, about 50% patients recover fully, about 20% show decrease in severity of symptoms, and about 30% show no improvement.

EVIDENCE-BASED TREATMENT OPTIONS

1. Setting: most patients with delusional disorder are treated in the outpatient setting. Hospitalization is indicated usually for safety concerns, such as a husband with jealous type delusions who threatens violence against his wife, or a patient with a somatic delusion of a disfigured body part who threatens to cut

off that part. Another reason for hospitalization may be if the patient's behavior is affected to the degree that he or she is incapable of taking care of their basic needs.

2. Pharmacotherapy: although there are no FDA-approved medications to treat delusional disorder, antipsychotics are often used. Other than the use of pimozide for somatic type of delusions, no specific antipsychotic agents have been shown to work better than others. In general, higher potency antipsychotics are preferred. Adherence to medications is a huge hurdle due to lack of insight.

3. Psychotherapy: establishment of trust is essential and can be difficult; empathizing with the patient's experiences often helps. Of course, the clinician does not want to agree with the person's delusion to establish rapport ("Of *course* Jill is having an affair . . .") but instead can empathize with the distress this belief causes. ("It must be very painful to have these thoughts about your wife.") It is also essential for the clinician to maintain a neutral stance and neither endorse nor directly challenge (especially not in a threatening manner) the person's delusional beliefs. Individual therapy has been used most often, and marital therapy may have a role for some patients. Group therapy is generally avoided. The lack of insight is a major obstacle to therapy.

CLINICAL COURSE WITH MANAGEMENT AND TREATMENT

Jeff is prescribed risperidone, starting at a dose of 0.5 mg at night and gradually increasing to 3 mg at night. He tolerates the medicine well and starts to believe that his wife has become faithful again. He never develops insight that this had been a delusion. After a couple of years, unfortunately, he stops the medicine and starts to have the same thoughts again. When Jeff is 48 years old, Jill files for divorce when she feels she "just couldn't put up with those accusations anymore."

REFERENCES AND RESOURCES

Practice guidelines by the American Psychiatric Association are available on the website www.psych.org.

The film *Fatal Attraction* (1987) features a female lead with a fixed, erotomanic delusion about the male lead.

CHAPTER 9

Autism

Felicity Adams, M.D.

CLINICAL PRESENTATION

Chief complaint: "Depression. . . . He argues with people."

History of present illness: Steve is a 28-year-old male with no prior psychiatric history who presents on referral from his primary care physician. The referral is to evaluate and treat for depression. There is a context of marital discord, and Steve comes to the appointment with his wife, Mary. They have been married for five years. It is the first marriage for each of them.

Steve describes feeling discouraged and constantly criticized by Mary, who he says is difficult to please. He says he never knows what she expects and has no idea why she gets upset with him. He doesn't know what to say when she describes a long day at home with their child.

Steve explains that although Mary is a nice woman, she can be emotional, and she makes many mistakes, which over time has been very frustrating to him. Even worse, he says, Mary continues to do things incorrectly even after he explains her mistakes to her.

Mary expresses concern that Steve often argues over trivial topics and gets upset if he is not allowed to win a debate. Though initially describing marital issues, Steve acknowledges that correcting others has also caused problems for him at work. Since his graduation with a master's degree in computer networking, he has worked in tech support for a medium-sized computer company. He explains that he performs well at work. He often stays late or goes in early to work on projects. Despite this dedication, Steve has never been promoted.

He explains that in his performance reviews he has been given feedback about arguing with others who suggest ideas different from his own. It has been suggested to him that he could allow others to do things in ways other than what he thinks would be best. He finds this request strange because he feels it could lessen the quality of the work they produce. Steve explains that he is polite to his coworkers but does best with projects he can do alone, because working collaboratively often presents challenges for him. If a coworker suggests an idea different from what Steve thinks is best, Steve may resist and insist that his way is better and right. If the coworker does not acquiesce and agree that Steve is right, Steve may feel unfairly treated. If more than one coworker is disagrees with him, he feels they are conspiring against him.

Mary says that the tendency to believe he is always right interferes with their marriage. At work, supervisors can assign Steve tasks he can do by himself. But living in a family requires some flexibility.

Steve and Mary are the parents of a daughter, who is three. While Steve works, Mary stays home with her. Steve's dedication to his work leaves Mary with a lot to do at home. But, she explains, things are easier while Steve is at work. She says that Steve prefers to do things in set ways, and his wife and young child interfere with the order and routine he prefers in the home.

When they are all home together, Steve often corrects Mary or tells her she is doing things improperly. She provides an example about the dishwasher. Steve believes Mary loads the dishwasher incorrectly, so he often unpacks it and reloads it, saying what she has done is inefficient and wasteful of water and soap. Steve agrees that this is true. He says he has tried for five years to teach Mary how to load a dishwasher and that despite his best efforts, she either cannot learn or shows total disregard for his teachings. His method, he says, packs the dishes to maximum efficiency, preventing water waste and the unnecessary waste of soap, which is best for the environment.

Mary relates that she feels anxious about getting the dishes washed and put away before Steve gets home each day, as it seems this is the only way to prevent being called into the kitchen for a recurring, loud, exasperated demonstration of the best way to load the machine. With the demands presented by running a home and caring for a child, worrying about having a dirty dish improperly placed increases the overall stress level unnecessarily, she says.

In the mornings Steve likes to keep to a fixed routine. Mary says that each weekday he gets up at the same time, gets himself ready alone, eats the same cereal for breakfast, reads his favorite sports updates, reads an online blog about computer networks, drinks two cups of coffee, and then goes to work. She says Steve prefers the house to be quiet while he does these things. If their daughter is crying, Steve may become upset and may get angry with her for making noise or angry with Mary for not quieting the child quickly. Mary reports that when he is angry, he often paces and then yells, and even at times flaps his lower arms slightly as he shouts for others to be quiet! Though usually a gentle person, Steve's anger happens suddenly and can be intense. If unable to complete his morning routine in peace, he may storm out the door having screamed at his family and slammed the door behind him on his way to work.

Steve admits he likes to do things a certain way, and says this is just the way he is and has always been. He doesn't see anything wrong with it. He thinks his wife should be more considerate and reasonable about doing things correctly, like keeping their child quiet for the few minutes he is home getting ready. He describes Mary as unreasonable, overly critical, and overly emotional and says she often exaggerates and is not precise in her language. For example, he says,

Mary reported that he drinks two cups of coffee before work at home, but in fact, he drinks one cup at home, and carries one with him in a travel mug in the car. This is one example of how Mary repeatedly misreports, distorts, and exaggerates things. She constantly gets things wrong. He says her imprecision is frustrating, and that he catches her in hundreds of similar lies all the time. He says she cannot be trusted. Mary says she feels constantly monitored by Steve. When they were dating, Steve did not insist that she follow set routines or constantly correct her, but that is the pattern now.

There are other concerns. Steve is worried that Mary is overly social with neighbors and friends and he is concerned about the nature of those relationships. Mary is friendly with a woman across the street named Robin, who is the mother of a toddler. The two mothers and their children get together during the day. At times, Steve has expressed vague concerns that he is jealous and does not understand the nature of the friendship. He tells Mary not to spend too much time with Robin, and asks her, "Why do you need to see *her* so much?" He feels anxious when Mary is with other people and says he doesn't understand why she would want to spend so much time with another person. Because Steve works long hours, Mary needs to spend time with other people, especially other adults. But when she does, Steve becomes suspicious and confused and accuses her of being unfair or even unfaithful to him. He does not relate to Mary's need to be with other people, and when she tries to explain it as normal friendship or companionship, he remains suspicious.

Other concerns are expressed, particularly about how to use the space in their house. Steve has a large collection of Star Wars memorabilia that he has kept since he was a boy. He is excited to share his passion for Star Wars with his daughter and talks to her about the characters. He gets frustrated when she shows little interest. Mary has explained that at age three, their child is too young for Star Wars, but Steve persists in talking to her about it. He has a lot of action figures that he has collected. His collection keeps growing, and the amount of space it takes up in the house is an issue. Mary would like to use the space in their home differently, but two rooms are completely devoted to Star Wars collectibles. Steve gets anxious and short-tempered when their three-year-old goes into the Star Wars rooms or touches his collection. Mary knew Steve was interested in Star Wars while they were dating, but she had no idea the interest was so strong or that it would dominate their lives to the degree that it does. She assumed that once they moved in together, the action figures would go to the basement. She points out that the collection takes up more room in the home than is provided to their daughter. Steve says it is not possible to store action figures in a basement or attic, because moisture, mold, insects, or fluctuations in temperature could damage them. He explains that the plastic the action figures are made from is best preserved at 68 °F. That is why the thermostat in the home must remain at a constant 68 °F. If Mary is cold, she can get a sweater. If she is hot, she can wear short sleeves.

With their daughter, Mary says, Steve is helpful when prompted but not generally able to anticipate needs. He will change a diaper or give a bath and can accomplish these things well. Where he struggles most is in playing with his daughter. He makes attempts to play with her in ways that would be better suited for an older child. Mary relates concerns that her child is too small for mini-lectures about Star Wars or to play video games with her father. Sometimes, rather than reading books to their child, Steve reads aloud from his favorite online blogs. He agrees that he is unsure what to do with young children. He says he loves his child, but that he feels at a loss when asked to get on the floor and play with a three-year-old. He says he just isn't sure how to do it. He looks genuinely uncertain, and says, "I am not good at making stuff up, or at pretending to be someone or something else. How am I supposed to act like a princess or a dolphin? I can't make myself do it. I watch Mary do it, but I just am not able to play the way she does. I am best at knowing about facts."

On direct questioning, Steve reports some difficulties with short-term memory, especially for information presented verbally. He says that if he is asked to remember a grocery list, for example, he easily gets confused and may forget things or even remember things as needed that were not. Even he finds this unusual, as he can remember huge volumes of information about topics that are of special importance to him, like sports statistics, computer-related information, and Star Wars trivia. This area of concern is one that Steve and Mary both agree on. Both wish his memory for verbally presented information could improve. Although his short-term memory is at times a problem, Steve has an ability to pay attention to details that is exceptional and usually serves him well. However, overfocusing on details also can be a problem, and Mary relates concerns that Steve becomes engrossed in thoughts about work or is on the Internet at times when she expects him to be supervising their child.

After talking over these other issues, the issue of depression was considered. This was the referring physician's concern, but it was not what Steve or his wife presented as their first concerns. In terms of mood, Steve reports that he is generally in about the same mood, which he describes as "usually at least fair," but he admits he has at times struggled with feelings of depression or low mood and that he gets tense or feels stressed very easily.

More than a severe and persistent depression, he is troubled by a constant sense of anxiety or of being "on edge." The feeling that he can never relax, or that he is "all wound up," rarely leaves him, and he struggles to feel peaceful. Insomnia can be a problem, too, and he feels like he cannot shut off his thoughts at night. When he tries to rest, he struggles to stop thinking about work at the end of the day. At times, he feels his coworkers may be treating him unfairly, and he wonders if they talk about him when he is not around. These kinds of worries and suspicions bother him and keep him feeling tense, as do his chronic anxieties about the nature of Mary's friendships. He says his appetite and energy are good. He has not recently lost or gained any weight. His focus and concentration are at his baseline, he says.

Steve denies any guilty ruminations or feelings of low self-worth. He denies loss of interest in things he usually enjoys. He says he sometimes does feel sad, especially about the way his coworkers and Mary seem to reject his good ideas but that when he is working on networking projects or reading about sports or Star Wars, he does not feel sad. He says he is not hopeless. He does not have suicidal ideation. He reports no periods of three to four days with excessive energy or high moods or periods of time when he did not need to sleep at all.

Steve says he has never been suicidal or attempted to injure himself. He is aware that at times he can get angry, but he does not think his temper is extreme. Mary, on the other hand, observes that he often gets overwhelmed and when he does his anger can be sudden, very intense, and involve shouting, slamming doors, smashing or throwing objects, and foul language. Steve says that although this is true, he thinks everyone acts the same way when angry. He is usually apologetic after a rage and will regret having broken things and try to make amends.

He denies any history of auditory or visual hallucinations. He does not think his worries about his wife or coworkers are overly intense or paranoid, but rather are valid concerns. His wife thinks he is too suspicious of other people and that he tends to attribute threat where there is none.

Steve denies any sensitivity to light, sound, taste, or touch, but Mary notices that he has an unusual preference for extremely deep pressure. Sometimes he will hug his child too hard, until she cries out for him to stop, and Mary reports that he will ask to be squeezed very tightly, in a way that would seem painful to her, but that Steve says he finds restful.

Psychiatric history: Steve has never seen a psychiatrist but did see a guidance counselor for about six months in high school after his parents expressed concern that he was not fitting in and had few friends. At that time his fascination with Star Wars was persisting longer than that of other children, and he seemed to want to talk about it more than others did, to a point that made others less likely to interact with him. He had not started dating and didn't seem to fit in with the other teens. However, he was a good student who did not have behavior problems and followed the rules. Teachers generally praised his careful work. If a teacher made an error, he could spot it and would point it out. In elementary school his teachers accepted this behavior and even told him he was clever, but by high school Steve noticed the same behavior made some teachers annoyed with him. He said he learned from the guidance counselor that sometimes people don't like to be corrected even when they are wrong. He says he still struggles to understand why this is so.

Steve has no history of inpatient hospitalizations or self-injury. He has no history of violence. He has no history of drug abuse. No history of alcohol abuse, but he does drink alcohol socially, and says this helps with his feelings of chronic anxiety.

Family psychiatric history: Steve's mother has been treated for depression and is described as a detail-oriented and organized person. His father likes sports statistics and has a large collection of baseball cards, which he keeps in alphabetical order arranged in specially sized filing cabinets. His father is employed in the computer industry, like Steve is. He has one brother who has been treated for ADHD, and a sister who was treated for anorexia. His paternal aunt had schizophrenia and a cousin's son has been diagnosed with autism. There are no completed suicides in the family.

Other medical history: Asthma was diagnosed in first grade, and he received breathing treatments whenever he had a cold. Eczema present as an infant and toddler is now resolved. He has frequent GI upset, intermittent stomachaches, and frequent headaches.

Other history (developmental, educational/occupational, family/social, legal): Steve reports that he has been told he was a planned and wanted child. His mother had a difficult pregnancy, during which she experienced significant nausea and vomiting. However, he was born on time by normal vaginal delivery. He was the first child for both of his parents. His father was 36 and his mother was 28 when he was born. He was formula-fed from birth and met all milestones on time or early. He had eczema and frequent respiratory infections as a baby. He says he does not think he had many problems with sensory integration as a child; he did not mind tags in his clothing or certain sounds. But he recalls not liking to finger paint and crying in school and hiding under his desk on days when finger painting was required. He says he did not like the way the paint felt on his fingers. He relates that his family has told him he was very smart and that he could name all the states and all their capitals by the time he was four years old. By six years old he knew every U.S. president. By eight he knew more baseball statistics than his father. He completed high school with good grades, two years of community college, and two more years at a technical college where he majored in engineering and information technology. He went on to finish a master's degree and never had significant academic difficulty, but he says he couldn't socialize and go to school at the same time so he focused on school.

Mary was a nutrition student at the same community college, and the two met in the library. She felt concerned after seeing Steve sitting in the same place day after day eating only peanut butter and jelly sandwiches on white bread, and she started bringing him oranges and bananas. The two struck up a friendship. Soon Mary was planning his meals. She was his first girlfriend. He reports that he always struggled to make close friends. He has never had any legal problems, and he denies any history of physical or sexual abuse.

Steve was raised attending a Methodist church with his family, and he and Mary now attend services there together with Steve's parents most weeks. They also participate in a Wednesday Bible study. Steve volunteers at the church by helping with the computers in the church office whenever needed. Resiliency factors include stable relationship with parents and siblings, ability to maintain employment, desire to participate in treatment, his faith, and his ability to focus on a task once he determines he wants to do so.

Mental status exam: This is an adult male who appears his stated age of 28 years, who is tall and thin with no dysmorphic features, dressed in casual business attire, khaki pants, and an oxford cloth shirt. His hair is cut short and neatly combed. He is wearing white cotton socks and tennis shoes with his other business attire. His gait is normal. He sits upright in the chair with a mildly stiff posture and is cooperative with the interview. His eye contact is fair. At times he looks out the window while he is speaking to the interviewer. His affect is mildly blunted. He describes his mood as "even and reasonably good today"; when asked to rate his mood on a scale of 1–10 with 10 being the best mood, he reported a 6.5. Speech is spontaneous, slightly loud in volume, but fluent and normal in rate and rhythm. No psychomotor disturbance is noted. Thought process is linear and logical, and thought content is negative for perceptual disturbances, suicidal or homicidal ideation. Attention and concentration are good in this context. Insight and judgment are grossly intact. Intelligence is above average. He is able to calculate change accurately from a $10 bill. He could correctly recall only two of three objects after a five-minute delay, but with a prompt did recall the third. He is able to abstract proverbs.

IMPAIRMENT IN FUNCTIONING

Impairment in functioning is considerable in this individual. He reports chronic poor sleep and daily anxiety. He is not progressing in his professional life and is at risk of failing to have an age-appropriate relationship with his child and also potentially having deterioration in his marital relationship if his interpersonal skills and insight do not improve.

DSM DIAGNOSIS

The clinician who interviewed this adult suspects he meets the diagnostic criteria for High-Functioning Autism. The clinical picture includes a mixture of multiple presenting problems, including argumentativeness, anxiety, obsessive compulsive personality symptoms, initial insomnia that is chronic and primarily the result of obsessive ruminations, sensory differences, mood symptoms (intermittent dysphoria/quick anger), social and communication problems, memory and attention problems, and possible thought-disordered symptoms (suspiciousness). The developmental history suggests that this pattern has been present since young childhood and has not changed very much over time. Autism is a complex neurodevelopmental disorder and individuals with autism often present with symptoms from all three symptom domains: mood, anxiety, and thought.

The tendency to argue with others or persist in defending a point of view without integrating the point of view of others suggests that Steve may have deficits in the ability to see or imagine other people's perspectives and potential reactions. The ability to imagine another person's point of view is an important part of social functioning, and people vary in the ability to do this. When a person is very poor at imagining the perspectives of others, this can cause deficits in communication and interpersonal relationships. The skill of imagining how another person will think about a situation and respond to it, has been described as "theory of mind." Theory of mind deficits are present to varying degrees in a number of psychiatric disorders; the concept was first described in relation to the psychopathology seen in autism spectrum disorders. Theory of mind broadly describes hundreds of interrelated processes of facial recognition, voice recognition, and higher order social thought processes that allow individuals to successfully navigate daily social interaction.

High-functioning autism is suggested as the best diagnosis for Steve, but it is also possible that he would meet criteria for one or more personality disorders. High-functioning autism was not included in the DSM until 1994. At that time, Asperger's disorder (autism without developmental delay) was introduced as a diagnostic category. Prior to then, individuals with this disorder first presenting for treatment as adults were recognized to have significant deficits in interpersonal relationships and occupational functioning but were not called autistic. Most of these individuals were historically diagnosed with personality disorders. Autism and personality disorders are both chronic, fairly stable conditions that typically present life-long impairments. One study found that adults diagnosed with high-functioning autism also met criteria for a personality disorder 50% of the time. The personality disorders diagnosed in high-functioning autistic adults were primarily cluster A and cluster C disorders. Within the group of high-functioning autistic people studied, the men were more likely than the women to also meet personality disorder criteria. Sixty-five percent of the adult men in the study group met full DSM criteria for one or more personality disorders, most commonly schizotypal.

A few different personality disorders share features with high-functioning autism, and adults on the autism spectrum may also meet criteria for schizoid, schizotypal, paranoid, obsessive compulsive, avoidant, or a mixed personality disorder. Though autistic adults do not usually meet full criteria for narcissistic personality disorder, the tendency to believe they are right can be perceived by others as narcissistic and grandiose. In addition, individuals with autism tend to think in rigid, precise terms, not allowing for much ambiguity. This "black and white" style of thinking is one of the diagnostic criteria for borderline personality disorder. However, people with autism rarely meet the full criteria for borderline personality disorder.

Patients who as children might have been diagnosed with high-functioning autism may first present for treatment in adulthood with features of personality disorders, particularly those personality disorders generally describe as "odd" or "avoidant" or "obsessive." Only a careful developmental history will clarify if features of an autism spectrum disorder have been present since early childhood.

Though the primary care physician referred Steve citing concerns for depression, that diagnosis alone would not accurately capture the wide range of elements present in the history of the present illness.

Schizotypy is a term describing a spectrum of traits ranging from normal creative and imaginative traits, to odd, unusual, or atypical beliefs to psychotic states. There is a relationship between schizotypy and autism, and many autistic adult men meet full criteria for schizotypal personality disorder. In DSM-5, shizotypal personality disorder is listed both in the personality disorders section and in the psychotic disorders section to acknowledge that schizotypy likely represents a milder phenotype of a schizophrenia spectrum disorder.

The working DSM diagnosis for this case is Autism Spectrum Disorder (historically Asperger's disorder). Steve also experiences frequent gastrointestinal upset and headaches. Stressors include marital discord and some conflict with coworkers.

EPIDEMIOLOGY

The epidemiology of autism spectrum disorder has been changing rapidly over the past few decades. Once diagnosed infrequently, since 1994 when Asperger's disorder was included in the DSM, the rate of diagnosis of milder forms of autism has rapidly increased. Autism is diagnosed more frequently in males than in females. Currently quoted figures are about 1 in 100 children and 1 in 88 boys on the autism spectrum. It is likely that numerous adults, particularly adult men, who had previously been diagnosed with a variety of personality disorders may meet criteria for mild autism spectrum disorder. An area of considerable debate is whether there is actually an increasing prevalence of autism spectrum disorder, or if individuals previously given other diagnoses such as obsessive compulsive and cluster A personality disorders are now more likely to be called autistic in young childhood so that there is a shifting of diagnoses away from one category to another.

DIFFERENTIAL DIAGNOSIS

Other than a personality disorder, which could be a synonymous diagnosis, several other diagnoses are considered. Obsessive compulsive disorder (OCD) comes to mind, but Steve's obsessions are not ego-dystonic and are more compatible with obsessive compulsive personality traits than with OCD. He is obsessive but has no corrective compulsions to stop his obsessing. His preference for order, routine, and sameness and his insistence on cleaning the dishes a particular way are personality traits more than anxious obsessions.

His collection could be seen as a kind of hoarding or obsession but likely is best understood in the context of the "special interest" that is very common in individuals with autism. Though obsessive traits and collecting are a part of the autism spectrum, about 25% of adults with high-functioning autism also have clear signs of OCD. However, when this is the case, the clinically impairing intrusive thoughts are often about different topics than those of nonautistic people with OCD. Nonautistic people with OCD often report intrusive obsessions about cleaning, aggression, sex, and religion. Autistic people who have obsessive worries are more likely to report these being about cleaning, being treated badly by others (bullying, teasing, maltreatment), being criticized, and making a mistake (Attwood 2007). At times the autistic tendency toward obsessive special interests can be joined with normal adolescent curiosity about sex, and some autistic teenagers or young adults develop obsessions with pornography that may persist and can be difficult to treat.

In this case, because Steve is not distressed by his preference for order and routine around the house nor by his collecting, his obsessive tendencies would be best characterized as a feature of his high-functioning autism, rather than as a separate diagnosis. It would be helpful to clarify how much time he is spending in obsessive worries and suspicions about his coworkers scheming against him or about his wife's social relationships. The obsessive suspiciousness is concerning because it begins to suggest a thought disorder. The clinician should try to determine if these thoughts are best understood as occasional worries, intense obsessive worries, paranoia, or delusions. At times, it is challenging to determine if a recurrent atypical thought is an obsession or a delusion.

Generalized anxiety disorder could account for Steve's report of feeling tense and anxious all the time, his irritability, and his sleep disturbance. However, the DSM criteria for generalized anxiety disorder preclude this diagnosis in the setting of a pervasive developmental disorder such as autism spectrum disorder. If the clinician suspects that autism is present, then the anxiety symptoms observed would be considered a feature of that disorder rather than a separate disorder.

The patient was referred for concerns about depressed mood, and he does acknowledge some periods of low mood with some difficulty settling to sleep at night, so he has some criteria for depression. However, he has not had other features typical of a depressive episode, such as changes in appetite or a change in his sleep pattern (the insomnia is chronic). He is not hopeless or suicidal and he is able to experience pleasure when doing things he enjoys. His distress is primarily interpersonal and seems to come from misunderstandings in communication with other people. There is no clear history of bipolar disorder, however, the report of intense anger might warrant further consideration of irritability as a feature of a mood disorder such as bipolar II.

Psychosis not otherwise specified could be considered to account for the suspiciousness and paranoia described in the patient's understanding of his coworkers motivations and his wife's relationships. He demonstrates poor ability to take the perspective that his concerns are likely unfounded, so it is possible that he is suffering from paranoia or delusional thinking. However, given the context of the other presenting concerns, it is likely his worries are accounted for by poor theory of mind, and that although he is somewhat paranoid, this state of mind is likely due to long-standing deficits in theory of mind and probably does not represent a newly emergent thought disorder.

Intermittent explosive disorder could be considered as a way of accounting for the extremes of temper described in which the patient sometimes destroys property and is intensely enraged for brief periods and then remorseful. There is no exclusion for pervasive developmental disorders in the criteria for intermittent explosive disorder. However, those who treat many individuals with autism are aware that intense flares of temper are often a problem in this spectrum of disorder, and a diagnosis of autism would account for some tendency to have "meltdowns" and intense tantrums. As with the other differential diagnoses considered, intermittent explosive disorder would not account for all the presenting concerns as well as would a pervasive developmental disorder.

ETIOLOGY AND PATHOGENESIS

Genetic disorders account for a small percentage of autism, but the higher functioning subtypes in which there is no developmental delay and no intellectual impairment are not typically associated with known genetic syndromes. There are known associations between maternal history of autoimmune disease and depression that may suggest immune or inflammatory links to the pathogenesis of mild autism spectrum disorder. Epigenetic modification of the genome seems a likely factor in the increasing rate of autism, and some have speculated that environmental toxins such as endocrine-disrupting chemicals could be playing a role in the rising prevalence of autism spectrum disorders. In addition, many families have reported a benefit to a gluten-free/casein-free diet for people with autism, and recent research suggests there may be a link between casein or gluten autoimmunity and a risk of psychiatric illness. Because this patient gives a history of frequent GI upset and headaches and had a childhood history of eczema and asthma, he may be at heightened risk for atopy and/or autoimmunity, and it might be reasonable to recommend further testing for food sensitivities or to offer a trial of an elimination diet. Elimination diets do not cure autism, but if a food sensitivity is the cause of gastrointestinal symptoms, avoiding that food can be helpful. Decreasing chronic inflammation may improve mood and decrease irritability overall. The possible contribution of chronic inflammation and inflammatory damage to autism is further supported by observations that children with autism spectrum disorders seem to have reduced antioxidant capabilities, and some small studies have shown that children show improvements in mood and decreases in autistic behavior while taking antioxidants.

NATURAL COURSE WITHOUT TREATMENT

Autism spectrum disorders are chronic and are considered neurologic and developmental disorders. Children with these disorders may show signs of decreased interest in sharing experiences with family members and friends and may show and sensory differences as early as within the first year of life. Mothers often report noticing differences in these children from very early in development. In particular, the children may show a decreased interest in other people and a preference for being alone or an increased ability to entertain themselves quietly. Many autistic children show intense interest in things that spin, and often they line toys up or organize them, rather than playing with them. Very young children with autism may favor one toy obsessively and need to take it everywhere they go. These kinds of behaviors are often the first concerns reported to a pediatrician.

However, if a child is firstborn, parents may be less able to spot differences in development simply due to their lack of experience. Children with high-functioning autism may tend to be content to play alone and may have comparatively less need to interact with their parents than do other children, but they do not show motor or language delays, and in some cases, they may have areas of precocious development, especially for language or musical skills.

Language and reading skills can develop quickly in high-functioning autism in a way that seems wonderful and amazing and may make family members think the child is a genius. In some cases, this is true. However, very often the early and excessive language development in high-functioning autism is part of a pattern of atypical development that may also include deficits in working memory and problems with fine motor skills, attention, facial recognition, and theory of mind.

Although the development of language is largely normal or exaggerated in high-functioning autism, often there are subtle differences in the production of speech. The tone of voice and melodic sound of speech is referred to as "prosody," and often there are prosody deficits in autism. This can be subtle and noted only as a person constantly talking too loudly or softly for the social context or it can be more pronounced. Some children seem to speak in accents different than their family of origin or may have a very flat monotonous or robotic-sounding voice. Alternatively or in addition, there may be an overly precise, overly formal, pedantic, lecturing quality to the speech of high-functioning autistic people. As children, these people are often described as "little professors" due to their tendency to lecture others about their topics of special interest, or "little policemen" due to their tendency to enforce rules on others even when doing so is socially awkward and makes it difficult for them to get along with others.

As development progresses, children are expected to become more independent from parents. In terms of social development, the older a child becomes, the less parents usually participate in the arrangement of social activities. By middle school children are generally expected to begin planning and organizing their own social experiences. Children with high-functioning autism tend to struggle with this transition to independent social competence and may be excluded by peers, who may see them as odd or annoying. It is not uncommon for children with high-functioning autism to go undiagnosed until middle or high school when their social competence issues become more pronounced as the social demands of adolescence become more complex.

However, not everything about the atypical development in autism creates disabilities. There may be special abilities that are created as well, and it takes specialized testing to document what many parents and families have known for years. High-functioning autistic people can do some amazing things with their minds! Raven's Progressive Matrices is an IQ test that is not time based and uses primarily geometric shapes rather than language. It is a single, self-paced test that limits the use of verbal directions and is not based on typical cultural experiences. Autistic individuals across a range of intellectual abilities score on average 30 points better on this test than they do on a Wechsler IQ battery, which is a standard measure of intelligence. Typical individuals show no such difference in IQ between test types, suggesting that using standard intelligence testing for autistic people may fail to capture their abilities and underestimate their talents.

Though intellectual delays are excluded in the diagnosis of high-functioning autism, many with this disorder show subtle deficits in working memory and attention and have features of attention deficit disorder (ADD). A good number of children with PDD are treated at some point in their development with medications to enhance focus and attention. Some individuals may benefit from special education plans to target organization and assist with modifying work to help them complete it with less difficulty, but many with high-functioning autism can excel in school without extra help.

Depression is more common in people with autism and many people with an autism spectrum disorder diagnosis will also have a comorbid mood disorder. Adults with autism spectrum disorders suffer in their lifetimes from a higher burden of psychiatric disorders that people without autism. Primarily overlapping diagnoses are major depressive disorder and anxiety disorders. A much smaller number of high-functioning autistic people go on to be diagnosed with psychotic spectrum disorders, such as paranoid schizophrenia. In one study of paranoid schizophrenics, 65% had met childhood criteria for PDDs based on retrospective interviews of family members.

EVIDENCE-BASED TREATMENT OPTIONS

For the presenting concern of mood-related symptoms, there is some evidence base for the use of selective serotonin reuptake inhibitors (SSRIs) in adults with autism, but less evidence for the use of SSRIs in children with autism. Atypical antipsychotics, particularly risperidone and aripiprazole are generally the drugs of choice in autism spectrum disorders as these are FDA approved for the management of mood symptoms, particularly the irritability often seen in children on the spectrum. Buspirone may be somewhat helpful as an anxiolytic, and there may be some role for anticonvulsants that act on the gamma-amino-butyric acid (GABA) and glutamate systems. The anticonvulsants could have the added benefit of possibly modifying some of the explosive temper that is a presenting concern, while also decreasing anxiety. There is also some evidence for the use of antioxidants such as omega 3 fatty acids in fish oils, and one recent study found benefit from N-acetyl cysteine for the reduction of irritability in children with autism spectrum disorder. Pharmacotherapy will not be entirely curative in this case, but it has the potential to be helpful.

Recently, social skills curricula have been developed to try to teach children with autism some better skills for working with and interacting with others by teaching skills for imagining other people's viewpoints. However, there are not much data to support the use of these kinds of classes for adults, and it may be that there is more flexibility in younger minds than in adult minds for this kind of skills training. More research will be needed to determine whether social skills curricula may be helpful for adults on the autism spectrum.

The diagnosis itself can be helpful for some individuals who may feel relieved to finally have an explanation for lifelong personality traits and social difficulties that previously were not understood. Two experts in the field, Tony Attwood and Maxine Aston, have studied the marriages of people with high-functioning autism and offer that if both partners can accept the diagnosis and learn about it, it may be possible for them to work around the problems that autism creates. However, the autistic individual will not be able to learn not to have autism. He or she may be able to learn skills to perform in some ways more typically, but the overall tendency to struggle to see other perspectives, have a preference for inflexible routines, have one or more special interests, and have excessive or pedantic speech will remain.

CLINICAL COURSE WITH MANAGEMENT AND TREATMENT

For adults with autism, finding out about the diagnosis late in life can be a relief or can be upsetting. Depending on Steve's reaction to the diagnosis, management may be very different. If he is accepting of the diagnosis, psychoeducation is the first step. Education can first come from his provider. Many higher functioning autistic adults also like to educate themselves and may take up autism as a special interest once the diagnosis is given. Fortunately, there are many resources available online for people with high-functioning autism and many find considerable support in online communities. Families of high-functioning autistic people can also find support online. Websites have been established to support families affected by high-functioning autistic members.

Proposed goals for treatment include improving sleep, reducing interpersonal conflicts, and reducing psychiatric comorbidity including decreasing overall sense of constant tension and anxiety, improving mood (both by lessening low-level depression and decreasing explosive anger), and decreasing chronic anxiety and suspiciousness of other people.

Improving sleep may be the easiest of the treatment goals to accomplish in the short term. Progressive muscle relaxation techniques and a bedtime routine may appeal to this patient, who is fond of routines. If needed, short-term treatment for insomnia could be added, but it would be preferable to teach a way to relax that helps him establish a normal sleep pattern and reduce anxiety without pharmacology.

Reducing interpersonal conflicts may be a challenge because these likely stem from his reduced theory of mind and preference for routine and order. It is likely he does not want to be in conflict with others and does not enjoy conflict, but nonetheless finds himself in repeated conflicts he does not fully understand. Working with a therapist who is skilled in autism spectrum disorders may be helpful, as will having the patient learn about autism and the ways it affects others who have the same condition.

Psychopharmacology could be helpful, and a trial of an atypical antipsychotic would be reasonable because these are approved for the treatment of irritability associated with autism spectrum disorder in children and should also be effective in adults. Given that this adult also presents with some features of pathological suspiciousness or paranoia, an antipsychotic may be helpful, and it may offer some mood-stabilizing properties as well. Steve's concerns about his working memory could lead a clinician to suggest a trial of an attention-enhancing drug like methylphenidate or amphetamine and dextroamphetamine, but these should be used with some caution in those with autism, especially where there is any concern for psychotic symptoms, as stimulants may worsen psychosis and may intensify irritability and mood symptoms.

These options were presented to Steve, who elected to try a combination of medication and psychotherapy. His medication regimen began with risperidone 0.5 mg orally qhs. This was gradually titrated to bid dosing. Initially, it was somewhat helpful for sleep but over time, as he became used to taking the medication, Steve no longer found it sedating. With his therapist, he learned a progressive muscle relaxation strategy and breathing techniques that greatly reduced his insomnia, and he did not require medication for sleep. He worked in therapy to learn skills for thinking about how others think. After about three months of taking risperidone Steve had gained 10 pounds. He was unhappy with this and concerned about side effects. His psychiatrist suggested adding topiramate 50 mg orally bid, which has been shown to have some efficacy in reducing symptoms in autistic children when added to risperidone and has the added benefit of tending to reduce weight gain from atypical antipsychotic medications. As an added benefit, topiramate is FDA approved for the treatment of migraine headaches. Steve noticed a reduction in the frequency and severity of his headaches when he began taking the medication. His overall anxiety levels were reported to be less after six months on the combination of medications, and he reported that he was getting along better with his wife and coworkers. His weight stabilized and he did not report other side effects to his medications. He continued to work in weekly therapy with a therapist skilled in recognizing the social and communication issues facing adults with autism.

SYSTEMS-BASED PRACTICE ISSUES

High-functioning autism is not commonly diagnosed in primary care settings or by general psychiatrists. The diagnosis is well known to child neurologists and child psychiatrists, but once an individual reaches adulthood, he is less likely to receive an accurate diagnosis because although awareness of these disorders has grown, the diagnosis is still primarily made in early or middle childhood. As a result, many individuals with milder forms of autism are likely diagnosed with personality disorders or are completely undiagnosed in adulthood.

LEGAL, ETHICAL, AND CULTURAL CHALLENGES

Legal and ethical issues with high-functioning autistic people arise because when these people break laws or act in ways that are socially inappropriate, questions are raised about their culpability due to their impaired ability to understand social norms. Impaired theory of mind may lead to impaired empathy, which in some cases may be a component of criminal behavior. The vast majority of people with autism, like the majority of people with mental illnesses, are not violent. However, there may be an increased rate of socially inappropriate behavior among those with autistic spectrum disorders. Particularly in the area of dating and intimate relationships people with autism can get very confused and may persist too long in showing interest or may make socially awkward attempts at indicating interest in another person. There have been case reports of stalking behaviors from individuals with autism spectrum disorders. Because high-functioning autism is a disorder in which intellect and planning can be preserved in individuals with impairments in empathy and social understanding, the potential for social misperception, inappropriate anger, misattribution of threat, and a resultant dangerousness does exist. However, the vast majority of individuals with high-functioning autism are not violent or criminal by nature.

Some individuals with autism offer unique insights into fields like music, science, math, and history. The DSM-5 removed the term *Asperger's disorder* in favor of autism spectrum disorder for all cases of autism, and many of those people who previously identified with the Asperger's label are disappointed by the change. They tend to think of Asperger's not as a disorder but as a way of thinking differently. Some with Asperger's refer to non-Asperger folks as "NTs" for neurotypicals and to themselves as "Aspies," taking on the mantle with pride. Tony

Attwood, a leading clinician and researcher in the field of high-functioning autism, describes that when he gives the diagnosis to a patient for the first time, he tells the client, "Congratulations!" because they have a different way of thinking.

TERMS

Refer to the DSM-V for major diagnostic criteria of *Autism spectrum disorder.* Some defining characteristics are:

- Lacking reciprocity or understanding in social and emotional human interactions
- Ineffectual production, interpretation, or integration of non-verbal communication
- Delays, deficits, or oddities in verbal communication and practical language
- Narrow range of interests, attention, and focus
- Rigid insistence on sameness and routines
- Repetitive impractical movements, actions, and speech (stereotypes)
- Hypersensitivity to environmental stimuli (tactile, olfactory, auditory, visual)

The above deficits are not sufficiently explained by intellectual disability. They must be persistent from an early age, across multiple contexts, and causing functional impairment at home, work, school, or play.

Personality disorder: an ingrained and inflexible pattern of behaving, feeling, perceiving, and thinking that is prominent in a wide range of personal and social contexts that causes significant impairment in life functioning or substantial distress. Historically in the DSM both autism spectrum disorders and personality disorders were coded on Axis II to emphasize their more pervasive and enduring patterns.

Cluster A personality disorders: Three personality disorders grouped together as sharing common features of odd behaviors and beliefs as well as features of reduced affective range. These disorders are often referred to as the "odd" or "eccentric" personality disorders. The cluster A personality disorders are schizoid, schizotypal, and paranoid.

- *Schizoid personality disorder:* apparent indifference to social relationships with restricted expression of emotions, and a striking lack of interpersonal warmth or concern.
- *Schizotypal personality:* interest in interpersonal relationships but with discomfort and reduced capacity for close relationships because of cognitive perceptual distortions and eccentricities of behavior.
- *Paranoid personality disorder:* a pervasive unwarranted suspiciousness and mistrust of people with associated hypersensitivity and emotional detachments.

Obsessive compulsive personality disorder: orderliness and perfectionism, interpersonal relationships, excessive devotion to work, relentless attention to detail, and a rigid cognitive style.

Sensory integration: The ability to receive and process sensory information. Most people have set points for sensory information, and those with autism seem to be particularly sensitive to light, noise, textures, and smell. For many on the autism spectrum, things can seem too loud, too bright, too scratchy or rough, or too smelly. Alternately, however, some people on the autism spectrum seem to have an underawareness of sensory input and may be somewhat insensitive to light or touch and may crave deep pressure. The same person may have some preference for deep sensations and other aversions or hypersensitivities to different sensations.

REFERENCES AND RESOURCES

Aston M, *Asperger's in Love: Couple Relationships and Family Affairs* (London: Jessica Kingsley, 2003). This is a comprehensive description of the impact of Asperger's syndrome on couples, families, and parenting relationships.

Attwood T, *The Complete Guide to Asperger's Syndrome* (London: Jessica Kingsley, 2007). This is the definitive resource for patients and families by the most popularly known clinician in this field. It is comprehensive and readable.

Chemerinski E, Triebwasser J, Roussos P, Siever LJ. Schizotypal personality disorder. *J Pers Disord* 2012 Aug 28.

Craig JS, Hatton C, Craig FB, Bentall RP. Persecutory beliefs, attributions and theory of mind: Comparison of patients with paranoid delusions, Asperger's syndrome and healthy controls. *Schizophr Res* 2004 Jul;69(1):29–33.

Jackson L. *Freaks, Geeks and Asperger's Syndrome: A User Guide to Adolescence* (London: Jessica Kingsley, 2002). Written by a British teen with Asperger's, this is a charming and helpful book both for adolescents and parents. The diction and text give interesting insights into the linguistic differences and abilities of people with Asperger's syndrome.

Lugnegård T, Hallerbäck MU, Gillberg C. Personality disorders and autism spectrum disorders: what are the connections? *Compr Psych* 2012 May;53(4):333–40. doi: 10.1016 /j.comppsych.2011.05.014.

Lugnegård T, Hallerbäck MU, Hjärthag F, Gillberg C. Social cognition impairments in Asperger syndrome and schizophrenia. *Schizophr Res.* 2012 Dec 21;S0920-9964 (12)00662-7. doi: 10.1016/j.schres.2012.12.001.

Soulières I, Dawson M, Gernsbacher MA, Mottron L. The level and nature of autistic intelligence II: What about Asperger syndrome? *PLoS One* 2011;6(9):e25372.

Whiteley P, Haracopos D, Knivsberg AM, Reichelt KL, Parlar S, Jacobsen J, Seim A, Pedersen L, Schondel M, Shattock P. The ScanBrit randomised, controlled, single-blind study of a gluten- and casein-free dietary intervention for children with autism spectrum disorders. *Nutr Neurosci* 2010 Apr;13(2):87–100.

Families of Adults Affected by Asperger's Syndrome, http://faaas.org. "This disability has profound effects on the family members and others in close contact with the Asperger's person. It is the spouses, parents, siblings, and children, of those with Asperger's Syndrome that experience the emotional pain, especially when the correct diagnosis has been delayed until relatively late in adulthood. Family members need validation and support. Feelings of rejection and loneliness play a major role in the lives of the family members of individuals with Asperger's Syndrome. Their feelings are not validated, acknowledged, or recognized by the person with this disability" (faaas.org).

In My Language, http://www.youtube.com/watch?v=JnylM1hI2jc. An impressive video by A. M. Baggs, a woman with autism and normal intelligence. The video is eight minutes long. At about 3 minutes and 15 seconds into the video, she uses voice-assisted computer communication to speak to the viewer about her condition and the ways she thinks about and interacts with the world. This gives a humbling reminder that neurotypicals may not fairly appreciate the hidden talents and abilities of people with autism and other neurodevelopmental differences.

CHAPTER **10**

Attention Problems

Thomas R. Milam, M.D., M.Div.

CLINICAL PRESENTATION

Chief complaint: "I just can't get anything done. I'm useless."

History of present illness: Kasey is a 34-year-old white female who is referred from her family physician for an initial evaluation related to problems with concentration, focus, anxiety, and insomnia. She describes herself as a healthy person with no significant past medical problems, but for the past several months she has noticed changes in her mood and her ability to get work done and stay organized. The only thing she says is different in her life is that she received a promotion at work earlier in the year. Although she is happy to have been promoted, she often feels like she is running behind and can't keep up with the demands on her time at work and home.

After college, where she studied sociology, Kasey took a job as a teller in a local bank. Though she enjoyed the job and outwardly appeared to be doing fairly well, inwardly she found it challenging to keep up with details and had to use a lot of lists and reminder strategies to stay organized. Her supervisor admired her use of these organizational strategies and four months ago, much to her surprise, she was promoted to assistant branch manager. Kasey was excited to receive the promotion and increase in pay, and she enjoys the people she works with. However, since her promotion Kasey has noticed significant problems with concentration, focus, and memory. She has forgotten several important deadlines and meetings at work. She has made a number of careless mistakes on loan applications and other important banking documents, and she has found it very hard to keep track of all the different things going on at work.

Recently she has started pretending to look busy when new customers come in so as to avoid them and avoid taking on any new work. She feels like she is more abrupt with her colleagues who interrupt her during the day and often wishes she could just close her door and get her work done in peace. However, even when she is able to find some quiet time to work, she often focuses on "sillier things," such as checking her email or looking at Facebook. She believes this

153

is wrong, but she frequently just cannot get started with her work and easily procrastinates. She feels like her life is falling apart and she wishes she could take a break, but she and her husband are now dependent on her higher income. She feels trapped.

In addition to problems at work, she is having significant problems at home. She reports being happily married and has two young children, though increasingly she finds herself getting more easily frustrated and irritated with her children and husband for no specific reason. She relates how one evening recently, during dinner, she thought her husband was making a negative comment about the meal she cooked, so she stormed out of the dining room, went to her bedroom, and slammed the door. She then refused to talk to her husband until the next morning. She worries about "going off" on her family again. Normally she relieves stress by going to the YMCA to work out or swim, but lately, since she has had to bring more work home, she has stopped exercising regularly and has gained eight pounds in the last six months. This is very concerning to her. She looks tired in your office and she begins to cry, stating that she feels like she is letting God and her family down and she doesn't know what to do.

Psychiatric history: Kasey denies having had any major mental health problems in the past. She reports that her grades in elementary and high school were generally above average. While seeing herself as naturally intelligent, she remembers having to struggle to stay focused and often got very emotional taking tests because she never felt fully prepared. She remembers her mother being very active in helping her get her work done and turned in on time. She laughs when talking about how her mother often read aloud and summarized books for her when she was fairly young just to get them done and to help reduce stress. She recalls having to study a lot more than most of her friends, which led her to feel somewhat socially isolated at times. Because her mother was integral to her success in school, she and her mother have remained very close. In fact she called her mother to discuss her problems prior to coming to the appointment to see if she remembered anything important about her childhood. Her mother reassured her that her early childhood was perfectly normal and that she had nothing to worry about. Such was the extent of her available developmental history.

Kasey reports that she often struggled with low self-esteem and feeling like she did not fit in, though she attributed this to always being the "new kid" due to her family's frequent moves for her dad's work. She remembers having had some normal fears as a child, especially a fear about her dad dying when he was away on tour in the navy. She says she always had trouble going to sleep, stating that her mind just always seemed to be awake and active and it was hard for her to shut it off at night.

Kasey reports being an average college student, having studied sociology because it was known to be an easier major, though she often struggled to maintain interest in what she was reading and in completing tasks that required a lot of mental effort. She found such tasks boring but necessary. She liked business and accounting but always worried she would not have sufficient mastery of these subjects to have a successful career, and sometimes she got overwhelmed trying to memorize a lot of data for exams. She often made careless mistakes on exams and frequently pushed major projects off until the last minute, finding it difficult to motivate herself to complete the work unless it was something she was really interested in. She found it easier to study in a cubicle in the library, but she took frequent breaks to check email and sometimes would spend more time doing social networking on the computer then studying.

Family psychiatric history: Kasey states that her child in third grade is having problems with concentration, focus, and sitting still in the classroom. His teacher has requested a meeting with Kasey and her husband about this, but so far she has been too busy to find a time to meet with the teacher. She is not sure about any other family members having any major mental health issues. She states her mom is a "worrier" and has some problems with insomnia. Her father works for a shipping company and is "always busy." She remembers that her maternal grandmother was an alcoholic, but she does not know the details. Her only brother is healthy and travels a lot in his work as a pharmaceutical sales representative.

Other medical history: Kasey reports that she is a reasonably healthy person currently. She takes antihistamines in the spring for seasonal allergies. She also reports that she was told that she has a very slight heart murmur, present since she was a young child, and she takes antibiotics before going to the dentist because of this. The deliveries of her children were uncomplicated. She denies any history of head trauma or concussions. She has never had surgery and has never been hospitalized, although she does remember spraining her ankle several times as a child while "goofing off."

Other history: Kasey has been married for 11 years and has two children, a daughter who is three and a son who is six. She and her husband met in college and got married right after that. Her husband has a good job in the manufacturing industry, though she is always worried about the possibility of his plant closing one day. She describes her family as "middle class" though she wishes they could be more financially secure. She and her husband argue most about money and family budget stuff. Despite both she and her husband working, she reports being the main parent who does the housework, cooking, and childrearing. She has tried to get her husband more involved in helping out in the evenings, though she says those discussions usually don't end up going very well—she acknowledges there is room for improvement in this area.

She rarely drinks alcohol, stating that it just makes her tired, and she has never smoked cigarettes or used any illicit substances. She has had a few minor "fender benders" and has had two tickets in the past six months for ignoring a stop sign. She says she was in a hurry to get to work and just was not paying attention.

Her daily routine consists of getting up at 6:30 am, fixing breakfast for her family, getting herself and the kids dressed for school, making lunches, looking over homework, and leaving in a rush by 7:45 am to get the kids to school by 8 am and herself across town and at her desk by 8:30 am. Her kids go to the same after-school day care and she picks them up between 5:30–6:00 pm. Her evenings involve getting dinner ready, getting dishes done, doing laundry, and getting the kids to bed by 8 pm "on a good night." After the kids are down she tries to get caught up on stuff she brings home from the office but is usually too tired and nonproductive. She does Facebook and email a lot at night, too. On the weekends she goes to the grocery store, does housework and laundry, takes the kids to activities, and occasionally takes a walk in her neighborhood with her dog. She feels tired a lot and always feels like she has not gotten enough sleep.

Vital signs: Blood pressure, pulse, temperature and respirations were all within normal limits.

Mental status exam: Kasey is nicely dressed in business attire appropriate for her occupation. She is well groomed. She presents in a pleasant and cooperative manner. She exhibits good eye contact. She has no problems with impulse control, and there are no psychomotor disturbances noted. Her speech is normal in rate, tone, and volume. She is fully alert and is oriented to person, place, time, and situation. Recent and remote memory are grossly intact. Attention and concentration are fair, though at times she seems a bit preoccupied. Intelligence is estimated to be above average. Her affect is fairly anxious, occasionally mildly labile and tearful, though appropriate for the situation. She describes her mood as "pretty stressed out." She does not endorse any suicidal or homicidal ideations, plan or intent. Her thought processes are linear, logical, and goal-directed. She is quite articulate and descriptive in her use of language and uses a wide range of vocabulary consistent with her level of intelligence. There is no loosening of associations, though she repeats parts of her story sometimes and then apologizes for having done so, indicating reasonable self-awareness. Her basic fund of knowledge and ability to perform simple calculations are appropriate for her age and intelligence. Her insight and judgment are normal. She reports no hallucinations, illusions, delusions, or any sense of depersonalization or derealization.

IMPAIRMENT IN FUNCTIONING

Kasey's initial presentation reveals a significant level of distress, a decrease in her general emotional well-being, and decline in functioning at home and at work. Since she reports that many of these problems came to a head after her promotion at work, her symptoms, though numerous, could indicate that she is simply not suited for the promotion she received. It is normal, developmentally, to try new things in life and to find out, by normal human trial and error, that one is simply unable to perform at the level he or she had hoped or expected, whether that performance is at work, in sports, parenting, finances, home life management, or some of the many other dimensions of normal human life.

From an Eriksonian psychosocial developmental model, Kasey appears to have reached the stage of adulthood fairly successfully, but may be appropriately struggling with the developmental conflict of generativity versus stagnation, where feelings of belonging and of being successful in one's personal and vocational lives lead to a sense of healthy pride and accomplishment. Her current feelings of failure could indicate psychosocial stagnation and warrant some intensive psychotherapy to explore her developmental growth through this, and even earlier, stages of development.

It is often quite hard to distinguish whether a person's current life stressors stem from psychological, social, interpersonal, developmental, or biological problems or deficits, as with Kasey. A biopsychosocialspiritual formulation is important to keep in mind when assessing a person's degree of emotional suffering, particularly when providing behavioral health care. Kasey's symptoms of inattention and anxiety may indicate that she is on the verge of a profound leap forward in her psychological growth and development, or they may indicate the cumulative effect of aberrant neurochemical functionality that is impeding her ability to experience joy and fulfillment in her chosen work and family life.

From a biopsychosocial formulation, the development of specific symptoms over a relatively short period of time, in the context of what appears to be an otherwise normal course of human development, may lead a clinician to see Kasey's symptoms as situational and time-limited. In such a case, a clinician may simply offer to correct the core, treatable symptoms of anxiety and insomnia by encouraging relaxation and stress reduction techniques, as well as reviewing sleep hygiene and healthy living patterns like exercise, nutrition, and limiting caffeine and alcohol. Using an over-the-counter sleep aid, or even prescribing a short course of a low-dose hypnotic or anxiolytic, may appear to be reasonable alternatives for the clinician to consider. The clinician considers whether Kasey's history and presenting symptoms indicate more than situational stress with insomnia. Here, the clinician functions somewhat like a detective while not losing site of the whole person presenting in distress and in need of care.

Kasey is a high-functioning, normally happy and healthy person who is presenting in significant distress. Were her distress manageable, she would be the type of person who would have managed it successfully, even if it took some time and work. Also her promotion at work, which she sees as a pivotal event or trigger, was something she hoped for and earned, not something she was made to do unwillingly or reluctantly. Thus her normal pattern of successful adaption to changes in her life, which heretofore she has navigated with great agility and ease, would lead her to believe she could do well and be happy with her new promotion. Her promotion is, in fact, a welcome event, consistent with a progressive and reasonable vocational plan. So the clinician ponders why she is having this problem, why at this time, and why such problems did not appear to cause more severe problems when she was younger. Perhaps it is not about work itself but about something in her that had helped her adapt so successfully in so many areas until now. Something has affected her work and family life and disrupted her emotional well-being enough that this highly capable person now sees herself as "useless."

The term *useless*, which Kasey uses to describe herself, implies a problem in functioning rather than a problem in mood (though Erikson might see the two as inextricably intertwined, as many thoughtful clinicians do). Looking at her symptoms and their severity categorically, diagnoses in several areas could be made relating to anxiety, depression, insomnia, and concentration/attention. A clinician could use various rating scales and other diagnostic measures to determine which categories best accounted for her collection of presenting symptoms and how severe each of these categories might be in terms of expected functional impairment. Kasey's symptoms are numerous and overlap several possible diagnostic categories. None of the individual symptoms she describes speaks to one major mental health diagnosis, but their overlapping nature and effect on one another lend themselves to a more dimensional formulation of her illness (i.e., her anxiety leads to insomnia, her insomnia leads to poor concentration and work performance, her poor work performance leads to irritability and mood problems). Her distress is then experienced not just at work but in many dimensions of her personal and family life, leading to her feelings of uselessness and being out of control. With so many overlapping symptoms, the clinician must understand the interrelationships prior to identifying what treatment modalities may best offer Kasey some relief from her distress and the ability to return to her normal level of function.

DSM DIAGNOSIS

As discussed, Kasey's numerous and overlapping symptoms present somewhat of a challenge in terms of a clear diagnosis and direction for treatment. In fact, patients often present with myriad symptoms that do not lend themselves to a clear categorical diagnosis. Their symptoms seem to present a cloud around them that makes normal daily functioning quite challenging. In Kasey's case, while she experiences the negative consequences of this cloud, she is sufficiently bothered by it and is highly motivated to both understand its origin and take concrete steps to be rid of it. Assessing a person's motivation for change is an important step in determining their course of and expected response to treatment.

A clinician's most useful tools for teasing out diagnostic elements are his or her ability to take a thorough but focused history and to know which screening or diagnostic measures or scales to use to narrow the diagnostic field. After going back through some of her history again in a more focused and targeting manner, the degrees, or dimensions, of her various presenting symptoms and their effect on her home and work life are better understood. Additionally, because her problems with concentration and focus at work and at home were significant (and may have been so throughout much of her life as indicated in her history) she was administered the Adult Symptom Rating Scale (ASRS). This is a brief, self-rated and easily scored screening tool designed by the World Health Organization to screen adults for attention deficit hyperactivity disorder (ADHD) and its basic subtypes.

Kasey's scores on the ASRS are in the moderate to severe range on the Inattention subscale. This should lead the clinician to reviewing the more specific diagnostic criteria for ADHD as found in the DSM, many of which form the basis for the questions in the ASRS. Although the age range for initial manifestation of

ADHD symptoms may extend into early adolescence, the DSM-5 states that significant symptoms of ADHD must be present prior to age 12 years (increased from the 7 years in previous editions). The patient must have six or more symptoms of inattention and/or hyperactivity-impulsivity that were persistent for at least six months and were maladaptive and inconsistent with the developmental age of the patient. Although many of these listed symptoms seem to apply more to child-onset ADHD, she endorses many of these symptoms, including making careless mistakes at work, having difficulty sustaining attention, being accused of not listening sometimes when a colleague is talking to her, failing to meet important deadlines at work, avoiding taking on advancement opportunities at work due to her fear it will take too much effort, feeling disorganized and frequently forgetful throughout the course of her day. While she often feels restless and fidgety at work, and at times has been accused of interrupting colleagues during meetings, she does not endorse significant symptoms of hyperactivity. ADHD symptoms must be present in two or more settings such as school, work, or home, and the functional impairment must be clinically significant enough to cause problems in social, academic, or occupational functioning. These ADHD criteria appear to apply in Kasey's case, are not better accounted for by some other type of mental disorder.

Diagnosing ADHD in adults can be quite challenging, especially if historical recollection of impairment in childhood is scant or anecdotal. In reviewing Kasey's childhood academic history, she does report some symptoms consistent with ADHD as a child prior to age seven or so. In some cases, when evidence for ADHD symptoms in childhood is not readily accessible for whatever reason, it may be prudent to collect more data from items such as old report cards or childhood schoolwork stored in a person's attic or basement. Talking to parents and even former teachers may help a person further identify childhood problems with attention, concentration, and impulsivity. Depending on available records and family members, this could be an unnecessarily burdensome and time-consuming task, though it might also prove clinically illuminating. Kasey's mother appeared to play a significant role in helping Kasey succeed academically, much more so than might be expected of an average parent. Such well-intentioned parents can mask a child's true deficits in attention and concentration, only to see such problems surface later when that parent is not around to provide a similar level of support and encouragement.

Taking into account the answers to Kasey's questions on the ASRS, their effect on her current home and work life, and the areas of impairment in attention and concentration shared in her educational, social, and occupational histories, Kasey is diagnosed with Attention Deficit Hyperactivity Disorder, Predominantly Inattentive type. Her symptoms of underlying ADHD, which were mild to moderate earlier in her life, have now become more severe and disabling given the significant demands on her at work and at home. While she has reported symptoms of stress, anxiety, insomnia, and depression in her history and current presentation, these could be manifestations of functional impairment solely related to her ADHD. However, the clinician keeps in mind the possibility of other distinct mental health diagnoses accounting for many of the other dimensions of her distress and functional impairment. Kasey's anxiety or depression may be significant factors, if not the main factors, leading to her current array of symptoms. Her insomnia may also contribute to impaired attention and irritable mood. These factors need to be explored by the clinician to make a definitive diagnosis. Screening for anxiety and depression in the clinic setting is straightforward, but trying to tease out such comorbidities in people like Kasey can be tricky. An evidence-based approach is best, in addition to sound clinical judgment.

EPIDEMIOLOGY

ADHD is generally understood to be a psychiatric condition that first manifests in childhood, though increasingly more and more adults who were not diagnosed as children are finding ADHD to be a significant cause of disability in numerous areas of life. Because of the evolving understanding of the impact ADHD can have on the lives of adults in addition to children, and because increasing number of adults are being diagnosed with ADHD, it makes understanding epidemiological issues related to ADHD somewhat challenging.

Recent literature reviews demonstrate highly variable worldwide rates of ADHD, ranging from as low as 1% to as high as nearly 20% among school-age children. In terms of adult ADHD, prevalence of current adult ADHD is estimated to be approximately 4.4%. Being male, previously married, unemployed, and non-Hispanic white were also significantly correlated with ADHD diagnosis. With more research under way on the importance of attention and concentration in regard to cognitive health in older persons, assessing for ADHD symptoms in older persons suspected of mild neurocognitive disorder or with early signs of dementia is very important.

Certainly, as people transition from childhood and adolescence into adulthood, their experience of ADHD and its effect on specific areas of life changes. Sitting at a desk in a classroom with 25 classmates in elementary school may not seem all that different from sitting in a meeting in a boardroom with 25 colleagues, but the effect significant ADHD symptoms might have on one's livelihood and family are much greater in the latter setting. Even mild to moderate ADHD that went unrecognized and untreated in a motivated and intelligent child may become a severe liability in adulthood as the demands of work, home life, and interpersonal communication increase in intensity and volume, having implications for the well-being of colleagues and family members such as children and spouses.

When one considers that up to 50% of children with ADHD will have symptoms that carry over into adulthood, adults who suspect that ADHD may be affecting their life should be encouraged to seek a clinical evaluation for this disorder. Some adults, like Kasey, put off seeking such an evaluation until the effect their illness has on their work and home life becomes quite severe. A keen clinician will keep in mind that although adults like Kasey may present with symptoms of depression, anxiety, or stress, an underlying diagnosis of ADHD should remain an active part of the differential.

DIFFERENTIAL DIAGNOSIS

Determining whether Kasey's symptoms may be caused by some other physical or mental health disorder is important. Also, other mental health problems like depression, anxiety, and substance abuse can coexist in an adult with ADHD and warrant concurrent treatment.

Kasey denies any significant problems other than those related to attention and focus prior to her advancement at work to a position for which she felt well qualified. Further explanation reveals that it is predominantly a matter of problems with focus, attention, time management, increased mental effort, and a significantly greater need for multitasking—all associated with her recent promotion at work—that appear to have led to the onset of her other mental health symptoms. She denies any prior history of anxiety, depression, insomnia, or other mood problems that might explain some of her symptoms, and she does not report having ever been tested for a learning disability as a child. She denies any significant symptoms of hyperactivity or impulsivity, though in regard to treatment approaches it may be important to determine diagnostically that she does not have one of the other two subtypes of ADHD including ADHD, Predominantly Hyperactive-Impulsive type or ADHD, Combined type. Hyperactivity in children frequently abates in adolescence, especially young girls, often giving the false impression that all ADHD symptoms cease in adolescence. This has left many males and many more females undiagnosed and untreated for a potentially disabling disorder.

In terms of the effect any substances may or may not have on Kasey's attention or focus difficulties, she reports that she does not use any alcohol, tobacco, or illicit substances. She does drink approximately three cups of coffee per day though rarely after 2 pm as it disturbs her sleep. She denies any significant current or past medical or surgical problems other than inner ear infections as a child.

Although anxiety and interpersonal stressors play a significant role in Kasey's presenting symptoms, her original complaint involved feeling like she could not complete tasks or maintain concentration and focus as well as she used to. Taking a thorough history is important in psychiatry because there are few clinically objective diagnostic tools to help make a diagnosis. This is quite unlike the lab work and images studies available to guide clinicians in other areas of medicine. However, there are some psychometric measures and screening tools that can help guide clinical decisions such as in this patient's case.

Kasey was administered the ASRS at her initial clinic appointment to screen for adult ADHD. Her scores on the ASRS reveal significant symptoms of ADHD,

Table 10.1: Commonly used screening tools for ADHD

Conner's 3 (Conner's 3rd ed.)
Swanson, Nolan, and Pelham IV (SNAP-IV) Teacher and Parent Rating Scale
Copeland Symptom Checklist for Attention Deficit Disorders (adults)
Vanderbilt Parent and Teacher Assessment Scales
Adult ADHD Self-Report Scale (ASRS)
Brown ADHD Scales

predominantly inattentive type. She actually laughed as she filled out the ASRS, stating that she saw so much of herself in the questions asked. Unfortunately, most of the existing screening and diagnostic tools used to assess for ADHD are geared toward the pediatric population rather than adults. This is consistent with the developmental understanding that ADHD is a disorder of childhood and adolescence that may persist into adulthood.

It is important for clinicians to familiarize themselves with the most common ADHD screening tools currently in use and to determine which ones are best suited to the clinician's patient population. Many current screening tools garner information from teachers and parents to help assess ADHD symptoms in children and adolescents, whereas screening and diagnostic tools that specifically address adult ADHD symptomatology are few. Typically teacher reports are more reliable because parents are more likely to minimize or exaggerate their child's symptoms. Some of these tools are public domain and can be found on the Internet; others are copyrighted and can prove costly. Table 10.1 lists some of the more commonly used screening tools for assessing ADHD.

There are additional neuropsychological tests that can be administered to assess for impairments in continuous performance, reading, learning, and other disorders that can overlap with ADHD. Additionally, formal intelligence (IQ) testing in children may demonstrate relative deficits in performance, especially in the subtests for arithmetic, coding information, and digit span. It is vital that a clinician not be too short-sighted when assessing persons who present with attention and/or cognitive deficits, no matter the person's age. Numerous etiologies and a wide differential should initially be entertained by the clinician, and then narrowed with a more focused clinical interview, a thorough development and family history, and the judicious use of appropriate screening and diagnostic tools.

ETIOLOGY AND PATHOGENESIS

Understand the multifactorial problems affecting Kasey's mood, sleep patterns, job performance, family well-being, and self-esteem can be quite complex. She endorses significant problems related to stress and anxiety that have led to weight gain, poor sleep, decreased exercise, and irritable mood, all of which could indicate separate, comorbid behavioral and medical health problems requiring different interventions and treatment strategies. It is important to determine why Kasey is presenting at this time. The time of initial onset, duration of symptoms, frequency, and when symptoms worsen or abate are critical to understanding the whole person and how best to guide their diagnosis and treatment. Kasey relates most of her symptoms as having started with her promotion at work. However she seems to have had some subclinical manifestations of insomnia or mood problems prior to her promotion, which are overshadowed by the intensity of her current symptoms. Although Kasey, like most persons who present for clinical evaluation, wants immediate relief of symptoms, spending time exploring specific questions about any symptoms present prior to her promotion is important.

Further exploration reveals that as a child Kasey had trouble falling asleep and she would frequently wake her parents up because she would get scared knowing that everyone in her house was asleep except her. Her parents often responded to such awakenings with frustration rather then empathy, and their reaction only added to her anxiety. She describes herself as a light sleeper, especially after the birth of her first child, though she has never seen it as a problem. She is not hampered with excessive tiredness during the day. She does not feel the need to take naps during the week or on weekends, even after nights when her sleep was more intermittent.

While Kasey believes that her promotion at work seemed to cause her current symptoms, exploring the onset and intensity of her symptoms in greater detail suggests that her promotion most likely exacerbated symptoms that were already brewing at home and in her prepromotion employment. She did recall some careless, infrequent mistakes in some of her work at the bank. She remembered customers who seemed to frustrate her to the point of causing her to be "snippy" with them, even before her promotion. She also described sometimes feeling overwhelmed and unprepared in large, organizational meetings at the bank. When she worked as a teller dealing one on one with customers in that controlled, highly regulated environment, she felt more of a sense of confidence and being in control. She stated that in fact she always did better in situations where she felt in control.

Regarding symptoms at home, there was a noticeable change in Kasey's ability to feel in control after the birth of her first child. She rightly thought this to be a normal part of being the parent of a newborn. On further exploration, she was able to recognize that ever since she had children she has felt slightly more anxious, often wondering if she is doing as good a job as a parent as some other moms she knows. She reports frequently feeling like most of the moms she knows seem to have it all together much more than she does, though she cannot state specifically what deficits she notices in her own parenting style. Her husband frequently praises her and reassures her that she is a wonderful, attentive mother and homemaker, and he often questions her as to why she doubts herself as a mom at times. All these "inadequacies" were present before her promotion at work, but she believes that they have gotten much more intense since her promotion.

When approaching Kasey from a biopsychosocialspiritual model, her symptoms contain meaning for her that can be easily overlooked by a hurried or problem-centered clinician. Her faith infuses her current crumbling self-awareness with numerous questions: Is God trying to show her that she is meant to do a different kind of work and develop different gifts? Maybe she should do some overseas mission work? Does God want her to see that she is too focused on material security and on being in control? Is she somehow letting God down at work or at home in a way she cannot yet see? While a clinician is not expected to answer these spiritual questions directly, it is important to be aware of the sense of meaning that Kasey perceives in her current symptoms, for good or ill, rather than seeing all her symptoms as pathological.

Additionally, maybe Kasey needs to change jobs, hire a housekeeper, or put the brakes on some of her family's extracurricular activities. Maybe she needs some psychotherapy to address the source of some of her shame and cognitive distortions. Or maybe she indeed has some underlying ADHD or other behavioral health problems that can be treated successfully with medications and psychoeducation. All these etiological factors influence the way Kasey experiences her current suffering. An experienced clinician continually keeps the whole person in mind, not just the illness or disease that has led the person to seek help. Maintaining such a holistic outlook can be challenging, especially given the numerous demands inherent in medical practice that can easily lead clinicians to treat the illnesses rather than the person.

One exciting and emerging area of research and clinical practice that has the potential to inform clinicians and patients in ways never before considered involves the field of genetics. From a purely biological basis, some people may possess certain genetic predispositions to developing certain types of behavioral or medical illness. Additionally, a person's genetics may inform how that person's illness may respond to certain forms of treatment. This is sometimes referred to as genomics. The fact that Kasey's son may be having similar symptoms related to problems with concentration and focus indicates a potential genetic basis for her symptoms as well. Such genetic evidence may guide clinicians more specifically in the future, though the diversity of human beings will never exclude the need for sound and thoughtful clinical judgment.

NATURAL COURSE WITHOUT TREATMENT

The majority of cases of adult ADHD appear to go untreated, and these same adults may present for treatment of other comorbid mental and substance disorders. Kasey did not see her symptoms as related to ADHD but to insomnia, stress, and possibly a mood disorder. In fact, comorbidity seems to be more the rule than the exception with adult ADHD. There appears to be a relationship between attention spectrum disorders and anxiety, impulse control disorders, bipolar disorders, major depressive disorders, and, most commonly, social phobia. Possible genetic linkages may eventually help elucidate the reasons behind these common comorbidities.

From a developmental perspective, attention problems in a child may lead to performance anxiety and low self-esteem in both social and academic contexts. With repeated failures in these settings, a child may get depressed or develop a defiant and oppositional manner, or both. Such behaviors, and the negative consequences that accompany them, can hide or distort a child's forgetfulness, inattention, or impulsive decision making.

The historical social struggles and the need for group identification in adolescence may foster gravitation toward more deviant peer groups who may use drugs and alcohol sometimes for self-medication. Marijuana may seem to improve impulse control in adolescents, but certainly lowers motivation and does nothing to improve attention. A bright child with ADHD may learn to compensate by expanding working memory through establishing rigid routines and adhering strictly to certain strategies. Some may even develop obsessive and compulsive personality traits. As the snowball of attention problems in childhood rolls down the developmental hill, layer upon layer of psychopathology may result in a huge accelerating and unstoppable sphere of emotional suffering.

The same pattern noted in children and adolescents is also reflected in many adults with untreated ADHD. Self-medicating with alcohol, marijuana, cocaine, and other drugs may temporarily bring relief to the stress and performance problems related to adult ADHD. Kasey did not report and drug or alcohol abuse, but one can surmise that a stressed, tired, frustrated adult is highly likely to use alcohol or other drugs to self-medicate the suffering they experience from untreated ADHD. It used to be thought that using stimulants to treat ADHD caused people to use more drugs and alcohol when they got older, though more current research has dispelled that myth. Untreated ADHD seems to be the true culprit rather than the medications used to successfully treat it.

If Kasey had not sought treatment for her disorder, one can only imagine the effect worsening mood and ADHD might have had on her family, her job, her faith, and her overall self-esteem. Clinicians fully appreciate how diagnosing and treating one diagnosis can prevent a whole cascade of negative consequences for a person and his or her family.

EVIDENCE-BASED TREATMENT OPTIONS

There are several classes of medications available for the treatment of Kasey's ADHD. What is clear from more recent research is that early diagnosis and treatment of ADHD promotes improved long-term outcomes in children and adults. The positive effect that ADHD treatment can have on adolescent and adult driving habits is emerging, though more long-term studies, especially those looking at long-term risks of stimulant treatments, are needed.

Atomoxetine is a norepinephrine reuptake inhibitor that is believed to increase the synaptic availability of norepinephrine by blocking its reuptake into the presynaptic cell membrane in cells that are important in the brain for concentration, attention and focus. Bupropion has a similar mechanism of action and can also improve concentration and focus, though it is FDA approved to treat depression, not ADHD. Both medications can take several weeks or more to demonstrate treatment benefits.

Stimulant medications such as methylphenidate and amphetamine salts tend to provide a more robust result and treatment benefit can be seen very quickly, often noticeable from the time of initiation of treatment. Though the side effects of stimulants are also greater, including appetite suppression, insomnia, anxiety, and irritability, stimulants are still seen as a first-line treatment for ADHD and are generally well tolerated. Adjusting the dose every four to seven days until remission of ADHD symptoms can lead to rapid and significant improvement in numerous areas as evidenced in the case of Kasey.

Generally the longer acting preparations of methylphenidate and amphetamine salts are better tolerated given the relatively short half-life and brief plasma concentration of the generic molecules. In terms of methylphenidate derivatives, Concerta is one of the most widely used brand-name medications, and there is significant research evidence documenting its benefit in the treatment of ADHD. Other commonly used brand names of long-acting methylphenidate preparations include Ritalin LA/SR, Metadate CD/SR, and Focalin XR. A topical patch form of methylphenidate can be beneficial for longer duration of action, especially for children who have gastrointestinal difficulties tolerating oral forms of methylphenidate or who have difficulty swallowing pills. There currently exists an extended-release stimulant in liquid form as well.

Long-acting preparations of amphetamine derivatives include the popular brands Adderall XR and Vyvanse, the former now being generic. Dextroamphetamine, in the long-acting preparation known as Dexedrine Spansules, is also a commonly used alternative. The amphetamine-based medications appeared to have a more robust effect for many patients, particularly adults, due to the fact that they are believed to directly increase the amount of dopamine in brain regions important for concentration and attention, such as the dorsolateral prefrontal cortex. Methylphenidate-based drugs do not appear to have this direct effect on increasing the production of dopamine; rather, they increase the availability and accessibility of existing dopamine to those important brain regions.

For reasons yet unknown, though likely related to dopamine and other catecholamine receptor sensitivities throughout the human body and brain, some people tolerate or respond better to one class of medications over another. At this time it is hard to predict exactly how a patient will respond to a specific stimulant medication, though research into genetic subtypes may lead to more advanced "custom tailoring" of many medications in the future. Currently clinical judgment, side effect profiles, cost, and provider preference are the main factors guiding a clinician's choice of initial ADHD treatment. In general, methylphenidate may be better tolerated (fewer side effects) than the amphetamine salts. Sometimes the long-acting stimulant preparations do not act long enough, leading to lack of clinical benefits and/or mild rebound irritability in the late afternoon or evening. Adjusting the time a stimulant medication is taken in the morning or augmenting with a lower dose of immediate-release stimulant preparation in the afternoon can be beneficial, although monitoring for appetite suppression and sleep disturbances, particularly in children and adolescents, is important when such augmentation strategies are used.

The alpha-1 agonists guanfacine and clonidine are often used for ADHD, particularly in regard to hyperactivity symptoms in children and adolescents. They are often used to promote better sleep in hyperactive children and adolescents. Both are currently available in the short-acting and long-acting preparations, though the cost of the longer acting preparations can be prohibitive. The alpha-1 agonists also serve as blood pressure–lowering medications predominantly in adults, but monitoring blood pressure and pulse in patients of any age taking these medications is recommended.

Nonpharmacological interventions exist and may be considered either prior to or in augmentation with medications. Cognitive behavioral therapy as well as training in techniques that help with organization, motivation, and time management are well documented. Cognitive behavioral therapy can also reduce anxiety and other comorbidities that can exacerbate ADHD symptoms. Clearly more research is needed regarding the role that therapy and supplements play in treating ADHD, as well as research exploring the effect that food dyes and diet regulation might have on ADHD symptoms.

CLINICAL COURSE WITH MANAGEMENT AND TREATMENT

Once a diagnosis is made, it is important to review both pharmacologic and non-pharmacologic treatment options available so that the patient can partner with his or her health care provider in designing treatment choices and goals. Although lifestyle changes, using basic organizational strategies, exploring patterns of nutrition and exercise, and psychotherapy are all important intervention strategies that should be offered to patients with ADHD and mood problems, Kasey tried many of these strategies without significant success. She simply found it hard to relax and focus without her thoughts and her frustration taking over. She also expressed a strong desire to try a medication before exploring the possibility of psychotherapy given her concerns about the time and financial commitments that psychotherapy would involve. Some clinicians insist that a patient get psychotherapy before starting a medication trial for ADHD. Although this may be warranted and beneficial in many cases where numerous comorbidities exist, it is not mandatory.

Both Kasey and her clinician hope that by treating her ADHD effectively, her stress level would go down and she would experience other significant benefits, including a more positive mood, better sleep, better work performance, and a return to a normal level of function at home. Kasey and her clinician explored the importance of lifestyle changes such as reinitiating exercise, limiting caffeine, improving nutrition, and finding ways to reduce stress at home and work. While it is not uncommon for persons to want a quick fix through the use of medications, clinicians should seek not only to reduce illness but to promote health in the whole patient, involving the biopsychosocialspiritual aspects of a patient's life.

When further explored, Kasey reported that in the past she had used yoga and meditation to work on stress reduction. This had worked for her to a degree many years ago, current attempts to reengage with these proved futile and frustrating. In developing her organizational skills, Kasey had become quite masterful at keeping lists of all the things she needed to get done—she used her mobile phone calendar and alarms to keep track of appointments, as well as a notebook calendar, a desk calendar, and, at home, a dry erase board on which she tried to keep up with all the children's and family activities. However, she found keeping up with all this quite overwhelming and exhausting, and she often felt discouraged by endless lists of things she needed to get done but somehow never fully completed. Given this clinical history, Kasey and her clinician agreed that further attempts at behavioral modification and time management strategies alone would likely not work for her given the severity of her problems.

After a thorough discussion of the risks, side effects, and benefits of both stimulant and nonstimulant medications used for the treatment of ADHD, Kasey consented to starting Adderall XR 10 mg daily with a plan to increase the dose by 10 mg each week until she noted significant improvement in her ADHD symptoms. Given that stimulant medications are broken down very quickly in the body and therefore have very short half-lives, the extended-release preparations have become more widely used, despite their greater expense.

A number of factors come into play when selecting an ADHD medication treatment in addition to determining whether to use a stimulant or nonstimulant. When symptoms are predominantly related to hyperactivity and impulsivity (key features of an ADHD presentation as often found in young boys), the use of alpha-1 agonists such as guanfacine and clonidine may be a good initial choice. Though sedation and hypotension can be potential side effects from these medications, they need to be dosed according to the general rule "start low and go slow." There are once-daily versions of these medications, but they are currently extremely expensive, and no strong body of data shows them to be any better than the much more cost-effective generics, though tid to qid dosing of the latter can lead to problems with adherence for some patients.

When the choice to start a person on a stimulant is made and the patient consents to treatment, long-acting stimulants are generally the first line of choice. Occasionally in very young children or in persons with certain medical comorbidities, an initial test dose or short trial with a short-acting generic methylphenidate or amphetamine formulation may be prudent. These medications begin acting as quickly as 10–20 minutes, though often cease to have clinical effect more than 3–5 hours, resulting in the need for a second or even third dose each day. Using short-acting stimulants as initial treatment may allow for the assessment of tolerability and side effects such tachycardia, nausea, headaches, appetite suppression, insomnia. For some patients these short-acting, cost-effective generic medications may be ample treatment for their mild ADHD symptoms, though long-acting stimulants are much more frequently used first line to improve adherence, reduce side effects, and prevent abuse or misuse of potentially addictive medications.

When choosing a longer acting stimulant, there are several forms available for the methylphenidate and amphetamine classes. The fact that they are longer acting often makes them feel "smoother" in their more gradual release, often leading to fewer side effects. They can, for some persons, be too long acting, at least initially, and lead to insomnia or anxiety. The other potential side effects are roughly the same as for their shorter acting formulations.

Some of the brand forms are quite expensive, and due to the complex processes and DEA oversight involved in making stimulant medications, even many of the current generic long-acting stimulant medications can be quite expensive. Given the high cost of all aspects of health care, clinicians should consider the cost of the medications they are prescribing and factor this into their decision making when selecting the best medication for each particular person they treat.

The additional decision was made to start Kasey on trazodone 50 mg at bedtime and as needed for insomnia. This medication is classified as an antidepressant but is widely used as a safe and nonaddicting treatment for insomnia. It does come in a brand-name form that is much more expensive than the generic form, so again an awareness of cost on the part of the clinician is important. There are numerous other sleep agents (hypnotics) that Kasey could have been started on, but using a non–habit-forming medication that has extensive clinical evidence for improving sleep in this particular person with significant insomnia is quite reasonable. As in most cases, using hypnotics for anyone with insomnia should be done with an initial goal of using them temporarily and on an as-needed basis. Any use of hypnotics should include a clinical review of sleep hygiene between the clinician and person seeking treatment. In Kasey's situation, she was advised to avoid excessive caffeine intake and to increase brief exercise activity, such as walking, in the early evening.

With the treatments initiated, Kasey noticed some improvement in her concentration and focus in the first few days of being on the stimulant medication, though this benefit was less noticeable by the end of the first week. Her sleep problems remained, and she noticed an increase in headaches and appetite suppression, leading to further worrisome weight loss. Attempts to increase Adderall to a higher dose resulted in only temporary improvement in her attention and concentration. She continued to have some worsening side effects, however, and her inability to tolerate a higher, possibly more clinically effective dose left her ADHD symptoms not optimally treated. She began to wonder whether any medication would help her, and her sense of discouragement and shame began to increase again.

After another review of her symptoms of ADHD and other possible treatment options, Kasey consented to try a slightly different stimulant called Concerta (methylphenidate). This would have been a reasonable initial treatment options as well, though the clinician must make the final call as to what he or she believes will be the best initial medication to prescribe. Kasey was started on Concerta 18 mg daily and ramped up to 36 mg daily after the first week. She noticed improvement in concentration, focus, and attention in many areas, though she felt that the medicine wore off early about 1 pm, leading to continued stressors at work and at home in the early evening. Her dose was increased to 54 mg daily and eventually 72 mg daily by the fourth week based on improving symptoms and no significant side effects. At this point she noticed significant improvement in her ADHD symptoms as well as in her mood.

Although Kasey continued to have some periods of initial insomnia helped by the occasional use of trazodone on an as-needed basis, she generally began to sleep better. Her appetite picked up and remained stable. Kasey began feeling happier and more engaged at work, and several colleagues noticed improvement in her mood as well as productivity and organizational skills. Over the following months, continued treatment of Kasey's ADHD resulted in less worry about losing her job as well as feeling much more capable of handling her present workload. She returned home after work each day feeling better about herself, which translated into more positive interactions with her husband and children in the evenings and on weekends.

At her two-month follow-up appointment, Kasey reported no symptoms of depression or anxiety, and her weight, appetite, and sleep returned to normal. She reported no side effects from the Concerta or trazodone, and she expressed immense gratitude to her clinician for helping identify and treat the underlying cause of her symptoms and despair. She stated that treating her ADHD has not only helped her at work but also improved her relationship with her husband and children and made their evenings and weekends together more peaceful and enjoyable. She only wishes she had sought treatment earlier in her life.

SYSTEMS-BASED PRACTICE ISSUES

Optimal treatment of a person with ADHD is hampered by at least two major system-based practice issues. The first involves the very existence of the diagnosis. Many children and adults have trouble with concentration and focus at times, especially when more is demanded of them at work or school. Learning to stay organized and maintain concentration amid distractions are fundamental aspects of human cognitive development. Modern society also provides a breeding ground of distracters, including television, email, texting, social media, advertising schemes, and more. Some people will be better adept at navigating such an environment, whereas others will struggle, which is consistent with the diversity of human cognitive and intellectual abilities. Many of those who don't succeed as well as others may get labeled with a diagnosis of ADHD. Just because someone who plays basketball does not make it to the NBA does not necessarily mean the person has a problem playing basketball that needs to be fixed or treated.

Human societies generally function with a set of standards regarding most aspects of human behavior. Numerous standardized tests and performance measures are developed over time in different human societies that help that society determine what is considered standard for them in terms of how a person learns or behaves. The use of scientific investigation applied to such standards often helps quantify what is standard and how close a person is in terms of meeting, succeeding, or failing that standard. This is referred to as standard deviation. In that regard, while there is great variety among how humans pay attention, focus, and maintain impulse control, impairment in these areas for some falls well outside the standard deviation of what is considered acceptable or functional. Certainly many of us have problems with concentration and focus sometimes, but not of such intensity or frequency to cause significant impairment as found in those persons diagnosed with ADHD. Just as it is normal to feel sad sometimes, not everyone who is sad is depressed. Many people continue to believe that ADHD is overdiagnosed or that the medical community overly pathologizes people whose impairments in concentration, focus, and impulsivity are not optimal. Even some experienced clinician may maintain that ADHD doesn't really exist or that they don't believe it is a real diagnosis. One major role for clinicians is to help determine what is considered normal function, what is not, and how to go about diagnosing, helping, and treating those whose behavior or function is problematic. This is ongoing work as human societies are constantly evolving and adapting new and revised standards regarding many aspects of human behavior and function.

A second system-based practice issue regarding ADHD involves its treatment. The use of stimulant medications is a very successful form of treatment for those diagnosed with ADHD. However, stimulants also can improve the concentration and attention abilities of people even without minor attention problems or a full diagnosis of ADHD. In fact, due to their ability to promote wakefulness and improved concentration, people without any significant problems in these areas may seek to use stimulants as performance-enhancing drugs to give them an edge over others, particularly in terms of academic or work performance. Some data show that nearly 50% of college students have access to these performance-enhancing medications to give them a competitive advantage in scholastic achievement. Coworkers in areas of employment that require high levels of concentration and attention to detail may accuse a colleague of taking drugs on learning that he or she takes prescribed stimulant medications. Though it is important to properly diagnosis and treat ADHD, there certainly are legal aspects to such treatment that clinicians must keep in mind to help prevent the misuse, abuse, and diversion of stimulant medications as addressed below.

LEGAL, ETHICAL, AND CULTURAL CHALLENGES

Given that stimulant medications are under strict control and monitoring by the DEA due to their potential for abuse and diversion, once an agreement is reached between a clinician and patient that stimulant medications are clinically warranted for treatment, written informed consent for the medication must be obtained from the patient. This consent needs to include the potential risks and side effects commonly associated with the medication being prescribed, as well as expected benefits of treatment versus continuing without treatment. The patient must be allowed to ask questions about the proposed treatment and be given information sheets about medications prescribed as well as access to any additional resources thought necessary for informed consent.

No medications are without risks, but the specific risks associated with stimulants, namely, abuse, dependence, and diversion, must be reviewed with the patient and documented in the chart. Clinicians can be held liable for continuing to prescribe potentially addictive medications to persons who knowingly abuse or divert their medications or other illicit substances. Many states use an online monitoring system for keeping track of prescriptions written for medications like stimulants that may have high potential for abuse or diversion. Such information can be invaluable when a clinician suspects abuse or diversion of prescribed stimulant medications for a particular patient. Some common scenarios may lead a clinician to suspect that his or her patient is abusing or diverting their prescribed stimulant medications. Instances where a person repeatedly reports that stimulant medication has been lost or stolen or when numerous early refills are requested might indicate that medication is being abused or diverted (sold or traded to someone who is not prescribed that medication). This presents important and challenging ethical and potentially legal problems that can impact the clinician–patient relationship. A clinician should be aware of the various resources available to guide him or her in this process, such as those available through state medical board agencies, the DEA (www.deadiversion.usdoj.gov), and the American Psychiatric Association website (www.psych.org).

Because different human cultures may have different ways of defining work productivity or academic performance, clinicians needs to maintain a degree of cultural sensitivity. While a person presenting for treatment for ADHD may be experiencing significant impairment at work or in school, the clinician, sometimes for cultural reasons, may not appreciate the degree of suffering experienced by the person seeking treatment, viewing it instead as normal problems. Being culturally sensitive to how issues such as ethnic origin, sex, and religion can bias clinicians as well as persons seeking treatment for ADHD is highly importance.

HISTORY

Although symptoms of ADHD have most likely been found in the human population for millennia, it can be surmised that since the Industrial Revolution, increased emphasis on productivity, education, and technology has led to an increase in people identified with problems that might impair their performance. In assessing and treating people with ADHD, clinicians need to be familiar with normal human development. Clinicians need to have a firm grasp of what is meant by terms such as *attention*, *cognition*, and *affect*, as these are quite different though they certainly overlap in all aspects of human existence. As humans we are creatures who sense, think, and who feel (among other brain activities) all at the same time, so impairment in one area can lead a person to sense more global impairment. Kasey's problems with attention and concentration led her to experience more global impairment in many aspects of her life.

With the growth of YouTube in recent years, many videos have emerged that claim to offer diagnostic and treatment for ADHD. Though most of these have to be taken with a grain of salt, a popular YouTube personality, Fred Figglehorn, brought to public awareness, in a humorous way, what it is like to be a teenager and young adult with ADHD. His YouTube video "Fred Loses His Meds" keeps viewers laughing as well as wondering about ADHD, its prevalence, and effect on one's life. In addition, many fans of the television cartoon sitcom *The Simpsons* cannot help wonder if Bart Simpson and his father Homer both have untreated ADHD.

Well-meaning friends, family members, and even clinicians can offer advice or guidance about the diagnosis and treatment of ADHD. Given the ability for nearly anyone to post unverified claims and even false information on the Internet, it is important for clinicians to know how to access relevant, evidence-based, and peer-reviewed information about ADHD. The American Psychiatric Association (APA) and the American Academy of Child and Adolescent Psychiatry are considered reputable, vetted sources of information about ADHD diagnosis and treatment. On the APA website (www.psych.org) there are Clinical Practice Guidelines that can be easily accessed to guide both clinicians and persons seeking information about ADHD.

Perhaps the most evidenced-based, peer-supported review to date of the treatment of ADHD in children and adolescents, which is also applicable in most respects to adults, is titled "Practice Parameter for the Assessment and Treatment of Children and Adolescents with Attention-Deficit/Hyperactivity Disorder" and is published in the *Journal of the American Academy of Child and Adolescent Psychiatry*. This practice parameter, the referenced articles in the next section, and a vigilant clinician well versed in the myriad presentations of ADHD will go a long way to promoting healing among those persons of all ages affected by this diagnosis.

REFERENCES AND RESOURCES

Barkley A. Major life activity and health outcomes associated with attention-deficit/hyperactivity disorder. *J Clin Psych* 2002;63:10–15.

Barkley RA, Brown TE. Unrecognized attention-deficit/hyperactivity disorder in adults presenting with other psychiatric disorders. *CNS Spectr* 2008;13(11):977–84.

Biederman J, Monuteaux MC, Mick F, et al. Young adult outcome of attention deficit hyperactivity disorder: A controlled 10-year follow-up study. *Psychol Med* 2006;36: 167–79.

Erikson, Erik H. *Childhood and Society* (2nd ed.). New York: W. W. Norton and Company, 1964.

Faraone SV, Glatt SJ. A comparison of the efficacy of medications for adult attention-deficit/hyperactivity disorder using meta-analysis of effect sizes. *J Clin Psych* 2010; 71(6):754–63.

Fredriksen M, Halmøy A, Faraone SV, et al. Long-term efficacy and safety of treatment with stimulants and atomoxetine in adult ADHD: A review of controlled and naturalistic studies. *Eur Neuropsychopharmacol.* 2012 Aug 20.

Ivanchak N, Fletcher K, Jicha GA. Attention-deficit/hyperactivity disorder in older adults: Prevalence and possible connections to mild cognitive impairment. *Curr Psych Rep* 2012;14(5):552–60.

Kessler RC, Adler L, Ames M, et al. The World Health Organization Adult ADHD Self-Report Scale (ASRS): A short screening scale for use in the general population. *Psychol Med* 2005;35(2):245–56.

Kessler RC, Adler L, Barkley R, et al. The prevalence and correlates of adult ADHD in the United States: Results from the National Comorbidity Survey Replication. *Am J Psych* 2006 April;163(4):716–23.

Knouse LE, Safren SA. Current status of cognitive behavioral therapy for adult attention-deficit hyperactivity disorder. *Psychiatr Clin North Am* 2010 Sep;33(3):497–509.

Lara C, Fayyad J, de Graaf R, et al. Childhood predictors of adult attention-deficit/hyperactivity disorder: Results from the World Health Organization World Mental Health Survey Initiative. *Biol Psych* 2009;65(1):46–54.

Mayes SD, Calhoun SL, Crowell EW. Learning disabilities and ADHD: Overlapping spectrum disorders. *J Learn Disabil.* 2000;33(5):417–24.

Newcorn JH, Weiss M, Stein MA. The complexity of ADHD: Diagnosis and treatment of the adult patient with comorbidities. *CNS Spectr* 2007;12(8 Suppl 12):1–14.

Polanczyk G, Silva de Lima M, Horta BL, et al. The worldwide prevalence of ADHD: A systematic review and meta-regression analysis. *Am J Psych* 2007;164:942–48.

Practice Parameter for the Assessment and Treatment of Children and Adolescents with Attention-Deficit/Hyperactivity Disorder. *J Am Acad Child Adolesc Psych* 2007;46(7): 894–921.

Safren SA, Sprich S, Mimiaga MJ, et al. Cognitive behavioral therapy vs relaxation with educational support for medication-treated adults with ADHD and persistent symptoms: A randomized controlled trial. *J Am Med Assoc* 2010 Aug 25;304(8):875–80.

Santosh PJ, Sattar S, Canagaratnam M. Efficacy and tolerability of pharmacotherapies for attention-deficit hyperactivity disorder in adults. *CNS Drugs* 2011;25(9):737–63.

Sonuga-Barke E, Brandeis D, Cortese S, et al. Nonpharmacological interventions for ADHD: Systematic review and meta-Analyses of randomized controlled trials of dietary and psychological treatments. *Am J Psych* 2013;170:275–89.

PART II

Mood Pathology

CHAPTER **11**

Depression

Tracey W. Criss, M.D.

CLINICAL PRESENTATION

Chief complaint: "I feel so bad that it is near impossible to drag myself out of bed."

History of present illness: Yvette is a 45-year-old mother of two who presents at an outpatient psychiatry office. She is an engineer and the chief executive officer for a local engineering firm and has suffered from severe depression for about three months. She reports that her brother, who is the vice president of the company, has noticed that she is not as functional at work and has inquired as to why her productivity and efficiency have dropped below their typical levels. Yvette has decided to take two weeks off to work on her health as she feels burdensome to the company. She reports that at home her two children and husband have also noticed changes. She says she made this appointment after one of her children asked if she just did not care anymore about his excelling on the football team.

She reports that she has had increased sleep and lack of interest and energy in doing anything, even the things that she normally enjoys. When she attempts to participate in an activity that she would typically look forward to with anticipation, she now feels a sense of burden and a lack of enjoyment. She has a lack of concentration when she tries to do anything, whether it is reading the newspaper, working on a project at her job, or following a recipe at home. She has gained about 10 pounds and describes her increased appetite as "comfort eating." She reports that she has had suicidal thoughts in the past but doesn't have any active thoughts now, though she does wonder at times "How long can I go on like this?" She has significant guilt associated with her lack of productivity and her lack of attention to her two children, ages 13 and 17, "They help keep me alive. I would never kill myself because of them." "My husband is a good guy but he is getting tired of carrying the weight of keeping our home running." As she softly described these issues, her emotional pain was palpable to the interviewer.

Past psychiatric history: Yvette has had one prior depressive episode at age 21 resulting in a psychiatric admission, has never made a suicide attempt, and has tried several antidepressants in the past. Her initial antidepressant, fluoxetine, worked well but caused sexual dysfunction. This medication was switched to venlafaxine which again was successful, but her blood pressure became elevated. After the venlafaxine was stopped, her blood pressure returned to normal and the depression did not return.

Past medical history: She denies knowledge of any major medical issues. She had a tubal ligation at age 34. She denies major medical issues such as diabetes, hypertension, seizures, hepatitis, thyroid, or cholesterol issues. She does not smoke cigarettes, does not and has not used illicit drugs, and rarely uses alcohol.

Family history: Her older brother committed suicide at age 39 and had suffered from severe depression. No one else in the family has any history of alcoholism, psychotic or mood disorders, or mental health counseling.

Developmental history/social history: The patient was born in a midsize Midwestern city and lived there until the age of five. The family then moved to a small Virginia city when her father relocated the headquarters of his small company, Her mother was a nurse and did outpatient work in a primary care office. The patient has one sister and two brothers (one alive, one dead by suicide) and describes the family as generally close. Family vacations were taken several times per year. She was not abused as a child in any way. She was actively involved in high school and played on the volleyball team and was a member of the student government. She attended college at Georgia Tech with a solid academic performance. Upon graduation, she worked at an engineering firm and later decided to branch out into her own company with her younger brother, who is also an engineer. She married her college sweetheart, and they have two children. She is a person of faith and her family regularly attends a local Protestant church. She does find some comfort in her faith. Her hobbies still include volleyball—she plays in backyard games—but her primary adult responsibilities have been to her work and to her children.

Mental status exam: On exam, Yvette is alert, coherent, polite, and cooperative, with good impulse control and no psychomotor agitation. Eye contact was fair. Speech is clear and fluent. She is fully oriented. Immediate, recent, and remote memory were intact. Attention and concentration are impaired as she had difficulty performing serial 7's. Language is appropriate though she mostly speaks when questions are asked, rather than with spontaneity. Affect is restricted and mood congruent. She denied suicidal or homicidal ideation, plan, or intent. Mood is "depressed, sad, like I am in a dark pit." Her thought processes are without looseness of associations or flight of ideas. There is no evidence of delusions or paranoia. Intelligence is above average as she answers multiple questions about the news and history. Insight and judgment are full. No hallucinations, illusions, or depersonalization are evident.

Collateral information: Hamilton Depression Rating score was 62. Beck Depression Inventory score was 50. Both tests are considered reliable, easily administered screens for depression.

IMPAIRMENT IN FUNCTIONING

The impairment in this patient's functioning is substantial. The acute issue is her significant mood problem and the dysfunction associated with it. She has a significant mood disorder and though she does not have suicidal thoughts, one has to be concerned about the family history of suicide given her brother's suicide. If she were to commit suicide, her death would leave behind a husband and two children with devastating effects on them. The issue of safety, as well as the issue of functionality, provide long-term challenges.

DSM DIAGNOSIS

The patient meets the DSM diagnostic criteria for an episode of major depression, most likely her second episode. She meets these criteria based on the number of symptoms as well as the required two week time frame of illness. She has symptoms of depression, including changes in her sleep, appetite, interest level, energy level, as well as a lack of concentration. She also has guilt, anhedonia, and has gained weight secondary to the change in her appetite. Though she denies any active suicidal thoughts, clearly she is feeling burdened by her perceived ineffectiveness at work as well as at home.

In the DSM-5, criteria for Major Depressive Disorder are essentially unchanged from earlier versions. A distinction is made between major depressive disorder where the primary feelings are a lack of pleasure or joy versus grief where the symptoms are of loss and emptiness.

EPIDEMIOLOGY

Major depression has a lifetime prevalence of about 15%. There is a twofold greater prevalence of major depression in women than in men. The mean age of onset is about age 40 and half of all patients have an onset between ages 20 and 50. It occurs most often in people without close interpersonal relationships or in those who are divorced or separated. No correlation has been found with socioeconomic status.

DIFFERENTIAL DIAGNOSIS

The differential diagnosis for major depression includes adjustment disorder, bipolar disorder, cyclothymia, dysthymia, postpartum depression, psychotic depression, seasonal affective disorder, and substance-induced mood disorder.

When evaluating a patient for a psychiatric disorder, and more specifically a mood disorder, the differential diagnosis includes medical issues that are associated with depression. Pancreatic cancer seems to be associated with higher rates of depression than other types of cancer. Neurological conditions such as multiple sclerosis, Parkinson's disease, and strokes—particularly in the frontal lobe—have higher depression rates. Endocrine diseases such as hypothyroidism and Cushing's disease are associated with higher depression rates. It is also of note that women with treatment-resistant depression have higher incidence of thyroiditis. Autoimmune disorders, such as rheumatoid arthritis and systemic lupus, have higher concordance with depression than do nonautoimmune disorders. Major depression develops in more than 10% of women in the postpartum year, and can result in great morbidity to the mother, family, and baby.

The physician needs to review a thorough history, conduct a physical exam, review lab data like thyroid function tests, review criteria for specific illnesses, and then determine a course of treatment based on a summary of all information gathered. In psychiatry, illnesses may be ruled in or out based on signs and symptoms, time frame of an illness, and/or concurrent medical issues. An example of this is that major depression has to have symptoms present for at least two weeks and the patient must have five of nine symptoms present with one of them being either a depressed mood or a loss of interest or pleasure. These issues must represent a change from previous functioning.

ETIOLOGY AND PATHOGENESIS

As with any illness, the clinician seeks to understand why this patient has presented in this particular way. By understanding the possible etiology of the problem, one can then determine how best to put the patient on a path to improved health and enjoyment of life.

For example, suppose Yvette's depression had come about after her brother's suicide a year ago and was a result of her losing her faith in God. The clinical intervention then might be very different than in a case where the person's depression was caused by a deterioration in thyroid function.

Dopamine, serotonin, and norepinephrine are all involved in the regulation of mood and anxiety. Dysfunctionality in some form of each of these major neurotransmitters is thought to be one of the etiologies of depression.

Dopamine is the principal neurotransmitter in the reward system in the brain and is involved in cognition, motor ability, reward, muscle tone, sleep, mood, attention, and learning. There are three major dopamine pathways in the brain. The first is responsible for cognition, reward systems, and emotional behavior and extends from the ventral tegmentum to the mesolimbic forebrain. The second is associated with movement and sensory stimuli and extends from the substantia nigra to the caudate nucleus putamen. The third helps regulate the hypothalamic-pituitary endocrine system and extends from the hypothalamus to the pituitary.

Serotonin is involved in the regulation of mood, anxiety, aggression, sleep, appetite, and sexuality. The main nuclei for serotonin are the rostral and caudal raphe nuclei. From the rostral raphe nuclei, axons project to the cerebral cortex, limbic regions, and the basal ganglia.

Norepinephrine can function in the brain as a neurotransmitter or in the peripheral nervous system as a hormone. It is also involved with reward, arousal, and mood regulation. The primary nuclei are the locus coeruleus and the caudal raphe nuclei. Axons from the locus coeruleus project to the frontal cortex, thalamus, hypothalamus, and limbic system. Nerves from the caudal raphe nuclei project to the amygdala and descend to the midbrain.

Other etiologies/associations of depression to consider are abnormalities of the hypothalamic-pituitary-adrenal axis. These abnormalities include hypersecretion of cortisol, diminished release of thyroid-stimulating hormone, decreased nocturnal secretion of melatonin, decreased prolactin release, and decreased testosterone in males.

Genetics also play an important role in the etiology of depression. Heritability has been shown to be 40–50% based on twin studies. Adoption studies also provide some support for a role for genetic factors. The relative risk is around two to three.

Psychosocial: Other issues long- thought to be related to depression include life events, environmental stressors, and premorbid personality factors such as dependent, obsessive compulsive, and hysterical personality types. Psychoanalytical factors, learned helplessness, and cognitive misinterpretations also are thought to play a role in depression.

The psychological aspects of the patient's current situation are profoundly disturbing. Intertwined with the bare clinical facts of the case is the fact that she feels guilty about her lack of ability to perform her duties at work and home. So, on top of feeling badly, she carries the burden of not feeling that she is leading the company as the CEO and not feeling that she is meeting her expectations of herself as a mother and as a wife. This burden is likely propelled by her innate drive to work hard, be productive, and succeed in all areas important to her. She has commented that her children are what keep her alive and in essence gives us a view into the window of thoughts that she likely has had at some point in time, that she might kill herself were it not for her children. With these emotions typically come poor self-esteem with thoughts such as "Why can't I just get over this? Other people have a lot bigger problems than I do. Some are homeless." Next come feelings of worthlessness and hopelessness and comments such as, "I know this is silly. It's pathetic." This type of thinking can build on itself and become self-defeating. Gradually the negative thinking combined with the depression leaves the patient without an ounce of energy to battle the mood problem. It is important to work extensively with the patient to try to avoid this lowest valley because this type of thinking could result in the worst possible outcome—death as a result of suicide. An important thing to remember is "Depression kills people."

We have discussed the patient's emotions about her depression. The social aspects of this also play a role in her work toward resolution of the mood disorder. Her home life has been affected in that she reports either directly or by implication that she feels she is not meeting her responsibilities/desires as a mother or as a wife. She also reports that her brother is aware of difficulties emerging within her business. Therefore, we can see that she has people and responsibilities around her that are playing a very important part in her journey with this illness. This is often seen in depression and can be used as a positive mechanism by which recovery can be achieved. The people who she feels are affected by her also are her supportive network, and having employment and a supportive unit can help move her in a positive direction away from any possible thoughts of death once she eventually has the emotional, physical, mental, and spiritual energy to use these strengths.

NATURAL COURSE WITHOUT TREATMENT

For many patients with major depression, the illness is an episodic condition. Some depressions come out of nowhere, whereas others may be caused by a precipitant. An episode typically lasts 6–13 months if untreated or about 3 months if treated. About half of all patients with an episode never have another episode, but episodes that recur tend to come frequently and last longer. Recurrence rates are higher in the first four to six months after recovery. Of those patients who have a second episode, 50% have a third one. Patients who have an episode are more likely to have future episodes if there is a history of dysthymia, substance abuse, or an anxiety disorder; if they have an older age of onset; or if they have a greater number of prior episodes. About 20% of patients with major depression become chronically depressed.

EVIDENCE-BASED TREATMENT OPTIONS

When a person presents with an episode of depression, one must consider what treatment is most likely to alleviate suffering. Possibilities include using antidepressant medications, specific psychotherapies, medications combined with therapy, electroconvulsive therapy, vagus nerve stimulation, transcranial magnetic stimulation, or alternative therapies. This section presents how some of these evidence-based treatments work and the evidence supporting their use.

Antidepressant response rates vary from 50–75% in clinical trials. Especially in severe depression, there is greater efficacy relative to placebo. Many studies and meta-analyses have been conducted to compare different antidepressants.

The heterocyclic antidepressants comprise tricyclic and tetracyclic antidepressants. These medicines mostly prevent reuptake or delay of reuptake of norepinephrine and some affect serotonin to a lesser degree. They affect histamine, cholinergic, and alpha-adrenergic receptors. Included in this group are imipramine, desipramine, trimipramine, amitriptyline, nortriptyline, protriptyline, amoxapine, doxepin, maprotiline, and clomipramine. Potential side effects are dry mouth, constipation, blurred vision, urinary retention, sedation, orthostatic hypotension, cardiac effects, decreased seizure threshold, weight gain, and sexual dysfunction. Younger adult patients may tolerate these better than geriatric patients due to the orthostatic issues. A person who has a prolonged QTc interval may not be a good candidate for a tricyclic antidepressant due to potential cardiac complications. TCAs are also considered more dangerous in overdose than some other categories of antidepressants due to cardiac toxicity. Hundreds of randomized controlled trials have shown that as a class tricyclic antidepressants are efficacious in the treatment of depression. The efficacy within the class appears to be comparable from agent to agent. Amitriptyline may have a slightly stronger effect.

Evidence also supports the use of specific psychotherapies in the treatment of major depression. Methods of therapies used include cognitive behavioral therapy (CBT), behavioral therapy, interpersonal therapy (IPT) psychodynamic psychotherapy, marital and family therapy, problem-solving therapy, and group therapy.

CBT has been extensively studied in controlled trials. When studies have compared the efficacy of CBT to either no treatment or minimal treatment, effect sizes have been near to or above one standard deviation on outcomes. When CBT is terminated at the end of treatment, the risk of relapse remains low, unlike when medications are discontinued.

Behavior therapy may be superior to brief dynamic psychotherapy and is comparable in efficacy to CBT or to pharmacotherapy based on the results of individual clinical trials.

IPT has also shown efficacy in a series of randomized clinical trials. In treating more severe forms of clinical depression, IPT had greater efficacy than pill placebo plus clinical management and was comparable to imipramine plus clinical management. IPT has also been found to be effective in treating pregnant and postpartum women with major depression. Also, in depressed HIV-positive patients, IPT or IPT plus imipramine showed greater improvements than supportive therapy or CBT.

The efficacy of psychodynamic psychotherapy in major depression has not been adequately studied in controlled trials. It has been widely used for the treatment of depression and is preferred by some patients rather than using other options, such as medications.

Individual studies suggest that the efficacy of marital therapy for depression may depend on whether marital distress is present. In one study, a greater proportion of depressed patients with marital issues responded to marital therapy rather than CBT, but among those without marital distress, the outcome was better for CBT. In one study, inpatients being treated for major depression were randomly assigned to treatment arms, and those who received treatment that included family therapy were more likely to improve and had significant reductions in suicidal ideation.

Modest improvement has been reported with mild depressive symptoms when problem-solving therapy is used.

Individual psychotherapies that work for treating depression have been studied mostly in Europe, and the research suggests that they also work in group format.

Many psychiatrists prefer to use a combination of psychotherapy and pharmacotherapy to treat major depression, but controlled studies conducted in the 1970s and 1980s did not find a significant advantage for combining therapies compared with one treatment provided alone. However, further evidence now indicates that the combination of therapy and pharmacotherapy is indeed quite helpful. Thase performed a meta-analysis looking at remission rates of about 600 patients using CBT, interactive behavioral therapy, and IPT combined with either imipramine or nortriptyline and found a modest advantage for combined treatment compared to CBT or IPT alone. In patients with less severe depression, there was a small advantage, but there was a fourfold difference in remission rates with more severe, recurrent depression. In the STAR*D trial, patients who did not have remission with an initial antidepressant could then add another medication or add or change to CBT. Results showed that CBT was as effective as adding another medication, but patients who opted to augment with a second agent responded faster. Overall, studies now demonstrate that combining pharmacotherapy with various forms of time-limited psychotherapies provides an advantage.

Electroconvulsive therapy (ECT) has a 70–90% rate of improvement. Compared to any other form of antidepressant treatment, it has the highest rate of response and remission. ECT has been associated with significant improvements in patients' health-related quality of life. It should be considered for use with those who have not responded to pharmacological and/or therapy interventions and who have significant impairment in functioning. ECT should be a first-line treatment option when patients have severe depression with psychosis, catatonia, risk of suicide, or malnutrition. Also, ECT should be considered a first-line treatment in patients who have previously shown a response or in those who prefer it (and are considered reasonable candidates for it). One benefit with ECT is that it works rapidly. One study conducted by the Consortium for Research in ECT showed that half of the 253 patients showed a response by the end of the first week of treatment and that suicidal ideation responded rapidly as well.

One of the interesting questions about ECT is the question of how it works. Dr. Max Fink, one of the leaders in the field, has advanced a neuroendocrine hypothesis of the mechanism of action of ECT. The neuroendocrine control of the hypothalamus/pituitary/thyroid and of the hypothalamus/pituitary/adrenal axes are disordered in patients with major depression, and ECT tends to affect these axes. Each seizure with ECT stimulates the hypothalamus to discharge both thyrotropin releasing hormone and corticotropin releasing hormone, which then stimulate the pituitary gland to discharge its thyroid and adrenal control hormones, which then inhibit the discharge of cortisol from the adrenal glands. After four to five treatments, the hypothalamic-pituitary-adrenal axis is reset. This occurs as the hormones have been "squeezed out," with changes in blood and cerebrospinal fluid levels being measurable within minutes.

Potential side effects of ECT include cardiovascular effects, cognitive effects, confusion, or fractures.

Vagus nerve stimulation (VNS) is a treatment in which an electrical stimulator is surgically implanted and the left vagus nerve is stimulated in the neck. VNS is approved for use in patients with treatment-resistant depression. There is no strong evidence of the effectiveness of VNS in the acute phase of depression. VNS has been found to be helpful in some and is tolerable, although some patients have voice alteration or hoarseness.

Transcranial magnetic stimulation (TMS) was FDA approved in 2008 for use in patients with major depression who have not had a satisfactory response to at least one antidepressant in the current episode. A magnetic coil is placed in contact with the head to generate rapidly alternating MRI-strength magnetic fields and produce electrical stimulation of superficial cortical neurons. Most but not all meta-analyses have found relatively small to moderate clinical benefits of TMS when looking at actual versus sham TMS. In comparing TMS and ECT, TMS has been found in randomized studies to be either less effective or comparable. In the latter studies TMS was more effective and ECT was less effective than is typically seen in clinical trials.

Alternative treatments for major depression include St. John's wort, S-adenosyl methionine (SAMe), omega-3 fatty acids, folate, light therapy, or acupuncture. Research on St. John's wort has yielded inconsistent results because a number of studies have shown superiority over placebo whereas some have not. A number of studies have found SAMe to be efficacious when certain dose ranges are used. Some benefit has been found with omega-3 fatty acids. Folate has shown benefit when used with fluoxetine. Light therapy has demonstrated benefit for seasonal and nonseasonal major depression. However, there were some flaws in the methodological methods used. Many reports of acupuncture are in an Asian language and are often overlooked by English-language searches. However, there have been few randomized, double-blind, placebo-controlled studies to support the use of acupuncture for depression.

CLINICAL COURSE WITH MANAGEMENT AND TREATMENT

One way to remember how to evaluate a patient's mood is by using the mnemonic DEPRESSING. Yvette is experiencing classic signs and symptoms of a mood disorder. We need to evaluate how to develop rapport with her and how to interpret what we are told. We have listened to her descriptions of involvement with her family and also her family psychiatric history. She has already mentioned her functional impairment in that she has had difficulty at work and has decided to take time off for two weeks. Obviously, the most important aspect of management to evaluate is to evaluate the issue of safety. Another important aspect of a patient's care is the maintenance of confidentiality.

DEPRESSING lists the major symptom criteria for a major depressive episode:

D: dysphoria (sadness)
E: energy (loss of)
P: pleasure (loss of)
R: retardation (psychomotor slowing or agitation)

E: eating (changes in weight or appetite)
S: suicide (recurrent thoughts of death)
S: sleep—any change
I: indecisive (poor concentration)
N: negative thinking
G: any guilty or hopeless feelings

A depressed person can sometimes be picked out in a group of people by appearance alone. There is an expression of sadness, with at times an inability to make good eye contact. The person may sit quite still and not move around much during the extent of the conversation, again due to the lack of energy. At times a depressed person may look disheveled due to chosen attire or lack of attention to personal hygiene. She may speak in a low monotone voice, exemplifying lack of energy or interest. Throughout the conversation there may be expressions or even ruminations of guilt, hopelessness, or worthlessness. There may be times where it appears that attentiveness to the conversation is less than maximum, as concentration may be impaired. The emotional pain felt by the person with depression is often evident early on in the interaction.

Generating rapport with a patient is vital to the process not only at the initial appointment but throughout the course of the treatment. When someone is depressed and needing to tell his or her story, knowing that there are eyes to look into when desired and ears to hear what are said are part of the generation of that rapport. Building rapport is believed to be the single most important factor in building a relationship. It begins to develop from the very first conversation the physician has with the patient. How does the listener help the patient achieve a comfort level with this? The listener needs to be aware of how the patient perceives him or her by judging not only verbal but nonverbal communication. By exemplifying energy, enthusiasm, empathy, respect, and an understanding of sensitive cultural issues from the start, the listener begins that process. The patient should feel that he or she is treated with respect and is a partner in the communication process. The patient's expectations of the physician are that he or she is competent and uses all knowledge and expertise in the patient's best interest. After the initial introductions, the clinician should begin the interview with open-ended questions, allowing the patient to tell her story and become engaged in the process. By asking follow-up questions, the listener demonstrates that he or she hearing the responses and also listening.

Assessment of suicidal risk is a very important part of any psychiatric interview, as safety is a primary goal with every patient. An assessment of the patient's response then leads the physician to either an inpatient or outpatient treatment plan at that particular time. Yvette denies that she has any current suicidal thoughts but reports that she has had suicidal thoughts in the past. As noted during the interview, her emotional pain is palpable, but she offers a reason she would not harm herself: her children. This importantly provides some reassurance to the interviewer, though it is not a guarantee of safety.

Asking about suicidal thoughts can be done in several ways. Asking about passive suicidal thoughts includes questions such as, "Have you ever thought that you would be better off dead or that the world would be a better place without you?" A follow-up question for active thoughts could then be "Have you ever thought about hurting or killing yourself?" Further assessment of the risk would then involve inquiring about a potential plan, details of a plan, and if the patient has begun implementing the plan.

In 2009, suicide was the tenth leading cause of death in the United States. The suicide rate is greatest for men over 45 and for those ages 15–24. Almost 95% of patients who attempt or commit suicide suffer from a mental disorder, with 80% of these suffering from depression. Females attempt suicide three times more often than males, but males are four times more likely to complete suicide. People who have attempted suicide in the past are more likely to commit suicide. Major risk factors include being male, older, unemployed, unmarried, living alone, having a chronic illness, substance abuse, and at least one major psychiatric diagnosis. These major risk factors can be remembered by the mnemonic SAD PERSONS. The mnemonic illustrates:

Sex: male
Age: older
Depression
Previous suicide attempt
Ethanol abuse
Rational thinking loss: psychotic
Social supports: lacking
Organized plan
No spouse
Sickness: chronic mental illness

Other risk factors include having a lethal method available, personality disorders, hopelessness, having an unambiguous wish to die, and having poor rapport with others. Yvette does not have any of these risk factors.

Inquiring about suicidal thoughts, assessing the risk factors for suicide, and making a decision about whether to hospitalize the patient are all part of interviewing the patient. Certainly if a patient has thoughts to commit self-harm, the potential need for hospitalization is assessed. The clinician must consider whether there is a plan and whether there is access to a means by which to commit suicide, such as a gun in the home. Access to an available lethal method is an important part of the interview, and many clinicians will ask for family members to remove lethal means, such as guns, from access by the patient during the course of the depression.

As noted, safety is a primary goal with the patient. Without safety first, no other issues really matter.

Another issue of importance is confidentiality. When a patient talks and looks into the listener's eyes, he or she assumes there is privacy to this process. Imagine how little rapport would be generated if the patient thought the physician would get on the phone after the interview and tell their neighbor the entire story! Confidentiality is demonstrated by closing the door during the conversation, discussing private topics only once the door has been closed, and by the absence of information being accessible by looking on one's computer or one's desktop in the office. Obviously, confidentiality doesn't end with the end of the interview. Information discussed during the interview process is not to be discussed with others outside of the room unless the patient gives permission by signing an authorization for release. Examples of others who may need information for the mutual care of the patient include therapists, primary care providers, or other specialists involved in the care of the patient.

Yvette clearly has multiple changes going on and also has stated that there is lack of enjoyment, or anhedonia. This patient has described classic symptoms of depression to the interviewer. At her first visit, the decision is made to start an antidepressant. Due to her reports of lack of interest and energy and her increased eating as well as weight gain, bupropion extended release is chosen. This medication is chosen not only for its side effect of increased energy but because of the low likelihood that it will cause sexual dysfunction as did the fluoxetine earlier in her life. She is to take 150 mg for three days, then increase the dose to 300 mg. She is scheduled to follow up about two weeks after her initial interview, and you learn from a phone call that she has begun to feel better about 10 days after the antidepressant was initiated and she has begun to feel an increase in her energy.

Yvette returns for a scheduled follow-up visit two weeks after the first visit and initiation of the antidepressant. During that visit, she reports that she is tolerating the medication without any side effects. Her energy level is higher and she has been able to stay out of bed and to do more around the house. Her husband and children have said to her, "You look like you are feeling better." You inquire about suicidal thoughts and she denies having any. She doesn't feel that she is at her baseline yet and would like to plan for a return to work in one week, rather than now. Though the patient is the CEO/co-owner of her firm, you recommend that she bring in short-term disability papers for you to fill out.

Yvette has started to improve and, more important, has an absence of suicidal thoughts. It is of note that she has begun to improve though she has only been on the antidepressant for two weeks. This is seen sometimes. It is important to remember that an adequate trial of any antidepressant is four to six weeks. Patients must be on the proper dose for the proper duration of time for a trial to be considered adequate. As noted earlier in this case, if improvement is not seen after an adequate trial, augmenting with other agents or changing to another medication are other options. Patients should remain on an antidepressant until they have been doing well (in other words, symptom-free) for at least 16–20 weeks. Stressors in the patient's life should also be under good control before consideration is given to stopping an antidepressant. It is important that you keep the patient informed of the potential risks and benefits at all times during their treatment. For example, there is a 50% chance of relapse if medications are stopped sooner than six months after symptom resolution. If depression is severe and frequent enough (more than two episodes), long-term antidepressant therapy may be indicated.

In seeing this patient on the second visit, you review with her that this is not her first episode of depression. Given that information and that her family has also noticed changes and are clearly feeling the effects of her depression, you suggest that she sees a therapist, and she agrees with this recommendation. You refer her to a therapist who is well trained, understands how to deal with those who have work pressures, and is willing to hold family meetings when there is a therapeutic indication for them. You believe that this patient will benefit from individual therapy as she deals with the stressors of her job. Also, the patient had reported to you that her husband, children, and brother had noticed changes, and you believe that one or two sessions will need to be held with the patient, her husband, and possibly her children. The value of involving the family cannot be overemphasized, and the evidence for this was mentioned earlier in this case. This is done for three reasons: to support the patient, to support the family, and to treat the family. Relatives should be informed about the facts of mood disorders, including symptoms, history, prognosis, and treatment. They should be counseled on how to respond to the patient in times of distress and to understand their limitations along with the importance of their support in alleviating suffering. The decision to include children of the patient depends upon the family constellation and the age of the children.

While the patient's care is continuing and once written authorization has been given for the health care providers to communicate, the psychiatrist and the therapist need to work together so that maximum benefit can be gained for the patient. Throughout the course of care, issues such as concerns of the family, concerns about medications, or concerns about safety may emerge. A good working relationship between providers can create a positive therapeutic environment for the patient as well as maximize the efficiency of the delivery of health care.

Yvette has mentioned a potential return to work. She has been off work for two weeks and would like to return in one week. Whether to work or whether to take time off work due to an inability to fulfill one's responsibilities is an issue that arises. This is a decision to be made with input from you and the patient. Difficulties may arise no matter what decision is made. For example, a person's employer may be upset if there is time missed from work or an extended time is taken away from work. From a medical standpoint, a person may be incapacitated to perform their responsibilities due to a lack of concentration, mood disturbances that result in crying spells, an inability to get out of bed and get to work, or other issues. As the health care provider, you can provide assistance for them by helping them come to a conclusion about this issue and then providing appropriate written documentation for them as required by their human resources department. If a patient has been off work for an extended time, it is reasonable to offer a few tips to them upon their return: possibly returning for half days for the first week or returning to work in the middle of the week so there is not the stress of facing an entire week before they find themselves struggling just to survive until the weekend arrives.

The importance of documentation is readily apparent. Being able to remember exactly what you have done at each session, why you recommended what you did, and being able to support the patient with these recommendations is highly important.

Part of the continuing educational process of anyone in health care is understanding the answer to "What exactly is it that we are trying to do?" In psychiatry, obviously safety is a primary goal. Along with that comes the reality that we are trying to help the patient establish and/or maintain functionality, not necessarily cure the issue at hand. Depression and other psychiatric disorders are treated, not cured. With our patient, we have taken steps to work on and maintain functionality. An antidepressant has been started, a referral has been made to a therapist not only for her benefit but for her family as well, and the issue of work has been discussed with recommendations made. As the therapeutic relationship continues, the issue of functionality will be addressed at each session as we evaluate her care from a biopsychosocial approach. Also, Yvette has mentioned that she is a person of faith and attends church on a regular basis. She is encouraged to continue this.

For the sake of completeness and to be thorough on a review of treatment options, suppose Yvette did not respond to bupropion over a 12-week trial at a maximum dose. Please note that augmenting agents for depression not responding to current treatment include lithium, lamotrigine, thyroid supplements, stimulants, aripiprazole, and buspirone. Also, antidepressants from different classes may be combined to relieve the suffering of the psychiatric patients. One must be cautious with monoamine oxidase inhibitors, however, because combining them with other antidepressant classes may cause potentially fatal elevations in blood pressure. Obviously, this should be done only while being aware of potential hazards and after a risk/benefit analysis of this strategy.

SYSTEMS-BASED PRACTICE ISSUES

Systems-based practice has become such an important topic that it is now considered a core competency in residency programs across the United States. Many citizens are faced with the diagnosis of major depression. Recently a patient confidentially stated that he would rather have cancer than depression. This is a startling comment on just how severely depression can affect a person's life and livelihood. Aspects of care that are important include how clinical services are delivered, who is going to pay for those services, and how those services are organized. Issues include whether a person will be treated by a psychiatrist or a primary care provider, and who will treat those who are institutionalized such as in jails. There are also advocacy groups for those with mental illness such as the National Alliance for the Mentally Ill and Mental Health America. Cultural competence is also an important issue given that the minority population in the United States is increasing. One of the areas being focused on in all of medicine right now is quality improvement. Included in quality improvement is the mind-set that physicians are never satisfied with the quality of the delivered care and that not only is effectiveness reviewed, but efficiency is measured as well. Cost, quality, and access are important considerations. Patient safety is part of reviewing for quality and a reminder of the Hippocratic oath: "Above all else, do no harm."

LEGAL, ETHICAL, AND CULTURAL CHALLENGES

The federal Family Medical Leave Act gives an employee of a qualifying company the right to take time off to attend to their own health issues or to support a family member in dealing with that person's health issues. In the United States judges or their designee's (often called special justices), are also empowered to give judicial authorization for the administration of certain types of psychiatric care in the event that the afflicted person cannot make his or her own decision.

Although major depression is seen and treated across cultural and ethnic groups, the incidence and prevalence may vary. Patients of different cultures may demonstrate their depressive symptoms in different ways, such as by somatic or psychomotor symptoms. Depressive symptoms may be thought to be secondary to a physical disease. The evaluation and treatment process may be influenced by factors such as religious beliefs.

Latinos and African Americans appear to be less likely to receive treatment for a mood disorder than is a Caucasian. Also, there is a lower frequency of the use of antidepressants and therapy in minority groups compared to Caucasians. Differences in the use of services may be due to several issues, including stigmatization and the preferences of individuals. An example of this is that studies have found that Hispanics are more likely to prefer counseling than are Caucasians, whereas African Americans varied in their preference for counseling versus medications. Financial constraints may also play a role in the use of services by minorities.

Another important note is that rates of metabolism, side effects, and responses to medications may affect the pharmacological choices made by patients.

REFERENCES AND RESOURCES

Thase ME, Greenhouse JB, Frank E, Reynolds CF III, Pikonis PA, Hurley K, Grochocinski V, Kupfer DJ. Treatment of major depression with psychotherapy or psychotherapy-pharmacotherapy combinations. *Arch Gen Psych* 1997;54:1009–15.

Over the past 20 years support groups for depression have grown throughout the world. Two of the better known are National Alliance for the Mentally Ill (www.nami.org) and Mental Health America (http://www.mentalhealthamerica.net).

Numerous movies feature characters suffering from depression, including *Ordinary People* (1980).

CHAPTER 12

Atypical Depression

Mark B. Detweiler, M.D., M.S.

CLINICAL PRESENTATION

Current complaint: "I have felt worthless since I left the military."

History of present illness: Joan is a 50-year-old married woman who has been depressed on and off for the past 30 years. Fired from numerous jobs and medically discharged from the army after two years due to chronic headaches, she gives a long history of impairment from her medical and psychiatric disorders. Joan feels depressed most of each month. She also reports low energy, weight gain, sleeping more than 12 hours each day, and a history of difficulty being around other people who she says judge her and make her feel uncomfortable. She says that during her brief attempts at employment, she has often felt disliked by her coworkers.

Joan has suffered headaches daily for many years. She relates the onset of her headaches to a time when she was a new army recruit participating in a gas drill. She recalls that during the drill her gas mask "did not fit right." After the exercise, she developed Bell's palsy (a usually self-limited, unilateral paralysis of the facial nerve). Though the Bell's palsy resolved, several weeks later Joan began having severe headaches. Now 30 years later, she has a headache almost every day. Many of her headaches are severe.

When Joan was asked to list her problems from the most important to the least, she first listed "I want my headaches to go away." Second was "we need more money," third was "I want some happiness," and fourth was "I want a life, I have not had a life for so long I can't remember when I felt like a normal woman."

It is notable that her mood was not listed first. Joan's headaches are her most impairing problem. However, she recognizes that she is quite depressed and she has insight that her life is not very rich or fulfilled. She is hopeful that treatment can help her.

On intake, the Beck Depression Inventory indicated a severe depression. Despite this, Joan stated that she felt "all right today," perhaps indicating that her mood can at times brighten in anticipation of positive events such as potentially receiving help for her condition. However, despite saying she felt all right, she also said she felt down and blue most of the time for at least 20 days of each month since 1976. She endorsed hypersomnia, sleeping 10–12 hours a day. She said she wanted "to sleep all day because I'm always so tired." She added, "I have felt tired for years." Regarding her interests, she stated, "I don't have any anymore. I can't do anything because I have no energy or interest." She acknowledged significant daily guilt, saying "I loved the military and wanted to stay in, but I could not. I feel guilty that I could not have an army career and that I have been unable to hold a job. I have no friends because I can't talk about my life without feeling ashamed." Her concentration has been chronically impaired: "I don't remember things." She reported hyperphagia, stating, "I eat more than I want to eat." Joan also endorsed feeling slowed down as if it was hard for her to move her body at a regular speed (psychomotor retardation, possible leaden-paralysis). She denied any suicidal intent or plan in the recent past; however, she wished that she could go to sleep and not wake up, stating "I don't want to live this way." Joan endorsed feelings of hopelessness, helplessness, worthlessness, and frequent crying episodes.

Past psychiatric history: Joan stated that she had seen mental health workers in the past, tried biofeedback, and also tried a variety of different medications. She remembered being on venlafaxine, fluoxetine, sertraline, bupropion, and many other medications which "don't work or worked at first and then stopped working." On reviewing the names of multiple medications that she may have taken in the past, it appeared that various tricyclic antidepressants, serotonin reuptake inhibitors, and serotonin-norepinephrine reuptake inhibitors were ineffective in resolving her chronic depression. At her telepsychiatry intake, Joan was taking citalopram 40 mg once daily.

She denied any suicide attempts or gestures and any past history of psychiatric admissions. She denied the use of alcohol or illicit drugs for the past 32 years. She denied use of any street drugs, illegal prescription drugs, or tobacco. She endorsed the consumption of three to four cans of caffeinated beverages each day.

Past medical history: Chronic migraine headaches, atypical chest pain, mixed lipidemia, tension headaches, abnormal weight gain, and hypothyroidism are listed in her medical history. For her headaches she had tried tricyclic antidepressants, anticonvulsants, triptans, migraine agents, NSAIDs, and biofeedback without lasting benefit.

Her gallbladder was removed in 2006. She has allergies to codeine, penicillin, and acetaminophen.

Joan reported, "I gave up on over-the-counter medications years ago, nothing helped." Her current medications are citalopram 40 mg once daily, diclofenac 75 mg once a day as needed for neck pain, lamotrigine 125 mg twice daily for headaches, levothyroxine 0.075 mg once daily for hypothyroidism, and simvastatin 40 mg once daily and niacin 500 mg once daily for hyperlipidemia.

Family history: Joan denied a family history of depression, anxiety, suicide attempts and gestures, or any other psychiatric illnesses. Her father was an "alcoholic," and this contributed to her wanting to leave home and join the army as soon after high school as possible.

Social history: Joan was born in Virginia. She was raised in a home with her two parents and a brother. She said her parents worked a lot and that she received most of her "mothering" from her grandmother. She felt her parents "played my brother and me against each other," and this left her feeling lonely and like she was constantly trying to get her parents' approval as a child. Joan participates in a church that has offered her personal and social support through many difficult years. She has been married for 27 years and has no children. She comments that "with the headaches and spending most of each day in bed, I couldn't take care of children. I didn't want to be a bad mother." She reported that "children were not a priority for my husband." She says that she feels "guilty and stressed" due to being sick all the time. Joan mentioned in passing, "sometimes I feel my husband is angry at me," then she stated that she gets along well with her husband.

During the early stages of her first interview, Joan denied any emotional, physical, or sexual abuse. However, as the intake continued, she shared that a neighborhood boy molested her when from ages 6 to 10. She could not remember any details of the incidents. She related that she was happy to hear that he died of cancer several years ago.

Joan denied any instances of military sexual trauma. She does not consider the sexual molestation experienced as a child to be significant in relation to her husband or to her past 30 years of poor health. She says she does not have any flashbacks or nightmares or other difficulties related to the childhood abuse.

Joan joined the Army Reserve right after high school. With the onset of the chronic headaches, she was medically discharged after six months of training and another year or so of waiting for her discharge evaluation. She achieved the rank of private first class and denies any disciplinary charges or reductions in rank prior to her discharge. Subsequently, she held many diverse jobs for short periods of time including stockroom clerk, textile company employee, salesperson, insurance representative, and floral shop assistant.

Joan denies any present or past legal charges with no report of driving under the influence or drunk in public charges. She is trying to have her army service connection (monthly payments) increased as she says "the headaches started in the army and they have kept me from having a job since I was discharged. I feel awful almost every day."

Joan keeps loaded pistols in her home, along with other weapons. She would not agree to have them removed from the house, as she said "we live in the country and we need to have guns to protect ourselves."

Laboratory results: A CBC, comprehensive metabolic screen, and urinalysis were within the range of normal. B_{12} was low = 199 pg/ml; but folate = 10.9 ng/ml was within the normal range. Thyroid-stimulating hormone (TSH) is at 2.821 mU/ml.

Imaging: Head CT was unremarkable.

Mental status examination: Joan is a well-dressed, Caucasian female, with neatly coiffed hair wearing a dress and carrying a purse. She is pleasant and cooperative, but she often cries during parts of the interview reviewing her army history. She has mild psychomotor retardation. At times she is motionless while sitting in her chair. Joan appears to be without enough energy to keep sitting up straight in the chair, as she often leans her head to rest on one outstretched arm. Her speech has a reduced rate, and there are long pauses as she considers even simple questions (response latency). When overcome by sadness, her speech becomes even slower. Her thought process is linear and logical, but at times she appears distracted by internal thoughts. She is not spontaneous and needs direct questions to elicit the needed information for the intake examination. There is no circumstantiality, tangentiality, looseness of association, or flight of ideas that might suggest mania or hypomania. Joan is alert and oriented to person, place, situation, and date. Her immediate recall is intact with correct recall of three of three unrelated words and five of six digits. Her intermediate recall is partial with correct memory of two of three unrelated words and four of six digits. Remote memory is intact—she can name four U.S. presidents since 1960 and she recalls the military event that occurred on December 7, 1941 (the bombing of Pearl Harbor). Her attention to performance commands is largely intact ("place your right finger on your left ear"). At times she is inattentive and answers some questions in an inappropriate way until she is reminded of the question being asked. Her concentration is impaired, as she can only perform two serial 7's correctly and she forgot one letter when asked to spell "truck" backward. Her use of English is congruent with her high school education. Her affect is depressed and moderately restricted. Joan describes her mood as "all right." She denies any suicidal or homicidal ideations, plan, or intent. However, she does have nihilistic thoughts of dying by natural causes "of just not waking up when it's my time." There is no evident thought content abnormality as Joan denies any paranoia. There is no evidence of delusions, and there are no signs of a thought disorder. She does not appear to be responding to internal or external stimuli and she denies auditory, visual, olfactory, and tactile hallucinations. She denies any illusions. Joan's abstracting ability ("what does 'a stitch in time saves nine' mean?") and her similarities intuition ("what are the similarities between a chair and a bookcase?") is average. When asked to perform a simple calculation ("how much is one quarter, two dimes, three nickels and four pennies?") her sum is correct. Joan's general knowledge is fair as she remembers two of five of the state capitals of states surrounding Virginia. Her knowledge of current events is average. Her judgment about managing her life is fair, and her insight about her psychiatric symptoms is poor to fair. There are no signs of depersonalization or derealization. Her impulse control appears intact.

IMPAIRMENT IN FUNCTIONING

Joan is a married Caucasian female who was sexually abused as a child by a non-family member for four years and reports emotional abuse by her parents. Her childhood was not rich with social experiences, school successes, or extracurricular activities. Home and social life appear to have been deficient for normal psychic maturation. She reports a 34-year history of disabling symptoms of major depression, recurrent, with atypical features versus a mood disorder with depressive features due to chronic intractable headaches and a vitamin B_{12} deficiency. The depression and unremitting headaches in this patient have been continual since her army experience at 18 years of age. The headaches were responsible for her discharge from the army and reportedly have interfered with all her successive job attempts. She has felt like a failure in life because she was not able to complete her army career, and she has not been able to hold a job due to the severity of the headache symptoms, which incapacitate her for many days a week, compromising her job reliability. She does not have children because she believed that the headaches would not allow her to be a proper mother. Her feelings of satisfaction in her marriage are compromised because she is chronically tired, has extreme fatigue, or is recovering from her recurrent headaches. These things have impaired quality time with her husband. Her functional impairment is considerable; she has not met typical adult goals in terms of work or family milestones and she continues to have a significantly reduced quality of life.

DSM DIAGNOSIS

The psychiatric diagnoses appear to be dysthymia starting in early childhood with major depression, recurrent, with atypical features, moderate severity beginning at least when she was 18 years old and undergoing army training. Joan's difficulty having friendships, participating in social events with a relatively reclusive life without work, suggests possible dependent personality disorder traits versus avoidant personality traits.

According to the DSM Joan does not meet criteria for bipolar disorder or posttraumatic stress disorder. She is already diagnosed with hypothyroidism and is taking lamotrigine for migraine headaches. There is a known association between hypothyroidism and bipolar type II, and it might be worth exploring if Joan has ever had two to three-day periods of higher energy or increased goal-directed activities. Antithyroid antibodies like those that cause Hashimoto's disease (autoimmune hypothyroidism) are associated with a higher risk of mood and anxiety disorders, especially bipolar disorders. Often patients with bipolar II do not report their periods of higher energy or irritability as a problem because they feel less depressed during those times. Bipolar II is primarily a depressive disorder with only occasional episodes of hypomania. It is more common in women with atypical depression and in women with migraine. By the history she gave, Joan does not yet meet full criteria for this disorder, but it may be that her illness is in that spectrum of disorders.

A severe headache syndrome in addition to a vitamin B_{12} deficiency of unknown duration requires consideration of diagnosis of pain disorder associated with both psychological factors and a general medical condition, chronic and mood disorder due to a general medical condition. Joan's comorbid medial problems include chronic migraine/tension headaches, vitamin B_{12} deficiency, mixed lipidemia, hypothyroidism, and history of atypical chest pain. Her psychosocial difficulties are nonemployability due to chronic medical and psychiatric symptoms, an unsatisfactory marital relationship, and poor social support.

The principal characteristics of major depression in the DSM are that there is no prior history of manic, mixed, or hypomanic episodes and that the depressive symptoms are not better accounted for by a substance-induced mood disorder, mood disorder due to a general medical condition, schizoaffective disorder, schizophrenia, schizophreniform disorder, delusional disorder, or psychotic disorder not otherwise specified.

Major depression may be classified as being a single episode or recurrent. In general, a recurrent episode is one that follows a period of two or more months with no signs of depression. As the depression progresses or recedes, the qualifiers mild, moderate, severe without psychotic features, severe with psychotic features, chronic, with catatonic features, with melancholic features, with atypical features, and with postpartum onset can be used. These specifiers may change as the disease varies over time.

Joan has had recurrent episodes of depression for more than 30 years. It was difficult for her to remember time during the past three decades when she was not depressed. She has had all the classic signs of depression, including depressed mood, lack of energy, loss of interest in all aspects of her life, and profound guilt about failing in the army in addition to failing at all her jobs due to the daily or weekly incapacitation of her headaches. She has gradually gained weight, perhaps due to a combination of eating and inactivity as she spends most of the day in bed due to fatigue, headaches, and depression.

EPIDEMIOLOGY

The prevalence of major depression is unrelated to ethnicity, education, income, or marital status. However, there are prevalence differences according to gender and age. Although estimates vary according to the study, women are estimated to have a higher prevalence of depression (10–25%) than men (5–10%). Several large genetic studies have reported a higher genetic susceptibility among female than male twins. The somatic symptoms of atypical depression such as hypersomnia, hyperphagia, and leaden paralysis (a heavy feeling in the arms and legs) are more often seen in women. Women may also reach the threshold for major depressive disorder and its qualifiers because they tend to report more symptoms than men.

Angst et al. studied the psychiatric and somatic characteristics in a population of subjects from 20 to 40 years of age. They compared four subgroups of major depressive episodes (MDEs); (1) melancholia or atypical depression combined, (2) pure melancholia, (3) pure atypical depression, and (4) unspecified MDE. The incidence rates were 4.1%, 7.1%, 3.5%, and 8.2%, respectively. Women were seen more frequently in the combined and atypically depressed group. In 47.9% of the cases, melancholia was longitudinally associated with atypical MDE. The finding that in many cases those with melancholic depression go on to have atypical depression fits with other work by the same researcher showing that many individuals initially diagnosed with unipolar depression may have broader bipolar phenotypes, especially when there are comorbid medical problems or personality disorders present.

DIFFERENTIAL DIAGNOSIS

Persistent depressive disorder (dysthymia) is defined as having a chronically depressed mood that occurs most days, more days than not, for at least two years. In children it may manifest as irritability. Joan admits to being constantly distressed by her parents' lack of support, and it seems she may have had lower mood as a child, but it is not possible to say for sure.

Social anxiety disorder is considered based on Joan's history of reported poor parental support, low self-esteem, and an apparent dearth of friends and social activities as a child, adolescent, and adult. She was living almost a monastic life when she arrived in the clinic for a telepsychiatry intake, and she described significant challenges with social relationships outside her marriage. Social anxiety disorder is described as marked and persistent fear of social or performance situations with the risk of being embarrassed in a social or work environment. Exposure to events or even the thought of exposure to such a situations results in persistent fear. This is typically followed by an avoidance of the feared situation or person. Adolescents and adults usually recognize that their fear is excessive, but children may not. In persons younger than 18 years of age, the fear must be present for at least six months before the diagnosis can be made. There is a fear of interacting in social situations and an aversion to participating in groups, dating, speaking to authority figures, attending parties and avoidance of taking leadership positions. These characteristics could describe Joan's life both before and after her army experience. The lifetime prevalence of social phobia is estimated at 3% to 13%. The fear of public speaking is the most common with some estimates as high as 20%. Less frequent are fears of eating, drinking, or writing in public or fears of using public restrooms.

It is also pertinent in this case that DSM describes social phobia generalized type and avoidant personality disorder as having greatly overlapping symptoms to the extent that they may be describing the same phenomenon. Joan's history suggests her temperament and early environment could have fostered dependent and avoidant personality traits. The relative self-isolation from all social activities starting in childhood and lasting into her middle adult years suggest a notable fear of social or performance situations in which embarrassment may occur (Criterion A). It can be inferred that there was sufficient anxiety to minimize her social performance as she describes herself as lonely as a child and she had few (if any) social contacts as an adult (Criterion B). Joan seems to understand that her isolation and fear of being in pubic is unreasonable; however, she is incapable of overcoming her anxiety (Criterion C). During the past several decades, she has made few attempts to initiate social engagements outside of having outings with her husband and mother-in-law due to anticipated stress (Criteria D). The hopes of having an occupational and social life may have been suppressed by chronic fear and avoidance.

At intake, Joan was more or less homebound due to her headaches, chronic fatigue, and depression. Finally, although she attempted many jobs after her army discharge, she finally gave up attempts to work as a result of her of continual failures in part related to her chronic and disabling headaches. Moreover, it can be reasoned that her fear of failing as a mother, given her own mother's failure in this role, has contributed to her avoidance of having children. This was complicated by the fact that her husband did not want children—after the marriage he continued to be his mother's main source of personal support at the expense of Joan's marital sense of being a loved partner. Joan noted that all activities with her husband included her mother-in-law. This subconscious partner choice may have replicated her role as a rejected child. She has more than four of the seven characteristics of avoidant personality.

The dependent personality disorder is characterized by a persistent and excessive need to be taken care of with fears of separation. The unconscious secondary gain is to foster caregiving from others based on the self-perception of being inadequate to function without assistance from other persons. Individuals with this disorder are submissive because they want other people to make decisions for them. In this case, Joan was unable to work, and she feared the responsibility of having children. She reports not feeling she had a strong maternal figure when she was a child. She failed all job attempts and relied on her husband to support her. Dependent personality disorder may be comorbid with serious medical conditions or disabilities. In these cases, the difficulty in decision making should exceed that normally expected for the medical condition.

The depressed patient often presents a wide variety of physical signs and symptoms. The physical complaints include chronic pain and headaches, sleep disturbances, severe insomnia and early awakening, appetite changes, anorexia and rapid weight loss, and a decrease in sexual activity, ranging at times to impotence in males and amenorrhea or sexual dysfunction in females. A headache secondary to depression is often considered a tension-type (muscle contraction) headache. But it is possible that the physical complaints are indicative of another medical condition that is also causing the depression or that depression is related to inflammatory changes that cause or worsen the physically painful sensations the patient notices.

The prevalence of mood disorder due to a general medical condition with depressive features is estimated to be found equally in men and women. The prevalence of mood disorders due to a general medical condition has variations depending on the underlying disease process. A study by Egede of thousands of adults with and without major depression examined the association between chronic condition status and health care utilization, lost productivity, and functional disability. The author reported that persons with depression due to chronic medical conditions had greater outpatient and emergency room visits, and greater functional disability compared to persons with chronic medical diseases but without depression.

Joan has had migraine headaches mostly without aura for more than three decades without relief. In more than 40% of cases there is bilateral head and neck pain. Bilateral pain is more common in persons who suffer from migraines without an aura. Pain in the back or top of the head is less common. Pain from frequent migraine and tension headaches has reduced Joan's quality of life significantly, and it could be that her depression is due to her headache condition.

A multitude of medical conditions can cause mood disorders due to a general medical condition, including cardiovascular, gastrointestinal, neurological, thyroid abnormalities (from which Joan suffers), infections, cancer, diabetes, and electrolyte abnormalities to name a few. In some cases the depressive symptoms may occur prior to the clinical appearance of the medical condition, such as in the case of some cancers, Parkinson's disease, cerebrovascular disease, or multiple sclerosis. More often, depression follows the diagnosis and treatment of diseases. Depression increases the risk of suicide, particularly when comorbid medical conditions are chronic and incurable such as Huntington's disease, spinal cord injuries, head injuries, and AIDS. There are four subtypes of mood disorders due to a general medical condition: (1) with depressive features, (2) with major depressive-like episode, (3) with manic features, and (4) with mixed features. Mood disorders due to a general medical condition are diagnosed when the mood abnormality is the direct result of the physiological effects of a medical condition(s). In this case these are chronic migraine headaches and a vitamin B_{12} deficiency and possibly also hypothyroidism.

Joan's clinical presentation resembles that of major depression. For major depression there must not be evidence from the physical examination or from laboratory results that the presenting symptoms are directly associated with a general medical condition(s). The depressive symptoms must not be better accounted for by another mood disturbance, such as adjustment disorder, psychosocial stressors, substance use, or delirium. The mood must result in significant disturbances of social, occupational, or other important aspects of the person's life. When a physical illness causes depression usually there is a temporal relationship between the onset of the general medical condition and the clinical appearance of the mood disturbance as is evident in Joan's case.

Also, in this case it is appropriate to rule out a pain disorder associated with psychological factors and a chronic general medical condition. This disorder is characterized in DSM by pain in one or more anatomical sites that is the focus of clinical attention and merits clinical evaluation. The pain causes significant distress or disruption of social, occupational, or other areas of function. Pain disorder ranks among the most prevalent conditions in the community setting. It is estimated that 10–15% of adults in the United States have some work disability due to back pain with an unclear percentage having pain disorder. Pain disorder associated with both psychological factors and a general medical condition is thought to be relatively common in clinical situations where chronic pain is the focus of attention, such as in pain clinics and for consult liaison services in hospitals and clinics.

In Joan's case, the almost daily treatment-resistant headaches and treatment-resistant depressive symptoms are the foundation for the diagnosis of pain disorder associated with both psychological factors and a chronic general medical condition. Fröhlich et al. noted that persons with pain disorder had significantly poorer quality of life, greater disability, and higher health care use rates compared to cases with pain below the diagnostic threshold. In his study, the majority of individuals studied had more than one type of pain, with excessive headaches being the most frequent type. The high prevalence of pain disorders in all age groups results in substantial disability and increased primary health care and emergency room utilization. Fröhlich and colleagues reported that the morbidity of pain disorders results in a greater health care burden than that for depression and anxiety.

Joan has no known family history of migraine headaches. Seymour Diamond, the executive chairman of the National Headache Foundation, has been studying the relationship between headaches and depressive reactions since 1964. He notes that the presence of minor depression is often missed, while major depressive episodes are more obvious. However, as the majority of depressed patients do not fit the classic DSM criteria, diagnosis of depression accompanying headaches may require an extensive biopsychosocial examination including the patient's marital relations, occupation, social relationships, life stresses, personality traits, habits, methods of handling tense situations, and sexual problems.

Before puberty, boys have more migraine headaches than girls. However, after puberty women have to three times more migraine headaches than men. Migraine frequency may diminish during pregnancy. Although there is not a consensus opinion about the origin of migraines, some authors suggest that it is a neuro-vascular disorder. Dodick and Gargus report that the probable mechanism involves increased excitability of the cerebral cortex accompanied by deficient pain control of trigeminal nucleus neurons.

Migraine headaches are a chronic, recurrent headache phenomenon characterized by autonomic nervous system disturbances, including nausea, vomiting, and photophobia. The pain may be pulsating and most commonly involves one side of the brain. The headaches may be very debilitating with durations from 2 to 72 hours. The symptoms are usually aggravated by sound, light, and physical activity. Approximately a third of persons experience an aura prior to the onset of headache symptoms; Joan usually did not experience an aura. The aura is transient and may include visual, sensory, language, and motor disturbances either singly or in combinations, which signals that the headache will soon occur.

Some of the symptoms present in this case could also be related to the vitamin B_{12} deficiency. Joan did not have any of the many lifestyles or disease states that may contribute to B_{12} deficiency, which are vegetarian diet, pregnancy with poor nutrition, chronic alcoholism, pernicious anemia, celiac disease, Crohn's disease, chronic antacid use, or past gastrointestinal surgery. One of the difficulties with assessing the role of B_{12} is that many of the symptoms associated with a deficiency state are common to other medical disorders. Moreover, there is no international consensus for the definition of B_{12} deficiency. At the Veteran Affairs Medical Center, the range for B_{12} blood levels is from 212 to 911 pg/mg, whereas the Japanese minimum recommended B_{12} blood levels is 500 pg/ml. Hence, in the contribution of a B_{12} deficiency is difficult to determine.

The length of time that Joan had suffered a deficient B_{12} level is unknown, however, it is could be that the deficiency is a contributing factor to her symptoms. Because it is easy to treat and may help her feel better, treatment is worthwhile. B_{12} (cyanocobalamin) deficiency is more common in persons following gastric surgery due to impaired absorption. It is also common in malnourished persons of all ages. However, it is most frequent in the elderly due to poor dietary habits and decreased absorption secondary to atrophic gastritis. Vitamin B_{12} deficiency may cause permanent damage to the nervous system if left untreated for prolonged periods. Reduced B_{12} levels can result in fatigue, depression, and memory deficits. In some cases, vitamin B_{12} deficiency can also cause symptoms of fatigue, agitation, irritability, confusion, disorientation, amnesia, concentration deficits, attention reduction, and insomnia. Depression may lead to altered dietary habits so that poor nutrition may be a result of depression instead of a cause. In Joan's case the most probable cause of the B_{12} deficiency would be poor diet based on her depression and lack of self-care. This was also compounded by the fact that the majority of her meals were made only for herself because her husband was out of the house most of the day and for multiple days at a time due to his job as a truck driver. Another common deficiency in depressed individuals who tend to stay indoors is a vitamin D deficiency. Joan's vitamin D was not checked, but most women in her age group can benefit from at least modest supplementation. Given her depression and likely lowered nutritional status, a solid multivitamin would be reasonable recommendation to supplement her care, as would replacement of B_{12}.

Standard assessment tools that may be useful to differentiate among possible diagnoses and resolve diagnostic uncertainty include the Beck Depression Inventory, second edition (BDI-II) and the Liebowitz Social Anxiety Scale (LSAS-SR) for social anxiety disorder. The Structured Clinical Interviews for DSM (SCID) can help distinguish between acute psychiatric conditions and personality disorders. A thorough medical evaluation, including laboratory work and imaging (MRI, CT, ultrasound, x-ray, etc.) as indicated by the presentation to determine possible physical causes of the pain.

ETIOLOGY AND PATHOGENESIS

Joan's difficulties probably began with dysthymic symptoms during her early childhood and continued through her brief time in the army. After her medical discharge, her headaches continued unabated despite treatment, and the dysthymia progressed toward major depression with atypical features. As her comorbid headaches and mood disorder continued untreated, she failed to achieve many lifetime goals, and her personality may have been affected.

The years of treatment-resistant episodes of depression have contributed to Joan's sense of worthlessness, helplessness and hopelessness, and ongoing guilt about her failure at becoming a productive employed person and having a fulfilling marriage. Moreover, she has been so debilitated by her headaches and the depression that she felt that she could not possibly be a proper mother and thus chose not to have children.

Personality disorders are precipitated by difficulties in childhood that are not adequately addressed in the context of the child's temperament, environment, and specific needs. Many children have resiliency factors that protect against difficulties and traumas, but some are sensitive to trauma and fare poorly when faced with it. From Joan's social history, it would appear that her problems started early in her life by perceived parental neglect and splitting of her and her brother. She reported that "my parents were always working. They played my brother and me against each other and this made me feel lonely as a child. I was constantly trying to get approval." She attributed her "real parenting" to her grandmother. She reported intermittent sexual abuse from a neighborhood boy from age 6 to 10. Joan did not report the abuse or ask for help. We have a picture of a child who was growing up in a family where she did not feel protected and could not ask for help. However, it is difficult to say how much her own temperament may play into these recollections. It is possible that a different child might have had a similar family and have recalled two working but loving parents; a loving, helpful grandmother; a healthy sense of competition with her brother; and exploratory but not damaging play with another neighborhood child. In understanding her report of childhood abuse it would be important to clarify the age difference between herself and the neighborhood boy who abused her. She may have been abused, but it would be helpful to have more information.

The trait of interpersonal rejection sensitivity is not present only during episodes of atypical depression but instead is present in individuals prone to the disorder and may tend to color how they perceive and report their experiences even at times when they are not depressed.

Therefore, extrapolation from the facts available about her childhood must be viewed with the qualification that these are speculations based on the patient's perceptions and recollections. After her failure to complete her initial army training and other failed attempts at employment, Joan became more secluded and her social contacts appeared minimal. Her original occupation as a soldier in the army involved multiple social contacts with the safety of the organization of interpersonal interactions as an enlisted soldier. Did this mandatory exposure to multiple people overwhelm her and create a stress that in turn precipitated somatic symptoms that would give her an acceptable withdrawal while saving face (medical discharge)? Her prior and subsequent history suggests an unwillingness to get involved with people unless certain of being accepted. It is not clear whether she shows restraint in her marriage because of fear of being ridiculed or shamed. It can be inferred that her social isolation may be caused by a preoccupation of being criticized or rejected and feelings of inadequacy, inferiority, and being socially inept. After her series of failed job attempts, it appears that she became reluctant to take personal risks or engage in new activities because they may have resulted in embarrassment. Also, by not having children, she could maintain a more childlike and dependent role in her marriage and possibly get her dependency needs met by her husband. However, these dependency needs were sabotaged by her husband's dependency needs with his mother, leaving Joan feeling alone and unfulfilled. She recalled the difficulty of having intimate time together on vacations "as my mother-in-law was always in a nearby room."

NATURAL COURSE WITHOUT TREATMENT

Joan's clinical course without treatment for her diagnoses would probably look even worse than what she has experienced for the past 34 years. It is difficult to imagine a worse situation than spending most of every day depressed, with extreme fatigue and anhedonia complicated by headaches. However, without antidepressants it is possible that Joan may have attempted or completed suicide. The prolonged and frequent migraine headaches may have been more prolonged and more intense without the ongoing use of prophylactic medications. Major depression has a high rate of completed suicide attempts. In general about 15% of persons with major depression die from suicide. This rate increases fourfold in persons older than 55 years of age. Risk of suicide is also higher within six months to one year after admission to a psychiatry ward and is higher among men and women without dementia.

Depression can be debilitating for the brain. Kemptom et al. studied healthy brains and compared them with those of persons having major depression and bipolar disorder. Persons with major depression and bipolar disorder had increased lateral ventricle volume and increased rates of subcortical gray matter hyperintensities when compared to healthy controls. The researchers found that when compared to healthy brain, the major depressive brain had lateral ventricle enlargement and larger cerebrospinal fluid volumes. Also, the depressed brains demonstrated reduced volumes for the basal ganglia, thalamus, hippocampus, frontal lobe, orbitofrontal cortex, and gyrus rectus. Persons in remission from depressive episodes often had larger hippocampal volumes than persons experiencing a depressive episode. Persons suffering from major depression had fewer deep white matter hyperintensities, increased corpus callosum cross-sectional area, and reduce hippocampus and basal ganglia volumes when compared with persons with bipolar disorder.

After onset, anxiety may portend a continuous lifetime of destabilizing disease. Social anxiety disorder may be insidious, initiating as shyness during childhood and progressing to social phobia in the mid-teens. However, it may have a sudden onset following a humiliating experience.

Personality disorder or traits usually start in infancy or childhood. The avoidant personality disorder can also be confused with dependent personality disorder. Both are characterized by feelings of inadequacy, an oversensitivity to criticism, and a frequent need for assurance. However, patients with avoidant personality disorder typically have such an intense fear of rejection that they instinctively withdraw until they are certain of acceptance. People with dependent personality disorder, in contrast, actually seek out contact with others because they need their approval. Dependent personality disorder and avoidant personality disorder are frequently comorbid and share symptom presentation. Both disorders are characterized by feelings of inadequacy, sensitivity to criticism, and the need for frequent reassurance. This case is complicated by Joan's social anxiety and interpersonal rejection sensitivity, which buttresses the fears of rejection. Without therapeutic assistance, she has remained relatively secluded for more than three decades.

EVIDENCE-BASED TREATMENT OPTIONS

For milder depression, either psychotherapy or pharmacotherapy alone can be used effectively. Combined psychotherapy and pharmacotherapy is best for moderate and severe depression. If there are indications of possible suicidality or homicidality, or the patient is showing rapidly progressing symptoms of depression with impaired judgment in the outpatient setting, the clinician needs to consider hospitalization.

The three most used psychotherapies for depression are cognitive therapy (CT), interpersonal therapy (IPT), and psychodynamic therapy. CT focuses on identifying the cognitive distortions thought to be responsible for the depression. Encouraging Joan to participate in weekly therapy would help her form a trusting relationship outside of her marriage, get her out of her home at least once or twice a week, and give her a venue for exploring some of her less adaptive personality traits with a professional trained to assist her to in meeting one of her stated goals of having more of a life.

Antidepressants are the most frequently used medications for the treatment of depression. Monoamine oxidase inhibitors (e.g., phenelzine, tranylcypromine) were among the first antidepressants and are still employed as a fourth choice in treated resistant patients. They may work best in patient with atypical depression but have significant side effects. Selective serotonin reuptake inhibitors also have efficacy in atypical depression. The Sequential Treatment Alternatives to Relieve Depression (STAR-D) study examined algorithms for treating depression in patients in primary care and psychiatric clinics. A number of other algorithms exist and can be helpful. Joan has already tried a number of agents for the treatment of her depression, so the psychiatrist will likely need to think creatively to help her.

Tufts University used a cut-off B_{12} blood level of 350 pg/ml and found that 39% of the 3,000 subjects studied had low B_{12} levels. Whereas Japan B_{12} standards have a lower limit of 500 pg/ml, Mitsuyama and Kogoh suggested 550 B_{12} pg/ml blood levels and Van Tiggelen et al. proposed minimum B_{12} levels of 600 pg/ml. In the present case the goal of treatment was to have Joan's B_{12} level increased to equal to or greater than 500 pg/ml, following the Japanese recommendations.

Joan's current TSH at 2.8 is higher than the optimal range suggested for patients treated for hypothyroidism. Those patients with known hypothyroidism are often treated until their TSH is less than 2, and some patients report not feeling better until the TSH is closer to 1.0. It is likely that individuals have a set point at which their body feels best for thyroid function and it is quite likely that Joan may be undertreated. This could account for her chronic depression, fatigue, hypersomnia, weight gain, hyperlipidemia, and headaches, all of which can be symptoms of hypothyroidism. Some hypothyroid patients feel better taking some levothyroxine (T4) and some liothyronine (T3). T3 is well established as an augmentation agent for the treatment of depression and is also sometimes mood stabilizing in rapid cycling bipolar disorder. It is possible Joan might respond to the addition of T3 to her levothyroxine.

CLINICAL COURSE WITH MANAGEMENT AND TREATMENT

Joan has had three decades of treatment for her headaches and depression with poor results. She would like to have a more intimate life with her husband. She is amenable to whatever treatment modalities would help her achieve these goals. Her depression is characterized as severe and treatment-resistant because she has failed to respond to many more than two biological interventions. An improvement in the symptoms of the major depression, recurrent, with atypical features would improve the quality of her life.

Joan had tried biofeedback without success. Electroconvulsive treatments could be used, but she did not want this option. Psychotherapy was indicated in this case, however, due to the very limited resources (see later discussion), this was not possible other than during the telepsychiatry clinical visits. Joan had received years of treatment for depression with some psychotherapy and multiple antidepressants, including tricyclic antidepressants, serotonin reuptake inhibitors, and serotonin-norepinephrine reuptake inhibitors, without resolution of her chronic depression. She was able to remember prescriptions for venlafaxine, fluoxetine, sertraline, and bupropion, but she could not recall the doses or the lengths of the medication trials.

Because the options of psychotherapy and electroconvulsive therapy were rejected by Joan as alternative treatment modalities, the decision was made to use medications. The cost of medications was not a factor in this case because Joan had all her medications paid for by the VA. This was due to the fact that her medical (headaches) and psychiatric (depression) problems were "service-connected" based on the problems she experienced in the army. She was evaluated by the army to be 90% disabled by the combination of these two maladies.

Joan had arrived at the clinic taking citalopram 40 mg once daily, and it was thought to maximize this serotonin reuptake inhibitor as the initial step. She was educated about the side effects of the medication, including nausea, agitation, insomnia, and anorgasmia. This case occurred prior to the FDA recommendations of limiting citalopram dosing according to age, with the QTc interval monitored with serial EKGs if higher doses were used. Therefore, the dose was increased to 60 mg for her depression. Later, sustained-release bupropion 150 mg in the morning was added to augment the serotonin action of citalopram with norepinephrine and dopamine reuptake inhibitor actions. The dose was titrated to 300 mg in the morning and 150 mg in the afternoon. It was next decided to augment the two antidepressants with immediate-release methylphenidate 5 mg bid to address Joan's fatigue, and hypersomnolence. The methylphenidate was eventually titrated to 15 mg bid as target symptoms were observed to improve with dose increases. Her energy increased with the methylphenidate titration, her hypersomnolence receded, and her libido returned. A serendipitous finding was the effectiveness of the methylphenidate for relieving her headaches. There is no supporting literature to predict this outcome. It was hypothesized that the action of methylphenidate on norepinephrine and dopamine was singularly responsible for the improvement in the depression and headache symptoms.

Treatment for B_{12} deficiency was initiated at intake to reverse the vitamin deficiency. Joan did not remember having any prior B_{12} levels being drawn. The clinical concern was about the risk of irreversible cognitive and peripheral nerve damage. Intramuscular injections are usually reserved for persons who have absorption defects. Joan had no indications to justify use of this route of B_{12} administration. So vitamin B_{12} 1,000 mcg and folic acid 1 mg daily were started with the goal of increasing her blood levels in the upper tertile of normal range (B_{12} > 500 pg/ml; folate > 12 ng/ml) based in Japanese standards. Joan's B_{12} level was kept between 500 and 900 pg/ml. Because she had no paresthesia of her extremities, and her attention and focus improved with the improvement of her headaches and depression, it appears that the vitamin B_{12} deficiency did not leave any major deficits.

Joan had multiple firearms in her home, and she was asked to have them removed to the house of a relative. However, she refused to remove the weapons, and she stated that she needed them due to her living situation. She stated that as she was relatively isolated in the country. Also, with her husband out on the road as a truck driver most days, she did not feel safe without the firearms. She denied any suicidal ideations, plan, or intent because this was contrary to her religious beliefs. As is customary at the end of all clinic visits, Joan was asked to call the clinic or hospital if any problems would occur. In the case of an emergency, she was advised to go to the nearest emergency room or come the more than 100 miles from her house to the VA Emergency Room where there is 24-hour psychiatry care available.

With the regimen of citalopram 60 mg in the morning, bupropion 300 mg in the morning and 150 mg in the afternoon, in addition to methylphenidate 15 mg twice a day, Joan's mood remained stable and euthymic with full range. She achieved great improvement of her headaches and felt some happiness. The hypersomnolence resolved. This was an exciting change for Joan and her husband. She was no longer sleeping excessively, and she took pleasure in doing activities both inside and outside the house. Her headaches were no longer debilitating. Joan described her residual headaches as few per week with shorter duration, less intense, and with a diminished recovery period. Moreover, she reported that the return of her libido had improved her marital relationship.

At Joan's most recent appointment, her appearance and dress were markedly improved compared to her intake presentation. She joked during her interview. Her dread of daily incapacitating headaches had resolved. She reported having enough energy and interest in her surroundings to spend an entire day fully awake and with multiple activities. Her quality of life, relationship with her husband, and self-esteem improved.

It appears that that Joan's mood and quality of life were most significantly affected by the onset and resolution of her headaches. The headaches were responsible for her medical discharge from the army, and they were the key element that led to her inability to hold a job. Moreover, the debilitation of the headaches made her feel unfit to be a mother. Thus the symptoms of major depression, recurrent, with atypical features seems largely a consequence of chronic intractable headaches and perhaps better diagnosed with mood disorder secondary to a medical condition with depressive features. The depressive features began after the onset of the headaches and became more profound as Joan experienced continual insults to her quality of life. Although the combination citalopram and bupropion improved her mood, the most remarkable mood and quality of life changes occurred with the resolution of her headache syndrome as methylphenidate was titrated to effect at 15 mg twice a day.

Joan had received many classes of medications for her migraines, including tricyclic antidepressants, anticonvulsants, triptans, migraine agents, and NSAIDs. Biofeedback sessions had failed. Her headaches had been described as migraine and cluster type. She had not used any alcohol for at least 30 years, which removed one possible headache trigger. She had received some preventive medications such as verapamil, gabapentin, and divalproex. She had also received medications for breakthrough headache episodes including aspirin, NSAIDs, ergotamine tartrate, Midrin (isometheptene, and dichloralphenazone), and multiple triptans over three decades. Methylphenidate is not a medication indicated for headaches.

In Joan's case, a trial of immediate-release methylphenidate gradually titrated to 15 mg bid, prescribed for treatment of chronic fatigue and hypersomnolence, resulted in the serendipitous dose-response reduction in the frequency, severity, and duration of her chronic headaches. The effectiveness if the methylphenidate was established as Joan accidentally stopped taking it due to confusing it with a second new medication that also began with "me-." The headache severity, duration, and frequency returned to nonmethylphenidate levels with the cessation of the medication and receded with the restart and titration to the precessation dosages. Eventual titration to 15 mg bid minimized headache symptoms. Joan did not experience methylphenidate adverse side effects, nor did she seem to abuse it or need to increase the dose for continued benefit over time.

SYSTEMS-BASED PRACTICE ISSUES

Psychotherapy may have played a more significant role in Joan's treatment but the Veteran's Affairs (VA) satellite clinic was more than 100 miles from the closest Veterans Affairs Medical Center (VAMC), where other services could be accessed. Initially, it was not possible for her to travel back and forth given her severe and almost daily migraine headaches and depression. Fortunately she was able to receive basic psychiatric services through telepsychiatry. This case was also complicated because the telepsychiatry clinic was small and significantly overcrowded with insufficient staff and office space for the client load. There was only one telepsychiatrist who provided less than two days each week to serve more than 1,000 veterans with mental illness. The number and frequency of visits was necessarily limited. There were plans for the VA satellite clinic to be replaced with a much larger clinic with two psychiatrists on staff five days a week, with several social workers and with at least one doctorate psychologist who provided psychological testing and psychotherapy. There have been several studies where psychotherapy was provided through interactive television both to individuals and groups. There are some websites that teach some of the coping strategies taught in psychotherapy sessions (e.g., https://moodgym.anu.edu.au/welcome).

LEGAL, ETHICAL, AND CULTURAL CHALLENGES

Gender is an important variable in depression. Major depressive disorder affects nearly 15 million Americans a year. Age is a risk factor as 49–54-year-olds have the highest rates of depression. Other major risk factors for depression include being female, being African American, and living in poverty. Regardless of nationality, race, ethnicity, or socioeconomic level, women are estimated to have twice the depression rate of men. Although men are more likely than women to die by suicide, women are twice as likely to attempt suicide.

Hormones may play a role in differences in rates of depression. Until puberty, boys and girls have similar rates of depression. Following puberty, girls have twice the risk for depression. Moreover, at menstruation, women may experience mood changes around the time of menstruation, and a small percentage of women suffer from a condition called premenstrual dysphoric disorder which can complicate preexisting mood disorders.

Epidemiologic and anthropological studies suggest that women are more prone to suffering based on social circumstances that contribute to depression, hopelessness, exhaustion, anger, and fear. These emotional states can be related to hunger, overwork, domestic and civil violence, entrapment, and economic dependence: "understanding the sources of ill health for women means understanding how cultural and economic forces interact to undermine their social status" (World Health Organization 2013). The World Health Organization (WHO) assists public health policy by developing the profile of problems in the domain of mental health that challenge policy makers committed to mainstreaming a gender perspective in health policy and state ideologies.

The WHO is notable for its concerns about the legal ethical and cultural issues of women. It notes that world and public health policy decision makers often consider the health of women to be related to their role of caregivers for children and family, with a focus on reproductive health and children's health and family planning (e.g., contraceptive distribution to reduce fertility). In the past decade, women have begun to exercise greater influence over health policy formation. They favor women's health policies that go beyond reproductive and maternal issues to also include mental and physical health across the life cycle. The WHO made be viewed as agreeing with feminist theorists about women's health policies, advocating that health care policy should not only address biological and reproduction but also by the effects of workload, nutrition, stress, war, migration, and women trafficking issues. Health care policy for both men and women should address both physical and mental health well-being across the life cycle. Consequently, as women disproportionately suffer from mental health disorders and are more frequently subject to social causes that lead to mental illness and psychosocial distress, women's mental health requires more attention and services worldwide.

TERMS

Major Depression in DSM-5 requires at least 5 of the following symptoms:

- D: dysphoria (sadness)
- E: energy (loss of)
- P: pleasure (loss of)
- R: retardation (psychomotor slowing or agitation)
- E: eating (changes in weight or appetite)
- S: suicide (recurring thoughts of death)
- S: sleep (any change)
- I: indecisive (poor concentration)
- N: negative thinking
- G: any guilty or hopeless feelings

Depression is defined as depressed mood that is reactive to external events and is characterized by hyperphagia, hypersomnia, hypersensitivity to criticism, and leaden paralysis (a heavy feeling in the arms and legs).

Atypical depression is more likely to have an earlier onset and chronic course with partial remission. It is more than twice as common in females.

Personality disorder: an enduring pattern of inner experience and behavior that deviates markedly from the expectations of the individual's culture, is pervasive and inflexible, has an onset in adolescence or early adulthood, is stable over time, and leads to distress or impairment. Historically in the DSM, both autism spectrum disorders and personality disorders were coded on Axis II to emphasize their more pervasive and enduring patterns.

Avoidant personality disorder: Because of extreme fear of being judged negatively there is social discomfort and withdrawal.

Dependent personality disorder: Because of a need to rely on others, the person passively relinquishes responsibility for major areas of their life.

Manic episode: a distinct period of abnormally and persistently elevated, expansive, or irritable mood with increased goal-directed activity or energy on a daily basis for at least one week according to the DSM. If the manic symptoms last for at least four consecutive days but not for one week, they qualify as a hypomanic episode. At least one lifetime manic episode is required for the diagnosis of bipolar I disorder. A diagnosis of bipolar II disorder requires at least one hypomanic episode and at least one major depressive episode.

Migraine headaches: common migraine headaches usually include a unilateral head pain with nausea, vomiting, and photophobia. Scotoma, paresthesias, and speech difficulties may be observed. Frequency is irregular. The pain may initiate at any point in the brain and precede with a pain crescendo from dull to boring, pressing, throbbing, or hammering in sensation. Approximately 25% of migraine sufferers have the classic presentation, which has a visual aura that precedes the headaches. Persons notice a small area of disrupted vision that has an irregular, scintillating, or colored outline.

Persistent depressive disorder (dysthymia): a chronic a pattern of down or low mood, outnumbering symptom free days for at least two years. Symptoms resemble those for major depression such as loss of appetite or hyperphagia; insomnia or hypersomnia; low energy; reduced concentration; and feelings of hopelessness, but do not include persistent or delusional guilt, nor persistent thoughts of death or suicide. Generally speaking the symptoms are less severe than those of major depression but are very chronic in nature.

Tension headaches: this is the most frequent headache type in the United States occurring in 30–80% of the adult population. They are usually triggered by environmental or internal stress. The causes for tension headaches are varied and not inherited. In some case, the tension headache results from tightened muscles in the posterior neck and scalp. They have episodic frequency, presenting once or twice a month. Approximately 3% of tension headaches sufferers have chronic daily tension headaches. Women have tension-type headaches twice as frequently as men do.

REFERENCE AND RESOURCES

Angst J, Dobler-Mikola A. Do the diagnostic criteria determine the sex ratio in depression? *J Affect Disord* 1984;7:189–98.

Angst J, Gamma A, Benazzi F, Ajdacic V, Rössler W. Melancholia and atypical depression in the Zurich study: epidemiology, clinical characteristics, course, comorbidity and personality. *Acta Psychiatr Scand Suppl* 2007;433:72–84.

Angst J, Gamma A, Benazzi F, Silverstein B, Ajdacic-Gross V, Eich D, Rössler W. Atypical depressive syndromes in varying definitions. *Eur Arch Psych Clin Neurosci* 2005; 256:44–54.

Detweiler MB, Halling M, Detweiler JG. Methylphenidate for chronic migraine and cluster-type headaches: A case report. *J Pharm Technol* 2011;27:84–86.

Dodick DW, Gargus JJ. Why migraines strike. *Sci Am* 2008;299:56–63.

Egede LE. Major depression in individuals with chronic medical disorders: prevalence, correlates and association with health resource utilization, lost productivity and functional disability. *Gen Hosp Psych* 2007;29:409–16.

Fröhlich C, Jacobi F, Wittchen HU. DSM-IV pain disorder in the general population. An exploration of the structure and threshold of medically unexplained pain symptoms. *Eur Arch Psych Clin Neurosci* 2006;256:187–96.

Gaynes BN, Rush AJ, Trivedi MH, Wisniewske, Spencer D, Fava M. The STAR*D study: treating depression in the real world. *Cleveland Clin J Med* 2006;75(1):57–65.

Grabe HJ, Meyer C, Hapke U, Rumpf HJ, Freyberger HJ, Dilling H, John U. Somatoform pain disorder in the general population. *Psychother Psychosom* 2003;72:88–94.

Kempton MJ, Salvador Z, Munafò MR, Geddes JR, Simmons A, Frangou S, Williams SC. Structural neuroimaging studies in major depressive disorder. Meta-analysis and comparison with bipolar disorder. *Arch Gen Psych* 2011;68:675–90.

Kessing LV. Epidemiology of subtypes of depression. *Acta Psychiatr Scand* Suppl 2007; 433:85–89.

Mota-Pereira J, Silverio J, Carvalho S, Ribeiro JC, Fonte D, Ramos J. Moderate exercise improves depression parameters in treatment-resistant patients with major depressive disorder. *J Psychiatr Res* 2011 Aug;45(8):1005–11.

Ortiz A, Cervantes P, Zlotnik G, van de Velde C, Slaney C, Garnham J, Turecki G, O'Donovan C, Alda M. Cross-prevalence of migraine and bipolar disorder. *Bipolar Disord* 2010 Jun;12(4):397–403. doi: 10.1111/j.1399-5618.2010.00832.x.

PubMed Health, http://www.ncbi.nlm.nih.gov/pubmedhealth/PMH0001941.

American Psychiatric Association Practice Guidelines, http://psychiatryonline.org/guidelines.aspx.

World Health Organization, http://www.who.int/topics/womens_health/en/.

OC87: The Obsessive Compulsive, Major Depression, Bipolar, Asperger's Movie (2010): Protagonist has onset of mental illness following college. After 30 years of treatment, despite ongoing symptoms, he initiates a movie about his life in which he is the subject and one of the directors. The movie about mental health recovery contrasts the protagonist's past (major depression and bipolar disorder) with his current diagnoses (Asperger's syndrome, obsessive compulsive disorder). In addition to his documentation of his life vicissitudes and struggles, he travels across the United States as he finds and interviews a psychiatrist, an actor, and a radio news anchor who relate their personal histories of mental illness and recovery. The protagonist struggles to reveal himself in the cinematic undertaking; however, he believes that the process will transform him, as well as the future viewers. The movie is described as "a testament to acceptance, change, and hope."

Other movies about depression: *Girl Interrupted, Manic, They Shoot Horses Don't They?, Ordinary People, 28 Days.*

CHAPTER **13**

Medical Illness and Depression

Guyton Register, M.D.

CLINICAL PRESENTATION

Chief complaint: "I have lost all my drive."

History of present illness: Robert is a 58-year-old male with no prior psychiatric history who presents in the company of his wife on referral from his primary care physician because of persistent lack of motivation. Three weeks ago he suffered an ischemic cerebral vascular accident (a stroke) affecting the anterior cerebral artery. MRI showed multiple ischemic lesions in the distribution of the left anterior cerebral artery with the largest defect in the left dorsolateral prefrontal cortex. Initially, the stroke caused paralysis of his right arm and leg. He was hospitalized for four days before being transferred to a skilled nursing facility. Some movement returned to both right extremities and the neurologist recommended physical rehabilitation to further minimize the sequelae of the CVA. Robert repeatedly refused to participate in rehabilitation and was discharged home from this facility because he was getting no benefit from his stay. He is now at home, confined to a wheelchair.

Robert's neurologist has explained to him that his prognosis for recovery based on the structural damage he sustained from the stroke and his premorbid functional state is quite good with rehabilitation. However, Robert has been refusing to participate in physical therapy. He notes that "I just don't feel like it. . . . I have lost all my drive." Similarly, he has been resistant to the idea of taking antidepressant medications, stating, "I can get through this on my own." He stated that "I should feel down. I had a stroke." Twenty years ago his father died suddenly from myocardial infarction at age 56 and Robert noted that "I was down then also, but I pulled through it."

Robert agrees that it would be best for him to work with physical therapy, but he cannot seem to find the motivation. All he wants to do is sleep. His wife and children have been commenting that he has been very irritable since the stroke. He states that he has no interest in anything. He had been an avid football fan, but has not watched a game in the three weeks since the stroke, despite the fact that his favorite team advanced to the playoffs. When asked about depression, Robert says "I am not sad, just tired." When asked about tearfulness, he says that he has cried several times since the stroke, but he has not felt particularly sad even then. He denied feelings of hopelessness, worthlessness, or guilt. He does feel a little helpless "being stuck in this chair."

Robert has been eating well, actually putting on about six pounds in the past three weeks. He has had residual right-sided weakness in his lower extremity and he feels "like it takes everything I have just to move." He feels fatigued and "in a fog." His concentration has been poor at best. He used to enjoy doing the newspaper crossword puzzle every Sunday morning. Last week, he threw the paper away after sitting at the kitchen table for four hours, having failed to get even a quarter of the way through the puzzle.

In regard to his stroke, Robert voices a feeling of personal responsibility. He notes that his doctor had told him he had a heart problem that put him at risk for a stroke, but he hated "having to take medicine." He had been erratic at best about taking the blood thinner he was prescribed. He plaintively states that he was "being fed rat poison." (Warfarin, used to prevent clotting in people who have had a stroke, is the active ingredient in some types of rat poison). Karen, his wife, notes that she did her best to keep up with his medications, but sometimes he just left them on the kitchen counter. He nods his head at this.

Robert has been the larger contributor to the family's income, having worked as an investment broker for a large financial firm. He notes some concerns over not being able to maintain his fiduciary obligations with the disability income he was drawing. His wife, who is 11 years younger than he is, works as a middle school teacher. She volunteers that their financial situation is stable and Robert has always been overly worried about finances. There has been some friction between them over his inability/unwillingness to engage in physical therapy, at home a couple of days a week. Robert notes that he is going to get better; he just needs time.

When asked specifically about his mood, Robert notes that he is neither happy nor sad. He feels "dull." He agrees that he has been more irritable since the stroke. He feels that his temper gets the better of him, and he gets disproportionately angry. He notes particularly that he will yell or slam things around the house. He has not broken anything or said anything overtly hurtful in his opinion. When asked to quantify his mood on a 10-point scale with 10 being the most happy and 1 being the most sad, he said it has been between 1 and 4 since the stroke.

Robert notes that he has been depressed before. After his father's death, he went through a period of depression that lasted three months. It was characterized by profound sadness. During that time he ruminated on things he had wanted to tell his father. He noted that he had felt a lot of guilt about ignoring his father, sometimes going a month or more without talking to him and not returning phone calls. He feels that he is "on the other end now" with his eldest son who left for college six months ago and has been distant in Robert's opinion.

Robert denies having ever experienced any auditory or visual hallucinations. He described feeling that overall he is "safe." He voices an understanding that his health care providers and family "want the best for me, but I just cannot do the things they are asking me to do." He had been highly functional prior to the stroke, working as an investment broker. He denied having any beliefs that others might find strange or bizarre. He never experienced any periods of persistently elevated or irritable mood.

Psychiatric history: Robert describes his psychological health as being "excellent." He has never received prior mental health treatment. He has never been on psychotropic medication. He revealed that his primary care doctor had offered him a trial of fluoxetine after his father's death, but Robert had refused. He describes himself as depressed for the three months following the death. He relates that he missed a week of work, the longest period of unscheduled absence he had ever had in his working life up until his stroke. He emphatically states that he only missed two days of work when he had been hospitalized with diverticulitis.

When questioned about affective symptoms in the three months following his father's death, Robert seems to be somewhat dismissive. His wife provides some encouragement for him to relate "how bad things really are." After this, he states that he had an increased need for sleep. He had found that his usual seven hours left him feeling "drawn and exhausted." He discovered he could "only really function with 10 hours of sleep, minimum." He describes his appetite as being "fine" during this period. He states that most of his problems revolved around "not being able to think clearly."

Specifically, Robert endorses feeling like he was in a "fog" then. His concentration was "gone." He feels that all he did was think about his father's death. If he tried to focus on anything else, intrusive and painful thoughts of loss and grief returned. He had no energy. He was not able to attend to his normally scheduled workout regimen. He felt that everything was pointless and stopped keeping up with the news and sports scores. Robert states that this was "the saddest point in my life." When asked about how that compares with his feelings now, he agrees that the affective components are all present in his life currently, but he adamantly denies persistent sadness. He volunteers, "I'm not sorry for myself. I am not sad."

Family psychiatric history: Robert's mother is suffering from late stage Alzheimer's type dementia. She was diagnosed five years ago when significant errors in managing her finances coupled with some spurious lending practices precipitated the loss of the family home. Robert noted that his father had been a "type A personality." Robert's father had been in the army in the Korean War, and Robert thinks he may have suffered from some form of post-traumatic stress disorder. His father drank heavily when Robert was young, but quit drinking entirely in his late thirties.

Robert describes his younger brother, age 52, as being "overly competitive." He describes one episode in which he and his brother both entered a foot race some years ago. His brother suffered a stress fracture while training for the race and still ran. Robert volunteers that "he didn't beat me." He describes his younger sister, age 50, as "the black sheep of the family." He notes she has a history of alcohol and illicit drug abuse. She left home at age 16 to marry her boyfriend, which ended in divorce after five years. Robert has a maternal first cousin who suffers from bipolar disorder and has been hospitalized once for this.

Other medical history: Robert has a history of paroxysmal atrial fibrillation on chronic warfarin therapy since age 51. He has stage II hypertension treated with hydrochlorathiazide. He is mildly obese with a body mass index of 36. He suffered a partial tear of his right rotator cuff a year ago that responded to conservative medical management. He has been hospitalized one time for diverticulitis five years ago.

Biopsychosocialspiritual history: Robert was born in Atlanta, Georgia. He was born via spontaneous vaginal delivery at 37 weeks gestation. The pregnancy was largely uneventful, without exposure to alcohol, tobacco, or drugs. He met all developmental milestones at anticipated ages. His mother has described him as a "little gentleman" during infancy.

Robert is the eldest of the three living children. He has a distant but "friendly" relationship with his brother, speaking to him every couple of weeks. He speaks to his sister maybe two or three times a year, but those conversations often last several hours. He feels that she "is really a good person . . . but she always has to learn things the hard way." His mother lost one pregnancy when Robert was five.

Robert was raised by both his biological parents. He identifies his mother as being the stronger parental influence. His father "worked and drank through my childhood." His father worked as a postal inspector. Robert's first memory from childhood is his father "yelling at me for something." He notes his father was much sterner with him than his siblings, but he would not classify this as emotional abuse. He denies any physical abuse, but he described substantial corporal discipline up until age 13. He denied any sexual abuse.

Robert says that he was a quiet, shy child. He was slow to speak to persons he was unfamiliar with. However, he had several close friends throughout childhood. He has maintained contact with a couple of them. He notes that he did well in school. He enjoyed all of his classes, excelling in mathematics from an early age. In middle school he began playing sports. By high school he had developed into a solid runner on the track team, enjoying football very much but usually held a back-up role in the teams he played for. He finished high school in the top 10% of his class, attending a major state university, where he lettered in track. After college, Robert attended business school where he graduated in the middle of his class.

He took a job as a loan officer at a bank. After five years, he was hired by a large financial firm as an investment broker. He has worked in that capacity for the past 28 years. He has been on leave from work since his stroke and is currently drawing 60% of his income from disability insurance. Although all of the household expenses are being met, he feels under financial hardship.

Robert has been married for 20 years. They have two sons, aged 19 and 17. His eldest son is attending Robert's alma mater, which is a 10-hour drive from where the family lives. Robert has not seen him since the stroke. He has talked on the phone with him three times in the past three weeks. His youngest son lives with

Robert and his wife. Robert notes that his youngest son has been very helpful around the house since the stroke. He states that he is very close to his youngest son, but things have become distant with his eldest since he left for college. He notes that "is just part of it, I guess."

Robert relates that he feels he has a strong social support system. He identifies his wife as being his "number one." He states that his brother is "a real pain, but he has always been there for me when the chips are down." He notes his youngest son has "been a godsend around the house." He says that he has one close friend from high school whom he speaks with three to four times a week on the phone. This friend lives five hours away. He also identifies his supervisor at work and his colleagues as being very supportive.

Robert notes that he "will not put this on my mom." His mother is alive, but in poor health, suffering from Alzheimer's type dementia. This has led to her being placed in a nursing home. He voices some reservations about "having to put her there, but I am glad we did it now that I am an invalid." As mentioned, his father died suddenly from myocardial infarction when Robert was 38. His father is buried in a secular cemetery local to Robert's home.

Robert notes that he is "not really spiritual or religious . . . but I believe in God." He was raised as a Southern Baptist. He is not a member of a congregation, and he has not attended services in the 20 years since his father's death. Prior to that, he had attended services usually around holidays five or six times a year. He does not feel that his faith has "anything to do with how I am coping." He denied having any spiritual beliefs that he could anticipate conflicting with medical treatment.

MENTAL STATUS EXAM

Robert is a 58-year-old Caucasian male who appears his stated age. He is mildly obese, with close cropped black hair and some graying beard stubble. He is somewhat disheveled in gray dress trousers, a blue long-sleeve dress shirt, and scuffed black oxfords. The shirt is open at the collar with two buttons loose, revealing a white undershirt. He is wearing a two-toned wrist watch and yellow gold wedding band. He sits in a wheelchair, and he was pushed in by his wife. He has a somewhat closed posture, arms folded in his lap. He does not use any gestures while speaking. He displays moderate psychomotor slowing. His demeanor is ostensibly cooperative, but dismissive. His eye contact is generally poor; he glances frequently out the window. His speech is slow in rate, decreased in volume overall, with regular rhythm. He has some very mild slurred dysarthria.

Robert is alert and oriented to person, place, time, and situation. He displays a working memory that is somewhat incongruent with his level of education. He could not recall the name of his neurologist. His remote memory is excellent. He is able to converse in detail about the last novel he read before his stroke. He describes the main characters, the plot, and how this novel compares to other works of fiction he has read. He maintains a pendulous conversational flow, concentrating on questions appropriately. He frequently looks out the window during the interview, indicating some mild deficit in attention.

His affect is blunted and congruent with a depressed mood. His current mood is 4 of 10. He refuses to use the words *depressed* or *sad* to characterize his mood, describing it as "dull and down." He adamantly denies any current, recent, or remote suicidal or homicidal ideations, intents, or plans.

Robert's thought content is without suicidal or homicidal ideations. There are no perceptual disturbances, paranoia, or delusions. He does have some persistent focus on his illness and loss. His thought process is linear and logically congruent, but flavored with consistent negativism. He has a good vocabulary, but displays some difficulty in word finding twice during the interview. He speaks in a tight, grammatically scrupulous fashion. He displays no paucity of ideas or thoughts. His use and interpretation of allegory during the conversation displays good abstraction. He has excellent calculating ability. His fund of knowledge is good. He displays no gross deficits in insight or judgment. He feels that he simply does not have the ability to participate in rehabilitation.

Robert denies ever having experienced any hallucinations. He is not prone to illusions. He denies any episodes of derealization or depersonalization. He has an excellent biographical memory.

IMPAIRMENT IN FUNCTIONING

Robert is suffering from significant impairment of functioning. His depression has become the chief obstacle in his recovery and rehabilitation from stroke. He understands that he needs to participate in physical therapy, but he is unable to find the motivation to follow-through on this. Given his high functional history and account of overcoming significant mood symptoms in the past after the death of his father, this inability is of concern to the provider. The critical period for rehabilitation that follows stroke provides a window of opportunity. Robert's depression has precipitated a change that poses significant risk of functional impairment going forward. It shows an erosion of his resilience and will to recover, which is the foundation of his effective rehabilitation.

DSM DIAGNOSIS

After the foregoing information is gathered, the mental health provider believes that Robert is suffering from depression secondary to his cerebral vascular accident. Overall, Robert impresses the interviewer as very depressed and with poor insight into his illness. His presentation with irritability and lack of motivation is not uncommon in depression. The interviewer's initial consideration of a primary major depressive disorder is less likely given Robert's pathognomonic left frontal lobe ischemia and the causal relationship that has been established with depressed mood.

In this case the predominant theme is "mood disorder." In the *Diagnostic and Statistical Manual* (DSM) the primary diagnosis is Depression Secondary to General Medical Condition.

It is important to distinguish the normal, transient feelings of discouragement which follow any acute illness or injury from depression due to a medical condition. The neurochemical changes triggered under the latter circumstances persist long beyond the actual effect of the injury and, in the long run, can be just as devastating.

EPIDEMIOLOGY

Depression affects roughly one-third of all stroke victims. Over half of all persons with a stroke affecting the left frontal lobe have been found to meet criteria for depression. Studies in the *Archives of Physical Medicine and Rehabilitation* indicate that male survivors of stroke are more likely to become depressed than are females. In addition, depressive symptoms are associated with less efficient use of rehabilitation services. It might be assumed that the deficit in cognition associated with depression would be responsible for this. However, the review of literature in this area indicates that this effect has a minimal role on rehabilitation. This may indicate that it is the motivational or sapping characteristics of depression that is most contributory to depressed patient's poor utilization of rehabilitation services. Similarly, a history of depression is associated with longer length of stay in rehabilitation facilities.

DIFFERENTIAL DIAGNOSIS

Robert's case exemplifies how physical and mental illness often overlap. Medical knowledge is advancing largely due to the increasingly detailed view technology provides into the engagement of anatomic and physiologic processes within the psychosocial environment. This has led to an understanding of illness on a spectrum rather a dichotomy of well and unwell. Additionally, it has increasingly blurred the lines between disorders of the body and mind.

Recently there has been a shift in paradigm of diagnosis away from the categorical and toward the dimensional. This broadening of diagnostic criteria is beneficial. It moves medicine toward inclusionary practice. Persons with significant functional impairment lacking the requisite check list of categorical symptomatology are no longer orphans of medicine. There is a paradox, however, in that such nuance makes the diagnostic process increasingly unapproachable. This is especially the case for novice clinicians. One of the strengths of categorical diagnosis is that it allows the clinician to build a schema of diagnosis that is fundamental to the practice of medicine. At the root of effective medicine is effective nosology.

Thus, the differential diagnosis is the key to beginning effective treatment leading to the most favorable outcome. The differential diagnosis in Robert's case begins and ends with his depression. Although he denies feeling sad, this is not uncommon in depressed men. It is his profound loss of interest and motivation that is the cardinal feature of his depression. Furthermore, he is suffering from hypersomnia, fatigue, psychomotor retardation, and diminished concentration. Together, these symptoms meet the criteria of a major depressive disorder under the DSM. However, it is incumbent on the mental health provider to explore other disorders that may be a more appropriate fit. It is important to note that the mood symptoms cannot be the result of a delirium. Although depression is an uncommon sequela of delirium, mania and anxiety are often notable affective clues.

Considerations in the differential diagnosis of the depressed person include depression due to physical illness, medication side effects, and substance abuse or dependence. The most common causes of medical depression include neurologic, endocrine, and cardiovascular conditions. Depression rates in Parkinson's disease, Huntington's disease, multiple sclerosis, and epilepsy approach 60%. It is also important to note that the diagnostic criteria for mood disorder secondary to general medical condition is less stringent than those for psychiatric mood or anxiety disorder.

Robert's case presents itself rather clearly under the categorical diagnostic model. His depressive symptoms are clearly better explained by the stroke than the possibility underlying psychopathology. There is a strong temporal relationship between the physical insult and onset of psychological symptoms. The medical literature is replete with cases similar to his outlining the effects of a lesion in the left frontal lobe on mood. Under the categorical model the provider would be well founded in the prescription of a serotonergic antidepressant and referral to follow-up some months hence. Perhaps what this case demonstrates most importantly is how necessary categorical diagnosis is, yet how insufficient it can be.

A dimensional approach enables the mental health provider to see how Robert is at a precipice with his disorder. The functional window for physical rehabilitation after a stroke is limited. During the period of remodeling that follows a neurologic insult, it is imperative that the stroke victim be able to participate fully in recovery. Robert's depression is clearly limiting his functional ability at this time. Untreated, his depression will lead to a poor rehabilitative outcome. In contrast, with effective treatment of his depression, his prognosis is quite good.

ETIOLOGY AND PATHOGENESIS

Post-stroke depression (PSD) has been identified as having a significant negative effect on stroke recovery. There are two major hypotheses regarding the etiological mechanism, although neither has been well established experimentally. The first is the biological hypothesis. The biological hypothesis of PSD includes four separate mechanisms: lesion location, neurotransmitters, cytokine-mediated inflammatory response, and genetic polymorphism.

Robert's case typifies the lesion location mechanism. Lesions of the basal ganglia and left frontal lobe are most associated with depression. Where Robert's case is somewhat atypical is the predominant apathetic flavor of his depression. Apathetic depression is more associated with lesions of the basal ganglion, particularly when bilateral. Left frontal lobe depression more commonly presents with affective depression—profound sadness. Robert adamantly denied sadness more than once, endorsing his symptoms as being motivational in nature.

The neurotransmitter mechanism is characterized by decreased serotonin and norepinephrine in the brain. High cytokine levels—particularly interleukin 1beta, IL-18, and tumor necrosis factor alpha—have been correlated with PSD. Also, recent genetic explorations show that there is a significant association between the serotonin transporter gene-linked promoter region and PSD This is specifically a short variant genotype polymorphism.

The second major hypothesis regarding the etiologic mechanism of PSD is psychological. This hypothesis suggests that stressors—both psychological and social—are the primary causes of depression. Thus, persons with the "perfect storm" of biological causes can present with no affective complaints whatsoever. Meanwhile, persons with relatively innocuous lesion mapping, adequate neurotransmitters, physiologic cytokine levels, and nonvariant transporter genotype can present with profound and debilitating depression. As is often the case in illness, PSD appears to be a complex biopsychosocialspiritual condition with multiple etiologic factors.

NATURAL COURSE WITHOUT TREATMENT

Persons with medically induced depression rarely get better without treatment. This is contrasted with a more favorable prognosis combing medication and psychotherapeutic management. Indeed, Robert's case runs a high risk of significant worsening due to his denial of illness in the face of impairment. Indeed, the stoicism and strength of will that has served him so well in the past has begun to show signs of fatigue and impending fracture. He characterizes his current physical state as being intractable despite his verbalized understanding that with participation in rehabilitation his prognosis is favorable. This is a particularly dark portent.

EVIDENCE-BASED TREATMENT OPTIONS

The two identified means of treatment for depression include psychotherapy and medication management. Robert's case poses some interesting psychosocialspiritual connections. In fact, it is unlikely that he will enlist in a biological intervention without some insight-oriented counseling. Such therapy should be focused on improving his understanding of depression as a mental illness rather than a character flaw. Once this enlistment is accomplished, a biologically based intervention would be the cornerstone of evidence-based treatment.

There are few controlled trials of antidepressant therapy in PSD. The available body of evidence with tricyclic antidepressants and selective serotonin reuptake inhibitors (SSRIs) show promise. Both agents have shown roughly equivalent response in PSD. However, the side effect profile of SSRIs is much improved over that of tricyclic agents. Among SSRIs there is no experimental evidence of agent-specific superiority. Robert's warfarin therapy in particular presents significant considerations. Sertraline and citalopram have both been demonstrated to be safe with warfarin. There have been some concerns raised regarding citalopram's potential cardiac effects in high doses as it can prolong repolarization of heart muscle. Thus, it would be preferable to use sertraline given Robert's family history of sudden cardiac death.

CLINICAL COURSE WITH MANAGEMENT AND TREATMENT

The mental health provider decides to counsel Robert using supportive and cognitive techniques with an emphasis on improving insight into his depression, its connection to his neurologic lesion, and the likely outcomes. Motivational therapy with an emphasis on medication initiation and adherence is indicated. This is of significant importance in Robert's case due to the medical etiology of his depression. Should he maintain his resistance to the suggestion of medication management in combination with therapy, the clinician makes the decision to forgo confrontation at this early stage in an effort to further build rapport.

Management of Robert's already injured ego during this initial session is a focus of the provider's attention. Care is taken to avoid narcissistic injuries to Robert, as it is clear from his presentation that his enlistment in treatment at this time is marginal. The clinician focuses on symptomatic goals that Robert will be more likely to resonate with. Emphasis is placed on expected improvements on his vigor, memory, and concentration with medication. The provider is also careful to set reasonable expectations, especially regarding the time frame of medication response. Also, psychoeducational goals are provided that contrast with the rather unfortunate natural history of medically induced depression versus the anticipated course of Robert's depression with treatment.

With treatment, mood disorders share an encouraging prognosis. In major depression, 60–70% of patients tolerating antidepressant medications respond to the first choice treatment. Studies of PSD have shown similarly favorably treatment figures. Unfortunately, between 5% and 10% of these patients have depression refractory to a series of interventions. There have been no convincing studies correlating areas of lesion in the frontal lobe or basal ganglia to those patients with treatment-refractory PSD. Theoretical consideration would argue that lesions in those areas most associated with depression are most refractory to treatment.

In Robert's case, the stroke has left him feeling relatively helpless. In some ways his refusal to participate in rehabilitative therapy and to take medication is a misguided assertion of his own willpower. The clinician recognizes this and involves Robert in the decision making. He presents three possible medications to Robert for his choice. He challenges him to use the skills he has learned as an investment broker to compare the three medications as though he were comparing three companies in which to invest. Sources of information on the Internet were suggested. Three days after this assignment, Robert called the clinician and announced that he had chosen one of the three medications and explained his reasoning. The medication was started with Robert's willing participation. The clinician suggested follow-up in a reasonable period of time and allowed Robert to choose a particular appointment time and whether his wife would accompany him.

Robert's wife drove him to this follow-up appointment but he asked her to remain in the waiting room. He discussed with the clinician his fears of becoming helpless, becoming a burden to his family, and dying young. He agreed with the clinician that it was worth fighting for a good outcome in his case and rescheduled neurological rehabilitative therapy.

Six months later Robert was still on the medication for depression and had completed the course of physical therapy. Strength had entirely returned to his right arm and over 95% to his right leg. Only when he was tired did he have a barely perceptible limp.

SYSTEMS-BASED PRACTICE ISSUES

Depression secondary to medical condition illustrates the importance of a good history and physical examination. History and physical exam are the tools a competent clinician turns to for investigation. Laboratory and imaging investigations should be initiated based on confirmatory merit rather than as a means of inquiry. The spiraling cost of health care has drawn the attention of society. Clinicians are entrusted with the responsibility of the parsimonious use of limited health care resources. Perhaps more important than the financial cost of indiscriminant diagnostic testing, such practice poses a very real risk of harm to the patient. Spurious diagnostic findings can trigger uncomfortable mechanisms of investigation or risky interventions.

Another area of systems-based practice that Robert's case exemplifies is the importance of the interaction between the mental health provider and the patient's primary care provider. This person recognized that Robert's depression was not characteristic of that seen in the more common major depressive disorder. This provider understood that there was some disconnection between Robert and the care delivery system. He was effectively failing what should be a very responsive physical recovery.

It is similarly important that the mental health professional maintain clear and updated channels of communication with Robert's other care providers. The increasing specialization in medicine has led to often fragmented delivery systems in which communication between the primary care provider and specialist is tenuous. In some cases, communication between specialists treating the same patient is poor. A patient suffering from depression or other mood disorder is often unable to manage the shuffle of information between providers.

LEGAL, ETHICAL, AND CULTURAL CHALLENGES

Robert's case illustrates a rather classic medical ethics paradox. This case is representative of what many would consider a conflict of autonomy on the part of the patient and beneficence on the part of the clinician. Robert seems to not want treatment for his depression, whereas the clinician feels such treatment would benefit Robert significantly. Such conflicts are best resolved by approaching the patient without having prejudiced decisions. After a review of Robert's medical record, even an experienced provider may make the mistake of jumping to a therapeutic conclusion—prescribe sertraline and a psychotherapy referral. This would likely end in Robert not taking the medication or attending to therapy.

Robert has had trouble keeping up with his blood-thinning medication. This is despite having his clotting ratio checked at regular intervals. Also, he has been unable to participate in physical therapy even with bedside visits and encouragement on a daily basis. The clinician is hoping to have Robert adhere to an antidepressant regimen and attend psychotherapy appointments in the absence of such monitoring or daily outreach. Nonadherence rates for antidepressant medications range from 29% to 46% in the general population. It is highly unlikely that Robert's chances of adherence would achieve even that level of mediocrity. The recognition of his probable difficulty prompts the clinician to consider the barriers to treatment adherence.

A fresh set of eyes and a willingness to listen often proves to be the difference for patients like Robert. By taking the time to hear the conflicts he presents with and realizing that the foremost problem in this case has to do with control over his life, the clinician can work to achieve his enlistment. This case emphasizes how even relatively common presentations and what appear to be straightforward decisions require thoughtful effort on the clinician's part. The prescribed treatment will be of little benefit unless the patient engages in it. Some might argue that it is inconceivable to provide true beneficence without a foundation of autonomy.

REFERENCES AND RESOURCES

Johns Hopkins Medicine: Neuropsychiatry of Stroke website provides an excellent primer on the neurologic and psychiatric implications of stroke. http://www.hopkins medicine.org/gec/series/neuropsych_stroke.html.

Aben I, Verhey F, et al. Validity of the Beck Depression Inventory, Hospital Anxiety and Depression Scale, SCL-90, and Hamilton Depression Rating Scale as screening instruments for depression in stroke patients. *Psychosomatics* 2002 Sept–Oct;43(5): 386–93.

Robinsin RG. *The Clinical Neuropsychiatry of Stroke* (2nd ed.). Cambridge: Cambridge University Press, 1998.

Yirmiya R, Weidenfeld W, et al. Cytokines, "depression due to a general medical condition," and antidepressant drugs. *Adv Exper Med Biol* 1999;461:283–316.

CHAPTER **14**

Bipolar Disorder

Anita Kablinger, M.D.

CLINICAL PRESENTATION

Chief complaint: "I have terrible mood swings . . . and I finally decided to do something about it."

History of present illness: Brian is a self-referred 37-year-old man with no previous psychiatric hospitalizations who presents to the outpatient clinic for evaluation and treatment of mood swings. He reports a long history of mood instability beginning in his early teens and continuing, worsening throughout his twenties and thirties. He describes significant periods of dysphoria in grade school, being irritable and easily frustrated most of the time. He recalls frequent fights with other boys "who would tick me off just by looking at me wrong." "It was difficult to make friends, though girls always liked me." In high school, Brian was often called "moody" but excelled at writing, science, and mechanical projects. Math was not his strong suit. He loved playing basketball, devoting hours to shooting practice and drills as well as flirting with the school cheerleaders. During his sophomore year, Brian had a "very tough time," "I felt blah the whole year, but especially at homecoming and during the winter basketball season." "It was awful, I couldn't get enough sleep and I was drained every day; my mom took me to the doctor because she thought I had mono."

Brian completed high school and entered a general studies program at a college in the Northeast. He describes his first year of college as "awesome," meeting a lot of new people, dating "three pretty girls at the same time," and going to a lot of parties. He was considered the "life of the party" and states he was "incredibly funny and could tell stories for hours and wrap others around my little finger." At the same time, his grades plummeted, and he lived on "chicken legs and ramen noodles" and four hours of sleep a night until the winter. In the spring of that first year, Brian found out that one of his girlfriends became pregnant and he decided to marry her "so she would not be the focus of gossip" and "for my religious parents." Once married, he quit school and began work as a salesman for a drink distribution company while his wife stayed home with their child.

Over the past 15 years, Brian and his wife had another child, and they both currently work outside the home. He has had two other jobs since college and describes himself "as a jack-of-all-trades" with abilities to fix, change, or build "anything." He describes his life as "only okay" and dreams of opening a family restaurant "to show everyone that I can make something of myself." He states that he has been more depressed and irritable over the past three months (sadness at 6/10 and anger at 8/10 most days), resulting in frequent arguments with his family and employer. He reports constant fatigue, poor focus, and lack of motivation in his daily activities. His wife berates him for frequent tearfulness, and he constantly thinks about his college days when life seemed so much better. He describes his wife as "cold" and "not interested in sex" any longer, a frustration that leads to frequent extramarital affairs.

Brian describes chronic sleep difficulties for the past three years and regularly takes two to three hours to fall asleep. Sleep duration is about four to five hours and is often restless and disturbed. He denies any nightmares or bad dreams. He uses marijuana to "calm down" twice a month, which he buys from a "friend." He states that he has "an amazing capacity" for alcohol, able to drink a case of beer and four vodka and tonics on Saturday nights without getting drunk. Despite this, he drinks only twice a month. Brian describes himself as frequently "clumsy" and has minor accidents on a regular basis—hitting his thumb with a hammer, cutting his hand while doing repairs, and dropping heavy objects, resulting in a broken toe. Opiate use in the past for dental work or other injuries "made me feel calmer and happy."

Brian denies any increased focus on body image (then showed the interviewer his biceps) and, though he eats minimally and rarely is truly hungry, does not binge or purge on food. He denies any panic attacks or superstitions and has never heard voices or had visions that others could not experience. Although math was never a strong subject, he denies the past diagnosis of a learning disability. His mother was worried about Brian's problems in grade school and a pediatrician once suggested that he may have attention deficit disorder, but medications or behavioral interventions were never initiated.

Stressors include the loss of his abusive father, marital conflict, financial difficulties, and a sense of personal inadequacy.

Psychiatric history: Brian has never been hospitalized for psychiatric illness and has never attempted suicide. However, he reports frequent thoughts of death in the past two months, especially when very depressed. He has multiple guns at home; shooting is a hobby. He denies the possibility of self-harm or suicide because it "would devastate my mother and children." He has never seen a psychiatrist prior to this evaluation but his primary care doctor has prescribed three different selective serotonin reuptake inhibitors (SSRIs) in the past five years to help with mood. Brian reports that the medications made little difference in his symptoms despite regular use for three or four months each.

Brian has never been involved in psychotherapy but did see his high school counselor on a number of occasions during his sophomore year, which he describes as "helpful—she really listened to me and what I was going through."

Family history: Brian's mother has been diagnosed with bipolar disorder and is currently in outpatient treatment. He describes her as "moody like me and very needy; I spend a lot of time helping her with her home and running errands for her." She is apparently stabilized on lithium and lamotrigine and follows up with her own psychiatrist. She also suffers from rheumatoid arthritis and requires daily medications for pain. Brian's father died of pancreatic cancer five years prior to this evaluation and was described as "a mean old man, abusing me and my brother every day of our lives."

Brian has one older brother who lives in New York with his wife and three children. He is extremely successful and wealthy—"I could never be as good as Michael."

Brian's maternal and paternal grandparents are deceased, but he recalls his maternal grandmother being very kind and warm—"one of the only people who treated me very well." A maternal cousin lives in the Southwest and has been in and out of the hospital "because she doesn't take her medications and ends up preaching on the street corner."

A paternal cousin has generalized tonic-clonic seizures and Brian's nine-year-old son takes methylphenidate for hyperactivity.

Medical history: Brian was born by C-section due to breech presentation and was a fairly healthy child. He obtained all vaccinations on time. He broke his arm when he hit a tree while skiing for the first time at age nine.

In his junior year of high school, he received a concussion after a collision on the basketball court, hitting his head on the gym floor. He did not lose consciousness, but the team trainer required him to miss two games due to the "seriousness of the hit."

There is no history of high blood pressure, diabetes, heart conditions, or hyperlipidemia. He does not smoke but occasionally chews tobacco.

Other history (developmental, educational/occupational, family/social, legal): Brian is the youngest of two boys. His mother had no complications during her pregnancy with him and did not smoke, drink alcohol, or use illicit substances during her pregnancy. Other than the C-section for breech presentation, the postnatal course was without problems and Brian went home with his parents appropriately after delivery. He is three years younger than his older brother, Michael. He met all his milestones on time.

Brian and his brother were physically abused by their father, who was an alcoholic. Brian reports that his father was very derogatory toward him and frequently beat him when he did not respond to demands quickly enough. He recalls one incident where his father would make him kneel on stones for 30 minutes because he did not take out the garbage. He remembers another time when he broke one of the house windows while playing ball and his father became very angry and spanked him with a wooden spoon in front of the rest of the family, made him take every penny out of his piggy bank to go buy a new window, and then threw away his favorite toy truck as a punishment. He does not recall his brother or mother ever stepping in "to save" him or provide protection.

Brian lives with his wife and two children, ages 16 and 9. His wife is a part-time waitress and is the primary caregiver for the children. His mother is 60 years old and lives in her own home three miles from Brian and his family. Brian's father stopped drinking two years prior to his death from pancreatic cancer. Brian reports that he has forgiven his father for the abuse, but they never had a conversation where his father admitted or apologized for his behavior.

Brian has a strong relationship with his mother and relies on her for emotional and financial support at times, especially for his children's school and extracurricular activities, which can be very costly. He has a very distant relationship with his older brother and feels that Michael has "made it big" and is very wealthy. Brian has a hard time understanding how Michael is able to "forget" the abuse he received as a child and envies his life and family.

Brian states that his marital relationship is "fine" but that there is no "connection or closeness" with his wife. She refuses to have sex with Brian because of a past affair that she discovered. His wife frequently puts him down and makes him feel as if he is worthless. Brian continues to try to "prove" to others (and his wife) that he is as good as anyone else. He describes his relationship with his children as "excellent" and focuses on giving them "the affection and love I never got." He is discouraged that his wife "does not believe in his mental problems," and she gets more cynical when he takes medications for any reason.

Brian describes his daily activities as consisting of "mainly working whether it's at home or at my job," with little time for his family or hobbies. He has many friends but does not interact with them much due to work restrictions. He is devoted to his car and maintaining the lawn around his home as well as building a gun collection and target shooting in his spare time.

Brian has never had any legal problems.

He is Christian but attends church only on special occasions. He does not consider spirituality or his relationship with God to be an important part of his life.

Resiliency factors: married with children, close relationship with mother, motivated to seek and maintain treatment.

Mental status examination: Brian is a well-developed, well-nourished white male, well groomed/cleanly shaven young man, wearing jeans, tie, and a baseball cap. He has a normal gait but demonstrates mild agitation—right leg shaking while seated and frequent readjustment of his cap and tie. He is cooperative and pleasant toward the examiner with intense eye contact and occasional tearfulness when discussing difficult times in his life. Speech is articulate and regular in rate and rhythm. He is alert and oriented to person, place, situation, and time. Both short-term and remote memory appear to be intact. Occasionally assessment questions had to be repeated due to poor attention. Mood is "down" with congruent and stable affect.

Brian's language is appropriate for his age and education and clear without any evidence of thought disorder. Thoughts are not sparse in production. He does not illustrate any persecutory, religious, or grandiose delusions. Abstraction was intact. Fund of knowledge is appropriate for education and age and he was able to perform simple calculations. He has adequate insight into his difficulties with fair judgment regarding daily situations. There is no evidence of perceptual disturbances including hallucinations, illusions, or depersonalization.

IMPAIRMENT IN FUNCTIONING

Brian's illness and past behaviors (including impulsivity and promiscuity) have had a significant effect on his life and continue to interfere in his goals. He had problems in elementary and high school and left college after one year likely attributed to mood instability and poor decision making (manic episode). He married young after his girlfriend became pregnant and the marriage is not stable, providing ongoing stress. Brian is dissatisfied with his life choices and feels inadequate, yearning for the lifestyle his older brother has achieved. The childhood physical and verbal abuse has contributed to a poor internal concept, and he has difficulty "measuring up" to those around him. Lack of effective interventions and treatment have contributed to frequent and chronic mood instability, further influencing his actions and self-esteem.

DSM DIAGNOSIS

The clinical picture includes multiple disruptions of mood (dysphoria, irritability, sadness), thought (worthlessness, inadequacy, focus on death), and behavior (poor sleep, frequent extramarital affairs, distractibility, impulsivity, childhood fights). For these reasons, a primary mood disorder was determined to be the main difficulty. It is imperative to recognize that Brian brings a will and motivation for getting well after years of mood dysregulation, "losses," and negativity and is determined that now is the best time in his life to care about himself and seek help.

The two sections for mood disorders in the DSM are bipolar disorders and major depressive disorders. In this latest version of the DSM, bipolar disorder is separated from other depressive disorders because of significant differences in genetics, family history, and symptoms. Brian appears to suffer from bipolar disorder with a previous manic episode during college (euphoria, irritability, decreased need for sleep, distractibility, an increase in goal-directed activity, and excessive involvement in pleasurable activities). In addition, the patient has experienced significant depressive symptoms at different stages in his life, including sadness, irritability, fatigue, feelings of worthlessness, poor concentration, and thoughts of death.

The DSM criteria for depression emphasize the importance of perceived distress and impaired functioning in a given syndrome as well as excluding any drug-induced or general medical condition as causation. Bipolar disorder is further delineated into type I or II based on the severity of the manic symptoms (type II involving hypomania and type I mania), and individual episodes may include depression, mania, or mixed symptomatology. Mixed bipolar disorder requires that a person experience or demonstrate both full criteria for a major depressive episode and full criteria for a manic episode during the same time period.

Finally, it is important to distinguish patterns and subtypes of bipolar disorder for optimum recognition of course and treatment planning. Those who have bipolar disorder may exhibit psychotic features, catatonia, melancholia, or atypical symptoms (these latter two during a depressive episode) as well as a seasonal pattern (with respect to the depressive episodes) or rapid cycling (four or more depressive or manic episodes within a one-year period).

Brian's working diagnostic profile includes bipolar disorder type I, most recent episode depressed, without psychotic features, as well as cannabis, nicotine, and alcohol use disorders. There is no strong evidence for a personality disorder, although the long-term effects of the bipolar disorder include some narcissistic behavior that might be diagnosed as narcissistic traits.

EPIDEMIOLOGY

Bipolar disorder type I is conservatively described as occurring in 0.8–1.6% of the population, and bipolar disorder type II is present in about 0.5%. These numbers are deemed conservative due to multiple issues, such as diagnostic uncertainty and spectrum disorder illnesses not meeting full DSM criteria. Recent epidemiological studies have indicated a lifetime prevalence of bipolar I and II disorders in 3.7–3.9% of the general population. Major depressive disorder has a much higher prevalence with 20–50% of affected individuals depending on the sampled group.

Culture and ethnicity have not demonstrated differences in the occurrence of bipolar disorders but age of onset and subtype tend to differ according to gender. Rapid cycling is more common in women. Men afflicted with bipolar disorder often develop a manic episode as the initial illness presentation as compared to women, thus often delaying a correct diagnosis and management plan. Regardless of gender, time between symptom manifestation and appropriate treatment or first hospitalization ranges from 5 to 10 years. Missed bipolar disorder diagnoses are common with a higher rate of psychotic disorders assessed in black and Hispanic individuals.

Bipolar disorder is highly heritable, and first-degree relatives with diagnosed or likely bipolar disorder are a significant aid in diagnostic assessment of individuals with mood difficulties. Age of onset is usually in the early twenties, but the diagnosis of bipolar disorder in children is common (almost 7% in a community sample). The majority of these patients do not meet criteria for specific type I or II illnesses and often are placed in the "not otherwise specified" (NOS) category. In addition, bipolar disorder NOS and attention deficit hyperactivity disorder (ADHD) have multiple similarities and co-occur very frequently in this age group.

It is rare for bipolar disorder to begin after the age of 60 and is more likely attributed to medical or neurological diseases as well as medication or substance use.

Brian has a positive family history of bipolar disorder as well as alcoholism, and he began having mood symptoms in his teens. He was given antidepressant medications by his primary care physician without benefit, likely due to a misdiagnosis of major depression.

DIFFERENTIAL DIAGNOSIS

The most common differential diagnosis in individuals with mood instability is major depressive disorder. Contrary to popular thought, depression and mania share some commonalities, including irritability or anger, physical restlessness or agitation, and sleep disturbances. "Racing thoughts" can occur in people with mania or in people with an agitated depression. This helps us understand the frequency of misdiagnosis in people who truly have bipolar disorder. In fact, bipolar disorder type II is often missed in the context of evaluations, and its documented prevalence is considered lower than the true number. Depression and mania may also be triggered by substance use including alcohol, stimulants, cocaine, opiates, sedative/hypnotics, hallucinogens, cannabis, and medications such as steroids. Other medical conditions (especially endocrine abnormalities, cancers) and neurological disorders (multiple sclerosis, HIV, strokes) can also cause secondary bipolar disorder and appropriate treatment approaches must be implemented for recovery.

Comorbid disorders are a rule rather than an exception in people who suffer from bipolar disorder. Alcohol abuse or dependence has been shown in approximately 46% of patients with bipolar disorder, compared with 13% in the general population, with substance abuse or dependence occurring in 41% of patients with this mood disorder versus 6% of the general public. Other psychiatric conditions also are found more frequently in patients with bipolar disorder, including anxiety disorders (especially panic disorder and obsessive compulsive disorder) and ADHD. Comorbidities often alter the course of bipolar disorder and often increase the complexity of treatment issues.

The risk of suicide for bipolar disorder patients (and other mood disorders) is higher than in those without mood disorders, specifically in depressed and mixed episodes and with psychotic symptoms. Approximately 10–15% of bipolar patients complete suicide during their illness.

ETIOLOGY AND PATHOGENESIS

The cause of bipolar disorder is multifactorial. Genetic transmission appears to be a strong component of etiology, given many epidemiological and twin study data. However, there is no specific mode of inheritance that has been identified.

Alterations or impairment in the hypothalamic-pituitary-adrenal axis and catecholamines have also been implicated. Environmental influences also account for episode initiation and duration, maintenance and relapse, and treatment difficulties.

Predisposing factors include positive family history of mood disorders, especially bipolar disorder, and substance use disorders; previous manic or depressive episode or juvenile-onset bipolar disorder; and childhood diagnosis of ADHD (controversial). Precipitating factors include stressful life events, especially in childhood; changes in sleep-wake cycle; antidepressant medications in at-risk populations; lack of full remission from previous mood episodes; and cluster B personality traits (increased risk of switching from depression to mania). Rapid cycling induction risk factors include female sex, the use of tricyclic antidepressants, stimulant abuse (including caffeine), alcohol/sedative withdrawal, bipolar disorder type II, menopause, subclinical hypothyroidism, and temporal lobe dysrhythmia. Exacerbating factors include alcohol or substance abuse; treatment nonadherence; and stressful life events. Perpetuating factors include stressful life events; chronic medical illnesses and medications (e.g., chronic obstructive pulmonary disease and intermittent use of steroids); lack of structure/routine in daily lifestyle; treatment nonadherence; and lack of support system.

Brian has two first-degree relatives with known risk factors for the development of bipolar disorder: his mother with diagnosed and treated bipolar disorder, and his father with alcoholism. Brian began having mood and behavior difficulties in grade school with an apparent major depressive episode in high school and a manic episode in college. Physical and verbal abuse, marrying early, and the death of his father were very significant events in his life that may have contributed to the onset, relapse, or maintenance of mood problems. Brian was treated ineffectively with three SSRIs and there is a possibility of alcohol, cannabis, and opiate misuse, all leading to the current state. In addition, he has severe sleep issues and a perceived lack of social support that may also influence his illness course.

NATURAL COURSE WITHOUT TREATMENT

Bipolar disorder is one of the most difficult psychiatric illnesses to confirm and treat because the manifestation of the illness varies according to age. Just as no two individuals with clinical depression are the same, those who suffer from bipolar disorder project multiple signs and symptoms in various combinations, and this variety greatly affects the clinician's treatment focus. Child and adolescent bipolar disorder shares many of the same cognitive difficulties and behaviors with ADHD. Similarities include impulsivity, hyperactivity, poor attention span, and racing thoughts. The treatment approaches are strikingly unique, and many researchers suggest that overdiagnosis and treatment of ADHD with stimulants has contributed to the extensive bipolar diagnosis in this age group.

Women, especially those with thyroid abnormalities and tricyclic antidepressants or oral contraceptive use, frequently experience rapid cycling. The concept of ultra-rapid cycling is also coming into usage, and difficulties separating borderline personality from bipolar disorder remains a challenge.

Lifelong bipolar disorder also continues unabated into older age with increased sensitivity to medication-induced mania and depression involving multiple somatic complaints.

Bipolar disorder must be considered a lifelong illness, usually episodic in nature but often with interepisodic symptoms that increase the risk for future delineated, full-blown episodes. Untreated patients with bipolar disorder may experience 10 or more episodes of depression and/or mania in their lifetime with the time between episodes typically shortening over the life span.

Men often present with mania earlier on in the course of the disease compared to women. Many women may develop multiple depressive episodes prior to having the first manic presentation. This difference may lead to a misdiagnosis of unipolar depression and inappropriate treatment, which complicates further assessment and outcome possibilities.

Complications of bipolar disorder include the development of a substance use disorder, requiring the need for separate and intensive treatment foci. Given the differing treatment options for mood instability and anxiety difficulties, such as panic attacks or obsessive compulsive behaviors, addressing bipolar disorder and an anxiety disorder can be complex and require additional resources.

Patients with bipolar disorder have an increased risk of suicide and generally a shorter life span than those without bipolar disorder, attributable to suicide or cardiovascular and pulmonary diseases.

EVIDENCE-BASED TREATMENT OPTIONS

The most important aspect in managing the patient with bipolar disorder is arriving at the correct diagnosis. Bipolar disorder is highly variable in symptom presentation, severity, and course. This places great emphasis on the need for accurate assessment to approach meaningful treatment plans. Screening tools such as the Mood Disorder Questionnaire may be helpful in identifying those requiring specialized evaluations. A complete evaluation including time course, family history, previous responses to medications, stressful life events, and level of functioning is of the utmost importance in the reliability of correct diagnosis.

There are two main therapeutic approaches to the treatment of bipolar disorder aside from accurate diagnosis: pharmacological and psychosocial/spiritual designs. A brief review of these approaches follows, and the reader is referred to references listed at the end of this chapter for a complete consensus.

The primary goal in the patient with bipolar disorder is to stabilize mood episodes and prevent future events. To that end, the number one focus should be to implement a mood stabilizer—a medication that is effective for depression, mania, or mixed states—prevent switching from one pole to the other, and protect against future episodes. Few medications provide all of these components.

First-line treatments for acute mania include lithium, valproate, and typical or first-generation antipsychotics (FGAs). Chlorpromazine is the only FGA to have FDA approval for this phase of the illness. Atypical or second-generation antipsychotics (SGAs) are approved for acute mania and are more frequently used in the United States. There does not appear to be a significant difference in efficacy between these SGAs, although acute patients are more likely to be prescribed a sedating medication while hospitalized. Recently extended-release carbamazepine has demonstrated efficacy and attained approval for the acute treatment of mania.

Lithium has been approved for the maintenance treatment of bipolar disorder since 1974, with the use of valproate widely accepted but not approved for this indication. Lamotrigine, olanzapine, and aripiprazole have received approvals for the effective maintenance treatment of bipolar disorder in recent times.

Bipolar depression has received less investigation over the years, but the primary treatment algorithm suggests lithium or lamotrigine as first-line agents with positive efficacy for quetiapine and olanzapine/fluoxetine combination, and Lurasidone recently receiving FDA approval for this illness phase. The most significant finding as related to the psychopharmacological treatment of bipolar depression is that antidepressants should not be routinely used. Mood stabilizing maximization with a combination of mood stabilizers is the current recommendation. Antidepressants may lead to switching from depression to mania (tricyclics > serotonin and norepinephrine reuptake inhibitors > selective serotonin reuptake inhibitor risk), destabilize mood, or lead to rapid cycling.

Anticonvulsants appear to be more effective in the treatment of mixed bipolar disorder, rapid-cycling patients, or those with comorbid substance use disorders, whereas lithium generally demonstrates superior efficacy in bipolar patients with a family history of bipolar disorder, classic features that include euphoria, grandiosity, and pleasurable, impulsive behavior.

Polypharmacy in the treatment of bipolar disorder is common, and many patients require combinations of medications to achieve stability. Current research into treatment-resistant bipolar disorder focuses on combinations of medications, stimulants or electroconvulsive therapy, as well as thyroid augmentation, omega-3-fatty acids, calcium channel blockers, and benzodiazepines.

Psychotherapeutic strategies have significant effect on patients with bipolar disorder and include family-focused treatment and cognitive behavioral therapy. Interpersonal social rhythms therapy has shown to be as effective as lithium in delaying the time to a future episode. Psychoeducation, which may include group therapy, also aids in minimizing relapse. Above all, structure, routine, and combination medications with therapy are extremely important for all patients with the illness.

CLINICAL COURSE WITH MANAGEMENT AND TREATMENT

Early identification and intervention in patients with bipolar disorder is warranted to prevent chronicity, more frequent episodes, and treatment inefficacy and to maximize quality of life. Effective management of a depressive, manic, or mixed episode producing complete remission of symptoms can decrease the chances of future events and impairment. The therapeutic goal of any physician must involve using the fewest medications necessary to produce euthymia and limit side effects and potential confounding medical illnesses. The best course of action typically involves pharmacotherapy and psychotherapy in addition to maintaining the patient in treatment and educating the patient and their family about prophylactic and ongoing care.

There are many patients with bipolar disorder who may experience a limited number of episodes given aggressive and continuous treatment, whereas others may require multiple medications, frequent hospitalizations, and intensive psychosocial support throughout the course of their illness. The rate of relapse and recurrence is very common in patients with bipolar disorder and the majority of time is spent in subsyndromal, especially depressive periods. The presence of comorbid illnesses including substance misuse, anxiety or personality disorders, as well as psychotic symptoms worsens the long-term prognosis and makes the illness more refractory to treatments.

Long-term use of medications is difficult to assess and the benefit-risk ratio must be individually scrutinized periodically to determine length of use.

Brian has a history of ineffective treatment with antidepressant medications and did not receive a diagnosis of bipolar disorder until his thirties. Good prognostic indicators include no prior history of hospitalizations, suicide attempts, or aggression and a strong desire to seek help. Unfortunately, his prior physical and verbal abuse, misuse of alcohol and other drugs, and marital strain place Brian in a difficult place requiring intensive management and education.

Brian reluctantly begins a course of treatment with a mood stabilizer in the form of quetiapine. He is scheduled for a follow-up appointment in two weeks which he cancels at the last minute by telephoning the receptionist. His wife calls the office the next day asking for a return appointment, which he is granted. On the return appointment, Brian is on time but announces that he can only stay for 15 minutes because of another engagement. He tells the clinician he took only two doses of the quetiapine because, "It blurred my vision, and besides, I don't think I really need it." Brian thanks the clinician and leaves after 10 minutes. He declines to schedule another appointment.

Six months later the clinician receives a subpoena from Brian's wife requesting records in divorce proceedings. Brian's attorney files a motion to quash the subpoena, and the clinician hears nothing more.

SYSTEMS-BASED PRACTICE ISSUES

Many practical issues become a focus in those affected with bipolar disorder. These include unemployment (despite frequent educational achievements), lack of adherence to medication and therapeutic regimens stemming from impaired insight or financial access, legal problems associated with impulsivity and comorbid substance misuse, and elevated divorce rates. Clinical care of these patients must be continuous and aggressive, decreasing the risk of relapse, psychosocial impairment, and treatment resistance.

LEGAL, ETHICAL, AND CULTURAL CHALLENGES

Patients with bipolar disorder face many challenges in the course of their illness, and studies have shown that the quality of life is greatly impaired, even during euthymia or remission. Such affected individuals also have high rates of relationship difficulties and occupational conflicts. A recent review of the National Epidemiologic Survey on Alcohol and Related Conditions demonstrates that those with mania (especially grandiosity, impulsivity, and excessive involvement of pleasurable activities as well as increased libido) experience a greater risk of being arrested, held by the police, or jailed.

Bipolar disorder is relatively common and the diagnosis of bipolar disorder has increased (especially in children and adolescents), but the mental health system has failed to adapt to ensure adequate care. Those who suffer from mental illness disproportionately receive less health care than those without mental illness. To compound this problem, the United States is estimated to have a current shortage of 70,000 psychiatrists.

REFERENCES AND RESOURCES

Bipolar disorder is also known as manic-depressive illness and has been described since the first century AD, but it was Emil Kraepelin in 1899 who solidified the concept of affective disorders called "manic-depressive insanity." Information about bipolar disorder has exploded in the past 30 years, including natural course of the disorder, pharmacological management, genetics, psychotherapeutic interventions, outcomes, and the concept of temperament.

Angst J, Marneros A. Bipolarity from ancient to modern times: conception, birth and rebirth. *J Affect Disord* 2001 Dec;67(1–3):3–19. Review.

Christopher PP, McCabe PJ, Fisher WH. Prevalence of involvement in the criminal justice system during severe mania and associated symptomatology. *Psychiatr Serv* 2012 Jan;63(1):33–9. doi: 10.1176/appi.ps.201100174.

Gitlin M. Treatment-resistant bipolar disorder. *Mol Psychiatry* 2006 Mar;11(3):227–40. Review.

Hirschfeld MA. Guideline watch: *Practice Guideline for the Treatment of Patients with Bipolar Disorder* (2nd ed.). doi: 10.1176/appi.books.9780890423363.148430.

Hirschfeld MA, Bowden CL, Gitlin MJ, Keck PE, Suppes T, Thase ME, Wagner KD, Perlis MD. *Practice Guideline for the Treatment of Patients with Bipolar Disorder* (2nd ed.). doi: 10.1176/appi.books.9780890423363.50051.

Maxmen JS, Ward NG, Kilgus M. *Essential Psychopathology and Its Treatment* (3rd ed.). New York: W. W. Norton and Company, 2009. Chapter 13, Mood disorders, pp. 331–72.

Scott JJ. Psychotherapy for bipolar disorders—efficacy and effectiveness. *Psychopharmacol* 2006 Mar;20(2 Suppl):46–50. Review.

American Psychiatric Association Practice Guidelines, http://www.psych.org/psych_pract/treatg/pg/prac_guide.cfm.

Depression and Bipolar Support Alliance, http://www.dbsalliance.org.

National Comorbidity Survey, http://www.hcp.med.harvard.edu/ncs/ncs_data.php.

National Institute of Clinical Excellence (UK), http://www.nice.org.uk/page.aspx?o=mental.

Texas Medication Algorithm Project, http://www.dshs.state.tx.us/mhprograms/TMA-Pover.shtm/.

Good Morning, Vietnam (1987; starring Robin Williams), *The Mask* (1994; starring Jim Carrey), *Frances* (1982; starring Jessica Lange), *Silver Linings Playbook* (2012; starring Bradley Cooper), and *Mr. Jones* (1993 starring Richard Gere). These films depict many features of mania such as rapid, pressured speech, rhyming and circumstantiality, impulsivity, euphoria, and distractibility, as well as the significant depressive phases that mark the cyclic nature of the illness.

PART III

Anxiety Pathology

CHAPTER **15**

Social Anxiety

Yongyue Chen, M.D., Ph.D.

CLINICAL PRESENTATION

Chief complaint: "I panic with people."

History of present illness: Nathan is a 19-year-old Caucasian male with a history of separation anxiety who is referred by his primary care clinician because of worsening anxiety. He describes his anxiety as "panic with people." Since early childhood, he has been uncomfortable in front of groups of people if asked to answer a question, make an announcement, or give a presentation. He becomes anxious when anticipating a social event. However, he has never sought mental health treatment. His parents label him as shy and anxious. He has a relatively small network of friends, though he desires more friends. He is afraid of being criticized or negatively evaluated. He did not join any sports or social groups in school for fear of experiencing "panic" in the group or embarrassment. He has not yet had any dating experience, and this is a source of embarrassment with his peers.

He experiences two to three panic attacks in an average day. It has been worsening since graduation from high school a year ago. The typical panic attack is characterized by a sudden onset of excessive anxiety, choking sensation, tightness of breath, palpitations, stomach cramping, hand shaking, and stuttering. These attacks usually occur in situations such as a class conference and small group discussion when there is the fear of being asked to speak. They may last tens of seconds and prevent him from participating effectively in class or group activities.

In anticipation of family gatherings during holidays or other events, Nathan is extremely anxious and even unable to fall asleep. He thinks about escaping the situation whenever he is greeted by extended family members whom he sees infrequently. His tendency to avoid family gatherings over the years bothers his parents. This causes relatively few connections with his extended family members. He had private piano lessons from age 7 to 16. Over that time he managed to avoid all but five recitals at the local church. He recalls being anxious and having difficulty falling sleep before every recital. He experienced a panic attack and was unable to play on the stage in four of the five recitals. About the one recital in which he performed he says, "I didn't even know what I was playing. It was horrible. I didn't get any official recognition of my piano accomplishments." He eventually canceled most of his recitals.

Nathan was also sent to a swimming training camp when he was 10 years old. He attended several days and quit with fears of being watched while swimming. He enjoys playing games at home by himself. He plays Xbox, Wii, and computer games. He is an active participant of an Internet forum about computer science. There are 60–70 people in the forum. They exchange daily posts relating to computers or other topics, and this activity never causes panic or excessive worry.

Psychiatric history: Nathan was diagnosed with "separation anxiety" by a school counselor when he started kindergarten at the age of five years. He refused to go to school for several months. He recalls that in school he was scared being around unfamiliar kids. He had difficulty eating in the school cafeteria and using public restrooms, but these problems have gradually improved. He did not receive any treatment for the separation anxiety. He has no mental health hospitalizations or outpatient treatment. He does not try any psychotropic medicine. He does not have any previous suicidal or homicidal attempts or physically aggressive behavior. He started seeing a school counselor at college for worsening anxiety. There has been no obvious change in his anxiety level. When he talked with his primary care clinician about his worsening anxiety, it was recommended that he seek professional assistance.

Substance abuse history: There is no use of tobacco, alcohol, marijuana, cocaine, opioids, inhalants, stimulants, hallucinogens, or prescription medicine.

Family psychiatric history: His father has obsessive compulsive traits and is strict about family rules and daily routine. His mother has generalized anxiety disorder and has been on sertraline treatment for years. One paternal uncle was alcohol dependent and died of "drinking too much in his forties." One younger sister has "similar anxiety as mine."

Medical history: Nathan had asthma in early childhood. He doesn't recall any asthma attacks or taking any medicine for asthma prevention. He was diagnosed with Marfan syndrome three years ago. He does not have any known cardiac problems. He doesn't take any medicine. He doesn't have a history of traumatic brain injury or seizure.

Developmental, educational, occupational, and social history: Nathan was born with no complications from a planned pregnancy. There was no intrauterine exposure to drugs, alcohol, tobacco, or illicit substances. He was delivered vaginally at full term and was released from the hospital on the day after delivery. He started walking at 10 months, speaking at 12 months, and potty training at 30 months. He achieved all developmental milestones. He was raised as a Catholic and baptized when he was three months old. There was no childhood sexual or physical abuse. He is the second child in the birth order with one older brother and two younger sisters, with approximately two years between each of the siblings. His older brother was bossy toward him. He has a good relationship with his younger sisters. His father is a physics professor, and his mother is a realtor. He had 10 years of private piano lessons starting from seven years of age. He began kindergarten at age five and completed high school in regular classes. He did not participate in any social organizations or student clubs during high school. He is currently a sophomore in a large state university majoring in computer science and engineering. He lives in a campus dormitory room by himself. He does not have any history of intimate relationships and has never been sexually active. This seems to bother him. He has a part-time job working for a software company, which he does alone in his dorm.

Mental status examination: Nathan appears his stated age of 19 years. He is a white male with slim body habit, light brown hair cut short, casually dressed wearing a long-sleeve shirt and blue jeans. He sits uneasily while constantly spinning a cell phone in his right hand and tapping the floor with both feet. He is cooperative with elusive eye contact. Speech is clearly articulated and spontaneous with normal rate, tone, and volume. He is alert and fully oriented to person, place, time, and situation. He is able to register and recall three objects after five minutes. His recent and remote memory is largely intact. He is attentive and able to concentrate during the session. His affect is anxious and congruent with expressed thoughts. He reports his mood as stable and euthymic without suicidal or homicidal ideation, plan, or intent.

Thought process is logical and goal-directed. There are no racing thoughts, loosening of associations, or flight of ideas. His thought content is without obvious delusions or obsessions. His intelligence seems to be above average based on fund of knowledge, comprehension, and vocabulary. In addition, he performs simple calculations accurately and quickly. Insight and judgment are grossly intact. He denies past or present auditory or visual hallucinations or any other perceptual abnormalities.

IMPAIRMENT IN FUNCTIONING

Several aspects of Nathan's life are substantially affected by social anxiety. Despite basic athletic competence, anxiety resulted in him quitting swim training. He did not join any team sports. Athletic activities and socialization through sports are necessary not only for his physical development but for building self-esteem as well. Physical fitness and competency is one of the core positive aspects of self-image in social interaction. Also, his inability to perform at piano recitals prevents the development of his artistic taste and competence. His poor classroom participation affects his academic achievement. Although he seems to be functioning adequately in college, he does not obtain the full benefit of certain educational opportunities, which may also have narrowed his career choices. Because of his performance and social anxiety, he is unable to tolerate a more competitive academic environment. He does not belong to any social groups and is mostly a loner. He does not have close friends or a romantic relationship. Socialization is one of the critical elements relating to late adolescent development of identity, independence, and eventually intimacy. Without a social life or peer influence, his cognitive maturation, moral development, self-identity, sense of belonging to certain groups, subcultures, and mainstream society is jeopardized. Obviously, Nathan is aware of the impairments in his development, and he is distressed.

DSM DIAGNOSIS

The essential feature of the clinical picture is a marked and persistent fear in class discussions, presentations, or recitals in which he is watched and may be evaluated. Participation in class discussion, presentation, or recitals mostly provokes anxiety or panic attacks. He recognizes that his anxiety response to the social situation is excessive and unreasonable. Although he does not circumvent school situations that provoke anxiety, he avoids piano recitals and sports activities. He is distressed about his situational anxiety. His intellectual, sports, and social potential are negatively affected by his situational anxiety. There is no obvious physical or medical condition that may contribute to his anxiety. He does not use drugs or alcohol.

The social phobia in this case is generalized because Nathan experiences anxiety in most social situations, including both public performance and social interaction. There are several psychological and physical features associated with social anxiety disorder: low self-esteem, hypersensitive to criticism or even regular evaluation, cold clammy hands, tremor, and shaky voice. Underachievement in academic endeavor, social status, and relationship development is the long-term social consequence of social phobia.

Nathan's clinical presentation is dominated by anxiety, and social anxiety disorder (previously called social phobia) is the clinician's initial diagnostic impression. If long-standing, social anxiety may result in an avoidant personality disorder, which is considered in Nathan's case. He also has Marfan syndrome and possibly reactive airway disease. Stressors seem minimal. There are multiple factors that might improve his prognosis and predict a positive treatment response. Nathan is from an upper middle-class family with solid financial resources and reasonable expectations. His intelligence is above average. His beliefs concerning the relationship between his personal interests and resources are realistic. His active learning and working behavior pattern shaped since childhood are assets. He has internal motivation adaptive to social and novel environments. He has a stable living situation where basic physical and emotional needs are met. His family is supportive and stable. These factors are likely to improve the prognosis of his social phobia and his response to treatment.

EPIDEMIOLOGY

Social phobia is a relatively common psychiatric disorder with lifelong prevalence of 5–12% and one-year prevalence of 7.1–7.9% in the United States. Nathan's clinic picture of social anxiety symptoms and signs highly suggests a diagnosis of social phobia. Considering the high prevalence of social phobia, it should be a default diagnosis until proven otherwise. Internationally, the lifetime prevalence of social phobia in developed countries is 6.1%, 2.1% in developing countries. It is higher in young, female, Native American, or low-income people. Being elder, male, Asian, Hispanic, black, or living in urban or more populated regions is lower in terms of risk. Mean age at onset is 15.1 years with a mean duration of 16.3 years. It is estimated that over 80% of individuals with social phobia do not receive any treatment. For those seeking treatment, the mean age at first treatment is 27.2 years. Lifetime social phobia is generally accompanied with generalized anxiety disorder, bipolar disorder, and avoidant or dependent personality disorders. The mean number of feared social situations among individuals with social phobia is 7.0, with the majority reporting anxiety in performance situations.

DIFFERENTIAL DIAGNOSIS

The core psychological features of anxiety disorders are excessive and ongoing worries and unrealistic views to one's spatial, temporal, and social environments. It includes not only psychological and cognitive features but also somatic symptoms and signs from head to toe.

- Head: headache, dizziness, sweating, pupil dilation, tinnitus, blush, or pallor.
- Chest: choking feeling, shortness of breath, chest pain, tachycardia, or heart palpitation.
- Abdomen: nausea, stomach upset, diarrhea, or frequent urination.
- Extremities: shaking or tremor, muscle tension, sweating, tingling, or numbness.

In psychiatry, anxiety disorders are among the most prevalent mental disorders with a 20–25% one-year prevalence in the United States. In DSM-5 anxiety disorders are now separated into four groups: fear-based, obsessive compulsive, trauma-related, and dissociative based on either etiology or symptomatic features. Anxiety may be secondary to a general medical condition or substance-induced. The core symptoms of social phobia are the excessive anticipatory and actual situational anxiety, which may or may not cause avoidant behavior. This is different from panic disorder, which is characterized by unexpected, not situational, excessive anxiety or panic attack. Recurrent and persistent concern about the recurrence of panic attack is also part of this disorder. Agoraphobia is extreme anxiety (with or without panic attack) about being in situations or places where escaping or help is not available. The avoidance only occurs in the situations with possible scrutiny in social phobia. This can help differentiate agoraphobia in which there is no scrutiny. Generalized anxiety disorder is characterized by constant worries without reference to any specific object, physical setting, or social situation. It can be ruled out because there is no worry in familiar, nonscrutiny situations. Separation anxiety is not in the differential diagnosis for Nathan's case, although he experienced excessive anxiety when separated from home or his mother (the attachment figure). With a familiar or attachment figure present, regardless of whether the situation is unfamiliar or involves possible scrutiny, the child would not experience obvious anxiety. That is different from social phobia. Anxiety to a specific object or physical setting is a specific phobia. Obsessive compulsive disorder is anxiety to perceived inappropriate and intrusive recurrent ideas, thoughts, impulses, or images—with repetitive behaviors or mental acts with the aim to prevent or reduce obsession-caused anxiety. Acute stress disorder is anxiety/arousal, avoidance, re-experience, and dissociation from environment, sensory, emotion, and memory following exposure to an extreme traumatic stressor. If these symptoms persist or arise one month after a traumatic experience, it is called post-traumatic stress disorder.

Situational anxiety and withdrawal may be one of the symptoms of other mental illness, such as dysthymia or major depressive disorder in which a distorted cognition causes situational anxiety. The significant depressive feeling, no enjoyment, or vegetative symptoms help differentiate it from social phobia. Schizophrenia involves delusional (usually paranoid) thought content (not obviously presenting in Nathan's case) and could manifest as social anxiety. Body dysmorphic disorder with specific delusional or distorted cognition of one's body image may also be associated with social anxiety. Usually no additional diagnosis of social anxiety is given if there is a comorbid major depressive disorder, dysthymia, schizophrenia, and body dysmorphic disorder. Pervasive developmental disorder such as autism spectrum disorders may manifest anxiety and avoidance in social situations. The difference is whether the patient gained age-appropriate social skill in childhood. In schizoid personality disorder, the patient has no desire for social interaction and anxiety may not be eminent. Avoidant personality disorder is not qualitatively distinct from social phobia. However, the avoidant behavior in personality disorder is more severe and generalized in social situations. Cognition of inappropriateness and sense of inferiority are prominent.

ETIOLOGY AND PATHOGENESIS

Nathan's father has obsessive compulsive personality traits, and his mother has an anxiety disorder. He and his sister have similar anxiety patterns. The genetic component predisposes Nathan's susceptibility to develop anxiety spectrum trait or disorder. A bossy brother and a strict father in his early childhood may have created a critical and harsh development condition, which sensitized his response to scrutiny or evaluation. His anxious mother models Nathan's anxious behavior pattern. He demonstrated an anxious temperament early in life as manifested by separation anxiety.

Separation anxiety interferes with the normal exploration that is necessary to establish a secure self-identity and self-efficacy. The early breakdown in sports and music performance reinforces his fear or expectation to failure. Nathan gradually develops a schema of failure with resultant performance anxiety and social avoidance. Through avoidant behavior he does not benefit from the practice of social skills, making the unavoidable future social interactions over the developmental course even more challenging. This ultimately presents clinically as social phobia or social anxiety. Repression and withdrawal are the two primary defense mechanisms he employs in response to overwhelming anxiety.

Fear in response to a threatening environment is an adaptive emotion, which prompts the fight-or-flight response. The sense of being scrutinized or evaluated is the cognitive awareness of a perceived threat. There are times when an individual should have an appropriate level of fear or anxiety as manifested by elevation of alertness and vigilance. Alertness and vigilance adaptively prepare the individual for a threatening environment to increase survival. When the fear or anxiety is excessive in magnitude and generalized in extent, the behavior responses are dysfunctional or maladaptive and reach the level of psychopathology.

Despite anxiety disorders running in families, no specific gene or environmental factor is reliably used to predict the onset, progress, or treatment response of social phobia. On the molecular level, neurotransmitter systems of serotonin, norepinephrine, and GABA are related to the chemical pathogenesis of social phobia. They are the targets of pharmacotherapy for social phobia. In the brain, the amygdala is the detector of salient environmental threats. Hyperactivity in this brain nucleus contributes to anxiety. Imaging studies also demonstrate hyperactivity of amygdala, locus coeruleus, and cingulated gyrus. How the interaction of different nuclei in the brain coordinates the onset of social phobia is unknown.

From a cognitive behavioral science point of view, post–social event rumination associated with negative self-appraisal and perceived negative consequences of a social performance, through direct social anxiety trait and indirect cognitive processes of inappropriate attention, are the major cognitive mechanisms of the etiology of social phobia. The person views a benign social situation as hostile or threatening. Cognition distortions can be conditioned by experiences. Cognitive behavioral therapy is based on this theme. Identifying and correcting the distorted cognitions is the principal cognitive behavioral therapy strategy for treating social phobia.

Psychodynamic theories view the social phobia as the result of conflict between the desire for success with the fear of failure, humiliation, or embarrassment. Psychoanalytic therapy resolves the conflict by bringing the unconscious desire and fear up to conscious through free association.

NATURAL COURSE WITHOUT TREATMENT

Nathan experienced separation anxiety at age five when he went to kindergarten. He was shy during childhood. The early signs of anxiety spectrum disorder were not treated. Social interaction increases with his development process. His anxiety symptoms and functional impairments expressed in social settings relate to his development stages involving the school classroom, sports program, music performance, and dating. Because of his stage in development, Nathan's impairment in functioning has not yet been obvious in the domains of career, family, and community. It is expected that without treatment, his professional career choices and performance may be negatively affected by his anxiety and avoidance behavior. It would be difficult for him to be a leader or a team player in tasks that require multiple human interactions. Avoiding social activity not only affects Nathan's early courting and family formation, it may also affect the quality of his family life.

About 15% of social phobia cases in adolescents remit, and a similar percentage of the patients still meet full diagnostic criteria after 10 years of follow-up. The rest have persistence of social anxiety in partial expression of symptoms. Early onset, generalized subtype, more anxiety cognitions, severe avoidance, co-occurring panic, impairment of functioning, and family vulnerability factors such as parental social phobia or depression, lack of warmth, or family dysfunction predict higher social phobia persistence and diagnostic stability.

Impaired functioning in social phobia has been well documented in literature. It is classified arbitrarily into three domains: work/study, social, and family. Increase of disability, financial dependence, underemployment, and impairment of education, romantic relations, friendships, and family relations are recognized. In general, social phobia reduces productivity and quality of life. Social phobia is among the five most impairing psychiatric disorders. Different subgroups may affect the functioning differently, that is, the generalized subtype has greater impairment.

EVIDENCE-BASED TREATMENT OPTIONS

The contemporary expert consensus is that both psychotherapy and medications have roles in the management of social phobia. There are more than 30 randomized trials of psychological treatments for social phobia. As with most anxiety disorders, exposure and response prevention are the important elements of successful treatment. Cognitive behavioral therapy (CBT) is the most examined psychotherapy modality. Some of the specific components of CBT (such as cognitive restructuring, relaxation, exposure, and social skills) are examined. Interpersonal psychotherapy and mindfulness-based stress reduction are the other two psychotherapeutic approaches with randomized trials. Although clinical trials in psychotherapy are always challenged by the standardization of the treatment protocols and the appropriateness of the placebo control, results in general favor psychotherapy regardless of the specific category of the therapies. Meta-analysis of available trial data in general suggests that psychotherapy is effective compared to control group. Efficacy is not significantly different between different components of CBT. It is a consistent finding that CBT is as effective, if not superior to, other psychotherapy approaches such as interpersonal psychotherapy and mindfulness-based stress reduction psychotherapy. The therapeutic endurance of psychotherapy is of significance in post-treatment follow-up as well. The encumbrance of psychotherapy is the cost and the availability of qualified therapists. There are two reports claiming that Internet-delivered CBT is equally effective to therapist-delivered CBT.

Pharmacotherapy remains the major modality of management of social phobia. Seventeen randomized placebo-controlled trials of selective serotonin reuptake inhibitors (SSRIs) are documented. Venlafaxine from the serotonin-norepinephrine reuptake inhibitor (SNRI) group has been studied in a randomized placebo-controlled trial. There are also several open-label trials of duloxetine. Phenelzine is the one in the monoamine oxidase inhibitor (MAOI) group with randomized placebo-controlled trials. There are also small numbers of randomized placebo-controlled trials in antiepileptic drugs, benzodiazepines, and second-generation antipsychotics. Paroxetine is the most examined SSRI, followed by fluoxetine, sertraline, escitalopram, and fluvoxamine. In general, all SSRIs examined are effective in the treatment of social phobia. The efficacy usually emerges in the fourth to sixth week and continues to increase to the 12th week after starting treatment. SSRIs are also effective in preventing relapse of social phobia. So is venlafaxine. Although there is no randomized trial in duloxetine, the open-label trial suggests its efficacy. Phenelzine is an irreversible MAOI and is the most effective medicine so far with randomized placebo-controlled clinical trial. However, its clinical use is limited by the necessity of strict diet control. An open-label clinical trial also suggests the effectiveness of tranylcypromine, a reversible MAOI. Interestingly MAOIs are also effective in avoidant personality disorder. Atomoxetine, a norepinephrine reuptake inhibitor, mirtazapine and nefazodone, which are antagonists of alpha 2 receptor and 5-HT receptors; all have had negative clinical trials.

Gabapentin and pregabalin, which are presynaptic voltage-gated calcium channel blockers, are effective in the management of social phobia, especially in higher doses for pregabalin (600 mg daily). The extra benefit of these two medicines is that they show early response to treatment—even in the first week of treatment. However, other antiepileptic drugs, such as valproic acid, levetiracetam, topiramate, and tiagabine, are ineffective. Clonazepam, bromazepam, and alprazolam are the three benzodiazepines that have been formally tested. They are all effective in acute control of the social phobia symptoms. There is only one randomized placebo-controlled trial with the combination of paroxetine and clonazepam, although it is a popular clinical practice to use both antidepressants and benzodiazepines in severe anxiety disorders. The conclusion is inconclusive as to whether the combined therapy is better than any monotherapy. Buspirone is not effective in a randomized placebo-controlled trial. The efficacy of the second-generation antipsychotics (olanzapine and quetiapine) is inconclusive from a limited number of clinical trials.

CLINICAL COURSE WITH MANAGEMENT AND TREATMENT

Nathan is started on sertraline 50 mg daily at his first office visit. It is obvious that medicine is the first choice based on its simplicity, his mother's favorable response to this medication, and its low cost compared to psychotherapy modalities. There is no evidence to support choosing one first-line antidepressant over another. Although there are more studies on the efficacy and safety of paroxetine in the treatment of social phobia, it does not necessary mean that this is better than other SSRIs or SNRIs. In clinical practice, paroxetine is usually not the first choice considering its relatively short half-life and possible withdrawal symptoms in a once-daily regimen.

Nathan tolerated sertraline with no obvious gastrointestinal side effects or increased agitation. However, even after gradually increasing the dose over many weeks to 200 mg, there was no obvious change in his social phobia symptoms or avoidance behavior after four months. With Nathan's high level of motivation for relief of symptoms, there was no reason to disbelieve his reports of taking the medication without fail. Next, the clinician decided to prescribe fluoxetine 20 mg and taper off sertraline over a few days. Nathan still reported feeling no relief from anxiety in social settings until fluoxetine reached 40 mg. Although still feeling anxious, he could at least tolerate social exposure without experiencing panic attacks. He has since continued fluoxetine 40 mg daily. He declines the offer of psychotherapy because of time constraints. CBT in a group setting might be most helpful.

Social phobia is treated by pharmacotherapy, psychotherapy, or a combination of both. Although both therapies are considered first line of treatment, the actual treatment implemented depends on whether the first encounter is with a psychiatrist or therapist. Even without medication, exposure and response prevention to social anxiety alone is effective in the motivated individual. The goal of therapy is the remission of anxiety symptoms. That can be objectively monitored using the Liebowitz Social Anxiety Scale.

SSRIs and SNRIs remain the medicine of choice. They follow similar principles to antidepressant treatment in depressive disorders except that the dose is usually higher for anxiety disorders. It is recommended starting with a low dose and gradually increasing to improve treatment adherence by avoiding the initial increase in anxiety on starting these medications. The response should be evaluated by the fourth or even the eighth week of treatment. Switching medicine should be considered if no benefit is seen in the sixth to eighth week of a medication trial at a typical therapeutic or maximum dose. Full benefit usually is seen over a period of months. Paroxetine is the most evidence-supported medicine for social phobia. Sertraline, venlafaxine, fluoxetine, citalopram, escitalopram, and fluvoxamine are other initial monotherapy medicines. Gabapentin, progabalin, beta-blockers, and benzodiazepines are usually used as adjunctive medicines to control acute exacerbation of dysfunctional excessive anticipatory anxiety before expected exposure.

Since first marketed in the 1960s, benzodiazepines have been increasingly used in a wide variety of medical practices. They are safe in general and effective in short-term (a couple of weeks) treatment of anxiety symptoms, although cognitive impairments and behavioral inhibition and aggressiveness may occur. They are controversial for long-term use due to the concern for tolerance, physical dependence, psychological dependence, and withdrawal syndrome on cessation. In combination with abuse of alcohol or opioid, or with suicidal behavior, benzodiazepines increase the risk of death or success of suicide attempt. In elderly persons, short-term confusion, long-term cognitive impairment, and risk of fall are very common. It is generally recommended to only use benzodiazepine if absolutely required in severe panic attack, dysfunctional excessive anxiety, or unable to tolerate antidepressant.

Propranolol is a commonly prescribed beta-blocker for the prevention of performance anxiety, although there is no supporting data from a randomized placebo-controlled trial. It is also a common practice that buspirone to be used as an adjunctive therapy for the social phobia even though randomized trials failed to confirm its efficacy as a monotherapy agent. Phenelzine, an MAOI, usually remains a latter pharmacological option for anxiety disorders considering the required diet control, its potentially dangerous interaction with a wide range of antidepressants and sympathomimetics, and high rates of side effects. Bupropion, the second generation antipsychotics, and valproic acid are also being used in clinical practice. They have either case report evidence or a small number of open-label study evidence to support their efficacy.

CBT is the treatment of choice in social phobia. There are several components in CBT that contribute to its effectiveness. Exposure is with the rationale to learn new responses or establish new adaptive behavior patterns when faced with the feared situation. Cognitive restructure aims to correct the biased or distorted perception of the social situation that provokes anxiety. Relaxation techniques, deep breathing, progressive muscle relaxation, or meditation can be invoked in anxiety-provoking situations. Social skills training with overpracticing reduces anxiety by expanding the repertoire of possible responses. The combination of medication and psychotherapy is likely to have the best therapeutic outcome.

SYSTEMS-BASED PRACTICE ISSUES

Functioning properly with no suicidal ideation and no psychosis, Nathan does not meet criteria for inpatient treatment in contemporary managed health care systems. Due to managed care addressing cost issues, the physicians who prescribe medicines are seldom able to provide psychotherapy, which Nathan definitely needs. It is likely that he will receive services from two separate clinicians, one for psychotherapy and another for medication. This imposes extra burden for time commitment and convenience. Consequently, he chose medicine management only and potentially will not receive maximal benefit from evidence-supported therapeutic modalities. Also, if seen first in a primary care setting, the busy practitioner may not be able to explore the anxiety and instead may attribute the shortness of breath from a panic attack to be asthma. The treatment for reactive airway disease using sympathomimetics may serve to exacerbate his anxiety.

CULTURAL ISSUES

The core features of social phobia are the marked and persistent fear of social situations in which embarrassment may occur due to scrutiny or evaluation. The scrutiny or evaluation is based on social norms or expectations, which is obviously culture-dependent. A person's reaction to social situations also depends on how he or she relates to others, and that is largely shaped by the culture in which the person is raised. The 12-month prevalence of adult social phobia is 7.1% in the United States and 0.8% in Japan. Similar differences are noticed in other countries with Western culture (such as 9.1% in Brazil and 6.4% in Chile) or Eastern culture (such as 0.2–0.6% in Korea and 0.2% in China). The presentations of social phobia are also culture-dependent. In Western culture social phobia is defined as the fear of embarrassing oneself. However, in Japan social phobia (Taijin kyofusho) is referred to as the fear of offending others. Social phobia is more likely in cultures that highlight individualism versus those that emphasize collectivism.

Regarding the treatment, there is no convincing evidence to draw any conclusion that culture, race, or ethnicity has any predictive value. Small numbers of reports suggest that whites, blacks, Hispanics, and Asians respond equally well to SSRI treatment or CBT.

HISTORY

Historically social anxiety disorder or social phobia was first used in DSM-III in 1980. Two categories were used in anxiety disorders then: phobic disorders and anxiety states. In subsequent editions of the DSM published in 1994 and 2000, the terminology was changed to social phobia followed by social anxiety disorder, emphasizing the recognition that there are cognitive components of fear (being judged anxious, weak, crazy, or stupid) and anticipatory fear (being humiliated or embarrassed in social or performance situations). There was the single specifier, *Generalized*, which acknowledges that the anxiety occurs in multiple social situations. In DSM-5, social anxiety disorder (versus social phobia) is considered the more appropriate term to use because the disorder is more obvious in cognition, awareness of fear, and anticipatory anxiety than specific phobia. Also, the avoidance in this disorder is more subtle in social situations than in specific phobia to objects or nonsocial scenarios. Elimination of the specifier *Generalized* is recommended with the new subtype specifier, *Performance Only*, for fear that is restricted to speaking or performance in public. Some experts have suggested a severity scale to reflect the continuum of social anxiety. The criterion A was changed from "fear of one or more social or performance situations" to "fear of performance, social interaction, and observation situation" in DSM-5. Although there is 42% comorbidity between social anxiety disorder and avoidant personality disorder, they remain as independent disorders to underscore the nature of developmental deficit of interpersonal relations in personality disorder.

TERMS

Anxiety: an unpleasant feeling of fear and concern. It is generally viewed as an emotional response to a perceived danger to the subject. Anxiety is a general concept with somatic, emotional, cognitive, and behavioral components. Proper anxiety is a normal reaction to the demands of the environment and prompts to manage it. Anxiety disorders are excessive anxiety states that compromise normal functioning of the affected individual.

Avoidance: a behavior performed to prevent an aversive stimulus from occurring. Avoidance behavior does not necessarily indicate anxiety. Anxiety may or may not evoke avoidance behavior.

Exposure and response prevention: confronting the subject with the thoughts, images, objects, or situations that induce anxiety and preventing the subject from escaping from the anxiety-evoking thoughts, images, objects, or situations. It is a CBT procedure for anxiety disorders including social phobia. Cognitively this procedure targets to the distorted cognition that a benign stimulus is perceived as a danger by the subject. Behaviorally, it is an example of Pavlovian extinction of a maladaptive behavior and establishment of an adaptive behavior.

Fear: a dreadful feeling about an intimidating object. *Fear* usually refers to specific threats, present focus, and short duration, while prompting escape from the threat. *Anxiety* is a more general word and refers to a vague threat, future focus, and long duration while instigating caution to the environment or approaching the threat.

Flooding versus graded exposure: confronting the subject with an extreme anxiety-evoking stimulus versus with serial escalating anxiety-evoking stimuli. Both exposures need to persist long enough to have the subject habituate to it. The difference is that the flooding evokes maximal anxiety response but the graded doesn't.

Gradual desensitization: diminishing emotional responsiveness from the least disturbance to the most disturbance to an anxiety-evoking stimulus. Gradual desensitization is more properly called "habituation."

REFERENCES AND RESOURCES

Amir N, Prouvost C, Kuckertz JM. Lack of a benign interpretation bias in social anxiety disorder. *Cogn Behav Ther* 2012;41(2):119–29.

Bögels SM, Alden L, Beidel DC, et al. Social anxiety disorder: questions and answers for the DSM-V. *Dep Anxiety* 2010;27(2):168–89.

Canton J, Scott KM, Glue P. Optimal treatment of social phobia: systematic review and meta-analysis. *Neuropsychiatr Dis Treat* 2012;8:203–15.

Liebowitz MR. Social phobia. *Mod Probl Pharmacopsych* 1987;22:141–73.

McTeague LM, Lang PJ. The anxiety spectrum and the reflex physiology of defense: from circumscribed fear to broad distress. *Depress Anxiety* 2012;29(4):264–81.

Stein MB, Stein DJ. Social anxiety disorder. *Lancet* 2008;371:1115–25.

Lars and the Real Girl (2007) is a movie in which Lars Lindstrom (played by Ryan Gosling), a sweet, quirky young man, has difficulty interacting and relating to his family, coworkers, and fellow churchgoers.

Social Anxiety, http://www.social-anxiety.org.uk, is a self-help website for social anxiety.

Social Phobia, http://www.ncbi.nlm.nih.gov/pubmedhealth/PMH0001953, is a page with concise and accurate information on social phobia.

CHAPTER 16

Obsessions

Delmar Short, M.D.

CLINICAL PRESENTATION

Chief complaint: "Please don't let me hurt her."

History of present illness: Matthew is a 62-year-old man who has been residing in a nursing home facility on the grounds of a hospital because he needs assistance with activities of daily living as well as his recurrent concerns about hurting himself. His main complaint is recurring thoughts of harming someone, including his grandchild. Twenty-two years earlier, at the age of 40, he gouged out his eyes in an attempt to avoid harming anyone. (It should be emphasized that this must have been enormous suffering to cause him to do this self-harm to protect others.) He reasoned that if he were blind, he would not be able to hurt anyone else. Due to his behavior he has been in and out of psychiatric hospitals since then; his family does not want him to return home.

Matthew has daily episodes, especially when he is depressed, of intrusive, unpleasant thoughts of physically attacking someone. These thoughts cause him marked anxiety and distress. He attempts to suppress or ignore these thoughts, but he finds it very difficult. He understands that these are internal thoughts in his mind and that they are not imposed from without, as in thought insertion. The patient denies any repetitive behavior, such as hand washing, ordering, checking, or mental acts, such as counting or repeating words silently that he feels driven to perform.

Matthew understands that these obsessions are excessive and unreasonable, but he nonetheless has difficulty dealing with them. Each day these thoughts occupy a good deal of his time, often at least an hour. Prior to being seen by a consultation-liaison psychiatrist he had been considered psychotic with a diagnosis of schizophrenia. He had been institutionalized for many years, in part due to his blindness but also because of safety concerns related to his self-harm behavior. He probably would not have needed to be institutionalized had his obsessions been aggressively treated earlier.

Matthew denies any hallucinations and shows no evidence of fixed delusions. He does not have disorganized, illogical, or incoherent speech, and his affect is not flattened.

He also reports periods of time that last more than two weeks of depression or sad mood as well as problems waking early in the morning and lying in bed worrying. He says his obsessions get worse during these depressive periods, but he still has some obsessions when he is not feeling depressed. His interest in things goes down during depressive periods and he feels especially bad about himself.

Matthew has a history of serious suicide attempts, including an attempt to hang himself while in the nursing home. He did this in hopes of ridding himself of the obsessions and to prevent himself from hurting anyone. Most often these obsessions are about harming a loved family member, not a stranger. These thoughts in his head are not audible voices; they are abhorrent (ego-dystonic), and he tries without much success to suppress them. He understands that the thoughts are unreasonable most of the time.

Matthew has never shown aggressive or violent tendencies toward others. In fact, he enjoys visiting others more handicapped than he in the nursing home. He does this especially with those that get no other visitors. Because of his blindness, he is particularly afraid to be on the acute psychiatry ward, where he has had to go on occasion.

Past medical history: Matthew's past medical history is significant for a multinodular goiter. In late life he developed proctalgia, which was thought to be due to a nonrelaxing pubo-rectalis syndrome. He did not have these symptoms until he was about 60 years old, and it was questioned whether these were related to his obsessionality. He actually was doing well with his obsessions at that time.

Psychiatric history: As noted, Matthew was treated as if he had schizophrenia for many years and was on an antipsychotic at the time of presentation to the consultation-liaison psychiatrist. He demonstrated mild tardive dyskinesia on examination using the abnormal involuntary movement scale.

Social history: This gentleman is married with one daughter and he also has grandchildren. His wife visited him in the hospital once a week for many years. His education included postgraduate work, and he worked as a teacher prior to becoming disabled.

Family history: He denies family history of psychiatric illness.

Mental status exam: Matthew is well groomed and sitting up in bed with dark glasses on. He shows some mild evidence of tardive dyskinesia with mild facial movements and mild hand movements. He is alert and oriented to person, place, time, and situation. His recall/recent memory is 3/3 with distraction. His registration and remote memory are intact. He is able to spell *world* backward and correctly does serial 3's without mistakes. His mini mental status exam is 30 out of 30. He shows no evidence of blunting or flattening of affect. He shows a full range of appropriate emotions.

His thought processes are logical and linear without looseness, flight of ideas, or circumstantiality. He is able to use abstract thinking and denies delusions. He also shows no evidence of delusions, thought broadcasting, ideas of reference, or magical thinking. He has a good fund of knowledge and good use of vocabulary. Matthew shows good insight into his problems. He understands that his obsessions are from within his own mind. He denies hallucinations and shows no evidence of paranoia or delusions.

IMPAIRMENT IN FUNCTIONING

Matthew's functional impairment is clear. He is a man tortured by his thoughts and obsessions which have physically taken his sight. His intrusive, unwelcome thoughts cripple him more than does his blindness.

DSM DIAGNOSES

Matthew's condition satisfies the DSM diagnostic criteria for obsessive compulsive disorder (OCD) with good insight, but he also shows symptoms suggestive of recurring major depression. He has no evidence of a history of manic symptoms or hypomanic symptoms. He shows no evidence of a personality disorder. He does have medical conditions including his self-inflicted blindness, goiter, and an old fracture of the right acetabulum. In the latest edition of the DSM, the diagnosis of OCD is tightly grouped with body dysmorphic disorder, trichotillomania, hoarding disorder, and excoriation disorder.

In capturing the character of Matthew's affliction, there are elements of mood, anxiety, and thought disorder. His extremely painful intrusive thoughts are as disabling as those experienced by a schizophrenic. His anxiety is paralyzing and at times his depression and remorse overwhelm him. The intensity of all three spheres of disturbance for this unfortunate individual is very high.

EPIDEMIOLOGY

OCD has a lifetime preference of about 2%. Genetics are likely involved, but there is also an association in children with group A streptococcal infections. It is important to note that there is little if any association between OCD and obsessive compulsive personality disorder.

DIFFERENTIAL DIAGNOSIS

Some patients with OCD are more along the line bordering between psychosis and OCD, whereas others are closer to the depressive line. Some are more in the anxiety spectrum, and the diagnosis has been classified in earlier versions of the DSM as an anxiety disorder. In the current version it occupies its own category. Along with it are four new disorders: hoarding disorder, excoriation (skin picking) disorder, substance/medication-induced obsessive-compulsive and related disorder, and obsessive-compulsive and related disorder due to another medical condition

Primary medical disorders can produce syndromes very similar to OCD. OCD is conceptualized as a disorder of the basal ganglia. This association derives from the similarities between OCD and disorders associated with the basal ganglia, such as Sydenham's chorea and Huntington's disease. It is important to look for such neurological illnesses in the differential diagnosis. OCD, like many psychiatric illnesses, has an age of onset usually before 30 years, so new onset of OCD symptoms at a later age should heighten the examiner's suspicions of neurological illness. As noted, there is an association in children between an immune reaction to streptococcal infections and either initial symptoms or an exacerbation of OCD. Also, patients with Tourette's syndrome often also have obsessive compulsive symptoms.

Patients with psychotic symptoms may have obsessive thoughts and compulsive behaviors that can be difficult to distinguish from a patient with OCD who lacks insight. Some of the keys in differentiating include the fact that psychotic illnesses are typically associated with a large number of other features, and patients with OCD almost always know that their symptoms are unreasonable.

Matthew's seemingly bizarre behavior of gouging his eyes out when he was 40 years old pushed some to believe he had schizophrenia for many years. He must have had enormous suffering from this. However, applying DSM criteria, using the acrostic mnemonic BADHI, the patient lacked evidence of the main criteria for schizophrenia. He did not show B for behavior that is disorganized, A for affect or flattening or blunting of affect, D for delusions, as he does not believe in thought insertion bizarre delusions like aliens are putting these thoughts in his head. He also has no H, for hallucinations; and his speech is not I (illogical and incoherent). He basically does not meet the main criteria for schizophrenia and yet he carried the diagnosis for more than 20 years.

Matthew does not have compulsive symptoms at all such as excessive washing, checking, ordering, or mentally repeating words or counting.

He also meets criteria for major depression at the time of presentation. Obsessions commonly occur during depressive illness, and his worsen during times of depression. But his obsessive symptoms occur even when he is not depressed, and this differentiates him from having unipolar depression. Looking at his history over time, he clearly has recurrent or unipolar depression, current episode depressed. An acrostic for depression to remember the criteria, may be used, such as the acronym DEPRESSING, with the D for depression, E for energy, P for loss of pleasure or interest, R for retarded psychomotor activity (or agitation), E for eating changes in appetite or weight, S for suicidal thoughts, S for sleep problems, I for indecisive or poor concentration, N for negative thinking, and G for guilt.

It is important to rule out any history, even on medication, of mania or hypomania, because it can influence treatment and overall course of the illness. Over the years, this patient never exhibited any hypomanic or manic symptoms. The symptoms of mania may be represented by the acrostic mnemonic DIG FAST, with D for distractibility, I for impulsiveness (pleasure-seeking), G for grandiosity (elevated self-esteem), F for flight of ideas (or racing thoughts), A for increased goal-directed activities, S for decreased need for sleep, and T for talkativeness or pressured speech. Patients with mania feel a decreased need to sleep. This is distinguished from problems with anxious or depressed patients who have trouble falling asleep or waking up early with inability to fall back to sleep. Matthew did not have any of these symptoms.

Generalized anxiety disorder (GAD) should be considered also when thinking about OCD. One of the differences is that the anxiety in GAD is about real worries or concerns that may be recurrent. With obsessions, the obsessions are almost like a reentry mechanism or recurrent seizure.

A screening or follow-up tool, such as the Yale-Brown Obsessive Compulsive Scale may be helpful in checking on progress and substantiating improvements with treatment.

ETIOLOGY AND PATHOGENESIS

The etiology of obsessive-compulsive disorder has been partially elucidated over the past several decades. Current theories focus on neurochemical and neuroimaging studies. Neurochemically, OCD appears to be a dysfunction of the anxiety-regulating systems of the brain, specifically tied to serotonin transmitting neurons. In many areas of medicine the underlying disorder can be elucidated by the mechanisms of action of beneficial medications. In the case of OCD, selective serotonin reuptake inhibitors and tricyclic antidepressants that specifically increase serotonin have been the most effective treatments.

Neuroimmune mechanisms may play a part as well; following streptococcal infection in childhood some people develop severe obsessive symptoms in a disorder called "pediatric autoimmune neuropsychiatric disorders associated with streptococcal infection (PANDAS)."

Neuroimaging studies strongly suggest the involvement of the orbitofrontal cortex, the caudate nucleus, and the anterior cingulate cortex.

NATURAL COURSE WITHOUT TREATMENT

OCD usually begins in adolescence or early adulthood but occasionally begins in childhood. Most patients with this disorder have a chronic course that worsens and subsides, with worsening related to distress or depression. About 15% show a progressive deterioration in occupational and social functioning. A small percentage of patients have an episodic course with no symptoms or minimum symptoms between episodes. Most patients with this disorder experience some daily distress due to it.

EVIDENCE-BASED TREATMENT OPTIONS

Cognitive behavioral therapy (CBT), involving exposure and/or response prevention, is useful and considered the first line for treatment for OCD. This is especially helpful in treating compulsions. Pharmacological intervention is also very useful. The first medication found to be very helpful for OCD was the tricyclic antidepressant (TCA) clomipramine. When comparing the effect size in double-blind, placebo-controlled studies for clomipramine versus more recent selective serotonin reuptake inhibitors (SSRIs), it would lead one to believe that clomipramine is superior in efficacy. However, head-to-head comparisons do not differentiate between SSRIs and clomipramine. This might be due to a population that was relatively untreated at the time of the studies with clomipramine. Recent studies involving SSRIs have likely been in a more treatment-refractory population also. This may also help to explain some of the lower differentiation between antidepressants and placebo in more recent studies. Some experts advise not giving up with pharmacotherapy for OCD until trying clomipramine. We usually start with SSRIs due to the benign side effect profile. We generally should push to higher doses, such as the maximum tolerated doses in some patients. Higher response rates and a greater magnitude of symptom relief are likely at higher doses.

After the foregoing methods have been tried at adequate doses for adequate periods of time, less well-supported treatment strategies may be considered. These include augmenting SSRIs with clomipramine, buspirone, pindalol, or even once weekly oral morphine sulfate. The latter should be avoided in patients with contraindications to opiate administration. If clomipramine is added, we need to be cautious about cardiac and central nervous system side effects from the combination—such as the serotonin syndrome. Less well-supported monotherapies include D-amphetamine, tramadol, monoamine oxidase inhibitors (MAOIs), ondansetron, transcranial magnetic stimulation, and deep brain stimulation. In very severe and treatment-refractory cases, ablative neurosurgery may rarely be indicated, but only at very specialized sites with experts in both OCD and ablative neurosurgery.

Why have we not discussed benzodiazepines as at least a potential augmenter in OCD? Long-term use of benzodiazepines along with long-term use of opiates in nonterminal pain are two of the most controversial issues in all of medicine. Clonazepam has been used as an augmenter, especially in cases of comorbid other anxiety disorders. However, it should be remembered that there are almost no psychiatric disorders where benzodiazepines are the first-line treatment of choice. Also, it should be noted that chronic use of benzodiazepines in disorders such as post-traumatic stress disorder is now considered to be relatively contraindicated or tends to cause more harm than good. One of the biggest problems with benzodiazepines (along with opiates) is their abuse potential and diversion potential, including diversion to young people in the home or on the street. In general, almost all experts agree that we should generally avoid long-term use of benzodiazepines in former drug abusers. Some recommend refraining from outpatient prescription of benzodiazepines for more than one month. They may be used short-term, except in sleep apnea, severe respiratory compromise, or with a history of alcohol, other drug abuse, or antisocial personality disorder. Patients with significant cardiac disease and anxiety may, however, benefit from longer term use of benzodiazepines. These medicines are relatively safe and helpful in the immediate post-myocardial infarction period. One of the most difficult problems is whether to withdraw a patient from benzodiazepines when they have been taking them for more than a year. There are published recommendations related to this, and we need to remember to taper a patient gradually, perhaps over an eight-week period, and slower during the final two weeks.

Similar to treatment for depression, it is important to continue pharmacologic therapy for 8–12 weeks before giving up on a medicine. Adjunctive medications have been found to be useful, especially antipsychotics, with the most evidence being for risperidone. Haloperidol, lamotrigine, and buspirone have found some effectiveness as adjunctive medications also. Switching between SSRIs is common, and at least one trial of clomipramine should be tried prior to giving up on pharmacologic therapy.

Why should we switch, and how do we switch between medications? It has become apparent in recent years that "somewhat better" is no longer good enough. Also, true failure rate is very low (<10%) if using an adequate dose for an adequate period. SSRI success at a higher rate, however, occurs at 3–8 weeks for depression and as long as 12–26 weeks for OCD.

When we switch between psychotropics, there are a few situations where we have to have a wash-out period. There are really three things we are trying to avoid:

- Hypertensive crisis
- Serotonin syndrome (probably on a continuum)
- Tricyclic toxic level, leading to conduction delay

A hypertensive crisis may occur with combinations with MAOIs, and therefore washouts are very important in the following switches:

- TCAs or SSRIs to MAOIs
- MAOIs to TCAs or SSRIs
- MAOIs to tranylcypromine

Note that all of these situations involve MAOIs.

The serotonin syndrome may include the following symptoms:

- GI: cramping, bloating, diarrhea
- Neurological: tremulousness, myoclonus, dysarthria, incoordination, headache
- Cardiovascular: including hyper/hypotension, tachycardia, cardiac collapse
- Psychiatric: including disorientation, confusion, mania

- Diaphoresis
- Elevated temperature
- Hyperthermia
- Hyper-reflexia

Also, stopping a short-acting SSRI may lead to a serotonin withdrawal syndrome with the following symptoms:

- dysphoria
- anxiety
- irritability
- hot and cold flashes
- nausea, diarrhea
- fatigue, lightheadedness, dizziness
- headaches, insomnia, vivid dreams

A washout is highly advisable also in the following situations: short-acting SSRI (e.g., venlafaxine, paroxetine) to TCAs or atypical antidepressants, and MAOIs to MAOIs (but see above for even more mandatory washouts).

Finally, we are concerned about residual fluoxetine elevating TCA levels. Fluoxetine has a very long half-life, and its residual may substantially elevate blood levels of desipramine, other TCAs, or vanlafaxine, sometimes leading to unexpected toxicity during switching. This is especially relevant in the elderly. How long should we wait after stopping fluoxetine to start an MAOI? The answer is a whopping five weeks!

Switching from one SSRI to another was studied (specifically fluoxetine to paroxetine), and the conclusion was that it is safe to do an immediate switch.

Switching from fluoxetine to sertraline was also studied, and the conclusion also was that an immediate switch was safe. Investigators also found better efficacy when the conversion ratio was 20 mg to 75 mg rather than 20 mg to 50 mg.

Some experts advise not tapering in the following situations in general:

- one SSRI to another SSRI (although others would taper with paroxetine)
- an SSRI to mirtazapine
- an SSRI to venlafaxine

In these cases, it is reasonable to stop the first SSRI one day and start the other medicine the next day.

When is it best to taper the initial agent while the dose of the new agent is gradually increased? This is helpful with relatively short-acting antidepressants, like venlafaxine and paroxetine.

Also, when going from a TCA to an SSRI, we probably should taper the TCA to avoid cholinergic rebound symptoms. We also should taper after a patient is on a drug with efficacy, to monitor for symptom return. We usually use a very slow taper for this purpose.

CLINICAL COURSE WITH TREATMENT

Matthew was seen weekly by a psychologist, and she attempted such methods as using a rubber band to snap his wrist to try to get out of the obsession. The patient didn't have any compulsions, which would have been more amenable to behavioral treatments.

The consult-liaison psychiatrist made the diagnosis of OCD and major depression. The patient was on thiothixene, and attempts to taper it due to his tardive dyskinesia were not successful because of recurrence of symptoms of obsessions. The first-generation antipsychotic was eventually cross-tapered and changed to olanzapine at a 10 mg dose. The patient was originally on imipramine, but this was switched to the SSRI sertraline and later changed to fluvoxamine, which was gradually increased to a higher dose. Over the course of treatment, clomipramine was briefly tried, but constipation was a problem due to the higher anticholinergic effects of this TCA. On a combination of the SSRI fluvoxamine and olanzapine, the patient had marked improvement in both his obsessions and his depression. Of course, antipsychotics may also be useful as adjunctive treatments in depression.

Over the course of many more years of follow-up, the patient only occasionally had obsessions and in general did very well. Discharge was attempted, however by that time the family did not want the patient home, and the patient had become quite institutionalized.

After Matthew had a hip fracture late in life, he lost his ability to ambulate independently. He was no longer able to visit others in the hospital and perceived himself more as a burden than as a help to others at times.

The patient was also put on lithium as an adjunct for major depression, and this seemed to help. When we attempted to taper the lithium, his depression returned, as did his obsessions; he would wake up early in the morning and start worrying again. Because of concerns about potential side effects, it was used at a relatively low adjunctive level. He usually ran a lithium level of about 0.5 or 0.6 mEq/L. In terms of adjunctive medicines for depression, lithium probably has the best evidence for efficacy. Thyroid augmentation, atypical antipsychotics, and buspirone have also been found to be helpful.

SYSTEMS-BASED PRACTICE ISSUES AND CULTURAL CHALLENGES

One of the striking things in this case was the stigmatization of mental illness and the difficulty that staff had treating the patient at times as a reasonable and reasoned individual. Even though he had a significant psychiatric illness, he would carry on normal conversations and interactions with family and others. He participated in music therapy, including playing an instrument and singing. He would perform with other patients at occasional events.

The patient's comorbid blindness and earlier diagnosis of schizophrenia contributed to him being institutionalized and having the family move on to other aspects of their lives. This made it very difficult, even after he was doing well at the end, to move him out of the institution. The hip fracture didn't markedly interfere with his ability to function in later life.

REFERENCES AND RESOURCES

OCD became very prominent in the public in the 1980s, and it was featured on a variety of talk shows. On some shows people have discussed some of their obsessions, but they did not meet the criteria for the disorder. There is a television series (*Monk*) that portrays a detective with severe OCD. One of the best films that demonstrate someone with obsessive compulsive disorder was, *As Good as It Gets* with Jack Nicholson as the person with OCD.

Short DD. Pharmacologic treatment for anxiety disorders. In: Hubbard JR (Ed.), *Handbook of Stress Medicine: An Organ Systems Approach*. Boca Raton, FL: CRC Press, 1997.
Somro GM. Obsessive compulsive disorder. *Clin Evid* (Online) 2012 Jan.

CHAPTER **17**

Military Trauma

Frank Tellian, M.D.

CLINICAL PRESENTATION

Chief complaint: "My wife says I need help."

History of present illness: Fred is a 64-year-old male who presents by himself to a specialized post-traumatic stress disorder (PTSD) treatment program. He has depressed mood most of the time coupled with considerable irritability. He denies any vegetative symptoms of depression. He has never had what he would consider a panic attack, but he does frequently have feelings of being closed in and feels compelled to go outdoors to find relief. He has suicidal ideation intermittently, but has never made an actual suicide attempt. He has thoughts of harming others almost daily, usually in response to his heightened irritability. He does not have any specific target of these feelings and has never made any attempt to actually hurt another person. He denies any psychotic symptoms, such as hallucinations, delusions, or formal thought disorder. He does not sleep well and awakens frequently during the night.

He has frequent episodes of intrusive thoughts about his combat experiences in Vietnam. The frequency of these increased when the war in Iraq started and he was exposed to news reports about the war. He tries to avoid watching any news coverage of the current war and avoids things that remind him of his military service in Vietnam. He has no hobbies or other things that he truly enjoys doing, and he has very few friends. The latter situation may be due in part to his general distrust of people and his efforts to keep his distance from others. He states that several people have referred to him as "emotionally cold." He has difficulty sleeping and frequent anger outbursts but tries to minimize these. He is seeking help because his wife threatens divorce if he does not go for treatment. He is unclear about exactly what he feels and is uncertain whether he is "normal." His wife describes him as "cold, short-tempered, not liking anybody, and having negative thinking." He feels very uncomfortable in crowds and always feels on guard. He usually sits with his back to a wall when eating in a restaurant. Several times in the past he has accidentally struck someone after jumping when startled because he was approached from behind.

Fred has not slept well consistently since his return from Vietnam. He has frequent nightmares and recently these have been increasing. A recurring theme in his dreams is being lined up with other soldiers against a wall and being shot by a firing squad. He often awakens from these dreams feeling anxious and sweating. During a typical night he will awaken about six times, and this number has been increasing recently. Rather than try to force himself to go back to sleep, he will watch TV until he calms down.

During the day he feels anxious and tense much of the time. He has intrusive memories of his combat experiences coupled with depressed mood, loss of energy, and loss of interest in things he used to find interesting. Years ago he enjoyed going out and being active, but recently has lost interest in this. He gets aggravated very easily. Years ago he would drink alcohol heavily to calm himself down, but he no longer does this.

Psychiatric history: Fred first sought psychiatric treatment six years ago. He was enrolled in group therapy for PTSD. The therapist was a woman of Asian descent. He came to an early group session with alcohol and a gun in his car. Before arriving he had phoned the suicide hotline and told them what he was bringing. Police searched his car, found the alcohol and gun, and charged him. He went to court and got three days in jail and two years probation. Fred has no memory of the event and says that he felt no ill will toward the therapist, only toward "the whole system." Two years ago he entered a seven-week residential treatment program for PTSD that emphasized cognitive recognition therapy.

He was drafted and served in the army from 1968 to 1970 with one year in Vietnam. He achieved the rank of staff sergeant, was awarded two Purple Hearts and a Bronze Star, and received an honorable discharge. He then served in the National Guard until 2003, where he retired with a final rank of major. While in Vietnam he witnessed multiple traumatic events that involved death, wounding, and seeing mutilated bodies. He was a platoon leader and had 33 soldiers under his command. Several of them died in combat. Particularly he remembers sending his best friend back to base to get help during an enemy attack. The friend was killed along the way, and Fred frequently thinks about him. He was repeatedly under fire himself.

Relevant to his psychiatry history, Fred began drinking at the age of 19 and continued heavy alcohol use until age 24. Typically he would consume a fifth of vodka daily. He gradually decreased his use and currently drinks one or two beers daily, with an occasional drink of vodka. He has never attended any substance abuse treatment program. There is no history of physical or sexual abuse, either during childhood or as an adult.

Other medical history: Four years ago he was diagnosed with adenocarcinoma of the prostate after a biopsy. He was treated with external beam radiation coupled with LHRH agonist injections. There has been no evidence of recurrence.

Developmental history: Fred is the sixth of seven children. He was born and raised on a farm and his parents had little money. He describes his childhood as happy and denies any developmental problems. He had a good relationship with his siblings. He did well academically, maintaining an A average. He was not able to participate in any sports or extracurricular activities because he had to work on the family farm every day after school. He reports that his parents taught him values of honesty, discipline, responsibility, and hard work. Both of his parents are now deceased. He described his father as a hard worker, fair with his children, and endowed with much "common sense." His mother was easygoing, friendly, and provided a good home environment for the family.

Educational/occupational history: He graduated high school at age 17 and went to live with his older brother, working in the construction industry. A year later he was drafted into the military. He has held more than 20 different jobs in a span of over 30 years. The longest time at any one place was nine years. Primarily these were in construction, and he considers himself a carpenter. He is currently retired.

Family/social history: Fred is married and has been to the same woman for the past 43 years. They have two adult daughters, who both live in other states. The marital relationship has been strained for many years with a history of three periods of separation, each lasting up to six weeks. He maintains a close relationship with one of his daughters, but has much less contact with the other. He has little contact with his siblings, all of whom are alive, even though they do not live very far away. He was raised in the Baptist faith, but does not currently attend church on a regular basis. When questioned about his religious beliefs, he expressed the feeling that "God hates me, so I'm angry back at Him." Years ago he enjoyed traveling with his wife, but they have not made any trips in several years. He states that his hypervigilance makes travel more difficult.

Legal history: Fred reports no current legal difficulties.

Mental status exam: The patient presents as a 64-year-old male who appears in no acute distress. There was no psychomotor agitation or retardation. He was appropriately dressed, and his personal grooming and hygiene were good. He sat calmly in the chair during the interview process. He is cooperative with the examiner and displays no bizarre behaviors. He maintains good eye contact. He spoke clearly without any evidence of speech impediment. He is alert and oriented to person, time, place, and situation. He is able to do the serial 7's without difficulty. The patient's ability to recall recent events is intact. His memory for events in the remote past is excellent. There is no evidence of any deficits in attention or concentration. His affect is rather tense and nervous. His mood is self-rated as anxious, with no current suicidal and/or homicidal ideation. His thought processes are logical and linear with appropriate word usage. His speech is logical and coherent. There is no evidence of pressured speech. The production and quantity of his thoughts are within normal limits. He shows no evidence of loosening of association or flight of ideas. He expresses no delusional ideation. His ability to think abstractly is intact. He is able to do simple arithmetic and has a good fund of information about current events, consistent with his level of previous education. His insight is limited and his judgment is good. He reports no hallucinations, illusions, depersonalization, or derealization.

IMPAIRMENT IN FUNCTIONING

Fred shows substantial impairment in functioning. He struggles with reexperiencing nightmares, which interferes with restful sleep. This compounds his low motivation, reduced energy, and limited productivity. He numbs himself by watching TV and uses it to "zone out." Because of hypervigilance he has a great deal of difficulty in developing interpersonal relationships. His anxiety and its concomitant body language make him appear very rigid in his thinking and attitudes and he communicates bluntly without finesse. The effect on social interactions is profound. He does not get along well with authority, which has gone so far as to get him into legal trouble in the past. He does many things in a consistent order and seldom varies from his routine. This is displayed in such activities as the sequence in which he brushes his teeth. He expresses the hope that he might someday be less regimented in his thinking. He notices that his relationships with his wife and daughters are strained and that he has few friends or activities that he enjoys doing.

DSM DIAGNOSIS

Fred experiences symptoms consistent with the diagnosis of PTSD according to the latest DSM-5 criteria (exposure, intrusion, avoidance, arousal, and negative mood or thoughts). First, there must be exposure to a life-threatening or violent event through direct experience or description by others. The traumatic event is re-experienced through invasive memories, dreams, flashbacks, physiological reactions or psychological distress. There is avoidance of internal or external stimuli that cue reminders of the trauma. The trauma experience has increased levels of arousal, vigilance and reactivity to the environment. Lastly, the traumatic event has negatively altered thoughts, emotions, and perceptions.

Fred has frequent upsetting memories of his traumas. He has recurrent dreams about the events. At times he feels as though aspects of the traumas were happening again (flashbacks). When current situations remind him of his past experiences, he responds with psychological distress coupled with physical symptoms such as elevated pulse, sweating, and breathing difficulty. This patient avoids thinking about and talking about his combat experiences. He does not watch news programs on TV if they are about war. He also tries to stay away from people of Asian descent. This patient has difficulty falling and staying asleep. He reports trouble concentrating on tasks. He is highly irritable and is prone to angry outbursts. He is extremely watchful and feels "on guard" at all times. He is easily startled.

In addition to PTSD, he has a substantial history of alcohol abuse. Medical problems include adenocarcinoma of the prostate, currently in remission. Stressors are a strained marital relationship, discord with siblings, and adjustment to retirement. However, Fred is willing to work on his present stressors through individual counseling and/or family therapy. He recognizes that they are affecting his emotional conditions. The initial working diagnosis is PTSD and alcohol abuse.

EPIDEMIOLOGY

Any event that poses a serious danger to the individual can be a potential trauma. Although Fred's case involves exposure to military combat and hostile enemy combat actions, other nonmilitary traumas may also lead to PTSD. These may include rape, personal criminal assault, serious physical illness or dangerous surgical procedures, automobile accidents, and disasters (both natural and man-made) such as earthquakes, floods, fire, and hurricanes. Prevalence rates for PTSD as reported in the literature have varied primarily due to methodological issues. A reasonable estimate is that in the United States, about 10% of people will show some symptoms of PTSD at some point in their lives. This coincides with a one-year prevalence of about 5%.

A number of factors have been associated with an increased risk of developing PTSD. Recent location of the individual in an area or country with considerable social unrest or civil conflict may increase the likelihood of PTSD. This would include combat zones. Other risk factors that influence the development of PTSD include a history of a previously diagnosed mental illness, poverty, a lack of social support (for children this may involve poor parenting, whereas in adults it may be reflected in few prior friends, lack of social involvements, etc.), and an initial reaction to the trauma that involved a very high level of emotional symptomatology.

Overall, women have a fourfold higher likelihood of developing PTSD than do men. Although women have a markedly higher risk of being sexually assaulted (and sexual assault constitutes the single most frequent trauma suffered by women with PTSD), men are more likely to develop PTSD after being sexually assaulted. But if the assault is nonsexual in nature, the risk for PTSD in men drops precipitously. For natural disasters and motor vehicle accidents, men and women display approximately the same rates of PTSD.

As in Fred's case, military combat may cause a delayed form of PTSD. Soldiers exposed to combat-related traumatic experiences may be more likely to display PTSD symptoms six months after the trauma than immediately following it. Thus an assessment for combat-related PTSD should be done about 6 to 12 months after the traumatic experience occurred. A study indicated a strong relationship between the amount of trauma exposure and rates of PTSD and with using stricter criteria, 18.7% of the Vietnam veterans met the criteria for war-related PTSD at some point and 9.1% still had PTSD when assessed 11–12 years later. It demonstrated the large prevalence and chronicity of this challenging condition. Fred is among one of the Vietnam War veterans who still suffers from this tenacious condition.

DIFFERENTIAL DIAGNOSIS

Adjustment disorder may be the more accurate diagnosis when one or more of the diagnostic categories for PTSD are not fully met. Thus a stressor that is not extreme (life-threatening) that leads to PTSD-like symptoms may be better labeled as adjustment disorder. This may also apply to an extreme stressor that does not produce the full picture of PTSD symptoms. A key issue requiring careful examination is the question of whether the symptoms, such as avoidance, increased arousal, numbing, and others, were present before the trauma occurred. To meet the diagnostic criteria for PTSD, all the qualifying symptoms must have their origin with the traumatic event. Pretrauma symptomatology points to a more likely diagnosis of a chronic anxiety and/or affective disorder.

Acute stress disorder involves the development of PTSD-related symptoms within one month of the trauma and their subsequent resolution within that same time period. A diagnosis of acute stress disorder may be changed to PTSD if the initial symptoms persist beyond one month.

Obsessive compulsive disorder may produce intrusive thoughts, but it may often lack the strong relationship to a traumatic event.

Reexperiencing aspects of the trauma (referred to as flashbacks) may be confused with the hallucinatory experiences of various psychotic disorders, such as schizophrenia, mood disorders with psychotic features, or delirium. The patient should be examined for the diagnostic criteria of those disorders.

Because the occurrence of a life-threatening stressor may subsequently involve legal proceedings or potential financial compensation, the possibility of malingering must always receive some consideration. An exposure(s) to trauma being a key element in view of differential diagnosis, it is important that the clinician should begin with broad questions about experiences, then move to more specific behaviorally anchored questions to obtain more reliable information. There are multiple assessment tools available to the clinician, the DSM-IV version of the Clinician-Administered PTSD Scale (CAPS) has been the "gold standard" assessment of PTSD and is now the most widely used diagnostic interview. Others are the Life Events checklist, the Traumatic Stress Schedule, the Traumatic History Questionnaire, the Traumatic Life Events Questionnaire, the Traumatic Events Scale, and the Posttraumatic Stress Diagnostic Scale.

ETIOLOGY AND PATHOGENESIS

The question of why some individuals develop PTSD when exposed to a traumatic event and others with the same exposure do not is an active issue of current research. There is strong interest in finding any variables that might serve as predictors of PTSD risk. In terms of neuroanatomy, MRI scanning has shown PTSD patients to have a smaller volume in the left amygdala, the anterior cingulate cortex, and the hippocampus compared to age-matched controls. When neurochemistry is examined, PTSD patients have been found to have lower levels of glucocorticoids and higher levels of norepinephrine than their non-PTSD comparisons. Along with these findings have come an expected up-regulation of the receptors for glucocorticoids and down-regulation of the receptors for norepinephrine in the central nervous system. In terms of brain functioning, studies have found a general trend for PTSD sufferers to show decreased left hemisphere functional ability compared to age-matched controls.

An interesting theory about the etiology of PTSD that has been garnering some research evidence in its favor is the sensitization model. In this theory the patient is subjected to multiple traumatic events throughout life. Initial exposures produce no overt symptoms but seem to lead to a lowered threshold for subsequent traumas to produce active PTSD.

Fred grew up in a farming family with six other siblings under hard-working parents. He had no known development issues as a child. His academic performance was more than average. He had no medical conditions as he grew up. Based on the historical information provided, it is reasonable to assume that Fred developed a healthy ego function. The major insult to his inner world was caused by the specific trauma of his Vietnam experiences. Despite his relatively efficient ego function, the trauma was significantly damaging enough for him to experience a mental breakdown. His PTSD symptomatology has caused significant impairment in his functional ability and interpersonal relationships and considerable load on his marriage. His initial symptoms of PTSD were probably precipitated by the news about the Iraq wars, exacerbated by concurrent depressive symptoms, and perpetuated by his heavy drinking and other unclear stressors at that time.

NATURAL COURSE WITHOUT TREATMENT

A traumatic experience or prolonged exposure to trauma produces profound changes in a person's inner world. As in traumatized children damaged by physical, emotional, or sexual abuse or abandonment, traumatic experience will grossly impede normative development and change the way the individual sees the world and him- or herself. When unresolved, the affected individual may experience abnormal or excessive reactions in the face of stress in the external environment. Once predisposed through a previous traumatic event, perceived stressors in current life may precipitate or provoke significant symptomatology that may be perpetuated by specific factors in the person's life, such as marital discord, medical conditions, substance abuse, and so on.

The course of PTSD is fairly chronic. The onset of symptoms usually occurs within a few months of experiencing the trauma, although as previously noted combat-related PTSD may only manifest itself after six months or longer. Some authorities on the disorder have speculated about the soldier's ongoing involvement in combat (if he is not severely injured) as causing a delay in the emergence of active symptoms until after his removal from the combat theater. Sometimes this may only become manifest after his discharge from the military and return to civilian life. While some studies have found approximately one-fourth to one-third of patients to be asymptomatic at one year, the course for the vast majority is a chronic one.

Occupational impairment due to PTSD can be severe. It may be marked by frequent conflicts with bosses and coworkers. This may result in repeated job changes, either voluntarily by the patient or imposed by the employer. Job satisfaction is typically low and the patient will try to force himself to work despite his symptoms. In general, PTSD sufferers do better at jobs where they have minimal exposure to other workers or the public.

Intimate relationships such as marriage may be highly problematic for a PTSD patient. Their heightened arousal level and avoidance behavior may severely stress the relationship. Spouses may find the process of accommodating the patient's symptoms (for example, sitting with his back to the wall at a restaurant) to be more than they can tolerate. Fear of crowds may preclude a PTSD patient from attending a child's sporting event and lead the child to feel that his parent does not care for him.

Social isolation is frequent in PTSD. The patient may have few friends and not engage in many social events. Interactions with neighbors can become strained. Some patients will move to remote rural locations to avoid social contacts.

Of those combat veterans who display symptoms immediately after the trauma, almost half may show spontaneous improvement after six months. If the trauma also involves actual physical injury to the soldier, the risk of developing PTSD increases significantly. Some studies have found traumatic brain injury to be especially highly correlated with PTSD. Approximately half of soldiers who sustained traumatic brain injury while in combat may be expected to go on to develop symptoms of PTSD. Also soldiers who exhibit PTSD symptoms are at increased risk for developing other psychiatric disorders several years later compared to their non-PTSD fellow veterans. These may include affective disorders, anxiety disorders (other than PTSD), panic disorders, and substance abuse problems.

Without proper therapeutic interventions, Fred is very likely to suffer from PTSD symptoms, which would further impair his social functioning and become taxing on his marriage. His condition may be also complicated by the above-mentioned psychiatric conditions. Self-destructive behavior can also be an outcome; however, with treatment, his resilience factors can be enhanced and might bring forth a positive outcome. The factors that he had a relatively normal childhood, strong work ethic, at least average intelligence, spiritual background, leadership role in military service, and so forth should be considered.

EVIDENCE-BASED TREATMENT OPTIONS

Both psychotherapy and medications have been used in the treatment of PTSD. Many patients are eventually treated with a combination of both. The majority of experts recommend that psychotherapy alone be the initial treatment of choice.

Out of the numerous psychotherapies that have been tried, the research litera-ture most favors the trauma-focused cognitive behavioral therapies (CBTs). These include exposure therapy, cognitive therapy, and training in coping skills. The underlying theory behind the psychotherapy of PTSD is based in behavior-ism. The traumatic event is an aversive unconditioned stimulus. The response to the original exposure to this event was fear. Certain current stimuli (which are conditioned stimuli) become associated with the original trauma. These may be things in the environment that remind the patient of the original trauma, includ-ing his own thoughts about it. The current stimuli elicit the same fear response the original trauma did. Under ideal conditions the individual would continue to expose himself to the conditioned stimuli. As they are repeatedly experienced without any accompanying danger, the linkage to the unconditioned stimulus is broken and the fear response extinguishes. In the PTSD patient, the avoidance behaviors act to prevent that extinction from occurring and the fear reaction remains linked to the conditioned stimulus. Experts have posited the emergence of a fear network that the patient seeks to avoid or escape from, which leads to the remainder of PTSD symptoms.

Therapy seeks to have the patient activate the fear memory. Then corrective information is presented to him that is not compatible with his symptom pic-ture. The patient learns to diminish and eventually extinguish his fear response in the presence of reminders of the trauma by realizing that exposure to the reminders does not lead to recurrence of the original trauma. Cognitive therapy seeks to change how the individual thinks about events in his or her life. Indi-viduals use their thoughts to affect their emotional state by the meanings they give to events. The therapist strongly encourages the patient to take a more real-istic approach in how he thinks about the trauma and his reactions to it. Studies of the efficacy of cognitive therapy in PTSD have generally been favorable.

An example of this approach is as follows. A patient was in combat, and he witnessed his good friend get shot and killed by enemy fire. He blamed himself for the death, feeling that he should have acted differently and his friend would have survived. The therapist works on getting the patient to realize that his actions were appropriate, that his friend's death was due to enemy actions, and that the patient could not have prevented it. By reevaluating his perceptions, the patient was able to stop blaming himself and subsequently was able to extin-guish the avoidance behaviors for the trauma.

Exposure therapy focuses on the patient reexperiencing the trauma in a con-trolled therapeutic setting. The absence of danger leads to a gradual lessening of the fear response. As the patient experiences his memories of the trauma again and again without any danger or injury, he eventually learns that they are not dangerous. This leads to a gradual reduction in the avoidance behaviors. Expo-sure therapy may be done using memories alone, may involve including some aspects of the original trauma experience (such as a photo of the location, a piece of military regalia), or may involve a dramatic portrayal of the trauma using sev-eral people. The patient, under guidance from the therapist, then processes his emotional reactions to the exposure. The therapist also questions the patient about his thoughts on the exposure, challenging and correcting maladaptive thought processes, especially as they relate to guilt, blame, or responsibility. The patient may also be encouraged to continue the exposure process after the formal therapy session through the assignment of homework, thereby further strengthening the extinction of the fear responses' connection to the memories of the trauma. Recently virtual reality technology has also been employed as part of the exposure process. This has been successfully used with combat-related PTSD patients. Studies of the efficacy of exposure therapy have found favorable results in all trials, although the extent of positive results has varied.

CBT incorporates both cognitive and behavioral aspects in the treatment of PTSD. It usually involves only the patient in therapy, but some trials have used it with couples. Data on couples therapy are promising. For PTSD patients it combines exposure to traumatic memories with cognitive therapy. Studies of the efficacy of CBT have generally found positive results, although there has been variability due to the various approaches that fall under this type of therapy.

Eye movement desensitization and reprocessing (EMDR) uses visual tracking to provide a nonfearful activity to the patient while he visualizes parts of the trauma and processes his emotions. He repeats the visual tracking and trauma recollection until his anxiety decreases. Studies of the efficacy of EMDR have produced mixed results. Further investigation is necessary.

Coping skills training and psychodynamic psychotherapy have been used in treating PTSD. Thus far, convincing evidence of their effectiveness does not exist.

Medications are widely used for the treatment of PTSD. In the treatment of many other psychiatric disorders, there is strong evidence that the earlier pharmacological therapy is initiated, the less likely the illness is to become chronic. Such evidence has not been found for PTSD. There appears to be no benefit to early initiation of pharmacotherapy for PTSD, and most authorities recommend that psychotherapy be tried first by itself. Medications have been most effective in improving mood and reducing hyperarousal. Results for the use of medications in the treatment of other PTSD symptoms, such as reexperiencing, emotional numbing, and excessive avoidance, have generally been less robust, although individual cases of positive results are reported. No consistently effective predictors of positive response have been identified thus far.

Selective serotonin reuptake inhibitors (SSRIs) are the most widely used medications for PTSD. Studies of their efficacy have generally been positive, but some have found little benefit, and the methodology of some has been less than ideal. Evidence of any kind of dose-response relationship in the use of SSRIs is lacking, so most experts recommend that initial dosages be at the lower end of the typical therapeutic range and advanced very slowly. In actual practice, many PTSD patients eventually end up on dosages of SSRIs at the upper end of the therapeutic spectrum. Therapy with a given drug should be continued for at least six weeks before it is considered a treatment failure. Patients should also be educated about the gradual onset of any benefits.

Serotonin-norepinephrine reuptake inhibitors (SNRIs) have been found to be superior to placebo for treating PTSD. No studies have directly compared this category to SSRIs for efficacy. Older antidepressants (tricyclic antidepressants, monoamine oxidase inhibitors, and atypical antidepressants) have not been shown to be effective in well-done studies. However, because of their significant sedation potential, trazodone and (to some extent) mirtazapine are often combined with an SSRI in an effort to facilitate sleep.

Atypical antipsychotics have been tried in many PTSD patients. The evidence that they are of direct benefit when used as sole therapy is less than impressive. The largest study of this class of drugs was done on combat-related PTSD, and efficacy for other types of PTSD has been based on fairly small studies. However, since the choice of medication options in PTSD patients who fail to respond to multiple SSRI trials is limited, the addition of an atypical antipsychotic medication as an adjunct to an SSRI is reasonable. Besides an improvement in mood, reexperiencing and hyperarousal symptoms seem the most likely to respond to this class of drugs.

Alpha-adrenergic receptor blockers seemed a reasonable candidate for treating the hyperarousal symptoms of PTSD. A few small studies did find benefit from using prazosin, especially for sleep and nightmares. Further investigations are under way. Of course, the impact of prazosin on blood pressure must be considered.

Benzodiazepines are frequently used in the treatment of PTSD, especially for the symptoms of anxiety and hyperarousal. This occurs even in the face of an overall lack of any objective evidence from well-controlled studies that this class of medications is of benefit for PTSD. Benzodiazepines may have a place in the emergency treatment of severe anxiety, but evidence that they are of benefit as a long-term treatment is lacking. But patients will frequently ask for this type of medication and insist that they cannot function without it. Of all the benzodiazepines, alprazolam seems to be the one most often requested by patients and may have the highest abuse potential.

Mood stabilizers are another category of medications that seemed reasonable to try for PTSD. Yet the evidence that they are effective has not emerged from the few proper studies that have been completed on them.

CLINICAL COURSE WITH MANAGEMENT AND TREATMENT

The treatment for Fred's PTSD was multifaceted. He was initially evaluated by a psychiatrist who opted for sertraline, one of the SSRIs, and simultaneously referred him to a therapist. He was started on 50 mg once a day, but it was gradually titrated to 150 mg once a day over a three-month period. Fortunately, he could tolerate this agent well without side effects such as sedation and nausea. He was also placed on mirtazapine 7.5 mg at bedtime for his chronic insomnia. Mirtazapine was selected because he already has a past history of substance and alcohol abuse and it doesn't cause tolerance or dependence. Also, it may stimulate his appetite. His therapist decided to provide CBT primarily because Fred was very motivated, intelligent, and able to grasp its goals. As his PTSD symptoms improved, he was more focused and invested in the assignments given by his therapist. When his symptoms were in fair control, he and his wife were referred to a family therapist. His wife thought the therapy was very educational and enlightening in the sense that she was able to understand the nature of Fred's condition and learned how to cope with his symptoms. Simultaneously, he started with PTSD group therapy. For the past six months, he has been almost symptom-free with this interdisciplinary treatment approach and was able to avoid inpatient treatment.

SYSTEMS-BASED PRACTICE ISSUES

Credentials for the trauma-based counselor are not clearly defined yet. In reality, most mental health counselors may seek educational opportunities through trauma-related lectures, seminars, or self-study materials. In the Department of Veterans Affairs system, combat-related PTSD patients benefit from the existence of a large and increasingly experienced system of health care, with treatment offered through local Veterans Outreach Centers, regional hospitals, and several national PTSD treatment programs. Most of the counselors are social workers and clinical psychologists by profession. Other types of PTSD patients in the community have more difficulty identifying therapists who are particularly qualified to treat this condition. Without experienced therapists, the interventions may retraumatize and cause more harm. Remember the endless abreaction of former PTSD groups over years and how a veteran in these groups developed a solid trauma identity that was more refractory to treatment. In terms of this challenging condition being commonly a cause of psychiatric disability, mental health professionals are keenly aware of the patient's primary and secondary gain. Astute clinicians should always pay attention to this issue that is inherent in this condition. Generally, the best way to tell malingered illness is to be firmly guided by the overall clinical picture that the individual brings.

LEGAL, ETHICAL, AND CULTURAL CHALLENGES

The role of the PTSD patient as a victim elicits various legal, ethical, and cultural issues. Soldiers are expected to be brave and fearless, making the admission of PTSD-related fear and avoidance difficult for many veterans to accept. Rape victims frequently question their own role in bringing on the assault and may blame themselves for the attack. Rescuers often need to continue working at professions where they will repeatedly be exposed to future life-threatening situations, and admission of PTSD symptoms may lead to the loss of employment or a lack of trust from other rescue workers. It is widely known that the complication of service-connected disability incentives for feigning PTSD is a challenging issue throughout various systems. It can be more challenging in the VA system largely because of the nature of the service that individual veterans provided to society. Nonetheless, it is a clinician's responsibility to firmly stand on his or her clinical judgment for the sake of the individual trauma victims.

HISTORY AND TERMS

In the early 19th century, military physicians started diagnosing soldiers with "exhaustion" after the stress of battle. This exhaustion was characterized by mental shutdown due to individual or group trauma. Prior to the 20th century, soldiers were expected always to be emotionally tough and show no fear in the midst of combat. The only treatment for this exhaustion was to relieve the afflicted from front-line duty until symptoms subsided, then return to battle. During the intense and frequently repeated stress, the soldiers became fatigued as a part of their body's natural shock reaction. Although PTSD-like symptoms have also been recognized in combat veterans of many military conflicts, the modern understanding of PTSD dates from the 1970s, largely as a result of the problems that were still being experienced by U.S. military veterans of the Vietnam War. Previous diagnoses now considered historical equivalents of PTSD include shell shock, battle fatigue, or traumatic war neurosis. The term *posttraumatic stress disorder* was coined in the mid-1970s and eventually added to the DSM-III, urged partly by the increasing recognition of the syndrome among the Vietnam War veterans.

REFERENCES AND RESOURCES

Clark AA, Owens GP. Attachment, personality characteristics, and posttraumatic stress disorder in U.S. veterans of Iraq and Afghanistan. *J Trauma Stress* 2012 Dec;25(6): 657–64.

Dohrenwend BP, Turner JB, Turse NA, et al. The psychological risks of Vietnam for US veterans: a revisit with new data and methods. *Science* 2006;313:979–82.

Hall T, Galletly C, Clark CR, Veltmeyer M, Metzger LJ, Gilbertson MW, Orr SP, Pitman RK, McFarlane A. The relationship between hippocampal asymmetry and working memory processing in combat-related PTSD—a monozygotic twin study. *Biol Mood Anxiety Disord* 2012 Dec;2(1):21.

Miller LJ. Prazosin for the treatment of posttraumatic stress disorder sleep disturbances. *Pharmacotherapy* 2008 May;28(5):656–66.

Morissette SB, Woodward M, Kimbrel NA, Meyer EC, Kruse MI, Dolan S, Gulliver SB. Deployment-related TBI, persistent postconcussive symptoms, PTSD, and depression in OEF/OIF veterans. *Rehabil Psychol* 2011 Nov;56(4):340–50.

Mohamed S, Rosenheck R. Pharmacotherapy for older veterans diagnosed with posttraumatic stress disorder in Veterans Administration. *Am J Geriatr Psych* 2008 Oct;16(10): 804–12.

Norrholm SD, Jovanovic T, Olin IW, Sands LA, Karapanou I, Bradley B, Ressler KJ. Fear extinction in traumatized civilians with posttraumatic stress disorder: relation to symptom severity. *Biol Psych* 2011 Mar 15;69(6):556–63.

Rothbaum BO, Rizzo AS, Difede J. Virtual reality exposure therapy for combat-related posttraumatic stress disorder. *Ann N Y Acad Sci* 2010 Oct;1208:126–32.

Shin LM, Lasko NB, Macklin ML, Karpf RD, Milad MR, Orr SP, Goetz JM, Fischman AJ, Rauch SL, Pitman RK. Resting metabolic activity in the cingulate cortex and vulnerability to posttraumatic stress disorder. *Arch Gen Psych* 2009 Oct;66(10):1099–107.

American Psychiatric Association's Practice Guideline (www.psych.org)

National Center for PTSD (www.ptsd.va.gov)

Regarding Henry (1991) focuses on a New York City lawyer (played by Harrison Ford) who struggles to regain his memory and recover his speech and mobility after he survives a shooting.

CHAPTER 18

Generalized Anxiety

Azziza Bankole, M.D.

CLINICAL PRESENTATION

Chief complaint: "I just can't stop worrying. I worry about everything."

History of present illness: Katherine is a 39-year-old woman who presents with complaints of increasing anxiety over the past year. She comes to her appointment alone. She reports that over the past year she has become increasingly worried about losing her job. Due to the current economic difficulties, a number of her family members and friends had been laid off work. However, the business that employed her remains economically viable and is even expanding its workforce. Despite this she continually worries about her job security. Katherine had no history of work-related problems or disciplinary actions. She had started to worry about meeting deadlines and completing the most mundane tasks. She experienced increasing stress at work and was unable to control her worries. One of her colleagues at work inquired if everything was okay because her work performance on a project had not been as good as it had been in the past.

Her anxiety has also extended to her home life. She has become increasingly worried about her family's finances should she lose her job. She has three children, and the oldest has just started high school. She worries that the family will never be able to afford college tuition for the children. Her husband is self-employed and his business has been slow. She has increasing conflicts with her husband over her continual anxiety. He has stated that she was "making mountains out of molehills."

Katherine is experiencing a number of physical symptoms, which leads her to worry about her physical health as well. She started having difficulty with initiating and maintaining sleep. She is unable to sleep because she is constantly thinking about her work, family, and finances. She provides a history of reduced energy levels and poor concentration. She feels tense with increased muscle tension, frequent headaches, palpitations, and shakiness. She finds it very difficult to relax. She used to enjoy needlework prior to the onset of her symptoms, but now she is no longer able to hold the needle steady. She has seen her primary care provider on a number of occasions with regard to these symptoms and various tests have been performed with normal results. At her last visit she was referred to psychiatry. Per the referral received from her primary care provider, Katherine was becoming increasingly disabled by her symptoms at work and at home.

Katherine feels anxious all the time. There is no history of discrete episodes of increased or profound anxiety. She denies any anxiety associated with being in a social environment or places where there were lots of people, for example, the mall or a supermarket. In fact, she has always enjoyed social situations. She had been feeling depressed on most days for most of the day until she started taking an herbal remedy that was marketed as helping reduce stress and improve mood. It had been recommended by a friend. A quick online search revealed that the herbal remedy in question contained St. John's wort, which could account for the reduction in her depressive symptoms.

Katherine denies having any suicidal or homicidal thoughts, intent, or plan. She did not have reduced interest in things but stated that she has not been able to enjoy her work as she had done in the past. She is afraid of heights and avoided certain bridges and roads as a result. There is no history of obsessive or compulsive symptoms.

There is no history of delusions or hallucinations in any modality. However, Katherine did mention that there were times when she felt she could see something just out of her visual field range and when she would turn to look there would be nothing there. She describes feeling on edge quite often. She has not experienced feelings about her thoughts being manipulated in any way or being able to do so to other people's thoughts. She also denies having ever received messages from different media. She has no history of manic or hypomanic symptoms. She did not use anything other than over-the-counter medications to help with her symptoms (acetaminophen for pain, diphenhydramine for insomnia, and the herbal remedy noted above). She quit smoking many years ago but has found herself thinking about starting again in response to her current symptoms.

Katherine really wants to get better and be able to get on with her life. She agreed to come for this visit because of the stress her symptoms have had on her marriage and her work.

Past psychiatric history: Katherine reports a history of depression in her early twenties, which was treated with psychotherapy over several years. There is no history of any suicide attempts or deliberate self-harm. She has never been hospitalized in a psychiatric facility.

Substance abuse history: Katherine used cannabis as a teenager. For the last two months, she has been drinking a glass of wine with dinner every night since realizing that this seems to calm her nerves a bit. She has not been increasing her alcohol intake. She believes that she should reduce her alcohol consumption but does not feel angry about others criticizing her drinking, feeling guilty about drinking, or ever needing an eye-opener. She has not had any blackouts, hallucinations, delusions, or withdrawal symptoms as a result of alcohol. She has not abused any other substances, either illicit or prescribed. She has never had any history of legal problems related to substance abuse.

Family psychiatric history: Katherine gives a history of depression in her mother, a maternal aunt, and a number of other family members. Her mother has received electroconvulsive treatment. There is also a history of anxiety in her sister who is currently stable on an antidepressant. Her paternal grandfather had alcohol dependence, as did one of her paternal uncles. There is no history of completed suicides in her family, but she did report a history of suicide attempts in an unknown relative.

Legal history: None reported.

Past medical history: Katherine does not have any chronic medical problems.

Social history: Katherine was born and raised in a two-parent family. She is the youngest of three siblings. She had an "okay" childhood and denies any history of physical, mental, or sexual abuse. She grew up not understanding what was going on with her mother at times. Her mother would leave home for a while and her father took care of the family in her absence. As an adult, she realized that her mother had been severely depressed at those times and had been hospitalized. Looking back, Katherine realizes that her father did a lot to help keep the family together and lessen the effect of her mother's depression on the family, especially on her and her siblings.

Katherine is a high school graduate. There is no history of bullying in high school, but she went through a rebellious phase when she smoked cigarettes and cannabis and drank alcohol during her sophomore and junior years. After high school she completed a two-year associate's degree program. She married her high school sweetheart at the age of 20 years. This is the first marriage for Katherine and her husband. They have three children—a daughter age 14 and two sons age 11 and 6. Her husband is self-employed. Katherine works as a mid-level manager in the health care industry.

Financially, Katherine and her husband have had some difficulties. Her husband's business is not as robust as it used to be, and they are contemplating remortgaging their home. This is another area of almost incessant worry for her.

She has good social support from her immediate family as well as her extended family. She is close to her sister, who has suffered from anxiety symptoms in the past. However, she is reluctant to talk in detail with her siblings about what she is going through. She has been contemplating talking to her sister about her sister's symptoms and how she had dealt with them.

Mental status examination: Katherine is a 39-year-old woman who appears her stated age. She is appropriately dressed, well kempt, and cooperative. She is restless and displays a fine motor tremor. She is not agitated. There is no psychomotor retardation present. Her gait is normal. She makes limited eye contact and at times appears to be making an effort to avoid eye contact. She sits hunched in her chair as if to protect herself. She appears to be distractible. Her speech is hesitant with average volume and speed. She speaks with an anxious tone. There is no latency in her speech.

Katherine is awake and alert. She is oriented in time, place, and person. Her registration is good but she displays some difficulty with immediate recall of three objects. This difficulty may be related to limited attention and concentration as a result of her anxiety. Her affect is of reduced range, stable, and increased intensity. Her affect is appropriate to content and situation. Her mood is anxious and low. She describes her mood as "really worried." She does not have any suicidal or homicidal ideation, intent, or plan.

Katherine has a good vocabulary. She displays an appropriate thought stream. Her thoughts are logical and goal directed. No delusions are elicited from this assessment. Her ability to think in an abstract manner is good. She expresses a number of preoccupations—potential for danger, financial ruin. She has some difficulty completing the serial 7's test. She displays an average fund of knowledge. Her insight into her illness is limited and her judgment is fair.

Katherine does not have hallucinations in any sensory modality. She is not experiencing illusions, depersonalization, or derealization.

IMPAIRMENT IN FUNCTIONING

Functional impairment tends to be worse in the presence of poorer adaptive supports. Katherine has been experiencing a substantial and increasing level of impairment in her functioning. The quality of her work has started to slip as a result of her constant worrying and the almost paralyzing effect it has on her ability to complete her work in the required time frame. Should her symptoms remain untreated, it is reasonable to envision a worsening situation with regard to her job security. This in effect would have a markedly detrimental effect on her finances, her feelings of self-worth, as well as her marriage.

DSM DIAGNOSIS

Katherine's clinical picture reveals a mixture of anxiety, depressive, and somatic symptoms. She does not present with any marked impairment in her thought process. At this time she meets the criteria for a number of DSM diagnoses but Generalized Anxiety Disorder (GAD) seems predominant and primary. Individuals with GAD are unable to control excessive worry about multiple life issues and situations. During a majority of their days they experience tension, distractibility, relentless irritability, fatigue, sleep problems, and numerous somatic complaints.

Katherine's stressors include concerns about work, especially her declining productivity and how this negatively impacts her finances and the effect of the previous issue on it, as well as interpersonal difficulties. She has good and stable support systems. She has been able to develop and maintain good relationships in different areas of her life over many years. She is employed and her position has brought her satisfaction. These factors, in effect, help increase the probability of Katherine responding to the prescribed treatments and therefore the probability of having a good outcome.

EPIDEMIOLOGY

GAD is a relatively common disorder and has been found to run a chronic course. Twelve-month and lifetime prevalence rates of 2.1% and 4.1%, respectively, have been reported in literature. GAD is twice as common in women as in men. As a woman, Katherine has a higher risk of developing GAD than would her brother. Onset of symptoms in GAD tends to be at a later age when compared to some other anxiety disorders such as phobias. Katherine is in her late thirties. In the national Comorbidity Replication study, Kessler et al. (2005) found the projected lifetime risk at age 75 years to be 8.3%.

DIFFERENTIAL DIAGNOSIS

It is often the case that a person meeting criteria for one anxiety disorder will also meet the criteria for other anxiety disorders. The differential diagnoses in Katherine's case include:

- Anxiety disorder secondary to a general medical condition, for instance, pheochromocytoma, hyperthyroidism. Katherine has undergone a thorough medical workup and no medical problems were reported.
- Substance-induced anxiety disorder, for example, caffeine-induced anxiety disorder. Katherine's history of increasing alcohol intake and smoking began after the onset of her main symptoms of anxiety, not prior. Long-term misuse/abuse of alcohol or illicit substances result in more complex symptomatology and a disorder that is much more resistant to treatment.
- Adjustment disorder with anxious mood. Time line is less than six months and symptoms occur in response to a specific stressor or within three months of the onset of the stressor. Katherine's symptoms have been present for at least six months, and there is no history of a specific stressor triggering her symptoms.
- Of course, other anxiety spectrum disorders. Specific phobia: Katherine does appear to meet criteria for fear of heights. Panic disorder: Katherine does not experience panic attacks, discrete periods of intense fear or apprehension that have a sudden onset and usually last for a few minutes.

Differential Diagnoses for Nonanxiety Symptoms

There is also concern about Katherine's increasing alcohol intake, but at this time it does not appear to have developed into a substance use disorder. Katherine would probably also meet the criteria for recurrent major depressive disorder and a specific phobia, in this case, heights. Further information about the onset of these fears, the effect on her, and other behaviors associated with it would be important to obtain.

- Alcohol abuse or dependence: as mentioned, Katherine does not meet the threshold criteria for either of these.
- Major depressive disorder: from the history provided, Katherine does meet the criteria. Her symptoms at present appear to have been partially attenuated by the use of St. John's wort.

Katherine was given the GAD-7 test to complete. This is a validated self-assessment tool for GAD and other anxiety disorders. Scores equal to or greater than 10 identify cases of GAD with a sensitivity and specificity of 89% and 82%, respectively. A score of 3 or more on the first two items, that is, the GAD-2, may be equally sensitive to the GAD-7. Other validated tools for GAD include the Penn State Worry Questionnaire and the Hospital Anxiety and Depression Scale. Katherine scored 13 on the GAD-7.

GAD is associated with multiple somatic symptoms. It is therefore prudent to ensure a thorough workup of the patient in the event that this has not been done already. A complete physical examination should be done and appropriate laboratory tests should be ordered. Such tests include complete blood count, complete metabolic panel, and thyroid-stimulating hormone. ECG should be considered for patients over the age of 40 who complain of symptoms such as chest pain. Other tests should be ordered depending on the history and physical findings (e.g., drug toxicology).

ETIOLOGY AND PATHOGENESIS

The expression of the phenotype that we diagnose as GAD is the result of complex interactions between genes and the environment. In a twin study of more than 1,000 female twin pairs, Kendler at al. (1992) estimated the heritability of GAD to be approximately 30%. Environmental factors are thought to play a larger role in GAD than in depression, for example. Risk factors for GAD include family history, stressful life events, and a history of childhood abuse and negative childhood experiences.

From the National Comorbidity Replication study, it was found that the presence and persistence of maladaptive family functioning such as parental mental illness, substance use disorder, criminality, family violence, physical and sexual abuse, and neglect have a significant but modest relationship to the persistence of anxiety disorders as well as with other psychiatric disorders (McLaughlin et al. 2010).

There is evidence of intra-amygdala abnormality and engagement of a compensatory frontoparietal executive control network in patients with GAD. Patients with GAD have also been shown to have significant deficits in the noninstructed and spontaneous regulation of emotional processing. Neurotransmitters thought to be involved in GAD include gamma-aminobutyric acid, serotonin, norepinephrine, and cholecystokinin.

Katherine has a genetic predisposition to both anxiety and depressive disorders. Her mother and sister both suffer from mood and anxiety spectrum disorders. Her sex is another predisposing factor in this case. As discussed, genetic predisposition is only part of the picture. Katherine's early life was associated with prolonged maternal absences. Negative childhood experiences also increase the risk of GAD. In Katherine's case, this risk was somewhat mitigated by the stable influence and presence of her father.

These vulnerability factors do not fully explain why Katherine's symptoms started when they did. For this we need to look closely into Katherine's current life. The downturn in her husband's business and the financial plight of a number of her relatives and friends compounded with the general difficult economic climate seem to have precipitated her symptoms at this particular time. The chronicity of the economic situation, the vicious circle of her symptoms on her work and confidence, and interpersonal problems associated with them have served to perpetuate Katherine's symptoms. Her clinical presentation is quite common in GAD. The focus of her anxiety is particular to her situation in life.

NATURAL COURSE WITHOUT TREATMENT

GAD has a fluctuating course with an increased rate of exacerbations in times of stress. Untreated GAD is associated with higher rates of medical comorbidities and health care costs as a result of the multiple investigations (invasive and noninvasive) and treatments (including medications and surgery), all of which have their own inherent side effects.

GAD is highly comorbid with other psychiatric disorders, especially other anxiety disorders such as social anxiety and specific phobias, depression, posttraumatic stress disorder, obsessive compulsive disorder, panic, and substance use disorders. The presence of comorbid psychiatric diagnoses worsens the prognosis with poorer responses to treatment modalities and more functional impairments.

The diagnosis of GAD is usually made during adulthood because this is the time that patients tend to present. The duration of symptoms prior to presentation is varied. GAD runs a chronic course and is unlikely to remit over time without treatment. Age may affect the content of the anxiety or worry. In older adults with GAD, the content of worry has been found to be quite similar to that seen in older adults without GAD.

GAD is associated with impairment in social and occupational function, increased health care costs, and comorbid psychiatric disorders.

EVIDENCE-BASED TREATMENT OPTIONS

The treatment options for GAD include psychotherapy and pharmacotherapy or a combination of both.

Psychotherapy for GAD

Psychotherapeutic options for treatment of GAD include cognitive behavioral therapy (CBT), psychodynamic psychotherapy, and a number of mindfulness-based therapies.

CBT is an effective treatment for GAD. There is a strong evidence basis for the use of CBT in patients with GAD. Patients with GAD display maladaptive thought patterns, for example, overestimation of the importance of negative events and the underestimation of the importance of positive ones and catastrophizing. In Katherine's case, even though her work has not been severely affected at the onset, she continually has thoughts that her work was of poor quality. These maladaptive thought patterns show up as judgment and attentional biases, for instance, frequently interpreting ambiguous events negatively and paying more attention to threatening stimuli. Katherine pays more attention to her thoughts about the poor quality of her work rather than to objective assessments provided by colleagues. Behavioral elements of GAD include avoidance and checking behaviors. Patients with GAD often develop reduced confidence in their problem-solving abilities. This is quite evident in Katherine's case.

CBT is able to tackle both the cognitive and behavioral disturbances associated with GAD. Cognitive restructuring plays a big role in the treatment. Other features of CBT for GAD include psychoeducation, self-monitoring, problem-solving techniques, time management, exposure therapy (imagery, immersion in anxiety-provoking situations), and progressive muscle relaxation.

Treatment response to CBT in patients with GAD has been found to last up to a year after treatment. The treatment usually involves 10–15 one-hour sessions. This framework may vary depending on severity, comorbid illnesses, and age. Computer-based models of CBT have also been developed and have shown promising results. They may serve as an effective and easily accessible treatment option for patients with GAD.

Studies have shown that the combination of CBT plus pharmacotherapy is better for GAD than pharmacotherapy alone. There are insufficient data comparing CBT and pharmacotherapy head to head in the treatment of GAD.

In psychodynamic psychotherapy, the focus of treatment is conflict and the resolution of that conflict. The therapeutic relationship should provide the basis for the patient to work through insecure attachments. Short term psychodynamic psychotherapy has been shown to be effective in the treatment of GAD, yielding large improvements at follow-up 12 months later. The evidence for psychodynamic psychotherapy in the treatment of GAD is not as robust as that for CBT. Other psychotherapies for GAD include Emotional Regulation Therapy, Acceptance and Commitment Therapy, and Zen Meditation techniques.

Pharmacotherapy for GAD

All pharmacotherapeutic options used in the treatment of GAD have been shown to be better than placebo. No one particular drug has been found to be superior to others. Escitalopram, duloxetine, paroxetine, venlafaxine, and buspirone are FDA approved for the treatment of GAD.

Selective serotonin reuptake inhibitors (SSRIs) have been shown to be the most effective drug treatment for GAD. SSRIs are, therefore, the first-line medications used in the treatment of GAD. Examples include sertraline, fluoxetine, escitalopram, and citalopram. There is little comparison data between the different SSRIs. Onset of action is usually within four weeks but may take up to eight weeks. Studies show that required dosages are similar to those required in the treatment of depression.

The choice of which SSRI should be used is largely determined by patient factors and potential side effects rather than the supposed superiority of any particular agent. Common side effects of SSRIs include gastrointestinal disturbances (especially nausea and diarrhea), sexual dysfunction (anorgasmia, reduced libido, etc.), agitation, weight gain, and an initial increase in levels of anxiety on starting the drug. If a patient shows no improvement in symptom profile after eight weeks on a therapeutic dose, switching to another SSRI or a serotonin-norepinephrine reuptake inhibitor (SNRI) would be prudent.

SNRIs, for example, venlafaxine and duloxetine, are efficacious in the treatment of GAD. They have been shown to have comparable efficacy with SSRIs in the treatment of GAD. Side effects of SNRIs include nausea, constipation, sleep disturbances, and elevated blood pressure in the case of venlafaxine.

Tricyclic antidepressants (e.g., imipramine) have also been shown to be effective in the treatment of GAD. However, they are associated with cardiovascular toxicity in overdoses and have less tolerable side effect profiles compared to SSRIs and SNRIs. Their prominent anticholinergic effects and nonlinear pharmacokinetics also precludes their use in elderly patients with GAD.

Other antidepressants such as mirtazapine, a noradrenaline and specific serotonergic agent, may be an option if insomnia is a particularly troublesome symptom. Weight gain and metabolic dysfunction are two worrisome side effects with this drug. It may be used alone as monotherapy or in conjunction with an SSRI. Buspirone is an azapirone that has been shown to be effective in the treatment of GAD. The onset of action is similar to that of antidepressants. Buspirone is mostly used as augmentation in patients already on an antidepressant.

Benzodiazepines may be appropriate for use at certain stages of treatment. They are most commonly used during the initiation phase with antidepressants to provide a more immediate relief of symptoms until the effect of the antidepressant becomes evident. Antidepressants are the preferred treatment if depression is a comorbid disorder. Side effects of benzodiazepines include sedation, impairment of motor function, and dependence and withdrawal with prolonged use.

Anticonvulsants, antipsychotics, and antihistamines have also been used to treat GAD. Pregabalin is an anticonvulsant that has been approved for the treatment of GAD in Europe. It has been shown to be efficacious in placebo-controlled trials. Similarly, gabapentin is often helpful although not officially approved. Antipsychotics have been used largely in patients with treatment-resistant GAD. Quetiapine has been shown to be effective in the treatment of GAD. Due to their side effect profile, antipsychotics should not be used as first-line or single agents in the treatment of GAD. They should be used as adjuncts. Hydroxyzine is an antihistamine and has been used in the treatment of anxiety symptoms for many years. Use is often limited by sedation. Other side effects include dry mouth, dizziness, and nausea.

Complementary/Alternative Therapies

There is a lack of randomized placebo-controlled trials to determine the efficacy of these therapies. Kava kava has been associated with acute liver failure. Other examples include valerian root and passion flower. People are often lulled into a false sense of security when using these therapies due to the belief that as "natural" substances they must be safe. Drug interactions are a possibility. For example, St. John's wort can cause serotonin syndrome when used with a prescribed antidepressant. The composition of alternative treatments has not been standardized. Dosing could vary from one manufacturer to the next and even with different batches.

Despite the foregoing warnings, alternative treatments can be used safely, and it is therefore important as clinicians to specifically ask our patients if they are using any of them to avoid or minimize any potential side effects.

Regardless of medication choice, effective treatment should be continued for at least 12 months. Patients have been shown to have a lower rate of relapse in a study using venlafaxine when it was continued for 12 months rather than 6 months. Long-term maintenance treatment should be considered in patients who have had two or more relapses.

CLINICAL COURSE WITH MANAGEMENT AND TREATMENT

After being presented with treatment options, Katherine chose to start CBT. She reported that she had a good experience with psychotherapy when she was younger and preferred this modality of treatment. She was referred to a psychotherapist knowledgeable in CBT for GAD and completed 12 sessions over a period of three months. Because psychotherapy is an integral part of Katherine's treatment plan, her motivation plays an important role in her improvement. She cannot be a passive observer in her treatment. It is important that she play an active role. She has voiced her willingness to this.

Katherine was more hesitant about pharmacotherapy. This led to a discussion about her experience with St. John's wort. The beneficial effects evidenced by the reduction in her depressive symptoms were noted. Katherine was educated about the similar mechanism of action with antidepressants. She consented to a trial of sertraline, and St. John's wort was discontinued. Dosing, side effects, onset of action, and duration of treatment were discussed. Sertraline was chosen due to its side effect profile and cost (this was a recurring theme of her worry). However, Katherine developed intolerable gastrointestinal side effects with sertraline, and it was discontinued. She was switched to escitalopram, which she tolerated well. Her symptoms improved gradually over time with these treatments. She experienced improvement in her quality of life and her level of function.

SYSTEMS-BASED PRACTICE ISSUES

In the primary care setting, screening for the presence of anxiety in patients may help increase accurate diagnosis. Early detection and treatment could potentially lead to improved overall health of patients with GAD and would also help reduce health care costs. Using a quick screening tool such as the GAD-7 or GAD-2 in primary care practices could help in achieving this goal.

LEGAL, ETHICAL, AND CULTURAL CHALLENGES

GAD, by itself, is not usually associated with legal issues. However, the increased risk of substance use disorders can cause impairment. Ethical concerns may be raised by the clinician when the patient's symptoms have a negative effect on their ability to function safely, for example, driving, use of heavy machinery, or in cases where other individuals may be at risk. The clinician must weigh the ethical principles of autonomy and beneficence and come to a decision as to which course of action to take. In Katherine's case, there is a risk of problem alcohol use but no history of driving under the influence or other such infringements. Also, her work is not associated with potential harm to others.

The National Comorbidity Survey Replication (Kessler et al. 2005) found that non-Hispanic blacks and Hispanics had a significantly lower risk of all anxiety disorders compared to non-Hispanic whites. Marital disruptions were found to be associated with anxiety disorders. The sex differences in anxiety did not differ across all the different age cohorts in the study. No significant relationship between racial/ethnic group status and indices in GAD symptom severity has been found. Differences between groups with respect to the predominant symptom profile have been observed. For example, one study showed that Nepali patients with GAD scored higher on the somatic subscale of the Beck Anxiety Inventory whereas North American patients scored higher on the psychological subscale.

TERMS

Agoraphobia: derived from Greek words *agora* and *phobos*, literally meaning "fear of the marketplace." This is anxiety associated with being in a place or situation from which exiting or escape may be difficult.

Anhedonia: an inability to enjoy or derive satisfaction from anything. There is a loss of pleasure.

Anxiety: feeling of apprehension caused by danger or the anticipation of danger. This feeling can become pathological when there is no obvious cause. Anxiety is said to be free-floating when it is not associated with any particular object.

Depression: a pathological feeling of sadness.

Distractibility: inability to focus.

Panic: acute episode of increased anxiety accompanied by an intense feeling of dread and physiological symptoms, for example, shortness of breath, palpitations, paresthesias, feeling faint, or dizziness.

Preoccupations: thoughts focused on a particular idea.

Psychomotor retardation: marked slowing of normal movement and is associated with slowing of thought and speech as observed in severe cases of depression.

REFERENCES AND RESOURCES

Grant BF, Hasin DS, Stinson FS, Dawson DA, June Ruan W, Goldstein RB, Smith SM, Saha TD, Huang B. Prevalence, correlates, co-morbidity, and comparative disability of DSM-IV generalized anxiety disorder in the USA: results from the National Epidemiologic Survey on Alcohol and Related Conditions. *Psychol Med* 2005;35(12):1747.

Kendler KS, Neale MC, Kessler RC, Heath AC, Eaves LJ. Generalized anxiety disorder in women. A population-based twin study. *Arch Gen Psych* 1992 Apr;49(4):267–72.

Kessler RC, Berglund P, Demler O, Jin R, Merikangas KR, Walters EE. Lifetime prevalence and age-of-onset distributions of DSM-IV disorders in the National Comorbidity Survey Replication. *Arch Gen Psych* 2005 Jun;62(6):593–602.

McLaughlin KA, Green JG, Gruber MJ, Sampson NA, Zaslavsky AM, Kessler RC. Childhood adversities and adult psychiatric disorders in the national comorbidity survey replication II: associations with persistence of DSM-IV disorders. *Arch Gen Psych* 2010 Feb;67(2):124–32.

Spitzer RL, Kroenke K, Williams JB, Löwe B. A brief measure for assessing generalized anxiety disorder: the GAD-7. *Arch Intern Med* 2006;166(10):1092.

Van der Heiden C, Methorst G, Muris P, van der Molen HT. Generalized anxiety disorder: clinical presentation, diagnostic features, and guidelines for clinical practice. *J Clin Psychol* 2011 Jan;67(1):58–73. doi: 10.1002/jclp.20743.

Mayo Clinic, http://www.mayoclinic.com/health/generalized-anxiety-disorder/DS00502.

National Institute for Health and Clinical Excellence (NICE), Guidelines for Treatment, http://www.nice.org.uk/CG113, http://guidance.nice.org.uk/CG113/Guidance.

NIMH, http://www.nimh.nih.gov/health/topics/generalized-anxiety-disorder-gad/index.shtml.

In popular culture, the movie *Analyze This* (1999), provides one portrait of GAD or panic disorder.

CHAPTER **19**

School Refusal

P. G. Shelton, M.D.

CLINICAL PRESENTATION

Chief complaint: "My son was suspended from school and will not return."

History of present illness: Sebastian is a 12-year-old young man who lives with his mother and attends the seventh grade at a local public middle school. He has a psychiatric history significant for attention deficit hyperactivity disorder (ADHD) and unspecified anxiety disorder. He presents with his mother to an urgently scheduled appointment to discuss concerns of increased anxiety following alleged bullying at school. Despite previous treatment for anxiety, he has continued to have significant symptoms that lead to occasional absences from school. This is more recently evidenced by three absences for alleged anxiety-related nausea during the first two weeks of school. Even with these missed days, Sebastian's grades have been exceptionally good during the end of last school year and the first few weeks of the new academic year. His mother believes Sebastian has experienced a period of relative success that led to some improvement in his self-esteem along with increased interaction with peers. He even made comments at the beginning of the school year about how much he was enjoying school.

After the first few weeks of the school year, two acquaintances posted slanderous comments on Facebook concerning Sebastian. This resulted in a brief episode of suicidal thoughts that resolved after an emergent evaluation the following evening. Two days later this alleged bullying culminated in an incident at the school in which Sebastian was pushed down from behind in a hallway in front of many peers. The fall resulted in multiple mild contusions and abrasions. Sebastian sought medical attention from the school nurse and reported the incident to her, but his mother was not notified until Sebastian told her later that evening. She was quite upset that the school administration did not notify the appropriate people, including herself, about the incident. She subsequently filed a complaint at the district and state levels to the Department of Education about this concern. Sebastian experienced increased anxiety around these events and returning to school, but he did so without further absences.

Several weeks later, there was another incident involving one of the same students harassing Sebastian while riding the bus home. During this event, a male peer pushed him several times before punching him in the abdomen. He retaliated by pushing this peer back, which was witnessed by the bus driver. Subsequently both young men were suspended from the bus for 10 school days. At that time Sebastian told his mother, "This is the last straw, I cannot take it anymore and I am not going back to that school." Due to her own health and transportation barriers and Sebastian's anxiety, his mother made the decision to subsequently keep him home during these 10 days, but requested that the teachers send his schoolwork to their home. Mother asserted that no schoolwork was ever delivered to her home. The school reportedly had offered to transport him on a smaller, separate bus during this time, but Sebastian was worried this would bring even more negative attention on him and as such, he and his mother refused to accept this transportation. Mother claimed that she attempted to contact the school to request homebound schooling during this time, but the school denies she made any such request.

At the time Sebastian presented to the clinician's office, he had apparently missed 12 consecutive days of school. During this time the clinician had not been contacted and informed of this situation, despite Mother requesting that the school send a request for homebound services to the doctor, which was never received. Sebastian's mother was apprehensive at the appointment because her son had continued to refuse to attend school since being suspended from the bus. This anxiety subsequently led to him missing a total of 15 consecutive days of school at one point. Upon time to return to school, Sebastian was very hesitant to go back. Mother observed that he appeared fearful of returning to school, and she questioned his safety there due to the "poor manner" in which she claimed the school handled the recent bullying incidents. Sebastian verbalized frustration for being punished when he stood up to one of his peers who was bullying him. Both Mother and Sebastian were further discouraged after they received a truancy notice with a judicial hearing from the school board over this incident. Mother claimed she felt the school was not only failing to act on the bullying in an appropriate manner but was filing a truancy report "spitefully" after she had complained to both local and state authorities on how the incidents had been managed.

The school was contacted briefly, after which time Mother withdrew consent for direct contact because she wanted to be involved in any conversation between the school and other professionals. During this one phone dialogue, the school staff revealed their opinion that Sebastian perceived the bullying to be much worse than it actually was. They even alleged that they had seen him instigating many of these situations and this is why they felt it was necessary to also suspend him from the bus. They said in the previous incident that one of the other students had been suspended, and all the students involved along with their parents had been brought into the principal's office. This particular school emphasized that they had a system-wide bully-prevention project that they participate in yearly and take all bullying claims seriously though they did admit that procedures to notify the parent had not been followed appropriately. Overall the school felt that Sebastian tended to exaggerate these incidents. Such exaggerations could be consistent with his background of being exposed to previous traumatic events.

Sebastian had been followed at the outpatient mental health clinic for some time but now presented for this appointment with the physician after numerous consecutive absences from school. His story was acquired from interviews with Sebastian, Mother, and a patient advocate who had assisted the family for the past two years. All were primarily concerned with Sebastian's long history of anxiety and the recent deterioration in school attendance and performance. Sebastian and Mother are observed to be codependent on one another as both had experienced significant loss and trauma over the preceding six years. Around the onset of his anxiety, Mother began to have health problems from a failing liver and developed diabetes. Father had a very inconsistent presence in the home, and as such, Mother was Sebastian's primary caretaker. There were times when Father and Mother attempted to reconcile their relationship, but it was terminated several years ago after Mother caught Father having an affair with a maternal aunt.

Beginning about five years ago, at age seven, it was reported that Sebastian had increasing separation anxiety concerning his Mother and would refuse to leave her alone. He was fearful of sleeping alone and often requested to sleep in his Mother's bed. At night when Mother attempted to return him to his bedroom, he would have tantrums and become anxious, often culminating in his return to Mother's bed. Whenever he was confronted by Father in the past, he would exhibit either oppositional behaviors or complain of somatic aches and pains, such as headaches or stomachaches. Around this time he began to miss numerous days of school and often stated that no one liked him there. At school he often isolated himself and on returning home would complain how mean other children were toward him. Sebastian would often be belligerent in the mornings when Mother attempted to get him to school, but once there he typically did fine. While he had experienced anxiety in the past, it was around this time that Mother first sought out psychiatric expertise, as it had become severely impairing at home and in the educational setting. Some degree of this separation anxiety still exists at present per Mother, but is nowhere near as impairing as it was five years ago. When Sebastian gets overly anxious at school, he often attempts to call his Mother at home as this is usually the most successful method in calming his anxiety.

On further investigation, it is clear that Sebastian has a long history of impairing anxiety. He worries in excess of his peers and is not able to control his worry. He worries about his performance in school, what peers think of him, Mother's health problems, and the family's financial situation. This "constant worrying" causes him to feel restless and easily fatigued. It often affects his concentration in addition to causing him difficulty with initiating sleep on occasion. Sebastian's worry is to the point that it leads to many somatic complaints that often make him miss school days each semester. On numerous occasions over the past five years, the family has been threatened by the school for excessive absences. The Department of Social Services has even been contacted in the past, and Sebastian voiced worry that this may lead to separation from Mother, his primary attachment figure. He can suddenly develop panic attacks that occur at least a few times weekly. These attacks last about 20 minutes and result in palpitations, shortness of breath, mild trembling, chest discomfort, nausea, and fear of losing control. No changes in his behaviors have been observed related to these attacks other than occasionally having to excuse himself from the classroom. These had improved the previous year but had returned at the time of his evaluation and worsened over the subsequent months. Sebastian does not have a persistent concern about having future panic attacks, though, nor does he worry about the implications of such episodes.

Sebastian may meet criteria for social phobia presently. Although he still has some symptoms of separation anxiety, it is difficult to ascertain to what degree this is responsible for his present severe level of anxiety symptoms. He has had persistent fears for many years, particularly in social situations, and always comments on how others do not like him in school. He fears his problems are evident to others when his anxiety manifests at school and in other social settings. He described a fear of humiliation and embarrassment at school and around acquaintances. It is unclear if this perceived or realistic judgment by peers provoked further anxiety and many of his panic attacks, but this seems probable. Upon discussion of individual incidents Sebastian had the insight to recognize the fear as excessive, but still attempts to avoid many situations, such as talking in front of the class. When the teacher addresses him in the classroom, he can lose his ability to even speak. Subsequently, he often does not participate in many activities and is not able to articulate to the teacher when he is experiencing severe distress and needs assistance.

More recently Sebastian has had several traumatic events occur in his life. The first occurred four months ago when a SWAT team forcefully broke into his home to seize his adult sister's boyfriend. This was quite distressing to both Mother and son, as the situation involved a forced entry with the family members being held at gunpoint for a short while until the SWAT team located their primary target. Mother said they later found out that this young man who had been living with them had been involved with child pornography before and while in their home. This led to further conflict in the family with regard to sister, who was later asked to leave the home about a month ago by Mother because her presence was unsettling the stability in the home. Sebastian appeared to have some symptoms of acute stress disorder at the time, but these symptoms had begun to mostly resolve before the more recent bullying incidents at school. Following the two incidents at school where he was pushed down and shoved numerous times on the bus, Sebastian began to develop many of the symptoms of post-traumatic stress disorder (PTSD), though full criteria for the disorder were questionable. He initially had recurrent and intrusive distressing memories of the incidents.

This later resolved within two to three weeks. Although he denies intense psychological distress and physiological reactivity on exposure to certain cues, his mother and patient advocate believe they had seen evidence of such on numerous occasions in the past week or more. He has made an effort recently to avoid returning to school and voiced at times that he did not feel safe and that he just wanted to quit going all together. He also has become even more withdrawn socially and has not been mingling with his peers to the degree he was earlier in the year. Finally, Sebastian has experienced difficulty falling asleep and had deterioration in his concentration. Mother has seen that he is more hypervigilant and believes he has an exaggerated startle response.

Sebastian has a long history of attention deficit hyperactivity disorder (ADHD) that was diagnosed by his pediatrician well before they sought out their first psychiatric care five years ago. Per record, both his mother and father reported symptoms consistent with combined presentation ADHD. He had always been a very active and impulsive child, though he appears less so over the years in part due to the inhibition caused by his anxiety. He continues to struggle with regard to inattentiveness in the educational setting. He tends to make careless mistakes on classwork and has significant difficulties sustaining his attention. He tends to not follow through on instruction and is disorganized and forgetful. When he is able to pay attention for periods of time he finds he is easily distracted compared to his peers. His family perceived that he obtained substantial improvement in these symptoms when placed on stimulant therapy. On this treatment, his grades improved dramatically and at present he is mostly an A and B student when he has been able to attend school regularly and keep up with his classwork.

Sebastian has had past difficulty with temper tantrums, but these are not a current problem. He denies any depressive, manic, or hypomanic symptoms and Mother confirms that he had not had any long-standing mood difficulties. When particularly stressed he can show some degree of excessive irritability. He has always been an "introvert" per Mother and had never had more than few good friends at any one time. Despite this, he has become more withdrawn recently, but Mother feels this is a result of his anxiety at school and in social settings. She and his advocate believe difficulties with his sleep, energy, and concentration are better explained by his severe anxiety. Sebastian often blames himself when things are not going well socially. He has expressed suicidal thoughts on at least one occasion recently after peers were ostracizing him on Facebook by calling him a "faggot." These thoughts were brief and have not occurred since. He has never experienced any symptoms consistent with a psychotic disorder. He denies paranoia outside of social situations and has never experienced any hallucinations, delusions, or ideas of reference. He has never met criteria for an autistic spectrum disorder as he seeks to share experiences with others, demonstrates adequate use of nonverbal behaviors and social/emotional reciprocity, and desires and attempts to develop peer relationships.

Psychiatric history: Sebastian has no history of suicidal attempts or gestures and has never been admitted to a psychiatric inpatient facility. He has been seeing a child clinician since age seven years and was diagnosed with ADHD two years previous to establishing psychiatric care by his primary care physician. The primary care physician prescribed methylphenidate 27 mg for his ADHD symptoms with significant improvement noted. He was also successfully placed on clonidine 0.15 mg at this time for primary insomnia. It was the occurrence of comorbid anxiety symptoms that led to the referral to psychiatry by the primary care physician at age seven. The anxiety around this time revolved primarily around difficulty separating from his mother and resulted in many temper tantrums and some limited school refusal.

Over the past five years he has had several waxing and waning periods of anxiety at times associated with brief absences from school. Relapses in symptom severity were often triggered after acute stressors such as past bullying, his father entering and leaving the home, and his mother's chronic illness. More recently it has been exacerbated by the incidents at school and with the SWAT team entering his home. At one time about three years ago it was felt that the stimulant medication controlling his ADHD symptoms may have been partly responsible for his severe anxiety and was briefly discontinued. Sebastian began struggling with academics shortly afterward, and the medication was restarted because little improvement was noted in his anxiety when it was removed. He has shown a partial response to citalopram but no other selective serotonin reuptake inhibitors (SSRIs) have ever been tried. Sebastian was tried on several different stimulant medications subsequently at Mother's request and the doctor's recommendation. He failed a trial of lisdexamfetamine due to increased anxiety and insomnia and Mother asked for a change from methylphenidate after it was not working at 20 mg daily. He finally ended up on extended-release dextroamphetamine/amphetamine starting about 20 months ago with his ADHD symptoms being stabilized without any significant side effects. The family has sought out services of a friend who works with an advocacy group out of state. This advocate has helped them significantly over the past two years in navigating the array of available services available to Sebastian in the region.

Sebastian and his mother deny any past or active substance use or concerns. His current medications include:

1. Amphetamine-dextroamphetamine extended release 20 mg, one tablet every morning.
2. Amphetamine-dextroamphetamine 5 mg, one tablet daily at 4 pm.
3. Citalopram 20 mg, one and a half tablets daily.
4. Guanfacine 1 mg, half tablet in the morning and evening daily.
5. Mirtazapine 15 mg, half tablet at bedtime for insomnia.
6. Promethazine 12.5 mg, one to two tablets as needed for anxiety and nausea.

Past medications include:

1. Methylphenidate up to 27 mg, one tablet every morning.
2. Clonidine 0.1 mg, one to two tablets at bedtime for insomnia.
3. Methylphenidate 20 mg, one tablet every morning.

Other medical history: Sebastian has a history of asthma and seasonal allergies.

Other history (developmental, educational/occupational, family/social, legal): Sebastian was born at 37 weeks gestation by way of cesarean section. Mother had no prenatal complications during the pregnancy and did not use any illicit substances or medications. Sebastian's birth was uncomplicated and he weighed six pounds, four ounces. Mother denies any perinatal or postnatal complications. Sebastian's infancy was fairly normal, and he did not have an overly difficulty temperament. His milestones were on time as was sitting at 5 months, crawling at 7 months, and walking at 11 months. He was able to say about 15 words at 18 months of age and was able to form two-word sentences at 22 months. Mother states by age three his language was fairly fluent. No early signs of anxiety such as separation difficulties were noted outside of age-appropriate norms until about the age of six years. He responds well to peers and his parents and seeks interaction with them routinely.

Sebastian is presently in the seventh grade and has an Individualized Education Program (IEP) with his primary disability being Other Health Impairment and his secondary disability being Emotional Disability. His most recent grades include an 89 in Art, a 91 in English, a 72 in Science, a 91 in Math, and an A in Health/PE. He apparently still has tests to make up in Science, which may help raise his grade. He has mostly incompletes for the first nine weeks of the school year because he did not attend school from October 11 to November 2. Sebastian is in the process of working on these incompletes but points out that the additional work is stressful to manage at times. His most recent mandatory end-of-grade testing resulted in scores of 494 in reading and 405 in math (scores above 400 are passing).

Sebastian's IQ testing was done by administration of the WISC-IV about two years ago. The results show that he is functioning within the low average range of cognitive ability (Full Scale IQ = 85). His verbal comprehension (93) and processing speed (97) skills fall within the average range, and perceptual reasoning (82) and working memory (83) were areas of relative weakness. Other testing showed that his visual memory skills were an area of relative strength: he scored 115 and 120 on the Visual Memory and Visual Recognition subtests of the Wide Range Assessment of Memory and Learning, 2nd edition. Despite this strength, his ability to form memories is likely impaired due to poor attention and concentration skills that were identified as an area of significant difficulty. Another area of relative weakness includes his scores of 71 and 74 on the subjects of Written Expression and Writing Fluency on the Woodcock Johnson III Achievement Test. Additional observations made by educational psychologists around this time revealed that Sebastian was demonstrating problems with anxiety, depression, somatization, and his adaptive skills in the home and educational environments. It was commented that this may have affected his testing in addition to having an ongoing effect on his academic performance in school.

Mother admits to a long history of an unknown anxiety disorder and mood difficulties. She says she has been diagnosed with Bipolar Disorder likely Type II, but denies any psychiatric hospitalizations resulting from such. Mother also has diabetes and a "fatty liver." She is on disability for both her medical and psychiatric illnesses. Sebastian's father is reported to have ADHD and likely bipolar disorder and is also on disability for these illnesses. He has made multiple attempts to hang himself in the past per report. There is one maternal grandmother with a history of an unknown depressive disorder.

Presently, Sebastian and his mother live together by themselves. His 20-year-old sister lived with them until the recent incident with her boyfriend. This led to increased conflict between Mother and daughter and to her demanding that her daughter move out of the home. He and Mother live in a several bedroom house and he has his own room. Mother used to be a health care professional, but has been on disability for three years due to her chronic medical illnesses.

Sebastian's parents separated numerous times during his life and last tried to reunite four years ago. This was unsuccessful and Father has had little contact with Sebastian over the past several years. Sebastian does not feel close to his father and does not care to see him routinely. For most of his life, Father was in and out of the home and never consistently kept in contact with Sebastian. At age four, Sebastian was kidnapped by his father for seven days. When he was finally located and brought back to the home, Father called the Department of Social Services and claimed that Mother was giving their son benzodiazepines. This resulted in Sebastian being placed back with his father for a month before Mother was cleared of these accusations. When Sebastian was nine years old he experienced his first major loss when his grandmother died, and he had more difficulty with this event than is typical of peers.

Over the previous summer, the home was invaded by a SWAT team subsequent to one of the home's residents, the sister's boyfriend, being involved with child pornography. The mother, client, and client's sister were reportedly unaware of these activities taking place in the home. Sebastian was quite shaken by this raid. Sebastian's father returned shortly thereafter for a period of three months to help Mother out due to her health problems. He left the home suddenly after cleaning out their bank accounts. Mother and Sebastian subsequently found out that Father had been having an affair while living with the two of them. A week later, he invaded the home and tied up the maternal aunt and allegedly raped her. The SWAT team was again called out to the home and the family removed from their home while they searched the woods nearby. Later they found Father, and he is presently in jail awaiting trial for this recent incident. Sebastian does not have any past diversion, legal charges, or involvement in the juvenile justice system.

Vital signs: Blood pressure 118/78, pulse 72, height 1.47 meters, weight 48.25 kg, BMI 22/24 kg/m^2.

Mental status exam: Sebastian is a 12-year-old Caucasian young man who appears his stated age. He well groomed and dressed in black sweatpants and a light blue sweatshirt. He has short dark brown hair and blue eyes and is of a large build but not obese. He appears to have some psychomotor restlessness during the interview as was evident by constant shaking of his lower extremities. At times he leans or even lies on his mother and appears to be comforted by this physical contact. He is cooperative but very inhibited during the session. He defers questions to his mother at the beginning of the session but becomes more vocal over the course of the appointment when Mother discussed consequences for set boundaries. Eye contact is good overall, but when any confrontation arises, or if he gets frustrated describing a situation, his eye contact along with his speech deteriorates and he defers further details to Mother for explanation. Speech is somewhat broken with low tone and volume to begin with but by the end of the session was of a normal rate, tone, volume, and latency. Sebastian is alert to his self, surroundings, situations, and date. His memory of recent events is intact when compared to third-person reports. Attention and concentration are age-appropriate and adequate for the session. Use of language is age-appropriate. Sebastian claims his mood is "frustrated and nervous," and his observed affect is congruent as it is quite anxious and apprehensive. He denies any suicidal and homicidal ideation.

Thought processes are linear and goal directed. There were no abnormal associations of thought. Thought content was negative for obsessions, delusions, perceptual disturbances. Sebastian possesses some ability for abstract thought, although most of his thinking is concrete. Cognition seems to be age-appropriate with regard to simple calculations, and fund of knowledge is average for his age. Insight is fair as Sebastian has some ability to understand his illness yet is unaware of many of the ways it manifests and causes him impairment. His judgment is fair as he often takes the path that in the short term leads to decreased worry and stress over that which will decrease his anxiety further in the long run. Perception and reality testing is intact.

IMPAIRMENT IN FUNCTIONING

There is considerable functional impairment in this case and many similar cases. Persistent absence from school can have many consequences on many aspects of a child's development. Academic performance and long-term education development can quite obviously be negatively affected. This may lead to problems making adjustments later in school life and adulthood. It is reasonable to be concerned that long-term complications with employment may develop.

Refusal to attend school may also interfere with social development as relationships with peers in this setting may be interrupted. This may lead to further anxiety around peers not just in the educational setting but in other nonschool situations because symptoms may generalize. Longer term difficulties in social adjustment may arise with school refusal and include avoidant behaviors of adulthood. Many similar children go on to develop agoraphobia and other anxiety disorders later in life. Many studies reveal that children exhibiting school refusal behaviors are more likely to have or seek care for a mental health disturbance decades later in adulthood. It is widely thought that the age of the child at the onset of school refusal symptoms is inversely correlated with the long-term prognosis.

DSM DIAGNOSIS

The clinician who assesses this person can easily be overwhelmed by the assortment of reported symptoms and disconcerted over the number of possible diagnoses. Further complicating the situation is the enigma to be solved over what diagnoses are the primary ones and which are later developed comorbidities. The vast majority of Sebastian's past and present symptoms appear to be internalizing in nature. Most of his reported symptoms best fit under the category of anxiety as the primary complaint and reason for his first presentation and functional impairment. From the DSM classification, numerous anxiety disorders could qualify from Sebastian's many symptoms. He first presented with severe separation anxiety and met criteria for this illness five years ago. He had excessive fear concerning separation from his major attachment figure, his mother. At present he still is most relieved of stress by calling or talking to his mother. He remains quite worried about Mother's health but is not overly concerned with losing her at present. Sebastian denies persistent concern over separation from his mother and does not express any anxiety or somatic symptoms when separation occurs.

It is likely that over time his anxiety has been displaced from a fear of separation from Mother to that of the fear of negative judgment by his peers. This is quite appropriate for his developmental level of early adolescence when moving into the Eriksonian stage of Identity versus Role Confusion. Part of an adolescent's identity is reflected in what he or she contemplates that peers think of him or her as an individual. Fears of being ostracized or separated from the peer group become substantial around this time. This is a fear that Sebastian has been experiencing for some time. When singled out in class by the teacher or in similar educational or social situations, he can become almost paralyzed by anxiety and often will lose his voice. This situation satisfies the DSM criteria for Social Anxiety Disorder (Social Phobia). He has learned to fear such situations, anticipating them in an apprehensive manner, yet recognizes this fear as excessive. Sebastian tends to avoid many social and educational activities in the classroom such as reading aloud and often will not interact with his peers so as to avoid anxiety-provoking situations that may arise. This results in him not being able to participate in some classroom activities, having few peer relationships, and most notably not attending school over the last 18 months. It is appropriate to diagnose Sebastian with social anxiety disorder because he fully meets criteria. It is protective that he has historically possessed both the desire and ability to relate with peers in an age-appropriate manner.

Sebastian's anxiety over time has generalized to many parts of his life and is not explained solely by past separation anxiety disorder and the more current diagnosis of social anxiety disorder. He has had an anxious temperament for a good part of his life, which has gradually worsened. He tends to worry about many things—Mother's health, his situation at school, what other peers think of him, his academic performance. He even worries about things that are not age-appropriate, such as financial problems overheard from his Mother. Sebastian admits that he cannot control this worry and recognizes it is excessive and as such meets the criteria A and B for a generalized anxiety disorder. Furthermore his anxiety is expressed in many ways. He describes being overly restless and keyed up, and this was present well before the two recent traumatic events. He also describes that the anxiety he experiences from his worrying affects his ability to fall asleep at night and leads to him feeling constantly fatigued. He also notes his muscles feel very tense, and his overall level of irritability waxes and wanes in correlation to his currently experienced anxiety. His concentration may likely be affected at times, he admits, but this is difficult to separate from his poor concentration as a result of his recent traumatic events and ADHD history. Even without difficulty concentrating, he meets five of the six criteria C, with only three being necessary for a diagnosis. His anxiety cannot be solely explained by his other comorbid anxiety disorders or other medical illnesses and so cannot be excluded. After taking into consideration the foregoing symptoms, this young man meets full criteria for generalized anxiety disorder. His anxiety could be protective from potential harm if it was not so excessive. If Sebastian was healthier, mild levels of anxiety could push him to strive for further academic achievements. Anxiety over being involved in the juvenile justice system due to his truancy may also serve to motivate him to attend school more regularly. Additionally, insight into the fact that his functional impairment could affect his mother's health further could both increase anxiety and motivate him to make appropriate changes.

The only other anxiety disorder this young man may meet criteria for is PTSD. Sebastian has experienced two recent traumatic events with the bullying and SWAT team incidents during which he felt his safety or well-being were threatened. He recovered fairly well from the first trauma, but it is likely that this along with past bullying led to a kindling effect that resulted in the expression of more severe symptoms after the recent bullying at school. In both the recent incidents Sebastian claims to have felt extreme helplessness. He has possibly been experiencing the event as a frequent intense psychological distress and physiological reactivity when he returns to the school grounds, as he feels this symbolizes the event. This recurrent experienced fear is consistent with two of the B criteria of PTSD. His avoiding going to school meets the C criteria requirements for PTSD. He has shown subsequent diminished interest in being around peers and friends. Mother describes a reduced range of affect recently. These two symptoms meet the threshold for the D criteria. Sebastian has also exhibited symptoms of increased arousal, category E criteria, since the most recent incident two weeks ago. He has increasing irritability, hypervigilance, difficulty concentrating, and an increased startle response. Despite having criteria A, B, C, and D, Sebastian has not experienced these symptoms for more than one month and as such would need to continue to have this degree of symptoms for another one or two weeks to be diagnosed with PTSD. Acute stress disorder criteria do not have this time requirement, but Sebastian lacks a reduction in awareness, dissociative amnesia, depersonalization, and derealization.

While this young man also experiences panic attacks, these seem to be triggered by associated social anxiety disorder or possibly PTSD. It is quite important to note that many young individuals with so many impairing anxiety symptoms would have developed the comorbidity of a mood disorder by now, but this young man denies any significant sustained mood symptoms. He does have a long history of ADHD, diagnosed around the age of five. From a description of his symptoms at the age of five years, past diagnosis from his primary care physician, and significant response to treatment of ADHD symptoms, it is fairly appropriate to concur with this past diagnosis and let it remain on the active problem list. Anxiety disorders happen to be one of the more common comorbidities of ADHD along with learning disorders. Additionally, any current ADHD symptoms would be difficult to distinguish from those of his anxiety disorder because the latter can cause many similar symptoms. As this is only a secondary concern at present, removing it and its past treatment, which has been deemed to be helpful, would likely only lead to further deterioration in this client. There has been evidence per past trials that stopping stimulants led to no improvement in his anxiety and an overall worsening in impairments. Finally, although there is a past report of possible learning disorders, Sebastian's achievement test scores are all within one standard deviation of his IQ score. By definition of the DSM, this cannot rule out a learning disorder, but it lowers the likelihood.

In summary, Sebastian seems to meet DSM diagnostic criteria for Social Anxiety Disorder, Generalized Anxiety Disorder, and ADHD (Inattentive presentation). Possible other diagnoses that could explain his symptoms include PTSD, Separation Anxiety Disorder, and Learning Disorder (unspecified). He has been diagnosed with asthma and air hunger related to reactive airway dysfunction that can cause anxiety. He has significant social stressors (perceived bullying and performance anxiety) and now truancy charges because of school refusal.

EPIDEMIOLOGY

School refusal prevalence is reported to be around 1% in school-aged children and 5% of all clinic-referred children. There are many reports in the literature of increasing rates of school refusal, but it is thought this may likely be due to a greater awareness and tendency to refer those who suffer with it for treatment as opposed to a true increase in incidence. School refusal is equally common in boys and girls throughout the educational age continuum. However there is evidence that there may be peaks between the ages of 5 and 7 years of age, at around 11 years of age, and a final peak around 13–15 years of age. Interestingly these peaks correlate with traditional transition periods into elementary, middle, and secondary schooling. Several studies suggest that school refusal may have a higher prevalence in preadolescence and adolescence as opposed to the early and middle childhood years. This has been the case with Sebastian—his school refusal did not begin in earnest until the middle school years. Studies have found maximum peaks in the prevalence of school refusal between the ages of 13 to 15 years. Sebastian, like many children who exhibit school refusal behaviors, has a fairly normal distribution in intellect. There is also a strong indication that learning disabilities are no more common in this population than in other similar aged peers. Additionally, socioeconomic factors do not appear to be correlated with rates as evidence for such is conflicting. Finally, evidence that school refusal is associated more with single-parent families is also contradictory. In cases of school refusal related to separation anxiety, there is often a primary caregiver who is struggling with medical illness or depression. In this particular situation, Sebastian's mother has numerous medical illnesses that impair her to the extent that she is on disability. Sebastian's case is quite typical in that most cases of severe school refusal involve severe anxiety symptoms and one or more anxiety disorders.

DIFFERENTIAL DIAGNOSIS

School-refusing children like Sebastian can have their impairment rooted in a variety of diagnoses. Often these children have had numerous previous psychiatric comorbidities by the time they become severe enough to present to the clinician in mental health. As such sometimes a more general psychological test such as the Child Behavior Checklist can be helpful in narrowing down in what spectrum of disorders the culprit illness may reside. Typically, disorders on the anxiety spectrum are the principal concern because a wide array of anxiety symptoms often accompanies those with school refusal. As such, several questions about all anxiety spectrum disorders should be asked to help tease out whether each may be possibly present before moving to a full symptom review in those identified as probable. More often than not, more than one anxiety disorder may be present, as is the case with Sebastian. Use of the SCARED (Self Report for Childhood Anxiety Related Disorders) or a similar anxiety rating scale every few months can be helpful for children such as Sebastian because it can help the clinician objectively and quickly evaluate the severity of anxiety symptoms.

Anxiety symptoms can be exhibited in cognitive, behavioral, and physiological domains. Cognitively, those with school refusal often possess irrational fears about their attendance at school. They often exaggerate the degree they will be judged and criticized by other peers while overstating the probability of anxiety-provoking situations occurring at school. Sebastian, like many similar cases, minimizes his own ability to cope with such anxiety-provoking situations and misjudges the severity of such events when they do arise. Behaviorally, these children will attempt to avoid what causes them the worst anxiety: school. They will often attempt to resist in many ways, some conscious and some unconscious. Sebastian does not seem to be consciously aware of all his attempts to avoid school, such as through the use of psychosomatic complaints. As evidenced by this case, refusal to attend can take many forms, such as remaining in bed, refusing to get ready, refusing to get on the bus or in the car to travel to school, missing the school bus, and refusing to get out of the car on arrival at school. Such behaviors often lead to significant conflict with the parent or primary caregiver. At times a child under duress of school attendance may cry, throw tantrums, and attempt to emotionally manipulate others. They can even threaten to harm themselves as Sebastian has done at times when frustrated and severely anxious. This is a key point in many cases and deserves additional attention by way of questioning and thorough risk assessment. At the physiological level, continued coercion can even trigger panic attack–like episodes. The mention of school can induce many psychosomatic complaints including abdominal pain, nausea, vomiting, dizziness, headache, diarrhea, and an assortment of other physical symptoms. The most common of these symptoms in children with school refusal are stomachaches and headaches.

Though in-depth evaluation of these young individuals often exposes one or more anxiety disorders, it should be noted that not all children who exhibit school refusal behaviors have an anxiety disorder. Additionally the vast majority of children and adolescents who suffer from anxiety disorders attend school on a regular basis with minimal absences due to their anxiety. Despite this there is a strong, well-cited correlation between anxiety disorders and school refusal. The more common diagnoses seen in these individuals include social anxiety disorder, separation anxiety disorder, generalized anxiety disorder, and adjustment disorders with anxiety. With the increasing recognition of bullying in the educational setting, PTSD is also being seen more in those with school refusal, though less so than the other above diagnoses. As explained in detail, Sebastian meets criteria for social anxiety disorder and generalized anxiety disorder while expressing many symptoms consistent with PTSD and separation anxiety, but not meeting full criteria.

Some age-linked trends exist among students with these diagnoses. For instance, separation anxiety disorder is much more common in younger children, whereas social anxiety disorder (social phobia) is more common in adolescents. Phobias of the school environment tend to be more specific to excessive fear of social and evaluative situations as opposed to fear of particular objects within the school. This young man does indeed possess the criteria required for social phobia while also meeting criteria for a generalized anxiety disorder. More recently bullying has been brought to the forefront at many schools, and this also can be a reason for school refusal. Although bullying may be more common in the young child, the severity and consequences of it tend to be much more severe in the older child and adolescent. These older students are more likely to develop post-traumatic symptoms after repeated bullying episodes. This young man exhibits many of these symptoms, but does not presently meet criteria for PTSD due to the requirement that symptoms last one month. Over the following weeks his post-traumatic symptoms waned to the extent that he would no longer qualify for the diagnosis.

Table 19.1. Primary Psychiatric Disorders among Youths with
School Refusal Behavior

Disorder	Prevalence
No diagnosis	32.9%
Separation anxiety disorder	22.4%
Generalized anxiety disorder	10.5%
Oppositional defiant disorder	8.4%
Major depression	4.9%
Specific phobia	4.2%
Social anxiety disorder	3.5%
Conduct disorder	2.8%
ADHD	1.4%
Panic disorder	1.4%
Enuresis	0.7%
PTSD	0.7%

Source: Kearney CA, The functional profiles of school refusal behavior:
diagnostic aspects. *Behav Modif* 2004;28:147–61.

Depressive disorders are also one of the more common psychiatric disorders found in children and adolescents who refuse to attend school. Although the prevalence of these disorders is not exactly known, some studies suggest that 13–21% of school-refusing students may have a depressive disorder or an adjustment disorder with depressed mood. It is thought that many more children, perhaps up to half, may show subclinical depressive symptoms, and this is more often than not associated with a comorbid anxiety disorder.

Conduct disorder symptoms are not characteristic of school refusal, although children who refuse to attend often may display stubborn, argumentative, and even aggressive demeanors when their parents pressure them to go to school. Oppositional symptoms, which can encompass some of the foregoing behaviors, have been reported in between 9% and 22% of anxious school refusing children. High externalizing scores in the absence of or in excess of internalizing scores on the CBCL may be a red flag that the child may in fact be truant and not a traditional school-refusing child.

In conclusion, school refusal can be quite diagnostically and symptomatically diverse and may include a wide range of anxiety, phobic, depressive, and oppositional disorder symptoms. The full spectrum of psychiatric disorders and their reported prevalence in one study are listed in Table 19.1.

ETIOLOGY AND PATHOGENESIS

Although development and progression of school refusal is multifaceted, the term itself can be quite confusing. It is best to begin by more accurately defining school refusal and describing its relationship further with other problems associated with poor school attendance, such as truancy. The two differ in several key ways. For example, most school-refusing children like Sebastian were often previously considered average to good students from an academic and behavioral standpoint. Such children often want to complete their schooling in the long run and have higher goals than the truant child does. The truant child is often one that is uninterested or dislikes school. They often exhibit poor academic performance and significantly more often have a diagnosis of conduct disorder.

Sebastian, along with many other school-refusing children, has a pattern of continuous absences from school. These periods can last from weeks to even months at a time and tend to be quite distressing to parents in addition to quickly coming to the attention of school staff and administration. During such periods they often first seek mental health care. This is different from the truant child, who often has a more discontinuous and irregular pattern of school absence. The truant child or adolescent often attempts to conceal their absences from their parents and school officials. Sebastian has never made any attempts to conceal his missed school days and often stays home with his mother. The truant child in such situations would typically not stay at home when he or she is in fear of discovery or confrontation concerning their nonattendance. Finally, truant peers often attempt to make others believe they are attending school by going part of the way there or leaving the school early.

The school-refusing child also tends to display severe emotional upset or will complain of severe somatic complaints consistent with a medical illness when pressured to attend school. This is the case with Sebastian, as opposed to the truant young person who would likely make his parent believe he was walking to school before taking a detour to participate in other, more interesting activities. If such behaviors do not exist as with Sebastian, one has to wonder if a reasonable effort is being made by the parents or caretakers to get the child to attend school. This may signal that some degree of possible parental irresponsibility may be perpetuating the condition. Finally, the truant child often has a history of some antisocial behaviors and conduct disorder symptoms. This was not the case with Sebastian and would not be with most school-refusing children. Although the school-refusing child can become resistant and even aggressive, this is almost always confined to the home environment and situated around resistance to attending school. They typically have little to no history consistent with conduct disorder. In the case of Sebastian, he has no history of legal charges or aggression until recently, when he has become belligerent at home toward Mother and been served with a subpoena concerning truancy charges.

Most children with severe and chronic school refusal possess some form of an anxiety and/or mood disorder. These children have often had an anxious temperament style from an early age and while not diagnostic, many have had difficulties with separating from their parents in their earlier years and often present to the doctor with an already long history of absences from school. Often the anxiety specific to the school setting or separation from a caretaker may have generalized by the time the youth sees a clinician. It is not out of the question for children who have been out of school for some time to learn that there are many advantages to not being present at the school on a daily basis (both primary relief of anxiety and secondary gain, such as increased parental attention). Subsequently, a learned behavioral component can develop over time that can further perpetuate the problem of school refusal and diminish the motivation of the client to return to the classroom. Further complicating the situation is the fact that sometimes a child may display symptoms characteristic of more than one type of attendance problem. For instance, if school refusal is not promptly treated it may lead to a frustrated and exhausted parent who begins to fail to apply appropriate pressure to their child to attend school. Over time this can allow a child to gradually move to more long-term homebound schooling and possibly even school withdrawal. This tendency for school refusal to escalate in severity fairly quickly makes it an urgent situation that should be tended to without delay.

In summary, cases such as Sebastian's can pose many quandaries concerning etiology and pathogenesis. A brief formulation of his case follows. Sebastian is a 12-year-old Caucasian male with a past history of several years of much milder school-refusing behaviors that have escalated in severity and frequency over the past 6 to 12 months. He has many predisposing biological risk factors, such as a family history of mental illness. Depression, anxiety, and possibly bipolar depression run on one or both sides of his family. His father has engaged in some antisocial behaviors resulting in incarceration. Sebastian has been exposed to several significant stressors during his life. His mother is battling several major physical and mental illnesses, which predisposes him to anxiety around her health and limits the resources she has both emotionally and financially. His father has been in and out of the home, and he has lacked a consistent second parental or male figure. This in addition to his mother's disabilities may have resulted in inconsistent boundaries being set at home due to Mother's lack of social supports and psychological guilt toward her son. Few social supports exist in the community, and Mother claims being "a proud person" makes her hesitant to engage available services at times. Sebastian's mother and home have been threatened by his father and his attempt to invade the home, in addition to the severe family conflict, has likely precipitated the recent worsening of his anxiety symptoms. Shortly after the incident resulting in his father's incarceration, Sebastian first began experiencing substantial bullying along with significant worsening of his anxiety symptoms.

These symptoms of fear have likely been further perpetuated over the past four months by his home being invaded by a SWAT team and the reoccurrence of perceived bullying in the educational setting. From a psychological standpoint he likely resents his mother's inability to protect him from these things in addition to her difficulty relating with him due to her chronic physical and mental illnesses. At times Sebastian may be attempting to mirror some of his mother's psychopathology, and this may perpetuate his illness. The two appear quite codependent from a psychological standpoint. This has created continuing problems with Mother setting and maintaining boundaries in the home. As Sebastian has missed significant periods of school, this has likely led to further social impairments and anxiety around his return to school. Recent truancy charges have begun to make him see school administration in a more adversarial role. Legal consequences and his mother leaking the possibility of his removal from the home have likely exacerbated his symptoms even further. His grades have dropped to the point that he reports being well behind his peers who are attending school. Falling behind at school probably further increases his worry around his return to the academic setting.

Protective factors include his average intelligence and relatively good health. Recently extra supports and boundaries have been put in place with the involvement of the juvenile justice system and social services. At school, he has an IEP which is protective, and Mother has been resourceful enough to obtain the free services of a stable long-term patient advocate. Previously he has had no history of violence and legal charges. His past history of average social skills may also benefit him as he begins his return to the educational and social environments.

NATURAL COURSE WITHOUT TREATMENT

School refusal can be symptomatically and diagnostically diverse. It can have an insidious onset, but as it evolves, it can result in a more chronic or acute reluctance to attend school and even progress to refusal to remain in classroom or a total refusal to attend school. Despite this, a more acute onset is possible, especially after a sentinel event or severe stressor. These symptoms often can wax and wane over the course of days and even hours. Subsequently the only mildly anxious child in the office can exhibit significant impairing anxiety when confronted with imminent return to the school or within the school setting.

Many school refusers have had difficulty with school attendance before, but of lower severity, only missing occasional days. Onset of school-refusing behaviors can occur gradually over years, as was the case with Sebastian. He had many more days absent from school when compared with other children in elementary school. These absences were often due to vague physical complaints and would occur during times of stress. When he began missing several days at a time over the past few years, his mother began to make attempts and negotiate deals to persuade him. Rarely removal from the home by social services sometimes is used as a last resort if the parent or caretaker is not able to or willing to apply the appropriate consequences and incentives considered reasonable to coax their child to attend school.

By the time mental health professionals became involved in Sebastian's case, the problem had become chronic in nature. Numerous studies have shown that school refusal is very much a chronic problem. Children with such refusing behaviors have a high prevalence of anxiety and depressive disorders earlier in childhood, though anxiety is by far more common. These children, like Sebastian, suffer from many somatic complaints. Such vague complaints occurred as a result of separation anxiety during Sebastian's elementary school years, but during his middle school years his avoidance of school began to serve as a way to remove him from the stress of perceived negative peer interactions. At first, his symptoms were worse in the morning and quickly resolved as the day progressed, but over a period of several years these vague complaints became more common, persistent, and intense. During this time his mother sought help from their primary care physician and specialists to treat these physical concerns. This resulted in unnecessary invasive workups and numerous medications to treat such symptoms as headaches and gastrointestinal distress. It took considerable rapport and assistance from professionals before Sebastian's mother could accept the symptom etiology being mental distress rather than signs of a genuine physical ailment.

School refusal can have significant consequences over the course of the illness. Sebastian had no close peer relationships, problems with bullying, family conflict, and most obviously poor academic performance as a result of his absences. Despite having access to Medicaid, the many doctor visits and legal consequences from school refusal posed further financial stressors for Sebastian's family. As his time out of school came to the attention of school administration, attempts were made to coax him back into attending school regularly. Refusal to attend school at some point ultimately resulted in reports of concern being made to the local truancy officer, who then attempted to place further pressures on Sebastian to abide by the legal requirements to routinely attend school. Legal charges are often needed in more severe cases and can motivate some children and adolescents to attend school more regularly. Despite this, some children end up progressing well into the juvenile justice system and in some cases can end up in juvenile detention for continued refusal to attend school.

If improvements in Sebastian's anxiety symptoms and school-refusing behaviors are not obtained, further comorbidities could develop, future employment difficulties could occur within the family, and academic failure or underachievement would likely be the outcome. Fortunately most cases of school refusal are not as severe as Sebastian's case. A considerable percentage of early school refusal situations will either resolve or improve suddenly with firm and consistent parental pressure and support. School refusal history of greater than two years, occurrence in adolescence, lower IQ scores, and comorbid depression are correlated with a poor prognosis. Sebastian has many of these poor prognostic indicators. Many children meet criteria for psychiatric disorders later in life in addition to having future social difficulties, marital difficulties, and problems maintaining employment.

EVIDENCE-BASED TREATMENT OPTIONS

Overall there is a lack of evidence for treatment of school refusal. This is likely due to the fact that many of the studies are either case reports or case series. There is good evidence that the longer the child is absent from the school, the more difficult it will be to get them to return to the classroom promptly. Ensuring that the parents and school staff are allied and on the same page in terms of their goal to return the child to school can be helpful. Communication between all involved parties is essential. If attempts to immediately return the child to the school fail, the primary treatments that must be considered include several different forms of psychotherapies and psychopharmacological agents.

Attempting to get a child into psychotherapy routinely takes some time if such a relationship has not been previously established. In cases such as this, when time is of the essence, it is important to attempt to advocate for the young person to help establish such care. The psychiatric physician may want to consider starting combined care, at least in the short term, as opposed to waiting the extra time to set up and coordinate split therapy. In most cases of school refusal, cognitive behavioral therapy (CBT) should be considered as a first-line treatment. The advantage of CBT is that it furnishes the child, the parents, and educational staff with a tool box of skills and strategies to help manage present symptoms and future complications. CBT also has the most research supporting its efficacy in school refusal in addition to being less costly and time consuming than many other therapies. CBT often begins with the teaching and practice of relaxation techniques followed by some form of graded exposure. Ultimately, as with most anxiety disorders, exposure and response prevention are essential treatment elements. Flooding desensitization can accelerate the exposure, is more quickly effective, and avoids prolonging the agony of worrying about returning to school. Family therapy is also thought to be helpful to further strengthen the family unit, which is often under immense stress subsequent to the child's behaviors. It is thought that only when children see that their parents are determined to ensure they return to school can measurable progress occur.

Pharmacotherapies for school refusal continue to be researched but have been used for decades to reduce underlying anxiety and mood problems. Typically psychiatric disorders are assessed, diagnosed, and individually treated with medications as deemed necessary. Although a critical component, pharmacotherapy is thought to be a second-line or adjunctive therapy for such children. Failure to participate in psychotherapies such as CBT may lead to inferior outcomes. The primary agents used in the literature are imipramine and SSRIs for anxiety disorders. SSRIs have the additional bonus of treating any underlying depressive disorders, whereas tricyclic antidepressants have not been shown to be effective in depressed children. Unfortunately, these medications can take weeks to begin to show any positive effects. This is inconvenient because several weeks is often not acceptable to these children and their families.

Within the psychiatric field, school refusal is considered one of the few true psychiatric emergencies. As such, prescribing clinicians are often forced to look at short-term use of quicker acting anxiolytic agents in addition to the foregoing treatments. There exists some limited evidence for anxiolytic medications, such as benzodiazepines. This is one of the few times such medications may be appropriate for this age group, but their use should be monitored closely and dosing should be either on an as-needed or short-term basis. Gabapentin, antihistamines, or alpha-1 agonist agents should be briefly tried before consideration of agents such as benzodiazepines. To summarize, although many treatment recommendations exists, little evidence is available to support the use of one over another. What evidence does exist favors the use of CBT in children with school refusal.

CLINICAL COURSE WITH TREATMENT

Because of the serious dysfunction and possible lifelong morbidity Sebastian could experience if his school refusal continues, such cases should be treated as an emergency, even including inpatient hospitalization to ensure safety if required. The primary focus on those similar to Sebastian should be on the identification and assessment of the issues at hand leading to the refusal behavior. Only then can the appropriate treatments be chosen and honed for success. The clinician begins with obtaining collateral information from parents and school staff. It is often not realistic to expect the child to identify factors that precipitated or are perpetuating their absence from school without first spending significant time building rapport. An initial step is to distinguish between children with school refusal versus the truant child because the approach to intervention is dissimilar. In those children with significant somatic complaints, arrangement of a brief medical investigation may be useful to reassure the parents there is no physical basis to their child's complaints and make them more receptive to psychiatric and psychological interventions. A more in-depth and costly workup should be avoided because often it can create more problems than it solves. Determining the history of school nonattendance can be useful in developing treatment because more sporadic and recent absences can often be treated with a quick enforced return to school while long-standing nonattendance in older children is often better addressed with a carefully considered gradual and graded return to school.

As soon as possible the clinician should do an in-depth exploration of the likely fears and anxieties around school attendance because they can vary significantly between children. Anxieties can include such things as fear of the toilets or locker rooms at school, participating in physical education, answering peer's questions about their absences, fear of separation from parents, and fear of being disciplined or singled out by school staff and administration. Identifying such fears can allow the clinician to implement immediate psychosocial interventions in addition to outlining the problematic areas to focus on for future psychotherapeutic interventions. In addition to perceived and exaggerated fears, the child may in fact be faced with some degree of actual challenges such as coping with bullying, learning difficulties, and social isolation. Sebastian faces all of these challenges on his return to school. The clinician can advocate that such experiences be swiftly abetted by prompt interventions on the school level. Rarely a change in school may be helpful for some situations like continued bullying, but this should typically not be the first choice because often problems can follow children from one school to another.

Finally, a thorough psychiatric evaluation is often warranted as continued refusal past several days is considered an emergency. Such an evaluation can look into other precipitating and perpetuating factors for the school refusal behavior and rule out complicating factors like comorbid mood disorders. When trying to quickly assess what factors are reinforcing school refusal, a scale such as the School Refusal Assessment Scale-Revised may be useful (Kearney 2006). This particular scale has 24 questions that measure the relative strength of four different reasons most children refuse to attend school. Versions are available for the child and the parent. The four reasons include two negative and positive reinforcers that commonly strengthen refusal behaviors. The school-refusing child often will not attend school to avoid particular situations or stimuli, as was the situation with Sebastian. He avoided school to avoid many social situations such as bullying and supposed negative interactions with his peers and teachers. He also had a past history of ADHD and a possible learning disorder per school reports. This likely leads to difficulty successfully completing the Erikson stage of Industry versus Inferiority, resulting in low self-esteem. Overall, his feedback was likely perceived as negative at school, and he may have been avoiding school over time to avoid such negative evaluations that are common to similar children. Sebastian may have been unconsciously attempting to pursue attention from significant others or to stay at home and avoid school work. At home he enjoyed playing video games for many hours daily and may have rightfully believed he would have more time to be involved in this gaming experience, one of his few voiced pleasurable activities, when he did not attend school.

CBT is a first-line therapy for school refusal and should be started as soon as reasonable in most cases. Despite recommendations to pursue a course of CBT, the family did not begin therapy until the behaviors had come to the attention of the truancy officer. Sessions to address school refusal can be more frequent than the traditional weekly meetings, because time is of the essence. As such it is realistic to consider twice weekly meetings. Although there is good evidence for the use of CBT in school-refusing children, the specific elements to the therapy that are the efficacious components are unclear. It is thought that it is the behavioral components, particularly exposure and flooding, which are most useful. As such, it is best that a wide array of basic CBT techniques is incorporated into the therapy. What makes CBT for school refusers unique is that it must heavily involve the parent and school to be successful. This was crucial in Sebastian's case, as Mother felt somewhat helpless with regard to her son's behaviors and had difficulty establishing and enforcing set boundaries. It is often the case that as much time is spent with the parent as with the child. Additionally, regular consultations with the school staff are thought to be helpful. Keeping both sides informed and working together often helps ally the parents and school. Sebastian's mother's refusal to allow school staff to talk directly with the psychiatrist and therapist were critical barriers to care. It was not until Mother was court ordered during the truancy hearing to sign appropriate HIPAA paperwork that this critical line of communication was reestablished. Communication with the educational setting should be a requirement of a continued relationship with these families.

Early on in therapy it is often appropriate to concentrate efforts on helping the parents and school staff develop pertinent coping strategies to help manage the young person. In this particular case, when the school and mental health professions were finally allowed direct contact, the client began to show improvement. If not successful initially through flooding, return to school typically should be attempted again throughout the course of CBT. Initial sessions with the child or adolescent focus on relaxation training and developing a tool box to help deal with anxiety symptoms before moving on to repeat attempts at exposure. The skill set should be developmentally appropriate to the child's or adolescent's age. These skills are taught primarily to give the young person a skill they can use to help combat physiological arousal later in the therapy and on the return to the school. In addition such skill sets offer the child a sense of further control over their experienced emotional states. Without this sense of control, the child will not be able to implement other CBT learned strategies.

Many different relaxation skills can be taught, but it is important to focus more on the ones that appear to be both easier and more useful for the child to employ. Common relaxation procedures include deep breathing, progressive muscle relaxation, and guided imagery, and less commonly techniques such as autogenic relaxation training and robot-ragdoll techniques for those who have difficulty sitting. In Sebastian's case, he was quick to refute the effectiveness of such strategies and would never practice such techniques at home without much hassle. Many other activities that the child enjoys doing and finds relaxing can be incorporated into the tool box and can help improve compliance. Such activities may include playing sports, listening to music, exercising, reading, and taking a bath. Role-playing can be used fairly effectively to help deal with expected social situations on returning to the school. The child can be encouraged to brainstorm likely questions and potential responses. He or she can then be exposed to question-and-answer situations through role-play with the therapist. This is especially important when school refusal involves social skill deficits and social withdrawal. The therapist can model examples for the child, but it is important that they come up with their own responses and not use the clinician's sample.

After being given a tool box of skill sets, the clinician spends part of the CBT sessions focusing on incorrect cognitions that may plague the young person. The school-refusing child often uses negative and anxiety-producing self-talk to support the absence from school. Common cognitive errors include an overestimation of the likelihood of negative events occurring, minimization of one's ability to manage particular situations, and appraisal of negative events as catastrophic. Sebastian's core belief system was perpetuated by all of these examples of cognitive errors. In challenging the young person to think about these foregone conclusions, the expectation is that the child will replace the negative self-talk with a more accurate and positive self-talk.

In the child who cannot be returned to the school promptly for whatever reason, it is important to begin talking about returning to school from the beginning of therapy and set realistic goals for such. Typically the reintroduction to school occurs around the middle of therapy. If the clinician and patient are meeting twice weekly, this would typically occur by week four to five of therapy. This is a flexible date but should include input from the physician and most important the parents and cannot be left to the sole discretion of the child. The child is not to be notified of the exact return date until several days before it occurs, but is given an approximate date at the beginning of treatment if possible. The introduction is usually graded and the timeline takes the patient's input heavily into consideration. School officials and parents are prepared and available to assist in the return. In setting up this return, it is always better to err on the side of moving slowly so as to improve the chances that the child will experience success. An initial successful return to school, even if only for minutes, can build confidence and motivation to continue working on return to the school. If the child experiences a relatively easy and problem-free return, he or she can always speed up the process as quickly as is desired. Successful steps in the child's return should be recognized, praised, and even rewarded while total refusal to cooperate on any level should be met with consequences.

Although a quick return is optimal, it can be difficult in those that have not attended in many weeks to months. In these cases, a too hastily planned return, if unsuccessful, can lead to a perceived failure by the child and damage the self-confidence and alliances that have been developed in treatment sessions. If such occurs, the clinician may quickly put the blame on the plan so as to remove it from the young person if appropriate. Setbacks should be expected and discussed in treatment before the return to school so as to normalize them. Subsequently, when an obstacle occurs, it can be dealt with more easily by all involved and not seen as calamitous by the child or adolescent. However, by not being able to tolerate school, the child will already feel inadequate and have the lowest self-confidence levels because of failure to accomplish what the vast majority of children are able to do. For this reason, and also to avoid prolonging the agony, some clinicians employ a more aggressive approach to returning to school and prefer flooding exposure to a graded approach. This can be immediately successful if the child realizes there are no other options. This behavioral approach requires careful planning and coordination with parents and the school. There is commonly an "extinction burst" of protest behaviors before settling back in school, and these behaviors can be potentially dangerous as the child ups the ante. Interestingly, in Sebastian's case, CBT was not helpful until after he was ordered by the court to attend school. He was comfortable with not attending and believed the consequences of attendance outweighed much of the stress created by his behaviors. As such, he was not motivated initially to participate as he was only at the precontemplation stage of change. Despite this, in those willing to participate, CBT should be considered one of the first lines of care.

When working with the parent, the satisfaction with the current school should be explored. Plans to work alongside the school can become unglued when parents lose confidence in their child's school. In the worst of cases, such as this one, the mother and school many even develop an adversarial relationship to an extent resulting in the client and their family not cooperating with school recommendations nor allowing sufficient communication between the school and mental health professionals. In such cases a change of class or school may be warranted, especially if there appears to be significant difficulties or conflict between the family and school.

Efforts to identify and reduce positive reinforcement for the child while he or she is at home should be accomplished. This reduces the secondary gain that may be perpetuating refusal behaviors. Many of these were present with Sebastian, and their removal proved quite successful after Mother began finally consistently enforcing boundaries after the truancy hearing. These efforts for Sebastian involved completing school work at home and denying access to the television, computer, and other forms of entertainment and media.

The parents and practitioner should discuss the child's return to school and set an approximate date but not notify the child of the specific date until shortly before the return to decrease anticipatory anxiety and extend the return over a much longer period of time. In the several days or more leading up to the return, a morning routine should be reestablished and problems with such addressed punctually. The parents should be made aware that enforcing the return to school may be difficult for them and that they may have to set instructions and boundaries around it. They also will need to be taught to ignore inappropriate behaviors, such as tantrums and somatic complaints. Parents will need to be prepared with some well-thought-out reinforcements to help fortify and shape appropriate behaviors. Specifically the parent should be prepared for the day of the return and for problems that may arise, such as the child not getting out of bed willingly, refusing to get into or out of the car, or running away. This preparation helps reduce anxiety and replaces it with some sense of control. Finally, anxiety-reducing strategies may need to be taught to those parents with more severe apprehension around this situation.

An alliance with the school staff and administration can be invaluable when working with the school-refusing child and parent. Poor communication or inability to communicate effectively with the school can pose many headaches for the mental health professional and result in poor therapeutic response. This was a critical area of deficit in Sebastian's case, as a patient advocate was the only person allowed to communicate between those involved in care. Ideally, appropriate school staff should be kept advised and informed of the ongoing progress and the child's pending return to the school along with any special needs they may require. On the first day of return to the school, the child should optimally be greeted by school staff at a place and time that would minimize any embarrassment. The first day the student may not even be able to associate with peers or complete any schoolwork. He or she may only stay in the guidance counselor's office becoming familiarized with the routine for that day or week as appropriate.

Expectations can be discussed this first day, and a plan should be arranged so that the child has supportive staff they can seek out if needed. Again it is important to emphasize to the school that expectations and goals should be set low initially. It may be required that the student be excused from certain situations on a longer term basis, such as performing or speaking in front of others. Over the first several weeks the attendance needs to be monitored closely and the child not excused from school if at all possible. Parents and the school will need to be aware of and supportive of continued attendance despite any voiced somatic complaints. During Sebastian's returns, he would often experience somatic complaints to the point of asking the school nurse to call his mother to come pick him up from school. It is helpful if any school staff is trained in relaxation techniques the client has learned so that they can reinforce their use during more difficult times. The school nurse and guidance counselor attempted to assist in this, but until the court date, Sebastian would not cooperate with such attempts to aid him if they did not comply with his desire to return home.

If the child should need to remove themselves, they should have work sent home with them and be expected to return the next day. Parents should attempt to put off picking up the child before the end of the school day to increase exposure, and a fairly difficult day may warrant the parent calling or taking the child to see one of the treating mental health professionals. If the child misses consecutive days, or has to be excused frequently, their absences need to be addressed promptly in therapy and the treating psychiatric physician should be notified by the parent and school. Ideally the school and parent can work and communicate with each other effectively and manage most problems without involvement of other professionals. Mediation by medical professions will decrease over time and be kept to a minimum.

Family therapy can be a useful adjunct for the family of a school-refusing child. It is only when the child realizes that the parents are determined to return to the child to school that real progress toward that goal can be made. Mother becoming determined to return Sebastian to school full-time was in fact the keystone in this case and can be in others. School refusal typically leads to increased stress within the family and its relationships. Although family therapy is often recommended, it is rare that it is suggested in isolation from other therapies. Additionally, there is no strong evidence to support the use of family therapy in school-refusing children and adolescents. Work with the family is often covered to some extent with CBT in these children. Despite this, in families where the dynamics are perpetuating the refusal behavior, family therapy may be a useful adjunct.

Many medications can increase anxiety in individuals such as Sebastian, and a solid review of the medication regimen can be helpful in determining if any part of the anxiety at school follows the use of a particular medication. Commonly used medications in children that can increase anxiety include albuterol and stimulant medications (amphetamine and methylphenidate products) used for ADHD. Although stimulant therapy can increase anxiety in select individuals, there also exists evidence that they can reduce anxiety in children with ADHD if many of their worries and situational anxiety are due to their ADHD symptom burden. In Sebastian's case, a brief trial of one to two weeks off the stimulant medication was attempted, which resulted in overall worsening of his ADHD and anxiety symptoms. Consequently it was concluded that the benefits of this treatment appeared to warrant restarting it at its previous dosing. Another option would have been to maximize the guanfacine for his ADHD symptoms, as it has anxiolytic effects. This was not pursued further because the client felt that higher doses were previously sedating and did not improve his ADHD symptoms to the extent that stimulant therapy did.

Pharmacological treatment is often needed as an adjunct to CBT in school-refusing children. It is typically recommended in children who cannot return to the education environment fairly quickly. Though thought to be effective, there is little evidence from solid clinical studies supporting its efficacy in school refusal. Still, due to its relatively quick onset of action and ease it is often tried first alongside psychotherapeutic approaches. In most cases only mild to moderate relief is obtained from medications. This is also commonly the case with anxiety disorders and why it is important to combine medications with other strategies. The two primary medications used are tricyclic antidepressants (TCAs) and SSRIs. TCAs have shown some efficacy in anxiety disorders and school refusal. Despite several positive studies, the evidence is mixed when looking at the handful of studies done with school refusers. In addition, this class of medications tends to have more side effects and TCA reviews have no evidence in treatment of depressive disorders in children, which often accompany school refusal behaviors. TCAs tend not to be as well tolerated by children because they have many anticholinergic and antihistaminic side effects. They also can rarely cause cardiac electrical conduction disturbances.

SSRIs have become the mainstream first-line care for anxiety and depressive disorders accompanying school refusal. This is due primarily to the fact they can treat both depressive and anxiety symptoms. Additionally, they are thought to be safer and have fewer side effects. There are no studies looking at the efficacy of these agents with school-refusing children, but they have been shown to be effective in many of the disorders that tend to accompany school refusal, such as social phobia, separation anxiety disorder, generalized anxiety disorder, and major depressive disorder. Sebastian had two trials of SSRIs. The first one was citalopram, resulting in mild improvement in symptoms. When complications resulted as his school refusal progressed, this agent became less effective and was abandoned for a trial of fluoxetine. Fluoxetine was chosen because there was question of some compliance issues. It is much more forgiving with regard to frequently missed dosing due to its long half life. He showed some improvement on fluoxetine, which was titrated up to 40 mg daily, but his improvement may also have resulted more from legal and environmental interventions that occurred around the same time.

Buspirone, β-adrenoceptor antagonists, and antipsychotics have been used instead of and to augment SSRIs. There is little evidence to support their use with children, and no evidence to support their use in school refusers specifically. When Sebastian began attending school routinely, he started having more frequent and severe panic attacks. At one point these attacks got quite severe and generated significant physiological arousal per parental and school reports and clinician observations. This would sometimes lead to aggressive posturing toward school staff and Mother. It also limited his ability to use the few coping skills he knew. Subsequently, we agreed to begin a trial of extended release propranolol to reduce the physiological arousal. This appeared to further reduce the severity of his panic attacks and helped him stay in the classroom for longer periods of time. Finally, there is some limited evidence as previously mentioned for the use of anxiolytic medications such as benzodiazepines that can cause disinhibition and associated self-injurious or suicidal behavior if associated with depression. Sebastian was given a very limited supply of low-dose clonazepam to use as needed to help him either get to or remain in school. This was helpful to him during the several days around his return to school. Benzodiazepines should be reserved as a last-line treatment and used short-term and sparingly because there is further risks of side effects and dependency on these medications.

Ultimately the involvement of the juvenile justice system was a turning point in this case. This typically is and should be one of the latter options, though it can be very useful. Sebastian's court date and experience served to motivate both him and Mother to participate in and remove barriers to care. The real threat of her child ending up in training school, detention, or under the care of social services helped invigorate Mother to enforce boundaries she set and personally deal with the psychological issues interfering with such. Legal repercussions persuaded Mother to also pursue follow-up with a mental health professional who has helped along with Sebastian's therapist to motivate her to begin to enforce the boundaries set in the home. These boundaries along with the legal repercussions of continued school refusal led to more effective care and participation by all involved. Despite continued difficulty with anxiety, over the following months Sebastian began regularly attending school and only missed about one and a half days over the first month he was back.

SYSTEMS-BASED PRACTICE ISSUES

Several systems-based issues exist within treatment of school refusal. Often a primary care clinician inadvertently colludes with the psychopathology by willingness to provide a physician's excuse for school absences. Although motivated by compassion, this intervention could prolong the agony and lead to greater dysfunction. It works at cross-purposes to what is known to be therapeutic and, even worse, may be pivotal in causing lifelong morbidity. The ethic of nonmaleficence ("do no harm") must rule the day.

The whole concept of school refusal requires the mental health professional to be proficient at communicating and working with educational systems. Communication was impeded by Sebastian's family during his course of care until permission for further contact was deemed necessary and ordered by a judge during the truancy hearing. Intervention requires a well-coordinated plan for exposure and response prevention including medications, relaxation techniques, social skills, and other techniques to effectively deal with negative emotions. In some cases of school refusal the juvenile justice or social services systems of care may become involved because school attendance is mandatory in most states to at least age 16 and some to age 18. Although these systems can be helpful, they also can become detrimental if poorly coordinated and seen as adversarial in nature from the perspective of the client's family. If at all possible, the mental health professional should maintain a supportive role during such proceedings so as to maintain a relationship with the child or adolescent.

Poor communication and knowledge of these systems of care leads to inferior treatments. The mental health clinician should help coordinate the systems of care involved, but without taking the primary lead for decision making in other systems of care. Advocacy for the child in these other systems of care can be invaluable and their primary goal should be to ensure that all parties are working together and not against one another for the child. Unfortunately school refusal behavior has often gone on for some period of time and multiple systems of care have been involved before the mental health professional becomes involved.

LEGAL, ETHICAL, AND CULTURAL CHALLENGES

During treatment and assessment of school refusal, several legal and ethical issues can arise. Numerous absences from school often lead to truancy officials being notified. This can result in the child and families being charged with truancy and the Department of Social Services can be subsequently notified and involved. Although this can be helpful for the truly truant child, it often can just further increases the experienced stress of the school-refusing young person. Such charges can create rifts between the school, the child, and the family, and in most cases it is entirely understandable that the physician, attempting to intervene and advocate for the young person, might offer documentation that the previously missed school days were missed due to underlying medical illness. Removal of the child from the home is contraindicated unless there is a significant truancy component to the school refusal behavior and the parent is thought to not be making a reasonable effort in enforcing boundaries around school attendance. At all times the focus should be on returning the child to the educational setting while strengthening the family and its supports.

The physician should attempt to mediate any conflict between the different systems of care involved, such as the parent, therapist, educational, and juvenile justice systems. Such conflict can prevent the young person from getting the services required for a successful return to school. The child and adolescent clinician is often in the best position and the best trained professional to deal with such conflict and help effectively coordinate systems of care when substantial problems arise. At all times, professionals should be grounded in person-centered care, which requires advocating and supporting the child or adolescent through this difficult time.

TERMS

School refusal: a difficulty with school attendance that often causes distress for the family and presents a challenge to educational and mental health professionals. As previously noted, the school-refusing child is often not deceptive, nor does he or she have any history of conduct disorder symptoms. The parent and all parties involved are usually aware of the situation, and there is no attempt by the child to conceal the absences. Typically the child with school refusal was previously at least an average student academically.

School withdrawal: equivalent to dropping out of school. This typically has to be done when it is legally possible, and the age it can be done varies from one state to another. Withdrawal of an adolescent from school can be done for many different reasons, such as boredom, pursuit of more immediate employment, and repeated academic failure with subsequent frustration.

Truancy: purposefully planned absence from school to avoid schoolwork and often to engage in what are perceived to be more enjoyable activities. It usually involves significant attempts by the child to conceal the absence, and when the child is absent he or she is usually not at home. Truant children have often previously struggled at school and may have exhibited some conduct disorder symptoms. Truancy is considered against the law and a status offense for youth.

REFERENCES AND RESOURCES

Fremont W. School refusal in children and adolescents. *Am Fam Phys* 2003;68:1555–64.

Heyne D, King NJ, Tonge BJ, Cooper C. School refusal, epidemiology and management. *Paediatr Drugs* 2001;3(10):719–32.

Kearney CA. Confirmatory factor analysis of the School Refusal Assessment Scale-Revised: child and parent versions. *J Psychopathol Behav Assess* 2006;28:139–44.

Kearney CA, Albano AA. The functional profiles of school refusal behavior: diagnostic aspects. *Behav Modif* 2004;28:147–61.

King N, Tonge BJ, Heyne D, Ollendick TH. Research on the cognitive behavioral treatment of school refusal: a review and recommendations. *Clin Psychol Rev* 2000;20: 495–507.

Wimmer MB. *School Refusal: Information for Educators.* Helping Children at Home and School II: Handouts for Families and Educators, 2004, http://www.nasponline.org/families/schoolrefusal.org.

AACAP Facts for Families, "Children Who Won't Go to School," www.aacap.org, Facts for Families No. 7.

AACAP Facts for Families, Bullying, www.aacap.org, Facts for Families No. 80.

U.S. Dept. of Health and Human Services, Stopbullying.gov website.

PART IV

Blended
Psychopathology

CHAPTER 20

Unexplained Physical Symptoms

Bush Kavuru, M.D.

CLINICAL PRESENTATION

Chief complaint: "My whole right side is numb. My arm, my leg, my face . . . I can't walk. I feel paralyzed. I can't feel anything."

History of present illness: Amanda is a 20-year-old single white female with a 4-year-old son who is admitted to a medical unit with a history of right-sided weakness and numbness over the past few weeks, with a waxing and waning course. Since onset, her symptoms have never entirely disappeared. She has been briefly admitted twice to the hospital. This is her third admission through the hospital emergency room for her recurring symptoms. Amanda's initial symptoms began a few weeks ago at her workplace, where she is a restaurant server. One day after a busy lunch shift she felt weak and tingly on her right side; when she returned home in the evening she could not move her right arm and leg, and the right side of her face felt numb.

She has intermittent burning urination and is not sexually active. She reports mild diarrhea for the past year especially when she eats greasy foods. Her sleep is fine; her appetite has been poor for a week. Because Amanda is not getting any better, her foster mother decides to bring her to the hospital for physical therapy and a second opinion.

During her first visit to the hospital her weakness worsened in the emergency room. Amanda's white blood cell count was 14.8, urine culture was negative, with no growth, and EKG was in normal sinus rhythm. She was admitted for three days with a completely negative medical workup; however, as her weakness slowly improved she was discharged. Amanda stayed home for two days after discharge and then went to back to work at the restaurant. She was on a light schedule for a day or two. She reported occasional spells of feeling "lost" at work and staring, while coworkers reminded her to get back to serving customers. She was eventually asked to work during a busy lunch shift. On that day while working, she felt sudden sense of weakness and within a few minutes could not move or speak. This resulted in her second visit to the emergency room and readmission to the hospital.

During her second admission, Amanda's numbness worsened and she was not able to feel most of her back. A neurologist noted that she had "flaccid paralysis of the right upper extremity and right lower extremity with a subjective sensory deficit in left lower and left upper extremity with normal grip strength. Mild swelling of the right arm and leg is noted in a lady with left-sided dominance." A differential of myoclonic epilepsy was entertained and outpatient workup was suggested. At discharge, Amanda was given a walker to assist in ambulation.

After returning home from this second hospitalization, Amanda continued to feel weak. She needed a walker to get around the house and was not able to perform her normal daily activities like caring for her son, doing dishes, and washing clothes. She started getting depressed about not getting better. She cried when alone, felt drained of energy, and felt physically weak. From home she spoke to her employer on the phone, who said her job was safe and they were waiting for her to come back.

During this third and current admission, Amanda was seen by a neurologist who suspected conversion disorder. Investigation included normal results for a CT scan of the head, MRI of the head, and EEG. Physical therapy was begun as Amanda has shown no symptomatic improvement for two consecutive days.

On direct questioning, she denies having any current major life stressors. She states her mood is sad now but then it is "okay" prior to the weakness. Sleeping is normal, and appetite has been poor. Energy reportedly is low. Self-esteem is good. "Confidence is good," she says. She denies feeling hopeless or helpless. She says she is looking forward to playing with her son, Joshua, after discharge from the hospital. She looks forward to going back to work and wants her full energy back. She denies any guilt, suicidal or homicidal ideation, and symptoms of mania or psychosis.

Amanda reveals that she has also been suffering from anxiety attacks brought on by new tasks or social situations. Her initial panic attack occurred two weeks ago at work. On that day, one of her coworkers fell sick and Amanda had to manage the cash register, serve, and clean the tables all in the same shift. As things got more hectic and busy, a sense of choking and fainting suddenly came over her "almost like a stroke." She went to the restroom, breathed slowly and deeply, calmed herself, and went home early.

Her symptoms have always occurred at work and come on rapidly. Amanda feels overwhelming anxiety in waiting tables during the lunch hour and describes her work as stressful. Apparently she never complains at work and feels she needs the job for her economic stability.

Amanda also expresses feelings of loneliness and missing lots of fun like other 20-year-old women. She experiences a sense of disappointment whenever she sees her friends going out together to socialize and she has to stay home to care for her son. She states that she does not feel bad about it all the time, because she loves her son so much, but sometimes wishes she had someone to babysit so she could socialize. She says her foster parents help take care of her son when she goes to work. She expresses a hope to become a nurse, get a good job, and provide a good life for herself and her son.

She says she is not necessarily looking for a boyfriend, but would love to have someone who can care for her without judging her. She describes herself as a caring and loving person. She reflects growing up without any love and affection. Amanda recollects sexual abuse from her family of origin until her move to a foster home. She is happy with her foster family and continues to live with them now.

After each hospital discharge Amanda's symptoms recur when she returns to work and are less apparent when she is home caring for her son. She feels compelled to work to fend for herself and the baby because the father of the child is in jail and is of no help. She gets support from her foster parents. Amanda says she is good at her job and looks forward to going back to work. Even though she expresses the concern about how her recurrent symptoms would affect her employment status, most of the time she appears indifferent to her physical disability.

Medically she has a history of seizure disorder and asthma. She denies other neurological symptoms like slurred speech, visual or hearing changes, or facial droop. She denies any recent seizure activity. She denies any new medicines. She denies any illicit drug use. Amanda's surgical history is positive for a classical cesarean section, tonsillectomy, and tympanoplasty.

Other history: Amanda was taken away from her biological parents around the age of 16; since then she has stayed with the same foster parents. Her history was positive for serious sexual abuse at the hands of her siblings and cousins. She does not have much expression when she speaks about her trauma and says it does not bother her now, and she is happy to move on with her life and leave the past behind. She says, "I love my foster parents; they are the best." She denies use of illegal substances or smoking tobacco. She consumes an alcoholic drink once in a while.

Her medication history includes sertraline 200 mg once a day, atomoxetine 120 mg per day, trazodone 50 mg at night, levetiracetam 100 mg twice a day, and albuterol inhaler as needed for asthmatic symptoms.

Mental status examination: Amanda looks young like a 20-year-old white female. She is moderately obese, she is in her own clothes, lying in the bed with little movement; she is cooperative with good communication skills. She makes good eye contact. Her speech is relevant, goal-directed, normal in tone, pitch, and volume and in prosody. She remains awake throughout her interview and is well oriented to time, place, and person. She has good attention and concentration. Her memory is intact. She is mildly anxious. Her thought processes are linear without any formal thought disorder and her thought content relates to her physical weakness and inability to walk. She denies feeling helpless or hopeless and denies any suicidal or homicidal ideation. She expresses significant frustration about her recurrent relapses and feels like a burden to her foster parents. She feels guilty for her inability to care for her son and wants to get better and be home with him. She displays good fund of knowledge and abstract thinking. She denies any paranoia or auditory and visual hallucinations. At times she talks matter of factly without any worry, especially when she is talking about her paralysis and numb feeling, suggesting the phenomenon of "La belle indifference."

During the session, she recollects a period of her life during her school years about getting sick with abdominal pain at school many times and being sent home, where she always felt better, without any pain. Looking back she is able to say school was always stressful and rough and she would get sick to avoid going to classes. These symptoms would not occur during summertime in absence of school and while she stayed at home. (The siblings and cousins who abused her were in the same school.) She shares that she was eager to graduate, and she did not pursue further studies after high school. She is able to see that her current physical sickness is a way for her to avoid the stress at work. She reflects, "I never thought about it that way and couldn't have guessed a link between them." Since finding a relation between work stress and onset of her weakness, Amanda is ready to address it and asks, "What will I do now?" With encouragement from the clinician that her mind can control her body, and her mind is dependent on her will, she agreed to test her will. She follows simple suggestive commands like shaking hands, flexing her knees, standing and walking. She stumbles in the beginning, taking some baby steps, and in a matter of minutes, she is able to walk up to the door and back, without any assistance. Her affect turns bright, with a smile on her face she says, "I am glad, I am able to walk." She also remembers that a few hours prior she could not move an inch and has been insensitive to painful stimulus. The improvement is significant and perceivable for Amanda.

IMPAIRMENT IN FUNCTIONING

Since her illness Amanda has not been able to bathe and feed her son, depending on her foster mother for taking care of him. She herself has not been able to drive around, carry groceries, or do laundry at home and has been asking her foster parents for help. She feels weak and helpless and has been missing work and not able to take her son to the playground or birthday parties. She needs rides to doctors' offices and hospitals. While in the hospital she needs help to go to the bathroom and clean herself.

DSM DIAGNOSIS

Somatization can be conceptualized as a process of understanding, experiencing and expressing psychological stress in a physical form. The treatment involves therapies to bring insight into the psychological origin of physical symptoms and helping the person learn adaptive and alternative coping skills that can lead to symptom resolution and prevent recurrence.

In this situation Amanda poses a challenge to the clinician in differentiating between conversion and factitious illness versus malingering to avoid working, while her foster parents take care of her child.

Her lack of concern on her disability during hospitalizations, absence of symptom exaggeration, and lack of manipulation or demands for new tests suggests malingering as the very least likely diagnosis. For it to be malingering, her symptoms need to be intentional, but her symptoms appear unintentional and unconscious in their origin.

Her current desire to go home and not wanting to be in the hospital and her willingness to go home in her prior two admissions do not support a sick role or support a diagnosis of factitious disorder.

Amanda does have an unexplained motor weakness with negative CT and MRI and sensory deficits, not conforming to an anatomical distribution, in the absence of a clear neurological or medical diagnosis. She is not able to state any stressors on direct questioning, but she shares her perception of stressors at work during an open-ended interview and eventually realizes the connection between her stressors and onset of physical symptoms, supporting a diagnosis of conversion disorder. Her ability to get up and walk in the same encounter confirms the diagnosis of conversion disorder, which is also called Functional Neurological Disorder in DSM-5.

By definition, *conversion* involves one or more symptoms of altered voluntary motor or sensory function. Clinical findings provide evidence of incompatibility between the symptoms and recognized neurological or other medical conditions. Psychological factors are judged to be associated with the symptoms or deficits.

Amanda's diagnosis is conversion disorder with motor and sensory deficits. The new edition of the DSM addresses some problematic aspects of the prior diagnoses of somatization disorder and conversion disorder. Under DSM-IV-TR diagnosis of these disorders relied heavily on "unexplained" medical symptoms, which were then attributed to the psychiatric disorder. Conceptually there is a problem with diagnosing an illness based on the clinician's inability to explain symptoms. In addition, many presentations of somatic complaints based on probable psychiatric illness did not neatly fit into any of the multiple subcategories of somatoform disorders. In DSM-5 the diagnoses are consolidated and simplified. The diagnosis of conversion disorder is retained and Amanda's presentation qualifies for this diagnosis.

EPIDEMIOLOGY

Somatization is common presentation in primary care. These persons present with physical symptoms that cannot be attributed to any physical disorder and are thought to be of psychological origin. Prevalence of conversion symptoms in the general hospital setting is around 20–25%, and 5% would qualify for a syndromal diagnosis. The percentages are higher in neurological and psychiatric settings.

According to the Epidemiological Catchment Area survey, the prevalence of DSM-III somatization disorder was 0.13% in the general population. Among a group of high utilizers in the primary care setting, Smith et al. (2005) found 23.3% prevalence of DSM-IV somatoform disorders.

DIFFERENTIAL DIAGNOSIS

There are many possible reasons for Amanda's symptoms. Is she faking these symptoms to avoid work and be home with her son? Does she get anxious with heavy work, especially during lunchtime? Can this be seen as secondary gain to consider a diagnosis of malingering versus factitious disorder?

Both malingering and factitious disorders involve conscious intent in feigning the symptoms, which differentiates them from conversion disorder. Malingering differs from factitious disorder in that the motivation for the symptom production in malingering is an external incentive, whereas in factitious disorder external incentives are absent. Evidence of an intrapsychic need to maintain the sick role suggests factitious disorder.

In clinical practice the Patient Health Questionnaire-15 (PHQ-15) is used as a standardized self-administered questionnaire with moderate reliability in diagnosing somatoform disorders. PHQ-15 focuses on somatic symptoms that are seen in primary care. It is part of the Primary Care Evaluation of the Mental Disorders (PRIME-MD.)

ETIOLOGY AND PATHOGENESIS

The etiology of the somatoform disorders is understood as an expression of unconscious wishes or conflicts through physical symptoms. This psychoanalytic explanation emphasizes the fact that the "conversion" of the psychological conflict into physical symptoms is beyond the awareness of the afflicted individual. The important aspect is that the subject is not producing the symptoms intentionally, as in the case of malingering or factitious disorder.

In Amanda's situation, she uses conversion as an adaptive defense mechanism whenever she is faced with perceived psychological stress. This is corroborated by her past history of recurrent abdominal pains at school, which improved when she was sent home and never occurred during the summer period when the schools were closed. It should be noted that her use of this defense mechanism is out of her awareness and is not volitional, distinguishing it from malingering.

Amanda feels unhappy over not having a social life like other girls at work. She says the reason for this is being a single mother and having no one to look after her son. It appears she also feels overwhelmingly anxious by comparing herself with other girls who were working more efficiently at the restaurant. These factors acted as perpetuating and provocative factors in eliciting Amanda's physical symptoms every time she was at work or when she thinks about going back to work.

NATURAL COURSE WITHOUT TREATMENT

Historically for most persons, acute symptoms of conversion disorders resolve within weeks. Among these people, 20–25% may have recurring symptoms within a year, often in association with a stressful life event. The outcome is very different among persons with conversion disorder that has been ongoing for longer than one year. For these persons, the persistence of symptoms is common and is often linked to significant psychiatric comorbidity. Usually the clinical course is linked with primary gain issues, where persons tend to hold on to the symptoms subconsciously as their primary gain is fulfilled and for fear of losing so-called benefits.

Conversion symptoms, if untreated, may resolve spontaneously or can become fixed. Conversion symptoms are mostly seen in histrionic and dependent styles of personalities, even though they can occur with any other type of personality traits or disorders. Without treatment, some persons can get worse and develop muscle contractures and develop decubitus ulcers and deep venous thrombosis. These persons may consent to various medical procedures even though they were given a possibility of psychogenic origin of their symptoms.

EVIDENCE-BASED TREATMENT OPTIONS

Cognitive behavioral therapy (CBT) and antidepressants were found to be effective in randomized controlled studies. CBT appeared effective in hypochondriasis and body dysmorphic disorder and less conclusively in conversion disorder. It cannot be ascertained whether antidepressants could improve comorbid depression and anxiety and in this way have a direct effect on somatic symptoms.

In many studies, clinical communication between a consultation liaison clinician and the primary care team about treatment strategies was found to improve the physical function of these persons, even though the somatic symptoms did not change.

CLINICAL COURSE WITH MANAGEMENT AND TREATMENT

In managing conversion symptoms, it is essential for the clinician to be sensitive to the person's perception about their physical nature of their illness. In general, persons presenting with conversion symptoms can become defensive if they are told "it's all in your head." These symptoms can be refractory to direct confrontation. Most of them perceive being seen as "fake" or "making up the symptoms" and get upset and feel angry and frustrated. Representing their symptoms as a disorder affecting their functionality and explaining how stress can affect bodily functioning through brain mechanism's gives them some face saving in accepting the psychological origins of their symptoms. Understanding this mind–body connection makes them ready for a change and to accept suggested psychiatric interventions.

In Amanda's situation, she is receptive to the idea of stress-induced physical symptoms and able to make a connection between stressful events at work and the onset of her symptoms. She is also able to come up with alternative thought processes and ways she can occupy herself with things of interest and not feel lonely or worthless. She feels she already has a "very important man" she dearly loves—her son—and she is not in any hurry to find a boyfriend. She recognizes the possibility of working and focusing on her educational goals and in spending time with her son to make him a better person in life. She shares that she has not been thinking right all along and now realizes that her work can be a source of strength for her economic freedom, her coworkers could be a help, and she should not think of them as adversarial.

Comorbidities like anxiety and depression are very common in subjects with conversion disorder, so it is very important to treat these conditions for the overall remission of symptoms and quality of life of the person.

Acute onset of symptoms with short duration with a recognizable psychological stressor indicate better prognosis in subjects with conversion disorder. Having a clinician who understands the psychological and behavioral origins of these symptoms can help the person in early symptomatic recovery. In this regard, a lack of awareness from the clinician can prolong the course of the illness. In general most of these subjects with conversion symptoms and psychogenic movement disorders are seen by a neurologist and perceived as feigning and malingering.

Shapiro and Teasell (2004) defined conversion disorder in a behavioral paradigm as maladaptive responses to life stress that are maintained with positive support from others and by physical disability to avoid the stressful life situations. Through a standard behavioral treatment modalities they have observed, that conversion symptoms that are acute in nature are quick to resolve with treatment and chronic symptoms would persist. In the same study 71% of persons with chronic conversion symptoms responded to strategic behavioral interventions, showing the usefulness of behavioral therapies using physical rehab as their main component.

Amanda has not discussed her problems with anyone prior to seeing this clinician. As she vents her issues in the session, she is able to recognize that she values herself as a mother and has goals to provide a good life for her son. Through Socratic questioning she is able to realize that to achieve her goals she needs a job, and her dysfunctional thought process of comparing herself with other girls and cognitive errors of minimizing her strengths are not healthy ways of thinking. During the session she recognizes that she is a responsible mother and a worker in the eyes of her foster parents and her boss and coworkers. This makes her feel good about herself. She is also able to develop alternative thoughts that work can be a place to show her merit, make money, and have her personal wishes fulfilled. Gaining these insights makes work an attractive place to go and not one to avoid.

As she participates in the cognitive therapy session, her mood improves and she develops insight that she may be expressing her psychological stress in physical symptoms instead of talking them out with someone she can trust and connect with.

SYSTEMS-BASED PRACTICE ISSUES

Most of the somatoform disorders are treated by primary care clinicians as medically unexplained symptoms; most conversion disorders and psychogenic movement disorders are treated by a neurologist, whose ability to address mental health issues is very limited, as is access to mental health services. These barriers can lead to prolongation of symptoms, delay in psychological interventions, and medical morbidity. For persons who are seen by a behavioral health specialist, reimbursements for CBT and psychotherapies is limited.

With the advent of electronic medical records, clinician communication between specialties like psychiatry and neurology and primary care can be improved to share lab reports and specialist evaluations and to come up with strategies of treatment as a team to improve patient care.

LEGAL, ETHICAL, AND CULTURAL CHALLENGES

There are instances when a person who has been given a conversion disorder diagnosis is later diagnosed with a demonstrable physical disorder. This can have medicolegal implications if there are any damages due to misdiagnosis or delay in medical diagnosis. Ethically it is challenging when persons showing symptoms of factitious illness or Munchausen syndrome try to subject themselves to high-risk tests and interventions, and it is also an ethical challenge to withhold some tests in strongly suspected cases.

Culturally somatization is reportedly seen more in rural, low socioeconomic, and less educated populations, but we need more data to support this.

HISTORY

Historically speaking, hysteria has been identified and studied for centuries. In the 16th century it was thought to be a manifestation of disease of the uterus, it was linked with witchcraft and demonic possession, and the subject's sensory symptom abnormalities of skin were called "devil's patches." Around the 17th century more psychological explanations were proposed, and it was considered to be a disease of the mind. In the 19th century Jean Martin Charcot studied it further with hypnosis and named it hysteria major. Later, similarly using hypnosis, Josef Breuer treated a young Viennese woman for her symptoms of convergent squint, paralyses, paresis of her neck muscles, and contractures.

REFERENCES AND RESOURCES

Allin M, Streeruwitz A, Curtis V. Progress in understanding conversion disorder. *Neuropsychiatr Dis Treat* 2005 Sept;1(3):205–9.

Feinstein A. Conversion disorder: advances in our understanding. *CMAJ* 2011 May 17; 183(8):915–20.

Kroenke K. Efficacy of treatment for somatoform disorders: a review of randomized controlled trials. *Psychosom Med* 2007;69(9):881–88.

Shapiro AP, Teasell RW. Behavioural interventions in the rehabilitation of acute v. chronic non-organic (conversion/factitious) motor disorders. *Br J Psych* 2004 Aug;185:140–46.

Smith R, Gardiner JC, Lyles JS, Sirbu C, Dwamena FC, Hodges A, Collins C, Lein C, Given W, Given B, Goddeeris J. Exploration of DSM-IV criteria in primary care persons with medically unexplained symptoms. *Psychosom Med* 2005;67(1):123–29.

Swartz M, Landerman R, George LK, Blazer DG, Escobar J. Somatization disorder. In: Robins LN, Reiger DA (Eds.). *Psychiatric Disorders in America—The Epidemiologic Catchment Area Study*. New York: The Free Press (Macmillan, Inc.), 1991. pp. 200–57.

Let There Be Light (1946), a film about Sigmund Freud and his early cases.

CHAPTER **21**

Pain

Justin White, M.D.

CLINICAL PRESENTATION

Chief complaint: "I had a seizure."

History of present illness: Sarah is a 26-year-old unemployed mother and married Caucasian female with migraine headaches and chronic lower back pain who presents to the emergency room for evaluation and treatment following a seizure. The patient had her first seizure about six weeks ago. She has been having one to two seizures a week, and her neurologist recently changed her medication regimen (from phenytoin to carbamazepine). She says that she has been adherent to this treatment plan, and laboratory studies confirm an appropriate level for the medicine.

This seizure was witnessed by her husband, who says it lasted about three minutes. She was lying in bed talking to him when suddenly she screamed and became unresponsive. Immediately she developed strong jerking movements of the head as well as the upper and lower extremities. There was no urinary incontinence, and some confusion was present as she regained consciousness. This new medical condition has had a profound effect on her life because she is not able to drive and is afraid to leave her home. While providing this history, Sarah becomes quite upset and reports feeling "overwhelmed." At one point she tells the triage nurse, "I wish I was dead and then all of this would just go away." Psychiatry is consulted and obtains the following information while waiting for a bed on the medical unit.

The patient says that she has been under considerable stress and is aware of anxiety and depressive symptoms that have become progressively worse over the past several months. She feels that her depression is directly related to lumbar physical pain that has been worse recently. She attributes the worsening pain to the particularly cold winter weather this year. She has had significant functional impairment from the pain and is upset that she is not able to be more physically active in playing with her children. With a slight smile and tears in her eyes she says, "Someone here should wrap me up in duct tape, because I'm falling apart . . . I feel like such an old lady sometimes."

Her husband has recently lost his job, and the entire family is experiencing stress. Finances are very limited to the extent that they may soon need to move to more affordable housing. Her primary care provider has been treating her depression and anxiety with a combination of citalopram and diazepam. She does not feel that this medicine is helping and is skeptical about seeing a mental health counselor. She is frustrated that she has seen a number of providers and does not feel that her general condition is improving. In an effort to educate herself about her medical conditions she is going to the library weekly and has been reading a number of self-help books in addition to reviewing various websites.

Regarding psychiatric symptoms, she describes sadness on most days of the week, and has experienced an increase in the number of tearful episodes over the past several months. There has been significant isolation to the point that she feels uncomfortable any time she leaves the home. Sarah no longer finds pleasure in previously enjoyed activities, such as knitting. She is aware of frequent irritability, and this is often directed toward her husband. She describes two to three physical altercations this past year toward him; fortunately no one was seriously injured, and no legal problems resulted from these events. One of her children has attention deficit disorder, and she is concerned about her poor frustration tolerance in addressing his behavior. She often feels that she is too loud and argumentative with him and then feels guilty when she calms down.

She finds that she is constantly thinking about her family and finances and has difficulty calming her mind. She constantly feels muscle tension, which triggers headaches and leads to worsening pain. Sleep has been poor and she estimates getting four to five hours of sleep per day. There is difficulty getting to sleep secondary to "racing thoughts," and she will often wake up early and stay in bed for hours. Poor sleep often leads to pain in the morning and difficulty with focus and distractibility that usually stays with her throughout the day. With the recent increase in stress she has started to have panic attacks and now has one to two a week. These usually occur in social situations and involve sudden and severe anxiety in the presence of shortness of breath, palpitations, and distal paresthesias lasting about 10 to 15 minutes. She was previously involved in a serious motor vehicle accident and does not enjoy driving. At one point she was experiencing nightmares about this event. Her pain became much worse since the accident.

Sarah clarifies her statement she made earlier in the evening suggesting the possibility of suicidal ideation. She would like to escape from her current set of stressors and physical pain but would never do anything that might hurt her children or husband. She also conveys protective spiritual beliefs. She denies having any access to weapons. She reports feeling safe in the hospital and denies active suicidal thoughts. In the emergency department a CT scan of the head shows no acute pathology, and there is no evidence for any significant arrhythmia per cardiac monitoring. Routine laboratory studies including electrolytes, liver function tests, glucose, pregnancy test, and a complete blood cell count are within normal limits.

Past psychiatric history: Sarah estimates having several major depressive episodes throughout her life and believes that the first episode was around the age of 12. She had some counseling in high school and was prescribed various antidepressants (clomipramine, fluoxetine, and sertraline) over the course of several years through her primary care provider. She acknowledges that as a teenager, her compliance with medicines was poor. As an adult she has had minimal outpatient psychiatric treatment but has required a previous inpatient psychiatric hospitalization. She was admitted to a state psychiatric facility when she was four months' pregnant for evaluation and treatment of suicidal behavior that involved numerous lacerations to the wrists and forearms.

Past medical history: Sarah says that she was born at term with a normal delivery and no complications. There were no known developmental abnormalities. She has struggled with obesity since her early teenage years and feels that this has contributed to a low self-esteem. Although she has tried a number of "crash diets," she denies any history to suggest an eating disorder. She has menorrhagia and has noted some worsening mood symptoms several days prior to her menstrual cycle beginning. A mild iron-deficiency anemia exists that is responding appropriately to iron replacement. Her previous surgical history includes molar tooth extraction, tonsillectomy, and tubal ligation. In her early twenties she had an elective cholecystectomy for recurrent right upper quadrant pain in the presence of gallstones.

Sarah recalls starting to experience some lower back pain when she was around 17 years of age. This pain did not lead to a significant level of functional impairment until approximately four years ago. Around that time she was involved in the motor vehicle accident. She was taken to the emergency department, and x-ray studies showed hypertrophic facet joints in the lumbar region. She had follow-up with her primary care provider and underwent several forms of conservative therapy. Her radiculopathy was initially treated with muscle relaxants and nonsteroidal anti-inflammatory medicines. She had physical therapy and has been using a transcutaneous electrical nerve stimulation unit, but she did not feel that these interventions were particularly helpful. Epidural steroid injections provide some partial relief, and the pain is reduced for about one to two weeks. An MRI later showed some evidence of disc herniation and foraminal stenosis. Eventually there was a neurosurgical procedure that involved a laminectomy. Over the first several weeks following her procedure she felt some benefit, but then began to feel worsening pain and says that now her pain is worse than it has ever been previously. She is scheduled for a trial of a neurostimulator in two weeks but is concerned that this would not be helpful and is now convinced that she will eventually need a drug pump.

Over the past six months she describes a daily headache that does not respond well to analgesic medicines. The pain is described as a generalized "throbbing" that may be a little worse on the right side. Sounds in the environment exacerbate the pain, and nausea is usually associated. It is common for her to have increased muscle tension in the neck and shoulders. There is no previous history of head trauma. She is aware that stress can cause worsening pain and will often "trigger a migraine." She also has been diagnosed with temporomandibular joint disorder and finds that there is some relationship with this and her headache pain. She has been taking analgesics as prescribed. The combination of carbamazepine and gabapentin has provided some modest reduction in the frequency and severity of headaches.

She also describes generalized soreness and muscle aches. She is quite upset as she describes how certain things that she is exposed to in her day-to-day environment that should not hurt cause her pain. In the evaluation and treatment of her pain, she has seen numerous care providers from many specialties, including physical medicine and rehabilitation, orthopedics, neurosurgery, rheumatology, emergency medicine, family practice, neurology, and psychiatry.

Medications: Prescribed medications that are scheduled include carbamazepine, celecoxib, citalopram, trazodone, ferrous sulfate, and gabapentin. Diazepam, hydrocodone/acetaminophen, and ondansetron are prescribed and used as needed. Herbal medications include a combination of ginger and curcumin. Occasional over-the-counter medications include Excedrin (acetaminophen, aspirin, and caffeine), diphenhydramine, and vegetable-based laxatives.

Allergies: Amitriptyline ("blisters"), artificial tears ("causes eyes to swell shut"), guaifenesin (breathing difficulty), tizanidine ("throat swelling"), varenicline ("severe mood swings"), latex (rash).

Social history: Sarah was born in Wisconsin in a rural town. She had two older sisters and one younger brother. Her mother died from complications secondary to melanoma when Sarah was five years old, and her father was the primary care provider for the family. Her father was a Methodist minister and was well respected in the community. She felt that her basic needs were met, but she did feel that he was somewhat emotionally distant, and often she felt lonely growing up. She did relatively well in school until the 11th grade. She remembers being sick frequently that year and consistently had trouble making up missed assignments. There were several fights involving other students, and she had few friends. She denies history of physical or sexual abuse. She became pregnant and was married in her senior year of high school. She dreamed of becoming a schoolteacher but did not feel that she had the support or finances to carry through with that and instead became a part-time clerk with a large railroad company. She was with this company for approximately four years. She felt underappreciated and was often upset with the work performance of her other colleagues. Currently she is on disability.

She describes having relatively few positive relationships in her life currently. She has three children with her husband, and they have been together for the past 10 years. She feels that her relationship with her husband currently is very strong and supportive. In his attempts to be available and care for her, her husband has been fired from several good jobs. One year ago he sustained a work-related injury while working as a cook and experienced a left lower extremity fracture. He has begun to have some chronic lower extremity pain. The patient feels that this has helped her to the extent that he is now able to have more understanding for the pain experiences she has been going through and is able to spend more time with the children. Her children are four, six, and seven years old. The oldest child has recently been diagnosed with attention deficit disorder. She has been concerned recently about her irritability toward him based on his behavior. She describes a good relationship with one friend in the neighborhood. This friend has been helping bring her to clinic appointments and has some depression and substance issues that she is struggling with.

Family history: The patient's mother died of complications related to melanoma. Her brother is heavily dependent on opiates, and she does not have much contact with him. One sister has previously had mental health treatment for generalized anxiety disorder and has a previous history of attempted suicide with psychiatric hospitalization. There is no known family history of bipolar illness or schizophrenia. There is no family history of suicide. The patient's maternal grandmother was diagnosed with Alzheimer's disease and is currently in a long-term care facility.

Substance use history: Sarah says that a few years ago she had several months where she found herself using alcohol in larger amounts than she originally set out to do. She found that this helps with the lower back pain and the anxious ruminations. During this time she does not recall having any social dysfunction related to her alcohol use, and she was able to quit without experiencing any significant withdrawal symptoms. She does not use any alcohol currently and has identified alcohol as a trigger for worsening her headache pain. Regarding pain medicine, she is aware of an unhealthy pattern where she will sometimes take extra hydrocodone when pain is very severe. She will then ration the remainder of her pain medicine and sometimes there are a few days before the next refill is available where she is completely out of opiate pain medicine. The husband indicates that he is aware of some emotional dysregulation related to this cycle. She has never purchased opiates from an illegal source. She clearly indicates that she does not take pain medicine "to get high." A few times per year she will smoke marijuana that is provided by her husband, who also smokes marijuana. She finds that this can sometimes help her with nausea, anxiety, and pain. Since she has been prescribed opiates, she has reduced her use of marijuana significantly and participates in random drug screening through her primary care provider. She denies any misuse of her gabapentin or diazepam. She appreciates that she has acquired some tolerance to the diazepam over the past year.

She says that her drug of choice is nicotine, and she has found it very difficult to quit smoking cigarettes despite having tried to do this many times. She started smoking when she was 17. She was able to quit for six months around the time of her first pregnancy but feels that numerous stressors eventually led to a relapse. She was also able to quit briefly around the time of her lower back surgery because this was a requirement for the operation. She is currently smoking one pack a day and is aware that this is expensive and harmful for her. She regrets her continued use and understands that she is not modeling healthy behavior for her children. She is concerned about cessation currently because she has gained some weight and finds that smoking does suppress her appetite. She has used bupropion in the past but did not find that it helped significantly with cravings. Anxiety was slightly worse, and fortunately no seizure occurred while on this medicine. A trial of varenicline resulted in significant emotional instability after one week.

Review of systems: The patient has not had any recent fever. She has unintentionally gained 20 pounds over the past six months, and she attributes this to less physical activity. She is unaware of any recent rash, new growths, or moles that have changed in size or color. She wears glasses, but has not had any recent changes in vision or eye pain. There has not been any recent hearing loss, drainage, ear pain, or tinnitus. She denies shortness of breath or cough and has not had any chest pain or palpitations. Her reflux has been slightly worse recently, and she does feel that this is related to her current medication regimen. During a panic attack she may encounter some brief chest discomfort. Constipation occurs when she takes hydrocodone in larger amounts. She has not had any pain with urination, hesitancy, or increased frequency. She bruises easily, but she denies the frequent bleeding of gums. There is some mild cold intolerance. She gets several upper respiratory infections a year, which she usually catches from the children. There is some pain with intercourse, and she feels that this is mostly musculoskeletal in nature. While the husband is out of the room, she denies any high-risk sexual behaviors and describes a monogamous relationship with him. She describes poor exercise tolerance and climbing up two flights of stairs is difficult, leading to pain and shortness of breath.

Physical exam: Temperature 98.2 °F, pulse 95, respirations 18 per minute, blood pressure 148/85, weight 205 pounds, height 64 inches, BMI 35, pain 7/10 (mostly localized to the lower back). Exam of the head and neck is within normal limits with the exception that the shoulders, neck, and scalp are tender to palpation bilaterally. There are no concerning skin lesions, and there is a small tattoo of the moon and two stars on the patient's left ankle and a tattoo of a brown bear on her back above her right scapula. Her chest is clear to auscultation bilaterally with normal heart sounds. Her abdomen is soft, nontender, and not distended with normal bowel sounds. There are some linear scars on the wrists and forearms, suggesting previous lacerations. There are surgical scars on the lower back.

Mental status examination: Sarah appears to be slightly older than 26 years of age. Her basic grooming and hygiene are appropriate for the clinical setting. She is slightly agitated and is frequently adjusting her position on the stretcher during the interview. With prolonged sitting she describes worsening pain and at one point walks to a nearby water fountain displaying an antalgic gait. She is wearing a hospital gown and visible jewelry includes a small crucifix on a necklace and a wedding ring. She is wearing her glasses, and her husband has placed a single-point cane by her bedside. There is a slight increase in psychomotor activity; she is mildly tremulous. She is initially reserved, focusing mostly on her husband, and eye contact is fairly poor, but this improves as she is telling her story. Her speech is normal in rate, tone, and volume with normal prosody and no latency. She speaks with a Midwestern American accent. The patient is alert and seems genuinely interested in discussing her history. Her fund of knowledge is fair. She is oriented to person, place, time, and situation. Explicit and implicit memory is intact, and there are no deficits with registration. She is able to recall three words after five minutes without prompting. The patient does not appear to be easily distracted. Sarah is tearful at times. There is a fine motor tremor of the outstretched hands. She describes her mood as "feeling over-whelmed . . . depressed" and affect is mood congruent and appropriate. Her thought process is mostly linear. When discussing her pain she is more circum-stantial, relaying excessive detail. There is no misuse of words, and she responds appropriately to the questions posed. There is no significant derailment. She does appear slightly impatient at times with direct close-ended questions and voices concerns about having her history documented correctly. She denies any suicidal or homicidal thoughts, and there is no evidence for any delusional think-ing. Her ability to interpret proverbs was somewhat limited, suggesting some mild impairment with abstract thought. Her processing speed for calculation is slightly slow, and there were some errors. Her judgment is intact per scenario testing. She denies any current auditory, visual, tactile, or gustatory hallucina-tions. She also does not describe any level of depersonalization or derealization.

IMPAIRMENT IN FUNCTIONING

In Sarah's case pain is a symptom associated with a number of specific medical conditions. One could also consider the potential conversion of emotional pain in this very depressed individual into physical pain. However, pain as an entity appears to be the primary focus of clinical attention and seems to represent a primary disorder of her mind. As her life centers on pain, the patient is not cur-rently able to meet many of the demands of her societal roles. She is finding it very difficult to work or socialize effectively and struggles with functional impair-ment in a number of areas of her life.

DSM DIAGNOSIS

This is a 26-year-old married mother with depressive and anxiety symptoms as well as chronic pain presenting for evaluation and treatment of seizures in the setting of acute psychosocial stressors and worsening physical pain. There may have been some genetic predisposition to developing psychiatric illness, and her sister clearly suffers from anxiety and depression. With the death of her mother at an early age, she experienced several developmental disruptions and invalidat-ing events that resulted in loneliness and depression as a teenager. She married a supportive individual who may currently be enabling some maladaptive habits and is also possibly adopting some pain behaviors in an effort to better connect with her. A number of environmental stressors continue to fuel her symptoms, and there appears to be some use of psychological defenses, such as somatization and repression. Although it is not certain if the seizures represent a form of conversion, the husband's recent job loss did increase the patient's stress level, and this may have been a precipitating factor. There is also evidence to suggest that pain has become a core part of her identity, and she may be adopting a sick role to address some unmet needs. Financial disability compensation may also play some role as a perpetuating factor in her illness. Her ability to tolerate frustration is impaired, and her interpersonal skills are dwindling. She is in a state of withdrawal, and her social support system has become increasingly limited to the extent that she only feels safe around her immediate family. She is able to communicate her distress to the medical community through numerous medical visits, seeing many different care providers, but still feels ignored and expresses her health and wellness as being in a steady state of decline.

The provisional DSM diagnosis in this case is major depressive disorder, recurrent, severe without psychosis, generalized anxiety disorder, pain disorder, and nicotine dependence. A possible conversion disorder, seizure type, requires further investigation. The presence of chronic moderate or severe pain colors virtually all aspects of life for people who suffer from it. They experience anxiety, demoralization, depression, and at times hopelessness and helplessness.

EPIDEMIOLOGY

There are not many epidemiologic studies examining the prevalence of pain disorder. One European study looked at the 12-month prevalence for pain disorder, and in the general population it appeared that 8.1% met criteria and 53% of this population also met criteria for comorbid mood or anxiety disorders (Fröhlich et al. 2006). Patients with a history of physical or emotional trauma appear to have an increased risk for developing pain disorder. The disorder frequently presents in adolescence. Women appear to seek treatment for this condition more than men do. There is also an increased risk of developing this disorder if there is a strong family history of pain.

DIFFERENTIAL DIAGNOSIS

Sarah has a complex history, as do many patients suffering from chronic pain. There is a strong possibility that the patient's Axis I diagnosis is somatization disorder. However, the clinical focus appears to be related to pain in a patient who has medical conditions that are known to be associated with pain. The patient has pain in a number of different systems, and given that there is a history of menorrhagia and the possible development of psychogenic nonepileptic seizures, it would be understandable to use a provisional diagnosis and list the primary condition as "possible somatization disorder." At this time the psychiatrist involved in this case felt that more time and investigation was needed to further evaluate the nature of the seizure disorder. Given a preoccupation with pain, the diagnosis of pain disorder appeared to be more appropriate to the provider than other disorders involving somatization, such as hypochondriasis or somatoform disorder. If in this case there is a strong suspicion of psychogenic nonepileptic seizure following an appropriate medical evaluation, somatization disorder would be an appropriate diagnosis rather than listing the presence of both pain disorder and conversion disorder.

Regarding the possible diagnosis of pain disorder, psychological factors appear to be closely linked to her pain. The timeline for her pain does not appear to be directly related or entirely circumscribed by a mood or anxiety condition. She has clearly met criteria for a major depressive episode in the past. In reviewing her situation, one might consider the diagnosis of major depressive disorder due to a general medical condition. A careful review of her previous depressive episodes illustrated that her depression was often linked to medical issues but was also sometimes strongly tied to social stressors. Also the patient appears to have developed her first major depressive episode in the absence of significant pain, and for this reason the provider chose to list this as a separate disorder.

In a similar way the patient suffered from an anxiety condition throughout her much of her life, and at times this was a distinct problem not entirely attached to pain or depression. She has panic attacks, but these appear to be directly related to her generalized anxiety. At this time Sarah is struggling with anxiety, pain, and depression, and these conditions are clearly connected and deserve individual focus and treatment. Regarding her cigarette use, she has developed tolerance and has had difficulty cutting back despite many attempts. Her inability to discontinue cigarette smoking despite her working knowledge of the damage this is causing suggests that the criteria are met for nicotine dependence. Her substance use disorder may be a secondary problem related to the other primary psychiatric conditions.

ETIOLOGY AND PATHOGENESIS

The experience of pain often requires a physical element, a cognitive component, and an emotional valence. At a basic level a nociceptive stimulus leads to the activation of a pain signal that travels to the dorsal root ganglia in the spine. This signal is transmitted to various areas of the brain from the thalamus, including the somatosensory cortex for localization of the pain. The signals also reach the frontal cortex for processing and understanding what the pain event means cognitively to the individual. The limbic system attaches an emotional significance to the pain. Pain can be experienced without tissue injury or inflammation. In pain disorder, psychological factors are evaluated to play an important role in the onset, frequency termination, or exacerbation of pain.

Patients who develop pain disorder often have a family history of individuals who suffered from this condition, and there is a theory to suggest the possibility that some pain behavior is learned. One psychodynamic theory suggests that the patient is experiencing underlying psychological stressors and this emotional pain is converted into physical pain. Mood disorders, anxiety disorders, and substance use disorders are common comorbid psychiatric conditions in patients who are dealing with chronic pain.

NATURAL COURSE WITHOUT TREATMENT

The natural course of comorbid severe pain and depression often results in permanent disability or death. The suicide rate for individuals with unremitting severe pain is high, as is the suicide rate for severe depression. Combining the two markedly augments the risk.

Experiments in pain perception with individuals who have depression indicate that a given stimulus not only causes more pain than a person who does not have depression, but that the distress and emotional meaning of the pain is worse.

Chronic pain is demoralizing and drives depression. Chronic depression makes chronic pain more intolerable. Together the conditions cause a synergistic feedback loop that is very destructive.

Individuals with chronic unremitting pain and depression often become apathetic and simply stop trying to function. The consequences of this surrender leads to a chronic invalid state that in itself is very demoralizing.

EVIDENCE-BASED TREATMENT OPTIONS

Patients suffering from chronic pain do need to be surrounded with many providers and supports. An optimally designed treatment team should incorporate health care workers from different specialties to meet the individual needs of the patient. A multidisciplinary approach to pain has consistently shown improvement in outcomes. An effective team for Sarah may include a nutritionist, a psychotherapist, case management, and a mental health clinician in addition to the medical providers she is currently established with. A primary care provider may need to provide assistance with rebuilding the team at various times depending on her status. For instance, Sarah probably does not need regular follow-up with rheumatology and orthopedics at this time, but neurology and psychiatry follow-up now may be needed given her recent increase in seizure activity and emotional dysregulation. When several providers are involved in a case together, frequent and effective communication is critical. Care providers may communicate with each other in a scheduled fashion (monthly basis) to evaluate which interventions are effective and adjust the treatment plan accordingly. This multidisciplinary approach can result in improved care, avoid unnecessary tests and procedures, and reduce compassion fatigue on individual providers. Although the cost may seem high, it will likely be less than the cost related to a number of hospitalizations and multiple visits to the emergency room.

In evaluating a patient and creating an effective treatment plan, neuropsychiatric testing can be very helpful in assessing a patient's strengths and weaknesses and is often underutilized. Many primary care and pain clinics continue to use the McGill Pain Questionnaire, which is a self-report assessment tool that measures the sensory, affective, and evaluative elements of pain. Various multidimensional assessment tools have been created such as the SF-36, the Brief Pain Inventory short form, and the Multidimensional Pain Inventory. It may be reasonable to use a combination of tools, and an example is using the Pain Disability Index for appraising the physical functioning along with the Patient Health Questionnaire-9 for evaluating emotional functioning. These are useful instruments that can often aid in composing a plan for psychotherapy. It is increasingly common that these tests are being used to identify patients that may benefit from psychological evaluation prior to a procedure. The Pain Patient Profile evaluates an individual for the presence of significant depression, somatization, or anxiety in those suffering from chronic pain. To use many of these assessment tools in clinical practice, it may be necessary to first register and complete a service agreement. Sarah completed a Pain Patient Profile evaluation, which did cost about $20. The report suggested that she would benefit from continued psychological assessment and treatment prior to another procedure such as the dorsal root stimulator trial that had been discussed as a future option in the treatment of her lower back pain.

One of the first steps in approaching this patient's care may be to gain as much collateral information as possible from other providers so as to reduce any unnecessary studies. Such patients have often had an extensive workup previously, and as the number of studies increases, so does the risk of having false positive laboratory studies and "incidentalomas" on imaging. In chronic pain states, a number of laboratory studies may be reasonable depending on the clinical setting, and common studies include CBC, comprehensive metabolic panel, thyroid-stimulating hormone, vitamins D and B_{12}, and erythrocyte sedimentation rate. Thyroid abnormalities, vitamin B_{12} deficiency, and electrolyte disturbances can often result in neuropsychiatric symptoms. Vitamin D deficiency can present with generalized pain, and many patients initially diagnosed as having fibromyalgia have been found to have this underlying diagnosis. A markedly elevated sedimentation rate or C-reactive protein may suggest the presence of a significant inflammatory process that warrants further medical investigation.

The psychiatrist taking care of Sarah searched the available chart information for these studies and also looked for the presence of elevated prolactin levels. This test can help in the process of differentiating between a psychogenic nonepileptic seizure and an epileptic seizure. Prolactin levels usually rise with an epileptic seizure but will usually not rise with a psychogenic nonepileptic seizure. A total creatinine kinase level is often less useful in determining the seizure type because patients can injure extremities and possibly fall, resulting in crush injuries with any type of seizure event. An EEG with video monitoring is very useful in assessing the character of a seizure and would probably be ordered for this patient while she is in the hospital.

Many patients like Sarah take complementary and alternative medicines for pain. The most commonly used herbs in pain management include devil's claw, ginger, boswellia, white willow bark, and bromelian. Many of these medicines appear to work by reducing cytokines and prostaglandins. Patients with chronic pain are often on a number of prescribed medications, and they should be warned about potential unknown drug interactions with herbal medicines that are not monitored by the FDA. Acupuncture has been used for centuries to help reduce headaches, back pain, and neuropathies. The analgesic effect is thought to be at least partly mediated by endorphins.

Various tools used in neuromodulation, such as electroconvulsive therapy and transcranial magnetic stimulation, have been shown to reduce pain. Although the exact mechanisms of action of these tools are poorly understood, it is clear that at a very basic level there is disruption in the neural networks known to be involved in pain. Many individuals have had some reduction in neuropathic pain with the use of transcutaneous electrical nerve stimulation (TENS). Many studies have shown only modest improvement in outcome with the use of TENS units. The mechanism of action is thought to involve pain signal inhibition at the level of the dorsal horn of the spinal column. Dorsal root stimulators are more invasive but are frequently effective for patients with chronic lower back pain who have had multiple surgeries and attempts are being made to limit the use of narcotics.

The treatment plan for this patient should include various forms of psychotherapy. In the initial interview the patient should be given the opportunity to tell his or her story, and there should be some acknowledgment that the pain and suffering that person endures is real. The first visit is an opportunity to build a strong therapeutic alliance. Some time will be spent discussing the pain history, but the majority of time is usually not spent focusing on pain but in taking an inventory to discover who the patient is and what environment surrounds them. There is usually a review of the healthy and maladaptive coping mechanisms the patient has used to address pain. The pain history may involve a description of the different types of pain and an examination of the effect the illness has had on the quality of life. There should be an evaluation for the presence of psychological factors associated with the pain.

An initial focus for therapy sessions is often on improving the patient's awareness of how stress and negative emotions may influence the pain state. Relaxation training can be incorporated early into the treatment plan. Targets for therapeutic intervention frequently include addressing low self-esteem, grief and loss, anger management, and improving interpersonal effectiveness. In individual therapy there is evidence to support the use of treatments such as cognitive behavioral therapy, cognitive hypnotherapy, and mindfulness-based therapy. Group psychotherapy using cognitive behavioral therapy techniques has been shown to be particularly effective for treating a number of chronic pain conditions. Pain groups provide an opportunity for patients to experience external validation from peers and improve in their level of social connectedness. Family therapy may be provided in an effort to provide education and examine and address the dynamics and various processes that may be reinforcing pain behaviors.

Sarah would likely benefit from family therapy because her husband is displaying a number of codependent behaviors and is probably unintentionally fostering the patient's isolation and focus on pain. She may benefit from a referral to a therapist who specializes in cognitive behavioral therapy for sleep. Another appropriate referral may be for biofeedback with relaxation training. Her primary care provider may use motivational enhancement therapy techniques to address her continued smoking. With the constellation of symptoms that Sarah is currently struggling with, she would probably do well in starting with individualized supportive counseling with the goal of eventually including her in group therapy. Patients with psychiatric illnesses that involve a high level of somatization tend to do better with a very structured environment and regularly scheduled follow-up appointments. This patient would also likely have difficulty following up with a number of therapists at one time, and it may be best to have focused, brief therapy interventions in a serially coordinated fashion.

Patients with pain disorders often struggle with adherence. Mental health support workers can be useful in helping improve adherence to treatment plans to which the patient has agreed. A mental health clinician can assist patients in getting to scheduled appointments and can help them pick up prescriptions and organize the medicine. Clinicians often support socialization, and in some circumstances can encourage and facilitate the patient's enrollment in appropriate exercise routines and other wellness activities. For example, if Sarah's treatment plan involves seeing a nutritionist to address her obesity (contributing to low self-esteem and osteoarthritis), a support worker may be able to help the patient complete food diaries and examine maladaptive shopping habits at the grocery store. If Sarah describes a desire to incorporate daily prayer or meditation into her treatment, a support worker may help her find ways to successfully achieve this and other goals.

Psychotropic medicines have some documented efficacy in treating patients with pain disorder. Medications that increase centrally available serotonin and norepinephrine are frequently found to be efficacious in reducing pain. These medications can also address comorbid mood and anxiety disorders. Medications that work on GABA (pregabalin, gabapentin) can also provide some mood-stabilizing and anxiety-reducing effects. Many antiepileptic drugs are still used for the treatment of neuropathic and headache pain (carbamazepine, valproic acid).

CLINICAL COURSE WITH MANAGEMENT AND TREATMENT

The prognosis for a pain disorder is relatively poor in many cases. One negative prognostic factor is active addiction. The presence of chronic pain can make consistent and effective work extremely difficult. However, chronic pain patients often do better if they are able to maintain healthy relationships and work. Although there is always hope for a cure, a standard treatment approach centers on using successful coping mechanisms and focusing on wellness strategies to achieve the best possible outcome.

Sarah was sent to a nutritionist and joined a low cost gym, where she could begin exercising, initially doing very mild water aerobics. She began to lose weight, which boosted her self-confidence and which also began to relieve some of the burden on her lumbar spine. Her pain diminished slightly. She was taught simple meditation techniques consistent with her spiritual beliefs and began to be able to experience her pain with less associated anxiety and despair. This also led to an easing of her symptoms.

Her antidepressant dose is adjusted slightly and, along with the other interventions she has undertaken, her pain ratings drop by 30% and her depression remits to a mild, intermittent occurrence.

SYSTEMS-BASED PRACTICE ISSUES

The skill sets necessary to treat pain and necessary to treat depression are different. Rarely does a clinician have equal aptitude in dealing with both. Individuals with morbid pain and mood symptoms are best treated in a specialized clinic by a treatment team composed of a pain specialist, a physical therapist, counselors, and a psychiatrist. Such clinics are rarely found outside major academic centers and are often at or near their limit on number of patients they can effectively treat.

It is difficult for practitioners in the community, not in such a program, to address the needs of these people. There are legal constraints on the prescription of opioid analgesics and there are time constraints in the practice of medicine that interfere with effective treatment.

LEGAL, ETHICAL, AND CULTURAL CHALLENGES

The communication of the experience of pain, as well as of depression, requires trust and rapport between the two individuals. Cultural attitudes regarding the expression of pain vary markedly. One cultural group may value the stoic tolerance of pain with little verbal communication. Another group may value the focal and emphatic expression of pain. A clinician from the first group may perceive a patient from the second group as "exaggerating" symptoms. Conversely, a second group clinician may minimize the pain suffered by a patient from the first group.

There are tremendous legal and ethical obstacles involved in the treatment of pain. Opioid analgesics have brought a great deal of relief to needlessly suffering people. On the other hand, in vulnerable populations, the use disorders caused by these medications may destroy lives far more than the underlying painful condition. A balance is difficult to achieve.

TERMS

When discussing the aspects of pain and in the process of reviewing the literature on the subject, it is necessary to understand some basic pain terminology. The International Association for the Study of Pain has defined *pain* as "An unpleasant sensory and emotional experience associated with actual or potential tissue damage, or described in terms of such damage" (IASP, 2013, 210). Health care providers who treat pain will often use descriptive terms such as *paresthesias*, *dysesthesias*, *allodynia*, *hyperalgesia*, and *hyperpathia*. Paresthesias are abnormal nonpainful sensations that may arise in the presence of pressure on a nerve. In describing paresthesias, patients may describe the sensation of experiencing "pins and needles" in an area. Dysesthesias represent the same phenomena but are described as being unpleasant. Allodynia is the situation where one is exposed to stimulus that is not usually associated with eliciting pain but experiences pain with this event. An example may be touching the skin with a paintbrush, described by the patient as painful.

Hyperalgesia occurs when someone is exposed to something that most would associate as being painful, but the level of pain is in excess of what one would normally expect given the nature of the stimulus. An example may be a needle stick that provokes a severe reaction of pain. Hyperalgesia could arise in the setting of a process called *sensitization*. With sensitization the repeated application of a stimulus can lead to amplification in the perception of a stimulus as being more painful over time. Understanding the nature of sensitization can remind us of the importance of addressing acute pain before it becomes a chronic problem.

Pain is usually considered to be chronic in nature when it has been present for more than six months. There is ample evidence to suggest that under treatment of acute pain is common (Edwards 1990) and can be a significant factor in the development of chronic pain. There may also be historical elements or personality traits present in an individual that can help us identify patients that have an increased risk for developing chronic pain. For instance, patients that have had a lifetime history of emotional trauma may be particularly vulnerable to developing chronic pain. A final pathway for pain could include a condition known as hyperpathia, in which an individual describes a state where everything is painful.

REFERENCES AND RESOURCES

Edwards, WT. Optimizing opioid treatment of postoperative pain. *J Pain Symptom Manage* 1990 Feb;5(1 Suppl):S24–S36

Fröhlich C, Jacobi F, Wittchen HU. DSM-IV pain disorder in the general population. An exploration of the structure and threshold of medically unexplained pain symptoms. *Eur Arch Psych Clin Neuroscie* 2006 Apr;256(3):187–96.

Hoffman BM, Papas RK, Chatkoff DK, Kerns RD. Meta-anaylsis of psychological interventions for chronic low back pain. *Health Psychol* 2007;26:1–9.

IASP: http://www.iasp-pain.org/Content/NavigationMenu/GeneralResourceLinks/Pain Definitions/default.htm#Pain

Leo RJ. *Clinical Manual of Pain Management in Psychiatry*. Washington, DC: American Psychiatric Publishing, 2007.

Melznack R. The McGill Pain Questionnaire: major properties and scoring methods. *Pain* 1975 Sep;1(3):277–99.

Melzack R, Wall, PD. Pain mechanisms: a new theory. *Science*, 1965 Nov 19;150(3699): 971–79.

Pendergrast R. Holistic Medicine MD—The Balance of Medical Science and Natural Health. 2012. Retrieved December 16, 2012, from Herbal Pain Relief, http://www.holistic-medicine-md.com/herbal-pain-relief.html.

Rasmussen KG, Rummans TA. Electroconvulsive therapy in the management of chronic pain. *Curr Pain Headache Rep* 2002 Feb;6(1):17–22.

Reiner K, Tibi L, Lipsitz D . Do mindfulness-based interventions reduce pain intensity? A critical review of the literature. *Pain Med* 2013 Feb;14(2):230–42.

Reyes-Gordillo K, Segovia J, Shibayama M, Vergara P, Morena MG, Muriel P. Curcumin protects against acute liver damage in the rat by inhibiting NF-kappaB, proinflammatory cytokines production and oxidative stress. *Biochim Biophys Acta* 2007;1770(6): 989–96.

Williams AC, Eccleston C, Morley S. Psychological therapies for the management of chronic pain (excluding headache) in adults. *Cochrane Database Syst Rev* 2012 Nov 14;11.

Wong C. *Herbs for Pain Management*. September 24, 2012. Retrieved December 16, 2012, from Alternative Medicine, About.com, http://altmedicine.about.com/od/healthconditionsdisease/a/pain_herbs.htm.

American Pain Society, http://www.ampainsoc.org.

How to Cope with Pain, http://www.howtocopewithpain.org is a very patient-center site that includes information on stress management and relaxation techniques along with a web log that allows for community collaboration.

International Association for the Study of Pain, http://www.iasp-pain.org.

CHAPTER **22**

Factitious Disorder

Karl Northwall, M.D.

CLINICAL PRESENTATION

Chief complaint: "I'm sick."

History of present illness: Oscar is a 38-year-old single male who was admitted involuntarily to the state hospital four years ago for his fifth hospitalization. His previous admissions started about 10 years earlier and were the result of court orders to evaluate him for competency or restore him to competency. This admission was a transfer of commitment from the state forensic hospital, where he had been for eight years after being found unrestorably incompetent on a felony charge of arson, having set fire to and burned down an apartment building. He had past diagnoses of schizophrenia and mild mental retardation. He was transferred on high doses of a depot antipsychotic and an oral antipsychotic. He was successfully tapered all the way off these medications in his first two years here, and there had been no evidence of any recurrence of psychosis. The episode under current discussion started after a period of several months when he had been doing quite well. He was on no psychotropics except valproate, which was being used to help with impulse control. He had a privilege level of being able to go for walks on grounds by himself up to half an hour at a time. He was regularly going to the Treatment Mall (a separate building that provides psychosocial rehabilitation with modalities such as talk groups, occupational therapy, music therapy, recreation therapy, and horticultural therapy), and even had a part-time volunteer job in the hospital making up packets of silverware and napkins for the dining room. His mother had been sending him some money regularly. It was his habit to purchase a can of a particular soda each day to drink in the evening. His mother quit sending him money, and he was unable to contact her. He was no longer able to afford his daily soda and became quite upset with this. He borrowed money from peers, which he couldn't pay back, and he tried to borrow money from the staff. While in a therapy group at the mall one day, he stood up and dramatically announced "I'm having a spell," laid down on the floor, and thrashed about. He would not respond to staff, and a medical emergency was called. He was taken back to the ward in a wheelchair. Vital signs and physical exam were normal, so he was allowed to lie down in his room the rest of the day. Valproate level was therapeutic, although that was not being used for seizure control. There was no loss of bladder or bowel control, and no clonic/tonic movements. He returned to the Treatment Mall the next day and did well for several days before a similar episode occurred. Metabolic studies, blood counts, and other labs were normal. Although his "spells" did not appear to be seizures, an EEG was ordered. He had another "spell" while this was being done, and the EEG was read as nonspecific. Consideration was given to this being a conversion disorder. These episodes began to occur each time he was in a therapy group, so he was restricted to the unit. He then began having episodes when at meals with other patients on the unit. A consulting neurologist decided that the diagnosis of a seizure disorder was based on clinical factors, not EEG findings, and he prescribed Levetiracetam.

Oscar told the staff that the neurologist told him that loss of bladder and bowel control happened with seizures, and he started having that also, although his physical movements could still be best described as thrashing about. He never had any physical injury from his spells. He had one of these spells one evening when a physician new to the facility was on call, and he was sent to the local emergency room and admitted to the medical service. Additional labs were done there, and he obliged them by having spells there also, and phenytoin was added to his medications. The hospital neurologist continued the diagnosis of a seizure disorder and returned him to the state hospital.

Psychiatric history: Oscar had been diagnosed as having mild mental retardation in grade school and had been diagnosed as having undifferentiated schizophrenia. He was hospitalized psychiatrically for the first time in his late teens and had been hospitalized at a different state hospital. He went to live with his mother after that and was given disability. He followed up outpatient at the local community mental health center. He was next hospitalized at the current facility in 1997. At that time he had a four-year history of drinking a six-pack of beer daily. He had gotten angry at his mother while intoxicated and set her home on fire, causing considerable damage. She would not let him stay with her anymore, and he was placed in an assisted living facility. While there he had ingested a jar of petroleum jelly in a suicide attempt, and wound up at the state facility. At that time he claimed to be depressed and wanted us to get his mother to let him stay with her again. He showed no evidence of psychosis during this hospitalization and was discharged on venlafaxine and risperidone. He started using cannabis daily, resumed drinking, and set fire to an apartment building when intoxicated. It burned to the ground, but everyone got out safely. He then had a series of two hospitalizations at his local state hospital and two at a state forensic hospital, related to criminal charges of arson, for evaluation of competency to stand trial and restoration of competency. The first time he was at the current facility for evaluation of competency, he said that his attorney did not want him to go to jail and wanted him to stay in a state hospital. He was, however, restored to competency to stand trial, and spent eight years in prison. He was released on parole to a group home, arrested on violation of parole, sent to the state forensic hospital in 2005 for evaluation of capacity to stand trial, and this time was found not to be competent and to not be restorable to competency. The criminal charges were dropped, and he was committed civilly to the state forensic hospital. When he was felt to be stable there, he was sent to the current facility. Of interest is the fact that he never displayed signs or symptoms of psychosis when here. When sent here this time from the state forensic hospital, he was on long-acting risperidone 50 mg IM q 2 weeks, and risperidone 8 mg at hs. He had evidence of tardive dyskinesia at that time. Over the course of two years, he was tapered all the way off the risperidone. There was no evidence of recurrence of psychosis. His tardive dyskinesia initially became somewhat worse, and then disappeared.

Family psychiatric history: Positive for schizophrenia in a maternal uncle.

Other medical history: Oscar had a history of recurrent pneumonias and had a thorocotomy with decortication of the right lung and removal of the right lower lobe for an empyema. He also had a history of renal calculi and had lithotripsy several times. There was a "possible" history of seizures, but EEG was normal at the state forensic hospital. There was no history of head trauma. He was allergic to aspirin.

Other history (developmental, educational/occupational, family/social, legal): Oscar was an only child, and the identity of his biological father was unknown. According to the community mental health center, mother had "intellectual limitations." He was in special education classes, and quit school in 10th grade at the age of 19. He worked briefly at fast food restaurants and grocery stores, but was unable to keep a job and was usually fired for being unable to do the job. There were no legal problems when he was a child, and there was no history of fire setting or cruelty to animals. There was also no history of attention deficit hyperactivity disorder or impulse control problems as a child. He started drinking heavily in his early twenties and experimented with cannabis and cocaine. He had never been in the military. He had never been married and did not have any children. His mother's involvement with him was tenuous at best throughout his incarceration and psychiatric hospitalizations.

Mental status exam: Thirty-eight-year-old male who is obese, unshaven, and short of stature. Eye contact is poor. He is lying in bed in a hospital gown. He has a coarse tremor of his hands, arms, and body. Voice is soft, and speech is poorly articulated. He appears sedated. He is oriented to person, place, year, month, and day of the week but not date. He will not cooperate with formal assessment of memory. Grossly there do not appear to be any memory deficits. He can do serial 3's but not serial 7's. He has poverty of speech and poverty of content of speech. "I'm sad because I'm not being taken care of." Affect is blunted and neutral. "I may as well die as let you take care of me." He denies wanting to harm himself or anyone else.

He is preoccupied with "something is wrong with me and I need to go to the hospital again. They took real good care of me there, better than you are doing." There were no delusions. His ability to abstract is poor. He denied thought insertion or withdrawal. General fund of information is poor. He knows the current president but not the previous one. His insight is poor, as is his judgment. He denies any auditory or visual hallucinations presently. He says he feels like "there is a motor in me making me shake." He denies feelings of depersonalization or derealization.

IMPAIRMENT IN FUNCTIONING

Oscar was quite disabled by this disorder. He was totally nonfunctional, refusing to do any activities of daily living and frequently exhibiting symptoms that demanded medical evaluation. Factitious disorder can cause significant morbidity and even mortality as ever more invasive workups and treatments are pursued. There have even been reports of procedures such as adrenalectomies being done in such patients. It can consume significant medical resources and produce emotional distress in caregivers and significant others as well as the patient. Chronic factitious disorder interferes with employment and social relationships.

Even though Oscar's baseline condition was such that he needed continuous hospitalization, the factitious disorder further affected his functioning. It impaired his relationships with staff and other patients. It impaired his ability to get his needs met.

DSM DIAGNOSIS

Oscar was intentionally producing physical symptoms. There was no external incentive for the behavior. He had no legal charges pending, he was not attempting to obtain any drugs of abuse, and he was not getting attention from his mother. The motivation was not unconscious, as in conversion disorder. The motivation for his behavior was to be a patient and to assume the sick role, and there was no external gain such as would be seen in malingering. Physical signs and symptoms were the predominate feature, so the diagnosis was Factitious Disorder with Predominantly Physical Signs and Symptoms. There could also possibly be a diagnosis of Factitious Disorder with Predominantly Psychological Signs and Symptoms when his physical symptoms ceased and he became aggressive. The DSM does not specify any particular duration of symptoms that is necessary for either diagnosis. It did not appear, however, that the production of psychiatric symptoms was gaining him the role of a psychiatric patient, as he was already an inpatient on a psychiatric unit.

In a review of what records we had of his past psychiatric history, it appeared that his previous diagnosis of schizophrenia came about during periods of grossly disorganized behavior, such as we were seeing. One might wonder if at that time those symptoms were being produced as part of malingering, a psychiatric disorder. There are no valid or reliable tests for factitious disorder. In DSM-5 the diagnostic criteria for factitious disorder are largely unchanged. A key component remains the demonstration that the individual is surreptitiously acting to demonstrate signs or symptoms of illness in the absence of obvious external rewards.

EPIDEMIOLOGY

It is difficult to gather data on incidence and prevalence. The nature of the disorder is such that cases may be missed, or conversely the same case may be counted multiple times. DSM estimates that it accounts for about 1% of persons in large general hospitals that get mental health consults. It is widely assumed that it is rare and is accompanied by extreme degrees of deception. The popular image of factitious disorder is Munchausen's syndrome, which is actually only about 10% of cases.

In Munchausen's syndrome (factitious disorder imposed on another), the person presents with dramatic and even life-threatening symptoms. They engage in pseudologia fantastica, pathological lying that may contain some truth that is very dramatic and is initially very engaging to the listener. It may appear that they believe what they are saying, yet when confronted by the truth, they may admit it. They may have repeated surgical procedures, as typified by a "gridiron abdomen" that has multiple surgical scars. They may call the nurses' station pretending to be a physician and order medications or tests on themselves. They are often extremely knowledgeable about the field of medicine. They may use this to influence the physicians' decisions about evaluation and treatment. They often wind up being very difficult for the nursing and medical staff and sign out of the hospital against medical advice, only to show up at the emergency room of another hospital in another city. When confronted, they disappear. Rather pejorative nicknames for such persons include pathomimia, "hospital hobos," "professional patient," polysurgical addiction, and "peregrinating problem patients." Munchausen's appears to be more common in unmarried men.

Persons with predominantly psychological signs and symptoms may take psychoactive substances to produce symptoms, such as amphetamines, hallucinogens, sedative hypnotics, alcohol, or cannabis. Their presentation reflects their understanding of the particular psychiatric syndrome they are feigning. Psychosis, bereavement with depression and suicidality, and dissociative identity disorder are among the disorders that may be presented. False claims of childhood physical or sexual abuse may be made. The presenting symptoms may be bizarre and defy classification. Medications that are used to treat such disorders will inexplicably prove to have no effect. Patients are usually very willing to be hospitalized psychiatrically. Because objective verification of many psychiatric symptoms is impossible, detection can be very difficult. They may be suggestible and add new symptoms when suggested by an interviewer. Such persons may claim bereavement with dramatic and tragic stories of relatives killed or injured.

Patients with predominantly physical signs and symptoms are usually women who have worked in the medical field. Presentation is highly variable. They may lie about or exaggerate their symptoms and medical history. Manipulation of diagnostic instruments may occur. This can include taping a small stone on the body to simulate a kidney stone or manipulating a thermometer by friction. Inexplicable laboratory results are very common, which can be caused by behaviors such as injecting insulin or taking thyroid hormone. They may deliberately injure themselves, inject themselves with feces to cause sepsis, put blood in urine samples, swallow batteries, or excoriate their skin. They may actually cause a disease. There has been a case reported where a person actually bled themselves to the point of severe anemia. Cases that involve only exaggerated symptoms are usually undetected. When persons are caught tampering with lab specimens, possessing syringes or drugs, or harming themselves and are then confronted, they become indignant, accuse the medical staff of incompetence, and leave the hospital. They tend to be very resistant to psychological inquiry and may not always realize that their motivation is to assume the sick role.

Five levels of factitious behavior have been proposed: (1) fictitious history, (2) simulation, (3) exaggeration, (4) aggravation, and (5) self-induction of disease. The odds of detection increase with the level of the behavior.

Factitious disorder by proxy would be diagnosed as factitious disorder not otherwise specified. This is defined as the intentional production or feigning of physical or psychological signs or symptoms in another person who is under the person's care. The motivation is to assume the sick role by proxy. External incentives, such as financial gain, are absent. This is overwhelmingly seen in mothers with "sick" children. This may be seen as a form of child abuse, and this diagnosis has been seen by some legal scholars as a medicalization of criminal behavior. The perpetrator seeks aggrandizement as a compassionate, concerned parent. They are outwardly caring and concerned but nonetheless cause illness in the child. The child may be poisoned, injected with pathogens, or even smothered episodically. The diagnosis is often made with the help of video surveillance. The child is typically two to five years old at the time of diagnosis. Mortality may be as high as 6–10%. Such cases, when discovered, usually result in removal of the child from the home. Children who survive this often have emotional disorders in adulthood.

DIFFERENTIAL DIAGNOSIS

Malingering and factitious disorder are similar in that both involve the intentional production of symptoms. In malingering, the person has a goal that is recognizable when the circumstances are known. Examples are avoiding prison, obtaining drugs of abuse, avoiding military duty, or obtaining compensation. Malingering is not a psychiatric diagnosis per se, but is a "Condition that may be a focus of Clinical Attention" (V Code 65.2). The intentional production of symptoms distinguishes factitious disorder from psychiatric disorders that have similar behaviors such as somatization disorder, conversion disorder, and pain disorder. The medical differential diagnosis includes functional somatic syndromes such as chronic fatigue syndrome and fibromyalgia. The distinction between factitious disorder and somatoform disorders—that in the former the motivation is conscious, whereas in the latter it is not—actually has no empirical support.

Persons with factitious disorder are usually agreeable to all kinds of diagnostic tests, whereas those who are malingering are reluctant to have more testing once they have been able to get the diagnosis they want, because additional testing may expose their malingering. Index of suspicion for factitious disorder should be increased if the presentation is dramatic and atypical, symptoms are present only when the person is being observed, there is disruptive behavior, there is rapid development of new symptoms, there is indifference to pain and painful procedures, there's a history of extensive traveling, or there are few visitors. The presence of any of these, however, is not diagnostic. It has been suggested that there is some overlap between antisocial personality disorder and Munchausen's, because both can involve pathological lying that does not have any clear external goal. Some forensic psychiatrists have argued that there is no empirical support for the use of consciousness and intentionality to distinguish factitious disorder and malingering from any other excessive illness behavior. It has also been argued that factitious disorder is just flat-out lying and does not deserve to be called a psychiatric disorder. If it is voluntary, then how is that really very different from malingering?

ETIOLOGY/PATHOGENESIS

The onset of this disorder in Oscar appears to be correlated with the withdrawal of caring from his mother and the experience of being cared for very intensively in the milieu of the medical floor. There has been little empirical research on factitious disorder. A basic barrier to research is the unwillingness of persons with this disorder to cooperate. Most research on deception in regard to illness has been on malingering. Psychodynamic explanations are plentiful, but etiology is not really known. Common historical factors are physical disorders as a child, a close relationship with a doctor in the past, a grudge against the medical profession, or a personality disorder. There are no consistent neuropathological findings. In the literature, the stressor of recurrent object loss or fear of loss is often mentioned.

NATURAL COURSE WITHOUT TREATMENT

Persons with this disorder cannot be relied on to give an accurate history or access to their medical records. The natural history is difficult to follow. In this particular case, the individual was involuntarily hospitalized and did not have the option of leaving. His factitious disorder resolved when he got angry that he was not able to obtain the role of a patient that he wanted. It is felt that the disorder is often intermittent. Munchausen's, in particular, may have a chronic course. Comorbidities, such as substance abuse disorders, personality disorders, eating disorders, or mood disorders, certainly can influence the course. Onset is usually in young adulthood, often after a hospitalization. Most cases are felt to be chronic.

In Oscar, the course of his disorder without any intervention would likely have been that he became an invalid who had to have total nursing care.

EVIDENCE-BASED TREATMENT OPTIONS

There is no evidence-based treatment for factitious disorder. The diagnosis must be confirmed, for a misdiagnosis may be disastrous and have legal implications. There is no universal agreement that treatment is deserved or necessary. Negative countertransference is common, and aggrieved medical professionals may well feel that legal charges are warranted, although difficult to implement. An internist once told a psychiatrist, "For you, this may be fascinating, for me it's a pain in the ass." Underlying disorders, such as psychosis, depression, borderline personality disorder, or substance abuse certainly can be treated. A prerequisite to treatment, however, is the cooperation of the person, and this is usually rare.

Persons must be protected from their own self-injurious behavior as well as the risk of iatrogenic harm. Most serious errors in the treatment of patients with factitious disorder occur when the patient exerts undue influence over the physicians' decisions. Cognitive behavioral techniques that help somatoform disorders might be beneficial. The possibility of strong negative countertransference should be realized and dealt with. Engaging in power struggles or publicly humiliating the person serves no useful purpose. Overidentification with the person or "rescue fantasies" are counterproductive and can reinforce the disorder. Generally it is felt that nonconfrontational approaches decrease the likelihood that the person will leave against medical advice. If possible, persons should be kept in the hospital, because the likelihood of engagement after they leave is low. It is very difficult to get the person to give up the sick role without losing face by admitting that they were faking.

Pharmacotherapy of comorbid disorders may be useful, but there is none that is specific for factitious disorder.

Mothers with factitious disorder by proxy are universally regarded as extremely difficult to treat. Management is usually coordinated and guided through the legal system. The safety of the child should be of paramount importance, and a report to Child Protective Services should be made.

CLINICAL COURSE WITH MANAGEMENT AND TREATMENT

Generally, it is felt that treatment starts with an element of confrontation. This is best done indirectly, and there is no expectation that the person will "confess." Generally, people leave treatment soon after they are confronted. Reports of successful treatment come largely from case studies. The possibility of successful treatment does exist. Treatment must be collaborative and involve all the treatment providers. These persons should be tracked through electronic health records and insurance databases. The disorder may improve with the passage of time.

We informed Oscar's mother of his medical hospitalization, but she did not resume her relationship with him. He began requesting to again be sent to the hospital, where they brought his food to him, fed him, bathed him, and had someone sit with him all the time. He began to claim to be unable to walk. When left alone in his room, he would walk out to the nurses' station, lie on the floor, and have a "spell." He would demand to be transported back to his room in a wheelchair and have a "sitter" with him "in case I have a spell." He then also developed a coarse tremor of his hands, arms, and upper body. It was present only when he was awake and was aware that staff was observing him. He claimed that he was unable to feed himself, bathe, or do any normal activities because of this tremor.

Oscar's peers tended to have one of two reactions to him. One group felt that there was something seriously wrong with him, and was upset and angry with the medical staff over not giving him proper treatment. The other group felt that he was faking his symptoms, and they would be verbally abusive to him at times. Either way, they were diverted from concentrating on their own treatment priorities and their progress in treatment suffered.

A case conference was held, and it was decided to manage his problems behaviorally. It was not felt that confrontation would be useful. We felt that clinically, he did not have a seizure disorder, and his seizure medications were discontinued. When he had a "spell," his vitals were taken, and he was taken to his bed to "rest." If he laid on the floor, he was moved out of the main traffic pattern, a blanket was placed over him, and he was left there until he decided to get up. He was given finger foods for meals. Vitals and physical examinations were done in a matter-of-fact manner with a minimum of verbal interaction. Any effort on his part to do things for himself were rewarded by increased attention from the staff. Despite these interventions, his symptoms did not diminish. After about a month of this, he started having episodes of anger where he would throw his meal tray, curse the staff, and become physically assaultive. His inability to walk disappeared, and he would chase staff down the hall while threatening them. At this point, he appeared to derive reinforcement from the attention he received when a behavioral code was called on him. He started to claim that the staff was talking about him and said he was paranoid of "everyone." He was much more verbally productive, and there was no evidence of looseness of associations. Somewhat surprisingly, he also started caring for and feeding himself. At this point, lorazepam was used as needed. Negative countertransference from the staff was much more of an issue during this behavior than while he was having physical symptoms.

After about a month of this behavior, he became calmer, asked to return to the Treatment Mall, and there were no further "spells," physical complaints, or "paranoia."

SYSTEMS-BASED PRACTICE ISSUES

In this person, the insistence of the neurologists that he had a seizure disorder helped perpetuate his behavior. It also led to the administration of a medication that was not needed. The diagnosis of a seizure disorder is indeed a clinical diagnosis and cannot be based just on the results of an EEG. The context in which the "seizures" were observed, however, was quite relevant, and a failure to look at the big picture led to an erroneous diagnosis.

Persons with a factitious disorder will usually leave the hospital or outpatient practice when confronted and then seek another provider elsewhere. They may go to a different city. In the most severe variant, Munchausen's, they may even use a different name with each encounter. It is often difficult to get any kind of continuity of care. With the advent of electronic health records, it will hopefully be easier to follow these persons and not duplicate expensive workups. It is useful to get previous records and corroborating information, if at all possible (and it may not be possible).

Negative feelings toward these people are common, and care needs to be taken that we do not do more or less than is indicated. Many of these people may be seen on consultation to a medical service, and discussion of feelings that are aroused by these people with nursing staff and with other physicians is useful.

The difference between factitious disorder and malingering is only the motivation for the behavior. Overlap between these is not uncommon.

The diagnosis of factitious disorder does not make a person immune from any real medical disorder. They can have legitimate medical problems as well. Most cases of overtreatment of persons with this disorder occur prior to the diagnosis being made.

Consideration might be given to making the person financially responsible for unnecessary tests and procedures, but this is very seldom done.

There is a dearth of research supporting this diagnosis. At this time, there are no biomarkers or tests to diagnose this disorder. There is also no evidence-based treatment. More research is needed in these areas. Munchausen's syndrome, although dramatic and colorful, makes up a minority of the cases of factitious disorder.

LEGAL, ETHICAL, AND CULTURAL CHALLENGES

Generally, when people are in the role of patient, it is assumed that they will give an honest history; that the symptoms result from accident, illness, or chance; and that they have the goal of recovering and will cooperate with treatment. Being a patient relieves one from social obligations; entitles one to the care and concern of family, friends, and health professionals; and exempts one from work. The individual with a factitious disorder violates these social expectations, generating feelings of anger, rejection, and betrayal in others.

Descriptions of persons who exhibited factitious disorder appear as early as the second century in the writings of Galen. The diagnosis of factitious disorder began in 1951 when Richard Asher, a British psychiatrist, published case reports of persons who went from hospital to hospital seeking admission with feigned symptoms and a greatly embellished personal history. He gave this syndrome the name Munchausen syndrome, after a German cavalry officer who was a world-class embellisher of his personal history. There followed numerous reports of persons faking almost every medical disorder. It turned out that this syndrome represented only a minority of cases, but the label captured the popular imagination. In 1977, the first report of factitious disorder with psychological symptoms was made. The first case report of factitious disorder by proxy was also made in that year. It was formally recognized in 1980 with the publication of DSM-III.

A famous case of Munchausen's was Wendy Scott of England, known as "The Woman Who Cried Wolf." She had over 600 hospital admissions and 42 major operations in 12 years. She was felt to be one of the rare people who recovered from this condition and became well known as an example of this disorder. Twenty years later she started going to doctors complaining of stomach problems, and they were understandably skeptical and did no tests on her. She became ill while visiting the United States two years later. She was found to have inoperable stomach cancer and died of that two years later.

In the age of the Internet, we are now seeing "virtual factitious disorder," where people claim to have illnesses and adopt a "patient's" role on the Internet, obtaining attention and sympathy from others. This would be called malingering if they are soliciting funds.

REFERENCES AND RESOURCES

Gabbard GO. *Gabbard's Treatments of Psychiatric Disorders* (4th ed.). Arlington, VA: APPI, 2007.

Hales MD, Yudofsky MD, Gabbard MD. *American Psychiatric Publishing Textbook of Psychiatry* (5th ed.). Arlington, VA: APPI, 2008.

Kilgus MD, Maxmen JS, Ward NG. (Eds.). *Essential Psychopathology and Its Treatment* (3rd ed.). New York: W. W. Norton and Company, 2009.

Krahn L, Li H, O'Connor MK. Patients who strive to be ill: factitious disorder with physical symptoms, *Am J Psychiatry* 2003;160:1163–68.

Rogers R. (Ed.). *Clinical Assessment of Malingering and Deception.* New York: Guilford Press, 2008.

CHAPTER **23**

Unreality after Trauma

William S. Rea, M.D.

CLINICAL PRESENTATION

Chief complaint: "My family says I went away that day and haven't come back."

History of present illness: Phyllis is a 52-year-old legal secretary who comes to a scheduled therapy evaluation in an outpatient office. She is a conservatively dressed black woman, neat, slender, and quite composed. She makes good eye contact and speaks softly but fluently.

Phyllis says that her life was "everything it should be" until six months ago. She enjoyed her job as a legal secretary in a high-profile law firm with over a dozen attorneys. She has worked with a particular senior partner for more than a decade and had a comfortable, collegial relationship. She considers herself fortunate in her marriage of 32 years, saying "I still love him and he still loves me." She has two grown daughters who are independent and successful, and two grandchildren with another on the way.

Six months ago just before lunchtime she was in the copy room scanning documents regarding a new case. She heard a male voice but could not make out what he was saying. The voice began to shout, and she heard a woman's voice raised. She could not make out the words, but the voices sounded angry and frightened. After another loud exchange she heard a gunshot and then screaming. She felt frozen. Two more gunshots rang out, followed by noises of people apparently trying to get away. Soon she heard another gunshot.

"I swear it felt like hours between the gunshots, but it must only have been a few seconds. I was paralyzed. I thought I was going to die." (The therapist notes that all of this is related in a calm, flat voice without emotion or much inflection.)

The corridor from the copy room led directly to the reception area, where she thought the violence was occurring. "I had nowhere to run. I didn't have my phone. I knew I was going to die." She closed the door to the copy room and tried to push the copier against it, but it was too heavy. She looked around for a weapon and picked up a stapler. She crouched down behind copier, terrified. Two more gunshots. Furniture being knocked over. Doors slamming.

She huddled down behind the copy machine, looked down, and saw her hand, knuckles white, clenching the stapler.

"I saw the stapler, and the hand, and I wondered, 'Whose hand is that?' It was as though I was outside my body or, not really outside, just at a great distance from myself."

She sighs, tilts her head slightly, and continues. "I don't even know how long I was in that room. Eventually someone opened the door, and it was the police and they took me out. I remember thinking, 'Isn't it strange that my legs are so cramped?'"

She and the other survivors of the violent incident were taken to the emergency room and she was released, apparently unharmed. An attorney and a paralegal had been killed and another secretary wounded by a former client who was dissatisfied with the outcome of his case. The client then killed himself.

She says, "Since then I have just been at a distance."

When asked if she thinks about the episode, she shrugs and answers, "Not much." When she does recall it, the memories are distant, fuzzy, and gray. "It was almost like it was a dream." She denies feeling depressed. She denies feeling anxious. She says, "I am not afraid it might happen again. He is dead." She denies nightmares or poor sleep. She denies feeling much distress but acknowledges she no longer feels much pleasure in her life. It had not occurred to her to come for psychological evaluation until her husband and eldest daughter told her that she was not acting like herself and that they were worried about her.

"I can see their point, but there's nothing to worry about. I am really okay; I just feel a little numb. They say my personality has changed. I guess that is probably true."

When asked whether her relationships had changed at work, she faintly smiles and says, "I think work will be different for all of us for a while." With a touch of humor she adds, "I volunteer to do all the copying and scanning now."

The patient denies flashbacks, nightmares, rapid pulse or breathing, anxiety triggered by going into the workplace, hallucinations, or fearfulness. She consumes about half a mixed drink once a year on New Year's Eve. She has never used drugs. She does not smoke. She has no family history of any psychiatric disorder and no medical problems.

IMPAIRMENT IN FUNCTIONING

Phyllis's functional impairment is subtle. She continues to quite competently do her job as a legal secretary. She has no impairment in her activities of daily living. She continues to help make a home for her and her husband, shop, and engage in normal social activities including going to the movies with him. She denies depression, anxiety, and paranoia and has no evidence of delusions.

The impairment that Phyllis is experiencing is a disconnection with living her life. She is no longer "present" in her daily activities. She describes this as being wrapped in a "wool blanket" and experiencing every moment as distant and emotionally neutral.

When asked about impairment, she says, "My family says I went away that day and I haven't come back."

DSM DIAGNOSIS

The clinician's impression of Phyllis is one of a completely neutral person. Not only does she have no increase in anxiety or depression, she has no decrement or impairment of thinking. Instead, it is as though she no longer has a personality. This phenomenon is described as depersonalization.

Depersonalization is described as the experience of feeling detached from one's body or life. Sometimes it is described as "not feeling like a person anymore." For true depersonalization as a diagnosis, rather than a description of an experience, there can be no immediate outside chemicals triggering it. For example, taking hallucinogens might cause the experience of depersonalization but does not warrant a diagnosis of depersonalization disorder.

Depersonalization can be a symptom of other mental illnesses, including various types of psychosis or intoxication. In Phyllis's case, there are no other symptoms and no evidence of any other mental disorder.

Depersonalization is one small aspect of a series of phenomena grouped under "dissociative disorders." Other dissociative experiences might include derealization, in which everything feels like a dream and hypnosis.

In Phyllis's case, a painting is not red, blue, or yellow. It is shades of gray.

In DSM nomenclature, Phyllis's diagnosis would be depersonalization/derealization disorder. There is no distinction made between the relative balance of derealization or depersonalization in a given individual. It is emphasized that—as in the case of Phyllis—reality testing is intact.

EPIDEMIOLOGY

Dissociative experiences in general are part of the normal human experience. There is a spectrum of dissociative experience in the same way that there is a spectrum of anxious or depressive experience.

A phenomenon called "normative dissociation" is quite common. One category of it is daydreaming. Most of us have had the experience of shifting our attention away from our environment into our thoughts and suddenly being aware that a period of time has passed. Another example often occurs when driving an automobile. Many of us have had the experience of driving some distance on a highway and realizing that we did not notice the passing scenery for the past several miles.

Dissociation and depersonalization can be normal, protective psychological defenses in the face of massive trauma. Dissociation and depersonalization are common, although estimates vary, in the face of natural disasters, war, and violence. Dissociation and depersonalization are especially common in children undergoing such horrible traumas. It is as though the mind takes itself off to a safe place. This can be quite adaptive, unless the mind has trouble coming back from that place.

In some forms of dissociation, particularly post-traumatic stress disorder, there may also be other symptoms of affect or autonomic arousal.

DIFFERENTIAL DIAGNOSIS

The differential diagnosis for Phyllis is straightforward. She has no history of alcohol or drug abuse. There is no evidence of neurologic phenomena that could be causing this, such as partial complex seizures, tumors, intoxication, or hormonal imbalances. In addition, the abrupt onset connected with such a dramatic traumatic event strongly urges us to assign causality to that event.

Post-traumatic stress disorder (PTSD) is certainly in the differential for this patient. However, she has no flashbacks, nightmares, exaggerated startle reflex, panic, anxiety, or mood disturbance.

ETIOLOGY AND PATHOGENESIS

The etiology of the depersonalization is practically self-evident in this case. Should Phyllis have not been in an office visited by a gunman on that particular day, it is likely that she never would have experienced depersonalization or any other dissociative symptoms. Sometimes, when something bad enough happens, it has an ongoing effect on a person's life.

There is evidence that early trauma and use of dissociative psychological defenses in childhood preconditions one to use those same defenses in later traumatic episodes. However, it is thought that virtually anyone can experience depersonalization or dissociation should the conditions be right.

Mental health interventions after natural or manmade disasters are largely oriented toward dealing with the mood and anxiety sequelae of those experiences. However, part and parcel of such interventions is also working on the ability to set aside the depersonalization when it is safe to do so.

Neurobiological analysis of people suffering from depersonalization disorder shows suppression of normal activity in the emotional regulatory part of the brain, the limbic system.

One aspect of depersonalization that is sometimes overlooked is "caregiver burnout" among health professionals. This experience shares some similarities with the numbness and disengagement that Phyllis describes.

NATURAL COURSE WITHOUT TREATMENT

The natural course of the dissociative disorders and depersonalization in particular is highly variable. Most people in most circumstances find that the dissociative symptoms gradually fade on their own without much intervention. However, there are many variables that influence this. Is the trauma likely to recur? Survivors of earthquakes will often confirm that the aftershocks, hours, days, or even weeks later, can return them to the similar shocked and paralyzed state of mind they suffered immediately after the initial quake.

Some people have great difficulty coming out of the depersonalization and derealization episodes. For these people, sequelae may be permanent.

EVIDENCE-BASED TREATMENT OPTIONS

Biological therapies have been tried for depersonalization disorder, especially when they have been associated with PTSD. Anticonvulsants have undergone many therapeutic trials with disappointing results. Selective serotonin reuptake inhibitor antidepressants have proven useful in a subgroup of patients. However, it is not clear whether the symptoms that are being addressed in this subgroup are primarily depressive ones. In that case the dissociative symptoms are improving as they are being "pulled along" by the improvement in mood symptoms. Some interesting research has been done with the use of opioid blockers like naltrexone or naloxone, but the trials have been of small numbers and the results mixed.

Multiple types of psychotherapy have been shown to be helpful in treating depersonalization disorders. In fact, it is likely that human engagement with the therapist conveys benefits on its own regardless of theoretic model. Some types of therapy borrow deeply from spiritual traditions. For example, dialectic behavioral therapy owes much to the mindfulness practices of South Asian meditative traditions.

In many ways, some of the spiritual practices throughout the world have the effect of helping practitioners discover meaning in their existence.

CLINICAL COURSE WITH MANAGEMENT AND TREATMENT

Phyllis and the therapist agree that she does not suffer from exaggerated mood, anxiety, or thought distortions. Instead, she suffers from the absence of normal mood, anxiety, and pleasure. She prefers, and the therapist supports, to not attempt pharmacologic intervention at this time.

Instead, she and the therapist outline activities to bring Phyllis back into engagement with her life. When the therapist asks what used to give her pleasure that she has not done for a long time, Phyllis says thoughtfully, "gardening."

Phyllis contracts to start a container garden on her deck because it is springtime. She and the therapist discuss the potential for her to become immersed in gardening and inadvertently perpetuate symptoms of psychological withdrawal and depersonalization. She leaves it to Phyllis to decide how to avoid this pitfall.

Phyllis invites her two daughters and her grandchildren to help her make a garden. They readily agree. The two preschoolers take pride in going with their grandmother to choose pots and seedlings to plant. Phyllis makes a conscious effort to pay attention to the children and her daughters and over the course of several weeks regains her natural resilience and liveliness.

After three months of therapy the therapist is surprised when Phyllis turns up at the scheduled session with her husband, one daughter, and a gift basket of homegrown tomatoes. She tells the therapist, and the family confirms, that she is better and will call the therapist again if necessary. She says, "I'm back now, and plan to stay back for a long time."

SYSTEMS-BASED PRACTICE ISSUES

Systems-based practice issues in treatment of dissociative disorders fall into two main areas of concern. The first is failure for health professionals to recognize that persistent lack of emotion can be a mental health problem in a different way than persistent excessive emotion. Many people with dissociative or depersonalization disorders have physical symptoms without emotional ones. The question of whether depersonalization or dissociation is present simply does not arise when they are talking with their primary care physicians.

In addition, massive natural or manmade trauma like hurricanes, floods, earthquakes, and war create large numbers of people who experience depersonalization, derealization, or other dissociative phenomena. When thousands of people are displaced, homeless, drinking contaminated water, starving, with the complete breakdown of social order, it is not unusual to consider the presence of dissociative experiences the least of their problems.

Dissociation and depersonalization can compound the population effects of natural disasters. When people are distanced from caring about their lives, they are more likely to be passive.

LEGAL, ETHICAL, AND CULTURAL CHALLENGES

When dissociation and depersonalization are alleged to compromise capacity to understand one's own actions in potential criminal acts, questions arise regarding being not guilty by reason of insanity. In general U.S. courts have not been receptive to dissociation or depersonalization leading to diminished responsibility for one's actions.

The acceptability of dissociation varies widely from culture to culture. This is especially true in religious observances. Some religious rights involve the practitioners going into dissociative states or "altered mental states." Anthropologists have studied this extensively in shamanistic traditions. It should be noted that such culturally sanctioned dissociation, even when it includes aberrant or anomalous experiences, is usually not a sign of psychosis.

REFERENCES AND RESOURCES

Butler L. Normative dissociation, *Psychiatr Clin N Am* 2006;29:45–62. An interesting examination of the normal scope of dissociative experience in our lives.

Frewen P, Lanius R. Neurobiology of dissociation. *Psychiatr Clin N Am* 2006;29:113–128. A review of recent imaging research about dissociation.

Many films use dissociative phenomena as a premise. For example, *Shutter Island* (2010) strongly features such a theme. *The Killing Fields* (1984) is a good depiction of the numbing and at the same time horrifying effects of manmade disasters.

CHAPTER 24

Dysphoria about Gender

Mark D. Kilgus, M.D., Ph.D.

CLINICAL PRESENTATION

Chief complaint: "I don't know why this happened to me, this is not the body I am meant to be in. . . . I am a victim of a terrible mistake."

History of present illness: Karl is a 15-year-old male with no previous psychiatric history who presents with his parents to discuss their concern and questions about his gender identity and anxiety. From a very young age, he has demonstrated a marked preference for feminine demeanor, clothes, and company, and more recently has talked about living as a woman and having gender reassignment surgery. He says "I don't have any desire to be seen in a masculine way. . . . I am not interested in the traditional male gender role." Karl believes that he can understand why his preference may make people uneasy because there is a "disagreement" between his natal sex and how he presents himself. He feels uncomfortable with expectations that he must dress and act in a masculine way and also feels anxious by his perceived lack of acceptance of who he is. He is most uncomfortable with how society treats him as an outlier, saying, "I don't have any desire to be an outlier." He has grown more reluctant to be in public by himself, and feels very self-conscious that even minor feminine attributes are noticed by strangers. In fact, he avoids most public places and recently would not even leave the car to pick up a pizza. He denies panic attacks. It is difficult for him to speak aloud for fear of scrutiny, and he describes low self-esteem. Sleep and appetite are unimpaired and he does not endorse other symptoms of depression.

Karl is particularly interested in speaking of fashion and dress because fashion is a career goal for him, and he is interested in how people can use their clothing to present themselves. He believes that women have more variety in the options with which they can present themselves to the world, including wearing traditional male or female clothing. He does not wear dresses to school because he thinks it would create too much of a problem. His T-shirts and pants are often purchased from the women's section of department stores. He describes his ideal wardrobe as feminine and all dresses. He does not wear female undergarments and says he has no history of doing so. He doesn't consider it something that is part of fashion and presentation; for him at this age they would be difficult to purchase. He's very interested in makeup such as foundation, blush, eye makeup, and mascara and describes makeup as an art form.

He describes his incongruent gender identity as an unfair and unfortunate situation as he should have been born a female but there was a "mistake" during development. He feels as though his family assigned him a gender based on their expectations and the clothes he was given. Most things that he is interested in are what one would usually associate with women. Karl sees himself as reserved and quiet, and unable to be a traditionally louder and more dominant male. He dislikes his traditional male name and is uncomfortable with pronouns of *he* and *she*. Interestingly, he thinks it may be easier for females to have different roles because women are considered less powerful, so latitude in their roles helps them assume power. When asked, Karl says he thinks that when people are young (early elementary), boys and girls start finding differences and fitting in to that "defines your mood." He believes that middle and high school are the most important times for this, and that it's easy to give in to presenting oneself in a way that is not true to oneself. He feels as though he fits in well with his group at the school and that they value diversity and appreciate someone different who does not fit into the norm.

Karl first remembers telling his father in preschool that he was a girl, but said it was a secret. Thereafter he suppressed those thoughts and was afraid that he wouldn't fit in. He later told his mother, telling her first about his gender preference because he thought she would be more understanding as a female. He thought his father would be less understanding as a man. Karl points out that his parents could be considered as people who do not follow completely traditional roles (mom played Little League baseball and still has little interest in fashion; stay-at-home dad). Beginning in April 2012, he also began speaking to his high school counselor, who has been supportive and does not try to influence his opinions. He says she stresses the importance of him eventually finding a place where he can be honest about who he is. They also talk about his social anxiety and sense of unease, and how it can affect his relationship with his mother. He feels defensive when his mother makes comments about wanting him to be friendly.

Karl says that he supposes he is attracted to men, but does not feel gay, as it is the more feminine part of him that is attracted to masculinity. He does not identify at all with his homosexual friends. He has not had romantic encounters of any kind with either sex. He does not engage in masturbatory fantasy. When asked to think about dating, he describes spending an evening doing whatever he was invited to do, such as dinner, conversation, and so on. He is unsure of how he would see the relationship progress, but also qualifies this line of thinking, saying that he has plenty of time to figure out relationships, and at this stage of life he also has to think about school and jobs. He does think that he would like to get married and have a family someday, with either medical intervention or adoption. He has considered gender reassignment surgery, and describes the process as having a psychiatric evaluation, being prescribed hormones, and living as the opposite sex for a time before having surgery. He also thinks about suppressing puberty and he shaves every day. He believes having a fully female body would help him feel more comfortable and have better self-esteem. Karl believes that being able to live in his own gender with a congruous body is equally important in private and in public, but most important to see oneself "in the most honest way possible, because that's the person you have to be with all the time." He says, "It's very hard to look in the mirror and see a body that is a little bit foreign to you."

Karl says he has considered the following potential drawbacks of a choice to have surgery: (1) that when he tells his romantic partner about his surgery they will break up, (2) making friends after a reassignment surgery and being considered a "third gender" or "token trans-friend," (3) that his job would not be secure, and (4) possible medical complications. However, he also says that he fears that if he doesn't go through with it, he won't be living a true life.

Karl admits that he can be moody and the mood usually ranges from 3 to 7 out of 10. It easily changes with a precipitating stressor. It was at the lowest last year (1/10) when he felt as though he was struggling with his identity, was having an argument with his mother, and was in the middle of school finals. He has never felt suicidal, but has felt as though life is too hard, and he imagines his future as being socially very difficult. The best he ever felt was when he was on vacation with his mother in Chicago last summer. He did not have much stress at the time, and he and his mother's interactions were positive. He felt optimistic seeing that there is a lot of diversity in such a metropolitan setting. He sleeps well and dreams often: sometimes that he is wearing clothes that he enjoys but is back at Christian school or in a public place. He denies a history of psychosis, eating disorder, and self-injurious behavior. Drugs and alcohol are not part of the present illness. Stressors include the father's dissatisfaction with the professional environment in the area and his career. Karl's family support system includes a close relationship with maternal grandparents, who are both in assisted living.

Psychiatric history: When Karl started kindergarten at four years old (nearly five) he was quite clingy and would not play with other children unless his father was present. At about that time, his parents noticed that he frequently awoke in a bad mood and was angry and argumentative; they had enough concern to talk to a psychologist. They describe him as socially awkward, a frequent questioner of authority, "intense and strong-willed," and "challenging to raise." Even today, he often speaks without thinking in social situations and seems socially unaware at times. As he grew older, he was able to separate with minimal difficulty to attend camps. They are proud to describe him as an "amazing violinist" and "exceptionally bright."

Karl has recently again seen a psychologist and continues to talk to his school counselor. He has no history of suicidal thoughts, self-harm, physical aggression, eating disorders, or drug or alcohol abuse. He is becoming more socially isolated. His parents think that the anxiety has worsened and give an example of him being very uncomfortable with the idea of using a male bathroom. He does not like to go to places alone because of concern that he will draw negative attention to himself, especially as he has changed his dress to a more feminine style. His parents have noticed that he will speak impulsively, to the point of unintended rudeness, but he is not hyperactive. They have noticed that he is increasingly fastidious in his dress and his expectations regarding the cleanliness of the house. He will not sit on a chair that appears dirty and comments on crumbs and filth at restaurants. Recently he appears more disorganized as his anxiety seems to be worsening.

Family psychiatric history: Karl reports that his sister is anxious, and that at the age of 11 she had struggled with an eating disorder, since resolved. His mother reports obsessive compulsive traits on the maternal side. She describes her father and older sister as "exercise fanatics." Her older sister, Karl's aunt, is described as having a very difficult time making decisions and is divorced. Maternal grandparents live nearby in assisted living, and the grandmother has dementia. There is a maternal nephew with Asperger's disorder. His paternal grandmother is thought to be depressed and socially avoidant. She has been having many health issues but "she magnifies it." Paternal aunt "is kind of wild, likes to run around with her friends."

Other medical history: Other than an appendectomy in first grade and receiving breathing treatments when he had a cold, Karl has had no significant medical problems. Records from the pediatrician indicate normal male external genitalia and a Tanner Stage V of physical development.

Other history (developmental, educational/occupational, family/social, legal): Karl is the result of a planned pregnancy complicated by preeclampsia and a renal stone. There was no intrauterine exposure to drugs, alcohol, or tobacco products, but he was born prematurely at 35 weeks (spontaneous vaginal delivery). He spent 10 days in the NICU. Mother worked most of the pregnancy (up to 30 weeks). Karl met all developmental milestones on time. As a child he usually preferred traditionally female toys and dress, such as playing with a Barbie house with his sister. He was a nurturing little boy who enjoyed playing with dolls, traditional girls' hobbies, and dressing up with items from his mother's closet. One of his mother's friends noticed that Karl was kind of girly and his mother was a little resentful that she herself did not pick up on it. His parents tried to enter him in sports and other activities with boys, but "he hated it all." In preschool and even earlier, he recalls having preferences for female clothes and roles and identifying with the female protagonist in movies. At one point the parents remember Karl declaring that he was a girl. He thinks his identification with his parents has changed over time. When he was younger, his father was home more than his mother was, so he identified with him. He describes his father as always gentle, nice, and loving. As he grew older, he identified more with his mother, as he thinks their personalities and ways of speaking are more similar.

When he was in third grade, Karl performed a song for a talent show impersonating a female singer. Not only did he win, he didn't want to take off the dress. He now prefers to wear clothes purchased from the women's department. He does not regularly wear a dress or a skirt. He wears cosmetics every day, and shaves his body daily. Since he was a young child, he has usually expressed himself with feminine gestures, rarely those of a male. Also when Karl was in the third grade, the family relocated for employment reasons. The mother is a local college professor, and the husband's major stressor is that he is currently unemployed because his employer, a pharmaceutical company, experienced huge layoffs. They have been married for 20 years with no previous marriages. Karl states that he "gets along" with his parents and that if he needs to talk to them, they will make time. He and his mother have a relationship that she describes as tenuous at times. There is more conflict with Mom because his personality is more like hers. He has a good relationship with his father. His mother says that Karl was at one time very close to her sister, his aunt, in Ohio but that changed a few months ago when she asked him some very pointed questions about his gender behavior. His mother also rarely speaks to her sister and thinks she does not accept that they left Columbus. Karl has a sister who is 13 years old. He gets along well with her, although they are very different people. He describes himself as organized but enjoys working alone and methodically, and she is less methodical and more social. His mother describes her relationship with her daughter as very good, and says they have a normal teenage–parent relationship. The parents disciplined their children by spanking, but there is no history of physical or sexual abuse in the family. The family is Christian and Karl attended a private Christian school from third grade until the ninth grade. Currently he does not go to church, saying he feels as though he has to make an extra effort to think about how he has to present himself when he goes to church. His parents describe their understanding of his presentation as that he is a male who believes he was born a male but prefers to live as a female. They recognize that their son is unhappy because he is ostracized for his behavior and does not have the opportunity to live as he wants to. They want to understand Karl and learn how they can help him, because they do "not want to make him something he isn't."

For the last two years Karl has attended a small private school, which he enjoys very much, as opposed to other schools he attended, where he perceived being snubbed and bullied by other students beginning around the fifth grade. He has never skipped or repeated a grade. He never really enjoyed school as he felt that students were making fun of him and would "stomp on his lunch." He tended to interact only with the girls. He was called "faggot" and teased but was never really physically harmed. The problems intensified as he grew older, and in middle school he began to feel ostracized even from his female friends because they were interested in dating and their boyfriends would make fun of him; consequently the girls no longer associated with him. He likes the kids at his current school but prefers girls because of common interests in fashion, shopping, makeup, hair, and so on. He has many girl friends. He uses masculine gestures infrequently and feminine gestures consistently. His hobbies are very feminine. He does not engage in characteristically male activities and just doesn't gravitate to boys and they don't gravitate to him, but he will talk to them. He hates his voice because it is too masculine. Although he has not tried to change his voice, his voice inflection and pace is sometimes like that of a girl. He does not like his name but has not requested to be called by a different name more associated with the opposite sex.

Now in the 11th grade at the smaller, more accepting school, he is earning excellent grades in honors classes. In addition to core courses, he studies art, drawing, photography, band, and music theory. His favorite subjects are reading and writing. Karl has been involved with some sports, including the swim team, when he was in elementary school and later, tennis. He says he didn't enjoy swimming, but his father was adamant that he try. He enjoyed playing tennis and exercising but not the competitiveness; he still plays recreationally. Karl tried golf lessons last summer and thought it was pleasant, but that is not something he would seek out. He plays the violin and enjoys baroque, classical, and romantic music. He volunteers at a local art museum and a charity fashion organization. He plans to go to college and thinks journalism might be another good option for his major.

He reports no deviant sexual behaviors and does not masturbate with cross-dressing articles. He dresses the way he wants to dress and is aware that he is not a girl but is a boy dressing like a girl because he "cannot be who he wants to be or he will be picked on, but if he isn't who he wants to be, he will be unhappy." He does desire a sex change operation and wants to start hormones immediately. He "wants to right this wrong terrible mistake." He does not express the desire for sex reassignment frequently. His mother's attitude toward the feminine behaviors and activities is: "I just don't know, that's why I am here . . . I want to get all of the information, input and help we can get so we know what we are dealing with and what we need to do. It is what it is, and I am not going to try to make him be something he isn't."

Mental status exam: This Caucasian male appears his stated age of 15 years and has a slim body habit without dysmorphia, with brown hair cut long, wearing a T-shirt and long pants and a pendant necklace. He is wearing light makeup. His gait is a bit stiff with short steps. He sits easily and calmly in the chair and is cooperative and pleasant. No psychomotor agitation or retardation is observed, and gestures are understated and subdued. Attention and concentration are very good. Speech is spontaneous, soft, fluent, and normal in rate and rhythm. His affect is somewhat restricted and congruent with reported euthymic mood as 5 on a scale of 10. He denies suicidal or homicidal ideation, plan, or intent. Thought process is without racing thoughts, flight of ideas, or loosening of associations. Thought content is without obvious delusions but is preoccupied with social anxiety and gender issues. He denies past or present auditory or visual hallucinations or other perceptual disturbances. Intelligence is above average. He is able to calculate change accurately from a $10 bill and name the three previous presidents. He is able to abstract proverbs. His three wishes are that (1) "my body would match my mind, as I think most of my social struggle would be solved," (2) "I was a faster learner, faster at analyzing," and (3) "I'll find the perfect career." He fears that if he becomes female that he would still not be accepted by other females or by other male partners if they find out he had sex reassignment surgery. Insight and judgment are grossly intact.

IMPAIRMENT IN FUNCTIONING

There appears to be substantial impairment in functioning. This adolescent changed schools twice and is avoiding the social interaction necessary for his normal development. Without social interaction he may not successfully negotiate individuation from his family and establish a separate, secure, and stable identity. He is not able to go to public venues, including restaurants, school events, and shopping malls. This avoidance will negatively affect his ability to live away from home and attend college. This will hamper his career goals and ability to earn a living in an occupation he enjoys and that brings him job satisfaction. Also, his desire to establish his own family is threatened.

DSM DIAGNOSIS

The clinician who interviewed this adolescent suspects that he may meet the diagnostic criteria for gender identity disorder. The clinical picture includes a mixture of multiple elements, including predominant anxiety, mood (dysphoria), and thought (potential fixed false belief about being of the opposite gender). Gender Identity Disorder (GID) is classified separately in the DSM-5 but, is now referred to as Gender Dysphoria. Two primary indications for a diagnosis of GID include intense and persistent cross-gender identification, and discomfort with one's sex or its associated gender role.

There is repudiation of one's own sexual anatomy in favor of the sexual characteristics of the opposite gender. There may be insistence that one is of the opposite gender or regularly expressed desire to be of the other gender. Also present are cross-gender grooming, dressing, recreation, playmates, friends, and fantasies.

Karl seems to meet these criteria. Although the presence of intersex conditions (disorder of sex development) is a predisposing factor for gender dysphoria, Karl does not have a physical intersex condition.

There is some concern that the DSM may not adequately differentiate GID from those children who merely show a pattern of extreme gender-nonconforming behavior. With the first symptom criterion, there is a blurring of the distinction between a child who desires to be the other sex (gender identity) and the child who merely shows signs of pervasive cross-gendered behavior (gender-discordant or gender-nonconforming behavior). DSM-5 emphasizes the incongruence between one's perceived gender and one's anatomical sex particularly in older children, adolescents, and adults. A strong desire to be the other gender must be present and will reduce the possibility of overdiagnosing children with extreme gender-variant behavior. The corresponding DSM-5 diagnosis of Gender Dysphoria emphasizes the distress the individual feels about the mismatch between anatomy and self-perception, rather than the mere fact of the mismatch itself.

DSM-5 divides GID into three categories: gender dysphoria in children, gender dysphoria in adolescents or adults, and other gender dysphoria. With gender dysphoria there exists a determination and motivation for change but also a rigidity (lack of flexibility and willingness to entertain other options) that may interfere with treatment and the most satisfactory resolution. Increased age, duration of cross-gender behaviors, and resistance to change these behaviors are more likely to be associated with real GID.

Karl is initially diagnosed with an anxiety disorder (most likely social phobia) and gender dysphoria. A personality disorder is not considered because at his age and developmental stage, patterns of behavior and thought are not yet locked in. He is struggling with identity issues and questions where he fits in society. His experimentation with identity and role behaviors as part of normal development is compromised by avoidance of social interaction and the ongoing perception of being picked on or bullied. Resiliency factors for Karl include a stable family and secure relationships, good friends, a supportive school community, therapeutic alliance with his school counselor, religious faith, and positive attribution of his gender identity as something that makes him a stronger and a more independent person.

EPIDEMIOLOGY

GID is a rare condition, although its incidence may be increasing somewhat. It is much more common to have cross-gender role behaviors and mannerisms than to really believe that one has a gender identity that is opposite natal sex. Although once considered rare, heightened awareness and increased openness in today's society has resulted in more referrals for gender dysphoria. The incidence of transsexuals who begin life assigned to one sex and at some time change to the other sex is currently estimated at about 1 in 15,000–25,000 and may be increasing. One in 25,000 males and 1 in 100,000 females become transsexual. The incidence of predominant homosexuality in males is about 5%, and two thirds of adult gay males report mild to intense gender variance in childhood. An unknown but probably much smaller number report some history of gender dysphoria. Very few predominantly heterosexual males report a history of gender variance, although one fourth describe themselves as being gentle boys.

DIFFERENTIAL DIAGNOSIS

The diagnostic possibilities include gender confusion in which the adolescent is uncertain about gender, such as a young male homosexual with a history of stereotypical feminine interests and behaviors including using makeup and dressing in girls' clothes. Often the gender confusion is substantially decreased after puberty with the reduction in cross-gender interests and activities and disappearance of dysphoric feelings. The desire for sex reassignment may reflect a lack of acceptance of homosexuality. If a gender-nonconforming youth experiences erotic pleasure and sexual arousal from engaging in cross-gender role behaviors, the diagnosis would more likely be a paraphilia (transvestitic fetish). Other adolescent males may fulfill the criteria for transvestite fetish, interpreting the desire to wear female clothing with or without sexual arousal as a sign of GID and need for sex reassignment. In adolescents it is difficult to know whether this is a permanent situation or just an experimental phase in someone who will never seek sex reassignment. In rare cases there is a wish for genital ablation in persons who prefer to be sexless but have no cross-gender identity, for example, male-to-eunuch identity disorder in males who seek castration voluntarily without wanting to acquire female characteristics. There are teens who attempt to integrate masculine and feminine aspects of the self and adopt an androgynous or gender-queer form of expression. This may signify incomplete gender identity development.

Family stress, whether a major change, loss, or some other trauma, may cause brief periods of cross-gendered behaviors. This may be pure delusional thinking as part of a psychotic disorder including schizophrenia, delusional disorder, or mood disorder with psychotic features (mania or depression).

Neurologic impairments across a spectrum of parietal lobe dysfunction could cause a variety of syndromes leading to dissatisfaction with one's physical body. Body integrity identity disorder may be grouped with body dysmorphic disorder or with paraphilias depending on the absence or presence of sexual arousal. In this disorder, otherwise sane and rational individuals express a strong and specific desire for the amputation of a healthy limb or limbs. Most date this desire to their early childhood, and not uncommonly the sufferer will attempt to obtain amputation of the specific limb. As few surgeons are willing to amputate healthy limbs, this often means that the patients themselves will attempt to irrevocably damage the limb in question, thus necessitating formal amputation. After amputation most report being happy with their decision and often state, paradoxically, that they are "complete" at last. This disorder has been studied for a number of years to determine whether it is actually neurological or psychological. Recent research has demonstrated there is a threefold increased desire to want removal of a left limb versus a right. This implicates damage to the right parietal lobe similar to those who suffer from somatoparaphrenia, where a stroke to deep cortical regions at the temporoparietal junction causes paralysis and the patient's delusional belief that the paralyzed limb does not belong to the body. In addition, skin electrical conductance response (a good indicator of sympathetic nervous system arousal) is significantly different above and below the desired line of amputation, which remains stable over time. The great majority desire a single leg removed above the knee. One study suggests congenital dysfunction of the right parietal lobe and, in particular, the right superior parietal lobule, which receives and integrates input from various sensory areas and the insula to form a coherent sense of body image. When this dysfunction is acquired, as in somato-paraphrenia the brain seems sometimes to rationalize the discrepancy by deny-ing ownership of the limb. When the dysfunction is congenital it leads to a feeling that affected area should not be there to begin with and thus a desire for an amputation. There are parallels in desire for amputation of limbs and genitalia in body integrity identity disorder and some cases of male-to-female GID, respec-tively.

Comorbid psychiatric problems may be a driving factor of gender dysphoria and desire for sex reassignment. One study revealed over half of GID children met criteria for at least one other psychiatric diagnosis. Perhaps 30% have an anxiety disorder. GID is significantly associated with measures of parental psy-chopathology. In Karl's case there is a family history of pervasive developmental disorder (PDD) and some characteristics including rigidity, social awkwardness, and obsessive compulsive tendencies. Some persons have poor genital develop-ment, and marked genital ambiguity is associated overall with a higher rate of gender dysphoria and patient-initiated gender change than the rate of trans-sexualism in the general population. Therefore clinicians who provide services for persons with serious problems of gender identity are likely to encounter some individuals with a disorder of sexual development among their patients and need to be familiar with the specific presentations and problems. Some chil-dren or adolescents with disorders of sex development and markedly gender-nonconforming behavior may become uncertain which gender they really belong to and may feel confused about it or even develop gender dysphoria and the desire to change their gender.

There may be an association with GID and autistic spectrum disorders possi-bly explained by the propensity for obsessions and restricted interests. Almost 10% have autistic spectrum disorders. It has been reported that individuals with PDD often have identity crises which sometimes include gender dysphoria. This phenomenon might be related to the so-called identity diffusion in youth. When they reach their young youth, it has been said that subjects with PDD realize their uniqueness and differences compared to others, and as a result, they may develop confusion of identity, which could be exhibited as GID. Taken together, PDD and GID seem closely related to each other. Some PDD persons assert GID symptoms in response to social isolation at school. Many of the clinical symp-toms related to gender dysphoria might be explained by the cognitive character-istics and psychopathology of PDD. It is important to consider an underlying diagnosis of PDD when encountering patients with gender dysphoria.

Helpful assessment questions specific to the differential diagnosis for GID include the following:

- In regard to clothing, cosmetics, behavior, gestures, gait, speech, voice inflec-tion, or mannerisms, does this child or adolescent present as male, female, or in-between?

- By what name does the youth prefer to be called (gender-neutral or of the opposite sex)?
- At what age and how did the youth first demonstrate signs of gender variance?
- Does the youth insist on wearing clothing of the opposite sex?
- What does the youth do when there is free time?
- What are favorite toys, games, books, movies, and songs?
- What is the relative frequency of stereotypical masculine versus feminine behaviors?
- With which adults, public figures, or entertainers does the youth most identify?
- How and to what degree is the youth like his mother and father?
- What types of undergarments are worn?
- How often does the youth feel to be of the opposite sex?
- How often does the youth pretend to be of the opposite sex?
- To what degree does the youth identify and feel comfortable with sexual organs?
- Is there acceptance of body changes in response to pubertal development, or is there disgust at breast development and menstruation or testicular development?
- Is there refusal to use bathrooms associated with the biological sex or a refusal to change clothes except in private?
- Is the youth well liked, accepted, isolated, withdrawn, or bullied by peers?
- Who are his or her friends?
- What percentage of time does the youth prefer opposite- or same-sex peers?
- How does this person define his or her sexual orientation?
- Is there dating with or any romantic interest in youth of a certain gender?
- What do sexual fantasies involve?
- Is the youth sexually active and what are the specific sexual practices?
- What are the significant religious or cultural views of transgender or homosexuality in the family?
- How is the youth's functioning (academic, creative, recreational, social, and family) affected by gender variance?
- Is there sufficient family, social, professional, or other support?
- How does the family respond to cross-sex behaviors?
- Is there active avoidance of masculine or feminine behaviors?
- Have preferences changed over time and become more gender-conforming or less so?

One caveat is that the foregoing questions follow a dichotomous model of gender identity that may fail to capture the complexity, diversity, and fluidity of the transgender experience.

Other specific measures for GID are the Parent Gender Identity Questionnaire for Children (GIQC) and Gender Identity Gender Dysphoria Questionnaire (GIDYQ) for adolescents and adults. The Parent GIQC is a 16-item screening tool that provides a mean score that dimensionalizes the degree of a child's cross-gender behavior and uses standard deviation scores compared to controls and other gender-referred children. Because this scale appears to be relatively impervious to age effects, it is possible to track the change in an individual score over time. For the gender-referred group a score of less than 3.54 was 95% specific and 87% sensitive. Karl's father provided the Parent GIQC that scored as 2.1.

The 27-item GIDYQ is a validated instrument that can guide clinician questions during the gender evaluation. Mean score of less than 3.0 is 90% sensitive for gender identity disorder and 99% specific for the controls. Karl scored 2.87 on the GIDYQ. This instrument formally assesses the degree of gender dysphoria.

Other psychological testing may point toward the existence of comorbid psychiatric conditions and psychosocial stability. Impairments in mental health functioning preclude individuals from being eligible for hormone interventions or sex reassignment surgery.

Psychological testing was conducted to help clarify the diagnosis and identify comorbid conditions. Karl's parents each filled out the Achenbach Child Behavior Checklist (CBCL). Karl completed the Achenbach Youth Self Report form (YSR), the computerized version of the Diagnostic Interview schedule for Children (CDISC), and the Personality Assessment Instrument—Adolescent (PAI-A). He was also give the Roberts Apperception Test (2nd ed.) (Roberts-II) and the Rorschach ink blot test. Intelligence testing from the school, neuropsychological testing with focus on parietal lobe was also considered.

When using the CBCL with children experiencing gender dysphoria, problems are at a level comparable to the clinic-referred standardization sample. Boys with GID generally show more internalizing then externalizing patterns on the CBCL, whereas internalizing and externalizing problems are more evenly distributed in girls. Children had less social competence. Boys with GID have also been shown to manifest traits of separation anxiety. An analysis of both parents' CBCL's and Karl's YSR indicates that Karl and his parents largely agree that he has internalizing problems with anxiety and possibly depression. It does seem that in scoring himself more in the clinical range for obsessive compulsive and post-traumatic stress problems, Karl is communicating that he views his anxiety symptoms as connected to specific clinical syndromes that his parents do not perceive.

On the CDISC, Karl endorsed all of the DSM-IV criteria for Dysthymic Disorder and Social Phobia. He also met one criterion for obsessive compulsive disorder (OCD) because he endorsed having compulsions causing marked distress. These included washing, checking, and counting rituals. He met one criterion for attention deficit hyperactivity disorder (ADHD) because he endorsed having had some inattentive or hyperactive symptoms prior to age seven.

In general, this PAI-A profile suggests that Karl feels pessimistic about his future and has had some intermittent suicidal ideation. He seems to live with chronic feelings of anxiety and depression. The depressive symptoms probably include feelings of sadness and anhedonia. The anxiety symptoms are more varied. They probably include tension and difficulty relaxing, fatigue, strong stress reactions in response to changes in day-to-day routine, fears that his impulses will get out of control, and distress in relationship to memories of past traumatic events that he may feel changed him in a fundamental way. Karl may somaticize his depressive and anxious symptoms, resulting in a lot of health worries. There are also indications that (1) Karl feels his moods can be unstable at times, and that at these times he feels uncomfortable with how angry he can get; and (2) he feels that he has made mistakes in the people he has picked as friends and feels he has been disappointed in his close relationships.

Because of Karl's presenting problem of gender dysphoria, the Roberts-II was administered using a combination of both male and female stimulus cards. In general, Karl's profile suggests that he understands interpersonal interaction much as others his age do. He may have an above average ability to perceive his own and others' mixed feelings in conflict situations. However, there are indications that he deals with chronic social anxiety, and sometimes feels helpless or inadequate to manage interpersonal challenges. As a result, he may understand the motivations of others but does not feel capable of following through with resolving conflict or making them feel secure. This may be due to his chronic anxiety, as well as feelings of apathy and inadequacy. These handicap Karl's ability to act on his knowledge of himself and others. When considering social interaction, he may imagine different roles and possibilities for himself, but cannot choose one. Thus there are indications from the testing that Karl may get "stuck" trying to process too much information in social situations and so cannot act. At the same time, he expects to end up victimized in conflict situations with his peers. This expectation contributes to his sense of social inadequacy. Although he fears being a victim of others' aggression, he also fears his own aggressive and sexual impulses. He worries that he will get in trouble over these impulses.

Because of the nature of Karl's presenting problem, the content of his Rorschach transcript was analyzed to determine if he produced any responses emphasizing female sexual characteristics. Typically on the Rorschach there will be more cross-sex responses in those with GID. One such response was found, as he described human figures in a response to card III as waif-like, with high-heeled boots. However, this content analysis was not part of the standardized Rorschach scoring using Exner's Rorschach interpretive assistance computer program (version 5), which produces a clinical report. Based on his Rorschach record, Karl probably has a good ability to form impressions about himself and others, anticipate the consequences of his own actions, and understand what constitutes acceptable behavior in most situations. The report notes that he can think logically and coherently and understands cause-and-effect relationships. He seems able to focus his attention and synthesize aspects of his experience better than many people his age. Despite these strengths, which seem closely connected to his baseline intellectual abilities, the report notes that Karl may tend to view his world (especially in its interpersonal aspects) with a narrow yet unconventional frame of reference. He tends to have little tolerance for ambiguity, and he may favor overly simple solutions to complex problems. Yet he also is comfortable looking at problems and events in a nonconformist manner. He is likely to have an avoidant interpersonal style and may default to keeping people at arm's length rather than get close to them. He probably feels socially awkward, which is part of the reason for his interpersonal distancing behavior.

Although not applicable to Karl, in the Draw-a-Person Test children are more likely to draw a person that matches birth sex unless they have GID, representing the gender with which the child most strongly identifies. If children of both sexes are drawn, the larger and more detailed drawing may also demonstrate stronger gender identification.

Testing for intelligence (IQ) was not performed because academic performance and mental status examination did not suggest any deficits in this area. However, it may have been interesting from a research standpoint to formally assess parietal lobe functioning because of the similarities between GID and body integrity identity disorder. The parietal lobes (particularly right parietal) are thought to be involved in visuoperceptual abilities, including spatial relationships. The neuropsychological tests that initially come to mind would be the Benton Judgment of Line Orientation, the Hooper Visual Organization Test, the Benton Right/Left orientation test, and the Benton Facial Recognition Test (although certainly faces are unique stimuli that are processed a little differently than are other objects). The Rey complex figure test is also a possibility, as well as block design. There is also a component of the Boston Diagnostic Aphasia Examination that is supposed to tap parietal lobe functions (finger agnosia, acalculia, etc.). Certainly many of these tests will involve other cognitive functions in addition to visuospatial skills (i.e., attention, executive skills) and therefore are not strictly parietal lobe tests. There are some specific body image distortion assessments that could be borrowed from the eating disorders literature (e.g., Body Image Distortion and Dissatisfaction Evaluation), and the clinician might do a literature review to explore whether any investigations of visuospatial processing have been done in that population.

Karl's psychological testing results suggest that he views himself as depressed, as well as socially anxious and inept. His parents generally agree with this view, as they rated him as having significant internalizing problems, such as slowed thinking, anxiety, and possibly somatization. A comparison of Karl's self-ratings with those of his parents shows a tendency for he and his mother to view his problems as somewhat more serious and for his father to place less emphasis on their seriousness. However, this should be understood within the general context that all three agree Karl has a problem with internalizing symptoms. The CDISC and the YSR can be seen as asking Karl directly what he understands about any DSM-IV symptoms he experiences. The results of these tests indicate that he views his anxiety as connected to social situations (which his parents already know), but also connected to OCD and PTSD symptoms. In particular, Karl seems to feel that compulsive rituals cause him real distress and associates his anxiety with past psychological trauma. Testing indicates that he may experience his depression and anxiety as somatic symptoms. His depression and anxiety have resulted in intermittent suicidal ideation, something he has acknowledged not only on test answers but also during interviews. The moderate elevation Karl obtained on the PAI Borderline Features/Affective Instability sub-scale should not be overinterpreted. However, along with some of his Roberts-II answers, it suggests that he may have trouble containing his anger when he feels disappointed by others.

The major theme in Karl's test results is his apparent discomfort with social situations. He seems to have an adequate understanding of social norms, but he (1) perceives conflicting emotions and motives and is not sure which ones to base his actions on; (2) has an overinclusive cognitive style by which he takes in too much information and looks at people's behavior from too many perspectives to be efficient; (3) is determined to view social relationships from a nonconformist perspective; and (4) feels frozen by his dysthymia and social anxiety. As a result of these factors, Karl experiences himself as socially inept even though he has the intelligence and reality testing ability to be socially competent. His creative, nonconformist perceptual style is particularly noteworthy because it has both a positive and a negative side. On one hand, he is capable of taking a broader view of the social norms with which he feels in conflict. On the other hand, he may perpetuate conflicts with others by rigidly sticking to his nonconformist view-point. These factors have a lot to do with Karl's tendency to be distant and unin-volved in his interpersonal relationships.

In addition to gender dysphoria, the patient does seem to meet all the criteria for social phobia. It does not seem from the interview that the patient has a core deficit in social reciprocity as would be typical of a PDD. Instead, there exists avoidance of social interaction of phobic proportions. His depression is not overtly psychotic (hallucinations of obvious delusions) but may be affecting his thoughts (more rigidity and fantasy). Cross-gender leanings have been present for years and predate depression. He does not meet criteria for a transvestitic fetish (paraphilia) or a disorder of sexual development.

For sake of discussion, a different clinical presentation may have included a brief admission to a psychiatric hospital at age 12 years because of cutting on his arms after being molested by an older adolescent male cousin. Perhaps fluox-etine 10 mg po qd was prescribed for one year and then discontinued with no return of cutting behavior. This would be an example of a single-incident sexual abuse with subsequent mood dysregulation. In such a scenario he is attracted to male adolescents perhaps in spite of the emotional traumatic experience where one would expect avoidance. This would not be identification with aggressive males because he claims to be female and have romantic attraction toward males although at a subconscious level an inclination could exist to be repeatedly vic-timized. This could be a repetition compulsion as deserving or expecting abuse, a desire for a corrective emotional experience, or manipulation for primary (reduce anxiety of recurrence) or secondary gain (control relationships). In such a sce-nario, gender identity issues predated the abuse and this would not seem to be post-traumatic psychopathology. Again for the sake of discussion, if the sexual abuse occurred repeatedly from age four to seven years by an older brother and his friends, the differential diagnosis would have expanded to include a post-traumatic gender dysphoria to either avoid traumatic reminders or repeat the expected abuse as a compulsive behavior to relieve the anxiety associated with the anticipation (likelihood) of future trauma.

Although psychopathology may be the result rather than the underlying problem of GID, being transgender may also be sought as a solution to nongender problems. Even experienced interdisciplinary teams find it is more complicated to accurately diagnose gender dysphoria in youth who are not functioning well in multiple domains. The validity of the evaluation in the face of self-presentation biases can be improved by interviewing multiple informants and by employing various methods to collect accurate clinical data.

ETIOLOGY AND PATHOGENESIS

Gender identity development is complex, and the interactions of mechanisms are poorly understood with unclear outcomes. The genetics–environment interactions responsible for gender identity are poorly understood. There are no associations with systemic hormone levels in adolescents and adults and GID or homosexuality. Prenatal sex hormones may affect gender role behavior and sexual orientation in adulthood. It has been hypothesized that prenatal androgen exposure promotes the development of attraction to females, whereas insensitivity or lack of exposure to androgens leads to male attraction. Antibodies to testosterone from previous pregnancies with a male fetus may lead to incomplete androgenation of the brain (consistent with the later birth order and more older male siblings). Also, androgen insufficiency may occur with fetal stress.

There are those who propose epigenetic explanations for same-sex partner preference, ambiguous genitalia, and transgender identity. Homosexuality does occur more frequently in families, but no studies implicate a specific gene. Epigenetics is the study of heritable changes in gene expression caused by mechanisms other than the underlying DNA sequence. DNA methylation and histone modification do not alter the underlying nucleotide sequence but may persist for multiple cell divisions and are sometimes passed to the next generation. These epi-marks may regulate the expression of certain genes involving androgen production or response to androgens during fetal development. Sex-specific epi-marks produced early in embryogenesis may protect each sex from the substantial natural variation in testosterone that occurs later in fetal development, that is, girl fetuses are not masculinized even under high testosterone conditions and boy fetuses are still masculinized even under low testosterone conditions. However, if these same epi-marks are transmitted to the next generation from fathers to daughters or mothers to sons, they would cause the reverse effects—masculinized girls and feminized boys.

Father absence may contribute to GID. Mothers of boys with GID have high levels of emotional involvement and lower criticism. Mothers' anxiety about violence from men, poor management of stress, and ambivalent or hostile relationships with the fathers could lead to parenting that promotes cross-gender behavior in sons. Sons may be anxious about maternal withdrawal and abandonment. There may be a lack of parental discouragement of cross-sex behaviors. As a child, when Karl first expressed his feelings of being different, he recollects that his father was not very sympathetic. By experiencing his father's response as rejecting, Karl may have gravitated toward his mother and identified even more strongly with her. The perceived lack of support by the father may have contributed to Karl feeling less protected and to more gender confusion.

The concept of what is male or female in most societies is deeply ingrained in culture and is largely dichotomous. There are individual variations in maleness or femaleness that challenge this dichotomy and, as with many of our diagnostic categories in the DSM, suggest a spectrum. Over time society can accept these individual variations. Extreme deviations from the norm are not pathologic by themselves but can lead to psychopathology (functional impairment). Substantial and unusual variation (outside the norm) in maleness or femaleness in behavior or identity is generally designated as cross-gender, gender-variant, gender-atypical, gender-nonconforming, or transgender. *Gender discordance* is defined as a discrepancy between anatomical sex and gender identity. Children and adolescents manifesting such variation are referred to mental health professionals for assessment and treatment. Gender nonconformity is not always accompanied by discordant gender identity. In the societal context, these variations may lead to gender dysphoria.

There seems to be a contemporary need for society to acquiesce to the desires of children with GID (and normalize children with disorders of sexual development). This may be motivated by the apparent fundamental human need to appear normal, perhaps to fill the social need of belonging to a group. Ironically, the desire to "fit in" survives despite telling our children to "be themselves" when the need to be accepted into the group is the issue and being like others is the goal. After adolescence this belonging to the majority group seems less important.

A desire to become a girl may have been an effort to avoid bullying from male peers or greater identification with nonmasculine traits. It may be a result of a lifelong avoidance of exploration because of an anxious temperament (association of less risk taking and strong attachment to the female gender). Also negative feelings about self may lead to gender dysphoria as an effort to cope with these feelings. If there was a history of abuse by a male perpetrator, the cross-gender identification may be post-traumatic avoidance as opposed to identification with the aggressor.

NATURAL COURSE WITHOUT TREATMENT

Gender constancy is established between the ages of two and seven years when the child is able to discriminate different gender roles and identifies accordingly. Children learn about boys or girls from authority figures and from social cues, and they apply this knowledge to themselves. As the child matures he or she becomes increasingly motivated to observe, incorporate, and respect gender roles. Although the idea of gender spectrum and gender fluidity has merit, it is easier for most children to have some clear sense of gender consistent with being either a boy or girl because our culture depends on gender to explain sexuality, society, and self. For some children, clarity about gender issues is just not possible unless it is defined strictly by anatomic sex or genetic constitution. So it is not surprising that gender-nonconforming children may struggle and experience prolonged gender distress.

By two years of age parents begin to notice gender-deviant behaviors, such as feminine interests in their boys. At this age children may have idiosyncratic ideas of what it means to be a boy or girl. By the time they enter preschool they have highly conventional, concrete, and rigid notions of boy versus girl behaviors. These gender classifications may generate confusion in a boy who is so different and uncertain about his gender identity. Although classified as a boy, he is not interested in the activities of other boys and finds girls to be more like himself. He does not realize that there are different kinds of boys who like girl things because they are uncommon. Also during childhood there is rehearsal of social sexual behavior that serves as the foundation for further development in adolescence and adulthood.

The boys exhibiting extremes of feminine behavior typically show a strong and persistent interest in the toys, play, and clothes of girls and a preference for girl playmates. There is an infatuation with hyperfemininity, including shoes, makeup, hairstyles, and anything feminine. He plays with Barbie dolls, not just baby dolls, because this is not about nurturing a baby. He also has an avoidance of rough-and-tumble play and at a young age he may verbalize wishing to be a girl. The boy's gender-variant behaviors seem to be playful expressions of creativity and fantasy. It is common for the expression of gender-variant behavior to decrease later in childhood around age 10, although it may re-emerge during adolescence. The typical gender dysphoric male who identifies as transsexual in adulthood reports having had an internalized feeling of discontent with being male and a desire to be female.

The vast majority of prepubertal cross-gender children do not become transgender in adolescence or adulthood. About one fourth of children referred for gender issues were still gender dysphoric in early adulthood. Although 80–90% of childhood GID desists by adulthood, GID rarely desists after the onset of puberty. Once adolescence is reached GID is far more likely to persist than in childhood. In fact, when GID persists into adolescence, puberty is often associated with a worsening of dysphoria and distress. When gender discordance presents before puberty, it persists into adulthood between 2% and 12% of the time. Both gender nonconformity and gender discordance are believed by some to be developmentally related to homosexuality. Gender-dysphoric girls referred in childhood are less likely to remit than are boys.

Adolescents with gender dysphoria may vastly differ in their ability to handle the complexities and adversities that often accompany gender variance. Some have such intense distress that they expect clinicians to immediately provide them with hormones and sex reassignment surgery as quickly as possible. Others are simply trying to find ways to live with these feelings of confusion or some unease. The gender dysphoria may have started long before puberty or be more recent. The environment can be accepting and supporting or rejecting. These individuals may present with a broad range of coexisting psychiatric problems. Gender-variant behavior and even the desire to be of another gender can be either a phase or a variation of normal development without any adverse consequences for a child's current functioning. Prospective studies show that gender variance in clinical populations is associated with later homosexuality or bisexuality as well as gender dysphoria in adulthood. Nonetheless, even in clinical populations in over 25% of cases, the gender dysphoria does not persist from childhood into adulthood. When presenting during adolescence, it seems much less likely that gender dysphoria will desist. Gender dysphoria can lead to such high-risk behaviors during adolescence as soliciting illicit hormones or silicone injections, drug and alcohol abuse, or suicide.

Peer rejection can be a major issue for the child or adolescent with gender nonconformity, leading to poorer social relationships in general. In childhood this is more of a problem for feminine boys than for masculine girls (tomboys).

There is no single clinical course for children with GID, although most children do not persist in their gender dysphoria. There is some evidence to suggest that those with more extreme measures of cross-gender behavior and gender dysphoria are more likely to persist. Of those who desist, some become homosexual in orientation whereas others become heterosexual. For boys with a pervasive pattern of feminine behaviors, meeting the DSM criteria for GID was more predictive of later homosexual orientation than of persistent cross-gender identity. Perhaps two thirds of children with GID develop a homosexual orientation in adolescence.

Of the 6,450 respondents in a 2011 survey of transgender or gender-nonconforming adults (*Injustice at Every Turn: A Report of the National Transgender Discrimination Survey*) 41% reported suicide attempts, 78% reported harassment, 35% reported physical assault, and 12% sexual violence during the school years with 15% leaving school. Fifty-seven percent experienced family rejection as well. Despite a probable selection bias of those transgender individuals willing to participate in the survey and the problems with retrospective data reporting, these respondents had significant functional impairment as indicated by a reported rate of unemployment and homelessness double that of the general population and a rate of poverty four times the national average.

Anxiety may be related to real or perceived rejection, hostility, and abuse because of the teen's transgender status or fear of being discovered. Transgendered teens have committed suicide, perhaps 50% have serious suicidal thoughts, and one third have actually made a suicide attempt. Suicide attempts are not correlated with childhood gender nonconformity but to parental physical and verbal abuse as well as to negative feelings about the body (especially in regard to weight) and how it was regarded by peers. Gender-nonconforming adolescents seem to have better psychological health than transgender adults. It could be that the stress associated with the desire to be of the other gender leads to socioemotional problems, including depression and anxiety. Also there may be social ostracism and rejection by same-sex peers. There is also research and clinical observations about how mental disorders may affect or be affected by intense gender-nonconforming interests and behaviors. Concurrent conditions such as attention deficit hyperactivity disorder, bipolar disorder, anxiety disorders, and autistic spectrum disorders may make a child more vulnerable to social ostracism or gender confusion. This helps explain some disturbing reactions, such as emotional hypersensitivity, severe mood swings, oppositional behavior, temper tantrums, attention problems, anxiety, and depression.

EVIDENCE-BASED TREATMENT OPTIONS

There is no universally successful approach because the evidence is lacking and treatment strategy is individualized as inferred from clinical reasoning and from one's best understanding of the person. The efforts to help children to fit in like everybody else must be tempered by a view of the uniqueness of each child. Gender-atypical behavior by itself should not be taken as an indicator for sex reassignment. A comprehensive psychological evaluation and an opportunity to explore feelings about gender with a qualified clinician are required over a period of time. It is important to remember that transient periods of uncertainty about one's gender are common in disorders of sexual development and in adolescents struggling with gender dysphoria, but should not be interpreted as a clear indication for sex reassignment. Gender uncertainty may arise from numerous factors, such as gender-atypical behavior and interests, atypical somatic development, social repercussions, chromosomal status, and so on. Supportive counseling in contact with support groups seems helpful, but there are no systematic intervention studies. Family therapy may be necessary to help resolve conflicts between family members. Parents may need guidance on how to relate to their child in a way that does not contribute to more gender dysphoria. Healthy boundaries and limits must still be provided by parents and will be tested by the gender-variant adolescent.

There are three general approaches to management and treatment for children with GID (gender dysphoria). The first approach offers no active intervention to lessen gender dysphoria or cross-gender behavior. This hands-off approach is based on the assumption that 80–90% of children even without treatment will have resolution of GID on reaching adolescence. The downside to this strategy is that the 10–20% who persist on reaching adolescence are more firmly established in their diagnosis and less responsive to interventions.

For prepubescent children, gender identity is fluid and its effect on families remains crucial to the clinical approach when the patient presents for treatment. There is no evidence-based approach to predict the adolescent outcome of a gender-variant child. This remains the hallmark dilemma in the treatment of these children. Proposed goals for treatment include reducing gender discordance, decreasing social ostracism, and reducing psychiatric comorbidity. Hastening the desistence, that is, fading of gender discordance, is the overarching treatment goal. This may be accomplished through eclectic relationship- and milieu-focused interventions. Encourage tolerance of gender discordance while setting limits on expression of gender-discordant behavior to the extent that these limits are necessary to decrease risk for peer or community harassment. Minimizing family disapproval and rejection helps reduce the risk for depression, suicide, and substance abuse. Families struggle emotionally and with making adjustments such as name or pronoun use. Increased levels of harassment and victimization by peers are related to increased levels of depression and anxiety and decreased levels of self-esteem.

Another approach attempts to lessen gender dysphoria by helping the child accept his biological sex and the associated gender identity. The child is assisted with expanding sex-role stereotypes and flexibility in both directions. Reducing dependence and enmeshment with the caregivers addresses the typical imbalance between attachment and exploration. In this case, separation anxiety was prominent in childhood and has contributed to social phobia in adolescence. Strategies to reduce peer rejection and ostracism can improve the social isolation and alienation that contribute to emotional distress. These include providing a safe place for the child to play, exploring same-gender activities, and reinforcing congruent gender role behaviors. Families are encouraged to be more accepting while reducing overt or inadvertent reinforcement of cross-gender behaviors. Punishment, ridicule, and criticism are avoided. The focus of these interventions is more on reducing the dysphoria than the gender role behaviors.

The third approach encourages a transition to the cross-gender role that is identity congruent. This approach requires a treatment team of professionals including psychiatrists, psychologists, endocrinologists, pediatricians, and surgeons. When GID persists to the onset of puberty, hormonal suppression of secondary sex characteristics is a treatment option. Sex reassignment must be based on thorough psychological gender evaluation because it implies major legal, social, and somatic changes for the patient. Reassignment profoundly affects the patient's family especially in regard to grief and loss. Educational and religious communities may require persuasion to accept the patient in the new gender role.

For transgender adolescents following this third approach, there are established phases of treatment both medical and psychiatric. It is not clear whether or how these three approaches affect the long-term psychosexual outcomes or overall psychosocial adjustment of the patient with gender dysphoria. As one would expect, without strong evidence to guide clinical interventions, there are diverse and controversial opinions. No systematic data are available on the effectiveness of these different treatment approaches.

There are no randomized controlled trials addressing efficacy of treatment. No one treatment to reduce gender discordance can be endorsed at this time. However, the following treatment principles are proposed according to the best evidence available and a consistent approach to addressing psychopathology in general.

1. Achieving greater gender flexibility is a major treatment goal and the clinician should offer education and resources toward that end. For example, it can be instructive to demonstrate changes in societal gender norms over the course of human history in regard to care, clothing, and jewelry. Patients would mark on a Likert scale or chart where their current identity exists along the spectrum from male to female and also record the percentage of the time they feel male versus female. This can be a more objective measure of treatment progress. Most children express relief when they can have a way of defining and understanding themselves as just a different kind of boy or girl. Educating parents and communities about expanding gender role and accepting cross-gender behaviors may complement this individual treatment goal.

The benefits of assuming a cross-gender social role in the school setting is controversial. It is not realistic to expect that everyone will accommodate cross-sex dress and behavior, and it may be best to help the transgendered child fit better into his or her environment. It is adaptive to figure out how to negotiate between expressing one's real self and acclimating to the real world, so we submerge aspects of ourselves depending on the context. There are alternatives for physical education that requires public dressing and undressing. There are also unisex bathrooms. It would be nice to embrace differences and strive to learn from and respect each other despite or because of our differences. So the best first approach may be to create as many safe spaces for feminine expression as possible. Paying special attention (even negative attention) to either gender role behaviors may serve to reinforce them. It is generally a good practice to provide positive attention independent of any gender-specific behavior. The overwhelming majority of gender-nonconforming children desist from their cross-gender identifications and behaviors by adolescence. A majority of these children will identify as sexual minorities as they become adolescents. The outcome does not seem to relate to severity of symptoms.

2. Especially early in development, one should avoid definitive labels on a person's cross-gender identity because it is still evolving. Many transgender children do not express or experience distress or dysfunction with their assigned gender, despite some having the desire to be the other sex. As mentioned earlier, 80–90% of children even without treatment will have resolution of gender identity disorder on reaching adolescence.

Psychological stability becomes the initial treatment goal. The clinician should initially treat underlying comorbidities that may be affecting gender identity and dysphoria. The comorbid psychopathology may be primary or the result of family and social rejection, psychological distress due to the real discrepancy between psychological and anatomic gender, or family psychopathology. Although psychopathology may be the result rather than the underlying problem of GID, sexual reassignment may also be sought as a solution to nongender problems. Even for experienced clinical teams, it is more complicated to make an accurate diagnosis of gender dysphoria in adolescents who are not functioning well.

3. There should be careful assessment and treatment of any comorbid psychiatric diagnoses. It is a challenge to disentangle the gender and autistic spectrum disorders. For example, environmental influences on the child's gender development, including school, peers, extended family members, siblings, popular culture, etc., and patterns of the child's coping strategies and resilience capacities should be thoroughly explored. An ongoing treatment relationship will expand the opportunities to understand the dynamic interactions between psychiatric comorbidities and various external influences on the child or adolescent, internal ego strengths, and coping patterns.

4. Psychotherapy should focus on assisting the individual in establishing gender identity that is congruent with biological and anatomical sex. As mentioned in the first treatment guideline, this is best accomplished by broadening the more narrow societal definitions of gender to allow for the patient's specific variation in gender role attitudes, preferences, and behaviors. In addition to validating feelings through peer support, group psychotherapy can extend the evaluation to discover important clinical information that was not initially apparent. It is not always possible to expose your child to another gender-nonconforming child. Such an opportunity allows access to someone who could truly understand. It would be nice to have a safe place for gender-nonconforming children to play with other kids without being questioned about their preferences. This is sometimes accomplished through activities in art, theater, music, and creative play.

There are few evidence-based treatment options but three general approaches: reducing gender dysphoria through cognitive and behavioral strategies (for example attempting to increase the child's comfort by expressing behaviors and identifications consistent with his or her natal sex), redirecting the child to neutral expressions of gender in an attempt to allow more time for the child to develop cognitively, emotionally, and socially, or facilitating ego syntonic cross-gender social transition prior to the onset of puberty. Each of these approaches has associated benefits and risks. The first option seems to have the least risk given the high desistence rates of gender-nonconforming behaviors and identifications in children.

Psychotherapy may focus on helping adolescents who experience shame about being different, guilt toward parents, or low self-esteem. They may need help dealing with social repercussions of being gender variant, such as exclusion and being teased or bullied, ridiculed, or harassed. Support groups are intended to offer a safe and informal social setting to meet peers. The object of the psychotherapeutic intervention is relief of the gender dysphoria. Some of the goals of psychotherapy in gender-nonconforming youth include improving adaptive ego strengths and resilience in the child, facilitate parental understanding and support of the child, address environmental factors that contribute to child in the validation, routine assessment of the degree of gender dysphoria persistence, facilitate positive coping strategies to varying degrees of environmental invalidation while minimizing components of environmental invalidation, and treat comorbid psychopathology within the context of gender identity.

Adolescents may resist therapy because of perceptions that they are psychosocially well adjusted except for their gender issues. The frequency of treatment is guided by the severity of associated psychopathology and the degree of functioning. Collaborative treatment with other provider's patients and families often view the mental health component of treatment as a means to achieving the medical interventions. Once achieving the primary goal, mental health follow-up is poor. Acute safety issues are dressed through psychiatric hospitalization. Psychomotor/play therapy may help youth who do not easily verbalize feelings. Treatment roadmaps and narrative medicine (writing and telling a story with drawings and pictures) may assist with the impatient adolescent.

5. Ongoing support of the youth and parents through the therapeutic treatment relationship is highly desirable. There are few experienced clinicians and little prospective evidence to guide treatment. Most parents initially question the diagnosis and whether the child is going through a phase or has been influenced by peers or social media or is otherwise exploring sexuality. There is also the concern that improvements in psychopathology following diagnosis and early treatment are transient and will return when experiencing ongoing discrimination, rejection, or disappointments. A more cautious clinical approach as opposed to strongly advocating for the presence and maintenance of the disorder is appreciated by most parents.

Parents often struggle with the conflict between validating the child's current stated wishes versus succumbing to the stigma that environmental influences may impose. Dealing with recommendations of other providers such as pediatricians, school psychologists, teachers, and therapists involved in the child's treatment may reflect inadvertent or blatant opposing ideas and biases. With adolescents who are gender-nonconforming, standards for establishing patient eligibility and readiness for treatment may be inconsistent across providers. Improving adaptation to the multiple external and internal challenges is necessary psychosocial treatment. Support groups may be helpful, but online and other resources cannot be relied on to give the best advice for any specific individual. Additionally this area has been highly politicized. An online discussion group through the Children's National Medical Center helps families know that they are not alone.

The social challenges for both the child and the parents are the hardest because our culture expects and is designed to support extremely binary gender roles. Parents are encouraged to share the facts first instead of the associated emotional difficulties along the way, such as "my child is nonconforming in gender role behavior and has been that way since an early age. He prefers female clothing, female play, and the company of girls." The message is conveyed confidently from a parent who loves his child and supports who he is and does not allow for second-guessing. It is parents who teach their children to be bullies. Instead of converting others, it is best to surround yourself with people who embrace the child and his or her nonconforming life.

Families often deal with grief and loss around losing a son or daughter and the normative hopes and dreams and expectation for their child's future. They grieve the loss of anticipated stability as their child grows older and progresses through normal development. They worry about reducing the reproductive possibilities. They are concerned about their child's succeeding at school, work, interpersonal relationships, and family formation. They worry about the physical and emotional safety of their child. They may respond with reduced expectations of the child's achievements and expectations around the household and failed to set appropriate structure and limits that all adolescents need. They may withdraw and fail to give the adolescent needed support. Most parents have encouraged their child to limit cross-dressing and other cross-gender behaviors that may be focus of negative attention in public and rather practice them in the privacy of their own home. Female-to-male cross-dressing is generally less hostile and more socially acceptable, as is the case with tomboys. Some parents believe that group participation may prematurely validate and actually promote a course of action that the child would not otherwise take; however, a group gives permission to discuss topics that may be difficult for single individual or family. Listening to the stories of others and talking about personal struggles contributes to developing insight and adaptive strategies, including anticipation. Family groups demonstrate acceptance, support, and collective problem solving.

6. Sex reassignment (also referred to as normalizing or gender-confirming procedures) is controversial and typically follows three phases: diagnostic phase, real-life experience as the other gender with prescribed hormones, and surgery to change the genitals and other sex characteristics. The diagnostic phase can take more than six years and includes some standardized instruments to assess psychosocial and psychosexual development. This includes intellectual abilities, coping abilities, psychopathology, self-esteem, sexual experiences, sexual attractions, sexual relationships, subjective meaning of cross-dressing, sexual fantasies accompanying cross-dressing, and body image. In addition to current cross-gender feelings and behavior, functioning at school, peer relations, and family functioning are also assessed (see number 3 above).

Much of the distress that transgender adolescents experience in puberty is related to the emergence of secondary sex characteristics. Pubertal suppression can buy some time and extend the diagnostic phase. However, puberty suppression will inhibit spontaneous formation of a gender identity corresponding to natal sex. Of course delaying treatment until adulthood may have its own psychological drawbacks, including the development of depression, suicidality, anxiety, and oppositional defiant disorders accompanied by school dropout and social withdrawal. So the rationale for early treatment is that transgendered youth may be spared the burden of having to live with irreversible signs of the wrong secondary sex characteristics and more surgical procedures. In recent years endocrinologists and mental health clinicians have been willing to consider puberty suppression or suspension (gonadotropin-releasing hormone analog) for early adolescence at Tanner stage II and cross-sex hormone therapy once adolescents reach the age of 16. Sex hormone suppression through the use of gonadotropin-releasing hormone analogs are used to reversibly delay development of secondary sex characteristics when decisions about sex reassignment cannot be deferred until adulthood or delay the need for treatment decisions until maturity allows informed consent and minimizes the later need for surgery to reverse them. A drawback would be insufficient penile and scrotal tissue to construct labia and a vaginal vault. Suppressing puberty does not give the adolescent the choice of freezing sperm prior to fertility. Gonadotropin-releasing hormone analogs may be used to suppress puberty, are reversible, and could be considered an extended diagnostic phase. Gonadotropin-releasing hormone initiates the secretion of gonadotropins by the pituitary gland and therefore secretion of sex hormones by the ovaries and testicles. Taking gonadotropin-releasing hormone analogs (e.g., luteinizing hormone–releasing hormone agonist depot triptorelin) causes down-regulation of gonadotropin secretion, thereby suppressing gonadotropins, testosterone, and estrogens. This can be considered when GID has intensified instead of decreased during early puberty and there are no serious psychosocial problems interfering with diagnosis or treatment. Such a determination must be made by a mental health professional with experience and training in child and adolescent developmental psychopathology, for example, a child and adolescent psychiatrist. In addition there must be exclusion of psychiatric conditions that are similar to or contribute to GID. Tanner stage should be confirmed by physical examination and hormone levels. It should be done at around Tanner stage II or III. Most gender-dysphoric youths choose to live in the desired gender roles simultaneously with the beginning of puberty suppression. Most who have had pubertal suppression at age 14 years to enable exploration of gender dysphoria still had gender dysphoria two years later. Medical treatment to suppress puberty is expensive, not routinely covered by insurance, and provides logistical hurdles that may not be affordable by the family. This may contribute to the adolescent's perception that his or her parents are unsupportive or rejecting. There are surgical, hormonal, and psychosocial consequences and protective laws may preclude such treatment in certain states or countries. Of course parents must be involved in treatment decisions prior to the age of legal consent.

Hormone therapy is the next step in sex reassignment and is considered at around the age of 16 years when there is sufficient maturity for independent medical decision making. It is an expectation that the social gender role change will occur simultaneously. It is desirable that gender-dysphoric patients undergo a prolonged period of living in the desired gender in most or all domains of everyday life as appropriate for the patient's age before undergoing any reversible medical treatment, such as cross-gender hormone treatment or gender-confirming genital surgery. Hormone therapy is easier and safer when following suppressed puberty. The resulting physical changes and effect on fertility are only partially reversible. Gender discordance presenting in adolescents or adults seems more likely to persist then when presenting in childhood, so treatment approaches often assume persistence of gender discordance. Treatment approaches focus on management of comorbid psychiatric issues such as depression, anxiety, and anger in addition to general behavioral and emotional problems in functioning (illicitly obtained sex hormones). Smoking and obesity seriously affect the effects of hormone treatment and surgical outcome. Other concerns relate to bone density, body height, and brain development. Most adolescents who have received hormonal therapy report persistent cross-gender identity and improved psychological functioning.

Surgery is considered at 18 years of age and only if there is a long-standing history of gender-atypical behavior and gender dysphoria and the desire to change gender being strong and persistent for a considerable period of time such as at least six months living as the desired gender. One must consider unrealistic expectations from genital surgery especially in females who desire change to male anatomy. The threshold for gender reassignment and surgery for those with developmental sexual disorders is understandably much lower than for gender-dysphoric children with normal anatomy. The surgery impairs orgasm. Cryopreservation of eggs and sperm is considered for loss of fertility. Parents and teens need to hear realistic descriptions of what hormones and surgery can and cannot do for a person seeking sex reassignment surgery. With a few exceptions, those who have had sex reassignment surgery do not express regrets, no longer report dysphoria, and self-report functioning well socially and psychologically. However, those patients selected for this treatment were the best-functioning from the start and may have done equally well with alternative treatment. There is little evidence to demonstrate actual improvement in overall functioning.

Education about the short-term and long-term costs and benefits of gender reassignment will help the adolescent have a balanced view. Realistic expectations of the neo-vagina and neo-phallus are necessary. Characteristics such as extreme shyness, lack of self-confidence, or perfectionism must be addressed to facilitate future partnerships. Adequate information about sexuality in general should be provided. There is the possibility of aggressive reactions when engaged in sexual encounters where the partner is not aware of the adolescent's natal sex. Adolescents may become frustrated at having to wait too long for sex reassignment, and even the slow results of hormone treatment may cause frustration that leads to social withdrawal.

Achieving congruence of gender identity and anatomical sex through reassignment surgery is an expensive and extreme intervention that potentially inflicts harm and dysfunction. It focuses more on appearance as a solution versus essence. To alter genitalia to conform to society's more narrow definition of gender must be carefully examined. The surgical procedure and hormone therapy may not achieve the acceptance or validation of gender identity that the person may be seeking. Identity is not really about appearance, so changing physical attributes does not change the identity or the essential genetic material. This reassignment approach defies reality and is inconsistent with the treatment of similar psychopathology such as body dysmorphic disorder or body integrity identity disorder, where noninvasive strategies are employed to reduce the patient's suffering. It seems that all other treatment options should be exhausted before a surgical solution is entertained to relieve psychological distress.

Unacknowledged homophobia-erotophobia by clinicians and parents may explain some decisions that encourage or allow the boy to transition to live as a girl or vice versa. Patients and their families perceive that they have almost no choice if they are choosing between a guaranteed low quality of life and the possibility of a more fulfilling life through sex reassignment. Based on the existing evidence, the clinician is ethically bound to avoid giving, even inadvertently, such an impression. Clinician neutrality regarding outcomes is often recommended to allow the youth to openly explore gender-dysphoric feelings and treatment wishes. This sounds good on the surface, but with the current evidence may not be on solid ethical ground.

CLINICAL COURSE WITH MANAGEMENT AND TREATMENT

In this particular case, Karl seems to meet all of the DSM criteria for social phobia. This condition seems to predate any gender dysphoria and must be primarily addressed and treated. The patient may be fantasizing that sex reassignment will magically improve his long-standing difficulty with social interaction. The SSRI antidepressant fluoxetine is prescribed initially at 10 mg and then increased after two weeks to 20 mg to target anxiety and mild depression. Gabapentin 300 mg up to three times daily as needed for acute anxiety may be added until the fluoxetine has its full effect in about two months. Assignments to walk around the shopping mall and visit other public venues are designed to expose the patient to anxiety-provoking situations where he perceives himself to be the object of scrutiny. Exposure and response prevention is the cornerstone of effective treatments for phobias. If necessary the exposure will be graded and coupled with training on relaxation techniques for greater tolerability.

As the clinician assists Karl with the treatment of mild depression (evident on psychological testing) and social phobia, the matter of gender identity is patiently explored. Self-acceptance and expanding gender role behavior are encouraged. When adolescents present with gender identity disorders, the clinician would do well not to rush to collude with young patients in the idea that unease and uncertainty are all related to an unclear vision of the most correct gender. Identity diffusion is a normal part of adolescent development. Although it may be that a broader conception of gender would be advantageous to some, and that any one individual may over the course of a life come to see him- or herself as more masculine or feminine, making a narrow determination of an incorrect gender in adolescence is shortsighted.

Adolescence is a time of uncertain, pluripotent possibility. Many aspects of identity are unsure and unknown. It is a time of questioning and should be honored as such. Clinicians treating adolescents with gender identity disorders might do best to recall the value of the holding environment and serve as a safe place for the exploration of a range of ideas and uncertainties, allowing the unfolding of a developing adult over time. The adolescent needs to form ideas about self, occupation, religion, and relationships to others and the community, in addition to perhaps determining a final comfort level with a postpubertal body. Some individuals may, later in adulthood, choose to transition to another gender, but likely not all who have had questions about gender identity would do so.

Questioning oneself is a natural part of the process of growing up. If we honor the identity diffusion and identity formation of adolescence we may help many patients become their best and most natural selves, and allow those who ultimately do choose to transition their gender role know that choice was made deliberately, with the benefit of adult maturity. The general problem reminds me of this quote from Rilke. He was writing to a 19-year-old who was unsure if he should try to be a poet or join the army:

> *Have patience with everything unresolved in your heart and try to love the questions themselves as if they were locked rooms or books written in a very foreign language. Don't search for the answers, which could not be given to you now, because you would not be able to live them. And the point is to live everything. Live the questions now. Perhaps then, someday far in the future, you will gradually, without even noticing it, live your way into the answer. (Rainer Maria Rilke, 1903, in* Letters to a Young Poet*)*

Twelve weeks after initiating treatment, Karl's depression and social anxiety lift to the point where he is again excited about plans after high school and visiting prospective colleges. One of those colleges has as part of its diversity program an acknowledgment of gender dysphoria and the opportunity to explore identity in a more accepting environment, including unisex bathrooms. Six months later, he acknowledges the wisdom of the therapist in not initially supporting his aggressive pursuit of hormonal therapy or sex reassignment. Without much fanfare Karl matter-of-factly shares his latest insight that he is homosexual in orientation.

SYSTEMS-BASED PRACTICE ISSUES

There are few child and adolescent psychiatrists in the United States who can be regarded as having some degree of expertise with gender-nonconforming children and adolescents. Other identified barriers to caring for gender-nonconforming and transgender youth include variability in clinical approach by community providers, a general lack of comfort and knowledge in gender identity issues, and multiple clinician (from various disciplines) involvement with poor coordination and disagreement as to what constitutes competent and comprehensive care. The latter relates to the lack of solid evidence to inform practice.

LEGAL, ETHICAL, AND CULTURAL ISSUES

Critics of the gender dysphoria (gender identity disorder) diagnosis contend that the behaviors of gender-nonconforming youth are not in themselves pathological but are labeled that way because of social intolerance and the associated distress to the person caused by the intolerance. In essence the diagnosis of GID may represent a medical accommodation of a social prejudice, where the distress and dysfunction are the result of that prejudice. Gender dysphoria theoretically would abate with more acceptance of androgyny versus the current societal preference for rigid gender dichotomy. Also, there are those who believe that cross-gender behavior is a normal developmental pathway to homosexuality and therefore not the basis for a valid diagnostic category. However, gender nonconformity is clearly not a precondition of homosexuality and does not necessarily lead to the same.

Any evaluation or consideration of intervention for a child with gender nonconformity is necessarily an ethical issue because the right course of action is in question. It is the responsibility of the clinician as expert in the field to weigh the scientific evidence and then decide what is ethical for each individual presentation. The evidence never directs the ethical decisions but informs what is necessary given the proper course of action. Although compassion, integrity, and fairness comprise the foundational principles of medical ethics, reduction to universal rules is elusive. For example, it is incumbent on the compassionate clinician to alleviate suffering in whatever way seems right. One recurring ethical dilemma in treating children is ascertaining whose suffering (parent, child, or even the clinician) ultimately determines the treatment and whose expectations define what is normal for the child. Legally the parent is responsible, and perhaps the best course of action is to give preference to the opinions of the parents because what children desire of themselves may be unlikely to satisfy them as adults. As clinicians it seems right to foster normal child development, but there is considerable latitude (individual variation) and the parent may have a different idea of normal (or desirable) compared to the clinician or the child. Also, the clinician is aware that gender-nonconforming children may experience conflicting desires over time within the bounds of normal development. With the long-term well-being of the person as primarily important, the clinician would avoid intervening in any way that could not be undone if the growing child, adolescent, or emerging adult sees herself as having changed (as distinguished from having developed). Also, promoting individuation as part of normal development allows the child to perform independent self-assessments that may contradict parents and other adults but should be considered and addressed in decision making. From a child's self-understanding grows an unambiguous identity and secure sense of self, the pinnacle of developmental achievement. Because of developmental constraints, young children may not be able or willing to verbalize cross-gender wishes or comprehend the implications. But regardless of any particular stage of development or theoretical interpretation, this underlying identity of the child must be considered wholly unique and carefully protected with definite standards of clinical care. Parents will look to the clinician for guidance. One may look to professional organizations for recommendations on standards of care but ultimately the clinician is personally responsible for the right course of action in each case.

Perhaps the major ethical dilemma for this case is the potential for doing harm where evidence is lacking. The more popular treatment options may lead to permanent irreversible harm and are inconsistent with approaches to similar clinical conditions. For example, the treatment of non–gender-related body dysmorphic disorder seeks to minimize surgical interventions and promote self-acceptance. There are those who express concern that sex reassignment is a form of sanctioned self-mutilation supported by the politics surrounding sexual identity and orientation and by a dichotomous societal preference regarding gender. They argue that a different approach would prevail for other similar but nonpoliticized clinical situations. For example, body integrity identity disorder denotes a syndrome in which a person is preoccupied with the desire to amputate a healthy limb. The desire to amputate seems related to a disturbance in the person's perception that the limb is not a genuine part of himself. Limb amputation can relieve temporarily the patient's feeling of distress without necessarily adjusting the patient's identity misperception. Persons with this disorder seek surgical correction, but the medical community is generally united in pursuing noninvasive treatment strategies to reduce the patient's suffering. The patient retains the most function and is thus best served by incorporating the limb as part of a fully integrated and unified whole identity. As with GID, the persons receiving the surgery express no regrets afterward, but have clearly lost some degree of functioning. They may also initially report less distress although the ambulation difficulties will undoubtedly provide new challenges with social and emotional consequences. Because of the reduction in functioning, this lack of regret seems insufficient for physicians to support the process of relieving psychological distress through surgery. Sex reassignment can be clearly distinguished from surgeries that are cosmetic, restorative, or reconstructive.

TERMS

Disorders of sexual development (intersex conditions): previously known as hermaphroditism and pseudo-hermaphroditism. These individuals have congenital abnormalities such as congenital adrenal hyperplasia, androgen insensitivity, 5-alpha reductase-2 deficiency, 17 beta hydroxy steroid dehydrogenase 3 deficiency, cloacal or bladder extrophy, penile agenesis, vaginal agenesis, mosaicism, and chimerism. There is controversy as to whether intersex children should receive nonessential genital surgical procedures involving sex reassignment prior to when the child is of an age to decide. The historical assignment to female sex at birth for persons with ambiguous genitalia was based on the reasoning that any neonate can be raised a girl, that boys without an adequate penis would struggle developmentally, and that XX neonates had the potential for fertility. Many children who were sexually reassigned at birth from male to female and later experienced transgender feelings commonly recognize that a switch has been made and that they in fact are the opposite sex. However, they are cognitively less rigid and typically do not reject their assigned sex. Because these children do not describe gender dysphoria, it appears to be a different phenomenon from GID. Prenatal exposure to effective androgen seems to be strongly associated with male typical behaviors in a dose-response relationship whereas in children with complete androgen insensitivity (testicular feminization) there is a distinct absence of gender discordance.

Gender: society's perception of a person's sex as male or female. Gender as a social, cultural, or family construct is more fluid and dynamic than one's sex.

Gender dysphoria: the subjective mood disturbance experienced by persons whose gender identity is incongruent with biological sex. This term replaces Gender Identity Disorder in DSM-5.

Gender fluid: a flexible approach to maleness or femaleness.

Gender queer: those persons who do not identify as fully male or fully female but somewhere along the gender continuum. *Gender queer, third gender, third sex, androgyne, bigender, gender outlaw, multigender, genderless,* and *pangender* are terms used by persons attempting to define themselves on the spectrum between male and female identity.

Gender identity: a person's inner perception of self as male or female, usually established by age three and concordant with biological sex and typical role behaviors. In young children at a preoperational stage of cognitive development, perception of gender identity and role is still changeable but as development progresses they become more permanent and remain stable over the lifetime.

Gender minority: those persons whose gender behavior or identity is nonconforming or discordant.

Gender role: a person's dress, grooming, speech, mannerisms, interests, activities, and behavior as expressions of conventional masculine or feminine norms accepted by society and prevalent culture.

Gender nonconforming: variation in gender role from conventional norms and is used interchangeably with *gender variant* or *gender atypical.* Examples of gender nonconformity include an aversion to rough-and-tumble play in boys and extreme tomboyishness among girls. Gender nonconformity is often associated with low peer status, poor self-esteem, and peer harassment that may lead to long-term mental health consequences. Childhood gender nonconformity may be associated with adult homosexual orientation, especially in males.

Internalized sexual prejudice or internalized homophobia: a syndrome of self-loathing in persons who have same-sex attraction, based on their adoption of antihomosexual attitudes, beliefs, and values. These persons struggle with sexual feelings that are discrepant from family and societal expectations. Consequently they may not successfully establish an independent identity with the incumbent increased risk for chronic anxiety, depression, substance abuse, suicide, and high-risk sexual behaviors.

Pansexual: persons who feel erotic attraction to all people regardless of biological sex or gender.

Sex: a person's biology, both the natal genetic makeup (XX or XY) and its anatomic expression.

Sexual minority: those persons whose sexual orientation differs from the heterosexual norm.

Sexual prejudice (homophobia): bias and hostility toward those persons who are homosexual or bisexual in orientation.

Sexual orientation: the sex to which a person is erotically attracted through patterns of sexual fantasy, physiological arousal, and sexual behavior as influenced by gender identity and role.

Transgender (gender discordant): persons with a gender identity that is discordant from biological sex (there is a spectrum of gender discordance). Transgender persons do not consider their attraction to people of the sex opposite their own gender identity to be a homosexual orientation.

Transsexuals: these people seek some degree of medical or surgical intervention to align their gender identity and biological sex (sex reassignment). These individuals identify themselves as members of the opposite sex.

Transvestite: persons who dress and groom in a way that is opposite to their biological sex and gender identity. *Drag* is a term applied to clothing and makeup worn on special occasions for *performing* or entertaining. A *drag queen* would be a man doing female drag; a *drag king* refers to a woman doing male drag. A transvestitic fetish is associated with erotic pleasure and therefore is a paraphilia.

REFERENCES AND RESOURCES

Deogracias JJ, Johnson LL, Meyer-Bahlburg FL, et al. The Gender Identity/Gender Dysphoria Questionnaire for adolescents and adults. *J Sex Res* 2007;44(4):370–79.

Grant JM, Mottet LA, Tanis J, Harrison J, Herman JL, Keisling M. *Injustice at Every Turn: A Report of the National Transgender Discrimination Survey.* Washington: National Center for Transgender Equality and National Gay and Lesbian Task Force, 2011.

Johnson LL, Bradley SJ, Birkenfeld-Adams AS, et al. A parent-report gender identity questionnaire for children. *Arch Sex Behav* 2004;33(2):105–16.

Pleak RR, Trivedi HK, et al. Gender variant children and transgender adolescents. *Child Adolesc Psych Clin N Am* 2011;20(4).

Practice Parameter on gay, lesbian, or bisexual orientation, gender non-conformity, gender discordance in children and adolescents. *J Amer Acad Child Adolesc Psych* 2012; 51(9):957–74.

Wallien MSC, Swaab H, Cohen-Kettenis PT. Psychiatric comorbidity among children with gender identity disorder. *J Amer Acad Child Adolesc Psych* 2007;46(10):1307–14.

Zucker KJ, Bradley SJ, Lowry CB, et al. A gender identity interview for children. *J Personal Assess* 1993;61(3):443–56.

Zucker KJ, Lozinski JA, Bradley SJ, Doering RW. Sex-typed responses in the Rorschach protocols of children with gender identity disorder. *J Personal Assess* 1992;58(2): 295–310.

Gender and Sexuality Development Program at Children's National Medical Center (CNMC) in Washington, DC (http://www.childrensnational.org/gendervariance) provides psychosexual evaluations and therapeutic services on an outpatient basis.

World Professional Association for Transgender Health (WPATH) is an international and multidisciplinary professional organization devoted to the understanding and treatment of gender identity disorders by promoting evidence-based care, education, research, advocacy, public policy, and respect in transgender health. http://www.wpath.org.

Guevote—The Way I Feel Is How I Am (1996) is a documentary film portraying the daily lives of a significant percentage of girls born in a Caribbean village who change into men at puberty because of a genetic variation that conveys androgen insensitivity.

Eating Fears

Delmar Short, M.D.

CLINICAL PRESENTATION

Chief complaint: "I can't concentrate. I am so wiped out."

History of present illness: Ashley, a 23-year-old female accompanied by her parents, comes to be evaluated for admission to an inpatient eating disorder program. Part of the assessment is to evaluate the readiness and ability of the patient to benefit from a costly and intensive service.

Ashley's eating problems began when she was 14 years old with binge eating and purging. She later alternated this behavior with restrictive eating without purging. She has not binged or induced vomiting for the last three years.

She reports that when she was younger, her parents drank heavily. In retrospect she believes controlling her weight was a way of controlling something in her life. She reports a significant fear of gaining weight or becoming fat. At one point she reported that she would rather be dead than fat. She does not see herself as being overweight or underweight, even though she appears emaciated to others. She has an extreme desire to be thin and perceives her body as too large. Ashley believes that if she even gains one pound, she is fat and is a "loser." Her self-esteem is greatly tied to her ability to control her weight. She has not had a menstrual cycle for several years.

Ashley is a very picky eater and rearranges her food on her plate in a certain order. She is not currently bingeing, but she has a history of self-induced vomiting and misuse of laxatives in the past. She also has almost no friends and isolates herself significantly. She is somewhat shy and uncomfortable in social situations. She has not had a boyfriend, partly because of fear of being rejected. She experiences fear in social situations and wants everything to go perfectly well or she worries about it. She has no unusual beliefs, ideas of reference, or thought broadcasting, nor does she report any special abilities like mind reading.

Five feet, 5 inches tall with a weight of 85 pounds, Ashley has a body mass index (BMI) of only 14. BMI was developed to give some guidelines for healthy weight at varying height. The formula is BMI = [weight in pounds/(height in inches × height in inches)] × 703. For Ashley, 85% of normal body weight for a female would be approximately 105 pounds. A healthy BMI is between 19 and 25.

Ashley also acknowledges that she regularly experiences lethargy, low interest, low energy, difficulty concentrating, poor appetite, and feeling bad about herself. She reported the recent development of recurrent grand mal seizures.

She ambulates with a slight limp on the left side. The electrocardiogram on admission showed a QTc interval of approximately 510 milliseconds, falling into the prolonged range.

Past psychiatric history: Ashley's parents brought her to a family physician a few years prior to this hospitalization due to concerns about excessive vomiting. Her BMI at that time was 19 and her weight was 112 pounds. At that time, there were no obvious physical findings, and laboratory tests were not done. Her blood pressure and pulse were normal. The primary care physician did not recommend anything further at that time.

Past medical history: She is now on phenytoin for her seizure disorder. She has a foot drop and QTc prolongation.

Social history: Ashley finished high school and has taken some junior college classes, but she has been very unmotivated recently and unable to concentrate on her schoolwork. She has not had any lasting jobs. It was noted previously that her parents are alcoholics but are now recovering. They have been trying to make amends for a difficult childhood, during which she was basically ignored. She was an only child, spent a lot of time alone, and continues to be uncomfortable in social situations.

Mental status exam/physical exam: Ashley is a very thin young woman with fine, blonde hair. She is somewhat psychomotor retarded. She ambulates with a slight limp on the left side. Her speech is slow and thoughtful. She is cooperative and wants to comply. She has good eye contact at times and looks down at other times. She is alert and oriented to person, place, time, and situation. Her recall/recent memory is 3/3 with distraction. Her registration and remote memory are intact. She is able to spell *world* backward and correctly does serial 3's and 7's without mistakes. Her mini-mental status exam is 30 out of 30. She does not have a blunted or flat affect. Her mood is subdued and depressed. Her affect is congruent with her mood, but shows some range.

Ashley's thought processes are logical and linear without looseness, flight of ideas, or circumstantiality. She is able to use abstract thinking, denies hallucinations, and shows no evidence of delusions, thought broadcasting, ideas of reference, or magical thinking. She has a good fund of knowledge and good use of vocabulary. Ashley's insight into the medical problems caused by her low weight is very limited, but she shows good judgment and insight in other areas of her life. She denies hallucinations or any history of depersonalization.

IMPAIRMENT IN FUNCTIONING

At the time of her hospital admission Ashley manifests serious symptoms and impairment in social and occupational and school functioning. On the other hand, she very much wants to comply and is motivated due to desire to feel better and function better in school. She very much wants to please others.

DSM DIAGNOSIS

In this case the overall pattern for Ashley's illness involves distortions in thinking (distorted body image), anxiety, and mood. DSM-5 concentrates on three primary criteria for anorexia nervosa. The individual must have significantly low body weight, a fear of getting fat, and a distortion of body image. In this particular person's presentation, all three "primary colors" are represented.

Ashley meets DSM criteria for anorexia nervosa that can be summarized with the mnemonic FADE:

F: fear of gaining weight or becoming fat,
A: amenorrhea, no menstrual period for several years,
D: disturbance in a way one perceives his or her body weight, as she does not see herself as overweight,
E: Stands for 85% or failure to maintain 85% of expected body weight. This would be about 105 pounds, and she's only at 85 pounds, with an extremely low BMI of 14.

There are specific subtypes to specify. She has been the binge eating/purging type in the past, but now she is only doing restrictive eating.

It is noted that at one time the patient met the criteria for bulimia nervosa, which can be summarized in the acrostic mnemonic BASTE, with

B: binge eating,
A: anorexia nervosa ruled out,
S: self of evaluation based on weight,
T: twice a week for three months, and
E: excessive exercise, emesis, enemas, and so on.

Another diagnosis to consider is major depression, as Ashley is very depressed. She has had some symptoms of depression for at least several months, including low interest, low self-esteem or guilt, low energy, low concentration, low appetite, and psychomotor retardation. She denies suicidal ideation, intent, or plan and does not have a sleep disturbance. However, we have to be careful about making the diagnosis of major depression initially, as starvation also has many of these symptoms. She denies any history of manic or hypomanic symptoms, which is important to rule in or out when considering depression.

Ashley exhibits symptoms of avoidant personality disorder. Common traits include: social inhibition, feelings of inadequacy, and hypersensitivity to the negative evaluation of others. She has no friends and isolates herself. However, unlike in schizoid personality, she actually would like to have relationships with others and feels a deep loneliness. She is not indifferent to the praise or criticism of others. She also has no odd beliefs other than those restricted to the eating disorder area, so she doesn't meet criteria for schizotypal personality disorder. Of note, cluster C personality disorders, such as obsessive compulsive personality or avoidant personality, are actually common in eating disorders.

Other medical problems includes grand mal seizure disorder, a left foot drop, and cardiac conduction delay, with a QTc of 515 milliseconds.

According to the eating disorders practice guideline by the APA, the clinician needs to be concerned about various things related to medical status that will lead to immediate inpatient hospitalization. These include such things as heart rate below 40, blood pressure below 90/60, any significant electrolyte abnormality such as very low glucose or potassium under 3 mEq/liter, or a temperature under 97 °F. Her electrolytes are normal; electrolytes tend to be more abnormal in bulimia.

Psychosocial environmental problems include parental nonsupport in the past but currently parents are supportive as recovering alcoholics. She is having difficulty with her education due to poor concentration, and she's unemployed. Her parents are not financially well off but are willing to use their available resources to help her in any way they can.

EPIDEMIOLOGY

Western culture has had a profound influence on people, especially women, to be thin. Some people's self-esteem is wrapped up in their appearance, and this is the case with Ashley. In 2008, the prevalence of anorexia nervosa was estimated to be 0.25%. Fifty to 70% get better in their twenties. Twenty-five to 30% of college-age women have at least tried self-induced vomiting, although a smaller percentage meets full criteria for bulimia nervosa. The lifetime prevalence of bulimia is 1–3% among women, which is 10 times the prevalence in men. Estimates in high school– and college-age women have ranged from 1% to 20%. One fourth of dancers and models may have an eating disorder. Dancers, models, gymnasts, and other athletes are particularly prone to eating disorders. In an online survey, 10% of women between ages 25 and 45 reported an eating disorder.

Anorexia nervosa is far more prevalent in industrialized societies. It is most common in the United States, Canada, Europe, Australia, Japan, New Zealand, and South Africa. Cases of eating disorders have been described, however, going back many centuries.

Greater than 90% of cases of anorexia occur in females. Anorexia is more common among first-degree biological relatives of anorexics. Ashley's parents do not have a history of eating disorders, but they have a history of alcohol dependence. There is also an increased risk of mood disorders among first-degree biological relatives. Eating disorders are far more common among monozygotic twins than in dizygotic twins. This is truly a biopsychosocial illness that very much illustrates the complexities of those interactions.

Additional diagnostic considerations: the diagnosis itself is not usually difficult in eating disorders. However, there are gray areas, and many patients who don't quite meet full criteria. In such cases, we may entertain the diagnosis of an eating disorder not otherwise specified.

Other possible causes of weight loss should be considered, especially when the onset of symptoms is over the age of 40. These include such general medical conditions as gastrointestinal disease, brain tumors, malignancies, and AIDS. Such patients do not have a distorted body image or a desire to lose weight.

Some patients with schizophrenia may have unusual eating behaviors along with weight loss, but such patients rarely demonstrate a fear of gaining weight.

Comorbidity should be looked into very carefully, because comorbid psychiatric illness may be very amenable to treatment; this may help greatly with the overall outcome. Look for medical conditions also.

DIFFERENTIAL DIAGNOSIS

Various medical disorders can mimic anorexia nervosa and the avoidance of food. Swallowing disorders including hypo-motility of the esophagus make eating and swallowing unpleasant. Hyperthyroidism may cause increased activity and energy, decreased perception of hunger, and decreased feeding with weight loss. Celiac disease and other gastrointestinal problems can lead to avoidance of certain foods and to weight loss.

Among the psychiatric disorders obsessive-compulsive disorder with rigid attitudes toward food can look very much like anorexia nervosa. However, these individuals do not have body image distortion. People who are very paranoid may also avoid eating food for fear of poisoning or contamination.

ETIOLOGY AND PATHOGENESIS

Eating disorders truly represent the complexities of the biopsychosocial spectrum of etiology and treatment. Ashley probably had some genetic predisposition for both eating disorders and depression due to both parents being alcoholic. We don't know the rest of the family history or if the parents drank due to mood disorders. Ashley was not well cared for in childhood and started using eating as an action she could control in an otherwise chaotic childhood. We do not know specifically about social pressures in her peer group, but that is often a very important factor in the development of eating disorders. Ashley had symptoms of avoidant and obsessive psychological defense mechanisms that are very common in eating disorder patients.

NATURAL CLINICAL COURSE WITHOUT TREATMENT

Long-term mortality among anorexia patients admitted to a university hospital is over 10%, making it one of the more lethal psychiatric diagnoses. Death most commonly results from suicide, electrolyte imbalance, or starvation. Medical complications and comorbidities are common in anorexia, and Ashley has a number of these issues. These may include cardiovascular and peripheral vascular disorders, central nervous system problems (including apathy), cognitive impairment, seizures, peripheral neuropathy, hypothermia, vomiting, abdominal pain, constipation, acute gastric distension, benign parotid hyperplasia, dental caries, glossitis, diarrhea, hair loss, dry and brittle hair, ipecac-associated myopathy, muscle aches, and cramps. Substance use disorders are common in persons with eating disorders (and note that in this case, Ashley's parents had substance use problems). Medical complications of bulimia include arrhythmias, enlarged salivary glands, seizures, constipation, rare cases of esophageal or gastric tears, and dental decay. Polycystic ovaries are also associated with active bulimia. Persons with bulimia have comorbid alcohol abuse about 23% of the time. Mood disorders are common in persons with eating disorders, and depressive symptoms may also be a consequence of malnutrition. Lifetime incidence of comorbid anxiety disorders was 71% in a large study.

The onset of eating disorders rarely occurs over the age of 40 and usually begins between the ages of 14 and 18 years. Earlier and later onsets have occurred. When eating disorders occur between the ages of 7 and 12, depression and obsessional behavior are common. Children often present with a variety of gastrointestinal complaints, such as nausea, abdominal pain, early satiety (feeling full early), or being unable to swallow. Each of these symptoms would need to be investigated. The weight loss may be rapid and serious. In children, the lack of normal weight gain over time is also of concern. A food avoidance pattern may also occur in children, called food avoidance emotional disorder, which is different from anorexia. These children, in contrast to children with anorexia, recognize that they are underweight and would like to gain weight.

Delayed growth is common in early onset anorexia. Osteoporosis and osteopenia are also common in early onset children. Bulimia, on the other hand, is rarely seen in children under age 12.

Some case reports and expert opinion note that as the Baby Boomer generation got older, there were more reports of eating disorders in middle-aged women. Incidence rates of anorexia in persons over 50, on the other hand, are less than 1% of newly diagnosed cases.

The course is quite variable, as is the outcome, with some recovering fully after a single episode, and some exhibiting a fluctuating course. There are also those who experience a progressively deteriorating course over many years. Even with treatment, symptoms such as restriction or purging may improve or resolve within a few months; other symptoms, such as body dissatisfaction or nonpurging compensatory behaviors, may take years to resolve. Patients with restrictive eating may develop bingeing and purging, or those who start off bingeing and purging may develop restrictive eating over time.

Some advertising agencies have increased their BMI goals for models due to concerns about the striving for thinness has on the models as well as those who observe them. Those involved particularly in the areas of ballet and gymnastics, as well as figure skating and distance running, should be especially aware of the increased risks in women in these fields. Those with a history of eating disorders who are now mothers may benefit from assistance with parenting skills.

EVIDENCE-BASED TREATMENT OPTIONS

Treatment involves making sure that acute medical situations are stabilized, such as low pulse, blood pressure, dehydration, and electrolyte abnormalities.

A *New England Journal of Medicine* article (Becker et al., 1999) included the following signs, symptoms, and medical complications of eating disorders: dental caries, enlargement of the parotid glands (sometimes called "chipmunk cheeks"), postural and nonpostural hypotension, prolonged QT interval (as in this case), U waves, sinus bradycardia, atrial and ventricular arrhythmias, decrease in left ventricle size (we had a patient with a severe eating disorder whose heart was so atrophied that the spinal column obscured the view of her heart on x-ray, so it appeared that there was no heart at all), esophagitis, hematemesis (watch for Mallory-Weiss tears), delayed gastric emptying, constipation, gastric dilation and rupture, elevated liver function tests, increase in serum amylase, hypokalemia, hyponatremia, hypomagnesemia, hypoglycemia, hypothermia, amenorrhea, oligomenorrhea, delayed puberty, arrested growth, osteoporosis, renal calculi, infertility, low birthweight infant, dry skin, hair loss, laugo hair, hand abrasions or calluses, peripheral neuropathy (which this patient had), reversible cortical atrophy, anemia, leucopenia, neutropenia, and thrombocytopenia.

After ensuring stable vital signs kidney, liver, and cardiac function are evaluated with a comprehensive metabolic panel that includes electrolytes.

Hospitalization is recommended for:

- Suicidality.
- Possibly < 75% of healthy body weight or acute weight decline with food refusal.
- Comorbid psychiatric condition requiring hospitalization.
- Unable to control multiple daily episodes without supervision.
- Medical: pulse < 40; blood pressure < 90/60; or temperature < 97 °F
- Glucose < 60 mg/dl; potassium < 3 mEq/L
- Hepatic, renal or cardiovascular compromise.

Treatment then includes nutritional rehabilitation, targeting two to three pounds per week for weight gain while in the hospital. Outpatients generally should gain between half to one pound per week. If the patient gains weight too rapidly, they may be afflicted with refeeding pancreatitis and fluid retention. Refeeding too rapidly can be medically dangerous and lead to death. Inpatients may be monitored and advised by nutritionists or dieticians during meals. Patients may also be watched for purging after meals to make sure they don't go into the bathroom and induce emesis.

In severe cases, where the patient refuses to eat or gain weight, he or she may need to be restricted to bed and only get privileges as they gain weight.

Nutritional rehabilitation should focus on the goals of restoring weight, correcting biological and psychological effects of malnutrition, normalizing eating patterns, and achieving normal perceptions of hunger and satiety.

In targeting healthy goal weights early on, we have to be cognizant of how fearful patients may be of gaining weight. This discussion may need to be delayed. One way of establishing a healthy goal for female patients is to target the weight at which normal menstruation and ovulation are restored.

In children and adolescents it is important to follow growth charts and be aware that failure to gain weight as appropriate can be a serious problem, not just losing weight. Growth charts are available from the Centers for Disease Control and Prevention at http://www.cdc.gov/growthcharts/.

For patients in inpatient or residential treatment settings, the target weight for discharge may vary and depend on the patient's ability to feed her- or himself, motivation, and ability to participate in outpatient programs. The closer the patient is to their healthy body weight prior to discharge, the better the outcome and less risk of relapse or having to be readmitted.

It is important to attempt to avoid control battles and not have punitive intentions when engaging in interventions that may be experienced by the patient as aversive. Positive reinforcers, such as privileges, and negative reinforcers, such as bed rest, exercise restrictions, and restriction of off-ward privileges, should be a normal routine of the program.

In inpatient programs, it may be difficult to obtain the cooperation of patients, especially if they do not wish to be there. Also, many patients have delayed gastric emptying, which may impair for a time their ability to tolerate more than 1,000 calories per day. In such cases, it may be important to begin with diets of 200–300 calories above the patient's usual caloric intake. A liquid feeding formula may be necessary in the early stages of weight gain, followed by gradually advancing the diet to include solid foods. Gradually increasing activity levels may be very effective in accomplishing weight gain.

Serum potassium levels need to be followed closely in patients who are inducing vomiting. Vitamin and mineral supplements may be of benefit, and hypokalemia may require oral or even IV potassium supplementation. Dehydration may need to be treated using IV fluids.

We can advise patients regarding what beneficial changes will likely take place as they start to gain weight. Apathy and lethargy should begin to improve in the early stages. Anxious and depressive symptoms, irritability, and sometimes suicidal thoughts may occur, however, as the patient gains toward some perceived important number that represents a "phobic" weight.

A number of medications have been tried in anorexia, and none show consistent research evidence of efficacy. Anxiolytic medications may be helpful before meals for the anorexic patient with anxiety before eating. There are case reports of successful use of olanzapine in patients with severe anorexia. The APA guidelines state that psychotropic medications should not be used as the sole or primary treatment for anorexia, but can be considered for the prevention of relapse in weight-restored patients or to treat depression or obsessive compulsive disorder.

A very important exception is that some patients may be treated successfully with medications if they have comorbid psychiatric illnesses. If the patient is extremely obsessive compulsive or depressed, medication may be helpful. Also, if the patient has some psychotic symptoms, antipsychotics may be of use.

In bulimia, antidepressants, especially selective serotonin reuptake inhibitors (SSRIs), have been found to be helpful. The tricyclic antidepressants (such as desipramine, imipramine, and amitriptyline), monoamine oxidase inhibitors, and buspirone are also more effective than placebo at decreasing bingeing and vomiting in patients with bulimia. However, the better safety and side effect profile of the SSRIs such as fluoxetine make these drugs more appropriate for first-line therapy.

Bupropion has been associated with seizures in eating disorder patients. Its original release to the market in the 1980s was delayed due to this problem. Further study showed that seizures were a relatively low risk, but about twice the risk of other antidepressants. Bupropion was not yet on the market when Ashley was treated, nor were SSRIs. Monoamine oxidase inhibitors are somewhat risky in eating disorder patients because of the need to restrict certain types of food. Two other drugs that may be useful in patients with bulimia are the antiepileptic agent topiramate and the selective serotonin antagonist ondansetron. Topiramate, at a dose of 25–600 mg/day (median dose 212 mg/day) in a randomized study of 61 outpatients (53 women, 8 men) with binge eating disorder (not bulimia) significantly reduced binge frequency and weight compared with placebo (94% versus 46% reduction).

Ondansetron (24 mg/day) was reported to reduce binge eating and self-induced vomiting in a small placebo-controlled study of 29 patients with bulimia. Other drugs that have been investigated for the treatment of bulimia include lithium and naltrexone; neither has shown to be of significant benefit (although in this case lithium was very helpful due to comorbid illness treatment).

In the specific diagnosis of binge eating disorder, escitalopram at doses from 10 to 30 mg was significantly better than placebo. Two anticonvulsants, topiramate and zonisamide, were also better than placebo; sibutramine, an appetite suppressant, was also effective.

After initial medical, nutritional, and behavioral interventions (or concurrently in some cases), family therapy may be an important component of treatment. A strong therapeutic alliance is important from the beginning, and individual psychotherapy may be necessary for a number of years. Group psychotherapy is often used, especially in inpatient settings. It is important to avoid having patients learn from others new maladaptive behaviors or compete with each other toward being the thinnest or the sickest member of the group.

Cognitive behavioral therapies or interpersonal therapies may be effective. Common cognitive or reasoning errors to address include "dichotomous reasoning," where the patient often sees things in extreme absolute, all-or-none terms. Food, eating, and weight are areas where this thinking is applied in patients with eating disorders. Patients often evaluate themselves in harsh or extreme terms, and yet view others more realistically. Other reasoning errors include personalization and self-reference, superstitious thinking, magnification, selective abstraction, overgeneralization, and underlying assumptions.

CLINICAL COURSE WITH MANAGEMENT AND TREATMENT

Ashley gained weight gradually in the hospital and over a period of time, her mood began to improve. Her concentration, interest, and energy all improved and she gained weight. However, it was noted that approximately every few weeks she relapsed into more severe depression, even as she was gaining weight and getting better. At the time of treatment SSRIs were not yet introduced into the market, and the only antidepressant that did not potentially cause cardiac conduction delay at that time was trazodone. However, trazodone is not considered to be an extremely effective antidepressant. Due to Ashley's somewhat cycling unipolar depression and the lack of other options in terms of cardiac conduction, the patient was started on lithium after a review of her kidney and thyroid function. Lithium has some risks in eating disorder patients, especially if they have renal damage, and careful monitoring of electrolytes and lithium levels is appropriate.

In patients with bulimia, lithium may be problematic because lithium levels may shift remarkably with volume changes. Also, lithium has not been found to be effective in the treatment of bulimia.

In this case, lithium was extremely effective in preventing further mood problems. The patient was also on phenytoin for her seizure disorder. She gained weight up to about 112 pounds, which is low normal for her height. She was followed twice weekly using psychodynamically oriented psychotherapy under the supervision of a training analyst. Behavior therapy and medical management were also used by the treating resident. The patient was weighed weekly at the therapy sessions.

After approximately one year of doing very well, phenytoin was changed to carbamazepine for her seizure disorder with the hope of preventing gingival hyperplasia. This continued to help prevent seizures, but it was decided that we would try to get Ashley off of lithium and see if the carbamazepine would hold her cycling mood disorder. Approximately 10 days after stopping the lithium, Ashley had her first major depressive episode in about a year. This did not resolve in spite of a psychodynamic interpretation of the issues and only resolved after the lithium was reinstituted. She did not have another mood episode for two more years.

Ashley continued to maintain her weight well, although at the low normal range. She went back to school to study to be a nutritionist and became more involved socially in church. She was no longer depressed and no longer restricted her eating. Her concentration and interest improved, and she showed a broader range of interests.

This case points out the importance of looking for comorbid diagnoses and treating those, as well as appropriately managing medical conditions. It also points out the importance of choosing psychopharmacology appropriately. Eating disorders also highlight the importance of a biopsychosocial approach.

SYSTEMS-BASED PRACTICE ISSUES

Anorexia nervosa is a rare but potentially fatal disorder that may require confinement and very strict control over the individual's activities for weeks or months. Psychiatric units are generally oriented toward crisis stabilization and discharge to a less restrictive level of care. Anorectics do not respond very quickly to treatment. Re-feeding may be necessary to correct nutritional imbalances and must be undertaken slowly. It takes time to reverse the rigidity and desperate control exerted by an anorectic person over everything to do with food. Specialized units are very staff intensive. For example, it may be necessary to observe each patient for a couple of hours after each meal to avoid purging in the restroom or frenetically exercising to lose the calories consumed. Insurers balk at paying the very large amounts necessary to sustain an individual in this type of specialized unit. Clinicians generally are strong advocates of patient autonomy and it is difficult to recognize the life-saving tight control needed for these individuals.

LEGAL/ETHICAL CONCERNS

The pressure toward thinness has changed dramatically in the United States since the 1950s and 1960s, when a more healthy BMI was popular. Although *peer pressure* sounds like an overused jargon term, there is an enormous amount of interaction between girls in school and other settings where they compete with each other about weight and value thinness enormously. We've even heard of girls at camps competing at how many sit-ups they can do and exercising obsessively.

Some of the early descriptions of bulimic symptoms appeared in Babylon between 400 and 500 BC. Descriptions of eating disorders occurred in the description of two patients in 1694 by Richard Morton. He described these persons as having nervous consumption, to differentiate them from persons with tuberculosis. William Gull rediscovered the syndrome in 1868 and in 1874 first used the term *anorexia nervosa*. Early in the 20th century, there was confusion between pituitary insufficiency and anorexia. Gerald Russell, in 1979 first used the term *bulimia nervosa* to distinguish these persons as separate from those with anorexia. The DSM-III came out the next year (1980) and defined bulimia separately from anorexia.

It is not known whether the extreme expense of an inpatient hospitalization is totally justified, and unfortunately it is currently unavailable to many patients with this disorder. We do not know if this patient would have gotten better if we had used less expensive options, although some had been tried previously. One of the major ethical and medicolegal issues that comes up frequently in treating patients with eating disorders is the dilemma of attempting to "force" treatment against the person's wishes. In ethics, the issue of beneficence, doing what is best for the patient or with the patient, may conflict with the principle of autonomy—doing what they want to do, even though their judgment may be impaired. Also, even though the person's behavior may be very detrimental to their health and possibly even life-threatening, it is hard to make a case for danger to self due to imminent suicidality to "force" treatment. This is a challenge when we are trying to get someone to gain weight, sort of against their wishes. Various means of behavior modifications, rewards, bed restriction, therapies, and gentle coercion may be used to help the person get better. Fortunately, in this case, Ashley was very compliant throughout treatment.

REFERENCES AND RESOURCES

Becker A, Grinspoon S, Klibanski A, Herzog DB. Eating disorders. *N Eng J Med* 1999; 340:1092–98.

Yager J, Devlin MJ, Halmi KA, Herzog DB, Mitchell III JE, Powers P, Zerbe KJ. *Practice Guideline for the Treatment of Patients with Eating Disorders.* (3rd ed.). Arlington, VA: APA, 2006.

The Famine Within (1992). This documentary explores the role of advertising and popular culture in the development of unrealistic ideals for women's bodies. Many girls become obsessed with food and are afraid of it, due to the pressure to look like someone they can never be. One statistic from this documentary notes that in the mid-1960s, the "ideal" appearance was only 8% thinner than the average woman. In the 1990s, the so-called ideal appearance was 25% thinner than the average.

Thin: Death by Eating Disorder (2005) is another film that features this type of psychopathology.

CRC Health Group's Eating Disorders website, http://www.eatingdisordershelpguide.com

Renfrew Center, specializing in eating disorders, http://www.renfrewcenter.com.

CHAPTER 26

Daytime Sleepiness

William S. Elias, M.D.

CLINICAL PRESENTATION

Chief complaint: "I get sleepy at times when I drive."

History of present illness: Wilbur, a 46-year-old male interstate truck driver, was referred to the sleep clinic mainly at the insistence of his wife for symptoms lasting three to four years. He admitted to occasional sleepiness in the morning and infrequently had awakened with a sense of air hunger and gasping for breath. These events were more likely to occur when sleeping supine. Although urged to come to the sleep clinic for some time, he finally agreed after he was suddenly awakened in his tractor trailer as he veered onto the rumble strip heading toward the median on a very busy interstate highway. His work schedule consisted of arising at 8 pm and starting his run at 10 pm from Richmond, Virginia, to the Baltimore, Maryland, area where he unloaded his truck, ate breakfast, and slept in his truck cab for a few hours. He then drove back to Richmond. While at home he attempted to sleep in the afternoon and early evening hours during the work week. On weekends he reverted to his family's schedule of night sleep and awake in the daytime with his wife and children. He seldom felt refreshed on awakening and in most situations, if given an opportunity, could fall asleep. His children were amused by his loud snoring, and his wife sometimes slept in an adjacent bedroom, but could still hear his snoring through the walls. He rarely slept more than a few hours before arising with an urge to void. He seldom recalled any dreams.

At this point the clinician should consider the known sleep disorders and what other history would be helpful before advising this patient. This patient has the symptom of hypersomnolence. It is important to know how long this symptom has been present and what other factors might predispose to the condition. The clinician must learn to search for causes of hypersomnolence, just as one would for a patient with abdominal pain. Considerations would be medications, both prescribed and illicit, alcohol, narcolepsy, circadian rhythm disorders, insufficient sleep time, insomnia, and obstructive sleep apnea.

Examination: Wilbur saw his primary care physician, who found no obvious abnormalities on his physical exam other than obesity and blood pressure elevation of 150/90. His body mass index was elevated at 35. Laboratory profile included a normal CBC, urinalysis, thyroid hormones, and borderline elevation of fasting blood glucose. Lipid profile was abnormal with elevations of total cholesterol, LDL cholesterol, and triglycerides. His HDL cholesterol was 30. He was placed on a weight reduction diet and referred to the local sleep center. He was directed to decrease coffee intake and discontinue smoking to stay awake. He should avoid energy drinks and explore the possibility of a daytime job. He was referred to a sleep-trained physician.

A sleep-trained physician noted a neck circumference of 18 inches, waist size of 40 inches, a deviated nasal septum reducing air flow on one side, an elongated uvula, and thick soft palate. It was difficult to see the posterior pharyngeal wall because of the excessive soft tissue. He recorded in his notes a Mallampati IV score and scheduled an overnight sleep study or polysomnogram.

During the first 180 minutes of sleep, snoring and periods of interrupted shallow breathing followed by arousals occurred. The events lasted 10 seconds or longer. The apneas and hypopneas were accompanied by declines in oxygen saturation. Longer duration apneas caused greater declines in oxygen levels. A tachycardia-bradycardia pattern on EKG monitor accompanied the irregular breathing. The apnea/hypopnea index (AHI) was 33 abnormal breathing events per hour of sleep, and lowest oxygen saturation reached 64%. The apneas were of longer duration and caused lower desaturations in rapid eye movement (REM) sleep than non-REM sleep. On being awakened, his blood pressure was 162/92. He was fitted with a full facemask and placed on continuous positive airway pressure (CPAP). He returned to sleep for another 240 minutes, during which time his sleep was more continuous and oxygen saturations remained above 90% on CPAP of 12 cm H_2O pressure. The AHI declined to three events per hour of sleep. Other remarkable changes after CPAP application were the appearance of more delta or slow-wave sleep and REM sleep. His heart assumed a steady rate in the upper 60s. On a morning questionnaire he felt refreshed and had slept much better than usual. In addition, he recalled dreaming and had no episodes of nocturia. It is interesting to note that patients with severe obstructive sleep apnea may not recall dreaming, suggesting that the sleep apnea disrupts REM sleep by causing frequent interruptions and fragmentation of sleep.

IMPAIRMENT IN FUNCTIONING

One should become familiar with the functions measured by the polysomnogram and also understand the difference between sleep apnea and hypopnea as defined by the polysomnogram testing. The AHI is a measure of the number of abnormal breathing events per hour of sleep. It is abnormal for adults if greater than 5 per hour and considered severe if greater than 30 per hour. Apneas and hypopneas are most apt to occur during REM sleep because of the skeletal muscle hypotonia that occurs in that stage and be more apt to occur when sleeping supine because of the tendency for the mandible to open and rotate backward, causing the tongue to be closer to the soft palate, thus narrowing the airway. There are significant electrocardiogram changes that accompany severe sleep-disordered breathing. Central sleep apnea appears to have a different morphology, etiology, and effect on the patient than obstructive sleep apnea.

Excessive daytime sleepiness leads to reduced reaction time and is related to transportation accidents. Psychomotor vigilance tasks are useful for demonstrating the relationship of sleep deprivation to inattention, diminished reaction times, and unsafe operation of vehicles while traveling. Chronic sleepiness often has a negative effect on mood and predisposes to depression. Persons whose sleep has improved by treating sleep apnea have reported how uplifting it is to awaken refreshed in the morning and often consider correction of obstructive sleep apnea to be a life-changing event.

EPIDEMIOLOGY

Obstructive sleep apnea has an adult male prevalence in the United States in various studies of between 4% and 9%. There is a lower prevalence in females, but postmenopausal female incidence rises and approaches that of males.

DIFFERENTIAL DIAGNOSIS

Obstructive sleep apnea is a sleep-related breathing disorder caused by intermittent partial or complete upper airway obstruction at the oropharyngeal level. The number and duration of the events determines sleep apnea severity by causing fragmented sleep, hypoxemia, and excessive daytime sleepiness. Several factors contribute to snoring and sleep apnea. The main pathophysiology is due to narrowing of the pharyngeal airway during sleep, especially when sleeping supine. Negative intrathoracic pressure during inspiration favors collapse of the nonrigid pharyngeal tissues if the collapse is not opposed by the pharyngeal dilator muscles, which maintain an open airway. Contributing factors are increased neck circumference; enlarged tongue, uvula, soft palate, tonsil, and adenoid tissue; and rigid structures such as narrow nasal passages. Retroposition of the mandible is a factor. Because the tongue is attached to the mandible, it will be closer to the posterior pharyngeal wall if the mandible is in a retroposition. Craniofacial developmental anomalies such as Pierre Robin syndrome, Treacher Collins syndrome, Down's syndrome, and Prader-Willi syndrome predispose to obstructive sleep apnea early in life. When you consider that our physiological drive to breathe diminishes when asleep and depends more on the responses to $PaCO_2$ and PO_2, then the anatomic variations assume great importance in the development of sleep-related breathing disturbance. AHIs may vary from patient to patient and do not always correlate with the patient's symptoms of excessive daytime sleepiness. Obesity and adenotonsillar hypertrophy increase the risk of obstructive sleep apnea in children.

ETIOLOGY AND PATHOGENESIS

Obesity is the most importance risk factor for snoring and sleep apnea. Over half of the individuals who have obstructive sleep apnea are obese, and among obese patients obstructive sleep apnea is more likely to develop and therefore should be suspected. The relationship between obesity and sleep-related breathing should not lessen your suspicion of apnea in nonobese subjects if symptoms warrant an evaluation. Obesity in males tends to be distributed more in the neck, trunk, and visceral locations, and in females in the lower body and extremities. This disparate fat distribution helps explain a higher prevalence of obstructive apnea in males because of fatty accumulation in the neck adjacent to the pharynx. Wilbur is definitely obese with a BMI well over 30.

Circadian and homeostatic processes have strong influences on our sleep–wake patterns. Our internal clock, the suprachiasmatic nucleus in the hypothalamus, is responsive to light and dark stimuli carried from the retina to the brain. During the night, wakeful stimuli are suppressed, melatonin is released by the pineal gland, and sleep onset occurs. This is aided by the sleep debt, also called homeostatic drive, which has gradually increased during the waking period or daytime. As we sleep, the sleep debt diminishes, waking stimuli gain dominance, and we awaken. These two main factors are constantly waxing and waning; circadian and homeostatic, rising and falling. This is an oversimplification of a very complex biological interaction in the brain. Shift work sleep disorder, which Wilbur experiences, is an example of a circadian sleep rhythm disturbance.

NATURAL COURSE WITHOUT TREATMENT

Adverse cardiovascular effects of untreated moderate to severe obstructive sleep apnea have been well studied. Complications include hypertension, myocardial and cerebral ischemia, and cardiac arrhythmias, most notably premature ventricular contractions and atrial fibrillation. A bradycardia/tachycardia pattern frequently accompanies intermittent apneas and hypoxemia. Alterations in vagal and sympathetic tone account for the variable cardiac rates. Those patients with profound hypoxemia and elevated PCO_2 values if untreated may develop pulmonary hypertension. Often chronic obstructive pulmonary disease may coexist with obstructive sleep apnea, requiring physicians skilled in pulmonary and sleep medicine to manage the cases. Overstimulation of the sympathetic nervous system by hypoxemia follows apneas and contributes to adverse changes in the vascular endothelium, predisposing to occlusion.

Metabolic changes of obstructive sleep apnea, if untreated, may include insulin resistance, suppression of leptin satiety effects, and elevated levels of ghrelin, an appetite stimulant. These changes may contribute to weight gain and development of the metabolic syndrome. Hypoxemia from repeated apneas and hypopneas affects insulin and leptin levels in a detrimental manner.

EVIDENCE-BASED TREATMENT OPTIONS

Several treatment modalities have evolved to treat sleep-disordered breathing over the past several decades. Good sleep hygiene is the mainstay of treatment of all sleep disorders, including obstructive sleep apnea. Sleep hygiene and lifestyle changes include avoiding smoking, excess caffeine, and alcohol near bedtime. Regular lights out and wake-up schedules, as well as avoiding prolonged daytime naps, are included in the good sleep hygiene measures.

More specific treatment for sleep apnea is that of CPAP, nasal and oral surgeries, weight reduction, avoidance of supine position, and oral appliances, all of which have a positive effect on sleep-related breathing. Depending on the findings of the polysomnogram and physical characteristics of the patient, one or more of these strategies are selected. Positive airway pressure (PAP) is the most frequently used treatment and is considered most successful in relieving symptoms and reducing morbidity from obstructive sleep apnea. PAP acts by preventing narrowing of the upper airway and retarding the tendency for the airway to collapse due to contraction of the pharyngeal muscles as the patient breathes. It affects both the pharyngeal and hypopharyngeal portions of the airway. The pressure can be applied continuously, as in CPAP, or as bilevel with an inspiratory pressure and a lower expiratory pressure, making it more comfortable for some patients. The optimal levels are determined during an overnight titration study while the patient sleeps with the unit on and breathing is monitored.

CLINICAL COURSE WITH MANAGEMENT AND TREATMENT

Wilbur was very compliant using CPAP. Family and coworkers remarked he seemed more alert and less likely to doze during conversations. His Epworth Sleepiness Scale declined from 21 to 4, and family members noted he was less irritable. He no longer had to snack to stay awake on his truck route, and he began an exercise program. Both of these behavioral changes helped him lose weight. Sexual performance improved, and his wife returned to the bedroom. Elimination of obstructive sleep apnea is known to reduce output of atrial natriuretic peptide and often nocturia improves once the patient is on PAP.

On his next visit with the occupational medicine physician, Wilbur had to present a compliance report generated by his CPAP unit verifying his use of CPAP for at least 4 hours per 24 hours over 70% of the time. Unless this standard is met, he will not receive his commercial driver's license.

SYSTEMS-BASED PRACTICE ISSUES

It is a wonder that the discovery of such an important clinical syndrome did not occur much earlier than it did. Discovery had to await development of the EEG to define sleep stages and the polysomnogram to explain pathological breathing related to sleep and changes in respiration, oxygen saturation, heart rhythm variations, and sleep fragmentation. Only then was it possible to relate chronic daytime sleepiness to abnormalities in breathing during sleep. With advancements in technology, monitoring can now occur in the comfort of one's own home as opposed to a sleep lab and screening for sleep disordered breathing is more accessible to all health care providers.

REFERENCES AND RESOURCES

Czeisler C, et al. Modafinil for excessive sleepiness associated with shift work sleep disorder. *N Eng J Med* 2005;353:476–86.

Drake CL, et al. Shift work sleep disorders: prevalence and consequences beyond that of symptomatic day workers. *Sleep* 2004;27(8):1453–62.

Epstein LJ, Kristo D, Strollo PJ Jr., et al. Clinical guideline for the evaluation, management and long-term care of obstructive sleep apnea in adults. *J Clin Sleep Med* 2009; 5(3):263–76.

Marcus CL, Brooks LJ, Draper KA, et al. Diagnosis and management of childhood obstructive sleep apnea syndrome. *Pediatrics* 2012;130(3):576.

Owens L. The overlap syndrome: not to be missed. Morbidity and mortality of overlap syndrome are greater than that for OSA or COPD alone. *Adv Resp Care Sleep Med* 2011 May:8.

Smith B, Phillips BA. Truckers drive their own assessment for obstructive sleep apnea: a collaborative approach to online self-assessment for obstructive sleep apnea. *J Clin Sleep Med* 2011;7(3):241–45.

Tragar S, Reston J, Schoelles K, Phillips B. Continuous positive airway pressure reduces risk of motor vehicle crash among drivers with obstructive sleep apnea. *Sleep* 2010; 33:1373–80.

Witmans M, Young R. Update on pediatric sleep-disordered breathing. *Ped Clin N Am* 2011;58(3):571–89.

Yaggi HK, Concato J, Kernin WN, et al. Obstructive sleep apnea as risk factor for stroke and death. *N Eng J Med* 2005;353(19):2034–41.

Young T, Finn L, Peppard PE, et al. Sleep disordered breathing and mortality: eighteen-year follow-up of Wisconsin Sleep Cohort. *Sleep* 2008;31(8):1071–78.

Young T, Shahar E, Nieto FJ, et al. Predictors of sleep-disordered breathing in community-dwelling adults: the Sleep Heart Health Study. *Arch Int Med* 2002;162(8):893–900.

Chapter 27

Sudden Onset of Sleep

William S. Elias, M.D.

CLINICAL PRESENTATION

Chief complaint: "I'm going crazy."

History of present illness: John, a 17-year-old 11th-grade student, thought he was going crazy. Excessive daytime sleepiness worsened, making it difficult to stay awake in class, and his grades declined. His teachers interpreted his behavior as lack of interest, and his parents accused him of being lazy and suspected drug or alcohol usage. For over a year he tried to hide another peculiar symptom he experienced. Whenever angry, frightened, or especially laughing hard at jokes, his strength seemed to leave for a few minutes, long enough to cause him to slump into a chair or crumble to the floor. There he would lie for a few minutes, awake and breathing, but unable to arise until the weakness subsided and he felt normal again. There was no jerking or urinary incontinence. He learned to avoid situations such as joke telling that precipitated the embarrassing episodes. Two other behaviors appeared a few months later. At night as he was falling asleep or on awakening, brief bizarre dreams occurred. Another symptom presented on awakening in the morning and that was his inability to move for one or two minutes no matter how hard he tried. Having no idea what was wrong with John, his parents took him to the health care provider, where his physical examination and routine laboratory work were normal.

John was born after a full-term pregnancy and uncomplicated delivery, weighing seven pounds, two ounces at birth. His APGAR score was 9 and he had no unusual problems with breastfeeding. His growth and development proceeded well, and he reached his motor and mental milestones to the satisfaction of his parents and pediatrician. His only significant injury was at age 12 when he fractured his clavicle while playing football. He was sociable and interacted with friends and an older sister very well. His schoolwork was above average, and there were no unusual disciplinary problems. The primary care clinician referred him to a specialist.

Examination: The neurologist observed a well-appearing 17-year-old youth who cooperated in the exam and answered questions appropriately. His speech was fluent and gave no suggestion of impaired cognition. He had no difficulty with calculations or abstractions. Knowledge of current events was good. His mood and affect did not arouse any concerns by the clinician. Recent and remote memory were not impaired. Cranial nerve, motor, sensory, reflex and gait testing were normal. The neurologist's evaluation suggested that this was not a psychosomatic disorder, although his examination was completely normal. A sleep-deprived electroencephalogram (EEG) awake and asleep showed no abnormal cortical discharges to suggest epilepsy, and antiseizure medications were not advised. He did suggest the youth not drive or play sports until a sleep disorder was investigated.

IMPAIRMENT IN FUNCTIONING

John's symptoms differed from someone with a seizure disorder. There were no episodes of falling unconscious, jerking, stiffening, tongue biting, or urinary incontinence to suggest major motor seizures. Knowing the characteristics of a partial or generalized seizure assist with understanding the differences between seizures and cataplexy. John was concerned that his teachers and parents would think that the symptoms were self-imposed and under his control. The lack of parent and teacher support might further increase his level of anxiety and contribute to more decline in school performance.

DSM DIAGNOSIS

Because of hypersomnolence, John was referred to a sleep clinic for an overnight study, a polysomnogram, and daytime nap study, the multiple sleep latency test. The results of the polysomnogram were remarkable only for early appearance and increased amounts of rapid eye movement (REM) sleep. His total sleep time exceeded 7.5 hours, of which 20% was in delta or deep sleep and 32% in REM sleep. His first REM sleep episode in the overnight study occurred 18 minutes after sleep onset, which was much earlier than usual during polysomnograms in normal individuals. In spite of an adequate amount of nocturnal sleep that night, the following morning he fell asleep quickly on each of five scheduled daytime naps two hours apart. The mean sleep latency of the five daytime naps was two minutes. On four of the naps he entered REM sleep shortly after sleep onset. This combination of findings indicates excessive daytime sleepiness and inappropriate REM sleep appearing during his daytime naps. A diagnosis of narcolepsy with cataplexy, hypnagogic hallucinations, and sleep paralysis was made.

Blood studies can be helpful in evaluating patients suspected of narcolepsy. Histocompatibility leukocyte antigens (HLA), also called major histocompatibility complex are examples of such studies. Many autoimmune diseases are associated with HLA patterns. Because narcolepsy with cataplexy is strongly associated with

HLA DQB10602 positivity, one would assume a positive test is diagnostic, but 25% of whites and 38% of African Americans without narcolepsy are also positive, thereby confounding the meaning of a positive test. A negative HLA DQB10602 is useful information that the diagnosis is not narcolepsy with cataplexy.

The main symptom of narcolepsy is hypersomnolence due to excessive REM sleep. The two cardinal signs of narcolepsy are sleep-onset REM periods and cataplexy. The disturbance in sleep architecture appears as an intrusion of REM sleep into non-REM sleep and wakefulness. The orderly cycle of REM and non-REM sleep is disrupted, which explains the early onset of REM in daytime naps, accounting for dreaming and hallucinatory behavior. REM sleep normally accounts for 15–20% of total sleep time and first appears 60–90 minutes after falling asleep, lasting several minutes before giving way to non-REM sleep. This alternating pattern of REM and non-REM persists, resulting in three to four REM cycles per night with each successive period growing longer. During REM, several physiological events occur. The most well known are dreaming and rapid eye movements. Activation of descending pathways from the pontomedullary area hyperpolarizes anterior horn cells in the spinal cord during REM and results in skeletal muscle hypotonia. Fluctuations in blood pressure, pulse, respiration, and core body temperature make REM an unstable autonomic state. Because of skeletal muscle weakness in REM sleep, including jaw and tongue muscles, disordered breathing such as found in obstructive sleep apnea may worsen. In REM sleep only the diaphragm and extraocular muscles maintain full contractile ability. Cardiac and smooth muscle are unaffected by REM sleep.

Cataplexy is a symptom and sign that is unique to narcolepsy and presents in most, but not all cases. The frequency and severity of cataplexy may vary from one affected individual to another. Over half of narcoleptic patients have cataplexy. Of the patients with cataplexy, heavy laughter is most likely to precipitate an attack of weakness. Less commonly, anger or fright may do the same. Of the anatomic sites affected in a cataplectic attack, weakness of legs and knees is most common followed by jaw and face, then upper extremities. At times the patient may slump to the ground, but consciousness is never lost and attacks last only a few minutes and are followed by full recovery. Narcolepsy may exist in either sex with or without cataplexy.

EPIDEMIOLOGY

Studies of the epidemiology of narcolepsy are restricted to the presence of narcolepsy with cataplexy because studying narcolepsy alone would likely include persons who are hypersomnolent for other reasons. When narcolepsy with cataplexy is studied, several countries (including the United States) report a prevalence between 20 and 30 per 100,000 population. Outliers are Japan at 160 per 100,000 and Israeli Jews at fewer than 1 per 100,000 population. A summary of prevalence studies can be found in the fifth edition of *Principles and Practice of Sleep Medicine* (Kryger et al. 2011). There the authors cite various methods used for arriving at the values. From my readings and attendance at lectures over many years, I have used the value of 4 per 10,000 without gender differences.

ETIOLOGY AND PATHOGENESIS

In the realm of genetics and inheritance, there is a small increased risk of transmission of narcolepsy to offspring, both male and female. This is variously cited as anywhere from 2% to 6% or 7%. There is not a high concordance rate in identical twins, suggesting environmental influences may play a role in whether narcolepsy appears at its usual time of onset in postpubertal adolescents.

In patients with both manifestations, several important discoveries have emerged that have facilitated our understanding of the pathophysiology of narcolepsy and cataplexy. Animal models (i.e., canine narcolepsy) have been well studied in Doberman Pinschers, Labrador retrievers, and dachshunds. Next, identification of a neuropeptide hypocretin produced by cells in the human and animal hypothalamus is reduced in the spinal fluid of affected patients. Narcoleptic patients with cataplexy have the lowest levels of hypocretin in cerebrospinal fluid. Narcoleptic patients without cataplexy have hypocretin levels in similar ranges as non-narcoleptic patients. Pathological tissue examination reveals loss of cells in the hypothalamic region that produces this neuropeptide without any accompanying inflammation. Hypocretin has extensive connections in the cortical and subcortical regions and causes alerting effects in the brain and normal alteration of the non-REM/REM cycles. Hypocretin deficiency in the brain reduces dopamine activity and enhances cholinergic activity, which leads to increased amounts of REM sleep. This neurotransmitter is not available to be administered to patients at this time. Cerebrospinal fluid levels can be measured in research laboratories, but testing is not available except in a few centers.

NATURAL COURSE WITHOUT TREATMENT

The course of narcolepsy is unrelenting with possible exception of some mild reduction of symptoms in elderly patients. There is no evidence for permanent remission of the disease. There may be variations in how the condition presents, but the usual sequence is hypersomnolence after puberty followed by one or all of the following: cataplexy in two-thirds or more, sleep paralysis, and hypnogogic hallucinations less frequently. The sleep episodes are usually brief, an hour or less, and followed by a sense of feeling refreshed. When asked to rate themselves, narcoleptics will indicate being excessively sleepy. Paradoxically, their nighttime sleep may be fragmented by brief awakenings, and they cannot consolidate their sleep into nighttime hours. If not properly treated, narcoleptics may have many problems in society including marital and social relationships, employment, education, and motor vehicle driving. Recognition and treatment of a narcoleptic will result in a most grateful patient.

EVIDENCE-BASED TREATMENT OPTIONS

Knowledge of neurochemical transmitters and their actions during REM has led to the rationale of medications chosen for treatment. The balance between brainstem cholinergic output and adrenergic, serotonergic, and dopaminergic output favors cholinergic activity during REM and the others during wakefulness and non-REM sleep. Stimulant compounds such as methylphenidate, amphetamines, and modafinil act by increasing dopaminergic output and promoting wakefulness. Adrenergic and serotonergic compounds act to reduce REM and cataplexy. These latter functions explain the benefit provided by antidepressants, which primarily block the reuptake of adrenergic transmitters at the synapse. Clinically protriptyline, desipramine, and venlafaxine are used for narcolepsy patients with prominent cataplexy. The REM sleep suppressant effects of these medications are thought to be due to anticholinergic and adrenergic reuptake inhibition properties. Newer FDA-approved treatments for hypersomnolence are available and include modafinil and, since 2007, armodafinil. The latter is the R-enantiomer of the racemic drug modafinil. They are Class IV compounds and have less addicting tendencies than methylphenidate and amphetamines which are Class II. Class IV medications are easier to prescribe, can be written in larger quantities, and be refilled without another prescription each month. The methods of action are not fully understood but are assumed to be by enhancing dopamine at the synaptic level.

An interesting compound is sodium oxybate, also known as gamma-hydroxybutyrate, and on the street as a "date rape drug." This compound is now FDA approved for narcolepsy with cataplexy. The exact mechanism of the beneficial effect on cataplexy is not known and because of its powerful effect on inducing deep sleep shortly after administration, the drug is closely regulated to prevent harmful overdose. Sodium oxybate also improves daytime alertness by its action to consolidate sleep into nighttime rather than short brief naps throughout the day, which is characteristic of narcolepsy.

CLINICAL COURSE WITH MANAGEMENT AND TREATMENT

The clinician considers the dangers posed by John's symptoms and what problems lie ahead if the condition is not effectively treated. Should he be allowed to drive or play sports? Will college and future employment be compromised? Will the symptoms improve as he grows older? How likely are his offspring to inherit his condition? The patient and his family were counseled about his newly identified diagnosis and treatment choices. As with all sleep disorders, good sleep hygiene and regular follow-up visits were stressed. Information from the American Academy of Sleep Medicine was supplied to the patient and family, helping them understand the condition and its course. Risks and benefits of medications were discussed and modafinil 200 mg each morning for hypersomnolence and venlafaxine 25 mg at bedtime to control cataplexy were begun. Scheduled brief naps once or twice daily also serve to treat excessive daytime sleepiness and may lessen the amount of stimulant medication prescribed. Driving was suspended until his response to medication could be evaluated.

The Maintenance of Wakefulness Test (MWT) is often used in sleep clinics to make decisions about safe driving. The MWT assumes that a patient's ability to stay awake in the laboratory setting will also apply to situations in the real world. However, there is disagreement that one can always rely on that assumption. The test is conducted by requiring the subject to sit or lie down in a dark room without outside stimulation for 40 minutes. If the person does not fall asleep, a score of 40 is recorded. After a two-hour break the test is repeated. The mean of four test sequences is then obtained, and a score between 30 and 40 assumes the person can maintain wakefulness in soporific conditions. However, the results have not been standardized, and some clinicians and industries place more reliance on the test than others. This author uses it and finds it is helpful when combined with a good history. John scored an average of 12 when he was initially tested.

SYSTEMS-BASED PRACTICE ISSUES

After medications were introduced and found to be effective, John was allowed to participate in sports and encouraged to pursue education and other long-term goals. Considering the progress made in understanding narcolepsy with cataplexy, both the neurologist and sleep-trained physician could be optimistic about his future. However, at present no cure for narcolepsy is on the immediate horizon. Some theoretical therapies being considered are replacement of hypocretin by some accessible route, developing a hypocretin agonist, or immunotherapy. Until better therapies are developed, stimulants that enhance dopamine, norepinephrine, and serotonergic pathways will be used to enhance wakefulness in conjunction with anticataplectic medications when indicated. Patients successfully treated may live nearly normal and productive lives because narcolepsy is a lifelong condition and seldom remits completely, and is not associated with a reduction in life span.

ETHICAL CHALLENGES

Decision making related to when it is safe to drive is among the most important and at times the most difficult decision the health care provider has to make. In some cases, driving restriction is quite obvious and easily accepted by clinician and patient. However, when the patient insists on driving for economic or other reasons and the clinician is hesitant to agree, some other resource is needed. Historical evidence of accidents or stories of recent near misses due to sleepiness make the decision easier. Patient questionnaires of degrees of sleepiness such as the Stanford Sleepiness Scale or the Epworth Sleepiness Scale are helpful but can be misrepresented by the patient.

REFERENCES AND RESOURCES

Aran A, Einen M, Lin L, et al. Clinical and therapeutic aspects of childhood narcolepsy-cataplexy: a retrospective study of 51 children. *Sleep* 2010;33:1457–64.

Aurora RN, Lamm CL, Zak RS, et al. Practice parameters for the non-respiratory indications for polysomnography and multiple sleep latency testing for children. *Sleep* 2012;35(11).

Boutrel B, Koob GF. What keeps us awake: the neuropharmacology of stimulants and wakefulness promoting medications. *Sleep* 2004;27:1181–94.

Cao M. Advances in narcolepsy. *Med Clin N Am* 2010;94(3):541–55.

Czeisler CA. Impact of sleepiness and sleep deficiency on public health—utility of biomarkers. *J Clin Sleep Med* 2011;7(suppl. 2).

Hoddes, E., Zarcone, V., Smythe, H., Phillips, R., Dement, W.C. Quantification of Sleepiness: A New Approach. *Psychophysiology* Volume 10, Issue 4, pp. 431–36, July 1973.

Johns, M.W. A new method for measuring daytime sleepiness: The Epworth Sleepiness Scale. *Sleep* 1991;50–55.

Kryger MH, Roth T, Dement WC. (Eds.). *Principles and Practice of Sleep Medicine*. St. Louis: Elsevier Saunders, 2011.

Mignot E, Lammers GJ, Ripley B, et al. The role of cerebrospinal fluid hypocretin measurement in the diagnosis of narcolepsy and other hypersomnias. *Arch Neurol* 2002; 59:1553–62.

Roth T. Narcolepsy: treatment issues. *J Clin Psychiatry* 2007;68(suppl. 13):16–19.

CHAPTER 28

Panic in Childhood

Lisa Rochford, Ph.D.

CLINICAL PRESENTATION

Chief complaint: "Pure panic." Caroline's mother describes her daughter's demeanor and facial expression during the attacks that have become as frequent as several times per week during the more difficult months of the year. "Help me, it hurts," Caroline tells her parents in the midst of her episodes.

History of present illness: This five-year, one-month-old girl with comorbid asthma and colitis is experiencing frequent, severe, and often unpredictable panic reactions. Her "meltdowns" often arise in response to wearing what she perceives to be tight or constricting clothing or having her seat belt snugly around her waist, but other times she has attacks without perceivable trigger. The attacks usually begin with an uncomfortable physical sensation, then escalate rapidly to a high level of distress and the feeling that she is going to die, rapid heartbeat, hyperventilation, stomach pain, extreme skin irritation, and a sense of impending doom. She usually screams and cries during the attacks. Distress usually peaks within 10 minutes but may last for more than an hour. In response to her fears, she has developed rigid and sometimes obsessive behaviors, such as requiring several toys or comfort objects with her when the family leaves the home. She dislikes leaving home, and this has resulted in oppositional behavior at school or when getting ready to leave home. Because she experiences an extreme physical reaction to the feel of certain clothing, she may strip naked during episodes while traveling in the family's van to school or immediately upon arriving home from outings. She cannot tolerate underwear, sleeps naked, and has only worn an open type of slide-on shoe for a year and a half, as she cannot tolerate any closed shoes. She prefers to go barefoot. She wears only slick, loose-fitting athletic clothing that is several sizes too large.

Because of these symptoms, Caroline's developmental pediatrician referred her for psychotherapy with a child clinical psychologist, with the goals of improving emotion regulation and reducing sensory processing problems. This pediatrician first suspected Asperger's disorder due to Caroline's sensory processing differences and rigidity, but discarded this diagnosis due in part to the child's strong social skills, use of humor, shared enjoyment with others, and deep empathy and concern for others. In meeting with the child psychologist, the parents requested diagnostic clarification as well as psychotherapy. Their goals for her included to develop better coping skills, transition more easily from activities and between places, reduce distress with the morning routine, and better control of meltdowns, obsessive compulsive behaviors, anxiety, and "worrying about everything." As therapy progressed, they also sought help in managing problems at school, including attention deficit hyperactivity disorder (ADHD) behaviors and learning problems.

Caroline's problems with emotion regulation and sensory defensiveness became evident at age two and grew much worse by her third birthday, when a steroid treatment for asthma precipitated her screaming for "the entire weekend" and made her quite aggressive. This episode occurred in the midst of heightened family stress shortly after a move to a new community. However, it was not an isolated incident; Caroline continued to exhibit extreme difficulty managing her emotions to the point that the family is now experiencing severe distress. One recent, especially intense panic attack was triggered by having to wear a wool sweater at Christmas. This attack lasted an hour and a half, caused Caroline to believe she was dying, and included hyperventilation, stomach pain, uncontrollable crying, and screaming. Typically she experiences greater distress, panic attacks, heightened rigidity, and depressive thoughts in the spring and fall, and less in the summer and winter, when her abilities to cope are stronger. Changes in the weather often result in regressions. Her mother reported worsened sensory defensiveness and aggression any time that Caroline is sick and if she has to take asthma or allergy medication.

Psychiatric history: Caroline's parents took her to the referring pediatrician when she was four and a half years old. The pediatrician connected the family with occupational therapy services, which included the Wilbarger brushing protocol for sensory defensiveness. The protocol consisted of brushing every two hours, and as a result Caroline briefly began wearing underwear, tennis shoes, and a nightshirt to sleep. She could also ride in the family van with less distress. These positive results were short-lived, however, with a regression that occurred when Caroline entered her first preschool and sensory stimulation and anxiety increased. In other attempts to help her, her parents removed processed foods from her diet and are taking her to a chiropractor who provides nutritional supplements. They believe both the occupational therapy and nutritional changes have helped, but say that Caroline is still experiencing panic attacks and a high level of distress. They had one consultation with a different psychologist before locating their current one for therapy.

Other medical history: Caroline receives medical treatment for asthma and colitis. She takes albuterol, budesonide, and beclomethasone for her asthma, and probiotics, polyethylene glycol, acetaminophen, and ibuprofen as needed for her colitis. She sees her pediatrician regularly and is also followed by a pediatric gastroenterologist for the colitis. She had a head injury at age two, but x-rays were negative. She has experienced no other major injuries or surgeries and has never been unconscious. She sleeps approximately 11 hours per night. She is allergic to dust and cats.

Other history (family, developmental, educational, social, strengths): Caroline is the younger of two daughters of a fast food manager and a retail salesperson. Her sister is two years older. Each of her parents attended some college and enjoys good health. The family is of modest economic means. They live in a rural area that requires at least a 45-minute drive to go to a grocery store, which has been problematic for Caroline due to her dislike of using a seat belt. Extended family live nearby, but this has been problematic, as well, because of these family members' views that Caroline simply needs spankings and other punishments when having a panic attack or refusing to wear certain clothes or her seat belt. In family psychiatric history, Caroline's mother reported obsessive compulsive tendencies and said that her husband has ADHD and dyslexia. Aunts and uncles have histories of substance abuse and problems with anxiety, including panic attacks. Caroline has never been abused or neglected and never experienced any major traumas of which her mother is aware. Two family friends who were not very close to Caroline died in recent months.

Nuclear family dynamics include that Caroline enjoys a close relationship with each of her parents. Attachment appears secure with both parents. Her mother assumes more of the disciplinarian role, and her father plays with her more. Parents expect good behavior and sometimes use behavior charts and incentives at times when the girls are not behaving as well. The parents expect both girls to perform chores and speak respectfully to adults. If Caroline misbehaves, she has extra chores and loses privileges she enjoys, such as attending fun outings and staying up late on the weekends. Her parents have attempted to curb her negative reactions to sensory stimuli and reduce her taking off her clothes by using negative consequences, but they find that Caroline is unable to change her behavior even with such punishments and that she feels quite guilty about her behavior after she has calmed down. When she has an attack, both parents attempt to distract her to other thoughts and activities, help her express what she is feeling, and help her find ways to calm down. They attempt to be proactive in situations that cause her distress, such as allowing her to play a video game in the van to take her mind off of her physical reactions. Because of the high level of emotion that Caroline expresses, they try to give her a great deal of "down time" to regroup after stressful experiences and allow her to avoid the sensory experiences that are the most problematic for her. To this end, they are allowing her to wear the clothes that are more comfortable to her and do not require her to wear the seat belt as it is meant to be worn. Due to her father's work schedule, her mother brings her to therapy most of the time, but her father sometimes comes as well or brings her if her mother cannot. Caroline and her sister have a normal amount of conflict but get along well overall. The sister, who tends to be quiet and calm, always accompanies Caroline and her mother to the sessions, waiting patiently in the waiting room. The sisters are never observed to fight while waiting.

Caroline was born without complications except that her mother experienced some contractions during the last three months of pregnancy. She was born at eight pounds, nine ounces when her mother was 23 years old. She walked and talked within normal limits but was not fully toilet trained until age four. After leaving the first preschool, where she began having much higher anxiety, Caroline is attending her second preschool, which she likes and where she has friends. She plays well with others but tends to wait until they approach her.

Caroline's strengths include a vivacious personality, delight in interacting with others, a kind spirit and sensitivity to others' needs, a strong desire to serve others in keeping with the family's highly religious background, a well-honed sense of fun and humor, and a close nuclear family that includes a sister who is invested in helping her. Multiple family friends are involved in her life, including a surrogate aunt who accompanies the family to some of the therapy appointments. She and her father enjoy a great deal of shared interests, including basketball and hiking. She enjoys playing tag with other children at church. Later in the course of her therapy, she joined local soccer and basketball teams, and symptoms improved with this participation. Her parents offer nurturing yet firm parenting and have read a good bit about child behavior management, sensory issues, anxiety, and ADHD. Caroline is aware that she is experiencing a greater challenge than many other children in dealing with her sensory defensiveness. She wants help and believes that she can feel better with assistance. She is involved in many church activities and draws on prayer and her faith as resources to make improvement. Of seemingly average intelligence, she is eager to learn at school, desires to please authority figures, and feels guilty for any bouts of misbehavior. She is anxious about certain experiences, including what her therapist will ask her to do, but is willing to make the effort asked of her to overcome her fears.

Mental status exam: Caroline presents as a Caucasian child of average height and weight for her age. She wears slick sports clothing with very few seams and slips off her slide-on shoes immediately on entering the psychologist's office. She keeps her arms crossed at her chest, which her mother says is to avoid accidentally touching anything in her surroundings. This is in keeping with the mother's report that Caroline recently began pulling her arms inside her dress or shirt at church as a self-soothing technique. She sits close to her mother on a couch, leaning in to her with her head on her mother's shoulder. She makes appropriate eye contact with the psychologist and warms easily to her. Caroline enjoys showing the psychologist items she brought from home and telling her about her experiences. Gestures are well coordinated with speech, which is fluent although overly loud at times in subsequent therapy sessions. Caroline is oriented to person, place, time, and situation. Short- and long-term memory appear intact. In later sessions, attention span varies depending on the type of sensory experience offered, with sand play holding her attention the longest. Also in later sessions, she sometimes behaves in an agitated way, such as dumping toys rather than playing with them or throwing an object in the examiner's face in response to a question about an experience that distressed her. She is more calm when she has spent the earlier part of the day at home than if she has been to school. She is sometimes observed to crack her knuckles.

Several different types of sensory experiences are offered as a way to begin determining what causes agitation for Caroline and what helps her become more relaxed. She enjoys a somewhat sticky squeeze ball with multiple arms, small rocks, water play, and sand play. She enjoys manipulating shaving cream and can tolerate tighter clothing for longer periods when engaged in this activity. In contrast, Caroline does not like the feeling of weighted objects such as bean-bag stuffed animals on her shoulders, being wrapped tightly in a blanket, and being flattened in pillows, all of which can be soothing to some children. Thus it is discovered that more constraining stimuli are bothersome to her, in keeping with her avoidance of tight clothing and her seat belt. However, she seeks the sensation of hard impacts, such as ramming into furniture, wrestling, and jumping off of objects. She prefers deep pressure touch over light touch and likes the joint compressions that are part of the Wilbarger brushing protocol in occupational therapy.

Caroline places her recent overall mood at approximately 4 out of 10, with 10 being the best mood possible, due to her recent distress regarding her panic attacks and sensory sensitivities. She denies suicidal or aggressive intent or thoughts, although her mother said that she has made two comments when quite upset that she wished she were dead. During the session she shows a range of appropriate affect congruent with the topic of discussion. Caroline has difficulty identifying any strengths or good qualities in herself, denoting a poor self-esteem.

She demonstrates the tendency to agree with adults if she thinks that is what they want her to do. Verbally expressed thoughts are linear with no unusual word usage noted, although she demonstrates a preference for "potty humor." Play sometimes appears disorganized, as she enjoys dumping toys. When she uses human figures with the sandbox provided in therapy, she will place them all into the sand without using them to interact with one another, sometimes burying them head-first because she finds this funny. No delusional thoughts are noted. Intelligence appears average, and fund of knowledge is developmentally appropriate. She expresses a wide range of interests. Sometimes she expresses what appears to be well-developed insight into her difficulties, describing how different stimuli and experiences make her feel, but this may be because of the excellent tracking and verbalization of feeling states that her mother has provided. More common to her age, she occasionally demonstrates free-floating anxiety and cannot identify a cause for the fear. No unusual perceptual experiences are noted beyond the heightened sensitivity to sensory input, such as the fabrics of certain clothing causing her to feel pain and the other physical symptoms of her panic attacks.

IMPAIRMENT IN FUNCTIONING

Caroline is apprehensive of future panic attacks and in addition to avoiding certain types of clothing and her seat belt, she has also begun avoiding going places where she might become uncomfortable or be made to do things that could disturb her. She prefers to remain at home, where she can control her environment, spending long hours playing outside, usually playing alone. She has begun to express that she feels different from other children and is showing signs of low self-esteem including some suicidal comments, such as "I wish I was dead." After she began preschool, which required a uniform that was difficult for her as well as a difficult 45-minute drive each way, her sensory defensive symptoms and emotional lability became extreme and she became highly disobedient with her teachers as well as parents. For these reasons, her parents withdrew her from this school and placed her in a new preschool closer to their home a week before they entered psychotherapy. Grooming activities including hair and teeth brushing cause her distress and lengthen the time needed to get ready in the morning. She often makes the family wait while she gathers items for distraction and self-soothing in the van. Her parents have tried to curb Caroline's negative emotional reactions by offering rewards and using spankings. Due to the difficulty of managing her behaviors, they stopped taking her to restaurants or other nonessential places. They are quite concerned about her safety given her severe reactions to wearing a seat belt properly. They have had conflict with extended family members over how to manage these problems.

Caroline's most impairing symptoms at present include extreme tactile defensiveness with anything that feels constraining to her, as described. She struggles also with unpredictable movement of long duration, such as riding in the family's van. When riding in the van, she wears her seat belt wrapped around the headrest and then looped loosely around her shoulders, and she has to have her seat in the family van set back and reclined as far as possible. Caroline struggles with managing sounds, smells, and many foods, as well. She becomes easily overstimulated in classroom environments and is a picky eater. She worries a great deal and fears car wrecks, her own death, and that her mother could be harmed. She demonstrates obsessive compulsive behavior that includes sorting and organizing materials, storing items such as the sticks she plays with outside, and panicking if she does not have certain toys with her when traveling in the van. Her mother described her as a sensitive child whose feelings are hurt easily. It takes her approximately an hour to get to sleep and she often feels "wound up" at bedtime. Caroline also has difficulty managing multistep tasks and has struggled with attention and learning at school.

DSM DIAGNOSIS

Clinical interviews and behavioral observations supported the psychologist's finding that Caroline is suffering from symptoms of multiple anxiety disorders, with the most pronounced being those of Panic Disorder (PD.) The hallmark symptoms Caroline is experiencing are the unpredictability of attacks of overwhelming panic, her range of distressing physical symptoms, and her dislike of leaving home. Although PD is typically not seen in children, Caroline is demonstrating a textbook case at a quite young age. A close examination of her symptomatology invites the question of whether PD is being underdiagnosed among the pediatric population, as many parents and teachers assume that children with similar behaviors are having temper tantrums and not thinking of the episodes as full-blown panic attacks. In addition to the matching symptom presentation that this case brings, several biological and familial markers give the diagnosis additional credence. PD is more common for individuals with asthma, which Caroline has, and more common for those with a family history of PD, which is also true in this case. A delineation of panic attacks and PD as described in the DSM is helpful here, to show how Caroline's symptoms fit.

Panic attacks constitute discrete periods of intense fear or discomfort, accompanied by heart racing or pounding, shortness of breath, choking, chest pain, dizziness, hot flashes, sweating, tremors, nausea, or other uncomfortable sensations or perceptions (like derealization or depersonalization). There may also be the fear of dying, losing control, or having another attack. The symptoms develop abruptly and reach a peak within minutes. Caroline's parents reported that she experiences heart palpitations, trembling, shortness of breath, and stomach pain. They said that she may appear dissociated or seem disconnected, which fits with the symptom of feeling de-tached from oneself. DSM criteria for PD include recurrent, unexpected panic attacks and at least one of the attacks being followed by a month or more of one or more of the following: persistent concern about having additional attacks; worry about the implications of the attack or its consequences (e.g., losing control, having a heart attack, "going crazy"); and a significant maladaptive change in behavior related to the attacks. Caroline worries that she is going crazy and her behavior has dramatically changed due to the panic attacks, inasmuch as she wants to avoid any provocation of another attack and thus limits (as much as she can) her participation in excursions from home and similar circumstances in which she has experienced panic in the past. She wants to avoid any clothing that she finds painful and constricting, and she wants to avoid any re-creation of circumstances in which she felt panic while riding in the family van, which includes, again, feeling constricted, such as with a seat belt securely around her waist and the seat set upright and pulled close to the seat in front of her. These avoidance behaviors are suggestive of a persistent concern about having additional attacks. Children as young as Caroline may not be able to express their fears verbally, but their avoidance behavior can demonstrate that anxiety.

As part of her PD, Caroline also exhibits elements of agoraphobia with heightened anxiety regarding being in places or situations from which escape might be difficult and in which help may not be available in the event of having unexpected or situationally predisposed panic symptoms and attacks. This was evident when she had a great deal of difficulty remaining at her first preschool. Agoraphobic fears typically involve characteristic clusters of situations that include being outside the home alone, being in a crowd or standing in a line, being on a bridge, and traveling in a bus, train, or automobile. Caroline's agoraphobia is mediated by the nearly constant presence of parental figures. However, as with most agoraphobics, she tries to avoid travel and when she does have to go somewhere, she often suffers marked distress and anxiety about having panic-like symptoms.

It is important to examine the symptoms of physical conditions and other psychiatric disorders, as well, considering them for the differential as well as comorbid diagnoses. Although Caroline is prone to constricted breathing and hyperventilation due to her asthma and abdominal distress due to her colitis, it is important to determine if the panic attacks she experiences include other physical symptoms and whether they occur outside of flare-ups of these conditions. For Caroline, this is the case.

It is important to rule out separation anxiety for children who display panic attacks. Separation anxiety did not seem to fit for Caroline, as her fears have more to do with various sensations she may experience than with separation from her attachment figures.

The case could be made that Caroline has multiple specific phobias of distressing sensory experiences, but the triggers of her panic are often unidentifiable and thus extend beyond simple phobic reactions. She does not appear to have social phobia, as she enjoys meeting new people, likes to be the center of attention, and is outgoing and extroverted.

Caroline demonstrates some seemingly obsessive compulsive behaviors, such as wanting to store up items like the sticks she plays with outside or adamantly requiring toys with her in the van. However, being "stuck" on certain thoughts or other signs of obsessive thinking are not present. The rigidity and seemingly compulsive behaviors in which she engages do not appear to be of the magnitude usually associated with OCD, but look more like transient stress reactions associated more with helping herself cope with the difficulty of going on outings away from home.

Post-traumatic stress disorder (PTSD) often co-occurs with PD. It is possible that a traumatic experience in the family van is related to Caroline's aversion to riding and being constrained by a seat belt in it. It actually became evident near the end of Caroline's therapy, when she was eight years old, that she may have endured such an experience. In the process of undergoing a few minutes of eye movement desensitization and reprocessing (EMDR), a cognitive behavioral–based therapy that encourages free association from one's feelings and thoughts of fear to other visual images, physical sensations, thoughts, and emotions, Caroline was reminded of an incident when she was three years old when the family went through an automatic car wash. Having never experienced a car wash before, she recalled that she thought that they had hit some water, such as falling in a river, and were being immersed. She thought the family was drowning, while she was tightly secured in her car seat. Her mother remembered this incident and confirmed that young Caroline had a terrified look on her face during it. This traumatic experience may help explain how confining clothing, a tight seat belt, and riding in the van create distress for Caroline. At such a young age, she could not verbalize how the experience affected her, yet vestiges of the experience appear to have remained. It was not until much later that she was able to verbalize it. The diagnosis of PTSD was not given partly because it was not clear if that experience was the main reason for her symptoms, which were much more pervasive than disrupting her ability to ride in the van. PD better captures the episodic, non–van-related panic attacks she has.

Generalized anxiety disorder (GAD) is the final anxiety disorder to investigate. Caroline's parents indicate that she has many worries: her own and others' safety, the possibility that she might do something wrong, and worries that she may encounter sensations that cause her distress. She also demonstrates problems sleeping, hypervigilance, restlessness, and physical tension, all symptoms of GAD. It appears, then, that GAD should be diagnosed as a secondary anxiety disorder. PD remains the primary one, as it is the most informative for those capturing her symptoms and most helpful in directing appropriate treatment. In addition, PD is needed in addition to GAD because of the noticeably episodic attacks of severe anxiety and physical symptoms.

Although it is a condition that does not appear in the DSM, Caroline exhibits what occupational therapists call sensory processing disorder (SPD), also known as sensory integration disorder. The disorder is conceptualized as a neurological disturbance in processing and integrating information from the five senses (vision, auditory, touch, olfaction, and taste) as well as sense of movement (vestibular system) and/or positional sense (proprioception). With normal sensory processing, individuals take in sensory information, derive coherent meaning, and are able to respond appropriately based on the given situational demands. With SPD, sensory information is perceived abnormally, causing confusion, distress, and often aberrant reactions. With SPD, sensations such as the noise of an air conditioner or fluorescent light, seams or tags in clothing, or textures of certain foods can be quite bothersome even though most people would not give them a second thought. Withdrawal and/or oppositional behavior are common reactions. Children with SPD may have problems with control of posture or quality of movements seen in low muscle tone or joint instability. They may have poor functional use of vision and problems with planning, sequencing, and executing unfamiliar actions, resulting in awkward and poorly coordinated motor skills.

Children may have only SPD or they may have another condition that includes sensory problems. Those with autism spectrum disorder, dyslexia, developmental dyspraxia, Tourette's syndrome, multiple sclerosis, and speech delays may have sensory issues. The condition is most often identified by an occupational therapist but is increasingly being diagnosed by developmental pediatricians, pediatric neurologists, and child psychologists. Although SPD was not accepted into the DSM-5 and is not listed in the ICD-9, sensory symptoms do appear in both manuals. They compose one of the four repetitive and restrictive behaviors listed for autism in DSM-5. In the ICD-9, several diagnoses are used to capture impairment from sensory processing problems: Unspecified Neurological Disorder, Sensory Disturbance of the Skin, Sensory Disturbance of Smell or Taste, Coordination Disorder for dyspraxia or bilateral integration disorder, and Subjective Visual Disturbance for visual perceptual dysfunction. In the *Diagnostic Classification of Mental Health and Developmental Disorders of Infancy and Early Childhood—Revised*

Edition (DC:0-3R), promoted by the late Stanley Greenspan and the Zero to Three organization, SPD is called Regulatory Disorder of Sensory Processing and it includes three types: (1) hypersensitive, which has two subcategories: fearful/cautious and negative/defiant, (2) hyposensitive/underresponsive, and (3) sensory stimulation–seeking/impulsive. For all types of this disorder, parents report a high level of impairment from sensory symptoms including that their children get upset easily, often lose their temper, have difficulty adapting to change, are overly sensitive, and/or have a difficult temperament. Other researchers have divided SPD into the following types: (1) sensory modulation disorder, which involves over- or underresponding to sensory stimuli or seeking sensory stimulation. Symptoms may include fearful, anxious, negative, and/or stubborn behaviors, self-absorbed behaviors, or inordinate seeking of sensation. (2) Sensory-based motor disorder, which results in disorganized motor output as a result of incorrect processing of sensory information. (3) Sensory discrimination disorder, which involves problems with sensory discrimination or incorrect processing of sensory information, such as visual or auditory input. Inattentiveness, disorganization, and poor school performance may result.

Caroline exhibits aspects of sensory defensiveness with a range of tactile, smell, taste, and vestibular input. She also exhibits some sensory seeking with her craving of proprioceptive input, including her love to crash or bump into things, frequent cracking of her knuckles, craving physical activities and enjoyment of contact sports, and high levels of energy and arousal. If she were diagnosed under the DC:0-3R, her symptoms would most closely fit the hypersensitive and sensory stimulation–seeking/impulsive types of regulatory disorder. She has exhibited both the fearful/cautious and negative/defiant reactions for hypersensitivity. She exhibits signs of both a sensory modulation disorder and a sensory discrimination disorder.

Caroline's primary diagnosis of PD calls for a more complete discussion of this disorder, especially as it manifests in childhood. PD is characterized by the repeated occurrence of discrete panic attacks. Between attacks, patients are often well, although after repeated attacks most develop some persistent apprehension, or anticipatory anxiety regarding the possibility of another attack. About half of these patients eventually develop agoraphobia. Children and adolescents with PD have unexpected and repeated periods of intense fear or discomfort along with other symptoms such as a racing heartbeat or feeling short of breath. Their panic attacks usually last only 5 to 15 minutes but can last for more than an hour. Panic attacks frequently develop without warning, usually coming on acutely, often within a minute, with rapid crescendo. After the attack most patients feel "shaken" and may feel drained and apprehensive for sometimes hours. The physical and cognitive symptoms of panic attacks may appear in any combination. A person rarely experiences all of the panic attack symptoms listed in the DSM during any one episode. The anxiety may take any of several forms. Some patients experience the classic "sense of impending doom" as if something terrible were about to happen. Some fear they are having a heart attack or a stroke, and this may occasion multiple visits to the emergency room. Some fear they will "go crazy."

PD in children can be difficult to diagnose. This can lead to many visits to physicians and multiple medical tests that are expensive and potentially painful. Children and adolescents with symptoms of panic attacks should first be evaluated by their family physician or pediatrician. A number of physical conditions produce symptoms that can closely resemble panic attacks, such as heart conditions, hypoglycemia, hyperthyroidism, pheochromocytoma, and simple partial seizures. If no other physical illness or condition is found as a cause for the symptoms, a comprehensive evaluation by a child and adolescent psychiatrist or psychologist should be obtained.

EPIDEMIOLOGY

Panic disorder has a lifetime prevalence of 1–2%. It is several times more common in females than males. The first panic attack generally occurs in late adolescence or the early twenties. However, later onsets up to the thirties are not uncommon. Rarely onset may occur in childhood or over the age of 40. Receiving a diagnosis of PD at age five, as Caroline did, is thus unusual, although she fits the epidemiological profile in terms of female gender.

Those who work with young children and especially children on the autism spectrum should be knowledgeable about sensory processing problems, as they are quite common for these populations and can result in extreme behavior problems that can be moderated with identification and proper interventions. Researchers estimate that between 5% and 13% of children entering school have significant sensory processing problems, with boys exhibiting greater impairment.

DIFFERENTIAL DIAGNOSIS

A few psychological measures were administered to gather data for diagnostic clarification. These tests were given over the course of the therapeutic process, as greater information about functioning became available and thus the need for more testing became evident. At intake, the Developmental Profile 3 (DP-3), the Achenbach Child Behavior Checklist (CBCL), and Miller's Sensory Over-Responsivity Scale Inventory (SORS) were provided. The DP-3 is completed by either a parent or a teacher and measures development in physical skills, adaptive behavior such as self-care, social-emotional development, cognitive ability, and communication skills. It was important to provide such a developmental screening due to the referring physician's initial concerns about a pervasive developmental disorder. The CBCL allows for a screening of a number of emotional and behavioral difficulties, including anxiety, thought problems, aggression, and ADHD. It offers different forms by age and informant, with versions for preschoolers and school-age children and adolescents, and versions for parents/caregivers, teachers, or oneself for children ages 11–18. This standardized screening of multiple disorders is helpful at the beginning of therapy as well as at the end to identify treatment effectiveness. The SORS offers an extensive list of sensory experiences including brushing hair and teeth, to allow for a parent, other observer, or the patient to pinpoint what is most distressing. This was important for Caroline due to the severe distress she was experiencing with various sensory experiences. More general sensory processing rating scales available online include the Sensory Processing Measure by Parham et al. and the Short Sensory Profile by Dunn.

Later in therapy, when Caroline was six years old and just told she would need to repeat kindergarten, additional psychological testing was provided to address the possibility of learning disorder and ADHD. Tests administered at that time were the Wechsler Preschool and Primary Test of Intelligence 4th ed. (WPPSI-IV), the Wechsler Individual Achievement Test 3rd ed. (WIAT-III), the Conners' Continuous Performance Test 2nd ed. (CPT), and the CBCL, this time with both parent and teacher input. The WPPSI-IV is administered to children ages two years, six months to seven years, seven months. The WIAT-III is used to test academic achievement in the broad areas of reading, math, writing, and oral language. The Conners' CPT is a 14-minute test of attention and impulsivity for the assessment of ADHD or neurological disorder that patients ages six and older complete on the computer. All measures except the SORS are well validated, widely used measures providing standardized scores based on comparisons of same-age children. The CBCL also accounts for child gender.

On the DP-3, Caroline's mother noted slight developmental delay with below average scores in social-emotional development and communication. Other developmental competencies were average. On the CBCL, she noted clinically significant emotional and behavioral difficulties including a high level of somatic complaints, withdrawal, affective problems, emotional reactivity, and pervasive developmental problems (due in part to the strange behavior she often exhibited and being disturbed by change, withdrawal, and distress from things being out of place that she sometimes experienced). The SORS showed that Caroline experiences stress from the following: the tactile experiences of elastic in clothing, hair brushing or combing, and getting dressed; the smells of perfume, cleaners, and strong-smelling food; the tastes of spicy foods, eating bread crust, and new/unfamiliar foods; sounds of alarms and someone talking when the child is trying to concentrate, the toilet flushing, appliances/small motor noises; and movement experiences of walking or climbing up open stairs, experiencing heights, and going on amusement park rides.

Results at age six indicated above average verbal intellectual ability but below average nonverbal intellectual ability, which was suggestive of a learning disorder. Her academic achievement in both reading and math were significantly lower than her verbal IQ, which suggested learning difficulty in these specific areas. Results of the CPT and the ADHD subscales of the CBCLs of both her mother and her kindergarten teacher showed clinically significant ADHD symptoms, as well, with both inattention and hyperactivity-impulsivity. Caroline's parents' CBCL indicated clinically elevated conduct problems, anxiety, depression, and thought problems (the latter due to storing too many things, sleep problems, and strange behavior and ideas).

As was explored for Caroline, panic attacks may be seen in separation anxiety, specific phobia, social phobia, obsessive compulsive disorder, and PTSD. In these disorders, however, the panic attacks always have a precipitating stressor that is the focus of the other anxiety disorder. For example, panic attacks can occur for the person with a snake phobia who has to approach a snake, for the social phobic who is asked to give a speech, for the PTSD patient who enters a situation reminiscent of the original trauma, or for the obsessive compulsive patient encountering a contaminated object. If, however, these patients have no panic attacks outside of their feared situation, a separate diagnosis of PD is not made. For PD, attacks do not follow such a logical and predictable pattern, but occur unexpectedly. Panic attacks are also seen with some frequency in patients suffering from a depressive episode either as part of major depression or bipolar disorder. In some cases the panic attacks may actually predate the onset of the depressive symptoms. In such cases, a separate PD is occurring in addition to the depressive disorder, and consequently, two diagnoses are given. If they only occur during severe depression, however, a depression diagnosis may be more appropriate.

As treatment progresses, it also becomes evident that Caroline has ADHD combined type (both hyperactive-impulsive and inattentive behaviors), as well as specific learning disorders in reading and math. Some of her ADHD symptoms are likely due to her avoidance behaviors arising from her anxiety and sensory problems, but the data from psychological measures and her family history offer strong support for adding this diagnosis, as well. As described, health concerns contributing to her symptoms are asthma and colitis. Thus, the revised diagnostic impressions include:

- Panic disorder with agoraphobia.
- Generalized anxiety disorder.
- Sensory processing disorder.
- ADHD combined type.
- Specific learning disorders in reading and math.
- Asthma.
- Colitis.

ETIOLOGY AND PATHOGENESIS

There is no single cause for PD. Biological, genetic, neurochemical, cognitive, and behavioral causes all contribute to its etiology. Higher rates of PD are seen with asthma and other respiratory conditions, hypoglycemia, hyperthyroidism, mitral valve prolapse, labyrinthitis, and pheochromocytoma. Of the anxiety disorders, PD has been the most extensively studied from a genetic standpoint. Results of family studies have consistently demonstrated that it runs in families, and twin studies indicate that genes contribute to this familiality. Various neurotransmitters have been investigated in PD research. The serotoninergic system is implicated not only by the undoubted efficacy of serotoninergic antidepressants in PD treatment but also by studies involving manipulation of brain serotonin levels.

For example, depletion of tryptophan, the dietary precursor of serotonin, increases the effectiveness of a panicogen (something that induces panic) such as flumazenil, whereas the administration of 5-hydroxytryptophan, which increases serotonin levels, will blunt the effectiveness of CO_2 inhalation as a panicogen. The GABAergic system is strongly implicated by the effectiveness of flumazenil as a panicogen and by the effectiveness of benzodiazepines in the treatment of PD. Some functional MRI studies suggest that the hippocampus and parahippocampal gyrus are abnormally activated in PD. It appears plausible to say that PD represents an inherited disturbance in the overall function of noradrenergic, serotoninergic, or GABAergic systems in one or more central nervous system structures responsible for anxiety. Candidate structures include the locus coeruleus, dorsal raphe nucleus, parahippocampus, hippocampus, and amygdala. Stimulation of limbic structures is well known to produce fear and anxiety. PD research has revealed certain important panicogens, which are substances innocuous to normal controls but which reliably produce panic attacks in patients with PD. The induced panic attacks are essentially identical to the naturally occurring ones and may be prevented by the same medications that are effective in preventing the naturally occurring attacks. Substances shown to be panicogenic include sodium lactate, inhalation of 5% or 35% carbon dioxide, cholecystokinin tetrapeptide, caffeine, yohimbine, isoproterenol, and the benzodiazepine antagonist flumazenil. Stressful life events including major transitions, stressful environment, and thinking in a way that exaggerates relatively normal bodily reactions have all been shown to contribute to the onset of PD. Often the first attacks are triggered by physical illnesses, major stress, or certain medications. PTSD patients show a much higher rate of PD than does the general population.

Caroline was biologically at risk for PD due to having asthma. Although sensory processing problems have not yet been studied in conjunction with PD, her tactile defensiveness also appeared to generate physically distressing symptoms that contributed to her panic. Second, she was genetically at risk for anxiety disorders in general and PD in particular, as her mother reported OCD tendencies and aunts and uncles had histories of anxiety, including panic attacks. Third, the family was no doubt stressed because they had just moved. Fourth, Caroline had experienced a crisis with her asthma at about the same time that necessitated steroid treatment, which precipitated a particularly difficult weekend of her being agitated and screaming. Finally, also at about the same time, near her third birthday, Caroline is believed to have experienced a traumatic event in the family's vehicle as it went through a car wash. Not understanding at her young age what was happening, and so fearing that she and the rest of her family were drowning, Caroline was terrified. This traumatic event could have precipitated her PD, because it was at about this time that she began to have the extreme "meltdowns" that the family now understands to be panic attacks. Thus, it appears that the combination of biologic and genetic risks, stress with transition to a new home, a period of physical illness, and a likely traumatic experience all contributed to the onset of Caroline's panic attacks, in keeping with research findings on the disorder's etiology.

NATURAL COURSE WITHOUT TREATMENT

With treatment, panic attacks can usually be stopped and complications such as agoraphobia, depression, and substance abuse can be avoided. If not recognized and treated, however, PD and its complications can be devastating. Panic attacks can interfere with a child's or adolescent's relationships, schoolwork, and normal development. Children and adolescents with PD may begin to feel anxious most of the time, even when they are not having panic attacks. Some begin to avoid situations where they fear a panic attack may occur or situations where help may not be available. For example, a child may be reluctant to go to school or be separated from his or her parents, and in severe cases, the child or adolescent may be afraid to leave home. Some children and adolescents with PD can develop severe depression and may be at risk of suicidal behavior. As an attempt to decrease anxiety, some adolescents with PD will turn to alcohol or drugs.

EVIDENCE-BASED TREATMENT

The goal of treatment in PD is to prevent future attacks and relieve anticipatory anxiety so that patients are enabled to overcome any avoidance behavior they may have developed. Cognitive behavioral treatment and medication have roles. When initiating pharmacologic treatment, one must impress on the patient's family the fact that medication cannot abort an attack once it has begun and so the thrust of medication is to prevent future attacks. The two groups of medications that provide effective prophylaxis are certain benzodiazepines and most of the currently available antidepressants. Benzodiazepines are effective for short-term stabilization and long-term management of panic symptoms, but do not appear as effective as cognitive behavioral therapy (CBT) and antidepressants. Benzodiazepines are used in adult populations much more frequently than in children and adolescents, perhaps due to the dearth of well-controlled clinical studies and the issue of dependence associated with long-term use. However, over a 10-year span there has been nearly a three-fold increase in the use patterns for these agents in the child population. Buspirone prescribed for generalized anxiety is not effective for panic anxiety. Four frequently used benzodiazepines shown to be are clearly effective are alprazolam, clonazepam, lorazepam, and diazepam. The benzodiazepines offer certain advantages. They have a rapid onset of action, generally few side effects, and often serve to reduce the anticipatory anxiety that most patients with PD experience. The total daily dose is gradually titrated up until symptoms are controlled.

Given the risk of tolerance (neuroadaptation) to benzodiazepines, many clinicians prefer to start with an antidepressant, choosing a selective serotonin reuptake inhibitor (SSRI), tricyclic, or monoamine oxidase inhibitor (MAOI). Antidepressants have been shown to be highly effective in reducing attacks and improving function, with SSRIs and tricyclics showing equal efficacy. The SSRIs are generally better tolerated than the tricyclics. The MAOIs, though often effective, are generally held in reserve given their more serious side effect profile and the need for dietary restrictions. Regardless of which antidepressant is chosen, it is generally prudent to start with a low dose. Once an optimum dose has been reached, a response may not be seen for weeks, and a full response may be delayed for up to three months. Given this potentially long delayed response, many clinicians will begin treatment with a combination of a benzodiazepine and an SSRI (e.g., clonazepam and sertraline) and then taper off the benzodiazepine once the SSRI has had a chance to become effective. Gabapentin is a more benign substitute for benzodiazepines and preferred in children. Among the SSRIs, the following have been shown to be effective in double-blind studies with adults: paroxetine, fluoxetine, fluvoxamine, citalopram, escitalopram, and sertraline. Of the tricyclics, imipramine is generally poorly tolerated over the long haul despite being considered quite effective. Nortriptyline, desipramine, and clomipramine are alternatives. Of the MAOIs, phenelzine is effective. Antidepressant therapy should continue for at least six months after the patient is symptom-free. When the antidepressant is discontinued, the patient should be gradually tapered off the medication and followed closely to detect recurrence of anxiety symptoms before they become debilitating.

Response to medical treatment is usually quite good. Most patients become completely free of panic attacks. However, a large percentage of patients still continue to have attacks, although with less frequency and reduced severity. Family physicians may wish to refer patients with PD to a cognitive behavioral therapist for 4–15 sessions of CBT, ideally with exposure techniques. CBT has been shown to reduce the frequency of panic attacks and effectively treat agoraphobia. Psychotherapy may help the child and family learn ways to reduce stress or conflict that could otherwise cause a panic attack. With techniques taught in CBT, the child may also learn new ways to control anxiety or panic attacks when they occur. Many children and adolescents with PD respond well to the combination of medication and psychotherapy.

CBT includes many techniques, such as applied relaxation, exposure in vivo, exposure through imagery, panic management, breathing retraining, and cognitive restructuring. Meta-analyses support the efficacy of CBT in improving panic symptoms and overall disability. Most of the studies included in these meta-analyses included 8–15 sessions of CBT, although a few studies have reported similar efficacy with only four sessions. Meta-analyses have found that specialized cognitive therapy, behavior therapy, and combined CBT approaches are superior to general emotionally supportive psychotherapy in patients with PD. In the CBT trials, an average of 73% of treated patients were panic-free at three to four months, compared with 27% of control patients, and 46% of treated patients remained panic-free at two years. Although these statistics are impressive, they represent studies in selected populations that may not reflect typical general practice patients. CBT appears to be effective over the long term, with trials ranging from six months to nine years. It remains unclear which component of CBT is more important: cognitive therapy (e.g., identifying misinterpreted feelings, educating patients about panic attacks) or behavioral therapy (e.g., breathing exercises, relaxation, exposure). However, the efficacy of exposure techniques alone, in which the patient repeatedly confronts the anxiety-provoking stimulus through imagery or in vivo, is well established in patients with PD, particularly in those with agoraphobia. When possible, referral to a therapist experienced in exposure techniques is preferred. Recent research is showing that breathing training requires that patients breathe in a way that is incompatible with hyperventilation, with paced, slow breaths. Deep breaths, if taken too rapidly, can actually provoke panic reactions as this mimics the process that occurs in hyperventilation by decreasing carbon dioxide levels. Other promising behavioral changes outside of therapy include exercise, as those who are involved in more physical activity experience reduced likelihood of panic attacks.

Although both antidepressants and CBT have been shown to be effective in treating PD, it remains unclear whether one treatment modality is superior to the other. Several meta-analyses suggest that CBT is more effective than antidepressants in reducing panic symptoms, but these studies have serious methodological flaws. A combination of antidepressant plus some form of CBT has been shown to produce the greatest benefit in meta-analyses of short-term studies, but in a longer term study, patients who used CBT alone or CBT plus placebo had better outcomes than those using combined CBT and antidepressants. Studies also are conflicting about how long to continue antidepressant therapy with or without CBT. Continued antidepressant therapy beyond six months did not decrease relapse rates in one study.

CLINICAL COURSE WITH MANAGEMENT AND TREATMENT

Although Caroline's parents had hoped to avoid using medication, shortly after her psychotherapy began her developmental pediatrician prescribed citalopram 1 ml (5 mg) once each night before bedtime. After a few weeks Caroline experienced major reductions in anxiety, sensory defensiveness, and panic attacks. A year after she entered psychotherapy, when Caroline was six years old, the pediatrician also prescribed methylphenidate hydrochloride extended-release, and this dramatically improved her ability to focus and learn at school. Dosages were increased at various points as she continued in psychotherapy.

Caroline was in weekly or biweekly psychotherapy from ages five through six, with maintenance visits at age seven and a short return to therapy at age eight due to familial stressors. Her treatment began in October, which is usually her worst month of functioning according to the patterns her mother recognized beginning at age three. It is notable that allergy and asthma sufferers like Caroline often experience more respiratory difficulties in the fall and spring. This was linked to increases in her anxiety, which is logical given that her PD also included breathing-related distress. After starting psychotherapy in the fall, Caroline began taking her citalopram in January. By mid-February, her panic attacks had decreased significantly and she was able to wear her seat belt loosely and keep her shoes on in the car, with her seat upright rather than reclined. Although regressions were frequent, overall she demonstrated a steady reduction in anxiety symptoms over time. By May, when she was usually feeling better anyway, she purposefully wore clothes that had distressed her in the past, saying that she wanted to "fight the enemy." She brought that same feisty spirit to almost every therapy session, trying assignments that were quite difficult for her, and this undoubtedly resulted in greater improvement. Her parents, sister, and family friends also provided a great deal of encouragement and positive reinforcement for each gain in functioning. As the therapy progressed, she became more able to tolerate a tighter seat belt for longer periods of time and able to wear a greater variety of clothing. She became more able to describe her bodily sensations, feelings, and thoughts. She developed the term "sticky monsters" to describe the fearful, irrational thoughts that would intrude into her experience of ordinary, nonthreatening events, and became adept at identifying these unhelpful thoughts and "bossing them back," a CBT technique used with OCD. She developed greater coping skills. In addition to learning to verbalize her feelings, she incorporated many self-soothing behaviors into her repertoire and drew heavily on these when starting to feel uncomfortable. These included prayer, singing, greater participation in sports, and many tactile experiences that soothed her, such as playing in water or with shaving cream.

Specific CBT exercises and therapeutic techniques used with Caroline in the 62 sessions she attended over a three-year span included the following:

- Several types of exposure therapy, including in vivo with the therapist while riding with her in her family's van. Relaxation exercises were used as well as distraction with items she had in the van to calm her fearful autonomic response. Positive reinforcement for her efforts, reframing her fearful reaction to the seat belt as a false alarm that her brain was setting off, using imagery of turning off that alarm and cognitive reframing of the seat belt as a hugging friend. After the session, Caroline called the experience "stupid" and was tearful about it the next day as well, and thus this flooding technique proved difficult for her. Imaginal exposure was also used, including setting up pretend van seats in the playroom with a scarf for a pretend seat belt. A parent was present with these exercises and helped generalize the experience as well as provide support. With a few minutes of EMDR, a trauma therapy, she also imagined being in a van seat, and this was when she recalled the traumatic experience of the car wash when she was three. The EMDR experience appeared to have the most profound effect of all of the exposure exercises in reducing her distress about riding in the van, as her symptoms dissipated almost completely in the months following this session.
- A fear hierarchy to identify challenging situations, denote how much distress they caused, and begin working on the least upsetting ones first to build confidence.
- Psychoeducation regarding the nature of panic attacks, sensory processing problems, and the body's fight, flight, or freeze reaction. Now that the book *The Whole Brain Child* (Siegel and Bryson 2012) has been published, it would

be an excellent tool in educating emotionally dysregulated and anxious children about the brain and neural processes that occur when they are afraid, as it even includes cartoons that children can easily understand.

- Cognitive restructuring of her dysfunctional thoughts and practice of new behaviors incompatible with the panic reactions, including discussions of how her feelings of danger would pass with time and how her panic feelings might grow if she reacted to them. Externalization of unhelpful thoughts and sensations as "sticky monsters" (her name for them) and bossing these back with alternative reactions was used, in keeping with CBT for OCD. One activity she particularly enjoyed was drawing the sticky monsters, cutting them out, and then setting them like paper dolls to shoot with darts. Such externalization of the internal process helps the child realize they can work against these unhelpful thoughts.

- Use of the child-friendly book *What to Do When Your Brain Gets Stuck* (Huebner and Matthews 2007) to normalize her experiences and illustrate the skills she could develop to combat faulty thinking patterns.

- Teaching her and her parents to identify problem situations, the physical signs heralding the onset of distress, and the use of positive coping statements and soothing behaviors in response. This gave her more feelings of control over her subjective experiences.

- Teaching of relaxation, including breathing, muscle tensing and releasing, and positive imagery. She chose to think about building a collection of sticks and pine cones, one of her favorite outdoor activities. Breathing training was for slow, shallow breaths.

- Use of reflection and naming of her feelings to build her competency with identifying her feelings and talking about them.

- Identification and extensive use of calming physical activity and tactile experiences to help her self-soothe. Playing outside in general, jumping on a trampoline at home, and playing with sand in sessions were among the most calming of the activities identified. Recommended *The Out of Sync Child* (Kranowitz 2005), which Caroline's parents found immensely helpful in understanding sensory processing disorder and learning about helpful activities. Use of a comforting "touch box" where she could keep items that helped regulate her emotionally.

- Encouragement of physical activity including time for her outdoor play and sports involvement, which had the added benefits of positive time with peers and improvement of self-esteem, as she was successful on the teams. One session was conducted outside, throwing a flying disc as the therapist and Caroline made up a song about a way she could cope and the positive self-statements she could make when distressed by riding in the van. The combination of physical activity and singing helped Caroline process the coping skills in a much deeper way than simply talking about it, and she reported that she used the song she had made up many times over the following weeks.

- Activities to promote a positive sense of self and greater self-efficacy, including taking photographs of her creations in the playroom for her to take home and videos of performances that she could watch that made her feel proud. Encouragement of independence and meeting challenges by completing challenging activities in therapy, to build resiliency and counteract anxiety overall.

- Highly engaging and interactive nondirective play and unconditional positive regard, which promoted a quite solid and trusting therapeutic relationship that promoted compliance and helped her build her capacity for seeking and accepting support at difficult times.
- Use of narrative therapy, with her creation of a book to help other children struggling with sensory issues. The therapist wrote down what she wanted to say, and she illustrated it.

Two years after Caroline began therapy, her mother wrote, "Caroline is doing so great! She has been sitting with the seat belt 'normal' for the past several months! She loves school and is doing so well with reading. She is even wearing her school uniform skirt that has shorts built in under it. Issues come every once in a while but don't seem to last too long." After the first year in therapy, with 34 sessions, it appeared evident that Caroline would meet this level of adaptive functioning when she dictated the following "book" at just six years old:

How Caroline Learned to Control Her Sensory Issues!

Sensory is . . . kind of bad.

It kind of feels like my heart is pumping really, really fast. And it's catching on fire.

It kind of feels like it's kind of drawing on my heart, and on Jesus too, like hurting me and Jesus, too.

It feels like someone writing on paper—fast, in a hurry, all over my body, on my bones.

[Picture of a robot here, marks coming out from it, with the description: Robot Me Having Issues!]

The way I deal with it is . . .

I say, "I can do this, I can do this, I can do this!"

It feels like God throws water on the fire that I was feeling, and it goes out.

When I'm thinking about my dad and my mom and my sister, going to the beach, and going on a cruise, that helps too.

That gets my mind off the sensory.

That's the way I control it!

I still have a little bit of issues (I call my sensory that sometimes.).

Like when I have to wake up early, and get dressed in my school uniform.

Another thing that helps me is if I do flips on the couch. That helps me every day.

Playing with mud is the best. I play with shaving cream or sand, too, or slimy gooey stuff, or dough or flour you bake with.

I don't know why that helps, it just does!

[Picture here of her swimming at the beach.]

So that's how I learned to control my sensory issues. You can get better too!

Then you can be like me—having fun being at the beach, having sleepovers and parties and doing good at school!

SYSTEMS-BASED PRACTICE ISSUES

In their search for a therapist for their daughter, Caroline's parents faced the challenge of finding one with knowledge not only of early childhood and anxiety disorders but also of sensory processing difficulties. Although awareness of sensory processing problems is growing nationally thanks to greater awareness in schools and clinicians' offices of the sensory needs of autistic children, many clinicians are still learning about sensory processing disorder because it does not appear in any versions of the DSM. Despite this lack of awareness, for therapists treating a child with sensory problems, it is possible to consult with occupational therapists who are the primary specialists for sensory dysfunction. Not only did Caroline's therapist have to be well versed in developmental psychology, especially the stages and needs of the kindergarten through second-grade ages, it was important for the clinician to be able to incorporate play into the work, as well, given that play would be Caroline's primary mode of relaxation to combat her anxiety. In many rural areas, especially, finding such a clinician may be difficult. The Association for Play Therapy (APT) has chapters nationwide, however, and families can sometimes locate therapists with these specialties more easily via the APT website. Excellent rapport between the child and therapist will be extremely important for the child to develop the trust and motivation required for dealing with such a high level of anxiety.

In terms of building a treatment team, parents whose children are suffering from debilitating anxiety would do well to start with their pediatrician, who may be able to refer the family to a competent therapist. Therapy will need to incorporate cognitive behavioral tenets as these are the most effective for PD. A pediatrician can also make a referral to a developmental pediatrician who can better assess for sensory and autistic symptoms, a child psychiatrist if medical treatment becomes complex, and/or an occupational therapist for sensory needs. Once the child is in school, the therapist can assist the family in knowing what types of services are needed and provide consultation to the school as needed. For many children with debilitating symptoms, the parents may need to request psychological and academic testing by the school system. This is done as part of a "child study" process to determine if the child should receive special education services via an Individual Education Plan (IEP). If the parents are not content with the findings of the school system's testing, they can request an independent evaluation in the community. The types of interventions that the school could provide for PD vary based on the child's individual needs, but could include the opportunity to take breaks during the school day to reduce stress or a modified work environment if sensory issues are a problem. Caroline was allowed modifications to her school uniform, for example. Allowing the child to go home because of a panic attack is likely to reinforce this response. Instead, school personnel should attempt to help the child recover and return to class if more serious medical conditions have been ruled out and the Panic Disorder diagnosis has been established.

Caroline and her family brought a number of strengths to the therapeutic process that enabled this remarkable child to make tremendous gains despite having severe symptoms of multiple disorders. Systems-based practice was vital for her improvement, as it is with many children, due to multiple parties involved in their lives, including family members, school personnel, and often other health professionals. The psychologist actively collaborated with Caroline's developmental pediatrician and received input from her occupational therapist and school personnel as well as the family. Throughout therapy, recommendations were provided to parents regarding ways to help improve functioning at home, in the community, and at school. The therapeutic process took time and required a variety of interventions including pharmacologic, CBT, psychoeducation, supportive therapy, and problem- or crisis-focused interventions.

LEGAL, ETHICAL, AND CULTURAL ISSUES

Ethical issues that have to be kept in mind include not stressing Caroline too much with the exposure therapy, but building up plenty of resources on which she could draw, to help her mediate the stress involved in overcoming her panic and sensory fears. Cultural issues included the need to be respectful of her and her family's strong religious convictions and incorporate these when appropriate into her therapeutic process. Therapy with this engaging child and her supportive family thus came to represent an evidence-based, culturally sensitive biopsychosociospiritual approach.

TERMS

Agoraphobia: abnormal fear of being helpless in an embarrassing or inescapable situation that is characterized especially by the avoidance of open or public places.

Cognitive behavioral therapy (CBT): a psychotherapeutic approach that addresses dysfunctional emotions, maladaptive behaviors, and cognitive processes and contents through a number of goal-oriented, explicit systematic procedures. The name refers to a combination of behavior therapy and cognitive therapy. Most therapists working with patients dealing with anxiety and depression use elements of both cognitive and behavioral approaches. CBT is problem-focused and action-oriented, with the therapist assisting the client in selecting specific strategies to help address problems.

Narrative therapy: involves a process of deconstruction and "meaning making" achieved through questioning and collaboration with the client, with the therapist helping the patient develop richer narratives via questions to generate experientially vivid descriptions of life events that are not currently included in the plot of the problematic story. The externalization that is part of the narrative process helps the patient gain greater mastery of possibly upsetting material, process experiences more deeply, and reduce negative reactions to them. The therapist's intentional inclusion of strengths and evidence of positive coping allows patients to engage in the construction and performance of preferred identities.

Panic attack: a sudden episode of intense fear that triggers severe physical reactions when there is no real danger or apparent cause.

Sensory processing disorder: also known as sensory integration disorder; conceptualized as a neurological deficit in processing and integrating information from the five senses (vision, auditory, touch, olfaction, and taste) as well as sense of movement (vestibular system) and/or positional sense (proprioception). This is common for children on the autism spectrum but also apparent with other disorders and otherwise normal children.

REFERENCES AND RESOURCES

American Academy of Child and Adolescent Psychiatry. Panic disorder in children and adolescents. *Facts for Families*, 2004;50. Retrieved from http://www.aacap.org/cs/root/facts_for_families/panic_disorder_in_children_and_adolescents.

American Academy of Child and Adolescent Psychiatry Work Group on Quality Issues. Summary of the practice parameters for the assessment and treatment of children and adolescents with anxiety disorders. 1997. Retrieved from http://www.aacap.org.

American Psychiatric Association Work Group on Panic Disorder. Practice guideline for the treatment of patients with panic disorder, 2nd ed. 2009. Retrieved from http://psychiatryonline.org/content.aspx?bookid=28&sectionid=1680635.

Beesdo K, Knappe S, Pine DS. Anxiety and anxiety disorders in children and adolescents: developmental issues and implications for DSM-V. *Psych Clin N Am* 2009;32(3):483–524. Retrieved from http://www.ncbi.nlm.nih.gov/pubmed/19716988.

Craske MG, Kircanski K, Epstein A, Wittchen H, Pine DS, Lewis-Fernande, R, Hinton D, and DSM V Anxiety, OC Spectrum, Posttraumatic and Dissociative Disorder Work Group. Panic disorder: a review of DSM-IV panic disorder and proposals for DSM-V. *Depression and Anxiety* 2010;0:1-20. Retrieved from http://www.dsm5.org/Research/Documents/Craske_PD%20Review.pdf.

Huebner D, Matthews B. *What to Do When Your Brain Gets Stuck: A Kid's Guide to Overcoming OCD*. Washington, DC: Magination Press, 2007.

Kranowitz CS. *The Out-of-Sync Child: Recognizing and Coping with Sensory Processing Disorder* (2nd ed.). New York: Perigee, 2005.

Ougrin D. Efficacy of exposure versus cognitive therapy in anxiety disorders: systematic review and metaanalysis. *Bio Med Cent Psych* 2011;11(200). Retrieved from http://www.biomedcentral.com/1471-244X/11/200.

Siegel D, Bryson TP. *The Whole-Brain Child: 12 Revolutionary Strategies to Nurture Your Child's Developing Mind*. New York: Bantam, 2012.

National Institutes for Mental Health on panic disorder, http://www.nimh.nih.gov/health/topics/panic-disorder/index.shtml.

Sensory Processing Disorder, http://www.spdfoundation.net/.

Play Therapy, http://www.a4pt.org/.

Analyze This (1999) A comedy film in which Robert De Niro plays the lead thug in a New York mafia group who develops panic attacks. He sees a psychiatrist (played by Billy Crystal) for treatment.

CHAPTER **29**

Complex Trauma

J. E. Vance, M.D.

CLINICAL PRESENTATION

Chief complaint: "I don't make apologies, and I don't talk about my feelings."

History of present illness: Scott is a 15-year-old African American boy who was born and grew up in a midsize town in eastern North Carolina, and was admitted to a locked residential treatment facility on a court-ordered petition. The clinician met with him initially in his dorm room, which was stripped bare except for a bed and desk bolted to the floor. He lay on a bare mattress, propped up on a pillow with his hands behind his head, while answering the clinician's questions. Scott appears as a very muscled young man, with dark brown skin and nearly black eyes that seem to glare; he was somewhat intimidating on first meeting. He is asked to relate the serious incident of assault on a group home staff member that had prompted his admission to the secure treatment center. This was one of several violations of his probation, and serious enough that he was committed by the court to a locked facility. He is unremorseful, stating that the staff member was "running his mouth." He had been playing a video game with another resident at the group home, when the staff member had joked about Scott losing the game, and Scott had told him to shut his mouth. The staff had then confronted him about being disrespectful and raised his voice, telling him to go take a time-out in his room, at which point Scott had thrown the game controller to the floor, breaking it, and headed toward the door to leave the house. The staff member had stood up to prevent his leaving, grabbing his arm, at which point Scott swung his other fist and landed several punches to the staff member's face, then ran out of the house.

The police were called and Scott was apprehended several hours later, hanging out with some other young men in a convenience store parking lot, smoking cigarettes and marijuana. The staff member had to receive medical care for a black eye and broken cheekbone. Scott had been at that particular group home for more than two months and had developed a pretty good working relationship with the staff person he had punched, but he expressed no remorse about the injuries he inflicted. When asked if he would be willing to talk about the incident, process it, and apologize to the victim, he stated, "I don't make apologies, and I don't talk about my feelings." At this point, the clinician calmly tells Scott that he is glad he has come to this facility to get some help, and that he hopes Scott will learn how to talk about problems and make apologies when necessary. He is silent and stares angrily out the window while the clinician expresses that he would return the next day to do a full psychiatric assessment.

The clinician is able to gather some of Scott's developmental, family, and treatment history from his case manager, but his guardian, the maternal grandmother, is unavailable for the initial assessment, living three hours away and having to care for two of her other grandchildren, including Scott's little brother. Scott is the firstborn to his mother, Marie, who was 17 years old and had dropped out of high school to have him. Marie had begun to use drugs and alcohol at 15 years old with her older boyfriend, who was Scott's biological father and was incarcerated soon after Scott's birth for selling drugs and assault with a deadly weapon. When she found out she was pregnant, Marie stopped drinking and using drugs until after Scott was born. At the time of his birth, Scott and Marie lived with her mother, his maternal grandmother, Nanny, for two years. After that, they moved in with Lashawn, Marie's new boyfriend. Marie's drug use escalated, and Lashawn was physically abusive to her and Scott, taking belts and sticks to the boy for discipline, and slapping and punching his mother, once pinning her on the floor with his hands around her neck until Scott jumped on his back, screaming for him to stop. When he was drunk, Lashawn would sometimes trash the apartment, breaking dishes and throwing furniture. The neighbors called the police to their apartment several times over the next couple of years. Marie left Lashawn several times, moving back with Nanny for brief periods, then back to Lashawn's apartment whenever Nanny would try to press her daughter to get sober. When Scott was four years old, his mother gave birth to his little brother, Derrick, Lashawn's child.

Scott and Derrick lived with their mother's addiction to crack and alcohol, and with Lashawn's violent temper for the next two years, no longer able to seek respite at Nanny's home, since she and Marie had grown emotionally further apart. Marie taught Scott how to feed Derrick a bottle and change diapers, and she would often go out, leaving them alone with the TV, or come home and pass out on the couch. The situation came to a head when five-year-old Scott was found by the police one evening, in the median of a four-lane highway, leading his brother by the hand toward a local convenience store to get some food. Child Protective Services intervened and placed the boys with Nanny as guardian, even though she was already raising two of her other grandchildren in her crowded home.

When he entered kindergarten from Nanny's home, Scott had already been identified as a high-risk student based on preschool behavioral problems, most notably aggression toward peers. He also struggled with problems in speech articulation, and quickly began to fall behind in academics, especially in reading, comprehension, and expressive language. His frustration and lack of skill in the schoolwork led to oppositional stand-offs against classroom assignments and power struggles with teachers, with frequent disciplinary problems. He was also noted to be fidgety, distractible, inattentive, and impulsive with peers, and frequently backtalked to teachers. Toward the end of first grade, a student assistance team recommended to Nanny that he be medically evaluated for attention deficit hyperactivity disorder (ADHD). Based on teacher checklists and Nanny's reports of disruptive and aggressive behavior at home, his pediatrician placed him on methylphenidate. Though it slowed him down some, the medication seemed to make him more irritable and unhappy, and he lost weight from his already skinny frame. It was stopped and dextroamphetamine/amphetamine was started, with much the same result, but it allowed him to maintain in school for nearly a year before everyone agreed it had "stopped working." His pediatrician referred him to a child psychiatrist, and a few months later he was evaluated.

In those same early elementary years at Nanny's, Scott and Derrick were required to make regular visits to see their mother and Lashawn as part of the long-term permanency plan. The family court ordered Marie to get substance abuse counseling and Lashawn to go to anger management classes. The visits seemed to go well at first, but it was suspected that their mother was still using drugs between visits, though she was at least sober during their time together. Sometimes, Lashawn would take them to the park and play football. During that time, when they returned home to Nanny's house after visits, the boys would be angry and escalate their behavior. Scott's behavior, especially at Nanny's home, seemed to worsen, with defiance, bossiness, and aggression toward his brother and cousins, poor sleep and bed-wetting, and a decline in his previous helpfulness to his grandmother. Nonetheless, the visits progressed to overnight stays, until a night when Lashawn lost his temper, slapped Scott in the head and threw him against the wall, after Scott had punched Derrick in a fight over a toy. The visits were suspended; this was around the time that Scott went for his first evaluation with a child psychiatrist.

The record of that initial psychiatric evaluation revealed a very different Scott than what is seen today: an eight-year-old boy who was long forgotten by the tough, callous, and violent teenager admitted to this residential facility. The eight-year-old Scott, who was initially brought to the child psychiatrist, had behavioral problems at school, including impulsivity, poor focus, and anger outbursts to teachers and other students. At home, Nanny had described him as stubborn and prone to anger outbursts, but often hyperresponsible and helpful, even loving to family members at times. At other times he was sad and worried, and recently more angry and defiant. He slept poorly, with nightmares about being chased by monsters or shot, and sometimes had bed-wetting accidents. He often asked Nanny about Marie's whereabouts and safety, and frequently checked to make sure all of Nanny's doors were locked at night. The family psychiatric history suggested untreated bipolar disorder and repeated incarceration of Scott's father, and a history of polysubstance abuse and probable post-traumatic stress disorder (PTSD) in Marie, based on sexual abuse as a teenager by a former uncle.

The psychiatrist diagnosed ADHD, oppositional defiant disorder (ODD), and nocturnal enuresis and prescribed an increased dose of dextroamphetamine/amphetamine, added clonidine three times daily, and imipramine for bed-wetting. Although there was mention of psychosocial and family adversity, there was no diagnosis of PTSD or mention of the effect of poor attachment, child neglect, or abuse effects. Nanny brought Scott to therapy and medication appointments for a few months, then became overwhelmed with her child care responsibilities and they dropped out of treatment.

As elementary school progressed, Scott continued to struggle with learning, especially reading and math, but had an Individualized Educational Plan (IEP) that offered him some extra help, and he was passed along into middle school. Over time, his aggressive behavior got him into more trouble, with angry outbursts in school, knocking over chairs and desks, and getting into fights with other students. He was eventually placed in a self-contained classroom, and finally in sixth grade he had a fairly successful year when his teacher was a seasoned, older woman, with great skills and patience, and he was assigned to a volunteer reading mentor for the year, through a special program for high-risk youths. The following year he changed classes and teachers, and the mentor was reassigned. Predictably, things went downhill again in school, and seventh and eighth grade were punctuated by suspensions for fights, property destruction, disrespectful and angry exchanges with teachers, and failing grades.

In spite of all his problems in middle school, he was passed along into high school, tried in mainstream classes, and his IEP was all but forgotten. Outside of school, he was being recruited by local gang members to be a "soldier" to beat up rival gang members. Smoking cigarettes and marijuana became routine for him, but he stayed away from alcohol and harder drugs after seeing what they had done to his mother and Lashawn. As a freshman, he was recruited to play on the school football team after an assistant coach had seen his natural athleticism playing street basketball. The coach met with Nanny and mentored Scott, trying to win him away from the hoodlums he was hanging out with. It worked for almost the entire freshman football season, and he even attracted a girlfriend. Unfortunately, he flew into a jealous rage and attacked another boy who was talking to her and was charged with assault and placed on probation in the juvenile justice system. For this, he was kicked off the football team and required to get anger management counseling.

The anger management group he attended had several boys he knew from the neighborhood, and they knew Scott well enough to avoid confronting him in the group. The group counselor was puzzled as to why no one else in the group would engage Scott to talk about his emotional issues, but all knew he was a member of the gang and was not to be messed with. He was disruptive and confrontational with the other group members and the counselor, and this was reported to his probation officer. He was drug-tested and tested positive for marijuana, and at his next court review, his probation was revoked and he was placed in detention. Outside the court building, as he was preparing for transport to detention, Scott saw Marie laughing as she and Lashawn pulled out of the parking lot. Soon after placement in detention, he got into a fight, breaking another boy's nose. He also required several physical restraints by staff, usually escalating his anger when directed by staff to change his behavior or comply with the detention center rules. After nearly three months, he stabilized somewhat, but his court review noted the multiple violations of his probation and remanded him to placement in the group home. There he assaulted the staff and was finally sent to the secure treatment facility.

Mental status exam: On admission to the treatment center, Scott presents as a well-developed African American teen, who appears his stated age, and has his shirt partially untucked and pants sagging low on his waist, in minor violation of the dress code. He is calm, without excessive motor movements or notable tics, and slouches in the chair, looking down at the floor, making only intermittent and fleeting eye contact. He is initially sullen and resistant to talk much, but eventually opens up. His speech is slow and reveals a lisp and mild dysarthria, at times difficult to understand, but not pressured. For the most part, he is alert and attentive to the interview, but easily distracted by noises outside the exam room, looking up quickly with a concerned look through the crack in the exam room doorway. He is fully oriented in all spheres, and his memory for current, recent, and past events is intact. His affect throughout the interview and in describing these events is remarkably blunted and nonreactive, though briefly negative and angry. He describes his mood as neutral, neither happy nor down most of the time, but with periods of anger that could last from minutes to several days. He denies any suicidal thoughts or intention, nor deliberate self-harm, though he had several times punched holes in walls and injured his knuckles. He denies current homicidal ideation, but admits in the past he had thoughts of killing Lashawn with a knife while he slept. He no longer has that thought, realizing he would end up in prison.

His thought process is coherent and relevant to the topics addressed, with no evidence of formal thought disorder, and with language and vocabulary that suggests borderline to low average intellect. Brief screening of his cognitive function revealed difficulty with mathematical calculations, serial 7's, making change, and limited fund of knowledge about current events, knowing only the current president and some recent sports news. His insight and judgment are very limited as to the cause and effect of what led him to his current situation, the need for him to change his pattern of behavior, and taking responsibility for his actions. There is minimal evidence of psychotic symptoms, such as persistent hallucinations or delusions, but he reports he sometimes thinks he hears his name yelled out when no one is around, and sometimes at night thinks he sees shadow figures outside his window or in his room. He does not report any paranoid delusions, but he consistently externalizes blame for his actions onto others, whom he portrays as hostile or unfair toward him. He denies depersonalization or derealization, but states that when he is in a fight, he will sometimes "black out" with anger and do violent things he would be told about later. He also admits to frequently thinking about past events in his life, describing several specific incidents that are the worst, including being picked up by the police when he was leading his little brother to the store, and the incident when he jumped on Lashawn's back, trying to stop him from choking his mother.

IMPAIRMENT IN FUNCTIONING

The development of antisocial traits and behaviors in the context of chronic abuse and neglect can result in a range of functional impairments. In the case of Scott and others like him, one of the most profound impairments is in the quality of interpersonal relationships. The many disruptions of attachment, incidents of neglect and lack of protection, and hostility, indifference, or aggression toward the young child are extremely damaging to the development of internal working models of relationships with others. Mistrust, hostile attributional bias, and problems with intimacy are common in both conduct-disordered youths and abuse victims. Even worse can be the development of aggressive, violent, or cruel behaviors that often mirror the treatment experienced by maltreated children. Relationships with caregivers, teachers, peers, and romantic mates can range from indifferent to hostile, manipulative, and controlling.

Behavioral impairments are common, and most often center around aggressive and destructive acts. Because emotions are poorly modulated, and easily triggered by trauma cues, these individuals have frequent anger outbursts, throwing and breaking objects, punching and kicking holes in walls and doors, and lashing out physically and verbally at those around them. Other antisocial behaviors are common—in Scott's case, lying to deny responsibility, stealing to procure necessities for survival, or simply taking by force from others to exert intimidation and control. Running away from home, staying away without permission, and skipping school may be acts of defiance, but also may arise from avoidance of traumatic environments where abuse, neglect, or dangers are present. School truancy in conduct-disordered youths may be a result of some combination of social awkwardness, difficulty accepting authority, incompetence as a student, and peer pressure to skip school. In any case, these behavioral problems may arise from post-traumatic roots and become established or habitual, and comprise conduct disorder.

One of the most common and devastating outcomes of serious conduct disorder is entry into the juvenile justice system. Though this system can provide mandated and needed habilitative services for many delinquents, it has also been shown that it can be detrimental to youth development to be immersed in treatment programs with other antisocial individuals. Some youths enter the system with minor problems and are exposed to more severely conduct-disordered youths while in the system, and thus become "socialized" into more antisocial norms. Group therapies of many kinds, such as "anger management" groups, have actually been shown to be detrimental when conducted with groups of antisocial youths. Unless such groups are highly scripted and conducted by experts, it is believed that groups of antisocial youths quickly establish covert group norms of intimidation, lying, minimization, and externalization of responsibility. For the half of all youths with conduct disorder who enter the adult justice system, this exposure effect is compounded, with the consolidation of antisocial behaviors and the common progression from nonviolent to violent crimes.

Cognitive and learning impairments have been observed in both traumatized children and in conduct-disordered youths. Large studies of maltreated children have shown a much higher rate of learning and cognitive disorders, lower IQ, and impaired school performance in relation to nonmaltreated children. It is also well known that antisocial individuals often have lower verbal skills or forms of dyslexia and are relatively stronger with hands-on and nonverbal tasks. Ironically, the diagnosis of conduct disorder is not officially recognized as an educationally impairing condition for purposes of special education, and is sometimes used to deny special educational services, with the view that the problem behaviors are under the youth's control and therefore don't qualify as a disability. Nonetheless, the frequent comorbid conditions of ADHD and specific learning disabilities among youths with conduct disorder enable them to get IEP services under other labels, and they tend to be overrepresented in special education programs.

Recent studies have shown that over half of multiply traumatized youths are at high risk to develop drug or alcohol use problems. It is also the case that over half of all youths diagnosed with conduct disorder have drug or alcohol abuse problems, with percentages as high as 70–80% among incarcerated juveniles. The developmental pathway through which substance abuse develops in this population involves several key mechanisms. One factor is very early exposure to cigarettes, alcohol, or marijuana in children who grow up in families with substance-abusing parents or older siblings and neighborhood youths who share substances with these children as early as 10–12 years old. Such early sensitization of the brain to substances dramatically increases the likelihood of subsequent abuse or dependence. Another powerful influence toward substance abuse among traumatized youths is self-medication. Many of these youths are suffering with untreated anxiety and mood disorders, related to chronic PTSD, and discover that drugs or alcohol effectively and temporarily relieve their symptoms. Of course, eventually they suffer the consequences of frequent or long-term use of substances by developing other problems. Finally, it has been shown that initiating cigarettes or other substance use is simply associated with beginning to engage in any other deviant or antisocial activities. If a youth is going to start engaging in antisocial acts, it is more likely he or she will also begin to use illegal substances.

The ultimate functional impairment is mortality as a result of the disorder. In this regard, severe conduct disorder has an extremely poor prognosis. A survey of previously incarcerated juvenile delinquents revealed that by their 25th birthday, the mortality rate of the group was 58 times the national average for individuals in their age group. It is also well known that the suicide rate among those patients with PTSD is markedly elevated. To suffer from both disorders is an extremely high risk combination.

DSM DIAGNOSIS

The constellation of symptoms that Scott's case presents involves a recognizable pattern of psychopathology with contributors from the realms of mood, anxiety, and thought. The history of trauma and attachment disruptions, coupled with the anger and aggression of his conduct disorder, has created for him a mood disorder that is labile, frequently provoked to hostility, and at times hopeless and dysphoric. The traumatic experiences of his childhood and the dangerous environments he continually creates or immerses himself in together perpetuate his underlying anxiety and hyperarousal, which is strongly defended against by his tough exterior and projection of blame onto others. Finally, due to trauma and neglect, his thought process is distorted by mistrust in relationships, sometimes to a level of paranoia, and he has developed the hostile attributional bias common in youths with conduct disorder. This combination of mood, anxiety, and thought problems has produced a recognizable pattern of behavioral and relational problems that include intimidation and reactive aggression; self-serving antisocial behaviors such as lying, cheating, and stealing; and a lack of empathy in all but his closest social relationships.

To address and reverse some of these psychopathological processes, Scott will need to first recognize how destructive and limiting his behaviors have become for him. In his case, being committed to a locked facility may be the only way to stop running from his problems and finally face them. He was able to see that he would rather be living freely with his family than in a series of locked facilities or eventual prison. This realization only came in the context of developing some of the first trusting relationships in his life, with the staff and therapists in the facility. In the context of truly helpful relationships in a safe environment, his anxiety diminished enough to drop some of his pathological defenses and begin to engage in honest interpersonal problem solving and taking some personal responsibility for his troubles. In a case of trauma like Scott's, it is helpful to validate the pain and suffering of the past, while moving the person to take responsibility for their current behaviors. It requires gentle but firm confrontation, and the eventual ability of the person to self-confront and begin engaging in self-soothing and affect modulation.

Narrative discussions of the past traumas, as well as required processing of current conflicts and incidents, forced Scott to correct many cognitive distortions and hostile attributions. After repeatedly processing such material, Scott was able to begin to understand cause and effect and put his traumatic past in the context of his mother's substance abuse, gaining some perspective and acceptance of what he had been through. All of this was accomplished as he was gaining some self-esteem with tangible skills in athletics and having some of his first academic successes in the program. His relationship skills improved with mentoring within the program, and his natural social support network was preserved with regular visits from Nanny and his brother, and eventually his mother.

Although different for the latest edition, the DSM has traditionally been a purely categorical and descriptive approach to the diagnosis and classification of mental illness, without regard to etiology. The criteria and description of conduct disorder are a good example of this. Conduct disorder is diagnosed when there is a pattern of behavior in which societal norms and the basic rights of others are violated, either by aggression, destruction of property, lying, stealing, or violating rules at home or school. This behavioral description gives no indication of the origins or developmental history of the disorder in a particular youth's life. Studies of youths with conduct disorder have identified a range of various biopsychosocial risk factors that contribute to the development of the disorder. In any youth for whom the diagnosis is made, it is crucial to document which risk factors are present and contributing to the maintenance of the symptoms. In the real world of practice, it is paramount to develop a working model of causation and understand the specific developmental context from which the conduct disorder emerged before effective treatment can be administered.

In contrast, PTSD, as described in the DSM, has been unique in that its diagnosis directly attributes causation to a traumatic experience. The diagnosis must arise following exposure to an actual or threatened death, serious injury, or sexual violence by directly experiencing or witnessing a traumatic event; learning about violent or accidental traumatic events to close family members, caregiver, or friends; or experiencing repeated or extreme exposure to aversive details of the traumatic event. Following exposure the patient has distressing, intrusive, and recurring memories, dreams, or flashbacks. There may be intense or prolonged psychological distress or marked physiological reactions at exposure to internal or external cues that symbolize or resemble the trauma. Consequently there is persistent avoidance of (or efforts to avoid) stimuli associated with the trauma such as the distressing memories, thoughts, or feelings (or the external reminders that arouse them). The negative alterations in cognitions and mood associated with the traumatic event include memory impairment, persistent and exaggerated negative beliefs or expectations, cognitive distortions about the cause or consequences of the trauma, persistent negative emotional states, diminished participation in significant activities, feeling detached from others, and persistent inability to experience positive emotions. Marked alterations in arousal and reactivity associated with the trauma include irritable behavior and angry outbursts with little provocation, reckless or destructive behavior, hypervigilance, exaggerated startle response, concentration problems, and sleep disturbance. The disorder develops over and persists for at least one month following a traumatic experience.

The diagnosis of PTSD has historically described a disorder that arises from a single severe trauma or a series of repeated traumas, such as repeated combat exposure or repeated sexual abuse. Revisions of the DSM face the challenges of more clearly defining the range of symptoms produced in multiply traumatized children, producing what has been called "complex PTSD." Complex PTSD refers to the array of psychopathology that arises from the results of repeated exposure to a wide variety of different developmental traumas. Problems commonly described in complex PTSD patients include extreme mood lability, aggression, self-harm, mistrust and instability in relationships, reenactment behaviors, anxiety, behavioral impulsivity, cognitive distortions, inattention, and substance abuse. In the current case of Scott and his brother, there were multiple traumas, including severe neglect, repeated physical abuse, and witness to life-threatening domestic violence, all occurring several times in the course of their development. In surveys of juvenile delinquents exposed to various kinds of trauma, the average traumatized youth has been subject to more than five different types of trauma. In such a developmental context, the potential for psychopathogenesis goes beyond the usual symptoms of PTSD and includes the development of multiple other problems. For example, in multiply traumatized delinquent youths, over half develop serious depression and substance abuse. Multiple traumas can also be found in the developmental history of many adult patients with borderline personality disorder, and many trauma theorists have suggested that borderline personality traits are often a manifestation of complex PTSD. Additionally, it has been noted that patients who develop schizophrenia have eight times the likelihood of having a history of severe trauma in early childhood.

The profound effect of trauma in contributing to the development of PTSD, mood disorders, borderline personality traits, substance abuse disorders, and even schizophrenia has lead some theorists to suggest a revision of DSM away from simple PTSD toward a concept of "trauma spectrum disorders" or "developmental trauma disorder." Such diagnostic frameworks would allow for the attribution of trauma effects to a range of disorders, including reactive attachment disorders, anxiety disorders, mood disorders, behavioral disorders including conduct disorder, trauma-generated psychotic and thought disorders, and substance abuse disorders resulting from self-medication. Critics of this approach point out that it is difficult to know which and how much symptomatology to attribute to the experiential effects of trauma, versus congenital or genetic characteristics that preceded the trauma. As more becomes understood about how trauma impacts on genetic expression, the DSM can evolve to incorporate trauma effects as a component of a variety of disorders beyond simple PTSD.

EPIDEMIOLOGY

During the course of normal development, as many as 50% of all teenage boys will engage in some of the DSM conduct disorder behaviors for some brief period of their adolescence. For the vast majority, this will be a passing phase or a brief, misguided association with "the wrong crowd." However, as many as 10% of boys will develop the full criteria with sustained patterns of conduct-disordered behavior.

If trauma is an important source of psychopathology, it is also extremely prevalent in our society and can almost be viewed as ubiquitous. As many as 60% of all children surveyed in one year were either exposed or subject to some form of severe violence or abuse. Of these, 46% were assaulted, and 10% were seriously injured. In the same large national survey, 10% were maltreated by caretakers, and 10% witnessed domestic violence. Among those surveyed, 11% had been victimized five or more times in a single year. A separate statewide survey of court-involved youths found that on average, these youths had been subjected to more than five major traumas. Over a million allegations of child abuse are substantiated in the United States each year.

Community surveys of children and young adults find a prevalence of diagnosable PTSD between 6% and 10%, with greater prevalence among urban and impoverished youths. This rate is amplified to between 15% and 20% among court-involved youths, and up to 30% of incarcerated youths, such as Scott.

Most studies have found that only about one quarter to one third of children will develop full-blown PTSD after a severe trauma, but it is also been found that others will develop symptoms of depression, conduct disturbance, personality pathology, and substance abuse. Given the history of repeated traumas and abandonment in Scott's life, as well as the early onset and persistence of conduct-disordered behaviors, the epidemiologic statistics strongly support the diagnosis of complex trauma effects with the emergence of aggression and conduct problems.

DIFFERENTIAL DIAGNOSIS

In arriving at the diagnosis of complex trauma effects and conduct disorder in Scott's case, several other sources of psychopathology need to be ruled out. In looking at the cognitive problems, it is important to consider whether ADHD is contributing to his impulsivity and aggressive behaviors, as well as his academic challenges. ADHD is very prevalent in conduct disorder, up to 50% comorbidity, and longitudinal studies suggest that conduct disorder with ADHD is a particularly persistent and severe form of the disorder, accounting for much of the lifetime mortality, morbidity, and criminality seen in conduct disorder. Standard ADHD checklists administered by teachers and parents (Connors, Vanderbilt, etc.), as well as the early childhood developmental and educational history can rule out ADHD. When considering ADHD in someone like Scott, it is important to rule out specific learning disorders as a cause of educational frustration and academic impairment and rule out underlying anxiety and paranoid hypervigilance as a cause of motor restlessness and cognitive distractibility.

Other common sources of the sort of problems presented by Scott include major mood disorders, such as recurrent or chronic major depression, bipolar disorder, or intermittent explosive disorder. Mood dysregulation is common in post-traumatic disorders, and can be distinguished from major depression based on severity and persistence of depressed mood, neurovegetative symptoms, impairment of school function, and social withdrawal. Nonetheless, periods of major depression can arise in the course of PTSD and can be comorbid and require treatment. Bipolar disorder can usually be ruled out by the absence of manic or hypomanic symptoms, such as decreased need for sleep, psychomotor acceleration, and grandiosity, but in cases like Scott, his intensely irritable mood, explosive rages, chronic sleep disturbance, and narcissistic projection of blame onto others can resemble bipolar features. The differentiation from bipolar disorder should be on the basis of episodic exacerbations in the case of bipolar mood, versus chronic or briefly intermittent mood disruptions in the case of youths like Scott.

A final type of mood disorder to consider is intermittent explosive disorder, characterized by dramatic episodes of rage and destructiveness, seemingly without much justifying provocation, and presumed to have some underlying neuro-psychiatric cause, such as a seizure disorder or neuroendocrine cause. It is vanishingly rare to determine a cause for such disorders, but EEGs and screening blood work for thyroid disorders are often performed. In badly traumatized youths, with episodic rages, it is not uncommon for them to "black out" and not recall what destructive things they say or do in the course of a rage episode. These blackouts may be a result of full or partial dissociation, based on PTSD, or more often represent severe cognitive and memory disruption commonly experienced during extremes episodes of emotional arousal, a sort of "affective storm." Usually, with patience and diligence, the person can partially or wholly reconstruct what happened during the incident and what triggered it, unlike the complete amnesia of an ictal episode.

Other considerations for differential diagnosis in cases of complex trauma include reactive attachment disorder (RAD) and disinhibited social engagement disorder (DSED). These disorders arise in the context of severe or repeated disruption of parent–child attachment in early childhood and result in a variety of problems mostly related to patterns of social interaction and relationships. Strictly speaking, RAD and DSED can be considered specific forms of complex trauma, with the essential trauma being the threat of or actual loss of the protective parental relationship, resulting in extreme episodes of anxiety or depression from abandonment. The variety of symptoms—including absence of social connection, excessive or inappropriate social connection, testing or trust violations in relationships, anxiety and mood dysregulation in response to relationships—often evolve over time in adulthood into antisocial, borderline, or even psychopathic patterns of social interaction. In many cases of complex trauma, such as Scott's, in which there were repeated incidents of parental neglect, abuse, or abandonment, there will also be elements of RAD and DSED to address without meeting the full diagnostic criteria.

It is also important to consider the possibility of co-occurring psychopathy in a case like Scott's. Although not fully described in the DSM, the characteristics of psychopathy have been well described in the criminology literature, and recent neurophysiological and brain studies of individuals with psychopathic or callous-unemotional traits have lent credence to the validity of this subset of antisocial personality types. In any assessment of a youth with severe conduct disorder, it is important to ascertain the likelihood of significant psychopathic traits, which are well captured in assessments such as the Hare Psychopathy Checklist, including characteristics like lack of remorse or empathy; glib, superficial affect; manipulative and deceptive behavior; narcissism; callous-unemotional reactivity; and lack of guilt. The presence of psychopathic traits predicts a much more persistent and potentially dangerous form of antisocial disorder, as well as treatment resistance. In cases like Scott, a history of complex trauma in early childhood can result in blunted emotionality, numbing, and a loss of empathy and remorse toward what may be perceived as a dangerous world. These symptoms are common reactions to trauma, and in the absence of deliberate exploitation or deception of others for self-serving reasons, they may not indicate psychopathy.

ETIOLOGY AND PATHOGENESIS

Scott presents as an angry and defensive young man, unrepentant about his very serious and violent actions, without the kind of remorse one would hope for, but typical of a youth who has been through significant abuse and exposure to violence. He is somewhat numb to violence, and remorse, if it exists at all, is reserved for his very closest family members, such as his grandmother and little brother. He is unemotional and indifferent when describing the significant traumas he suffered as a child. He is hostile and suspicious of the clinician at first, showing the kind of mistrust typical of abuse victims, but also typical of the classic trait of hostile attributional bias (HAB), described by Ken Dodge and colleagues in many youths with conduct disorder. This type of pervasive mistrust in relationships falls short of being paranoid in a psychotic sense, but certainly impairs the development of happy and healthy relationships. As a result, many conduct-disordered youths form alliances or associate with other antisocial youths, rather than developing close friendships. Association with other antisocial youths often leads to normalization or sanctioning of deviant behaviors such as truancy, theft, vandalism, intimidation, fighting, and substance abuse.

Large studies of populations at risk for either conduct disorder or childhood maltreatment have revealed significant overlap in the prevalent risk factors contributing to each. For example, parental problems such as substance abuse, mental illness, teenage or single parenthood, high school dropout, poor parenting skills, and parental criminality have all been associated with both maltreatment and conduct problems. Genetic influences and familial patterns have been shown to predict mood disorders, criminality, and PTSD. In Scott's case, his biological father was a substance abuser, with violent and criminal tendencies, in and out of jail and prison for most of Scott's life, and thought to have possibly untreated mood disorder. His mother, Marie, has a history of early and severe substance abuse, often associated with bipolar disorder in females, and also has a history of childhood sexual abuse. Because Marie has been resistant to referrals for treatment, these disorders have not been officially diagnosed or treated.

Beyond genetics, shared environmental influences are even more potent predictors of externalizing and antisocial behaviors, and PTSD is by definition caused by an experiential trauma. So Scott's exposure to adversity at the hands of Lashawn and his mother were likely strong contributors to his problems. It is also becoming increasingly clear that gene–environment interactions, such as epigenetic processes (experiential or environmental insults that act to modify genomic expression) can preferentially "push" certain haplotypes in the direction of psychopathology. For example, individuals with early life maltreatment who also possess certain genetic monoamine oxidase (MAO) haplotypes are more likely to develop conduct disorder later in life than are maltreated individuals who possess a different genetic MAO haplotype. The relevance of MAO haplotypes to PTSD and conduct disorder arises from the knowledge that monoamine neurotransmitter abnormalities have been found in anxiety, mood, aggression, and impulse control disorders. In Scott's case, treatment with antidepressant medication initially improved his mood and decreased aggression, but over time was discontinued because he felt it was no longer necessary.

To explain the fairly significant genetic contribution to antisocial behavior, as seen in adopted away twin studies (40–60%), as well as the fairly high prevalence of antisocial behavioral traits in the population at large, evolutionary selective forces have been suggested by some theorists. It has been noted in ethologic population studies that the competing social-behavioral strategies of reciprocal altruism versus cheating will both be maintained by evolutionary selective pressures to some degree in social organisms over time. Specifically, certain antisocial behaviors, including lying, cheating, stealing, and aggressive behaviors can be maintained and perpetuated in a large population of reciprocators, until the antisocial individual is discovered and rejected, forcing him or her to move to a different group of reciprocators and resume his or her deceptive behaviors until discovered and excluded from the group again. Nonetheless, antisocial individuals are thus able to mate and procreate their genetic package without much investment, then move on to deceive the next mate.

Other risk factors that are commonly found in populations of conduct-disordered youths and antisocial characters are various cognitive and educational impairments, most notably low IQ, and language disorders, such as dyslexia, speech, and reading disorders. Scott had speech impairments and reading delays and was suspected of having ADHD, another risk factor for serious conduct problems. These attentional and language impairments are particularly challenging in the school and classroom environment and often result in educational frustration or failure, increasing the likelihood of school dropout. Educational failure in turn increases the risk of social marginalization of the youth, and development of substance abuse and affiliation with other marginalized or antisocial youths. Many youths like Scott are identified with special educational needs and placed in special classes for help, and although some may benefit, others succumb to the negative influences of congregating disruptive disorders into special classes or separate schools.

Another perspective from which to view the development of certain antisocial behaviors is by understanding them to be survival strategies developed in certain stressful contexts. In the case of Scott, stealing and hoarding food and money might have arisen in part as a response to his early deprivation and neglect of his needs by his mother, who was impoverished and preoccupied with her substance abuse, leaving Scott and his brother to fend for themselves. Habitual lying can arise in situations where effective deception can help one avoid receiving a severe beatings or harsh punishment. The use of intimidation and bullying can arise in environments where power, authority, loyalty, or compliance is maintained by threats or aggression, rather than love or strong attachments. Chronic anger or hostility, and hostile attribution bias projected onto the surrounding world can arise as a protective strategy, based on chronic mistrust in unreliable relationships within chaotic or abusive families.

Aggression or violence may be the most concerning symptom to emerge out of the development of PTSD into conduct disorder. As a behavioral symptom, severe early childhood aggression has been shown in longitudinal studies to be one of the most enduring problems in psychiatry. Aggression and violence have also been shown to be self-perpetuating, creating cycles of violence in families and communities that are extremely hard to break. Theorists have tended to divide aggression into two separate types: reactive aggression and proactive (planful) aggression. Reactive aggression is thought of as emotionally driven, most often a defensive response to a threat or a perceived threat. Brain studies have shown that defensive and aggressive reflexes involve a cascade of neural responses, starting with an activated amygdala, which sends signals to activate the fight or flight response through the hypothalamic-pituitary-adrenal (HPA) axis and sympathetic nervous system (SNS), while temporarily inhibiting the prefrontal cortex (PFC) and the parasympathetic nervous system. Reactive aggression is a normal emergency response system with important survival functions, but the system can become dysregulated as a result of severe or repeated trauma.

Proactive or planful aggression, sometimes called "instrumental" aggression, seems to have a different behavioral function and has been shown to have different underlying brain mechanisms. Theorists have thought that instrumental aggression arose in the context of hunting for prey and other organized types of aggression, such as dominance displays and organized warfare. In instrumental aggression, brain studies have shown minimal activation, or even suppression, of the amygdala, the HPA, and the SNS. This allows for the use of the PFC and cortex to plan, problem solve, and remain "cool-headed" in such situations. In certain antisocial or conduct-disordered individuals, planned aggression can be used excessively or deliberately to gain power, control, or resources that should be attained by prosocial means. In the extreme case of psychopathic individuals (a small subset of antisocial individuals), brain studies have shown that they have underreactive amygdalas, HPA, and SNS, and as a consequence have very little response to even very emotionally charged stimuli. It is believed that this hyporesponsiveness may explain the callous-unemotional personality trait seen in psychopathic individuals. Unfortunately, the lack of emotional reactivity may also explain why psychopaths seem to have no empathy and are capable of terrible, planned, interpersonal aggression with little or no remorse.

The amygdala serves to attach emotional salience to experiences, most notably fear. It is believed that the amygdala may play a role in the development of guilt in healthy individuals, who learn to "fear" the loss of an important relationship if they violate the social contract. This has clear implications for the development of healthy attachment behavior. In psychopaths, and to a lesser degree in other antisocial individuals, a less reactive amygdala may generate less fear about mistreating others in interactions, and hence less guilt and weaker or indifferent attachments. It is not known whether chronic or repeated abuse might weaken or blunt the reactivity of the amygdala, with a similar result. It certainly seems possible, as it has been shown that HPA and cortisol reactivity is decreased in repeatedly traumatized individuals. It is likely that either nature or nurture might result in a less reactive amygdala, with resultant consequences.

It may be even more common for victims of abuse and conduct-disordered individuals to have hyperaroused and excessively reactive neuroendocrine systems. Excessive arousal is often manifested by sleep disturbance, almost ubiquitous in this population, with or without nightmares. Startle response is often elevated. Hypervigilance and subpsychotic paranoia are often present. Measures of 24-hour cortisol secretion are elevated in some subpopulations of trauma victims and suppressed in others. Ironically, it may be that an excessively reactive HPA system is preferable to a blunted system. As noted, an excessively blunted neuroendocrine system may manifest itself as an individual who is cold, unemotional, poorly attachable, or even psychopathic. One study of early intervention with oppositional defiant–disordered children showed that the more behaviorally impaired children had less reactive HPA systems and that behavioral improvement with the intervention was correlated with increased HPA reactivity.

In the case of Scott, as in most individuals with aggression, there is some mix of reactive and planned aggressive behaviors. This is not surprising, given that he was clearly a victim of early neglect and abuse, causing the development of emotional reactivity, as well as growing up in a family with Lashawn as a model for how instrumental aggression can be used to intimidate and control others. As he grew up, Scott had plenty of examples of reactive aggression, with frequent fights at school, anger outbursts resulting in property damage, and eventually serious assaults on staff in treatment programs. He also used instrumental aggression at times, being recruited by local gang members to beat up rival drug dealers in his home town and confronting and assaulting a boy in high school who had been talking to his girlfriend. Both types of aggression are important to treat but have different underlying mechanisms, and thus require different treatment approaches.

NATURAL COURSE WITHOUT TREATMENT

The natural course of conduct disorder in the context of complex trauma begins with the interaction of early developmental risk and protective factors. For example, congenital infant temperament types, such as difficult temperament or inhibited temperament, can pose risk for or protection from the development of conduct disorder, respectively. Ironically, these two temperament types serve as risk and protection for the effect of early childhood trauma as well, but in the reverse direction. In Scott's case, early temperament was neither particularly difficult nor inhibited, though he had a single, teenage mother, poor attachment, and an antisocial father to begin his burden of risk factors.

The onset of conduct problems often begins in early latency age children, in the form of oppositional defiant disorder (ODD). Subtypes of ODD include children with comorbid ADHD, and more recent studies have suggested a subtype with a significant dysphoric and irritable mood component. Not surprisingly, these comorbidities worsen the course of problems. In spite of this, as many as 50% of children with ODD remit as they mature, whereas the other half progress to the development of conduct disorder. Early onset of conduct disorder, as opposed to adolescent onset, has a worse prognosis and is more likely to persist into adult antisocial behavior. As with ODD, comorbid ADHD with conduct disorder is a particularly persistent form. Nonetheless, as many as half of all youths diagnosed with conduct disorder in childhood will not go on to develop adult antisocial personality disorder.

The morbidity and mortality of untreated conduct disorder is high, with higher rates of mood disorders, substance abuse, and suicide than comparison populations of youths. Progression to antisocial personality disorder and incarceration occurs in half of all of those with childhood conduct disorder, and comorbid callous-unemotional (psychopathic) traits predict a particularly persistent form of antisocial disorder. Longitudinal studies of antisocial personality disorder have shown that for many men, antisocial patterns of behavior decline dramatically as they reach 40 years of age, but this is not the case for those with psychopathic traits. Naturalistic longitudinal studies have also shown that two common pathways to the desistence of adult antisocial behaviors include pursuit of a military career or entering into a stable, committed marriage.

The course of untreated complex trauma is a bit less well understood, in part due to the lack of a discrete diagnosis and the divergence of outcomes. However, the morbidities of untreated PTSD include significant anxiety and mood disorders, substance abuse, increased rates of suicide and suicide attempts, and severe personality disorders, such as borderline personality disorder. Large reviews of patients with schizophrenia have revealed eight-fold rates of childhood abuse compared with control populations, suggesting a role for trauma in the development of psychotic disorders. It is also well documented that PTSD symptoms are extremely persistent, often continuing to manifest in elderly patients.

EVIDENCE-BASED TREATMENTS OPTIONS

For extreme cases of complex trauma and conduct disorder with violent or aggressive behavior, it is often the case that youths are briefly admitted for psychiatric hospitalization or admitted to longer term residential treatment. This is often prompted by the need to attain safety and security while the necessary outpatient treatment elements are put in place. Treating conduct-disordered youths in group settings, also known as "congregate care," seems to make sense from the perspective of economies of scale and centralizing resources and expertise to work with this challenging population. However, a number of problems emerge from this approach. First, removal of a youth from their home and community, even if it is a dysfunctional setting, has been shown to act as an additional risk factor for the youth. Placement among other antisocial youths, in group settings, no matter how skilled and structured the treatment providers are, creates hazards for exposure to unsavory new behaviors and accommodation to antisocial norms and habits. Some experts refer to this deleterious effect of group treatment as "deviancy training." Also, in rural areas, placing a child at a distant treatment center makes it very difficult to engage in regular family or in-home treatment, due to transportation limitations. Finally, many outcome studies have concluded that behavioral gains made in residential or hospital treatment centers do not easily generalize to the home and community, so that a youth's "institutional adjustment" is not necessarily a good indicator of prognosis in the real world. Nonetheless, group and especially secure treatment settings for severe conduct disorder are a permanent part of the treatment continuum and may be the lesser of two evils when the alternative is a dangerous lifestyle in the community.

On a more hopeful note, treatment efficacy studies have shown that arranging for treatment in the home or community is more effective than use of inpatient or residential treatment, though many communities lack the comprehensive array of outpatient services needed to treat this complex group of youths. One exemplary mode of evidence-based treatment, known as multisystemic therapy (MST), specifically and intensively targets the risk factors that contribute to and perpetuate antisocial behaviors. For example, MST provides an in-home social worker several times a week to identify and target such risk factors as parental substance abuse, hostile-coercive parenting, youth association with negative peers, lack of communication with school personnel, and lack of connection to existing community resources. MST also provides case management to coordinate between the family and needed mental health services, schools, social services, and so on. Follow-up studies of MST and comparable approaches, which build resilience and protective factors by targeting the youth, their activities, family function, and garner helpful resources for the youth's life, have shown lasting improvement in function and a decrease in recidivism to the juvenile justice system.

Other discrete, less comprehensive interventions have also shown evidence of efficacy for conduct-disordered youths and families. Parent management training (PMT) is an evidence-based treatment for disruptive and conduct-disordered behaviors, which relies on working with parents to improve their parental behavioral modification skills. It includes defining acceptable and unacceptable behaviors, teaching parents to give active attention and planned ignoring of undesirable behaviors, how to praise, improved rule and limit setting, and how to maintain consistency in rewards and punishments, such as brief time-outs. The effect of parent training is increased with younger children with ODD, which is sometimes a precursor to more serious conduct problems. A variety of studies on parent behavioral training programs that have incorporated the key elements of PMT show clinically significant improvements in as few as three training sessions, and improvements comparable to medication effects for children with ADHD. Interestingly, parent training interventions with ODD children have been shown to enhance cortisol reactivity in the children, which correlated with behavioral and interpersonal improvement. Effective parent training approaches have been encapsulated in several popular books including *1-2-3 Magic* (Phelan, 2010).

Another effective set of discrete interventions, with a broad evidence base, is the range of social problem-solving interventions. As early as the 1970s, Spivak and Shure had shown that teaching three- and four-year old children how to come together, with a peer and a teacher or parent, and talk about feelings, problem solve, and make apologies, can have a profound effect on the behavior of these children, even years later in middle school. Since that time, many similar interventions targeting social problem-solving and conflict resolution have been shown effective in decreasing problem behavior and aggression, improving socialization, and even enhancing academic performance. Certain social problem-solving interventions, which also include skill building for stress coping and affect regulation, are especially well suited to address many of the problems in traumatized, conduct-disordered youths. These types of interventions have borrowed cognitive behavioral therapy (CBT) elements from dialectical behavioral therapy, pioneered for borderline personality disorder by Marsha Linehan. Some advantages of these types of interventions is that they can be administered in any setting, including the home, clinics, schools, treatment centers, individual, or group modality. Not surprisingly, studies of resilient children have shown that those who have the ability to rise above adversity have naturally good problem-solving skills, good social skills, empathy, likeability, humor, and the ability to get along with others.

Cognitive behavioral approaches to directly address antisocial behaviors have a historically poor track record of success. Many of these interventions have been tried in prisons with adult antisocial personalities, and have most often been unsuccessful or even worsened the behaviors. One exception is a cognitive behavioral approach developed by Stanton Samenow and Samuel Yochelson, which relies on the voluntary participation of habitual offenders in an intensive CBT program, which involves identifying and confronting cognitive distortions that lead to criminal thinking and behaviors. Modifications of this approach have been adopted for use with adolescents and in correctional settings, as well as with substance abusers, with some success. The intervention focuses on helping individuals self-identify their thinking errors and engage in relapse prevention to avoid resumption of self-defeating and harmful behaviors. A significant limitation of these cognitive behavioral and relapse prevention approaches is that they require highly motivated participants who are ready for change. Many antisocial individuals are unwilling or unable to abandon their long-established patterns of feeling, thinking, and acting.

For Scott and others with active symptoms of PTSD, in addition to behavioral and social problem-solving interventions, evidence-based psychotherapy for trauma is indicated. The gold standard for child and youth trauma victims is Trauma-Focused Cognitive Behavioral Therapy (TFCBT), developed by Cohen, Deblinger, and Mannarino. TFCBT is a highly adaptable and modular approach to treating PTSD in children and incorporates elements of psychoeducation, traditional CBT, narrative therapy, prolonged exposure therapy (Edna Foa), parent–child psychotherapy, and safety education. A maximum benefit for this particular type of psychotherapy relies on the involvement of the parent or key adult to engage in conjoint therapy sessions and to "bear witness" as the youth discloses the effects of the trauma on his or her life. For simple PTSD, the entire package of TFCBT can be administered by a trained clinician in 10–15 sessions. For complex PTSD, such as Scott, with other comorbidities, a full course of TFCBT may take up to six months.

Treatment for attachment problems is an important component to overall approach to cases like Scott's. It has been shown in early intervention studies that training new mothers in healthy, secure attachment techniques can positively affect developmental outcomes. These findings have been replicated even in intervention studies of therapeutic parenting of severely neglected, adopted infants. Efficacy studies are far less clear for attachment interventions for older children with attachment-related problems, but invariably include elements of psychoeducation, parent skills training, collaborative problem-solving techniques, and stress management for the parents. Controversial approaches, such as regressive parent–child psychotherapies, holding and restraining techniques, and residential treatment centers for attachment are not well proven and may be countertherapeutic. In Scott's case, the treatment center used an assertive mentoring approach to develop a trustworthy working relationship with him as he engaged in a range of competence building activities and required ongoing discussion and cognitive processing of disruptions or hostility in the working relationship. He also had the benefit of his longtime attachment relationship with his grandmother, which was fostered and maintained during his stay, while his troublesome relationship with his mother was normalized and contextualized for him over time.

To fully address the treatment needs of conduct-disordered youths with complex trauma histories, consideration of medication is often warranted. As with most medication approaches in child psychiatry, the priority targets are identifiable diagnostic syndromes, which may be comorbid or contributory to the clinical picture. For example, Scott had elements of ADHD that were identifiable back into early childhood and was treated with stimulants for years. Over time, mood and anger problems became more prominent, and treatment providers rightly began to consider the use of mood stabilizers and atypical antipsychotic medications to decrease aggression and improve impulse control. In the course of Scott's problems, the emergence of antisocial behaviors and aggression effectively masked his significant underlying depression and anxiety and the traumas that created it. In this context, the antidepressant and anxiolytic medications are often passed over, due to lack of self-report of depression, as well as a well-founded fear that selective serotonin reuptake inhibitors may either activate or exacerbate any underlying mood disorder. He developed strong psychological defenses against feeling the pain, and therefore never reported it to evaluators, and he became seen as a cold-hearted, remorseless, aggressive conduct disorder.

Nonetheless, certain medications have been shown in various studies to have beneficial effects on aggression and impulse control. These include stimulants and alpha-2 adrenergic agonists for aggression and impulse control with comorbid ADHD, as well as lithium, valproate, carbamazepine, and certain atypical antipsychotics for mood-driven aggression. Risperidone in particular has shown benefit for aggression in youths with pervasive developmental disorders and cognitive impairments. In traumatized youths and those with hostile attribution bias, the antipsychotic/antiparanoia effect of low-dose atypical antipsychotics may be helpful. There is some promise in the evolution of a class of antiaggression medications, known as "serenics" (eltoprazine, fluprazine), blocking or agonizing certain serotonin receptors, but these have been under study for over 20 years without coming to market.

CLINICAL COURSE WITH MANAGEMENT AND TREATMENT

Due to the extreme and dangerous levels of aggression shown by Scott as he was placed in increasingly structured and restrictive placements, it was ultimately decided he would require secure treatment. Without the specialized secure treatment center available, he would likely be placed into a juvenile correctional facility. Although less restrictive and more community-based options are shown to generate better clinical outcomes, Scott's level of dangerousness requires initial stabilization in a secure setting. Brief stabilization in a psychiatric hospital might be considered in a case like his, but his potential dangerousness toward staff and other patients might result in refusal to admit him, while his long-term treatment needs related to chronic trauma, attachment problems, and antisocial behaviors seemed best treated in a secure setting.

During the first few months of his stay at the residential facility, Scott was very defensive and aloof from nearly all of the staff, particularly the male staff, but he eventually began smiling and joking with the nurse, who was a soft and buxom, big-hearted woman, Ms. Fuller, whom the boys called "Ma." While tending to their medical ailments and delivering the medications to the residents, she would tease and joke with them, convincing the most resistant to take their needed medications. She would ask Scott about the trouble he was causing on the unit and began to get him to talk about the conflicts he frequently got into with the staff and peers. He nearly always projected blame onto others, never taking responsibility, and claiming injustices were perpetrated against him. She wouldn't judge or confront him, just offer some words of encouragement and give a big hug for the day.

The treatment facility had a behavioral level system based on staff trust in the safety and predictability of each resident's behavior on a week-by-week review.

The overarching behavioral approach of staff was guided by the principles of "Positive Discipline," developed by Jane Nelsen, incorporating a humane interpersonal approach and social skill–building techniques. When Scott was confronted for his problem behaviors or frustrated with rules or limits set by staff, he was capable of extreme aggression. Once, when he didn't make his behavioral level, he left the treatment team meeting and ran into the copying room and turned over the copier, smashing the glass screen and destroying the machine. He was in several fights with peers, giving one a black eye and another a broken wrist. He required physical restraint by staff on several occasions during his stay, and it often took three or more staff members to subdue him and transport him to the secure quiet room, where he would punch the concrete walls, once breaking a knuckle, requiring a cast. As part of the treatment program, after each of these major incidents, he was briefly isolated until safe, then received the consequence of a loss of some privileges, and he was also required to write out a detailed recounting of the incident, what led to it, what thoughts and feelings he had, how it affected others, and make apologies and restitution to those involved. This recounting, analysis, and interpersonal conflict resolution was called "cognitive processing." Scott refused to engage in it at first, but he soon realized that the restoration of his privileges depended on participation in processing the incident. The first few times he did a poor and superficial job of the written and verbal processing, but over time and with repetition, his processing was more thorough and genuine.

In the context of processing incidents of extreme anger, he began to realize that he was having reenactments and flashbacks of past abuse during some of these incidents. After several of his conflicts with peers and staff, he would initially say he "blacked out" and couldn't recall what he said or did during the fight or restraint. With careful processing of the incident, however, he was usually able to reconstruct what had triggered his strong emotional reactions. He also began to notice that he would sometimes hear Lashawn's voice or see brief flashes of his face in the voices or faces of the staff who yelled at him or had to restrain him. At these times he would become rageful and lose control of his behavior and emotions.

In addition to his episodes of extreme out-of-control, emotional aggression, Scott also engaged in deliberate antisocial behaviors. He was involved in sneaky, planned assaults on other residents, hiding in wait for a time to attack someone he felt had wronged him, or he was put up to it by other peers, as part of a group or gang-type rivalry. He also stole repeatedly, taking food from the resident snack shop or intimidating and stealing food from peers, then hiding or hoarding the food in his room. He would often lie and deny behaviors he was known to have done or lie to cover up for others in his group or gang. He was well aware that it was unacceptable to be a "snitch." These antisocial behaviors were confronted and sanctioned in a process that incorporated principles of restorative justice, requiring taking responsibility and making face-to-face amends with those people harmed by the actions.

Schoolwork was a challenge for Scott at the treatment center, as he struggled with reading and language, but he progressed with small class size and plenty of one-on-one help. Like many youths with his background and problems, he had been coded as a special education student, and had an individualized educational plan (IEP) that included supplementary help with his delayed reading and speech therapy for his dysarthria. For the first time in many years, he made academic progress, advanced his reading level, and proved to himself (and others) that he could function in the student role, without academic frustration or acting out. He also proved himself talented at nearly all sports and excelled on the various teams within the program.

Over time he developed productive mentored relationships with some of the male staff members around sports and vocational activities, but was consistently better when working with older female staff members. The mentoring relationships were a foundational component of the program and fraught with interpersonal conflicts when treating youths like Scott with serious attachment and mistrust problems. He was repeatedly required to process incidents of hostility, conflict, and aggression in the context of the mentor relationships, and he became better at taking some personal responsibility, understanding the effect of his actions on others, and being able to describe his own thoughts and feelings around such incidents.

He was engaged in individual psychotherapy that focused mostly on the very difficult and traumatic childhood he had. He was able to recognize the effect of his painful relationship with his mother, the violence he was exposed to by Lashawn, and the warm and positive relationship with Nanny. Through the course of psychotherapy, he and his therapist wrote a journal of his life history, detailed his traumas and his troubles, and wrote a hopeful plan for his future. They sat together with Nanny before he left, and shared it with her. Although his individual therapist was not formally trained in TFCBT at the time, she engaged in prolonged exposure therapy by repeatedly processing his past traumas with him, while also working on his current affective control and coping skills, all of which are key elements of TFCBT. In the end, Scott had awareness that some of his current feelings and behaviors were unduly influenced by negative past experiences that he no longer needed to respond to.

On admission to the facility, Scott was being treated with lithium, valproate, and quetiapine and had been doing poorly at his previous placement. He presented as dysphoric, irritable, excessively sedated at times, and impulsively aggressive. One benefit of a long-term, secure treatment center is the ability to simplify medication regimens and reassess underlying symptomatology in cases like Scott, whose treating outpatient psychiatrist may have been doing everything in her power to stabilize him. We were able to taper and simplify his medications by substituting relatively low-dose risperidone for aggression and mood stabilization and guanfacine for impulsivity and decreased autonomic arousal. Like many youths with his history, Scott had significant underlying symptoms of anxiety and depression that had never been treated medically. In part this is a result of these symptoms being masked by defensive anger, aggression, and acting out, which prioritize other medication choices but also reflect a hesitancy on the part of prescribers to use antidepressants in youths who may have comorbid bipolar disorder. The latter concern is often unwarranted, and Scott eventually benefited greatly from the addition of sertraline, which improved his mood and decreased his irritability and reactivity. Eventually, risperidone was discontinued, though he continued to benefit from guanfacine for focus and distractibility in the school setting, though he was not formally diagnosed with ADHD.

A year later, Scott, Nanny, and Derrick attended the annual reunion for the treatment facility. Scott had avoided hospitalization or incarceration and had had only one minor street scuffle. He said he was dealing with his anger by going into the back yard to cool off. He was a senior high school student in an alternative vocational school, studying automotive repair, and was thinking about enlisting in the army after high school. Nanny was asked how she managed to keep Scott on the right path, and she stated that she required him to help with chores and was firm with discipline, but her husband often accused her of "loving too much." She told me that when Scott first arrived home, the family was preparing to go to church and he asked her if he had to go, to which she responded, "not this time, but you'll need to go sometime." As they were driving away, he came running after the car and has been going to church ever since. She also told me Scott had said, "Nanny, people have told me I'm a bad person," to which she responded, "God doesn't make bad people, you're a good person who's had a hard life." Nanny expected Scott to finish high school and get a good job, and expected highly of all of the grandchildren she has helped raised. Derrick was now playing football with the coach who had tried to keep Scott on the team a few years before. Scott and Derrick frequently played catch football to enhance Derrick's skills. They visited with their mom on occasion, but both realized and accepted that their safe and dependable home was with Nanny.

Over time, with the development of a therapeutic alliance with mental health providers and staff at the residential facility, Scott was able to talk about his painful past, he got better at processing and taking responsibility for his problem behaviors, and his aggression diminished. After leaving treatment, he was able to consolidate his supportive relationships and engage in protective activities that played to his strengths to increase the odds of a better long-term life outcome.

Perhaps the most important overarching principle to embrace, when developing a treatment plan for a youth like Scott, is to tailor the interventions to the varying individual needs of the particular youth. This can only be done effectively if there has been a thorough assessment and accounting for all of the youth's risk factors and disorders, as well as the existing strengths and resilience factors that are present. In Scott's case, this includes the risk factors of poor early maternal attachment, split family, maternal substance abuse, paternal criminality, exposure to family violence, physical abuse, affiliation with negative peers, involvement in the court system, out-of-home placement, substance abuse, diagnoses of ADHD/learning disability, PTSD, and mood disorder. With all of his problems, Scott also has a number of strengths and protective resiliency factors. He has a strong and loving attachment to his grandmother and, based on this, was able to form healthy attachments to other treatment providers and staff. He is likable, with good social skills and a broad smile once he gained some trust. He is athletic and excelled at a number of sports, later playing on recreational teams in the community. He is good with hands-on learning and skills, even though his language and communication skills are limited. This allows him to do well in learning automotive repair, even though he limped to the high school finish line academically just to please Nanny. His faith is growing, his attendance at church has become regular, and the pastor has become a sort of mentor to him. He talks in therapy enough about his mother and Lashawn to come to some tolerable acceptance of what he has been through with them, as well as accepting their limitations as supportive relationships. He is happy to get his social support elsewhere. His plan and hope is to enlist in the military, and this may be a good choice for him as he accumulates other protective factors to keep him on a positive life path. (Sampson and Laub have done longitudinal studies of conduct and criminality and found that a stable marriage or a military career is a common pathway to desistence from criminality).

SYSTEMS-BASED PRACTICE ISSUES

One of the major challenges for youths like Scott is to find good-quality, evidence-based treatments within the juvenile correction system. Most treatment programs include a structured behavioral program with minimally trained safety officers, supplemented by consulting ancillary mental health providers, who may or may not be providing evidence-based interventions. Most of these programs are congregate care, many combine principles of isolation or strict discipline (wilderness, boot camps), all of which have been shown to be minimally effective or even harmful in studies of their efficacy. Alternatives such as intensive in-home, multisystemic-type therapy, and therapeutic foster care have been shown to be less expensive and more effective than any form of congregate care, but the correctional system often defaults to the forces of economies of scale and tends to favor group settings.

Within the array of juvenile services systems, there are a very limited number of secure facilities that are also structured to provide a high-quality treatment environment. In general, juvenile correctional facilities are considered to be more "therapeutic" than adult corrections, but the adequacy of treatment resources varies widely from state to state and facility to facility. It has often been argued by treatment advocates that correctional facilities of all types are by nature cold, inhospitable, neglectful, unsafe, and generally untherapeutic if not traumatic for most (if not all) residents. This is undeniable in the case of certain facilities and has spawned lawsuits by inmates and youth advocates against state agencies in a number of cases. On the other hand, it is certainly possible to find adequate facilities, providing safe and effective treatment for this difficult subset of people. Ironically, in the case of Scott and some others, the safety, structure, and stability of a secure treatment environment may be much better than the unsafe and unpredictable environment in which they were raised. It is important for the consulting clinician to weigh these complex issues in determining the appropriateness of a treatment or rehabilitation setting.

LEGAL, ETHICAL, AND CULTURAL CHALLENGES

Scott's case raises some common legal and ethical dilemmas involved in the care of youths with complex trauma that has evolved with associated severe aggression and conduct disorder. Fundamentally, there always exists a tension between the priorities of the legal system to hold offenders accountable and exact justice, and the priorities of the treatment system to habilitate or rehabilitate the person with mental illness. The dilemma arises most commonly with violent offenders, who also suffer from a serious mental illness. Scott is a young man who clearly needs treatment, but he has developed a set of behaviors that are absolutely unsafe in an unlocked setting. Although it can be argued that many of his violations have arisen in part as a result of his mental illness, he would almost certainly not meet adult criteria for criminal insanity. He not only needs treatment, he also needs to be adjudicated to a secure setting for an adequate period of treatment to safely address his aggression, which in some sense holds him accountable for his violations by depriving him of his freedom. In some cases of particularly egregious crimes committed by juveniles, the person may be committed to a treatment facility until they reach the age of legal adulthood, then be transferred to adult corrections for an additional period of incarceration, though the treatment resources in adult corrections are more limited and in great demand.

HISTORY

The recognition of the effect of trauma goes back to descriptions of "hysteria" in ancient Egypt, and around 400 BC Hippocrates incorporated stress and disruption into his homeostasis theory of illness. The concept of hysterical reactions in response to perceived sexual traumas or fantasies figured prominently in Sigmund Freud's conception of mental illness, but it was his colleagues, Pierre Janet and Abram Kardiner in the early 20th century, who drew direct connections between actual childhood or combat-related traumas and the development of PTSD-related psychopathology. Since the emergence of PTSD as an official diagnosis in 1980, conceptions of etiology have largely returned to homeostatic disruptions of anxiety, mood, cognitive preoccupations, neurotransmitters in response to past traumas. Complex PTSD was described by Judith Herman in 1992, and it implies severe and chronic forms of interpersonal trauma, when the victim is trapped in an inescapable situation, including the dependency of childhood. Bessel Van Der Kolk has described children growing up in these situations as having "developmental trauma disorder." Current deliberations on the DSM diagnosis of PTSD include trying to account for the wide variety of manifestations of trauma effects over the course of the life span.

REFERENCES AND RESOURCES

Understanding the deleterious criminogenic and neurobiological effects of early trauma and attachment problems are well described in these seminal articles:

Kaufman J, Plotsky PM, Nemeroff CB, Charney DS. Effects of early adverse experiences on brain structure and function: clinical implications. *Biol Psychiatr* 2000;48:778–90.

Lewis DO. From abuse to violence: psychophysiological consequences of maltreatment. *J Am Acad Child Adolesc Psych* 1992 May;31(3):383–91.

Phelan TW. *1-2-3 Magic: Effective Discipline for Children 2–12* (4th ed.). Glen Ellyn, IL: ParentMagic, Inc., 2010.

Valliant GE. Sociopathy as a human process. *Arch Gen Psychiatry* 1975 Feb;32(2):178–83.

An excellent discussion of the risk factors associated with antisocial behavior, and how to differentiate transient versus persistent forms of conduct disorder, for purposes of prognostication is contained in:

Moffitt TE, Caspi A. Childhood predictors differentiate life-course persistent and adolescence-limited antisocial pathways among males and females. *Devel Psychopathol* 2001;13:355–75.

A comprehensive survey of the putative mechanisms of psychosocial resilience in the face of trauma is found in the following article:

Charney DS. Psychobiological mechanisms of resilience and vulnerability: implications for successful adaptation to extreme stress. *Am J Psychiatr* 2004;161:195–216.

The *Journal of the American Academy of Child and Adolescent Psychiatry* produces practice parameters for the evaluation and understanding of a variety of childhood disorders, and a recent one exists for PTSD (vol. 49, April 2010), and a more dated version for conduct disorder (vol. 36, October 1997, with a newer version in progress).

Parenting With Love And Logic (Updated and Expanded Edition) by Foster Cline and Jim Fay (Apr 19, 2006) Nav Press.

Freedom Writers (2007), is a film that captures well the common transformation of traumatized youths into conduct disorder. Hilary Swank stars as a rookie schoolteacher assigned to a class of high-risk students in a slum high school of a gang-ridden southern California town. After she is frustrated by classroom violence and truancy in the face of traditional teaching approaches, she coaxes the students to begin writing and submitting anonymous personal journals, creating a complex tapestry of written exchanges. The narrative exchanges, with their growth and healing power, illustrate the well-known principles of trauma therapy, that narrative disclosure and processing of trauma in the context of a safe relationship can be therapeutic. The range of traumas in the lives of the students is astounding, and the developmental consequences of these traumas come to life in the here-and-now of this ultimately uplifting film.

CHAPTER **30**

Competency to Stand Trial

Conrad H. Daum, M.D.

CLINICAL PRESENTATION

Chief complaint: "I can't remember what happened." Lamont states that he took his girlfriend to the park for a picnic. He says they drank beer as they ate. He can't remember how much they drank, but he thinks that he consumed the majority of a 12-pack of beer. He doesn't remember confronting the victim. He remembers the park police putting handcuffs on him. "The next thing I remember is waking up in jail."

Present illness: An attorney calls about his client, who is in jail without bond. The summary of the facts of the case come in a letter sent to the clinician's office. The defendant is a 27-year-old African American male who was at a picnic area at a nearby park with his girlfriend and had consumed between them about 12 cans of beer. At the table next to them was a couple with their infant son. The infant's father was drinking beer while his wife was feeding the child baby food. A sudden gust of wind blew the heavily soiled bib onto the face of the defendant's girlfriend. The defendant became angry and confronted the father. An argument ensued and the defendant punched the victim, breaking his jaw. Lamont did not resist arrest when the park rangers came and charged both men with public intoxication. In addition, the defendant was charged with felony unlawful wounding. The defendant claimed no memory of the argument or the assault. This is the major reason for his attorney requesting the psychiatric evaluation, to explore a possible insanity defense.

The attorney requests a list of the evaluator's standard fees to do the evaluation at the jail. The attorney describes who would pay and when. The standard fees include an hourly rate from the time of departure from the office until return; the mileage charge is the IRS business tax deduction rate. The attorney agrees that testimony, record review, report writing, discussions with lawyers, and witness interviews will be billed the same way.

The attorney then obtains a judicial order for the evaluation at the jail. When the judicial order arrives, the evaluator's office schedules a time for the clinician to see the defendant in the jail that does not interfere with meals or security procedures. The schedule allows for the trip to the jail each way, the entry into the jail, the exit from the jail, and an evaluation time of two hours.

The day of the evaluation, the evaluator's office calls the jail medical department and arranges a visitation time. The nurse provides information about any medical and behavioral problems the inmate has had. The nurse also faxes the list of medications and treatments administered.

At the jail parking lot, lighters, knives, cell phones, and other prohibited items belonging to the clinician remain locked in the car. Brought into the jail are materials to make notes, the court order, and a driver's license for identification. The jail personnel screen for prohibited items, and then provide an office for the interview.

The defendant comes to the interview in handcuffs. The guard states that he will have to stay in the room because the defendant is on security precautions for fighting with another inmate. The defendant is informed of confidentiality issues as well as the purpose of the visit. The defendant learns that the visit is for an evaluation only. Any medical treatment would be provided by jail personnel. The defendant receives instructions on how to obtain treatment at the jail. The defendant then signs a release of information to the attorney, the jail medical officers, and other parties who would share with the defense any information about the case.

Legal history: Lamont has previous convictions for one count of possession of marijuana, one count of driving while intoxicated, and two counts of assault while intoxicated. He has no felony convictions. He was on probation for the last assault charge when he was arrested. He reports no juvenile offenses. He's been in jail "a few times" for child support problems.

Psychiatric history: There has been no previous mental health or substance abuse treatment except for court-ordered alcohol abuse classes associated with the DUI offense. Lamont reports having suicidal thoughts from time to time, but he denies any suicide attempts. He reports multiple episodes of depression lasting weeks at a time. These episodes included insomnia, fatigue, problems concentrating, suicidal thoughts, and feelings of worthlessness. He describes having irritable mood swings with racing thoughts, distractibility, and impulsive actions that lead to serious consequences. These episodes frequently last for a week or more. The Mood Disorder Questionnaire score at the interview is 10/13; this score indicates possible bipolar spectrum disorder problems. He acknowledges using alcohol and various street drugs to help calm down. He has used drugs and alcohol this way since adolescence. He smokes about one pack per day of cigarettes and expresses no interest in reducing his tobacco consumption.

Medical history: Lamont had an overnight hospital stay for a concussion suffered in a bar fight. Otherwise he has no medical or surgical problems. He reports taking no medications prior to incarceration. The jail reports that he has taken no medications while there.

Family history: Lamont has two healthy daughters, ages three and seven, by two different mothers. He seldom visits his children. He has two older brothers and no sisters. Both brothers have a history of alcohol and drug problems. Both have spent time in jail for misdemeanors. His father died two years prior of a myocardial infarction. His father had lost his driver's license due to a habitual offender conviction for driving while intoxicated with alcohol. The father had a history of poorly controlled hypertension and diabetes. His mother is living with good general physical health. She has been treated for many years as an outpatient for chronic anxiety and depression.

Social history: Lamont was born, raised, and lived his entire life in the local area. He reports no history of physical, emotional, or sexual abuse. He completed the 10th grade, then dropped out of school at age 18 because of repeated failing grades in reading and writing. He acknowledges numerous trips to the high school principal for fighting and disturbing the classroom. He denies ever being suspended from school. He was never married. He has no history of military service. He lost his driver's license because of failure to pay child support. He has been making regular payments to the court clerk in an effort to regain driving privileges. He works as a construction laborer. He's been fired from numerous jobs for arguing at work. He has not attended church in many years. He gives his address as the same as his girlfriend and her two daughters. They have lived together about two years. He has no medical insurance.

Review of systems is negative for allergies, seizure symptoms, and current health problems.

Mental status examination: Lamont is a black male appearing his stated age. He is clean and wears the jail clothing appropriately. His gait, psychomotor actions, and mannerisms are appropriate. He is alert and calm. He is pleasant and cooperative. His responses to questions are appropriate. His speech is clear and understandable. The Mini Mental State Examination score is 26/30. He indicates an awareness of the nature of the interview and its implications for his case. He is able to discuss events about his recent jail fight. He is aware of the reason for his current security precautions. He knows why he is in jail. He had some problems stating the date but not the year or month. He has a good ability to discuss the events of his past history and to discuss the events surrounding his incarceration. His concentration and attention on the questions are fine during the one-hour interview. His answers are expressed well. His use of English words and phrases are satisfactory. His affect is neither anxious nor irritable. His mood is mildly depressed, and it is congruent with his thought content and current situation. His thought processes are logical and coherent. He has realistic expectations about possible punishments. His associations are intact. There are no signs of delusions or hallucinations. The abstract reasoning is consistent with his educational achievement. He has trouble with the Mini Mental State Exam calculations. He does not indicate much interest in current events. He acknowledges memory lapses in the past during times of heavy use of alcohol. He recognizes that his use of alcohol is associated with the current incarceration. He expresses an interest in getting help with his irritable mood swings and alcohol abuse. He does not exhibit signs of hallucinations, illusions, or derealization in the interview. He does not express any current thoughts of suicide, or of hurting others. The Sheehan MINI suicide risk score is 6/33. He expresses chronic frequent thoughts of suicide on close questioning.

IMPAIRMENT IN FUNCTIONING

The *Dusky* case listed in References and Resources discusses the criteria for competency to stand trial. During the evaluation, the defendant indicates a risk for unmanageable courtroom behaviors because of his recent jail fight. Based on behavior during the interview, he seems to be able to control himself in the courtroom if he chooses. The defendant appears able to relate to an attorney, weigh defense options, work with an attorney to plan the legal strategy, and consider a plea bargain. He accurately discusses the role of the judge, prosecutor, and other participants in the trial. He indicates an awareness of courtroom procedures and how to challenge witness statements. He appears able to testify relevantly and is motivated to help himself. He understands the charges, penalties, and possible outcomes. The examination shows that he has "sufficient present ability to consult with his attorney with a reasonable degree of rational understanding and a rational as well as factual understanding of the proceedings against him." He presents with a capacity "to assist in preparing his defense." The conclusion is that he is competent to stand trial.

In the sanity evaluation (assessing criminal responsibility), the only significant mental disorder during the offense was self-imposed intoxication. In virtually all jurisdictions this is not a diagnosis compatible with an insanity defense. The start and end times of the face-to-face encounter are noted, and the interview is concluded.

DSM DIAGNOSIS

The clinician arrives at a primary diagnosis of Alcohol and Nicotine Use Disorders (formerly abuse and dependence), and a provisional diagnosis of Bipolar Disorder NOS (Not Otherwise Specified). It is suspected that he has Intermittent Explosive Disorder. Other problems include a history of a Specific Learning Disorder in Reading and Written Expression. He reports no allergies. He is unable to sustain employment, and he has active legal charges of unlawful wounding. The bipolar disorder NOS diagnosis fits his clinical presentation. There is the self-report on the Mood Disorder Questionnaire of hypomanic episodes. The defendant has a history of irritability. The examination contains signs of major depression. What is not clear is the etiology of the hypomanic episodes. Are the episodes primary, due to medical problems, or due to substance abuse? For the forensic conclusions, the etiology is not relevant. For clinical purposes the etiology is important.

EPIDEMIOLOGY

Attorneys frequently request a competency or sanity evaluation during the pre-trial phase. The defense attorney is required to provide a zealous defense. This defense often includes exploring for mental illness as a cause, or partial excuse, of the criminal behavior. The majority of evaluations do not find information to completely exonerate the defendant. Even if there is no insanity defense, mental examinations can provide information helpful at sentencing. The forensic conclusions can provide reasons to divert the individual to a community-based sentence rather than require lengthy incarceration.

U.S. National Institutes of Health surveys have found lifetime prevalences of over 13% for alcohol misuse disorders, over 6% for other drug misuse disorders, and over 28% for comorbid addiction and mental disorders. The prevalence of lifetime substance misuse is about 75% in persons with a history of incarceration. The case of *Powell v. Texas* (listed in the References and Resources section) discusses how courts manage criminal acts associated with intoxication.

ETIOLOGY AND PATHOGENESIS

The pathogenesis of Lamont's problems is a combination of family genetics, family milieu, poor impulse control, temper outbursts, and use of alcohol to cope with dysphoria. His father had alcohol problems. His mother has a history of anxiety and depression. His siblings have had their own problems with substance misuse and the law. The diagnoses of bipolar disorder NOS with alcohol use disorder address the importance of treating the mental disorder and alcoholism concurrently.

NATURAL COURSE WITHOUT TREATMENT

Lamont presents with a lack of awareness of social resources to develop behaviors that conform to requirements of the law. Without treatment he is likely to experience a lengthy incarceration followed by repeated legal offenses. Some defendants have no desire to change their lifestyle. Other defendants like Lamont express a motivation to change. Judges are often willing to lessen incarceration time if the terms of probation and parole include some rehabilitative treatment plan that reduces the probability of criminal recidivism.

EVIDENCE-BASED TREATMENT OPTIONS

The treatment options are limited by available medical resources and the person's motivation. If Lamont will cooperate with the treatment plan, the jail social worker and the probation officer can help him obtain resources for treatment in the jail and in the community. The most successful treatment for this patient will consist of substance abuse counseling that also addresses biological, psychological, and sociological relapse triggers associated with his mood swings. Contingency reinforcement is an accepted modality to treat addictions. Lamont has the motivation to reduce his time of incarceration by cooperating with mental health and substance abuse treatment. The contingency of freedom from incarceration is a strong reinforcer. This reinforcer can keep him motivated to participate in the months and years of therapy he will likely need. It is important to view addictions as diseases of frequent relapse. The treatment should provide patient education for Lamont on how to avoid turning a temporary lapse of sobriety into a full-blown relapse. The therapy should address his anger management problems. Relapse prevention also can include an exploration of psychodynamic causes of his depression.

CLINICAL COURSE WITH MANAGEMENT AND TREATMENT

The management and treatment are facilitated by the defendant's cooperation. The defendant expresses a willingness to comply with a recommendation in the report for outpatient treatment of probable bipolar disorder NOS and alcohol use disorder. This provides an option for community diversion from lengthy incarceration. The defendant is willing to ask the jail doctor to evaluate him for suitability for treatment of the mood symptoms. The jail guard agrees to help the defendant fill out the necessary paperwork for the medical request. The case of *Estelle* (noted in the References and Resources section) discusses the obligation of the jail to provide medical care for prisoners.

SYSTEMS-BASED PRACTICE ISSUES

Issues confronting the examiner include the slightly different criteria for sanity and competency depending on the legal jurisdiction. The examiner must be familiar with the definitions and how they are applied in each territory. The qualifications for the examiners are set by law. In some cases, a social worker may give the legal opinion. In other cases, especially those requiring testing, only a psychologist has the expertise. If the defendant has pertinent medical problems, a psychiatrist may be needed. The options to treat defendants vary by the legal jurisdiction's resources and the defendant's personal resources.

LEGAL AND ETHICAL CHALLENGES

Jurisdictions vary on the confidentiality of information in criminal evaluations. These issues include whether the prosecutor can subpoena the guard to reveal what was said in the interview and the limits of confidentiality for an attorney's agent, such as the examiner. The examiner has an ethical duty to report or otherwise clinically manage any signs and symptoms of dangerousness to self or others.

A big challenge in performing forensic evaluations is to avoid bias. The best attitude to take is that of a friend of the court to help the judge or jury decide the verdict. An attitude of a "hired gun" can bias the legal fact finder against the consultant's testimony. Each defendant and crime is different, and each case deserves to be looked at from many different perspectives. Each defendant is guaranteed due process under the law by the U.S. Constitution. The examiner's job is to help provide the due process necessary to keep the constitutional guarantee.

REFERENCES AND RESOURCES

Dusky v. United States, 362 U.S. 402 (1960). The U.S. Supreme Court ruled that for trial competency the defendant must have the ability to consult with his attorney. The defendant must also have a rational and factual understanding of the proceedings.

Estelle v. Gamble, 429 U.S. 97 (1976). The U.S. Supreme Court ruled that "deliberate indifference" to an inmate's medical needs is cruel and unusual punishment barred by the Constitution.

Folstein MF, Folstein SE, McHugh PR. Mini-Mental State: a practical method for grading the cognitive state of patients for the clinician. *J Psychiatr Res* 1973;12:196–98.

Hirschfeld R, et al. Development and validation of a screening instrument for bipolar spectrum disorder: the Mood Disorder Questionnaire. *Am J Psychiatr* 2000;157:1873–75.

Lipsitt PD, Lelos D, McGarry AL. Competency for trial: a screening instrument. *Am J Psychiatr* 1971;128:105–9.

Powell v. Texas, 392 U.S. 514 (1968). The U.S. Supreme Court held that self-imposed intoxication alone is not sufficient to excuse criminal accountability.

Rosner R. *Principles and Practice of Forensic Psychiatry*. London: Arnold, 2003.

Sheehan D, et al. Mini International Neuropsychiatric Interview. *J Clin Psychiatr* 1999; 60(suppl. 18):45. This is a screening instrument for severity of suicidal thinking.

CHAPTER **31**

Disability or Malingering

Conrad H. Daum, M.D.

CLINICAL PRESENTATION

Chief complaint: "Back pain."

History of present illness: Allison is a 37-year-old divorced Caucasian woman who is referred to the office for evaluation and treatment by her workers' compensation insurance case worker. About six weeks prior to the referral, she injured her back lifting a bag of grass seed. At the time she was working as a cashier at a local hardware store. After the injury, the store manager drove her to the store's occupational medicine clinic. The clinic evaluated her and sent her to an orthopedic surgeon. Initial physical exams and x-rays showed no abnormal findings except for exquisite pain to palpation in the left lumbrosacral area. She was prescribed tramadol with acetaminophen and physical therapy. She was given a six-week medical leave of absence. On reevaluation two weeks prior to the referral, she again had no physical findings except some mild lumbrosacral pain on palpation. She insisted to the physician that she had problems with walking, standing, sitting, and lying down for more than an hour or two. She stated that her sleep was punctuated by frequent nocturnal awakenings when she turned over in bed. The orthopedic surgeon prescribed duloxetine 60 mg daily for the pain. He switched her from tramadol to codeine with acetaminophen because of possible side effects with the tramadol and duloxetine combination. An MRI of the lumbrosacral area found no abnormalities. The orthopedic surgeon diagnosed the pain to be of psychiatric etiology. She was then referred for psychiatric evaluation.

Psychiatric history: Allison reports no prior mental health treatment except for a few months of counseling when her husband separated from her five years before. During the separation and divorce, her family physician prescribed several different antidepressants; she does not recall their names. She recalls stopping several of them because "they made me feel more nervous than I already was." She describes feeling chronically anxious since the divorce. The symptoms include feeling on edge, frequent nocturnal awakenings, and irritability. She says that the anxiety associated with the antidepressants was "different." She is a nonsmoker. She drinks a glass of wine with dinner two or three times a month. She never had any problems associated with heavy alcohol use. She smoked marijuana a few times in high school. She stopped marijuana when she decided that it caused her to feel dysphoric. She never experimented with other illegal drugs. She denies misusing prescription drugs. Her legal history is negative except for two speeding tickets. She denies thinking about suicide. There is no history of suicide attempts by her or other family members.

Medical history: Allison has received treatment for hypertension with hydrochlorothiazide for the past year. She had two normal pregnancies with two normal deliveries. She had a bilateral tubal ligation following the delivery of her last child. She denies any other surgeries, illnesses, or hospitalizations. She takes a generic multivitamin daily. She denies taking any other over-the-counter drugs except for an occasional aspirin.

Family history: Allison has a 14-year-old son and a 16-year-old daughter. Her son is being treated with methylphenidate for attention deficit hyperactivity disorder that was diagnosed at age seven in the second grade. During his kindergarten and first grade years, Allison had numerous visits to the school for his conduct problems and failing grades. Since starting methylphenidate, her son has had no major conduct problems at school but has consistently low average grades. Occasionally her son refuses to take the medication. During these times school conduct problems and grades are clearly worse. She thinks her daughter is using cigarettes and marijuana. Allison has been unable to confirm or disprove that suspicion.

She has two younger sisters who live out of state. She talks with them by telephone every few weeks. She sees her sisters and parents at family gatherings at the parents' home, about 150 miles away. Both of her sisters and their families have no major health problems. Her father is 68. He stopped working at his factory job at age 60 because of back pain. He was denied disability; he began Social Security retirement at age 62. Her mother's health is good except for arthritic joint pain. Her mother worked as a homemaker her whole life. The parents lived on savings and the proceeds of a refinanced home mortgage while her father was unemployed and not eligible for Social Security retirement. There are no other legal, psychiatric, or medical problems in her family.

Social history: Allison describes her childhood as "average." She was an average student. She recalls no significant childhood physical or psychological trauma. She met her former husband in high school. They did not begin seriously dating until a few years after her graduation. He is three years her senior. She had worked as a cashier after high school until her first child was born. Her husband worked in a local factory that closed about six years prior to her injury. The family moved to their present location when he was offered a job at a reasonable but lower wage. She and her family consider themselves Christian. They occasionally attended church at Christmas, Easter, and special occasions.

Allison noticed problems with her marriage after the family moved to their present community. Initially she attributed the problems to the stress of the relocation and the stress of her husband's new job. She had no hint that he would leave her until he moved out of the home and filed separation papers. A few months after their divorce, he remarried. Only after his remarriage did Allison learn about an affair that started soon after they moved to the current community. Her ex-husband visits the two children regularly. He pays child support directly deposited from his payroll check into her checking account. The child support income is not enough to cover her expenses. She began work with her current employer about four years prior to her injury.

Review of systems is pertinent for the back pain and problems sleeping. She reports no allergies. Allison experienced weight loss after the injury. Her appetite has returned, and she has regained the weight. She prides herself on not being over or under weight. Her menses have been irregular since the injury. As a part of the orthopedic evaluation Allison had a thorough physical examination. This included negative findings for diabetes, thyroid problems, heart problems, and anemia. When extremely anxious, she occasionally experiences a rash and itching.

Mental status examination: Allison is an appropriately groomed middle-age Caucasian woman of average build. She is alert and cooperative. She is able to relate to the clinician with good eye contact. There are no unusual mannerisms or posturing. Her articulation is fine. She is aware of her surroundings. She came on time, having driven herself to the appointment. Her memory for the events surrounding the accident and the sequelae is good. She is attentive during the interview. Her affect is calm throughout the interview. Her mood is mildly anxious and depressed. She indicates no current thoughts of harming herself or others. She reports she would not consider suicide as long as her children "were around." She reports wishing she were in "a different place."

Her use of English words and phrases is satisfactory. Her answers to questions are appropriate for thought coherence and relevance. She stays on topic with out extraneous associations. Her responses do not indicate delusional thinking. Her intelligence appears average. The Mini Mental State Examination is in the normal range with a score of 28. She can do the calculations well. She talks about current news events in a way that indicates an interest in the news. She is able to discuss her situation from her view as well as from the view of the workers' compensation regulations. She has good insight into her chronic psychological problems. She describes episodes of irritability and mood swings; these range from mildly euphoric to mildly depressed. She reports these have been a problem for her since high school. These episodes of irritability are associated with racing thoughts, sleeplessness, and hyperactivity. She believes these mood swings have contributed to marital, childrearing, and job problems. On the Mood Disorder Questionnaire she responds "yes" to 9 of 13 items. This indicates the possibility of a bipolar spectrum disorder. She does not report hallucinations or episodes of derealization.

IMPAIRMENT IN FUNCTIONING

Allison reports no response or side effects from the duloxetine. She agrees to continue the medication for a full six-week trial of therapy. She emphasizes that she does not feel ready to return to work because of her pain and sleep problems. There are serious symptoms related to her expressions of wishing to "be in another place" related to her mood swings. These symptoms require treatment. A feeling of not wishing to be alive can progress to concrete thoughts of suicide. The no-suicide contract she made about wanting to live for the sake of her children is temporary. The no-suicide contract is unenforceable anytime she chooses not to honor it.

DSM DIAGNOSIS

The clinician suspects that Allison meets criteria for bipolar II disorder and pain disorder associated with both psychological factors and a general medical condition of back pain. She also has generalized anxiety disorder. Medical problems include lumbar back pain and hypertension. The episodes of irritability and euphoria described in her mental status examination and by the Mood Disorder Questionnaire suggest that Allison experiences hypomanic episodes. Her other symptoms meet diagnostic criteria for major depressive disorder and generalized anxiety disorder. The Differential Diagnosis section discusses the possible diagnosis of malingering. The important feature of a pain disorder diagnosis is that the severity of symptoms requires treatment.

EPIDEMIOLOGY

Disability from pain disorders is common with an estimated 10% of adults afflicted in any given year. The incidence of malingering can range from less than 1% in clinical practice to over 10% in criminal cases, military service avoidance, and court cases claiming pain and suffering.

DIFFERENTIAL DIAGNOSIS

Diagnosing malingering or factitious disorder requires a high degree of certainty to rule in or out those disorders. To testify under oath in a workers' compensation deposition, there must be a reasonable degree of medical certainty about the diagnosis. At the least, there should be an opinion that some other respected experts in the field would agree with the diagnosis; otherwise, the clinician is open to professional board complaints or even civil suits by persons angered by the diagnostic conclusions. Pain disorder focuses on the pain as the primary clinical problem. Factitious disorder implies the intentional production of pain symptoms to assume the sick role. Malingering (a person feigning illness) implies the production of pain symptoms for gain, financial or otherwise. Diagnosing malingering requires a suspicion that the disorder exists in the patient. Then the evidence for and against the diagnosis is evaluated. Often a team approach is beneficial. A person who is malingering may show one set of symptoms to an evaluator. The same person in other situations may show symptoms indicating no handicaps. An important issue includes looking for symptoms that do or don't fit known disease patterns. In Factitious Disorders the psychological gain is the sick role itself. In Allison's case the unconscious gain from being sick is probably minimal. She speaks of duties to her children; she speaks to the need to pay her bills. These problems cannot be solved by simply withdrawing into a role requiring nursing care. The gains in malingering can come from both conscious and unconscious mental processes. Consciously she needs money to meet expenses. We can hypothesize that unconsciously she desires help to manage her difficulties. Her history does not suggest any "significant others" she can rely on for help.

ETIOLOGY AND PATHOGENESIS

Perception of the intensity of the pain in pain disorder can be exaggerated by psychological problems that are associated with preexisting disorders or problems arising from the pain. Sometimes individuals feign symptoms with the hope of monetary or other secondary gain. In Allison's case, the pain is likely exaggerated by the financial, psychological, and social stressors. She is confronted with pain that limits her ability to work. She is confronted with an inability to get disability benefits or long-term workers' compensation benefits. She is confronted with stresses of raising her children. She is also confronted with having to depend mainly on herself to solve those problems. The development of malingering can come from a person's perceived lack of options to cope with overwhelming stressors. Allison may focus on imagined social and financial gains from others, accepting an exaggerated severity of the illness. This way she could hope to solve problems imposed by both limitations from her current physical pain and her financial difficulties.

NATURAL COURSE WITHOUT TREATMENT

The experience of Allison's father illustrates the socioeconomic limbo that can occur in these cases. He had back pain that limited his ability to work. His medical handicaps were not severe enough to qualify for Social Security disability. He had to rely on savings and budgeting to meet his expenses until he could apply for early Social Security retirement benefits. Some unfortunate persons spend many years feeling too ill to work, being denied disability, and being too young to retire. In Allison's case, the reality of having to try to get permanent disability promoted the need to find other ways to cope with her dilemma. Unless a patient develops motivation to overcome handicaps and not exaggerate illness, psychotherapy is ineffective.

EVIDENCE-BASED TREATMENT OPTIONS

The treatment plan will depend on the individual physical, financial, motivational, and psychological resources available to each person. Allison is fortunate to have insurance from workers' compensation. This allows her to access to medical, psychological, and physical therapy treatment. Duloxetine is a medication indicated by the FDA for musculoskeletal pain, depression, and anxiety. Physicians often prescribe this single medication to patients with the combination of physical and psychological problems exhibited by Allison. The primary treatment modalities at this stage for Allison are psychotherapy and job modification. The psychotherapy focus is to help her see options other than permanent disability to deal with her problems. The focus of job modifications is to let her return to work as soon as possible without creating more back injury.

CLINICAL COURSE WITH MANAGEMENT AND TREATMENT

Allison has a probable bipolar spectrum disorder. She was warned about the risk of hypomanic mood swings being precipitated with duloxetine and instructed to call the answering service if she experienced any worsening of symptoms. She scheduled a return appointment in two weeks.

Based on the report, the workers' compensation insurance company authorized eight treatment sessions. Her insurance company also authorized an additional six weeks of paid medical leave.

A few days after her appointment, Allison called the answering service about worsening sleep and anxiety. She received a prescription for risperidone 0.5 mg tabs to be taken once or twice daily for the presumptive hypomanic symptoms. Allison understood that risperidone is not approved for bipolar II depression treatment, but that it usually works to help stabilize mood swings. She was informed that in susceptible persons, antidepressants can precipitate hypomanic symptoms. She agreed to take the prescription.

When Allison returned for her next appointment, she reported that she was "sleeping a little better." She said the pain was "about the same." She said her anxiety currently felt more like the chronic anxiety that she had experienced for many years. She said that the acute anxiety and mood swings had responded to the risperidone. She said that the acute anxiety felt like the symptoms that she had experienced with other antidepressants. There followed a frank discussion about the pros and cons of applying for permanent disability. She accepted a suggestion to consult with an attorney specializing in disability law. She agreed to return to the office in two weeks.

On the next visit, Allison reported that the disability attorney told her she did not have a strong case. She reported that the sleep and pain were "somewhat improved." She said she felt anxious about returning to work because she was worried that she would reinjure her back. During the session she requested reasonable job modifications such as a stool to sit on and no heavy lifting. She agreed to return a few days before her medical leave of absence would expire. She reported no suicidal thinking.

On the next visit Allison stated that she would like to try to return to work. The workers' compensation rehabilitation worker had previously discussed her work modification requests with her manager and the store had agreed to them. Allison reported no suicidal thinking. She said her sleep and pain continued to improve. She explained that she still felt chronically anxious. Exploring that problem, she uncovered a number of psychosocial stressors. She stated that she was afraid of ending up like her father, who was unable to work and unable to get disability. She described her fear that "something else would go wrong." She traced the origin of that fear to her marital separation and her realization that she was on her own. She agreed to a return appointment a couple weeks after her return to work.

On the visit after her return to work, Allison reported that the work situation was "okay." She said that she had minimal problems with sleep and pain. She reported no suicidal symptoms. She wanted to continue discussing her anxiety about her future. She agreed to use the remaining authorized visits for symptom relapse prevention by focusing on her chronic situational problems.

SYSTEMS-BASED PRACTICE ISSUES

Allison's case illustrates some common problems encountered in the evaluation and treatment of workers' compensation referrals. Often there are numerous personal stressors that the patient feels able to control until the accident upsets the psychological equilibrium. Managed care imposes a limit to therapy visits. There is a limit to the number of days off from work to recover from the medical problems. A patient's psychological defenses can easily become overwhelmed, and the patient can retreat into ineffective coping styles. Fortunately workers' compensation health benefits do not end on return to work. In Allison's case, this permitted treatment to continue during a period of work readjustment.

Another issue is the countertransference of the therapist. A therapist can hold a belief that the patient is trying to take advantage of the disability system. This belief can lead to a poor therapeutic outcome. A more helpful attitude is for the therapist to view the patient as being overwhelmed by their circumstances and helping the patient find ways out of their dilemma.

LEGAL AND ETHICAL CHALLENGES

The workers' compensation laws vary by jurisdiction. The regulations may seem arbitrary. They represent a synthesis of rights of the injured party, the employer, and society. According to the American Medical Association's Code of Medical Ethics, "In general, when physicians believe a law is unjust, they should work to change the law." A therapist who sees unethical practices by workers' compensation insurance personnel should work through the professional societies and local legislators to change those practices. In Allison's case, it is important to assure that her health care benefits are not prematurely terminated by managed care. It is an ethical obligation of the therapist to not use an excessive number of treatment sessions simply to fill an appointment schedule.

REFERENCES AND RESOURCES

Americans with Disabilities Act, 42 U.S. Code, sections 12101 et seq. (1990). This act requires reasonable work accommodation for persons with mental and physical handicaps.

Carter v. General Motors, 361 Mich. 577 (1960). The Michigan Supreme Court ruled that eligibility for disability compensation includes illness related to stress from the job.

"Code of Medical Ethics," American Medical Association, Chicago, 1998, p. 1.

Daubert v. Merrell Dow, 61 U.S.L.S. 4805, 113 U.S. Supreme Court 2786 (1993). The Supreme Court set standards for expert opinion testimony.

Folstein MF, Folstein SE, McHugh PR. Mini-Mental State: a practical method for grading the cognitive state of patients for the clinician. *J Psychiatr Res* 1973;12:196–98.

Hirschfield R, et al. Development and validation of a screening instrument for bipolar disorder: the Mood Disorder Questionnaire. *Am J Psychiatr* 2000;157:1873–75.

Rosner R, ed. *Principles and Practice of Forensic Psychiatry*. New York: Oxford University Press, 2003, pp. 270, 292. The "eggshell" doctrine is based on common law. The defendant must take the victim as she is. This implies that preexisting conditions exacerbated by the injury are legally relevant to the current disability.

Chapter 32

Alcohol Use

Lauren Lehmann, M.D.

CLINICAL PRESENTATION

Chief complaint: "I need detox."

History of present illness: Bennett is a 64-year-old man with a 48-year drinking history. He typically drinks in a pattern of four-day binges every two weeks, drinking 12 to 18 12-ounce beers each day during the binge. He has done so for the past eight years since he retired as a contractor; before his retirement he was drinking four beers daily. The recovery period following each drinking episode is increasing in duration and severity. He reports that he needs more alcohol to achieve the effect he desires and that he has tried unsuccessfully to decrease the quantity he consumes. He reports no history of drug use, blackouts, seizures, or delirium tremens. His last drink was eight hours ago, and he complains of tremulousness, anxiety, headache, mild nausea, and diaphoresis.

He has a 15-year history of hypertension, and he was diagnosed with diabetes and hypercholesterolemia 5 years ago when he was briefly hospitalized for detoxification. His surgical history is remarkable for tonsillectomy at age 5 and an appendectomy at age 18. The youngest of three boys, Bennett began drinking at age 16 with his peer group and began smoking cigarettes, which he has done since. He has no alcohol-related legal problems, and has had three speeding tickets over the past 40 years. He was an average student, and he obtained a high school diploma. He enlisted in the army at age 18 for 4 years and served in Germany, where his drinking increased. He achieved the rank of corporal, had no disciplinary problems, and was not involved in combat. He was married in his early twenties for 10 years, which ended in divorce. He has two adult children with whom he has regular contact. His second wife of 12 years is supportive of his efforts to stop drinking and works outside the home. They previously attended religious services together, but now his wife goes alone because Bennett chooses to not attend. His father and two of his uncles have a history of alcohol problems. He denies a history of mood, anxiety, thought, and cognitive disorders and has never had psychiatric treatment of any kind. He reports that he has been to a couple of AA meetings in the past with a friend but that he did not think at the time that he "needed" AA and that he could cut back or even stop drinking on his own. He acknowledges at least moderate craving, which typically heralds the onset of another drinking binge.

Mental status exam reveals an appropriately dressed man who appears to be of stated age, diaphoretic but in no distress and with slight psychomotor agitation. He maintains good eye contact throughout the interview. His speech is normal in rate, rhythm, and pattern. Cognitively, he is alert and oriented to person, place, time, and situation. His remote and immediate memory are intact as he provides historical information throughout the interview and recalls seven digits forward and four in reverse. He recalls 3/3 objects at five minutes. His affect is appropriate, congruent to mood, and full-range. His mood is anxious, and he denies suicidal ideation and homicidal ideation now and at any time in the past. Thought processes are linear, logical, and goal-directed. He demonstrates no idiosyncrasies of speech. He denies delusions and gives abstact proverb interpretations. He performs simple calculations with no errors and demonstrates an above averge fund of knowledge. He has fair insight and judgment. He denies auditory, visual, or tactile hallucinations and has no illusions.

Physical exam revealed heart rate 110, blood pressure 150/100, respiration rate 20, and temperature 99.6 °F. He is overweight, but the physical exam is otherwise normal. Routine chemistry, liver enzymes, and CBC results are pending. Thiamine 100 mg was administered orally.

IMPAIRMENT IN FUNCTIONING

Bennett also acknowledges that since his wife continues to work, he has a considerable amount of free time, which he spends on projects or watching TV. He has a few friends with whom he socializes occasionally, but since he retired he tends to avoid social contact. He states that he and his wife "don't communicate as well as we used to" and "don't do things together as much as we used to." He has limited contact with his children from his first marriage, though he reports his relationships with them as "close." He reports that he is dissatisfied with his life, particularly since retirement, and that his interest in his projects is waning. He thinks his drinking might be contributing to his lack of motivation and communication problems with his wife, but at this point, he feels helpless to stop drinking.

DSM DIAGNOSIS

Although the characteristic physiological manifestations of withdrawal described above are unique to alcohol and other drugs that act on gamma amino-butyric acid (GABA) and can be accompanied by significant autonomic hyperactivity and hallucinations when severe, mild withdrawal can be mistaken for anxiety. This may be what brings the person to the clinician, and the clinician who neglects to inquire about alcohol and benzodiazepine use may mistakenly diagnose and treat what he believes is an anxiety disorder. Withdrawal is one of the criteria that may be used to diagnose alcohol dependence and typically is present to at least some extent.

Bennett suffers from an Alcohol Use Disorder, with some degree of severity. Previous versions of DSM emphasized withdrawal as one of the primary criteria for substance dependence, which caused diagnostic problems in dealing with substances that are not abused but do cause withdrawal if stopped abruptly, such as phenobarbital for epilepsy. The criteria of "repeated legal involvement" was completely dropped from the current system because it made applying the criteria internationally, with patchworks of laws, difficult. A new criteria of craving was added. Bennett's diagnosis of Alcohol Use Disorder falls into the severe range based on the number of criteria endorsed.

EPIDEMIOLOGY

According to the most recent data available, half of the world's population consumes alcohol, though men (55%) are more likely to drink than women (34%). 75% of the alcohol is consumed by 30% of the population. In the United States, the greatest consumption is by men in the 18–25 years age group. Non-Hispanic whites consume the most alcohol, followed by Native Americans and Hispanics, non-Hispanic blacks, and Asians, though Hispanics and Native Americans have a greater prevalence of problem drinking. The prevalence of heavy drinking, defined as five or more drinks on five or more days of the previous month, is 7% in the United States. More educated people consume more alcohol than less educated people. The prevalence of alcohol abuse and dependence in the United States is 8.5% (Ruiz and Strain, 2011, pp. 140–41).

DIFFERENTIAL DIAGNOSIS

Anxiety disorders, particularly generalized anxiety disorder and panic disorder, should be included in the differential diagnosis, particularly when the person complains of tremulousness, fatigue, insomnia, concentration difficulties, and restlessness and can provide a history of these symptoms during a period of extended sobriety. The presence of particularly auditory hallucinations with a clear sensorium suggests the possibility of alcohol-induced psychotic disorder, which typically occurs when the person decreases the amount he or she has been consuming. Multiple somatic complaints that accompany withdrawal may be confused with somatization disorder. Finally, alcohol can produce symptoms suggestive of depression, which may be considered alcohol-induced mood disorder unless the mood symptoms occur during a period of extended sobriety or the patient has a family history of depression, at which point a diagnosis of dysthymic disorder or major depression can be considered.

ETIOLOGY AND PATHOGENESIS

The emergence of the alcohol withdrawal syndrome has biological, psychological, and social elements. Biologically, there is growing evidence that genetic factors may predispose humans to severe withdrawal symptoms, including seizures and delirium tremens (Ries et al. 2009, pp. 561–62). Hence, not only should the clinician obtain a family history of substance use, he should also inquire whether any family members developed severe withdrawal symptoms. Additionally, multiple withdrawal episodes expose the person to the "kindling" phenomenon (Linnoila et al. 1987; Becker and Hale 1993), which is the increased risk of seizures developing over time and with multiple withdrawal episodes as the brain adapts to the absence of alcohol.

Psychological elements typically contribute precipitating and perpetuating factors to the development of the alcohol withdrawal syndrome. In this case, Bennett's retirement led to an increase in his drinking. The clinician explores the meaning of retirement to him, including a possible response to a change in his role as provider, as well as his view of losses that accompany the aging process. His chronic medical problems may reinforce his sense of vulnerability. His retirement may have triggered the expression of an unresolved conflict regarding self-worth, and he may have increased his use of alcohol as a result. A lack of meaningful activities and sense of purpose at this stage of his life may contribute to low self-esteem as well. Because these issues are ongoing, they become a perpetuating factor in Bennett's current situation. He is unable both to resolve the conflict he is experiencing and accomplish the tasks of this stage of his life. That he presents now for treatment of alcohol withdrawal offers an opportunity to begin to explore these issues with him.

Social elements, particularly the number and quality of his interpersonal relationships, provide potential protective factors for Bennett's alcohol withdrawal. His wife is supportive of his efforts to obtain treatment for the withdrawal symptoms, and she and other family members should be interviewed, with Bennett's permission, to determine their perceptions of his drinking and the extent of their willingness to support his recovery efforts.

NATURAL COURSE WITHOUT TREATMENT

Although age, gender, and duration and extent of alcohol use are less robust predictors of a complicated course of alcohol withdrawal than previously thought, Bennett's repeated episodes of withdrawal at home between binges, his medical comorbidities, and his current autonomic hyperactivity do convey at least a moderate risk for more severe withdrawal. Although he has never had seizures or delirium tremens, the fact that either or both could occur dictates an aggressive treatment approach. Likewise, since he currently has symptoms of withdrawal that need to be relieved, the clinician must decide both the setting for the detoxification (inpatient or outpatient) and the regimen. Another element to be addressed later in this episode of treatment is assessment of his interest in recovery. This detoxification provides an opportunity to engage him in additional treatment once the withdrawal symptoms resolve. The classification of subtypes of alcohol dependence has evolved over the past few decades. Moss and his co-researchers delineated five subtypes (Moss et al., 2007): young adult, which is the most prevalent and characterized by no concomitant drug use, mental health issues, or family history; young antisocial, noted by early onset, a family history, mental health problems, and drug use; functional, with onset in middle age and a strong family history of both alcohol problems and mood disorders; intermediate familial, also with a middle-age onset and a family history of alcohol problems; and chronic severe, which is the least common and characterized by early onset, antisocial personality disorder, criminality, drug use, and a strong family history of alcohol problems.

EVIDENCE-BASED TREATMENT OPTIONS

The first goal in alcohol withdrawal treatment is amelioration of the symptoms, which typically are the opposite of those produced by alcohol, followed by prevention of both seizures and delirium tremens. The primary neurotransmitter systems involved in the appearance of the alcohol withdrawal syndrome are the GABAergic, glutamatergic, and noradrenergic systems, though the dopaminergic, opioidergic, serotonergic, and cholinergic systems are affected as well. At the cellular level, alcohol increases the chloride influx of the inhibitory GABA neuron, enhancing the effects of the GABA neuron with acute administration and suppressing its effects with chronic administration. However, during sudden alcohol abstinence, the inhibitory effects of GABA are reduced, producing anxiety, seizures, and agitation. The neurons of the glutamatergic and autonomic systems, up-regulated and inhibited during chronic alcohol use, are suddenly unopposed, resulting in the symptoms of sympathetic hyperactivity such as tremor, hypertension, hyperreflexia, diaphoresis, hyperthermia, and tachycardia. The appearance of these symptoms typically begins within 12 hours of the last alcohol ingestion and may include visual, tactile, and/or auditory hallucinations in a clear sensorium, accompanied by insight that the perceived events are not real. Seizures occur within the first 48 hours after the last drink and are generalized and tonic-clonic in character. Delirium tremens is a later manifestation, usually occurring between 36 and 96 hours after the last drink, and although it no longer carries the 15–30% mortality rate of several decades ago, it continues to be frequently missed or misdiagnosed. The hallmarks of delirium are a waxing and waning level of consciousness, impaired cognition, and/or the development of hallucinations in addition to persistent autonomic hyperactivity (Ruiz and Strain, p. 157).

The use of the Clinical Institute Withdrawal Assessment of Alcohol Scale, Revised (CIWA-Ar) and similar measures to reliably and objectively assess the severity of symptoms of alcohol withdrawal has led to the development of clinical pathways, more uniform treatment of the syndrome, and fewer complications. Typically, a CIWA-Ar score of less than 10 indicates mild withdrawal, which may be managed with supportive care alone or a symptom-triggered treatment regimen wherein benzodiazepines are given on an as-needed based only. Scores ranging from 10 to 18 are considered moderate withdrawal, and scores above 18 are indicative of severe withdrawal (Ruiz and Strain, p. 563).

Some cases of mild alcohol withdrawal syndrome can be managed on an outpatient basis, provided the person is well supervised and can return daily for evaluation. Factors putting the person at relative risk of a complicated withdrawal and thereby requiring inpatient admission include lack of social support (e.g., housing), pregnancy, previous seizures and/or delirium, and significant medical or psychiatric conditions.

Because they are cross-tolerant with alcohol, act on the benzodiazepine receptors of the GABA neurons, and have a high index of safety, benzodiazepines are the mainstay of treatment of the alcohol withdrawal syndrome. However, the manner in which they are used and the provision of adequate dosing have changed somewhat over the years. Sellers et al. (1983) reported the use of a diazepam loading regimen that works well for most patients, typically administering 20 mg every two hours until sedated. Because diazepam is rapidly and reliably absorbed orally and has a long half-life, usually no additional benzodiazepines are required, and the patient continues to metabolize the medication for several days. In these times of managed care, the five- to seven-day detoxification is a thing of the past unless the patient develops complications. The shorter acting, renally excreted agents oxazepam and lorazepam should be used for those over age 65, those with cirrhosis, and those with severe emphysema, either in a loading regimen or scheduled taper. Relatively recently, off-label adjunctive treatment with the anticonvulsants carbamazepine (600–800 mg daily), valproic acid (20 mg/kg daily), levetiracetam, and gabapentin (900–1,200 mg) have been used to decrease the required dose—and the concomitant sedation and memory impairment—of the benzodiazepine while providing seizure protection and reducing postwithdrawal craving and relapse risk.

Project MATCH was a multisite study conducted about 20 years ago that examined the efficacy of three main types of substance abuse treatment—12-step facilitation, cognitive behavioral therapy, and motivation enhancement therapy. Because of the Project MATCH finding that no model was clearly superior with respect to the other two for the initial treatment of patient groups, many treatment programs today use a combination of the three approaches. Often, motivational interviewing techniques can be used to address a patient's ambivalence about changing his or her behavior related to alcohol use. Once committed to recovery, the patient's preference regarding acceptance of the tenets of the 12-step facilitation or the cognitive behavioral model can guide subsequent treatment.

Approved in 1994 for alcohol craving and relapse prevention, naltrexone, which interferes with opioid action in the nucleus accumbens, is an adjunct for persons for whom craving is a major contributory factor in drinking. Studies have shown that naltrexone 50 mg daily when taken orally or 380 mg monthly intramuscularly may increase the number of days until the first drink and decrease both the number of drinking days and the amount of alcohol consumed. The duration of treatment is flexible, though most recommendations are for at least the first 90 days of abstinence when the relapse risk is greatest. The only relative contraindication is significant liver disease, so baseline and quarterly liver function testing is advised. Side effects include nausea, insomnia, and headache, and, because it blocks the action of opioids, naltrexone can precipitate withdrawal in patients taking opiates or tramadol. Acamprosate, an alternative to naltrexone, primarily acts at glycine receptors in the nucleus accumbens, interfering with dopamine release, and has some antagonist effect at the N-methyl-D-aspartate receptor. At a dose of 666 mg three times daily, acamprosate also has been shown to increase the time to the first drink, decrease craving, reduce alcohol consumption, and reduce the number of drinking days. It is renally metabolized, so patients with renal impairment require a lower dose. Acamprosate's side effects include nausea and headache (Ruiz and Strain, pp. 478–85).

Behavioral couples' therapy also has been shown to be an effective means of reducing alcohol consumption by helping couples achieve greater satisfaction with their relationship. Community resources such as Al-Anon can be useful for family members to gain a better understanding of alcohol dependence and support for themselves and their challenges as they deal with a family member with alcohol dependence (Ruiz and Strain, p. 153).

CLINICAL COURSE WITH MANAGEMENT AND TREATMENT

Bennett's CIWA-Ar score on hospital admission is 12. He consents to a course of diazepam 20 mg every two hours with valproic acid 1,250 mg daily. He requires 40 mg diazepam over four hours before his repeated CIWA-Ar score is 6. The next day, prior to discharge with a five-day course of valproic acid and a continued decline in his CIWA-Ar score, he is willing to discuss the next steps in treatment. He reports that he has been to a couple of AA meetings in the past with a friend but that he did not think at the time that he "needed" AA and that he could cut back or even stop drinking on his own. He acknowledges at least moderate craving, which typically heralds the onset of another drinking binge. Also, he acknowledges that since his wife continues to work, he has a considerable amount of free time, which he spends on projects. His wife reports growing family concerns about Bennett's drinking to the point that they had considered meeting as a family with Bennett to discuss it. Although his wife has heard of Al-Anon, she has never attended because she had thought Bennett eventually would be able to control his drinking. She is relieved that this detoxification episode has allowed her to voice her realization that his drinking is beyond his control and that help is available for him—and for her.

Having completed the acute detoxification phase of treatment, Bennett is now in a position to be approached by the treatment team to assess his readiness to change his behavior and his willingness to explore pharmacologic aids to assist him. The clinician must decide who will undertake this next step with Bennett and how, while other team members are available to discuss his wife's concerns about the drinking and to assess the level of support she is willing to provide him. In addition, the team will determine her understanding of the nature of alcohol dependence and its effect on the family system and her willingness to obtain both additional education and support for herself.

SYSTEMS-BASED PRACTICE ISSUES

Alcohol dependence has been described as a systems illness such that treatment ideally involves all elements of the person's life, particularly the family. As the family with an alcohol-dependent member progresses through the developmental stages, often role shifts occur such that others in the family assume responsibilities previously held by the alcohol-dependent person, whose drinking serves to more firmly establish the changes in family dynamics, which then become difficult to reverse. If the alcohol-dependent person enters treatment while the family is still intact, however, the family also becomes a focus for treatment, which often significantly improves the prognosis. Although the process of role reestablishment takes time as familial relationships are redefined and strengthened, enlisting the assistance of the family provides a valuable opportunity to examine problematic family processes. Consequently, a multidisciplinary treatment team is well suited for this task, which often involves person-requested contact with the legal system in addition to an employer, school, and other clinicians outside of the team. In addition, Al-Anon may become another source of support for family members just as AA may be beneficial for the alcohol-dependent person.

LEGAL, ETHICAL, AND CULTURAL ISSUES

Through the nineteenth and early twentieth centuries, people with alcohol use disorders were regarded as having a moral deficiency. A great premium was set upon willpower during the Victorian era and alcoholics were believed to be sadly lacking in this area. With the founding of Alcoholics Anonymous in 1935, alcohol use disorder has gradually been more accepted as a biological and psychological illness.

Part of the quandary in conceptualizing any substance use disorder is that the primary behavior appears to be volitional. Surely an individual who recognizes the problem with alcohol in his life should be able to simply decide to not drink. Even now many health professionals will privately express distaste for working with those who have substance use disorders.

Part of the evidence for the disease model of use disorders is genetic and part biological. When two people are exposed to the same supposedly innocuous stimulus (e.g., a glass of beer or wine on their 21st birthdays), one may go on to develop the dysfunctional patterns associated with the use disorders and the other may not.

Because alcohol use disorder generally follows a relapsing/remitting course, it is not uncommon for people suffering from it to have extended periods of recovery followed by bouts of drinking. In the United States the average number of treatment episodes before entering stable recovery is approximately seven.

Imagine that we treated diabetes as we sometimes treat alcohol use disorders. A diabetic man may have good control of his illness for a period of time and then have an elevated blood sugar in response to forgetting to take his diabetic medication, a dietary indiscretion, or a failure to exercise. If we approached his period of hyperglycemia as a "failure" or relapse the way we sometimes do with alcoholic individuals, he would be reluctant to let us know about difficulties controlling his glucose and demoralized by our disapproval.

REFERENCES AND RESOURCES

Becker HC, Hale RL. Repeated episodes of ethanol withdrawal potentiate the severity of subsequent withdrawal seizure: an animal model of alcohol withdrawal "kindling." *Alcohol Clin Exp Res* 1993;17(1):94–98.

Linnoila M, Mefford I, Nutt D, et al. Alcohol withdrawal and noradrenergic function. *Ann Int Med* 1987;107(6):875–89.

Moss HB, Chen CM, Yi HY. (2007) Subtypes of alcohol dependence in a nationally representative sample. *Drug Alcohol Depend* 2007 Dec 1;91(2–3):149–158. Epub 2007 Jun 26.

Myrick H, Malcolm R, Randall PK, et al. A double-blind trial of gabapentin versus lorazepam in the treatment of alcohol withdrawal. *Alcohol Clin Exp Res* 2009;33(9):1582–88.

O'Brien C. Addiction and dependence in DSM-V. *Addiction* 2010;106:866–67.

Ries RK, Fiellin DA, Miller SC, et al. *Principles of Addiction Medicine* (4th ed). Philadelphia: Lippincott Williams and Wilkins, 2009.

Ruiz P, Strain E. *Substance Abuse: A Comprehensive Textbook* (5th ed.). Philadelphia: Lippincott Williams and Wilkins, 2011.

Sellers EM, Naranjo CA, Harrison M, et al. Diazepam loading: simplified treatment of alcohol withdrawal. *Clin Pharmacol Ther* 1983;34(6):822–26.

Days of Wine and Roses (1962), directed by B. Edwards, produced by M. Manulis, Warner Bros.

CHAPTER 33

Cocaine Use in Adolescence

David W. Hartman, M.D.

CLINICAL PRESENTATION

Chief complaint: "I need something to make this craziness stop. I know I am a drug addict."

History of present illness: Marie is a 16-year-old female who is brought to the psychiatrist's office by her paternal grandparents. She presents with a serious cocaine addiction, which came as something of a surprise to her grandparents because although they knew that she had previously smoked marijuana, they were unaware of the cocaine abuse.

Marie has been primarily raised by her father's parents, who are present during part of the psychiatric evaluation. When she was six years of age, Marie's parents divorced. Her mother, suffering from severe chronic back pain, had been mostly bedridden throughout Marie's childhood. She recalls returning home from kindergarten to find her mother lying on the couch watching TV. The house was always dirty and unkempt. There was never any food in the kitchen, and her mother showed little interest in what happened at school or in her personal life. Her father was described as an alcoholic who had many extramarital affairs. Marie remembers spending time with him rarely and says that he was always out late at night. On weekends, her father would often show up intoxicated. When the parents did spend time together, they frequently argued about her father seeing other women, her mother saying that he could never be trusted. Whenever her father did promise to spend time with Marie, he often did not show up. When the divorce occurred, it became apparent that Marie could no longer be cared for by her parents. The Department of Social Services got involved, as well as the courts, and her paternal grandparents were given custody as her legal guardians. She moved in with them.

Marie has trouble sleeping and toward the end of the interview, when her grandparents are not present, she admits to having nightmares about drowning, waking up in a sweat, and trembling until she realizes that it was "just a dream." She says she doesn't expect to be alive after these dreams; it surprises her to not just die during these dreams. She is not suicidal, but she would not be surprised at having a short life. She describes anhedonia, not much pleasure is experienced—she has looked for relief by seeking to use cocaine. She thinks life might get better after treatment and if she and her boyfriend can get away and start their own lives together. She shrugs as if she doesn't really believe she can get off drugs. She considers the possibility that she might be happy just using marijuana if she can stop the cocaine.

The grandparents do not have a detailed recollection of Marie's early childhood, but they believe she met her developmental milestones as expected. They know of no incident of hospitalization, but they are quite confident that the household was neglectful and trauma-ridden with violent fights occurring between her parents that Marie would have witnessed. The mother's disability, her father's alcoholism, and the history of a neglectful childhood led the judge to award custody to the grandparents when Marie was six. The grandparents think it is very possible that Marie may herself have suffered trauma, but that it was never disclosed to them and was never given medical attention. Her father had a history of violence against the mother and has been charged with assault several times by other parties, as well. Marie will not speak about her father except to say that she has no interest in a relationship with him.

After moving in with her grandparents, Marie proved to be a difficult child; she was described by her elementary schoolteachers during the parent–teacher conferences with the grandparents as being excessively active in the classroom, often getting into fights with her peers. These misconduct events occurred as early as the third grade, when the client was eight years old. At age 11, she was picked up by the local police for shoplifting and at age 14, she became pregnant. The grandparents are presently helping care for the patient's 10-month-old child. Marie says her grandparents are too old to raise a teenager and claims they are excessively controlling. She feels that her grandparents never trust her, thus there is no reason for her to be trustworthy. She talks about her grandparents wanting to know every minute where she is going and with whom she will be spending her time.

Marie first tried smoking marijuana at age nine, when she visited her mother. Apparently, her mother had been smoking pot for several years to help control her pain and she thought that it might help her daughter's problem with attention deficit disorder. Marie continued to smoke marijuana and had increasing problems at school with inattention, falling grades, and truancy. One of her friends gave her methylphenidate to try and Marie found that it calmed her and made her feel euphoric. She continued to smoke pot but now interspersed it with methylphenidate. She bought the methylphenidate from classmates. Within a couple of months she tried snorting it rather than swallowing it and quickly found that taking it this way provided a much more rapid and rewarding effect.

When she became pregnant at age 14, a urine drug screen revealed the presence of the marijuana but not the stimulant, as she had not used that for over 48 hours. The obstetric nurse practitioner spoke with her and her grandparents and Marie promised to stop smoking pot. She did so, but her use of methylphenidate increased. Because she knew when her obstetrical appointments were scheduled (and hence the drug tests) she avoided taking any stimulants for a few days prior to the appointment. Her grandparents believed that she had given up all drugs and were pleased with her. The pregnancy was of concern for many reasons, among which were failure to gain weight.

Mental status examination: Marie is a young woman appearing a little older than her stated age, sitting quietly in the chair during the interview. She seems to have diminished spontaneous movements and sits quite still. Eye contact is poor. She is oriented to person, place, time, and situation. Her connection with the interviewer is somewhat reserved and a little distant. Her affect is constricted and her mood appears depressed. Because of the decreased spontaneous movement she does not appear to be anxious but says that she is. She denies thoughts of suicide, self harm, or harming anyone else. Her concentration and attention are mildly diminished. Her short-term memory is intact but with a slightly slow response. Long-term memory, fund of knowledge, and gait are all normal. Speech is soft but fluent. Thought processes are linear and logical. Insight and judgment are fair. She acknowledges intermittent strong cravings but denies their presence during the interview. Arithmetic calculations are performed flawlessly albeit slightly slowly.

IMPAIRMENT IN FUNCTIONING

Marie initially has difficulty identifying negative consequences to her cocaine use. She identifies the primary problem as her grandparents not trusting her. The cycle of emerging drug abuse that has gripped her has altered her relationship with her grandparents, causing her to lie to them at times, and causing them to mistrust her. Her perception of their mistrust then becomes a reason for her to continue to use drugs because "it does not make any difference anyway." In addition to the functional impairment in her closest family relations, the use of cocaine has also caused impairment in Marie's sleep, appetite, and mood and anxiety regulation. She has panic attacks and nightmares and finds herself progressively doing and justifying activities that previously she would have avoided.

DSM DIAGNOSIS

Cocaine and other stimulants do not have much in the way of severe physiological withdrawal. Stopping cocaine abruptly does not cause seizures, elevated blood pressure or pulse, or other major physiological changes. For this reason, withdrawal is not always apparent to people near the individual who has abruptly stopped using stimulants. Often the primary symptoms of withdrawal are irritability, sleeping too much, moodiness, and depression. However, physiological tolerance and withdrawal are only two of multiple signs of a substance use disorder. In many ways, a better gauge of dependence is simply the answer to the question, "Is the person's life better or worse as a result of using the substance?"

Using this criterion, one person who happens to suffer from attention deficit disorder may experience increased focus, self-esteem, and improved academic performance with use of the stimulant. Another person using exactly the same drug may find it impossible to control the use and may find that use of the drug has led to deterioration in performance of many roles in his or her life. In this case Marie qualifies for a DSM diagnosis of cocaine use disorder. Her mood and anxiety symptoms may also justify a diagnosis of cocaine-induced mood or anxiety disorder. One way of evaluating this is to simply see what happens when she stops using the drug. If her mood, sleep, anxiety, and nightmares all improve, then de facto she did suffer from a substance-induced disorder. However, many people find that prolonged or severe drug use may cause disruption of mood and anxiety regulation that persists long past cessation of the drug.

In this case, the pattern-recognition skills of the therapist have a critical value in assessing the minimization Marie is applying to her problems and her readiness to address change.

In the current version of DSM, cravings and loss of control have been emphasized. Both of these symptoms are present in Marie's case.

EPIDEMIOLOGY

Since the mid-1980s a federally funded program called Monitoring the Future has surveyed middle and high school students for use of abusable substances as well as their attitudes about the substances. Questions are asked of a large number of teenagers about such issues as, "Is using cocaine once harmful?" "Is using cocaine frequently harmful?" "How easy is it to get cocaine?" Questions are also asked about whether the teenager disapproves of people using these drugs. (The Monitoring the Future project publishes its data online at www.monitoringthefuture.org.)

The results of these surveys show that there is some variability over time in whether teenagers of various ages have used drugs. Not surprisingly, in years in which more students say that using a particular drug even once is harmful, they report a lower prevalence of use of that drug in the past month. Not surprisingly, considering a drug more harmful makes adolescents less likely to use it.

For cocaine, perceived risk during the 1980s was relatively low and many 12th-grade students reported having used it. In the most recent data, perceived risk has been higher and in 2012 only 2.7% of 12th-graders reported current use.

DIFFERENTIAL DIAGNOSIS

The differential diagnosis of cocaine use disorder is obviously narrowed greatly if the afflicted individual acknowledges using the drug. In the absence of such acknowledgment, symptoms of mood, sleep, and anxiety disorders have a vast differential diagnosis, including primary psychiatric disorders like generalized anxiety disorder and major depression or bipolar disorder, as well as medical conditions such as hyperthyroidism.

As is the case in every area of mental or physical health treatment, the most useful diagnostic tool is the sensitive history taken by a professional. However, people are often reluctant to acknowledge abusing substances. To get an accurate history the clinician must establish rapport and trust in a nonjudgmental supportive atmosphere.

In addition, given Marie's chaotic and unfortunate early childhood, consideration must be given to the possibility of post-traumatic stress disorder. However, it is almost impossible to evaluate this or most mood and anxiety disorders in the context of acute intoxication or withdrawal.

ETIOLOGY AND PATHOGENESIS

It is fairly unlikely that most individuals who end up with substance abuse problems start by resolving, "I would really like my whole life to revolve around a drug." Instead, virtually all use begins recreationally. All drugs of abuse affect chemical functioning in the brain, and most generally chemical functioning of the reward pathway. This pathway leading from the ventral tegmental area and nucleus accumbens to the forebrain is our natural route for reinforcing behavior. When we are hungry and eat, the neurons in this pathway light up and reinforce the act of eating. When we experience pleasure in the company of others, happiness, and even the rewards of arousal in sex, this pathway is involved. The neurons involved do their work through dopamine. Cocaine and drugs like it hijack the pleasure pathway by substituting for the dopamine. Stimulant drugs of abuse can either bind directly to dopamine receptors, cause dopamine neurons to release the chemical prematurely, or prevent the inactivation of dopamine that is already in the synapse. Over time the brain becomes dependent on this exogenous drug to produce even a normal tone of dopaminergic transmission. Over a relatively short period of months a cocaine user will find that heavy use of cocaine no longer leads to a "high" but that he or she must simply use to feel the least bit normal and function at a rudimentary level. At this point virtually all the behavior of the individual becomes directed toward ensuring and maintaining the supply of the drug.

NATURAL COURSE WITHOUT TREATMENT

The natural course of severe cocaine use disorder without treatment is usually catastrophic. Depending on how the person uses cocaine, her collapse may be extremely rapid or a little slower. In the 1980s Mark Gold, a substance abuse researcher and clinician, set up the 1-800-COCAINE hotline for people to call in and get information about local treatment resources. The operators on this hotline would ask basic information such as how the individual was using the drug and how long they had been using it. If a person snorted cocaine, it took on average about three years to call for help. If he or she smoked crack or freebase, the deterioration was accelerated and the call came within six months.

Although many people who abuse cocaine experience severe physical complications, including cardiac arrhythmias and death, in many ways the damage done to their lives is worse than the purely physical effects. Cocaine destroys the plans and dreams of the people who use it. It erodes their self-esteem, the meaning in their lives, and becomes all-consuming. This consumption of life leads people in recovery to talk about any drug addiction as being a spiritual disease. Cocaine abusers will minimize their drug use and, while desperately attempting to control or reverse it, nonetheless deceive the people they love the most.

EVIDENCE-BASED TREATMENT OPTIONS

In considering biopsychosocialspiritual treatment options for a pervasive disease like drug addiction, it makes sense to use whatever works in each sphere of those options.

Biologically, as we have noted, people withdrawing from cocaine are not at high risk for physical complications. However, the withdrawal is often associated with extreme cravings and impulsivity that immediately puts the relapsing individual in harm's way. Withdrawing cocaine abusers sign out of treatment, seek out dangerous individuals to get the drug, and do whatever is necessary to get high. To diminish withdrawal we often use drugs that help reequilibrate the dopamine reward system. None of these drugs are addictive in humans or animals. One category of drugs (represented by bromocriptine) substitutes directly for dopamine and markedly ameliorates the unpleasant psychological aspects of withdrawal, including cravings. Another medication group called presynaptic dopamine blockers fool the neurons going to the forebrain into acting as though they need to make new dopamine faster. Amantadine is the prototype of this category. Finally, dopamine reuptake inhibitors in the form of antidepressants are often used to ameliorate withdrawal symptoms. These drugs have some risks, however. The two most studied are bupropion and desipramine. Although they are very effective in lessening withdrawal symptoms, they have potential side effects which, when combined with cocaine, can be dangerous. Both cocaine and bupropion can lower the seizure threshold so that if an individual who has been detoxified using the antidepressant relapses soon after leaving the hospital, he or she is at risk for having a seizure. Similarly, both cocaine and desipramine impede the heart's ability to repolarize after a beat; when these agents are used together, it might lead to irreversible cardiac arrhythmias and death. Amantadine and bromocriptine are generally safer to use.

With respect to the psychological treatment of cocaine or other addictions, many therapies have been studied and shown to be useful. Changing the person's thinking about drugs using cognitive behavioral therapy works quite well, as does motivational enhancement therapy. There has been quite promising research about desensitizing cocaine abusers to the cues that previously triggered strong craving. This gives a useful set of tools to fight cravings when they occur. By far the most widely applied type of therapy for any form of substance abuse is that embodied by 12-step programs like Alcoholics Anonymous, Cocaine Anonymous, or Narcotics Anonymous. These programs are more widely available because they are peer-driven and do not require a specially trained therapist. In addition, they are free.

These programs also address both the social and spiritual consequences of substance use. Some of the steps in these programs involve making amends to those who have been harmed by the substance abuser's actions and doing a searching moral inventory. Some people do equally well immersing themselves in a community religious congregation.

CLINICAL COURSE WITH MANAGEMENT AND TREATMENT

In Marie's case, the clinician spends some time while her grandparents are out of the room discussing Marie's fears about "coming clean" with them. Initially Marie focuses on issues of who is "right" about the mistrust between them, but she is able to acknowledge that their opinion of her is important to her and that she fears losing all their respect. With support from the therapist, she says that she will think about honestly acknowledging her substance use. A return visit is scheduled for three days hence.

At that visit Marie opens by announcing that she has a confession to make. She talks about her substance use and the extent to which she has hidden it from everyone. She is in tears and seems relieved when her grandparents praise her for her courage in acknowledging the problems. A comprehensive treatment plan is set up with Marie and, with her permission, her grandparents.

She is to attend a semiweekly support group for adolescents in various stages of recovery, individual therapy with the clinician, and biweekly family sessions. She is also encouraged to attend some teenage 12-step meetings. She is begun on a low dose of bupropion and cautioned regarding concomitant use of cocaine. She is coached on proper sleep hygiene and is encouraged to begin a journal which she may or may not share with the therapist.

Over the next six weeks Marie's sleep and mood normalize and her anxiety markedly drops. The bupropion seems to be helping with her concentration and attention as well. At first somewhat tentative in her participation in the adolescent group, she has begun to emerge as one of the more supportive teen leaders. She begins attending Alcoholics Anonymous meetings. Her functioning improves in all areas of her life.

At six months of recovery, at her request, the bupropion is tapered and stopped.

She feels her mood to slip over the next months with more negativistic thinking. She finds herself being more irregular in her attendance at her support meetings. When members of the group gently confront her with their concern, she is able to reflect on her own behavior and decides to restart the bupropion.

After another year she has gradually decreased her attendance, although she continues to go to recovery meetings a few times a month. She is able to taper the bupropion, this time without relapse to the depression.

The evidence-based treatment recommended by the Substance Abuse and Mental Health Services Administration (SAMHSA) for adolescent addiction is the Adolescent Community Reinforcement Approach combined with Assertive Continuing Care. Although the evidence to date involves studies with cannabis dependence and cocaine, these best practices are considered promising for other forms of addiction. This treatment program embraces several key concepts, including the use of reinforcement to support the adolescent's participation and promoting prosocial activities. Therapeutic strategies include motivational interviewing and cognitive behavioral therapy leading the patient to develop healthier thought patterns and resiliency skills, such as anger/stress management, problem solving, and communication skills. Including the grandparents in at least four sessions is part of the evidence-based model. This family-centered approach is relevant to the sixth assessment dimension of the American Society of Addiction Medicine (ASAM) PPC-2R criteria for treatment planning: the recovery environment, especially the family's characteristics. Relapse prevention most importantly relies on nonusing behaviors by the family members and the provision of an environment that supports protective factors such as rewards for prosocial behaviors, school engagement, appropriate boundaries and limits with reinforcers for compliance, and consequences for misconduct.

The Adolescent Community Reinforcement Approach is most effective when combined with assertive continuing care. Assertive continuing care is based on a model that is "assertive," shifting the burden of ongoing engagement to the provider working in partnership with the family and the client. Continuing care includes home visits and provision of transportation services as needed.

SYSTEMS-BASED PRACTICE ISSUES

Often the options available for treatment of adolescent substance abuse are purely determined by availability in the area. Equally important, if there is not a strong recovery community locally, it is difficult for adolescents to go against peer pressure when many of the people they know are using drugs, and go into recovery themselves. These factors also help determine why AA meetings are so important because of their pervasive availability, the fact that they are free, and that they are anonymous. A recent strong factor for recovery also is now the Internet, with anonymous recovery support groups available to anyone with a computer and Internet access.

LEGAL, ETHICAL, AND CULTURAL CHALLENGES

Many legal systems protect vulnerable populations. Depending on the jurisdiction, children and adolescents may or may not expect confidentiality with regard to their parents or parental substitutes being entitled to know what goes on in their therapy. In addition, U.S. federal laws regarding disclosure of substance abuse information are also even more stringent than those regulating mental health information.

Given the fact that substance abuse often contaminates family systems, it can be difficult to negotiate the pitfalls and barriers of communication and disclosure within the recovering family. Very often multifamily support groups, in which adolescent substance users and their families come together, can lead to role modeling by the more "experienced" families with accelerated progress available to the newer families.

In addition, some substances of abuse carry more societal opprobrium than others. An adolescent is less likely to feel comfortable confessing snorting heroin than drinking beer.

REFERENCES AND RESOURCES

Doweiko H. *Concepts of Chemical Dependency* (8th ed.) Belmont, CA: Brooks/Cole, 2012.

Friedman AS, Utada A. A method for diagnosing and planning the treatment of adolescents drug abusers (The Adolescent Drug Abuse Diagnosis ADAD instrument). *J Drug Educ* 1989;19(4):285–312.

Godley SH, Meyers RJ, Smith JE, et al. The adolescent community reinforcement approach for adolescent cannabis users (DHHS Publication No. SMA-01-3489). Cannabis Youth Treatment Series, vol. 4, Rockville, MD, Center for Substance Abuse Treatment, Substance Abuse and Mental Health Services Administration, 2006. Available at http://www.chestnut.org/li/cyt/products/acra_cyt_v4.pdf.

CHAPTER **34**

Opioid Use

Anjali Varma, M.D.

CLINICAL PRESENTATION

Chief complaint: "I feel terrible; I stole my clients' medications."

History of present illness: Kelli is a 33-year-old female social worker who presents to the emergency room of a tertiary hospital reporting pain in her lower back. She recently moved to the area from another state with her seven-year-old son after she met "a wonderful man" on the Internet. She describes her back pain as 7 out of 10 in intensity, burning in character; it radiates from her back to her ankles. She says, "I have had this forever, but it has gotten worse over the last few weeks." She reports that she had been scheduled for an MRI but moved prior to the appointment. She states that her doctor always gave her hydrocodone and oxycodone for the pain because "they worked best." She reports being allergic to acetaminophen and ibuprofen. She is evaluated by the emergency department physician; physical examination shows some tenderness and tension in her lower back, and spine x-rays are relatively unremarkable.

She receives an injection of ketorolac (a strong, non-narcotic anti-inflammatory and analgesic) and is referred to a primary care doctor. Kelli repeatedly tells the emergency staff, "This isn't going to do it," and pleads, "Why don't you give me what works? I'm in so much pain." She is informed that narcotics are not provided in the emergency room for her condition. She denies any suicidal or homicidal thoughts; however, she begins to yell and scream at not being "treated right." Because of her behavior, a psychiatrist is asked to consult, but she leaves prior to being seen.

In three weeks she has her initial appointment with her new primary care doctor who thoroughly evaluates her condition and decides to give her hydrocodone 10 mg three times daily after she signs a pain agreement. During this meeting Kelli mentions having mood swings and is scheduled to see an outpatient psychiatrist. She is also scheduled for a follow-up appointment with primary care in six months.

After two months Kelli calls the primary care office reporting a fall that has caused worsening of her pain and requests an increase in the dose of her hydro-codone because "this is not working." She calls twice for early refills of opioid pain relievers and once gives a urine drug screen showing benzodiazepines (not prescribed for her), she is told that she is in violation of her pain contract and will no longer receive narcotics from the primary care doctor.

Kelli is seen in the psychiatric outpatient clinic of a buprenorphine provider. She admits to using pain pills to get high. Her use of pain medications first started at age 23 after she injured her back in a fall. She received a prescription for four weeks of oxycodone without refills. She liked the way the drug made her feel and went through the entire prescription in two weeks instead of four. How-ever, she did not seek out a continuing supply of pain pills at that time. After her son was born by cesarean section when Kelli was 26, she received morphine for analgesia; the "buzz" she had previously experienced with hydrocodone returned. She regretfully admits to stealing pain pills from family members and even her clients when she made home visits as a social worker. She admits that it has become a "huge problem" over the past two years and "I can't function without those pills." She reports that she had been discharged from the practices of sev-eral local pain doctors in her prior state of residence for running out of prescrip-tions early and going to multiple doctors. She has been buying prescription pain pills off the streets regularly for the last two years. She spends about $75 a day on pain pills (hydrocodone or oxycodone) but more when she has more money. With this amount of drug she is able to "just function" and reports that she no longer gets much of a high/buzz at this dose. She typically snorts the crushed pills while her son is at school and after he goes to sleep at night but has at times taken a few pills in front of him for "bad backaches." For the last two years she has stopped socializing with her friends from the mom's group that she belonged to when her son was first born. Kelli feels that the little time she has between work and taking care of her son after school is taken up by driving long distances to multiple doctors and more recently street dealers to get her pain pills. At work, she travels some to her clients' homes and uses in between visits. She tries to stay to herself and does not chitchat much with coworkers for fear of her col-leagues finding out about her use.

Without the pills she has withdrawal symptoms, including runny nose, watery eyes, gooseflesh, yawning, abdominal cramping, bone pains, and loose stools. To avoid this she ensures that she never runs out of pills. Her route of use is snort-ing or oral. She has never done intravenous drugs as she is aware of the risks of infections and other complications. She has never used heroin.

When she cannot get pain pills she uses two to three alprazolam 1 mg pills a day to reduce withdrawal symptoms. She has, on a few occasions, bought "this new pill called Suboxone" off the streets when pain pills were not available to handle withdrawal. She reports needing two or three of the "big ones" to com-pletely take care of withdrawal. Suboxone brand-name drug that is a combi-nation of buprenorphine (an opioid partial agonist) and naloxone (an opioid blocker). Her last dose of opioids was the morning of presenting to the psychia-trist.

Kelli sobs throughout the interview, says that she feels guilty about using and that she has made several attempts to cut back on her own but cannot stop because of withdrawal symptoms. She knows about methadone clinics but never dared to go to one, as some of her clients used to go there. She feels that she would not fit into the patient population. She reports having sleepless nights when she has no pain pills, has lost weight (about five pounds in the past two years), and has often felt depressed but has never let anyone know. She tries to function at a high level at work and at home as a single parent "to get it all done."

She has continued to keep her job as a social worker for family services up until recently when she decided to move to Virginia for the new relationship. Kelli thinks that no one at work ever knew or found out about her drug use. The father of her son divorced her five years ago and continues to pay child support and alimony. Kelli thinks that he suspects her of abusing pain pills but has never brought it up and is unlikely to do so, as he would not want to take custody of their son due to his own new marriage and baby.

Psychiatric history: Kelli was sexually abused as a child from ages 8 to 10 by her mother's boyfriend. When her mother identified the abuse, she kicked the boyfriend out. Kelli has a history of cutting herself (superficial scratches with a blade) once at age 14, after her mother disapproved of Kelli's first boyfriend. After sessions with the school counselor, she never repeated the cutting or any self-injurious behavior. She had induced vomiting to lose weight on two occasions after she had eaten too much of "a sinful dessert." She did not repeat this behavior though, as she did not like how it made her feel. She has always watched what she eats, is within normal limits of weight, and has never met criteria for an eating disorder.

She has always had a tendency to easily become frustrated and lose her temper, and she acknowledges that she is overly sensitive to the opinions of others. She had her first boyfriend at age 14 and has been sexually active since age 16.

She has never been admitted to a psychiatric hospital and has never attempted suicide. Kelli has only once been prescribed any psychotropic medications, when she was given sertraline after becoming depressed after a break-up with a college boyfriend. She never filled the prescription or took the medication because her mood improved on its own.

Substance abuse history: Kelli first experimented with cannabis at a weekend party in high school. Sporadic use continued until she entered college. She once tested positive for cannabis when tested at her part-time job in college. She denies using cannabis since.

Kelli took her first alcoholic drink in high school but did not like the taste. She did drink at times in college on the weekends "mainly to blend in with the crowd." "Alcohol was never my thing." Now she takes a glass of wine for a special occasion like a birthday or New Year's celebration.

Kelli's opioid use is described. She does not smoke.

Other medical history: Kelli has a childhood history of asthma and has had low back pain since age 23. She has tested negative for hepatitis, HIV, and syphilis.

Other history (developmental, educational/occupational, family/social, legal): Kelli was the product of a full-term normal vaginal delivery; her mother smoked throughout the pregnancy. She was a planned and wanted pregnancy. Her mother had a master's degree and her father was a construction worker. They had fallen in love while he had been working in her office. Soon after Kelli was born, marital discord worsened and parents divorced when Kelli was two. Kelli was born in Tennessee and was mainly raised by her grandparents, who were a "good Christian" family, while her mother worked.

At age six when her grandmother died, Kelli went to live with her mother and her boyfriend. There was ongoing sexual abuse by the mother's boyfriend from age 8 to 10. Kelli was a quiet girl in elementary school, shy, had few friends but made fair grades, "B's and C's." She had a fairly close relationship with her mother after the departure of the mother's boyfriend until Kelli's own interest in dating developed in her teens. In her teen years she had frequent arguments with her mother over her social life but continued to do fairly in school. She graduated from high school and went to college to get a bachelor's in social work. She enlisted in the military for one year, where she met the father of her son and moved to a Western state with him. She married at 24 and had her first baby at 26. Kelli reports having nursed her son for a full year. She returned to work as a social work assistant in the community with a local family services agency. She could do that then because she had the help and support of her then mother-in-law, who watched her son for her. She describes her son "being her life" and providing him with whatever he has ever asked for. She divorced when she was 28 because "things were just not working out." She reports that after her divorce she had been focused on her job and her son and did not care much about men until she came across her current boyfriend, with whom she is living, on a dating site. He works for a car dealership and does not use drugs or alcohol. He is supportive of Kelli seeking help from the psychiatrist for her pain pill abuse.

Kelli's father was an alcoholic. She had no contact with him growing up. There is no history of any other problems with drugs or alcohol in any other family member. No history of chronic mental illness or suicides.

Kelli has never had trouble with the law at any time other than two speeding tickets.

Mental status examination: Kelli presents as a tall, attractive, fashionable blonde, carrying a designer handbag. She speaks with animation and has clear, well-articulated speech with linear goal-directed thinking devoid of acute suicidality, homicidality, formal thought disorder, or perceptual abnormality. She reports her mood to be "okay" and has normal affect. She is alert and oriented to time/place and person and is judged to be a fairly intelligent person being aware of current events and quick at doing simple math tasks.

However, Kelli has presented differently at different points in time. During her initial ER visit, she had presented in pain and was argumentative and agitated, yelling and shouting when the emergency physician declined to give her pain medication. During her first visit with the psychiatrist, when she admitted to her prescription pain pill abuse, she expresses guilt and is appropriately tearful during the interview.

IMPAIRMENT IN FUNCTIONING

This working female parent shows substantial impairment in functioning. She has been spending a great deal of time procuring, consuming, and recovering from the effects of the prescription opioids. She has been socially withdrawn both at work and at home, has not been out with her friends to avoid people, and fears that they would find out. Driving large distances seeking different doctors and drug dealers to obtain the pain pills had become a routine for her. She had thus far not run into any legal trouble but has had several close calls. His work entails making home visits as a social worker and she had stolen pain medications from her clients.

DSM DIAGNOSIS

A clinician seeing Kelli for the first time would have an impression of prescription pain medication misuse which is classified in the DSM taxonomy as an opioid use disorder. In this case, the patient has symptoms of tolerance and withdrawal, taking larger amounts over longer periods of time than intended, persistent desire and cravings, and unsuccessful efforts to cut down on use. This patient has been spending a great deal of time in activities necessary to obtain the substance, giving up important social, occupational, and recreational activities despite the knowledge of the problems associated with the substance use. She has also been stealing medications to get the drug. In this case a DSM diagnosis of opioid use disorder is made with further qualifiers present once she is on maintenance therapy.

This patient does present with some sadness, regret, and tearfulness at initial presentation to the psychiatrist, but these symptoms seem to be directly related to the ongoing substance use and its effect on her life rather than substance-induced symptoms. Some of the mood and anxiety noted at different points in time may also be part of her personality framework with some cluster B traits that have been evident through the course of her life. In longitudinal follow-up in the outpatient clinic, depressive/anxiety symptoms that are noted are transient at best. Because of her erratic, impulsive, and affect-laden behavior in the emergency room, consideration is given to whether she might also suffer from borderline personality disorder. However, it is important to realize in the context of acute drug abuse and withdrawal that behavior becomes much more erratic and may not be indicative of the person's long-term coping skills.

EPIDEMIOLOGY

As of 2010, the estimated prevalence of current opioid use in the United States is nearly 18 million people (5.9% of the population), and 1.9 million individuals are dependent on prescription pain medication for nonmedical use. In contrast to Europe, Asia, and Africa, where heroin is the most prevalent illegally consumed opioid, in North America, prescription opioids are the primary opioids of abuse. However, a surge in prescription opioid abuse has been reported worldwide in the past decade.

The Drug Abuse Warning Network (DAWN) provides estimates of the health consequences of nonmedical use of individual drugs, including opioid medications. DAWN indicates that opioid analgesic misuse is being encountered more frequently in ERs in the United States over the past decade. In 2005 and 2009, hydrocodone and its combinations accounted for 51,225 and 86,258 ER visits respectively. Oxycodone and its combinations resulted in 42,810 visits to the ER in 2005; this number increased to 148,449 visits in 2009. According to the National Survey on Drug Use and Health, there were 140,000 new heroin users older than 12 years of age in 2010.

Lifetime nonmedical users of pain relievers grew from 31.8 million (13.2%) in 2004 to 34.8 million (13.7%) in 2010 and a 250% increase in oxycodone-related hospital admissions from 2004 to 2009 was witnessed. At least 24 million Americans have ever used a hydrocodone product illicitly. Some studies estimate that as many as 20% of the individuals in the United States have used a prescription opioid for nonmedical purpose at least once during their lifetime.

The greatest misuse was among individuals 18–25 years of age, and the incidence was higher in men than women of all age groups, except among those 12–17 years of age. Male-to-female ratios of lifetime heroin-only users and lifetime heroin and oxycodone users are similar. However, lifetime oxycodone-only users are more likely to be females (43.7%) than either of the other two groups. Male opioid users are more likely to also abuse other prescription drugs. There is a high incidence of mood/anxiety disorders among opioid users, and this incidence is significantly greater among women than men. A recent national study indicates that illicit drug use is 16.2% among pregnant teens and 7.4% among pregnant women aged 18–25 years.

Racial and ethnic distribution of lifetime nonmedical use of pain relievers is predominantly white (15.2%) and Native American (19.3), with Asians being the least (6.3%).

The increase in opioid analgesic abuse is particularly troubling because respiratory depression and death can result from the doses at which these agents are frequently abused, especially when mixed with other central nervous system depressants such as sedatives and tranquilizers.

DIFFERENTIAL DIAGNOSIS

In Kelli's case, opioid use disorder is one of the fist diagnoses to be considered. It may be considered an iatrogenic initiation, given that her first intake was from prescription.

Kelli's mood swings, anger, and irritability were initially found to be related to cycles of opioid intoxication, withdrawal, and the lifestyle associated with being an opioid addict. It is not uncommon to come across addicts who have significant depressive symptoms associated with drug use. For the sake of discussion, if her mood symptoms had persisted, a differential of opioid-induced mood disorder depressive type would also be entertained.

Patients with underlying bipolar illness are more prone to substance use, and bipolar disorder with opioid dependence should be considered and ruled out in such cases.

During her second trimester of pregnancy, Kelli needed an increase in her buprenorphine maintenance dose. This is expected in the second trimester and is attributed to the physiological increase in plasma volume. However, an astute clinician would constantly keep watch for signs of relapse to illicit drug use in opioid-dependent patients even in pregnancy. A possibility of diversion of buprenorphine should also be entertained. Use of random urine drug testing under observation and random pill counts help minimize the diversion of controlled substances.

ETIOLOGY AND PATHOGENESIS

Opioid dependence is best described as a central nervous system disorder characterized by neurobiological changes leading to compulsive drug-taking behavior.

Most opioids exert their effect by mimicking the naturally occurring endogenous opioids peptides or endorphins. There are four distinct families of classical opioid peptides: enkephalins, endorphins, dynorphins, and the most recently discovered nociceptin/orphanin. The endorphins and opioids produce their effects through activity at four major receptor subtypes: mu, kappa, delta, and ORL-1. These are transmembrane G protein–coupled receptors linked to adenylate cyclase.

Most opioid therapeutics, and all opioids with abuse potential, are selective for mu receptors (see Tables 34.1 and 34.2). Opioid agonists have several common physiological effects including:

- Analgesia.
- Sedation.
- Disruption of neuroendocrine function leading to decreased plasma concentration of testosterone and cortisol.
- Respiratory depression at high doses.
- Constipation and urinary hesitancy.
- Pupillary constriction.

The diverse biological effects of opioids are manifested through specific opioids receptors distributed throughout the central and peripheral nervous system. A detailed discussion of the molecular basis of dependence is beyond the scope of this text. However, opioids are known to exert their positive and nega-

Table 34.1. Specific Opioid Drugs

Drug: Full Agonists	Characteristics
Heroin	Diacetylmorphine
	Highly potent
	Prodrug rapidly metabolized to 6-monoacetylmorphine
	Rapid action after IV or intranasal use
Codeine	High oral bioavailability
Tramadol	Synthetic codeine analog
	Weak mu receptor agonist
	NE and 5HT reuptake inhibition
Meperidine	Limited use because of metabolic toxicity risks
Fentanyl	Synthetic opioid
	Fast action
	Potent
	Widespread use in chronic pain as transdermal patches
Methadone	90% oral bioavailability
	Long but variable half-life up to 80 hours
	Drug interactions related to CYP 3A4
	Tissue binding and accumulation—peripheral reserve
	QTc prolongation
	Dose for maintenance treatment 60–100 mg/day
Hydrocodone	Semi-synthetic codeine derivative
Oxycodone	Potent analgesic

tive reinforcement of mu and kappa receptors by the mesolimbic dopaminergic reward pathway.

Opioid withdrawal is a syndrome that emerges in physically dependent individuals following discontinuation of opioids or administration of an opioid antagonist such a naloxone. Signs and symptoms of opioid withdrawal include:

- Dilated pupils.
- Rhinorrhea.
- Lacrimation.
- Piloerection.
- Nausea.
- Vomiting.
- Diarrhea.
- Yawning.
- Muscle cramps.
- Restlessness.
- Elevated vital signs.
- Dysphoria

Onset of withdrawal symptoms depends on the half-life of the mu agonist being used. These are monitored using scales with the Clinical Opioid Withdrawal

Table 34.2. Mixed Agonist-Antagonist

Mixed agonist- antagonist	Mu	Kappa
Buprenorphine	p	−
Butaophanol	p	+++
Pentazocine	p	++
Nalorphine	−	+
Nalbuphine	p	

p: partial agonist, +: full agonist, −: antagonist.

Scale being the most commonly used. Typically heroin withdrawal begins approximately 8 hours after the last dose, peaking at about 48–72 hours and gradually tapering after 4–7 days. For opioids with longer half-life, like methadone, withdrawal symptoms may not set in until the fourth or fifth day after the last dose, depending on individual metabolism.

Risk factors for opioid abuse/dependence:

- Persons abusing alcohol/cannabis.
- Having first-degree relatives addicted to alcohol/drugs.
- Having friends/associates indulging in alcohol/drug use or other high-risk experimentations.
- Increase in the number of prescriptions for opioids written in the United States and the overall way medicine is practiced.
- Internet access to prescription drugs.
- Concurrent mental illness.
- Risk of fatal overdose rises in older, unemployed users of heroin or prescription opioids via intravenous route with concomitant use of alcohol or benzodiazepines.

Early exposure to opioids in adolescent users may cause neurobiological changes and behavioral consequences that differ from adults. Individuals who use nonmedical prescription opioids before 13 years of age are more likely to become addicts than those who initiated use at 21 years of age or older.

Over the recent years iatrogenic dependence, that is, dependence to opioids that are initially prescribed for a medical condition, mainly among chronic pain patients, has been a growing problem. Strategies to minimize this iatrogenic dependence include:

- Minimizing the use of opioids for non–cancer-related chronic pain.
- Use of alternate pharmacological and nonpharmacological strategies for pain control.
- Screening for dependence risk potential based on personal and family history of substance use.
- Minimize the duration of treatment with opioids.
- When opioid treatment is essential, use of narcotic treatment contracts.
- Constant monitoring and surveillance using drug screens/pill counts.
- Exercising extreme caution with regard to aberrant behaviors.

NATURAL COURSE WITHOUT TREATMENT

The natural course of opioid use disorder from initiation to daily use with physical and psychological dependence may vary in terms of time in different individuals; however, the stages are clearly delineated.

During the initiation phase, acute reinforcement of the initial drug effect is mediated by mu-opioid receptors and dopamine in the ventral tegmental area and nucleus accumbens, resulting in conditioned responses and drug craving. During the continuation phase, various neurotransmitters are involved, including dopamine in nucleus accumbens, corticotropin-releasing hormone in the amygdala, and glutamate in the frontal-cingulate circuit.

Tolerance refers to the decrease in the effectiveness of a drug with repeated administration. Tolerance to opioid effects is encountered in both the clinical use of opioids for pain relief and in recreational use of heroin. As tolerance develops, the dose and route of administration often change , with progression to intravenous use a frequent outcome. Short-term receptor desensitization may underlie the development of tolerance, probably involving phosphorylation of the mu and delta receptors, whereas long-term tolerance is believed to be associated with increase in adenylyl cyclase activity.

Glutamate and norepinephrine in the locus coeruleus are primarily involved in causing the symptoms associated with withdrawal. The orbitofrontal cortex, anterior cingulate gyrus, and amygdala are the brain regions implicated in relapse to opioid use.

Chronic relapsing nature of opioid dependence must be taken into consideration when considering any treatment option.

Kelli had made several attempts to give up opioids on her own, and she had been reluctant to seek help in a methadone clinic because several of her clients were in treatment there. Refusal to seek help due to the stigma associated with opioid abuse and its treatment is frequently a reason for opioid use disorder going unrecognized and untreated in the community.

When no treatment is rendered, it is common for opioid users to progress in their loss of control and role deterioration to the point that they face grave legal, social, and medical consequences. Role deterioration leads them to undertake behavior that is not characteristic of their premorbid values and personality. They may "steal, deal, and hook" to get money to pay for their drug. In addition, there are a host of medical problems resulting from chronic self injection of opioids including bacterial endocarditis, hepatitis, cellulitis, and blood clots. Opioid-dependent pregnant women may frequently be unrecognized and undertreated. Several barriers to treatment can be identified:

- Stigma of substance use during pregnancy.
- Patients may attempt to quit opioid use on their own once the pregnancy is detected.
- Fear of mandatory reporting to social services.
- Low socioeconomic and educational status.
- Abusive relationships.
- Ongoing legal problems.
- Early signs of pregnancy such as nausea/vomiting and fatigue may be confused with opioid withdrawal symptoms.

Ongoing opioid use during pregnancy may be related to several medical and obstetric complications. Medical complications include:

- Anemia,
- Bacteremia,
- Endocarditis,
- Cellulitis,
- Hepatitis,
- Phlebitis,
- Sexually transmitted diseases,
- Pneumonia, and
- Cystitis/pyelonephritis.

Obstetric complications may include:

- Placental abruption,
- Chorioamnionitis,
- Placental insufficiency,
- Fetal growth restriction,
- Spontaneous abortion,
- Hypoxic brain injury,
- Premature labor and delivery,
- Miscarriage,
- Low birthweight, and
- Neonatal abstinence syndrome.

EVIDENCE-BASED TREATMENT OPTIONS

Principal treatment modalities offered for opioid dependence include detoxification, agonist maintenance, and antagonists. At present there are no direct interventions that are capable of reversing the effects of drug dependence on learning and motivation systems.

As discussed, detoxification is frequently followed by early relapse to opioid use and is successful only in highly motivated patients.

Opioid maintenance therapy with an agonist aims to reduce or eliminate illicit opioid use, associated health risks, and stabilize an unhealthy lifestyle. After a patient is tapered off the short-acting opioid agonist, a long-acting opioid agonist such as methadone or a partial agonist such as buprenorphine is introduced to tide over withdrawal and cravings. Results of short-term therapy with agonists followed by rapid taper have shown increased risk of relapse, whereas long-term maintenance is associated with greater retention in treatment. Some patients may remain on these agonists on a long-term basis—sometimes lifelong—depending on individual needs. Methadone and buprenorphine act by eliminating withdrawal and reducing the craving for opioids, thus reducing illicit opioid use and producing very strong positive health outcomes as measured by decreased mortality, improved mental and physical health, and reduced risk of disease transmission.

The modern use of methadone as a opioid maintenance treatment (OMT) pharmacotherapy started with in the 1960s. Since that time, there has a been a stigma associated with OMT among physicians, patients, staff, and the general public that may pose a barrier to treatment. However, methadone remains the most inexpensive and empirically validated agent available for opioid replacement therapy. Studies have shown one-year treatment retention rates of 80%, with significant reduction in illicit opioid use. Treatment is provided in federally regulated specialized OMT programs requiring initial daily visits. Initial dose of 25–30 mg/day of methadone is titrated in 5–10 mg increments a day to a desired range of 60–120 mg/day. Lower dose treatment is associated with less positive outcome.

Buprenorphine is a partial agonist at the mu opiate receptor and an antagonist at the kappa receptor and has a very long half-life. For opioid dependence a sublingual tablet containing a combination of buprenorphine and naloxone is frequently used. The naloxone (opiate antagonist) component is inactive when used sublingually but prevents the parenteral recreational use of the drug (see Table 34.3). The unique pharmacological profile of the drug makes it an ideal treatment option in some ways. It is now increasingly being used as a first-line maintenance treatment for opioid dependence due to its safety, efficacy, and convenient usage compared to methadone. A DATA 2000 waivered physician may prescribed buprenorphine in an office-based setting.

Medication is currently available in pill and film form to be taken sublingually. Most providers use a treatment agreement or contract similar to a narcotic contract used in pain clinics to clearly lay out rules of treatment. Induction dose of buprenorphine 4–8 mg is given on the first day, increased to 16 mg the second day and thereafter titrated up depending on level of cravings. Most patients are stabilized on 16–24 mg/day, 32 mg/day being the highest possible dose. However, given the ceiling phenomena, higher doses are not typically more beneficial.

Frequently noted side effects with buprenorphine include nausea, headaches, sedation, insomnia, constipation, urinary hesitancy, dry mouth, and sexual side effects. Some patients may get a transient high on the medication when it is first

Table 34.3. Methadone and Buprenorphine

	Methadone	**Buprenorphine**
Schedule	Schedule II	Schedule III
Receptor profile	Pure agonist, NMDA receptor antagonist-neuropathic pain	Partial agonist-antagonist-analgesic ceiling effect
Treatment setting	Only in clinic/daily visits	Outpatient—variable visits
Efficacy	Well-documented/standard of therapeutic comparison	May be first-line for certain patients
Safety	Abuse and overdose potential high	Lower abuse/overdose potential
Pregnancy	Standard of care since 1970s	Not enough evidence

started, but most patients report feeling normal on buprenorphine. Once stabilized, patients may be maintained on a monthly basis. Ongoing monitoring with random urine drug screens and pill counts is an essential part of office-based buprenorphine treatment to prevent abuse and diversion. Office-based treatment is almost always combined with individual and group therapy for addiction.

Detoxification from opiates is generally not recommended during pregnancy because studies have shown that these women who have been withdrawn from opioid maintenance are likely to relapse to illicit drugs. For the majority of these women, opiate substitution programs combined with psychosocial treatment offer the best chance of stabilization of their addiction and opportunity for a sustainable recovery. Methadone has been considered the gold standard for treatment of opioid dependence in pregnancy. As more data regarding safe use of buprenorphine in opioid-dependent pregnant patients continues to be collected, clinicians and researchers are slowly getting comfortable with the use of buprenorphine in pregnancy.

In Kelli's case, she is already enrolled in the buprenorphine clinic when she gets pregnant. Since she has had good experience on buprenorphine for over a year, after consultation with her psychiatrist and obstetrician she makes an informed decision to continue treatment. For patients in the community who may be identified as opiate addicts by the obstetrician or family practitioner at the time of initial screening in pregnancy, women should be offered immediate and appropriate referral for substance abuse treatment. Most pregnant women are already in the contemplation stage of behavioral change and are readily motivated to take appropriate action.

General objectives of opioid agonist treatment:

- Prevent opioid withdrawal signs and symptoms.
- Provide a comfortable induction onto the agonist medication.
- Block the euphoric and reinforcing effects of illicit opioids while attenuating the motivation (craving, social interactions) to use illicit opioids and other drugs.
- Enhance treatment retention and prenatal care.
- Create a more optimal environment for behavioral and psychosocial interventions.

Compared to methadone clinics that require daily attendance to receive medication, buprenorphine offers greater privacy because it can be prescribed during a physician's office visit and may be combined with routine obstetric care. However, women with long-standing addiction to high-dose intravenous opiates are at higher risk for relapse and should be considered for referral to a methadone clinic.

Though in clinical practice buprenorphine is used in combination with naloxone, a mu antagonist that is inactive when taken sublingually and prevents intravenous misuse, the general consensus is to use buprenorphine monoproduct and avoid naloxone in pregnancy. Though literature was limited until recently, there is a now growing evidence regarding the safety and efficacy of the use of buprenorphine in pregnancy. A multicenter study in 2010 (MOTHER trial) comparing opioid-dependent pregnant patients maintained on methadone versus buprenorphine showed that the rates of maternal medical complications, overdose potential, rates of neonatal abstinence syndrome, and duration of newborn hospitalization were substantially lower in the buprenorphine group, although the retention rates were variable (and controversial) and birthweight was equivalent or higher in the buprenorphine group. For patients like Kelli, when provided with this information, buprenorphine was quite an obvious choice.

A detailed discussion of management of labor and postpartum pain control is beyond the scope of this chapter. Additional analgesia may not be necessary in many instances, and the maintenance dose of buprenorphine given in divided doses may provide sufficient analgesia. NSAIDs and acetaminophen are frequently adequate for mild to moderate pain. However, additional augmentation with short-acting injectable opioids should be added as needed, especially for postoperative pain following cesarean section. Need for additional opiates may be necessary due to inadequate analgesia provided by buprenorphine, patient's tolerance to buprenorphine, and opioid-induced hyperalgesia (decreased pain threshold resulting from prolonged opiate use). However, most opioid agonists will not displace buprenorphine from the opioid receptor. Fentanyl, an extremely potent opioid, is the exception. Awareness of some of these key principles of judicious opioid use in this patient population among family practitioners and obstetric providers is pivotal in providing these patients with optimal care they need and deserve.

Neonatal abstinence syndrome (NAS) is a drug withdrawal syndrome in newborns after birth, most commonly occurring in the context of antepartum opiate use. A wide array of signs and symptoms include central nervous system hyperirritability and autonomic nervous system dysfunction: excessive crying, tremors, poor sleep, hyperthermia, tachypnea, poor feeding, irritability, and vomiting. A modified Finnegan scale is used to monitor for symptoms of NAS every four hours. Various opiates or phenobarbital (especially with concomitant benzodiazepine abuse) are used in management of NAS. Infants are usually kept in the hospital for five to seven days to monitor for the delayed appearance of NAS symptoms and longer if treatment is necessary. Breast milk of mothers on methadone may be insufficient to prevent NAS, and infants still may require opioid agonist treatment. Treatment of the infant with an opiate may continue after discharge, as was the case of Kelli's baby.

Although breastfeeding is not recommended for mothers who are taking buprenorphine per the package insert, there is increasing evidence that breastfeeding with buprenorphine maintenance may be safe. Studies show that infants receive less than 1% dose per kilogram of the maternal buprenorphine and its metabolite, norbuprenorphine, in breast milk. The risk of breast milk–induced buprenorphine addiction in the infant appears unlikely, and there is no reason to time breastfeeding to avoid peak levels of buprenorphine in maternal plasma.

Naloxone is compatible with breastfeeding, and thus in the postpartum period women should resume the buprenorphine/naloxone combination and most providers encourage breastfeeding even for infants being treated for NAS.

Naltrexone is an opioid antagonist that acts by blocking the mu opioid receptors, thus preventing the reward from the problem opioid drug. However, it does not stop drug cravings, leading to overall low retention rates. Naltrexone treatment has been found to be successful in relapse prevention only in patients with stable social situations and who are most highly motivated, such as health care professionals. It is available as a pill and as a once-monthly extended-release injectable formulation. There is limited and equivocal data regarding naltrexone in pregnancy.

Pharmacotherapy must be offered in a comprehensive health care context that also addresses the psychosocial aspects of dependence. Opioid dependence patients may frequently suffer from physical and psychiatric disorders, making targeted interventions of psychiatric comorbidity an essential component of treatment for improving outcome for these patients. Polysubstance use is the rule rather than the exception in opioid dependence, and concurrent use of other substances should be carefully monitored and treated when necessary.

There are no current data to support psychosocial interventions as a sole intervention for opioid dependence. Psychosocial interventions when added to opioid agonist treatment have been found to significantly improve the outcome of treatment and improve retention and follow-up rates.

Therapies may be broadly classified as

- Interventions that were first developed for treating depression and anxiety and were later adapted for treating persons with addictive disorders, for example, cognitive behavioral therapy, supportive expressive therapy, and interpersonal therapy. Readers are referred to specialized texts for details of these therapies.
- Therapies that specifically developed for persons with addictive disorders, for example, motivational interviewing, motivational enhancement, contingency management, and 12-step/self-help programs such as NA.

Motivational enhancement therapy (MET) is a counseling approach that helps individuals resolve their ambivalence about engaging in treatment and stopping their drug use. This approach aims to evoke rapid and internally motivated change, rather than guide the patient stepwise through the recovery process. This therapy consists of an initial assessment battery session, followed by two to four individual treatment sessions with a therapist. In the first treatment session, the therapist provides feedback to the initial assessment, stimulating discussion about personal substance use and eliciting self-motivational statements. Motivational interviewing principles are used to strengthen motivation and build a plan for change. Coping strategies for high-risk situations are suggested and discussed with the patient. In subsequent sessions, the therapist monitors change, reviews cessation strategies being used, and continues to encourage commitment to change or sustained abstinence. Patients are sometimes encouraged to bring a significant other to sessions.

The contingency management approach of treatment emerged from the behavioral therapy tradition. Desirable patient behaviors—such as submitting negative drug screens and adherence to program rules or treatment plans—are rewarded. Medication take-home privileges is a form of contingency management frequently used in methadone maintenance treatment. Patients are permitted to "earn" take-home doses of their methadone in exchange for increasing, decreasing, or ceasing certain behaviors.

Twelve-step programs for opioid abuse and dependence include Narcotic Anonymous (NA) and Methadone Anonymous (MA) and are modeled after Alcoholic Anonymous (AA), an abstinence-based support and self-improvement program that is based on the 12-step model of recovery. The 12-step model emphasizes acceptance of dependence as a chronic progressive disease that can be arrested through abstinence (but not cured). Additional elements include spiritual growth, personal responsibility, and helping other addicted persons.

CLINICAL COURSE WITH MANAGEMENT AND TREATMENT

Kelli is accepted in the outpatient buprenorphine clinic of the psychiatrist after she signs a treatment agreement that details clinic guidelines such as:

- Lost and stolen prescriptions are not replaced.
- Patients are subject to random urine drug screens and pill counts.
- Female patients need to use birth control while on this medication.
- To inform other providers that she is maintained on buprenorphine especially prior to painful procedures.
- Concurrent use of benzodiazepines is prohibited with this medication.
- Violation of clinic rules may lead to discharge.

She is asked to present in mild to moderate withdrawal and receives an induction dose of buprenorphine/naloxone 8 mg/2 mg the first day and then 16 mg/4 mg the second day. She reports no cravings or withdrawal and some benefit in back pain, and is stabilized on 20 mg/5 mg daily of buprenorphine/naloxone. She attends weekly groups in the clinic, is compliant with rules, and all her urine drug screens are clean. She is gradually switched to a biweekly and then a monthly schedule.

Her "mood swings" initially reported to the primary care doctor are noted to have been mainly related to use of drugs and possibly due to low-grade personality issues. These are monitored but not treated with medication.

She does well in the buprenorphine clinic for over a year. Besides decreased sexual drive, Kelli reports no side effects with the medication. During this time of routine follow-up visits and groups, she denies sadness/anxiety or mood swings and shares having a stable relationship with her boyfriend.

She presents one morning for an unscheduled visit and reports being pregnant. She states that she had been using birth control as advised but failed to use barrier protection "just one time" and has now had two pregnancy tests that have been positive. She does not know what to do and is crying, asking for help. She wants to have the baby but is afraid of relapse to opiate abuse if she stops the buprenorphine.

An interdisciplinary team meeting is set up with the psychiatrist and her obstetrician who have a detailed discussion with Kelli and her boyfriend regarding treatment of opioid dependence in pregnancy and various options. Long-term evidence about using methadone in pregnancy and more recent literature regarding use of buprenorphine is discussed. Risk of neonatal abstinence syndrome is reviewed. Kelli asks a few questions that are answered to her satisfaction, and she signs an informed consent and agrees to continue treatment with the monoproduct buprenorphine during pregnancy.

Other than the nausea and sickness of first trimester Kelli has a relatively unremarkable pregnancy.

In response to her reports of increased cravings in her second trimester, her psychiatrist considers increasing the dose of her buprenorphine to 24 mg/day but does not do so because of lack of evidence of improved effect over 16 mg and possible increased risk to the baby. Instead, Kelli increases her contact with supportive friends within the recovery community. She continues to take her buprenorphine until the day of her scheduled cesarean section as advised by her anesthesiologist. She receives spinal anesthesia using bupivacaine during the procedure. After the baby is delivered, she is switched back to a combination buprenorphine/naloxone product and the dose is increased to 24 mg buprenorphine to handle her pain. (Consideration was given to using a stronger opioid agonist for pain, but the buprenorphine would have prevented its action.)

Kelli's baby girl weighs 7.5 pounds and on the second day after birth is noted to have signs of neonatal abstinence syndrome in the form of irritability, poor feeding, and loose stools. She is treated with methadone and kept in the neonatal ICU for five days after birth. She is finally discharged home after seven days on a tapering dose of methadone with weekly appointments in the neonatal outpatient clinic for monitoring. The baby is completely tapered off the methadone after 17 days of treatment.

Kelli did initially try to breastfeed the baby and had a detailed discussion with her neonatologist as well as her psychiatrist about the safety of use of buprenorphine/naloxone in breastfeeding. She later elected for bottle feeding.

Kelli's baby girl is now one year old and is doing very well in terms of timely achievement of milestones. Kelli married her boyfriend and father of her daughter when the baby was three months old. However, she and her husband have problems related to finances and caring for children. She has felt close to relapse in times of stress, but she has not actually used drugs again.

Patients with opioid dependence may present in various settings, including emergency rooms, primary care clinics, pain clinics, OB/GYN clinics, and psychiatric clinics. After being identified and correctly diagnosed, the next step is a thorough assessment of patient's knowledge and acceptance of the problem with opioids. For less motivated patients, MET may be used for several sessions before patients are more accepting of the treatments offered. As discussed, agonist treatments may be offered first along with psychosocial interventions. The decision of which agonist agent (methadone versus buprenorphine) should be used must be decided on a case-by-case basis. Psychosocial interventions when used in combination with agonist treatment help in retention and relapse prevention.

SYSTEMS-BASED PRACTICE ISSUES

Long-term opioid agonist treatment has been shown to have a positive effect on public health by significantly reducing overdose deaths, criminal activity, and spread of infectious diseases. As of 2008 only 260,000 (10% of all opioid-dependent) patients in the United States are enrolled in opioid replacement therapy. Methadone maintenance has been found to be cost-effective. A study of Veterans' Affairs patients showed that the six-month costs are about $21,000 for an untreated drug abuser and $1,750 for a patient enrolled in methadone maintenance program. A recent study suggests that office-based buprenorpine/naloxone treatment for clinically stable patients may be a cost-effective alternative to no treatment at a threshold of $100,000 per quality of life–adjusted life years) depending on assumptions about quality-of-life weights.

One recent retrospective cross-sectional study of nationally representative sample of newborns evaluated the incidence of NAS and the associated health care expenditure between 2000 and 2009. The incidence of NAS among newborns increased from 1.2 (95% confidence interval 1.04–1.37) to 3.39 (95% confidence interval 3.12–3.67) per 1,000 hospital births a year (p for trend < 0.001). Mean hospital charges for discharges with NAS increased from $39,400 (95% confidence interval $33,400–45,400) in 2000 to $53,400 (95% confidence interval $49,000–57,700) in 2009 ($p$ for trend < 0.001).

LEGAL, ETHICAL, AND CULTURAL ISSUES

Morphine and heroin were first synthesized and used medicinally in the 19th century and recreational and illicit use soon followed. Due to the powerful reinforcing effects of the opioid drugs and several patient and environmental factors, treatment of opioid dependence has been very challenging with high relapse rates after detoxification. Over 45 years ago methadone was introduced as replacement therapy in the treatment of heroin addiction. This was a breakthrough treatment at the time. The goal was "harm reduction" to reduce the social effect of opioid dependence in terms of crime, prostitution, and increased incidence of infectious disease. Later in the 1980s, the rise of hepatitis and HIV infections due to needle sharing reiterated the need for harm reduction, and needle exchange programs were started alongside of methadone programs. Over the years treatment of opioid dependence has grown with the advent of 12-step programs of Narcotic Anonymous and psychosocial interventions to augment the agonist replacement therapies.

Opioid use disorder remains a chronic relapsing disorder characterized by compulsive drug seeking and use. Given the high rate of relapse after detoxification, maintenance therapy with an agonist is now considered the mainstay of pharmacological treatment of severe relapsing opioid dependence along with lifelong psychosocial interventions focusing on recovery.

Several legal, ethical, and cultural factors are increasingly becoming highlighted as the discussions and controversies regarding use of opioids for management of chronic pain increase. Opioids are the pharmacologic *sine qua non* of pain management in life-limiting illness and should be prescribed based on the severity of pain and its functional and psychological significance. The highly addictive nature of opioids, propensity to development of tolerance and dependence, and risk of respiratory depression are increasing concerns that are now leading to cautious prescribing of opioids for non–cancer-related pain.

With increased diversion of scheduled drugs, more and more states are opting to use prescription drug monitoring programs (PDMPs), state-run databases that store and distribute information regarding federally controlled substances. These serve health care workers as well as law enforcement agencies and support legitimate medical use of controlled substances while limiting abuse and diversion. Pharmacies that dispense controlled substances are usually required to register the filling of such prescriptions with the database.

Though, PDMPs may help curb the problem to some extent, widespread availability of opioids over the Internet continues to fuel the growing epidemic of prescription drug use. An understanding of opioid dependence and its various effective treatment options is vital to medical and mental health, and other health care professionals in a variety of settings as the number of people afflicted with this addiction continues to rise.

TERMS

Abuse: the definition varies depending on the context. *Abuse* is defined as the use of prescription medications beyond the scope of sound medical practice. *Abuse* and *misuse* often overlap when referring to prescription medication. The American Psychiatric Association defines *abuse* as "maladaptive pattern of substance use leading to clinically significant impairment or distress as manifested by one or more behaviorally based criteria." The Drug Enforcement Agency defines *abuse* as the use of a Schedule II–V drug in a manner or amount inconsistent with the medical or social pattern of a culture.

Addiction: defined by the American Society of Addiction Medicine as "a primary chronic, neurobiological disease, with genetic, psychosocial, and environmental factors influencing the development and manifestations. It is characterized by behaviors that include one or more of the following: impaired control over drug use, compulsive use, continued use despite harm and craving."

Dependence: a confusing concept with regard to substance use disorders. It can refer to a normal physiologic accommodation to an external substance. Someone treated with an opioid for pain over a long period of time will become physically dependent on it.

Misuse: patient's incorrect use of a medication, including use of an unintended purpose, exceeding the prescribed amount, or taking the drug more frequently or for longer than prescribed.

Pseudoaddiction: drug-seeking behaviors iatrogenically produced in pain patients by inadequate pain treatment.

REFERENCES AND RESOURCES

Alto WA, O'Connor AB. Management of women treated with buprenorphine during pregnancy. *Am J Obstet Gynecol* 2011;205(4):302–8.

Jones HE, Johnson RE, Jasinski DR, et al. Buprenorphine versus methadone in the treatment of pregnant opioid-dependent patients: effects on the neonatal abstinence syndrome. *Drug Alcohol Depend* 2005;79(1):1–10.

Jones HE, Kaltenbach K, Heil SH, et al. Neonatal abstinence syndrome after methadone or buprenorphine exposure. *N Engl J Med* 2010 Dec 9;363(24):2320–31.

Miller SC, Fernandez L, Soria R. Opioid use disorder during pregnancy—non judgemental identification and treatment can maximize maternal/fetal outcomes. *Curr Psych* 2011;10(3):35–45.

Schackman BR, Leff JA, Polsky D, Moore BA, Fiellin DA. Cost-effectiveness of long-term outpatient buprenorphine-naloxone treatment for opioid dependence in primary care. *J Gen Intern Med* 2012 Jun;27(6):669–76.

The Man with the Golden Arm (1955), a film from the novel by Nelson Algren, tells the story of a heroin addict who gets clean while in prison and struggles to remain clean after release.

CHAPTER 35

Ingestion of an Unknown Substance

William S. Rea, M.D.

CLINICAL PRESENTATION

Current complaint: incoherent muttering.

History of present illness: Sunday at 1:30 AM a young, disheveled man is brought to the local emergency department by two other young men, who leave him in the waiting room and run back to their car and speed away. The person sits in the waiting room, giggling and muttering to himself. He is sweating profusely. He is blinking rapidly. The emergency department staff quickly triages him to a cubicle near the nurses' station. The nurse who takes his vital signs notes that he startles and tenses at every loud sound or overhead announcement. His eyes dart constantly. His pulse is 120, respirations 20, and blood pressure 150/94.

Speaking in soothing tones, the staff obtains blood and tries to obtain a urine sample but he does not seem to understand what is requested.

Examination of the contents of his pockets shows university identification and a driver's license. His name is Travis and he is 19 years old. The home address is a dormitory at a local college. A telephone call to the campus police is made to attempt to contact anyone who knows Travis or who knows anything about what happened.

A stat psychiatric consult is requested and he is examined within 45 minutes. The blood laboratory results have returned by this time and show normal electrolytes, liver function tests, and complete blood count (indicating an infection to be unlikely). Travis's blood alcohol concentration is 0.066% by volume. (Most states consider the person to be legally intoxicated at an alcohol concentration of greater than 0.08% by volume.)

The psychiatrist is unable to get much information from Travis. The initial giggling described by the emergency department staff has disappeared, and now he appears frightened and paranoid. He cringes away from every motion by the clinician. He makes no eye contact, except for fleeting glances at the clinician's face. His muttering is incoherent and at times turns into grunting.

The clinician returns to the nurses' station and learns that the campus police have found a phone number for the resident advisor from the dormitory. The RA says that Travis has shown no behavioral disturbance in the past. He is an above average student with no academic difficulties. He is part of a clique that is known to use marijuana and frequently binge on beer on weekends. He has had a stable relationship with a girlfriend for the past four months. The clinician asks the RA to try to find someone who has been with Travis this evening.

After hanging up, the clinician sees Travis bolt from his curtained cubicle, knock over an IV pole, and stumble down the hall. A security officer grabs him, and other staff assist to restrain him. Travis is thrashing around, screaming, and trying to bite people. He is restrained by all limbs to a gurney in a more isolated cubicle to minimize his stimulation. With the psychiatrist's advice, the emergency physician administers 2 mg lorazepam intramuscularly. It has no apparent effect. Fifteen minutes later, another 2 mg are given, and the patient gradually quiets. When he is asleep, a straight catheterization of his bladder obtains urine for a drug screen. The screen is negative for all drugs of abuse, except cannabis. A CT scan of the head is completely normal.

Travis is clearly in need of a safe environment to protect him. Equally clearly, he has no capacity to understand and consent to psychiatric admission and treatment. A temporary detaining order is obtained from the local magistrate, permitting admission to the psychiatric unit of the hospital. Within two business days a judge will examine the case and decide whether to commit or release Travis. His transfer to the psychiatric unit is uneventful, although he remains extremely sedated.

IMPAIRMENT IN FUNCTIONING

The cause of Travis's condition at this point is a puzzle. What is known is that he is completely incapacitated at the moment. He does not seem to be able to process information or communicate. His behavior is impulsive and aggressive. He has gone from being a highly functional individual to being extremely impaired in one evening.

DSM DIAGNOSIS

There are three primary reasons to make a diagnosis: first, to predict the natural course of the disorder; second, to rationally choose the best treatment options; and third, to determine the cause. To make a diagnosis, the clinician needs information. In mental health treatment as in other areas of health care the most useful source of information is the history the person relates to the clinician. Travis cannot coherently relate anything. We are reduced to using observable measures and collateral history obtained from other people. The resident advisor tells us that this is a completely new behavior for Travis. There was no evidence of a gradual deterioration, but rather of an abrupt onset. Travis previously functioned well vocationally (in his case, academically) and socially, with friends and a significant other. He has no history of aggression. Observable information includes his vital signs, behavior, examination, laboratory findings, and the results of the CT scan.

His examination shows a high stress response. He is sweating, restless, with elevated pulse and blood pressure. This is common to psychosis in general, whatever the cause.

From the laboratory studies, we know that he does not have an elevated white blood cell count as a reaction to an infection (e.g., encephalitis) and does not have a metabolic disturbance, and the only drug that appeared in his urine test was cannabis. His urine was negative for cocaine, amphetamines, phencyclidine, opioids, methadone, and tricyclics. Psychosis is not uncommon in use of cocaine, amphetamines, and phencyclidine, so their absence is useful information. His CT scan was normal, ruling out a brain tumor.

At this point the working diagnosis is psychosis, not otherwise specified. This is a generic diagnosis that will be refined as the treatment team obtains more information and history.

The overall impression at this point is of a person with a catastrophic, abrupt onset of thought and anxiety symptoms.

The DSM diagnosis would be brief psychotic disorder (assuming it resolved within a month). This diagnosis emphasizes the brief duration of the episode. This diagnosis may account for up to 1 in 11 of all first psychotic breaks. If the episode were precipitated by a drug, the diagnosis would be substance-induced psychotic disorder.

EPIDEMIOLOGY

How do we determine the prevalence or incidence of people using a certain drug in the population when we do not know what the drug is? In emerging use of drugs, which are common in Western Europe and the United States, there is a common pattern that shows use rising from zero (prior to the introduction of the drug) to a peak level as it spreads through the population and then gradually decreasing to a lower prevalence. In some ways the graph of population use of these drugs is similar to what is seen when an infection goes through a naive population. Many people are initially infected, and some of them develop a chronic problem. Many others seem to recover.

The two primary examples which we have seen in the 21st century of the emergence of unknown drugs has been MDMA or "ecstasy" in the early part of the century and then "bath salts" at the end of the first decade. MDMA (3,4-methylenedioxy-N-methamphetamine) is a drug similar to amphetamines with some hallucinogenic properties. In 2013 there has been a resurgence of MDMA abuse, now in a powder form ("molly") rather than pill ("ecstasy"). Similarly, bath

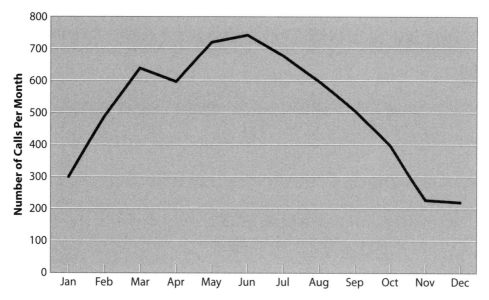

Figure 35.1. 2011 Bath Salts Exposure Calls

salts (often MDPV or methylenedioxypyrovalerone) are stimulants and halluci-nogens derived from the khat plant of eastern Africa. These are called cathinones.

Poison control centers in 2011 showed rapid tripling of the number of calls for bath salts within a few months which then fell to a lower baseline level (see Figure 35.1). It is likely that these calls correlate with the number of new cases (incidence) of bath salt users. Because cathinone users tend to have severe conse-quences for ingesting the drug, their use would not be expected to continue over a long period of time. Word will get out on the streets about its dangers so both the incidence and prevalence (all cases) of use will decline. When the perceived risk of using a drug is low, the prevalence remains high, for example, marijuana.

DIFFERENTIAL DIAGNOSIS

The differential diagnosis for new-onset psychosis in a 19-year-old person is broad. The psychosis could be due to a brain infection, an endocrine imbalance (for example, marked hyperthyroidism or thyroid storm), a frontal lobe tumor, or an acute cerebrovascular event (stroke). It could also be due to sudden onset of schizophrenia or manic psychosis. However, by far the most likely diagnosis is psychosis due to drug ingestion.

But what drug? We know that Travis had used marijuana within the past few weeks. Tetrahydrocannabinol, the active drug in marijuana, is heavily absorbed into fatty tissues in the body and may be detected up to a month after use. Although marijuana can cause psychosis, the question in this case arises as to why now? Travis has been known to have smoked pot in the past without such obvious ill effect. One problem with this particular question is that unlike pharmaceuticals regulated by the FDA, street drugs like marijuana and cocaine have little or no quality control in their production and distribution. It is not unusual to find other drugs contaminating marijuana. One possibility, then, is that Travis had a bad batch of marijuana with a contaminant that triggered the psychosis.

However, as he awakens Travis tells us that he indeed had ingested bath salts by snorting them with some friends. The diagnosis then becomes substance-induced psychosis.

ETIOLOGY AND PATHOGENESIS

The etiology of hallucinations from drugs of abuse involves a complex interaction of multiple neurotransmitter systems, especially dopamine, serotonin, and probably acetylcholine. The exact pathogenesis probably varies for each unique chemical.

Common questions that arise regarding psychosis after drug use can often be distilled into three possibilities. First possibility: the psychosis is purely drug-induced and will disappear when the drug leaves the body. Second possibility: the drug has induced a psychosis that will persist following excretion of the drug. Third possibility: the drug has released or precipitated an underlying psychosis, which will then proceed according to the natural course of illness of that type of psychosis.

Given that the first possibility (of the psychosis leaving with the drug) is fairly common, often the treatment of an acute drug-induced psychosis is very conservative. The person is put in a low-intensity environment without much in the way of stimulus to excite or aggravate him. He is kept safe without access to any means of harming himself or anyone else. He may be sedated with a benzodiazepine to alleviate evident distress. All interactions with other people are designed to reassure and soothe him.

NATURAL COURSE WITHOUT TREATMENT

Given that the half-life of most exogenous hallucinogens in human beings is measured in hours rather than days, the precipitant of the psychosis is usually gone within a couple of days. For those individuals who get better by letting the drug get out of their system, they will usually do so within two to four days.

Some individuals, however, find that the use of the drug has precipitated an ongoing psychosis, which can be tremendously debilitating.

EVIDENCE-BASED TREATMENT OPTIONS

Often in the first 24–36 hours after ingestion of a hallucinogen, the individual is sedated with benzodiazepines while the drug is being cleared naturally from his system. Emergence from the psychosis for most of these people is gradual, unlike the onset, which is usually abrupt.

Should the psychosis persist despite passage of time and clearance of the presumed hallucinogen from the body, treatment with an antipsychotic is warranted. Most often atypical antipsychotics, which have less risk of movement disorders associated with them, are chosen. There is a delicate balance to be achieved in how aggressive to be with these medications. Using them too tentatively unnecessarily prolongs the psychosis and distress of the afflicted individual. Using them too aggressively exposes the individual to unnecessary side effects.

Once the person has (hopefully) completely cleared from the psychosis, intervention regarding the potential ill consequences of using such drugs must be addressed. In fact, given that the quality control on street drugs is not terribly reliable, the argument is often made that the person should refrain from all drugs of abuse. Surely the risk of potentially permanent psychosis outweighs the benefit of getting high.

CLINICAL COURSE WITH MANAGEMENT AND TREATMENT

Travis showed gradual emergence from the psychosis over a four-day hospitalization. The campus police were able to find his friends who had dropped him at the emergency department and to recover a package labeled "rose food: not for human consumption." Forensic examination at a state law enforcement laboratory revealed the presence of hallucinogenic cathinones. These drugs had been classified by the state legislature as illegal to sell after July 1 of that year. However, Travis and his friends acknowledged that they had bought the packet from a truck stop early in June, so there was no criminal recourse available against the seller.

Travis became less frightened and paranoid and the benzodiazepine was gradually reduced. He was no longer hallucinating and no longer had an exaggerated startle reflex. However, he continued to experience occasional bright flashes of light in his peripheral visual field. He was unable to determine what made these flashes more or less likely to occur. They gradually diminished over a six-month period and disappeared.

SYSTEMS-BASED PRACTICE ISSUES

The primary systems-based issue in this sort of case has to do with the acutely emergent nature of the problem. The affected individual is psychotic. Because of this he is unable to care for himself. In addition, he is often suicidal or homicidal. Containment for his own safety is imperative. Because of the psychosis he has no capacity for understanding the consequences of consenting to treatment on a psychiatric unit. Invariably this situation leads to a civil commitment.

LEGAL, ETHICAL, AND CULTURAL CHALLENGES

Attempts to put up legal barriers to access to emerging drugs have been well intentioned but largely ineffective. This is because the same advances in technology that permit relatively rapid development of therapeutic medications equally permit rapid development of illicit drugs. The legal system is usually one step behind the street in addressing dangerous drugs.

In many ways the critical interventions should be made educationally in early to mid-adolescence to help teenagers learn that even a single use of these drugs is potentially permanently life-changing. By doing this sort of prevention, we may prevent cases of psychosis that otherwise we would be less effectively treating.

In the late 1990s MDMA ("ecstasy") showed rapidly escalating use among adolescents. An extensive campaign was directed at this age group to educate of the hazards of this drug. As a result, for the next few years ecstasy use markedly abated. However, in 2012 and 2013, MDMA once again made a more frequent appearance among this population. Now it was called "Molly" and was in powder form rather than a pill. It is clear that the inoculation effects of education diminish as people grow into the vulnerable age population.

Regrettably, popular culture often glorifies and glamorizes drug use. Although we are familiar with numerous examples of recent celebrity drug use, we should remember that in the early 19th century Samuel Taylor Coleridge romanticized the use of opium. More recently, Hunter S. Thompson, in *Fear and Loathing on the Campaign Trail '72*, has described the alterations in perception and anxiety caused by substance abuse.

REFERENCES AND RESOURCES

Schwartz RH, Miller NS. MDMA (ecstasy) and the rave: a review. *Pediatrics* 1997;100:4 705–708

The website www.monitoringthefuture.org is a valuable resource to track trends in adolescent substance abuse.

PART V

Pervasive Psychopathology

CHAPTER **36**

Narcissism

Ritu Chahil, M.D.

CLINICAL PRESENTATION

Chief complaint: "I don't know, I was referred to you."

History of present illness: Seth is a 38-year-old male who was recently discharged after a brief hospitalization on an inpatient psychiatric unit. He presents stating that he was referred for treatment by his inpatient psychiatrist but he is not sure how the therapist could help him. He attributes his recent hospitalization to how his wife had treated him. He states, "My wife wants to separate and I can't believe that I have to leave the house, my own house, and she gets to stay in it." He has been feeling depressed and angry. Conflict has escalated in their married life over the past year and finally his wife asked him to leave. Subsequently he feels depressed, has nowhere to go, and expresses homicidal thoughts toward his wife and the man with whom she was having an affair. It is with these homicidal thoughts that he presented to the emergency room and was recommended for hospitalization. He had grudgingly agreed to hospitalization although he did not think he had any issues that needed it; however, because he had no money and did not want his relatives to be aware of his current homeless state, he had agreed.

He is not sure what led his wife to pursue separation especially since he has been such a great husband. He discusses his role in the marriage as the one being the breadwinner and caregiver for their four children. He says, "She does nothing to help with the children or the finances, instead I am convinced she is going out with other men." He adds, "I can't believe that she has even convinced her father against me." He believes his wife has ruined his reputation with his father-in-law, with whom he had enjoyed a good relationship, even better than with his own father. In addition he is upset at her for defaming him and bringing to light their issues for other people in the community to see. Moreover he is soon going to run for sheriff, and he just could not tolerate the way she was talking to her friends about him. He misses his children and does not think that his wife is capable of taking care of them. He wishes to return to his house. When asked why he could not return, he notes that his wife has obtained a restraining order against him. This is a result of their last fight, when there was physical violence toward each other. "I can show you the scratch marks she has made on my chest." However, he notes that he became angry only when his wife attacked him and that he was acting in self-defense. He is now preoccupied with the fact that his wife has mentally poisoned their children against him.

He reports low mood and insomnia and remains preoccupied with staying in the house that is rightfully his and desires that his wife leave. He is also angry at his wife for demanding child support. He denies any mood swings, and for the most part, enjoys socializing with his friends, with whom he occasionally uses recreational drugs. He enjoys going to the bar and playing a round of golf with the mayor of the town. He denies symptoms of ever experiencing a manic episode. With regard to psychosis Seth denies experiencing any auditory/visual/olfactory/gustatory hallucinations or other perceptual abnormalities. He denies any thought insertion, thought broadcasting, or magical thinking. He also denies any organized persecutory/hyperreligious/grandiose delusions. He has always been wary of other people's motives and has difficulty trusting anyone whose intentions are not clear to him. He has always sensed that people in their interactions and dealings had a certain agenda to fulfill for their own benefit. However, he gets along well with people and is a respected man in the community.

Past psychiatric history: Seth denies any previous psychiatric contacts prior to being hospitalized last month. He emphasizes that he did not think he needed the treatment and had stopped taking the medications that were prescribed. He plans to attend the marital sessions with his wife with the hope that he could return to live in his house.

Record review from hospitalization: Seth presented to the hospital because of homicidal ideation toward his wife and her lover. He also reported intense anger toward his wife, along with ruminations and preoccupation with hurting the person he thinks is her lover. The following information was noted in the family meeting with his wife during the hospitalization. Seth's wife, Nancy, had obtained a restraining order against him after the last incident of domestic violence. She noted that she had started to see a therapist after discovering that Seth had multiple affairs over the years. She had only found out in the previous year after receiving a phone call from one of his ex-girlfriends who was angry at him and wanted to get even. She noted that her husband was gone for days at a time from the family with the pretext of working and bringing home a "sizable check." Even when he was at home he rarely contributed to the household but was demanding and became angry when he was asked to help. He had convinced his wife that because of his hard work she needed to drop him off and pick him from the bar most nights since he needed to relax. With his children, he claimed to be involved in their schoolwork and sports; however, his participation was largely superficial and revolved around being present at events where he could be seen socially. Later in the privacy of his home, he would accuse the children of performing poorly and making him look bad. He had a great relationship with his father-in-law and brother-in-law and had become a shareholder in the family business. They were in utter disbelief that Seth could have cheated on his wife and had been violent toward her. Nancy reported that during their last fight when he accused her of cheating on him, she sustained fractured ribs and he left a big hole in the wall. She reported that she was trying to work out her issues in therapy, especially since her husband had constantly accused her of being the reason for his multiple affairs. When she disagreed with him over issues he would experience fits of anger. He was also envious of her on how easy it was for her to make friends. He knew multiple people but had no deep friendships and was constantly preoccupied with how many people he knew. He demonstrated a lack of empathy in his relationship toward his wife and children but did express remorse for having affairs. During hospitalization he was started on an antidepressant to help with mood symptoms. He was initially hesitant to a trial of any medication but eventually agreed. At the time of discharge he was not experiencing any homicidal thoughts toward his wife but was preoccupied with wanting to move back to his house which rightly belonged to him and letting the kids know "how their mother had destroyed the family." He denied any previous contact with mental health professionals.

Substance abuse history: Seth denies any consistent use of alcohol but described himself as a social drinker. He used cocaine recreationally in his early twenties, but denied any current use of cocaine or alcohol since he started taking medications. His urine drug screen during hospitalization was positive for cocaine. He denies gambling and vehemently denies that the extramarital relationships were a sex addiction.

Developmental history: He reports that his childhood was "average," but he is unable to provide any description of his childhood or his relationship with his parents. He notes "everything was fine growing up." The inpatient psychiatrist had noted that during a family meeting Seth's sister described being raised in a chaotic environment; his mother was sexually promiscuous and the children raised themselves. Seth left the house at age 16 and the other siblings had not heard from him for several years. Despite the chaos at home Seth did well academically and achieved a college degree.

Interpersonal relationships: He describes himself as fairly popular in the community; however, he could not call on any close friend or relative to help him during the hospitalization.

Spiritual beliefs: Seth does not wish to disclose his religious beliefs and states that he could not understand how it was relevant to his treatment. He exhibits a general distrust toward giving this much personal information.

Legal history: There is no legal history other than the current restraining order.

Mental status exam: This is a well-developed African American male who appears his stated age. There is no evidence of psychomotor agitation or retardation or other abnormal psychomotor activity. Overall he appears suspicious with failure to make eye contact. Speech is normal in rate, volume, and content. He is alert and oriented to time, place, person, and situation. Immediate, recent, and remote memory are intact. He is able to attend and concentrate throughout the interview. There is appropriate use of language and words are clearly articulated. Affect is restricted in range and congruent with mood described as "irritated." Seth denies any feelings of suicide or homicide. He is angry at his wife but perceives himself to be a victim in this marital conflict. Thought process is without flight of ideas, racing thoughts, or loosening of associations. There is no evidence for religious, grandiose, and persecutory delusions; however, Seth appears to be cynical of people's intentions. He is able to abstract proverbs and perform simple calculations. Intelligence is average based upon fund of knowledge, vocabulary, and comprehension. Insight is absent and judgment grossly intact. He denies hallucinations or other perceptual abnormalities.

IMPAIRMENT IN FUNCTIONING

Seth has significant impairment in functioning. He has difficulty accepting that he is homeless and financially troubled. Although he is unemployed, he reports that he would have no difficulty getting a job and that his wife is the limiting factor because he had to take care of the children. His contact with mental health services was precipitated by an ultimatum from Nancy, who at that point was focused on pursuing a divorce. His relationships with other family and friends are superficial and he cannot rely on anyone to help him in this time of need. Although his sister felt a sense of responsibility toward helping him, she noted that her husband and Seth cannot get along. Therefore he is unable to live with them even temporarily. His recent crises has precipitated a depressive episode and escalated his substance abuse issues, both of which caused further impairment in functioning.

DSM DIAGNOSIS

Seth is diagnosed with an adjustment disorder with disturbance of emotion and conduct versus major depression and cocaine and alcohol use in the context of marital discord with resulting legal difficulties and unemployment. He has the following features that are suggestive of Narcissistic Personality Disorder:

- The "special" individual or sense of entitlement: He had convinced his wife that he was special with regard to the money he brought to the household and needed to be dropped off at the bar every night where he could relax and enjoy himself. He could not understand how his father-in-law had reacted strongly against him since he had a special relationship with his wife's father and felt that Nancy had fabricated stories again him to destroy that relationship.
- Interpersonal exploitation: While he actively pursued his wife during courtship, he was soon disinterested in her and spent most of his time away from

home. He was noted to have convinced his father-in-law of his exceptional talents and had gained a foothold into the family business. He had also used his father-in-law's contacts to establish himself with the "movers and shakers" of the town to further his own career as a potential sheriff, and now his wife had destroyed it all for him.

- Grandiose self-importance: Seth informed the clinicians of his financial achievements and the high-paying jobs he had held over the years that required travel out of town. His wife confirmed that most of this information was exaggerated. Her father had often supported them financially and currently they were in financial crisis.
- Envy: People with narcissistic personality disorder are often envious of others or believe others envy them. Seth was envious of Nancy's friends and how she receives support from her family.
- Lack of empathy: He expresses anger at his wife and he presents with lack of empathy toward her and their children. While he expresses remorse at his lifestyle choice of multiple affairs, he quickly accused his wife of cheating on him. He is unable to identify with the feelings and needs of his wife and children and how his behavior has led to the interpersonal difficulties. Although narcissistic persons lack empathy, they usually have remorse. This is in contrast to the antisocial personality disorder, which is characterized by lack of empathy as well as lack of remorse.
- Lack of insight: Seth believes that the precipitating factor for his hospitalization was his homeless state and intense anger toward his wife. He does not think he really needs any psychiatric help. People with narcissistic personality disorder often do not have much insight and are usually forced to seek psychiatric care on account of interpersonal difficulties, usually in a relationship or at work.
- Narcissistic rage: The patient is prone to intense anger when he perceives slights or feels challenged. This is exemplified by his anger toward his wife, escalating to the point of domestic violence.
- Hypervigilance: Narcissists are very sensitive and closely watch people's reactions and emotional responses, sometimes to the point of appearing paranoid. During the mental status exam, Seth appears to be overly attentive to what the clinician asks or says, as if the clinician is going to get him to agree to or acknowledge an error that he has made in life.
- Eye contact: Eye contact is noted to be impaired in these individuals, and often there is gaze aversion.
- Humiliation and shame: These individuals are often prone to feeling shame. Seth expressed how his wife humiliated him when she discussed their marital issues with their friends.

The initial proposal for DSM-5 excluded narcissistic personality disorder as an independent personality disorder type, but ultimately it is retained as one of the 10 previously established personality disorders as well as the six specific personality disorder subtypes presented as an alternative to the categorical approach.

The newly proposed essential features of a personality disorder are impairments in personality (self and interpersonal) functioning and the presence of pathological personality traits.

Although the reformulation of narcissistic personality disorder has helped include more phenotypic variations of this disorder, an outline of the internal resources that the patient brings should be added to help guide treatment. Seth presents to the therapist with the following internal resources. He is motivated to be the perfect father to the children and wishes to win over Nancy's affection with the final goal of gaining control over his house again. Also, he was curious about the fact that he is invariably suspicious of other people's motives. In addition, he is motivated to seek treatment for coexisting disorders, particularly cocaine and alcohol abuse. His acceptance of promiscuity coupled with a desire to stop these maladaptive behaviors are factors that prompted Seth to seek treatment.

EPIDEMIOLOGY

Prevalence is varied in different studies and ranges from 0% to 5.3%. It is the least prevalent personality disorder represented in the current DSM. There is a significant male preponderance with this personality type. Narcissistic personality disorder in youth has been identified with many of the characteristics being similar to adult narcissistic disorder. It is not uncommon for narcissistic patients to seek help during an acute crisis or interpersonal failure. More recently studies indicate a lifetime prevalence rates of 7.7% in men.

DIFFERENTIAL DIAGNOSIS

Grandiosity in bipolar mania can present as narcissistic personality. Manic patients can often present as attention seeking and entitled. Given phenotypic variations of narcissistic personality disorder, it can easily be confused with the other cluster B personality types including antisocial, histrionic, and borderline personality disorder. Because both lack empathy, the key to differentiating from antisocial personality disorder is that narcissistic individuals do express remorse, while antisocial persons lack remorse or shame and humiliation associated with their behaviors. Although both antisocial and narcissistic individuals present with interpersonal exploitativeness, the narcissistic individual's exploitation of others is based on his or her sense of entitlement. With regard to borderline personality disorder, Kernberg identifies narcissism as a subset of borderline personality disorder with greater ego strength and a more integrated sense of self. Of note, the narcissistic individual lacks the impulsiveness and affective lability that is characteristic of borderline individuals. They both use primitive defense mechanisms including splitting, idealization, devaluation, and denial.

With regard to psychological testing, the patient can be referred for a Minnesota Multiphasic Personality Inventory. The Narcissistic Personality Inventory (NPT; Raskin and Terry 1988) has scales to assess narcissistic symptoms such as exploitativeness, entitlement, superiority, exhibitionism, and vanity and has been demonstrated to correlate closely with the construct provided by DSM-IV.

ETIOLOGY AND PATHOGENESIS

The pathology of narcissistic personality disorder (NPD) is not clearly defined. Most of the empirical explanation is from psychoanalysis. Phenotypic expression of narcissistic personality disorder is considered to be a continuum with grandiose, exhibitionist on one end and hypervigilant, vulnerable on the other end. Although there are several phenotypic labels, they can be broadly classified into two themes: grandiose and vulnerable types. Some of the adjectives used for their description of subtypes are oblivious versus hypervigilant (Gabbard 1997), pathological malignant (Kernberg 1975), horizontal split and vertical split (Kohut 1971), and arrogant and shy (Ronningstam 2000). The current DSM criteria emphasize the grandiose theme, while the vulnerable themes have been included in the associated features.

Kohut employs a psychodynamic theory of self psychology. He notes development of NPD as a "developmental arrest." This arrest is ascribed to parents' empathic failures, lack of validation and admiration, and lack of models worthy of idealization—hence the constant need for a soothing, and validating selfobject. Kernberg uses internal object relations to explain the development of NPD and notes better ego functioning in the presence of primitive defenses (splitting, projective identification, devaluation, denial). Thus he considers it a subset of borderline personality disorder.

Seth presents as a hypervigilant narcissist. His lack of self-esteem is covered by his self-enhancement. He is extremely sensitive to feedback, which is perceived as disrespect. His cognitive distortions, externalizing behaviors of drug use and promiscuous relationships, lack of insight with no legal issues have led to failures in social and occupational functioning as well as significant impairment in close relationships. With regard to his childhood, Seth reports that he was raised in a caring, loving environment by his parents. This is in direct contrast to his wife's input; she reports that his parents are deceased. Seth's sister had stated that while Seth did not know who his father was, his mother was noted to have been a prostitute. Seth reiterated that Nancy was lying and this was not the case. Per his sister, the children had raised themselves. Kohut's theory of developmental arrest can very well be applied to Seth. In addition there is some evidence that narcissism tends to run in families, although Seth denies family history of mental illness, his sister confirmed that several of the other siblings suffered from drug-related issues.

NATURAL COURSE WITHOUT TREATMENT

Patients with narcissistic personality often present as likable and empathic individuals in initial meetings. Developmentally adolescent narcissistic presentation is not substantially different from adult presentation. These individuals often come into contact with psychiatry for crisis intervention. Often significant impairment in relationships later in life prompts these individuals to seek help; more often their partner has given them an ultimatum. For others it pursues an unrelenting course and they develop a variety of secondary acute psychiatric illnesses as a result of their dysfunctional traits.

Substance abuse issues, major depression, and anxiety often coexist/develop in narcissistic individuals. Of note here, both substance abuse and depressive symptomatology are present in Seth. Narcissistic persons experience a difficult and protracted course with and without treatment. The consequences of narcissistic aggression, self-enhancement, cognitive distortion, impaired relations, and a profound lack of insight and failure to build a therapeutic alliance lead to poor outcomes. Often these patients have visited several different practitioners and are unsatisfied with their interventions. They first present for help either due to external pressures forcing them into treatment or the sense of emptiness and feeling lonely and unloved in their midlife. They also have difficulties around aging and might find themselves in extramarital affairs with younger individuals. In general, left untreated in their older years, they are often seen as bitter and lonely individuals.

EVIDENCE-BASED TREATMENT OPTIONS

Most narcissistic patients do not voluntarily seek treatment. They are often referred for treatment due to issues in employment, confrontations, and ultimatums by significant others/family members (as in Seth's case). In some cases they are diagnosed when they seek mental health treatment for other disorders. The recommended treatment is individual psychoanalytic psychotherapy. However, treatment of narcissistic pathology poses certain challenges. Narcissistic individuals' lack of insight, reluctance to accept treatment, and resistance to change prevents them from seeking active treatment. Moreover it is difficult to establish a therapeutic alliance given their essential mistrust in relationships, shame associated with treatment, and their own grandiosity. As noted, Seth presents without a chief complaint, and his purpose of treatment is to get his own house back rather than to focus on personal growth and building healthy relationships. It is now popular to integrate the foregoing with other forms of therapy, including supportive and cognitive behavioral approaches that incorporate education, validation, and identification of target behaviors. Schema-focused therapy (Young et al. 2003) has also shown benefit. Although there is no strong evidence to support the use of medication to treat this personality disorder, patients are encouraged to seek treatment for comorbid disorders.

To summarize, the treatment of NPD remains a challenge. However there is evidence to support the benefit of the aforementioned treatments. An integrative approach using different modalities and skills in psychotherapy with attention to building an empathic alliance, as well as understanding maladaptive defenses and complex countertransference issues, is recommended.

CLINICAL COURSE WITH MANAGEMENT AND TREATMENT

Treatment in narcissistic individuals is a challenge. Because insight is lacking, these patients often fail to continue with treatment. In addition, developing a therapeutic alliance is always challenging and the therapist needs to be mindful of the countertransference issues that develop.

In Seth's case, crisis stabilization was achieved through inpatient hospitalization. Seth maintained that he did not need treatment but needed to work on housing options and employment. The inpatient team was able to use his motivation for employment to encourage sobriety through referral to a substance abuse counselor. He also started an antidepressant to help with the dysphoric symptoms and insomnia. The initial focus of treatment was to target the comorbid acute psychiatric disorders while trying to develop a therapeutic alliance with him. Therapy was initially focused on psychoeducation and self-assessment, however, Seth had very low tolerance and often reverted to blaming his wife for all the issues. The therapist's aim was to gently redirect focus on the devaluation of his wife toward his aims and goals for treatment. A consistent, nonconfrontational approach allowing for active collaboration to establish a shared understanding of Seth's internal feelings and perceptions were critical for a gradual alliance building to effect change in behavior.

Therapy with Seth was a challenge, requiring a very attentive and flexible approach. Attention to his internal emotions and changes in self-esteem and perception of the help he was receiving was always critical in terms of motivation to continue treatment. Progress was slow and incremental. This patient was seen in a practice setting where there was unlimited access to services without the patient having to pay out of pocket. In other cases, cost of therapy can be expensive and can be a major limiting factor. Usually these individuals participate in treatment when a crisis arises and in family counseling sessions. Higher functioning narcissists presenting during midlife of their own volition tend to choose private pay practice settings, although they usually have fired several providers in the process of seeking help.

SYSTEMS-BASED PRACTICE ISSUES

Psychoanalytic psychotherapy with three to five sessions a week in the current system of health care and patient lifestyle is difficult to administer. A more successful approach in keeping with current health systems and time constraints is the use of an integrative and flexible psychotherapeutic approach.

LEGAL, ETHICAL, AND CULTURAL CHALLENGES

Historically across cultures, violence and abuse, hate crimes, and dictatorships have been led by individuals with narcissistic and antisocial personality disorders. These individuals use their social charm to draw others into their belief system to perpetuate their own self and cause. Psychotherapists have to be vigilant during the course of treatment and constantly monitor their own countertransference. A narcissist can often trick the therapist into believing that the patient is special and consequently entitled to special accommodations. One has to be always mindful of this manipulation and attempts to execute control over the therapist during treatment. Clinicians should not hesitate to refer to a more skilled therapist if needed.

HISTORY

Diagnosis of narcissistic personality disorder was first introduced in DSM-III. More recently the DSM-5 workgroup initially considered removing the diagnosis of narcissistic personality order; however, significant feedback and epidemiological evidence of existence of the disorder has resulted in retaining the diagnosis of NPD with revised criteria to attempt to capture the phenotypic variability of this disorder.

REFERENCES AND RESOURCES

Gabbard GO. Psychotherapy of personality disorders. *J Psychother Pract Res* 2000;9(1): 1–6.

Gabbard GO, Lazar SG, Hornberger J, et al. The economic impact of psychotherapy: a review. *Am J Psychiatry* 1997;154:147–55.

Kernberg O. *Borderline Conditions and Pathological Narcissism.* New York: Jason Aronson, 1975.

Kohut H. *The Analysis of the Self.* New York: International Universities Press, 1971.

Raskin R, Terry H. A principal-components analysis of the Narcissistic Personality Inventory and further evidence of its construct validity. *J Pers Soc Psychol* 1988;54:890–902.

Ronningstam E. (Ed.). *Disorders of Narcissism: Diagnostic, Clinical, and Empirical Implications.* Washington, DC: American Psychiatric Press, 2000.

Ronningstam E. Narcissistic personality disorder: a clinical perspective. *J Psychiatr Pract* 2011 Mar;17(2):89–99.

Ronningstam E. Alliance building and narcissistic personality disorder. *J Clin Psychol* 2012 Aug;68(8):943–53.

Ronningstam E. An update on narcissistic personality disorder. *Curr Opin Psychiatr* 2013 Jan;26(1):102–6.

Young JE, Klosko JS, & Weishaar M. *Schema Therapy: A Practitioner's Guide.* New York: Guilford Publications, 2003.

A Streetcar Named Desire (1995) film of the Tennessee Williams play about the destruction of an attractive but lonely Mississippi widow Blanche DuBois (Jessica Lange) by her brutally outspoken brother-in-law Stanley Kowalski (Alec Baldwin), who tears down her pretensions of virtue and culture that thinly veil her delusions.

CHAPTER 37

Emotional Overreactivity

Robert Dean, M.D., Ph.D.

CLINICAL PRESENTATION

Chief complaint: "My director said I had to come."

History of present illness: Rebecca is a 24-year-old woman who presents to the office after coming straight from work. She is short with delicate features and bright red hair. She is dressed in a blouse and jumper; the jumper has an enormous bow and the overall effect is that of an eight-year-old child from an English novel. She tells me that her supervisor at the day care center where she works referred her for a psychiatric evaluation. She seems somewhat baffled by this but appears to write it off as another example of her director's irrational behavior. She works at a day care center for a large corporation and describes her director in scathing terms, making clear that she knows more about running a daycare center than her director does. Rebecca reveals that although she is committed to her work, she has already been through several positions because she couldn't get along with her supervisors. With some difficulty the clinician directs Rebecca to her own experience of herself, and she admits to some struggles. She is easily angered and views all authority figures, including the clinician, with deep suspicion. Then she abruptly shifts from this grandiose evaluation of herself as a teacher to seeing herself as flawed, broken, unloved, and unlovable. She looks down and appears to cry. At times such as these, she thinks of suicide, although she has never attempted it. Sometimes she loses a sense of who she is and feels lost, hopeless, and alone. The only thing that seems to help her with these experiences is pain. So she heats up her oven and presses her arm against the baking rack. She shows me, with a certain amount of pride, the results of her intervention on her forearm: a series of parallel superficial burns.

Some nights Rebecca buys a bottle of liquor after work and goes home and drinks it until she passes out. She shares that it is very hard to be alone, but at the same time beginning a relationship feels overwhelming. She describes how some nights she would find herself with some man that she had picked up in a bar and whose name she couldn't recall. She smiles when she tells me this. Whenever she claims some outrageous behavior, she becomes vague and evasive as the clinician probes further. Without alcohol she says her sleep is usually poor and sometimes she will stay up all night doing things, but without any sense of euphoria or enjoyment.

Past psychiatric history: Rebecca has always felt that there was something wrong with her and had reached out in the past to her minister and later to the college chaplain at her religiously affiliated college. In college she started intermittently drinking heavily, but generally she has been isolated and lonely. She was unable to participate in an exploration of her sexual history and once again became vague and evasive as to her experiences. Since college she had attempted to see a therapist on at least two occasions. Because the therapists were women, she stopped after one or two sessions. Although suspicious of all authority figures, she is especially disdainful of women. She had never previously seen a psychiatrist or been psychiatrically hospitalized. Her primary care physician with whom she did feel quite comfortable (interestingly, a woman) had prescribed fluoxetine 20 mg for some time, but Rebecca seemed unsure as to whether this has been of any benefit, and she had stopped taking it months ago.

Medical history: Rebecca is in good physical health with no history of medical hospitalizations or surgery. She denies ever being pregnant, but acknowledges sexual activity. Onset of menses was around 12 years, and her periods are regular. She is on no birth control medication. At this time she is on no medications and has no allergies.

Personal history: Rebecca was born into an intact family in a rural area in a Southern state. She is the youngest of three children, and her older siblings are male. The family owns a large tract of land and her father had retired to operate a small farming operation. Her mother never worked outside the home. Her older brothers are married and live in houses on the family land. A similar piece of land has been set aside for Rebecca, but she has fled to the city and not returned there to live. It was very difficult to get a clear picture of her childhood. She speaks of this time as lonely and unhappy. She presented these years as anxiety-provoking and fearful but cannot give a coherent account of any incidents she can clearly remember. She regresses to a childlike state when she attempts to talk about this. When I ask her about sexual abuse history, she becomes anxious but denies any such abuse occurred. Her worst clear memory about her childhood is of her mother abruptly leaving the household for unknown reasons and being gone for long periods without explanation. She herself ascribes her distrust of women to these abandonments.

In school, Rebecca had been an excellent student and a star of her track team, becoming the all-state champion of her event. She remembers running as her "escape" from her childhood. But once again she could not really say what she was running from. She continued to do well academically. She did not appear to have any important relationships with peers and denies having a boyfriend in high school. In college she continued her pattern of social isolation. While in college she became very involved in contemporary Christian music. She lived for a time with a musician and his wife. Apparently Rebecca had a sexual relationship with him and possibly with his wife as well. She experiences this as abusive but cannot talk about it with any clarity.

Rebecca's religious faith is clearly important to her. She had grown up attending the family Baptist church, but was never comfortable in that setting, seeing it as an extension of her family, as small rural churches often are. In college and afterward she had attended church and always sought a relationship with the pastor. At the same time it is very difficult to get a sense of whether her faith was a source of comfort for her. The relationship with the male pastors, however, is an important source of support and these men have always tried to be helpful. She experienced these relationships as safe and supportive.

In her quests to connect, Rebecca has transitory relationships with a number of men she meets in bars and elsewhere. She presents these liaisons as if she were not responsible for meeting them, that she would simply find herself with them. When asked about safe sex practices, Rebecca ignored the question.

Mental status exam: Rebecca presents as an attractive but somewhat sullen young woman. There is no psychomotor agitation or retardation. She has poor impulse control. She is clearly uncomfortable in the interview and has difficulty making eye contact. In general she views the clinician with distrust. Speech is fluent and articulate, and she normally expresses herself well except when she shifts to a more noncommunicative state and becomes nearly mute. Rebecca is very alert and fully oriented, with a good understanding of the purpose of the conversation. Memory is certainly intact, and she can be quite coherent except when discussing emotionally laden events in her past. Intelligence is above average and although her fund of knowledge is consistent with her education, she shows little curiosity. Attention and concentration appear unimpaired. Her affect is full range, but at times quite labile, and when she becomes anxious she can shift into a depersonalized state. She admits to chronic suicidal impulses but is quite evasive as to whether she has a plan. She does deny current suicidal intent or any violent ideation or impulses toward others. She regularly self-injures but does so in an attempt at emotional regulation. She describes her mood as "depressed" but more often appears angry; at the same time she can seem quite anxious with the questioning. Affect, thought content, and behavior are congruent. Her thoughts are well organized, logical, and goal-directed, and she can be quite animated and engaged when talking about her work with children. She shows no loosening of associations or pressured speech. The content of her thought shows an appropriate reality orientation and she is free of any delusional thinking; her distrust and guardedness are anxious rather than paranoid. She shows little empathy or understanding of other people and is quite self-absorbed. At the same time she shows limited insight to her own feelings and behavior. Day-to-day judgment is often appropriate, but at times can be severely impaired, with her impulsive sexual behavior and substance abuse. Perceptually she is usually reality based without hallucinations or illusions but is vulnerable to episodes of depersonalization, even in the course of the interview.

IMPAIRMENT IN FUNCTIONING

Despite having completed college, being consistently employed, supporting herself, and living independently, Rebecca has significant functional impairment. She has been unable to sustain a relationship, hold a job for more than a year, or maintain a therapeutic relationship. She abuses alcohol, engages in unsafe sex, and performs self-injurious behavior. Her self-concept shifts between grandiose idealization and a more consistent sense of herself as worthless and injured. Taking her account at face value, she suffers from dissociative episodes that are confusing and frightening.

DSM DIAGNOSIS

The clinician's immediate impression of Rebecca is that she has a personality disorder. Personality disorder is defined as an enduring pattern of inner experience and behavior that deviates markedly from the expectations of the individual's culture, is pervasive and inflexible, has an onset in adolescence or early adulthood, is stable over time, and leads to distress or impairment. The 10 identified personality disorders in the DSM have been grouped into three subcategories: odd or eccentric-unusual; dramatic, emotional, or erratic-externalizing; and anxious or fearful-internalizing. Rebecca fits best in the second category—the dramatic, emotional, or erratic type, which includes borderline personality disorder (BPD). To meet criteria for this disorder in DSM-5 the patient must exhibit at least five of nine characteristics. Rebecca shows a pattern of intense interpersonal relationships often characterized by devaluation, significant identity disturbance, impulsive behavior with respect to alcohol and sex, self-mutilating behavior, and affective instability, chronic feelings of emptiness, and severe dissociative symptoms. It is not immediately evident that she displays frantic efforts to avoid abandonment, but it is revealed later that she struggles with this vulnerability as well.

In DSM-5, the 10 personality disorders are maintained, but there is an alternative approach offered that considers dimensions of personality running across all the disorders (as well as normal people) with a primary emphasis on the experience of the self and of others. The dimensional model includes the goal of integrating descriptions of impaired personality functioning, with separate definitions of pathological personality traits within five broad domains (and 26 specific trait facets). Disturbances in self and interpersonal functioning constitute the core of personal psychopathology.

There is substantial overlap between personality disorders, and it is not uncommon for a patient to qualify for more than one. Rebecca is stubborn and rigid and disregards the competence of others. Excessive devotion to work is common with obsessive compulsive personality disorder, and her isolation and avoidance of close relationships as well as her difficulty enjoying herself in social settings is characteristic of avoidant personality disorder, but again she does not seem to fully meet the criteria for anything but BPD. Comorbid acute psychiatric disorders are also very common and may be targets for treatment. So far the clinician recognizes dysthymic disorder, alcohol abuse, possible dissociative disorder not otherwise specified, and BPD with obsessional and schizoid traits. Current stressors include conflicts with her work supervisor, isolation, and alcohol abuse.

At the same time one could argue that Rebecca has some real strengths. She has been able to complete college (although not graduate school) and has been able to remain employed. Her stubbornness may in some ways be seen as a strength, and with some reluctance she sees her mood states and behavior as a source of problems for her. Although her appointment was required by her employer, she expresses a sincere desire for treatment. The big question in the initial appointment becomes will she be capable of maintaining a therapeutic relationship?

EPIDEMIOLOGY

The prevalence of BPD in the general population is estimated at 5.9%, but its impact on the health care system is substantial. People with this disorder have a high rate of suicide attempts, completed suicides, psychiatric hospitalizations, mental health visits, and general medical visits far out of proportion to the problems. They may account for 25% or more of all psychiatric admissions and 15% or more of outpatients. The gender ratio in treatment settings is heavily weighted toward women, but in community surveys the gender ratio is equal. People with BPD also tend to be high consumers of general medical services. It is likely that these numbers are underestimates, because as Gunderson (2008) discusses, clinicians are often reluctant to make the diagnosis. On most psychiatric admissions the personality diagnosis is put down as "deferred." Certainly the high rate of psychiatric comorbidities complicates the picture. This high prevalence of BPD in treatment settings supports the clinician's diagnosis. It is the most common personality problem in persons seeking treatment.

DIFFERENTIAL DIAGNOSIS

Not only are comorbid acute psychiatric disorders commonly associated with BPD, many patients may meet criteria for more than one personality disorder. There is substantial overlap with other cluster B personality disorders: antisocial, histrionic, and narcissistic. In the clinician's experience, the combination of impulsivity, intense vulnerability to abandonment, and high emotional lability are always present in BPD. More controversial is the relationship between BPD and the bipolar disorders, particularly bipolar II disorder. It has been suggested that BPD is a form of bipolar disorder and a stable bipolar patient may also meet criteria for this personality disorder. Distinguishing between these conditions requires, on one hand, the abandonment sensitivity associated with BPD, which is not expected with bipolar disorder, and, on the other hand, the presence of more prolonged hypomanic or manic episodes, which are associated with bipolar disorder.

There are no office-based assessments tools for personality disorder diagnosis, although there are several instruments used in research. There are some key questions that are worth asking: are your mood swings in response to relationship changes? Do you find it hard to be alone? Are you sensitive to abandonment? Is expressing anger aproblem for you? Do you tend to be impulsive?

ETIOLOGY AND PATHOGENESIS

Formulation of this case is complex and involves genetic vulnerabilities and life history events. A coherent and generally accepted model of the etiology and pathogenesis of BPD is lacking. We know from studies of infants that there are significant differences in capacity for attachment, emotional regulation, anxiety, novelty seeking and tolerance, and impulsivity. Infants who struggle with attachment, emotional regulation, and impulsive behavior may well be at risk for developing BPD. Parents who are patient, loving, and consistent may exert a powerful corrective effect. It is no accident that most patients with BPD did not grow up in such loving and supportive households. Characteristically they are reared in environments that are chaotic or openly abusive. At the very least a temperament mismatch between parent and infant may lead to ineffective parental emotional responses and difficulty with self-soothing in the infant consistent with adult relationship behaviors in BPD. Too often parents may be absent, inconsistent, abusing substances, or in other respects unable to maintain a safe environment for the child.

Dramatic shifts in mood, usually in response to real or imagined abandonment, help generate unstable relationships as well as an unreliable sense of self, thereby enhancing underlying vulnerabilities. Periods of significant depression may be demoralizing, and brief psychotic symptoms reinforce a sense that the world and others are unsafe.

The DSM diagnostic criteria include nine attributes, of which five are needed to make the diagnosis. This allows for 256 different combinations. There is little research to support consistent subtypes of BPD, but clinical experience suggests the following presentations. Patients with significant trauma histories tend to be lower functioning, more consistently anxious, and more frequently hospitalized. Comorbid post-traumatic stress disorder may also be present. Another group may present primarily with unstable mood states and may meet criteria for bipolar II as well; the precise relationship between BPD and the mood disorders remains unclear. Significantly, however, the mood shifts are usually driven by interpersonal events. A third group responds to the interpersonal challenges by becoming isolated and avoidant. Recent research is now identifying neurobiological correlates of BPD symptoms, such as impulsivity and emotional reactivity. Also significant is the high prevalence of childhood and adult trauma in the lives of about 60% of BPD patients. Chronic unstable mood, perhaps clinically unrecognized or unsuccessfully treated, probably reflecting underlying neurobiology, may result in a more pervasive pattern of behavior than is recognized as a personality disorder of the borderline type.

Rebecca's vague reporting of her childhood suggests parents who were unavailable and at times abandoning. Her most vivid childhood memory is seeing her mother leave the house and feeling that she would never return. There are hints of sexual abuse as a child and more definitely as a young adult. With this environment and history and a child with an anxious temperament and limited internal resources for self-care and modulating her mood states, we have fertile ground for adult difficulties. However, it is premature to endorse any real theory of pathogenesis in this disorder.

NATURAL COURSE WITHOUT TREATMENT

Impulsive behavior, relational instability, and problems with mood regulation can certainly occur in adolescence as the brain continues to develop executive functioning. In BPD we see an intensification of such symptoms into young adulthood, and the most florid symptoms tend to occur at that time. Treatment, if it occurs at all, is usually the result of concerns of family or comes about through behavioral difficulties, such as suicide attempts. As BPD patients reach their thirties, some will seek treatment on their own as they become aware of their failure to achieve the usual milestones of education, employment, and committed relationships. Some studies suggest a gradual damping down of the impulsive and risk-taking behavior (in the survivors). Older patients are more likely to complain of chronic feelings of emptiness, boredom, and depression. Although the more severe behavioral disturbances may be less common in older patients, significant functional impairment often remains. Significant borderline symptoms may be seen in geriatric patients. Suicide and deliberate self-injury are a significant concern. The lifetime risk for suicide in patients with BPD may run as high as 10%, and such patients may account for 9–33% of all suicides. Self-injury, such as cutting and hitting, are very common in this group. Eating-disordered behavior, primarily bulimia, is common as well. Substance abuse can also be a significant barrier to treatment of BPD, but patients are appropriate for standard treatment protocols and may find the structure very helpful.

Rebecca was pushed into treatment in her late twenties and continued in treatment on her own. She was employed in childcare, a very common finding for those with BPD. Others may pursue careers as elementary schoolteachers. It seems that they find the world of the child easier to comprehend than the world of the adult. Rebecca's job instability was the result of her inability to relate appropriately to her adult coworkers and supervisors. Without treatment it is likely that she would enter a downward spiral toward unemployment, substance abuse, suicide, or death as a result of other impulsive behavior. Treatment of BPD can be lifesaving, although this may not be clearly evident when one is in the thick of it.

EVIDENCE-BASED TREATMENT OPTIONS

The best supported model for the treatment of BPD is intensive team-based treatment that lasts for at least a year. Several different approaches have been studied, including dialectical behavior therapy (DBT), a cognitive-based group and individual treatment. However, transference-focused psychotherapy has also been shown to be effective and superior on some dimensions in a head-to-head study. Other effective treatments include mentalization-based treatment, group therapy, and case management. By and large studies have not shown any modality to be uniquely helpful, and patients improved with all of them. As Gunderson (2008) discusses, there are some significant common features. All provide a stable treatment framework, target self-destructive behaviors, are actively engaged with the patient, and are attentive to the patient–therapist relationship. In addition, residential treatment or at times inpatient treatment may be necessary and useful. In Rebecca's case, treatment that incorporates her spiritual attachment and that includes her pastor in the treatment team may be helpful and can do much to build a treatment alliance.

The reality is that these specialized treatments for BPD are not available in many areas. More common is for the patient to see a psychiatrist and a therapist; in some cases, a case manager may be involved as well. Gunderson's (2008) case management approach works well with this but requires open communication between all the treating partners to avoid conflicts. Studies suggest this may be comparably efficacious compared to more costly and often unavailable treatments.

Medications may be modestly helpful, but are not life-changing. Reasonable targets include depressed mood, emotional instability, impulsivity, and psychotic symptoms. Studies suggest low-dose antipsychotics may be the most helpful, followed by mood stabilizers (such as divalproex and lamotrigine), and finally selective serotonin reuptake inhibitor antidepressants (Gunderson 2008). Although patients with BPD often complain of high levels of anxiety, benzodiazepines are not indicated because they may be disinhibiting and are often abused. Many patients end up on complex medication regimens for which there is little evidence of utility. Many psychiatric medications bear a significant risk of weight gain, problematic for borderline patients, who are often obese and not uncommonly bulimic. When prescribing medication for patients with BPD, the clinician must be wary of the possibility of an impulsive overdose. For this reason it is necessary to avoid highly toxic medications such as tricyclic antidepressants.

The borderline patient poses special challenges to the treatment team. The source of the challenge is, of course, the intense emotional responses of the patient to the providers (transference) and the often equally intense responses of the providers to the patient (countertransference). Patients anticipate mistreatment by caregivers and thus behave in provoking ways to bring about that very response! Alternatively, they may harbor nearly magical fantasies about the therapist's skill and feelings for the patient, inviting boundary-violating contact outside the office. Perhaps most frequently, the desperate demands for support and attention may exhaust and anger anyone involved in the patient's care. "Splitting" describes the patient's primitive idealization or devaluation of others, and this process can produce significant splits on the treatment team, with different members viewing the patient's prognosis and behavior in radically different ways. Open communication is essential to avoid victimizing the patient through dysfunctional relationships among caregivers. Brief sessions directed toward medication can stir up intense transference fantasies in the borderline patient. If anything, patients may have particularly powerful fantasies about physician efficacy or insensitivity. What works is to stay calm, be straightforward and human with the client, and communicate freely with others on the treatment team. It is often helpful to talk to patients about BPD; knowing that they have an illness that their doctor understands and knows how to treat may be an enormous relief.

CLINICAL COURSE WITH MANAGEMENT AND TREATMENT

Perhaps the most exciting development in the care of patients with BPD is the discovery that treatment can be very effective. Mental health clinicians often respond to BPD patients as hopeless and frustrating cases, but the research literature has shown surprisingly good outcomes. In one study 93% of BPD patients attained a significant remission of symptoms with some recurrences; those achieving a sustained remission were able to maintain it. Treatment studies establish significant sustained improvement with a variety of treatments. It is also true, however, that remitted BPD patients still struggle with some symptoms, including emotional dysregulation and feelings of emptiness.

All the treatment protocols have had a real effect on suicidal and self-injurious behavior, regulation of emotional states, impulsivity, and other parameters of the borderline condition; these results have been sustained over time even when the most intense phase of treatment ends. Because such patients make enormous demands on the health care system, even expensive treatments may be cost-effective. Treatment can be expected to provide substantial support and relief for these patients and needs to be ongoing because symptom relapse can occur.

In Rebecca's case, insurance considerations left the only DBT program in the area unavailable, so a psychodynamic supportive model that also involved basic case management was chosen. Weekly sessions were negotiated. As treatment started, it quickly became clear that Rebecca had difficulty making it from session to session without any contact. The clinician allowed her to leave voicemail messages; often she did not need a callback and found hearing the clinician's voice in the outgoing message to be helpful and reassuring. Like many persons with BPD, Rebecca felt victimized by her emotional shifts, and an early goal of treatment was to help her reach some understanding that the shifts were in response to things going on in her life. The clinician addressed her self-injurious behavior and alcohol abuse, but she adamantly refused to attend AA or consider other treatment options. She and the clinician explored the inner experiences that provoked self-injury, and she found this helpful as she developed other strategies for coping with dissociation, anxiety, and abandonment. Over time in treatment, self-injurious behavior became significantly less frequent until it finally died away altogether. She continued to have dissociative episodes that were frightening and most often lead to a phone call. She had one significant exacerbation of suicidal thinking which almost led to hospitalization, but when confronted with that reality, she was able to put together a workable safety plan with the clinician. Although the clinician could understand Rebecca's areas of difficulty as reflecting internal conflicts around victimization, anger, assertion, and helplessness, she showed little ability to respond to conflict-based interpretations. What was helpful was a steady and reliable therapeutic interest in her life with confrontation of significantly problematic behavior. Medication management alone will never be particularly helpful in patients with BPD. Because of consistent complaints of depression and anxiety, the clinician initiated a trial of fluoxetine 20 mg and subsequently sertraline 50 mg later increased to 100 mg daily. There was no discernible benefit from either medication. Because of Rebecca's chronic sleep disturbance, she was eventually prescribed clonazepam 1 mg qhs, which was significantly helpful. By and large regular use of benzodiazepines should be avoided because of their disinhibiting effects. The biggest concern was her episodic and increasingly infrequent alcohol abuse. Rebecca remained in treatment for over a decade and showed substantial improvement over that time. She was able to marry, have a child, settle into a job that she was able to hold for an extended period, and stopped the self-injurious behavior. She continues to struggle with periods of identity disturbance. Also, she was able to give up the alcohol abuse and the impulsive sexual behavior. This is not atypical, and today she no longer meets criteria for BPD, but continues to struggle with episodic identity problems.

The question of hospitalization in patients like Rebecca is thorny. It is quite clear that the hospital may represent a sanctuary from the difficulties of life outside and in some patients may be eagerly sought. Extended hospitalizations are rarely helpful and tend to lead to regression and power struggles that may involve the entire hospital staff either condemning or advocating for the patient. However, if the patient is clearly unsafe, the hospital may be the best possible intervention with a step-down partial hospitalization as soon as the patient improves. Under some circumstances, going directly to a partial hospitalization or day program may be adequate to avoid a more serious event. It should also be mentioned that some patients will regress in psychotherapy and feel they need to maintain the sick role to have access to the therapist. This leads to the important question of when therapy should stop. Not infrequently patients with BPD will break off treatment in response to some slight they experienced from the therapist. At the same time, the treating practitioner may become exhausted or overwhelmed in efforts to contain the patient's behavior and emotional storms. Fortunately the clinician never reached this point with Rebecca but did seek consultation with experienced providers on several occasions, which were found to be enormously helpful. These issues are discussed further later.

SYSTEMS-BASED PRACTICE ISSUES

In our current health care systems, most BPD patients may have treatment split between a number of practitioners, such as the psychiatrist, a nonphysician therapist, a case manager, a group leader, and a primary care physician. Patients may also shift around between different systems and levels of care that do not always communicate well with each other (e.g., hospital, residential treatment, jail, and so on). It becomes essential to communicate with all the caregivers, and it is probably best if one clinician assumes responsibility for directing the overall plan of care. This is very difficult to achieve in most care systems. Many psychiatrists have limited understanding or interest in the patient's internal dynamics and may be blindsided by the patient's intense response to them. Also, there is either reluctance or simply a failure to make the diagnosis of BPD, resulting in misguided and misdirected treatment. Complex medication regimens may be used in a generally fruitless chase of elusive mood and anxiety disorders. If the frequency of BPD is inaccurately reported or perceived, appropriate resources are less likely to be available.

LEGAL, ETHICAL, AND CULTURAL CHALLENGES

Many clinicians are reluctant to take on patients with BPD because of the frequent behavior problems and other demands such patients may place on caregivers. They may overtly overvalue or devalue the clinician, resulting in strong countertransference responses from the clinician. It may be difficult to establish and maintain therapeutic boundaries; patients with BPD often demand extra time or have frequent crises that can exhaust caregivers. Therapeutic boundaries are established at the outset of treatment to protect both the clinician and the patient. The psychiatrist negotiates how often to meet with the patient, makes clear the need for payment, and states how available he or she will be outside the scheduled session. Patients may push for extra sessions, more frequent sessions, or meetings at a coffee shop. The task of the clinician is to maintain boundaries. It can require a great deal of patience and consistency to stand firm in the face of repeated demands. Patients may do less well with more frequent visits. Learning to tolerate the therapist's absence between sessions is one of the goals of treatment.

Patients with BPD tend to be treatment seeking, yet optimal treatment is often unavailable in many areas. The patient may consult a psychiatrist for medication management yet refuse or be unable to obtain a therapist. They may not qualify for case management. Clinicians with training in group interventions such as DBT are often not available outside of metropolitan areas. What is the most ethical stance when what you have to offer may not be enough?

A clinician treating patients with BPD, even from a primarily pharmacological approach, must be attentive to his or her own emotional state. It is essential for clinicians to recognize their limits and care for themselves as they care for their patients. Limiting the number of demanding patients, getting additional training, pursuing peer or professional supervision are appropriate interventions that may preserve the clinician's own mental health as well as the patients.

Another challenge is treating comorbidities for which the doctor or other clinician feels unprepared. Eating disorders and substance abuse come to mind. Should the clinician take on such a patient when other support is not available? Rebecca's religious faith was important, and treatment must at the very least be respectful of her beliefs even if the beliefs of the treating clinician are very different. It is crucial to respect the value systems of patients, even when they may be rigid and punitive. Simply attacking beliefs is never helpful. Reframing a patient's self-assessment and offering alternative value systems may be life-sustaining.

In spite of these concerns, the treatment of patients with BPD is often rewarding to both the clinician and the patient and can be an opportunity for both to grow and prosper in the therapeutic relationship.

TERMS

Borderline: the border between psychosis and neurosis; neurosis referring to less severe disturbances of personality that one might treat with psychotherapy alone. The diagnosis comes from psychoanalytic work with disturbed patients and first gained currency in the 1930s. It was included in the DSM-III in 1980 and has become the most frequently diagnosed personality disorder in clinical practice. There has been substantial evolution in the concept to include neurobiological, psychosocial, and life history factors.

Countertransference: the emotional responses of the clinician to the patient, particularly those that interfere with appropriate treatment. These also may be rooted in past relationships of the clinician.

Psychotherapy: any form of metal health treatment that involves a relationship between the patient and the clinician directed to relieving the patient's distress and bringing about change. It has been referred to as the "talking cure." Medication management is a particular form of psychotherapy that also involves prescribing medication. There are many types of psychotherapy, but those of which psychiatrists are most aware are: cognitive behavioral, psychoanalytic, interpersonal.

Therapeutic boundaries: the framework in which therapy occurs, and the limits of the relationship between clinician and patient.

Transference: the emotional responses of a patient to their caregiver. Originally these responses were seen as coming from past impaired relationships, but the broader definition is more useful.

REFERENCES AND RESOURCES

Clarkin JF, et al. Evaluating three treatments for borderline personality disorder: a multiwave study. *Am J Psychiatry* 2007;164:922–28.

Gunderson JG. *Borderline Personality Disorder, a Clinical Guide* (2nd ed.). Arlington, VA: American Psychiatric Publishing, 2008.

Kreisman JJ, Straus H. *I Hate You—Please Don't Leave Me. Understanding the Borderline Personality Disorder* (rev. ed.). New York: Penguin, 2010.

Silbersweig D, et al. Failure of frontolimbic inhibitory function in the context of negative emotion in borderline personality disorder. *Am J Psychiatry* 2007;164:1832–41.

Stanley B, Siever LJ. The interpersonal dimension of borderline personality disorder: toward a neuropeptide model. *Am J Psychiatry* 2010;167(1):24–39.

Zanarini MC, et al. Time to attainment of recovery from Borderline personality disorder and stability of recovery: a 10-year prospective follow-up study. *Am J Psychiatry* 2010; 167:663–67.

National Education Alliance Borderline Personality Disorder (www.borderlinepersonalitydisorder.com) and BPD Central (www.bpdcentral.com) offer information and support for patients, family, and health care providers.

Girl, Interrupted is a 1999 drama film based upon the memories of an 18-year old diagnosed with BPD as portrayed by Winona Ryder who checks herself into a psychiatric hospital after taking an overdose of aspirin.

Young Adult (2011), directed by Jason Reitman, is a dead-on portrayal of a woman with BPD, with all the self-destructiveness and charm that one can imagine.

CHAPTER **38**

Perfectionism

Gary Curtis, Ph.D.

CLINICAL PRESENTATION

Chief complaint: "I am being fired from my job, and my wife is leaving me, but I do not know why these things are happening to me."

History of present illness: Tom is a 52-year-old married but separated physician who is referred to an outpatient psychiatrist by his primary care physician. He has a long history of being a hard worker and sees himself as a caring, loving husband, but he appears to be failing in both of these life situations. He describes himself as an intense worker, who frequently works 12 or more hours a day taking care of his patients, and making detailed notes in their records. He admits that he is a perfectionist, and this results in his constantly worrying about making mistakes. He also admits that too often he demands the same perfection in his staff and medical students that he supervises. He recalls a recent discussion with a nurse, when he told her that she needed to wash her hands between seeing patients and also every time she touches the patient. Thus during one visit he expected her to wash her hands about five times, since she checked the patient's weight; then she took his blood pressure and later took his pulse. Tom also complains that the nurse (who is paid a yearly salary and not hourly) should be willing to stay three to four hours into the evening to ensure that the work gets done correctly. Tom feels that one of his strengths is talking directly to patients about their problems. He states to me that one lady who is overweight and complains about her knee hurting is "fat, fat, and fat." She is a "beached whale" and needs to lose the weight.

Tom is confused about why his wife wants a divorce. He has always been a good provider and she has never wanted for anything. He knows that he often gets home about 10 pm, but she must understand that his work is important and that he does not feel anyone else could ever take care of his patients as well as he does. He admits that he usually works every weekend, and he is available every night even though there is a physician on call for his practice. He claims that he has been a good husband, putting up with her inability to cook a good meal or adequately clean the house. They have been married for five years; he feels that she has never complained that he was not a good husband. Her leaving has been a major shock to him. He confesses that they have not made love in four years, saying there is never enough time. Anyway, "sex," he says, "should not be a significant part of a good marriage." The patient admits to being depressed since he lost his job and his wife. He is not sleeping and is losing weight. He can no longer concentrate. He has periods during the day when he questions whether life is worth living. He strongly denies any suicidal thoughts, but says that if he was suddenly diagnosed with a terminal illness, he would be relieved. He feels a sense of hopelessness and worthlessness. He has always identified himself as a physician who treats patients. Since he was told that he no longer has a job, he lacks purpose and direction. He had hoped to work long into his seventies, and now finds himself without work.

Past psychiatric history: Tom experienced a severe depression when he was in medical school after he had failed an exam. At that time he was depressed for several months. He was unable to sleep, could not eat, and had trouble concentrating. He saw a medical school psychiatry professor, who successfully treated his symptoms with an antidepressant (possibly amitriptyline). He did not require a hospitalization. He has never been suicidal and has never attempted to hurt himself.

Substance use history: Tom has never been a heavy drinker, describing himself as a social alcohol consumer. He is careful never to drink and drive. He is shocked when he sees colleagues get intoxicated and is often the first to confront them the next day at the office. The patient has never used cocaine, opiates, marijuana, or any other illegal drug. He does not use tobacco products.

Legal history: He has never been arrested or engaged in any criminal activity.

Medical history: Tom is in good physical health, except for an elevated blood pressure and elevated cholesterol. He takes hydrochlorothiazide 12.5 mg a day and is trying to lower his cholesterol through diet and exercise. He works out at the gym five days a week, both walking on the track and using the weight machines. He has no known drug allergies.

Family history: His parents stayed married but never appeared to have a romantic life. He says he cannot remember his parents ever kissing or showing any form of affection. His father was a successful engineer and often worked long hours. He cannot recall ever doing anything fun with his dad. His mother was chronically unhappy. He recalls seeing her crying at night. His father was extremely strict and would become physically abusive if Tom ever misbehaved. He remembers bringing home a report card with a C, and his father becoming enraged. He said his father made him give up playing baseball so that he would never get another C on his report card. The patient had an older brother who hung himself several years ago when his wife discovered he was having an affair. Tom has a younger sister who is very overweight and constantly complains about her inability to find a man who would marry her. This sister frequently drinks too much and then talks about how miserable her life is.

Social history: Tom was raised in Boston. He was always a good student and enjoyed sports. Unfortunately, his father was never interested in his athletic activities, and often used participation in sports as a way to discipline him. He worked hard on his schoolwork and might stay up late at night to be sure his homework was completed in the best possible manner. He graduated at the top of his class and was devastated when he was not accepted to Harvard University. He ended up attending Tufts and earned a 3.8 GPA. He then went to Yale Medical School, where he found himself excited about practicing medicine. He entered an internal medicine residency at Brown University, where he proved to be the hardest-working member in the residency program. During this time he was encouraged to talk to a psychiatrist about his tendency to work too hard. He could not understand why he would be encouraged to get help for working hard and doing a good job. He later moved to Virginia to join an internal medicine group. During the first year of general medical practice, he met his wife. She was a nurse in the hospital where he was an attending. They had a short romance and got married. They had two children; both are doing well. Unfortunately, his wife started having an affair 10 years into their marriage. She claimed that they never spent time together, and she wanted more from a marriage; they eventually divorced. The patient spent a number of years single. He felt very poorly treated by his first wife and called her a slut and a whore. About seven years ago he met his present wife, who also worked as a nurse in the same hospital where he practiced. She is about 10 years younger than he is, and she was very passionate about their relationship. As noted, she is now in the process of leaving him.

Mental status: Patient is well groomed and in good physical shape. He has no evident psychomotor impairment. He is obviously an individual who eats well and exercises regularly. His speech is coherent and goal directed, and normal in rate and prosody. His sensorium is intact and he is oriented times three. His short-term and long-term memory are good. Tom denies suicidal ideation, plan, or intent but endorses depressed mood. His thought content is free of hallucinations and delusions; it also displays continuity and good logical interrelationships. He has no active suicidal or homicidal thoughts. His fund of knowledge is above average, and his abstract thinking ability is intact as can be seen by his discussion of his life circumstances as well as his response to proverbs. He performs simple mental calculations accurately. His insight is poor, because he is totally confused about why his wife would leave him and his colleagues would have asked him to resign the practice. His impulse control is good and his judgment is fair. His assets are that he is bright and capable of learning, though one might have anticipated that he would have an appreciation for why his wife is leaving, since this is the second marriage to fail. He notes that he ruminates constantly about the recent setbacks in his life. He feels betrayed and complains that his wife and colleagues do not appreciate the efforts he has made. When he is asked about his compulsive behavior at work, he describes it as an appropriate way to meet the highest professional standards. He attributes his tendency to check his own pulse and blood pressure at work as due to increased anxiety.

IMPAIRMENT IN FUNCTIONING

A review of Tom's clinical presentation provides evidence of the kind of functional impairment that occurs with obsessive compulsive personality disorder (OCPD). He has lost his job; his second marriage is on the rocks, and his first ended in divorce. He is currently depressed and was in the past after a professional setback. His current depression does not involve outright suicidal ideation, but he has had episodes of hopelessness and nihilistic thinking. His marital problems seem to hinge on his partner feeling ignored. Overall, he is stuck in life, due to barriers that may be of his own making.

DSM DIAGNOSIS

The clinical picture includes a mixture of multiple elements including pervasive anxiety from early development with conditioned thoughts designed to alleviate the anxiety. The clinician who was working with Tom suspected that he was not only depressed but also met the criteria for OCPD. A personality disorder is defined as an enduring pattern of inner experience and behavior that deviates markedly from the expectations of the individual's culture, is pervasive and inflexible, has an onset in adolescence or early adulthood, is stable over time, and leads to distress or impairment. When personality traits are inflexible and (as a result of this inflexibility) cause distress and/or functional impairment they constitute a personality disorder.

In the DSM, the personality disorders have been divided into a taxonomy of three clusters in which one grouping is made up of disorders characterized by a odd or eccentric interpersonal style; one grouping is made up of disorders characterized by a dramatic or emotionally reactive interpersonal style; and one grouping is made up of disorders characterized by a fearful or anxious interpersonally style. OCPD is in the latter grouping.

The specific personality disorder that Tom's clinician suspects is OCPD. Obsessive compulsive personality disorder is currently defined in the DSM as an enduring pattern of preoccupation with orderliness, perfection, and rigidity (mental and interpersonal control). To best determine if Tom meets criteria for OCPD, the clinician must have an understanding of some theoretical issues pertaining to the diagnosis of personality disorders in general and OCPD in particular. There are different methods for understanding and evaluating criteria for a personality disorder. The first involves a categorical decision about whether a patient meets personality disorder criteria. Another method that has been tried is to consider personality traits as dimensional. In one version of this model, the enduring personality patterns that make up personality disorder symptoms delineated in DSM are viewed as existing on a continuum. In another dimensional personality theory model, there is an attempt to discover several fundamental personality dimensions (not necessarily connected to the DSM criteria) that underlie the continuum of normal to pathological human personality functioning. In one

2005 study Skodol and colleagues tested individuals determined to have various personality disorders (according to semi-structured interviews) for the presence of personality dimensions from proposed three- and five-factor models of personality functioning. Subjects were then rated on a number of domains of psychological functioning. The results were that there was a stronger relationship between both the categorical and the continuum-based methods of measuring DSM-based personality disorders and the study's domains of psychological impairment, as compared to a weaker relationship between those domains of functioning and either the three- or five-factor personality dimensions. Skodol and colleagues concluded that the DSM personality disorder criteria should be retained but thought of by clinicians as existing on a continuum.

In clinical practice, diagnosing a personality disorder depends the most on whether there is evidence of these enduring and stable maladaptive traits that impair functioning. However, it still needs to be conclusively demonstrated that such traits are actually stable in the population. In 2004, Grilo et al. examined the stability of four personality disorders over a two-year period. Subjects were given semi-structured interviews at baseline, 6, 12, and 24 months. The results suggested that personality disorders may be characterized by maladaptive traits that are structurally stable but can change in severity over time. In 2005, McGlashan et al. studied a sample of 474 patients diagnosed with four personality disorders over a two-year period. Blind follow-up assessments after 24 months found that some diagnostic traits were more stable in the sample and some were more changeable. For example, for the OCPD subjects in the sample, cognitive rigidity and problems delegating were stable over the period whereas miserliness and moral rigidity were not. McGlashan and colleagues suggested the results favored a hybrid model of personality disorders in which some diagnostic criteria are more trait-like and enduring than others. To summarize, recent trends in the study of personality disorders suggest that some enduring maladaptive personality traits are more stable and others more changeable. Other current research suggests that it is useful to think of the traits comprising the various personality disorder as existing on a continuum rather than being either/or. Typically the traits themselves are ego-syntonic and cause more distress for others who interact with the person. However, resulting losses of relationships and employment do cause distress and clearly demonstrate impaired functioning.

These trends in the research on personality disorders appear to be gradually generating a greater sense of theoretical clarity in the field. However, overall there are still a number of unresolved conceptual questions about how to define a personality disorder. These were summarized by Stone (2012). First, many clinicians think of personality disorders as existing on a continuum ranging from quirks to outright pathology to a more disease-like cluster of symptoms on the opposite end of the spectrum. But the problem with a continuum is: how do you determine where on the continuum a qualitative cut-off point may lie? Second, the general agreement as to what a normal personality is varies greatly between cultures. A third problem is again a continuum issue, this time within the diagnoses themselves. Some personality disorder symptoms can vary in severity over time. In addition, some symptoms are inherently more severe, which can easily be seen by an examination of the different symptoms that make up antisocial personality disorder. Accordingly, the continuums present within each personality disorder diagnosis can lead to more confusion. Diagnostic confusion can also arise because many patients may have overlapping symptoms from two or more personality disorders at the same time. A converse problem can arise because the names of the various personality disorders may be discussed as if they represent either/or labels. This can be a real problem during legal proceedings, because attorneys on one side or the other may use either/or labels to support their arguments. Thus although the continuum point of view in defining personality disorders creates one kind of theoretical confusion, the either/or categorical approach creates another.

An additional problem arises from some recent multifactorial models of personality that now exist. As of now it is still unclear how the narrower trait descriptions covered by the definition of the various personality disorders relate to the more fundamental personality factors described in these models. Then there is the problem of inherited temperament, which can predispose an individual to be more adventurous on the one hand or more harm-avoidant on the other. This issue leads to confusion about how to distinguish personality disorder symptoms from inherited temperament, which may be immutable. Finally, there is the fact that a personality disorder diagnosis focuses on maladaptive, negative traits (as does most medical diagnoses). Thus the diagnostic process tends to ignore the study of groups of positive traits, which may be what determines whether treatment for a personality disorder is successful. Stone's article suggests that a lot of theoretical and empirical work needs to be done to help sort out these conceptual confusions. He concludes that in the meantime, clinicians should focus more on pathogenesis and individual etiology as a way of diagnosing personality disorders.

The DSM-5 attempts to address some of these issues. The new personality disorder criteria try to bridge the controversy between continuum-based and categorical diagnostic criteria by revising the overarching criteria. An alternate hybrid model of classification is offered that includes five broad areas versus the previous three clusters of supposedly related personality disorders. There are several proposed common factors that all of the disorders will share. The new definitions emphasize somewhat different traits for each personality disorder. However, the basic diagnostic concept of personality disorders depending on enduring personality traits continue in the new edition. At this time the conceptual problems raised by Stone and others are quite broad, and the revised definitions leave many of them unresolved.

It should be noted that in line with the research suggesting that personality disorders are extreme representations of normal personality traits, OCPD could be seen as an extreme expression of a rigid, stubborn, moralistic, and perfectionistic approach to life. In general, the goal of most activity in individuals with OCPD is to experience a sense of emotional control through a rigid, stubborn, perfectionistic, and miserly approach to life in general and interpersonal relationships in particular.

EPIDEMIOLOGY

OCPD is not a rare condition. In 2012, Grant et al. summarized results from that year's National Epidemiological Survey on Alcohol and Related Conditions. The survey places the lifetime rate of OCPD as 7.8% of U.S. adults. The results of this survey are particularly notable because of the large sample size of 43,093 adults. OCPD was found to be significantly less common in Asians and Hispanics, and more common in individuals with a high school education or less. According to this survey, the disorder occurs at an equal rate in men and women. The latter result differs from some a number of other studies, which found significantly higher rates of OCPD among males than females (see Golomb et al., 1995).

DIFFERENTIAL DIAGNOSIS

Some of the demands Tom makes on his colleagues could reflect frank obsessive compulsive disorder (OCD) symptoms. The fact that he tends to stay at the office an unusual amount of time, asked a nurse to wash her hands five times, and checked his own pulse and blood pressure while working might indicate that he has compulsive behaviors. In OCD, intrusive thoughts or feelings of being compelled to take certain repetitive actions both create anxiety and are an attempt by the patient to manage such anxiety. However, the intrusive thoughts or the compulsive actions are experienced by the person as ego alien. This contrasts with OCPD, in which the enduring maladaptive traits are ego syntonic. Tom's clinician must take a careful history and ask him to describe whether his compulsive behaviors are ego syntonic to determine whether Tom meets criteria for OCD. The clinician may also use one of several available structured interview techniques to help make this determination.

In general, Tom's complaints are in line with OCPD. He seems to display the following traits: perfectionism, a preoccupation with details, overconscientiousness, a reluctance to delegate, and excessive stubbornness. His poor personal adjustment at work and in his marriage demonstrates the practical negative effects that can result from this diagnosis. His job loss is likely because he is controlling, demanding, and perfectionistic in his interactions with colleagues. Tom's comments that his compulsive behaviors at work are due to his high professional standards suggest that the behavior is ego syntonic. At the same time, the presence of at least some compulsive symptoms suggests that he could meet criteria for a hypothesized subtype of OCPD in which the patient also has OCD symptoms. (Research relating to this possible subtype is referenced later in the discussion of comorbidities between OCPD and anxiety disorders.) It appears that he is suffering from an acute relapse of major depression disorder (MDD) as well, since he has sadness, nihilistic thinking, weight loss, sleep disturbance, and impaired concentration. One possibility is that his MDD symptoms have increased his anxiety and led to classic OCD symptoms that he does not have when he is functioning better. Thus Tom's clinician will probably have to wait until his depression improves to determine if his baseline functioning includes OCD as well as OCPD symptoms.

ETIOLOGY AND PATHOGENESIS

To draw conclusions about the individual etiology of Tom's personality disorder, it is best to first understand some proposed general explanations for the causes of OCPD. Theories about the etiology of OCPD have varied widely, from psychodynamic formulations to explanations based on social learning theory to complex genetic and environmental factor analytic studies. There are many psychodynamic explanations of the formation of personality disorders in general and OCPD in particular. The first psychoanalytic treatment was undoubtedly Freud's description of the anal character. The more modern psychoanalytic approach was summarized by Glen Gabbard (2000). Individuals with OCPD feel unable to please at least one parental figure, thus seeing him or her as rejecting. In this situation the person increasingly strives to please the rejecting parent, while building up a reservoir of rage due to frustrated dependency needs. As these individuals mature, they develop an ego-syntonic tendency to control their need for social validation because they feel that interpersonal sources of nurturance may disappear at any time. Avoiding intimacy through overwork and controlling oneself and others by insisting on rigid standards serves the function of keeping them at a distance. In this way the obsessive compulsive personality continues to strive for parental recognition, while at the same time defending against feelings of anger, loss, and frustration. Tom's description of his father seems consistent with this theory. Karen Horney (1950) proposed three neurotic types: the compliant, the aggressive, and the detached. These represent broad drives to move toward others, move against others, or move away from others. Obsessive compulsive personality can be seen as a subtype of the compliant group. Horney (1950) described the dynamic underlying pathological overconscientiousness (a key characteristic of OCPD) as resulting from the striving to attain an unrealistic ideal self-concept. Her chapter titled "The Tyranny of the Shoulds" is a good description of this process.

Learning theory explanations of the pathogenesis of OCPD focus on the idea that the child imitates and learns inflexible and overconscientious behavior observed in parents or other important figures. In 1995 Mischel and Shoda updated this basic understanding by proposing that stable personality traits result from inferences individuals make about others' reactions to their own possible behaviors. These inferences are inductive conclusions gleaned from previous social experience. Thus stable personality traits result from learned theories about what behaviors will produce social rewards. If formative social experience was often with rigid, over-responsible individuals the data collection leading to this social inference process would be skewed accordingly, resulting in OCPD traits.

Recent factor analytic studies, which are influenced by developments in genetics, provide some of the most up-to-date etiological ideas. In 1986, Cloninger proposed a model that relates levels of three neurotransmitters (dopamine, serotonin, and norepinephrine) to the strength of drives toward seeking novelty, avoiding harm, and seeking reinforcement or reward. This line of research suggests that genetically determined efficiencies in the production of these (and perhaps other) neurotransmitters influence the development of personality traits, particularly those associated with approach-avoidance decisions. In 2010, Reichborn-Kjennerud summarized some newer literature in the genetics of personality disorders. A multivariate study of DSM-IV personality disorders using data from an Axis I–Axis II twin study produced a 27% heritability estimate for OCPD. Only 11% of the variance in OCPD was accounted for by common environmental and genetic factors, suggesting that OCPD is for the most part etiologically distinct from the other cluster C personality disorders. Joyce et al. (2003, cited in Reichborn-Kjennerud, 2010) found an association between both avoidant and obsessive compulsive personality features and polymorphism in the dopamine D3 receptor (DRD3). This finding was replicated in a second study and in a meta-analysis. So it does seem possible that the DRD3 gene plays a role in the development of OCPD. Reichborn-Kjennerud viewed the current evidence as demonstrating OCPD (as well as the other personality disorders) to be moderately heritable.

In 2011, Taylor published an analysis of 307 mono- and dizygotic twins' scores for obsessive compulsive symptoms, obsessive compulsive personality traits, and two markers of emotional distress. Matrices of environmental and genetic correlations were produced and factor analyzed. The analysis of these matrices showed that obsessive compulsive symptoms and traits were etiologically related through a more fundamental, nonspecific genetic factor linked to negative emotionality. Taylor viewed these results as supporting a clear clinical distinction between OCD and OCPD; he did not feel their results supported a continuum hypothesis, in which OCD and OCPD are seen as on the same spectrum. In addition, Taylor suggested that further research into environmental factors could focus on early experiences leading the child to acquire an overdeveloped sense of responsibility. In a 2009 study that touched on both genetic and environmental themes, Calvo et al. studied parents of both OCD children and healthy controls. Structured interviews were given to both sets of parents, and personality dimension scores and OCPD criteria were compared for the two sets of parents after excluding parents with frank OCD from the analysis. A higher incidence of OCPD was found in parents of probands; hoarding, perfectionism, and preoccupation with details were more frequent in parents of OCD children. In OCD children compulsions to count, order items in the environment, and clean predicted a higher probability of perfectionism and rigidity in their parents.

Studies such as the ones described here hint at a future in which the relative contribution of genetics to the etiology of OCPD can be determined more exactly than is currently possible. At the same time, learned factors such as an overdeveloped sense of responsibility are still important, whether conceptualized through psychodynamic or social learning theory. In Tom's case, learned behavior (whether explained psychodynamically or through social learning theory) and genetics are probably important factors in the development of his OCPD. From what is known about his strict, demanding, and at times physically abusive father, he could have had OCPD, OCD, a mood disorder, or all three. Thus Tom's father's genetic legacy and his behavioral example probably both factored into the development of Tom's OCPD.

NATURAL COURSE WITHOUT TREATMENT

Patients with OCPD are at risk for a number of other disorders. Some of the most common are the depressive disorders such as adjustment disorder with depression, dysthymia, and MDD. Tom currently has depressive symptoms, probably secondary to abrupt changes in his life circumstances; he had a previous depressive episode while in medical school. Several studies have focused on comorbidity between affective disorders and personality disorders. In 2004 Schiavone et al. gave structured diagnostic interviews to samples of inpatients diagnosed with either unipolar or bipolar affective disorder. The most frequent personality diagnoses among the unipolar group were borderline personality disorder (BPD) at 31.6%, dependent personality disorder at 25.2%, and obsessive compulsive personality at 14.2%. Among the bipolar group, the most frequent personality disorders were BPD (41%), narcissistic personality disorder (20.5%), dependent personality (12.8%), and histrionic personality (10.3%). Statistical analysis revealed that unipolar patients had a higher frequency of recurrent OCPD than bipolar patients. In general, cluster C disorders (of which OCPD is one) were more frequent in the unipolar group, whereas cluster B diagnoses were more prevalent in the bipolar group.

In 2010 Morey et al. employed six-year outcome data from the multisite Collaborative Longitudinal Personality Disorders Study. They found that clinical outcomes after six years for patients with comorbid MDD and personality disorders were similar to the outcomes of those with personality disorder only, but significantly worse than the outcomes of the patients with MDD only. At follow-up, patients initially diagnosed with both a personality disorder and MDD were more similar clinically to other personality-disordered patients. The results suggest that a personality disorder diagnosis leads to poorer clinical outcomes in depressed patients. The authors concluded there is little cause for concern that personality symptoms may be transient results of MDD. Instead, the symptoms tend to endure, consistent with the DSM definition of personality disorders. It appears that personality disorders made treating depression more problematic, not vice versa. The results also were said to reflect the increased risk that personality-disordered patients have of developing MDD.

In 2010 Grilo et al. studied 303 patients with MDD at baseline who were part of the Collaborative Longitudinal Personality Disorders Study, using structured diagnostic interviews. The results were that those who had personality disorders when joining the study were at greater risk of relapsing into another depressive episode. BPD and OCPD had the most significant association with relapse. In 2011 Skodol et al. analyzed structured interview data for 1996 individuals in the 2001–2 and 2004–5 National Epidemiologic Surveys on Alcohol and Related Conditions. They found that OCPD-diagnosed individuals had a 25.40% risk of MDD over the course of the study. Notably, other personality disorders had stronger associations with MDD. The strongest predictors of lack of remission in MDD were BPD and schizoid personality. Overall these and other studies suggest that having any personality disorder tends to worsen the prognosis for MDD. The relationship with MDD for specific personality disorders varies depending on the study. There is a tendency personality disorder diagnoses that were in the old clusters A and B to be associated with a greater risk of more severe affective disorders. However, at least some studies also name OCPD as a factor that makes remission from MDD more difficult.

Other researchers have looked at the potential comorbidities between OCPD and anxiety disorders. The DSM notes that individuals with anxiety disorders are at increased risk of having OCPD. In 2011, Ansell et al. published a study following 499 patients in the Collaborative Longitudinal Personality Disorders Study who had been diagnosed with anxiety disorders. Sample members were given structured diagnostic interviews at yearly intervals for seven years. Specific personality disorders were statistically associated with relapse and with new episode onset of anxiety disorders. In particular, OCPD was found to be associated with a relapsing or chronic course of OCD, generalized anxiety disorder (GAD), and agoraphobia.

A number of researchers have examined the prevalence of OCD in OCPD patients and discussed what this association might mean. In 2006 Eisen et al. analyzed 629 participants in the Collaborative Longitudinal Personality Disorders Study. Specifically, they looked for prevalence of the eight OCPD criteria in OCD subjects. The OCPD symptoms of hoarding, perfectionism, and preoccupation with details were significantly more frequent in OCD subjects than in those without OCD. This contrasted with nonsignificant relationships between the OCPD criteria and either other anxiety disorders or MDD. They suggested that this kind of symptom-level analysis might clarify the relationships between acute mental health disorders and personality disorders. In 2010 Garyfallos et al. looked for evidence of comorbidity between OCD and OCPD in a sample of 146 outpatients. Almost a third of the OCD patients met criteria for OCPD. Patients with both disorders had more severe obsessive compulsive symptoms; their histories showed that these symptoms began earlier in life. Patients with both disorders also had lower Global Assessment of Functioning scores and a higher rate of comorbidity with avoidant personality disorder. The authors concluded that these associations support the idea that comorbid OCD and OCPD represents a specific subtype of OCD. In 2011 Lochner et al. published similar research but interpreted the results differently. They measured 403 OCD subjects with and without OCPD on a range of genetic, demographic, and clinical characteristics. Their results indicated that OCD with and without OCPD have similar distributions in terms of gene variants, gender, and age of onset. OCD patients with OCPD are more likely to have obsessive compulsive symptoms associated with the OCPD criteria (such as hoarding); they are likely to have more severe symptoms. The authors concluded that instead of defining a specific subtype of OCD, OCD with OCPD is probably an indicator of more severe illness with greater functional impairment. In 2005, Mancebo et al. came up with similar conclusions in their review of contemporary literature on the relationship of OCD and OCPD. They noted that although there is evidence of a linkage between the two disorders, neither is a necessary or sufficient condition for the other.

In summary, there seems to be evidence that OCPD is associated with a higher risk of MDD than seen in the general population and also complicates recovery from MDD; that OCPD is more often associated with unipolar as opposed to bipolar affective disorder; that when it occurs with a cluster B personality disorder it is less determinative of the clinical presentation; that OCPD can be less debilitating than some of the other personality disorders (such as BPD, schizotypal personality, and schizoid personality); that OCPD does raise the risk of co-occurring anxiety problems; and that OCPD patients with comorbid OCD are likely to be more severely impaired than those without this co-occurrence. Although the association between OCD and OCPD is still being investigated, such comorbidities may mark greater severity rather than a distinct subtype.

EVIDENCE-BASED TREATMENT OPTIONS

Medications are used for more acute consequences of OCPD but have not demonstrated efficacy by themselves for personality disorders in general. Monoamine oxidase inhibitors (MAOIs) seem to be effective for avoidant personality disorder which may be closely related to social anxiety disorder. However, there are a number of different psychotherapeutic approaches to treating personality disorders. Two of the most frequently used approaches will be outlined. In 2005 Appelbaum described a common psychodynamically influenced model. The basic strategy is to provide a supportive environment in which the patient can work with the therapist on overcoming obstacles to a more adaptive interpersonal adjustment. The supportive focus is defined as "maintaining a reflective state" (Appelbaum 2005). In this way the patient feels safe enough to explore his or her difficulty with affect regulation (which Appelbaum sees as a fundamental problem in personality disorders) and experiences a positive transference toward the therapist. However, Appelbaum notes that when doing such supportive therapy with patients who have not integrated strong emotions into their personalities, deep exploration of the transference relationship is not advised. Instead, she advises the therapist to reinforce the appearance of a quiet, alert state in which the patient is open to new learning. Interestingly, this state seems to be related to that sought in meditative practice. She also suggests that the therapist reinforce verbal expression of thoughts and feelings and find aspects of the patient to respect and appreciate. Appelbaum believes that this approach is the treatment of choice especially for the initial phase of therapy. However, she notes that for high-functioning OCPD patients, treatment after the initial phase would need to focus more on helping the patient have insights into his or her behavior and using those insights to improve social adjustment. This means a transition from a more purely supportive therapeutic approach to an expressive one. In this expressive phase the patient's transference wishes and fears are more openly discussed. In Tom's case, his current depression and marital separation, the damaged relationship with his father, and his brother's suicide all suggest the need to start with the reflective/supportive approach and only gradually move into a more expressive, insight-oriented phase.

Psychotherapy for OCPD can also be in the form of cognitive behavioral therapy (CBT). In 2010, Matusiewicz et al. provided a good literature review of the application of CBT to various personality disorders. The authors view CBT as well suited for treating personality disorders because these disorders persist due to a combination of maladaptive hypotheses about self and others, features of the social environmental that reinforce maladaptive behavior, and interpersonal skills deficits. CBT can apply a variety of tools to treat these three factors. These include psychoeducation, social skills training, cognitive restructuring, behavior modification, and exposure hierarchies (although some of these tools are more commonly used for treating cluster A or B personality disorders).

The general CBT approach to personality disorder treatment emphasizes the development of a supportive therapeutic alliance, in which the therapist presents himself as the patient's consultant or collaborator. In traditional CBT, the initial focus is on orienting the patient and developing a cognitive formulation of their symptoms. Later sessions focus on identifying and altering negative, maladaptive thought patterns and reducing self-defeating interpersonal behaviors. Work with the patient on negative thinking patterns may include thought monitoring, teaching the patient to engage in Socratic dialogue with him- or herself, and practicing techniques for self-reassurance and disputing irrational beliefs. In the subtype known as schema-focused CBT, the therapy targets more fundamental maladaptive interpersonal belief systems that may have originated in childhood. As such, the content discussed with the patient sometimes resembles discussions of transference patterns in psychodynamic therapy. There is usually liberal use of homework assignments, such as daily charts of negative thoughts or moods; bibliotherapy; practicing meditation, relaxation, or other calming activities that lower anxiety; graduated exposure to anxiety-provoking situations (while at the same time practicing such anxiety-reducing techniques); and planned social exercises for which the patient prepares through coaching and anxiety reduction work in the therapy session.

Both psychodynamic therapy and CBT for personality disorders have produced good results in therapy outcome studies. In a 2004 study, Svartberg et al. compared the effectiveness of 40 sessions of dynamic psychotherapy to the same amount of CBT for a sample of cluster C personality disorder patients. Patient responses to treatment were measured at the beginning, middle, and end of therapy and up to two years after the end of treatment. Both treatment groups showed significant reduction of symptoms on all of the personality measures used. Two years post-treatment, 40% of the patients in each group had significant improvement in their interpersonal functioning. Although a somewhat higher percentage of the psychodynamic therapy patients had significant individual symptom relief (54% versus 42%), both of these treatment effect sizes were noteworthy.

CLINICAL COURSE WITH MANAGEMENT AND TREATMENT

Earlier in his life, when he experienced his first episode of MDD, Tom responded well to a tricyclic antidepressant. It was reasonable to treat the depression at that time and then stop the medicine after he was in remission for six months. His expected recurrence rate was 50%. Now that he is experiencing a second episode of depression, the possible recurrence rate is at about 75%. Thus when he is once more brought to remission, he may need to be maintained on an antidepressant. Since his first episode new antidepressants have emerged; these medicines are safer and have fewer side effects than the amitriptyline he was initially given. Therefore, he might be given a drug such as fluoxetine. Since fluoxetine is now generic, its cost is very low. Further history might be obtained to rule out a manic episode, since the administration of an antidepressant in an individual who has a bipolar disorder might cause him to have rapid cycling, thus worsening his condition. His compulsive symptoms will need to be discussed with Tom as he improves, with the goal of determining whether he has these symptoms at baseline or whether he is simply being overly detail-oriented (which would be consistent with OCPD). To get treatment started while these questions were being assessed, Tom was started on fluoxetine, generic, and offered psychotherapy.

Tom could be a good candidate for psychotherapy for several reasons. He is bright, articulate, and in good physical shape. His overconscientious nature may prompt him to work hard in therapy; the fact that he is moralistic may make him reliable if he is asked to agree to a safety contract. Tom may want to please his physician, who to him probably represents an authority figure. In fact, if he makes progress in treatment and receives positive feedback from his psychiatrist, that could serve as a counterexample to his inability to win his father's praise and thus be a corrective emotional experience.

Tom returned in a week and indicated that he was still very depressed and disappointed that the medicine had not started to have an effect. More realistic expectation for the medication was facilitated through education about how antidepressants work and the typical time frame of about six weeks. He was able to talk freely about his childhood and how strict his parents were. He never felt that he could complete a project to his parents' satisfaction. If he mowed the lawn, his father would claim that he missed the corners and become verbally abusive, saying he was "lazy and always wanting to cut corners." His father claimed the patient would never amount to anything, if he continued to cut corners. As the patient vented, he began feeling less stressed and experienced approval from the therapist.

During the next session several weeks later, Tom was able to reaffirm his purpose to be a physician, and although his coworkers in his practice asked him to leave, he continues to be a doctor and can find a new group to join. By now the fluoxetine had started to have a positive effect, and he was able to begin seeing a light at the end of the tunnel. He admitted that initially that light seemed like an oncoming train, but now it seems like a ray of hope. Several weeks later, the therapist was able to help him begin to compare how his father treated him and how he often treats his wife and coworkers. He began to acknowledge that this approach seems to push people away, rather than draw them closer to him. Thus there seemed to be insight and some motivation to change.

At the next weekly session, Tom was helped to reexamine his work habits. He was encouraged to reflect on his inability to let others take call and relinquish his patients' care to the people who are covering for him. The psychiatrist helped him identify his need for control and explored ways to rethink his decision not to let others help him. During the next session, Tom indicated that he was able to have a satisfactory interview with a new group of doctors. He was pleased with their response to his visit. He started feeling hopeful about this new opportunity. In addition, he had dinner with his wife and was able to share with her that he was beginning to appreciate his critical nature. He acknowledged that he was becoming harsh and demanding like his father. His wife seemed to be open to the idea of marital counseling.

The psychiatrist is pleased with his progress so far. However, certain aspects of his history suggest that the quick improvement in his symptoms is too good to be true and that he might be at risk for relapse in the future. In particular, his previous depressive episode and divorce, as well as his brother's suicide, are warning signs of potential relapse. Accordingly, Tom's psychiatrist will spend some time thinking about the best approach to treatment going forward.

SYSTEMS-BASED PRACTICE ISSUES

The systems issues that arise in this case are the same as those that arise when treating physicians in other contexts. When treating a physician, especially one who is obsessive, the clinician should be aware that the person being treated knows enough about diagnosis and treatment in general that explaining the proposed treatment to him can give rise to more than the usual amount of anxiety. The person may challenge the treatment plan after having read some of the literature about the diagnosis. Thus it will be important to answer patient questions clearly and with reference to accepted practice guidelines. In addition, if Tom is seen by a clinician in the same hospital system he has worked in, providing good treatment while maintaining confidentiality can be difficult. Some of the specific issues regarding confidentiality that often arise when treating physicians are described in the next section.

LEGAL, ETHICAL, AND CULTURAL CHALLENGES

There are important ethical and legal challenges for the psychiatric or psychotherapeutic treatment of a physician patient. The treating clinician must learn whether the physician is currently seeing patients and whether in fact he or she is competent to do so. If the patient is unable to make good treatment decisions in his or her specialty, it is important to address this. Sometimes a clinician must have a delicate conversation with a physician patient who is too impaired by his psychiatric symptoms to practice, reminding the patient of the prospects of improvement and a return to work, while at the same time pointing out that making treatment decisions while psychiatrically disabled could lead to unethical behavior on the patient's part and end his or her career permanently. In Tom's case, he is between jobs and also is responding well to treatment to date, so the issue has not arisen.

Another important legal and ethical challenge in a case like this arises if the treating clinician or others in the clinician's practice know the patient. It is always important to review confidentiality procedures with the person being treated during the first session. However, if the physician-patient is a member of the same hospital system as the treating clinician, maintaining confidentiality will be more difficult; this fact should be brought up directly with the patient. If the clinician's or the office staff's degree of knowledge of the patient is minor or peripheral, then treatment can proceed while being careful to follow appropriate confidentiality guidelines. Some hospital systems make this easier by adding an extra level of restriction regarding access to medical records for patients who are also hospital employees. This can be done with paper records by storing them separately and with electronic records by programming in administrative warnings and monitoring access to such records. However, if the physician-patient is too well known to the clinician or the office staff, it is best to refer him or her to a trusted colleague at the beginning of treatment.

REFERENCES AND RESOURCES

Ansell EB, Pinto A, Edelen MO, et al.The association of personality disorders with the prospective 7-year course of anxiety disorders. *Psychol Med* 2011;41(5):1019–28.

Appelbaum AH. Supportive psychotherapy. *Focus J Lifelong Learn Psychiatr* 2005;3(3): 438–49.

Calvo R, Lazaro L, Castro-Fornieles J, et al. Obsessive-compulsive personality disorder traits and personality dimensions in parents of children with obsessive-compulsive disorder. *Eur PsychiatrJ Assoc Eur Psych* 2009;24(3):201–6.

Cloninger CR. A unified biosocial theory of personality and its role in the development of anxiety states. *Psychiatr Devel* 1986;3:167–226.

Eisen JL, Coles ME, Shea MT, et al. Clarifying the convergence between obsessive-compulsive personality disorder and obsessive-compulsive disorder. *J Pers Dis* 2006; 20(3):294–305.

Gabbard GO. Psychotherapy of personality disorders. *J Psychother Pract Res* 2000 Winter;9(1):1–6.

Garyfallos G, Katsigiannopoulos K, Adamopoulou A, et al. Co morbidity of obsessive-compulsive disorder with obsessive-compulsive personality disorder: does it imply a specific subtype of obsessive-compulsive disorder? *Psychiatr Res* 2010;177(1–2):156–60.

Golomb M, Fava M, Abraham M, Rosenbaum JF. Gender differences in personality disorders. *Am J Psychiatr* 1995;152(4):579–82.

Grant JE, Mooney ME, Kushner MG. Prevalence, correlates, and co morbidity of DSM-IV obsessive-compulsive personality disorder: results from the national epidemiologic survey on alcohol and related conditions. *Jo Psychiatr Res* 2012;46(4):469–75.

Grilo CM, Sanislow CA, Gunderson JG, et al. Two-year stability and change of schizotypal, borderline, avoidant, and obsessive-compulsive personality disorders. *J Consult Clin Psychol* 2004;72(5):767–75.

Grilo CM, Stout RL, Markowitz JC, et al. Personality disorders predict relapse after remission from an episode of major depressive disorder: a 6-year prospective study. *J Clin Psychiatr* 2010;71(12):1629–35.

Horney K. *Neurosis and Human Growth: The Struggle toward Self-Realization.* New York: W.W. Norton & Company, 1950.

Joyce PR, Rogers GR, Miller AL. Polymorphisms of DRD4 and DRD3 and risk of avoidant and obsessive personality traits and disorders. *Psychiatr Res* 2003;119(1–2):1–10.

Lochner C, Serebo P, der Merwe L, et al. Co morbid obsessive-compulsive personality disorders in obsessive-compulsive disorder (OCD): a marker of severity. *Prog Neuro-Psychopharmacol Biol Psychiatr* 2011;35(4):1087–92.

Mancebo MC, Eisen JL, Grant JE, Rasmussen SA. Obsessive compulsive personality disorder and obsessive compulsive disorder: clinical characteristics, diagnostic difficulties, and treatment. *Ann Clin Psychiatr* 2005;17(4):197–204.

Matusiewicz BA, Hopwood CJ, Banducci AN, Lejuez CW. The effectiveness of cognitive behavioral therapy for personality disorders. *Psychiatr Clin N Amer* 2010;33:657–85.

McGlashan TH, Grilo CM, Sanislow CA, et al. Two-year prevalence and stability of individual DSM-IV criteria for schizotypal, borderline, avoidant, and obsessive-compulsive personality disorders: towards a hybrid model of axis II disorders. *Am J Psychiatr* 2005;162(5):883–89.

Mischel W, Shoda Y. A cognitive-affective system theory of personality: reconceptualizing situations, dispositions, dynamics, and invariance in personality structure. *Psychol Rev* 1995;102(2):246–68.

Morey LC, Shea TS, Markowitz MD, et al. State effects of major depression on the assessment of personality and personality disorder. *Am J Psychiatr* 2010;167:528–35.

Reichborn-Kjennerud T. Genetics of personality disorders. *Clin Lab Med* 2010;30:893–910.

Schiavone P, Dorz S, Conforti D, et al. Co morbidity of DSM-IV personality disorders in unipolar and bipolar affective disorders: a comparative study. *Psychol Rep* 2004;95(1):121–28.

Skodol AE, Grilo CM, Keyes KM, et al. Relationship of personality disorders to the course of major depressive disorder in a nationally representative sample. *Am J Psychiatr* 2010;168:257–64.

Skodol AE, Oldham JM, Bender DS, et al. Dimensional representations of DSM-IV personality disorders: relationships to functional impairment. *Am J Psychiatr* 2005; 162(10):1919–25.

Stone MH. Disorder in the domain of the personality disorders. *Psychodynam Psychiatr* 2012;40(1):23–46.

Svartberg M, Stiles TC, Seltzer MH. Randomized, controlled trial of the effectiveness of short-term dynamic psychotherapy and cognitive therapy for cluster C personality disorders. *Am J Psychiatr* 2004;161:810–17.

Taylor SS. Etiology of obsessive-compulsive symptoms and obsessive-compulsive personality traits: common genes, mostly different environments. *Dep Anx* 2011;28(10): 863–69.

Les Miserables (2012). In this film, the policeman Javier represents the diagnosis of OCPD in his motives and personality as he obsessively pursues Jean Valjean.

CHAPTER **39**

Lack of Empathy

Hilton R. Lacy, M.D.

CLINICAL PRESENTATION

Chief complaint: "I have a problem with a bad temper."

History of present illness: JD is a 41-year-old single male referred to the prison psychiatrist for evaluation and possible treatment. JD has spent the previous 10 years in state prison following a conviction and 20-year sentence for accessory to murder. During this time he has had continuing difficulties, which he attributes to his temper, resulting in many fights with other inmates and verbal conflicts with prison guards, leading to disciplinary actions. His most recent difficulty was after being moved to a new facility. When he sat down to eat at his first meal there, a large, muscular prisoner put his finger in JD's food, then asked what he was going to do about it. JD proceeded to eat his meal, but as he was leaving the dining room, he slammed his serving tray into the other prisoner's head. He said he did not recall what happened next, as he was unconscious for several days after the other prisoner had finished beating him in retaliation. He feels that his temper often gets him into many similar life-threatening and difficult situations. He has become concerned that he will not be able to get more privileges, move to a lower security facility, or be eligible for early release if he does not learn to manage his temper.

JD describes his life as always having been filled with similar challenges, including conflicts with authority. He feels these problems are related to his upbringing. During his childhood, he moved back and forth between his parents, who divorced when he was three years old. He describes his mother as a "good woman" who was loving and supportive but "had trouble keeping me in line." He recalls that usually whenever she would try to discipline him, he would lose his temper and become extremely agitated, resulting in her giving up her attempts to set limits on his behavior. She was often gone from the home or emotionally unavailable, being involved in one of a multiple series of romantic relationships. Her boyfriends often stayed in the home for short periods of time, and some of them were physically abusive to JD.

He describes his father as "really strict" during the times he stayed with him. He describes one visit during which he accidentally spilled a soda. His father became so angry that he beat JD extensively with a belt, resulting in multiple bleeding areas on his torso and buttocks. He reports similar situations occurring several times throughout his early childhood, which he never reported to his mother or to any authorities. He said the beatings stopped when "I got too big for him to put his hands on me anymore." When he was 13 years of age, his father was sentenced to prison for selling heroin. They have had little to no contact over recent years.

During late elementary and middle school, JD was frequently disciplined at school for disruptive behavior in class. This included arguing with teachers or getting in physical altercations with peers. He was also brought to his home by local police on occasion for trespassing or minor shoplifting, but never had any formal legal consequences resulting from these episodes. The police would release him to his mother after she would promise to monitor him more closely. As a teenager, he discovered that he could make money shoplifting and then selling the goods at a local flea market, but he was eventually caught and arrested. During a six-month incarceration at the age of 20, he met a 45-year-old man who had been arrested for domestic violence. JD was impressed with this man's apparent calmness during stressful situations, as well as his ability to influence other people and get them to do what he wanted. The two developed a friendly relationship. After they were released, JD began to spend time regularly with this man. The friend related that he was in a bad marriage, and claimed that his wife wanted to divorce him and take their child with her, as well as all of his money. He persuaded JD to agree to help him to confront and threaten the wife, with the goal of forcing her to share custody of their child and split their assets. JD talked frequently with this friend about how to set up such a situation and helped locate firearms to use in the confrontation as well. Unfortunately, the friend from prison actually intended to kill and not merely threaten his wife; JD was present at the time of the wife's murder. Later JD discovered that the friend may have been involved in other murders for which he had never been arrested. The fact that the friend had been raised in a supportive, intact family and had been a regular churchgoer was confusing to JD.

Other than his chronic "temper," JD does not describe any chronic or intermittent sad or elevated mood or any anxiety. He denies any problems with his sleep, energy, or appetite. He says he "just sees red" and "blacks out" and does not remember the details of what happens during his physical altercations. He otherwise says he does not have any problems with his memory or concentration. Although he hopes to be able to stay out of trouble and earn more freedom and privileges, he feels that in general he is "just doing what I have to do to stand up for myself" during the fights or conflicts and does not express any particular guilt or disappointment in himself for his actions. Other than believing that people in general are overall untrustworthy and are usually "just trying to get what they want, same as everybody," he does not describe any specific paranoia or delusions, and does not describe any unusual sensory experiences such as hallucinations. While he feels that "the whole world might be better off if some of them [the other inmates] were dead," he does not endorse any homicidal ideation toward any particular person and has never felt suicidal. He does not endorse any recurrent intrusive thoughts or efforts to avoid any.

Past psychiatric history: At age 12, JD was psychiatrically hospitalized for aggressive behavior during an argument with his mother, when he had threatened her with a kitchen knife and she called the police. During that hospitalization he was given a trial of lithium, which seemed to help his behavior for a while, although he did not follow up with treatment after discharge. At 14 years of age, he was placed in a residential setting for six months due to chronic truancy from school, violation of curfew, fighting, and other criminal behavior. After an initial period of adjustment, he eventually did well enough in the program to be released and continued to do well for several weeks after his discharge, but soon his behavioral problems returned.

Substance use: He started to smoke marijuana when he was 11, using it daily by age 13, primarily with his peers. He experimented with alcohol but never really liked the way it made him feel. He tried cocaine, mainly snorting it, but eventually decided that he would be better selling it rather than using it himself and began to do that on a regular basis. He smokes a pack of cigarettes a day. When he has the limited opportunity to get drugs while incarcerated, he prefers to trade them for extra food and personal favors in the prison than imbibe them himself.

Legal history: He is likely to complete the remaining full 10 years of his sentence for his conviction for accessory to murder. He had several earlier arrests for shoplifting, with one relatively short period of incarceration; he had one charge for selling drugs, but this was reduced to possession, so he did not serve any time for this.

Past medical history: He reports having been in fairly good health. He has had several emergency room evaluations for lacerations, fractured bones, and brief periods of unconsciousness after past fights. He has early symptoms of chronic obstructive pulmonary disease secondary to smoking.

Allergies: No drug allergies.

Family history: His parents were divorced when he was young; he spent most of his time with his mother, but stayed with his father fairly regularly. His father had chronic problems with his temper, as well as dependence on cocaine and marijuana, but never engaged in any treatment and was eventually incarcerated himself. His mother was treated for depression, and attempted suicide on one occasion about 20 years ago, with one psychiatric hospitalization. She also had trouble sustaining relationships. A psychiatrist who had treated her had expressed concerns that she had a borderline personality disorder. An older brother is in prison for armed robbery and also has a history of heroin dependence. An older sister works as a nurse and has no psychiatric problems. He has limited contact with his family.

Social history: JD grew up in a small town in an economically depressed area of the state. In addition to behavior problems, he failed and repeated two grades in elementary school. Later he was frequently truant. At age 15, his mother (his father being absent) gave up trying to keep him in school; he made an agreement with her that he would get a job if she let him drop out, although he made most of his money shoplifting and selling the items. He has never married and has no children. He has dated sporadically, but his romantic relationships were brief and transient, primarily being involved with girls or women who helped him in selling his shoplifted goods or later selling drugs. One of his longest relationships was in his mid-twenties with a teenage girl. She helped him steal from a discount store where she worked part-time. His mother had pets, a dog and cat, but he never liked them and would play tricks on them, such as stepping on their tails and watching them struggle to get loose. He admitted that once he set some of his mother's belongings on fire and loved to watch things burn. Whenever his family had a cookout, he always volunteered to start the charcoal.

Mental status examination: JD appears a bit older than his stated age of 41 years. He presents to the interview in a short-sleeved prison jumpsuit; a variety of tattoos (a mixture of apparently being created by professionals and amateurs) are visible on his forearms and neck; he is noted to be missing one upper and two lower teeth. He often leans forward and drums his fingers on the table during the interview, but is not otherwise impulsive or hyperactive and has no abnormal movements. He seems mildly excessively familiar, saying "How you doin' today, bud?" as he enters the room; eye contact at times is excessively direct and seems mildly challenging. Speech is notable for a heavy regional accent; he also occasionally seems not to understand questions and asks to have them repeated or explained. He is fully conscious and oriented to person, place, time (although he does not know the correct date), situation, and setting. Registration is somewhat limited given that he sometimes asks for questions or instructions to be repeated or explained; immediate recall and recent and remote memory are intact. Thought processes are logical and goal directed, although occasionally somewhat circumstantial responses are given, possibly related to misunderstanding questions. Thought content is generally restricted to his concern about managing his temper and gaining more privileges, but he does express some concern that he could lose his temper and hurt someone if they were to "get in my face," leading to more legal problems. He feels that he has gotten a "bad rap" for his incarceration, and claims he was unaware that the friend intended to kill the woman during the planned confrontation; he insists that if he had known that the friend intended to kill her, he "never would have even hung out with the man." There is no evidence for hallucination or delusional thinking. His thinking is somewhat concrete, in that when asked to describe similarities between objects, he refers only to their physical characteristics. He is able to make simple calculations such as correctly making change for hypothetical purchases. His fund of knowledge about recent current events is limited; he says, "I just don't keep up with that stuff in here." His insight seems somewhat limited, given his feeling that his temper is the only reason for his current difficulties. His judgment for hypothetical situations is poor. When asked what his response would be if he found an envelope full of money on the street, but which had a name and address on it, he stated "that sounds like a pretty lucky day for me," while smiling. Historical judgment is also poor given his current placement. Perceptual disturbances such as delusions, hallucinations, or dissociative experiences are absent. Specific suicidal or homicidal thoughts are emphatically denied. His mood is generally euthymic in the interview; affect is mildly labile, with his becoming transiently angry, raising his voice and his face flushing briefly, when discussing how he was misled into his current incarceration. He denies any anger, however, and generally discusses his history in a somewhat detached, unemotional manner.

IMPAIRMENT IN FUNCTIONING

Functional impairment is typically described in relation to severity of a person's reported symptoms, or by problems identified in other areas of life, such as school, work, relationships, and legal problems. JD's subjective distress is rather minimal, more specific to his situation, and his behavior leads to a lack of possible material or personal gain, rather than general and pervasive distress. However, he has chronic and severe impairment in nearly every other life domain assessed. He obviously has legal difficulties that have led to the penal consequence of long-term confinement. Impairments exist in occupational functioning (no work skills or previous employment outside of criminal endeavors) and in social relationships (chronic conflicts including physical aggression, no apparent close interpersonal relationships, including with family). His educational achievement is low. Medical problems include the multiple emergency medical evaluations due to injuries resulting from his physical altercations.

DSM DIAGNOSIS

JD meets sufficient criteria primarily for a diagnosis of antisocial personality disorder (ASPD). This includes symptoms occurring since before the age of 15 (and likely meeting criteria for conduct disorder (CD) at that time). He has repeated failure to conform to social expectations for lawful behavior, leading to him being arrested and incarcerated. He also has chronic irritability and aggressive behavior, engaging in repeated physical fights. He also expresses no apparent remorse, indicated by rationalizing his behavior and social interactions. His relationship with the teenage girl involved in his shoplifting enterprise is evidence of his deceitfulness and manipulation in interacting with others. His history also suggests a consistent failure to plan ahead, if not chronic impulsiveness, and consistent irresponsibility is evidenced by his early truancy and having no work history other than selling shoplifted merchandise or drugs. He is also over the current age criterion of 18. In addition to his symptoms being chronic, there seem to be no other diagnosis that would better explain his symptoms, particularly schizophrenia (i.e., hallucinations, delusion, or grossly disorganized behavior) or manic episodes of bipolar disorder (BPD), with episodic sustained euphoria, grandiosity, insomnia, racing thoughts, and so on.

JD's primary motivation for change is to achieve primarily external, relatively materialistic goals of increased privileges and early release. He does not seem to have a desire for any internal change, such as subjective thoughts or feelings like sadness, regret, remorse, or a lowered opinion of himself as a result of his actions, at least in this assessment. This is often the case with ASPD, in which the reason for seeking treatment is to obtain such external incentives, relief from family pressure, or avoidance of punishments such as legal consequences. His resources and potential for improvement are limited by factors often associated with ASPD, like his low educational background, possible language difficulties, lack of family support or any significant other, or having no apparent occupational skills. The external structure and relatively concrete incentives provided by his incarceration seem to be the only factors that could potentially contribute to his improvement.

Personality disorders are in general considered to be patterns of inflexible and maladaptive behavior that deviate from normal cultural and social expectations, are present by the time an individual is an adolescent or early adult, are persistent and enduring, result in subjective distress or observable impairment in functioning in multiple contexts, and are not believed to be due to another mental health or medical condition. They can have typical manifestations in mood and its expression, behavior, thought processes, social interaction, and other areas. As with personality, they may develop early in life, and although by definition they are persistent and enduring, these disorders are also subject to modification over time.

The approach to diagnosing personality disorders continues to evolve with accumulating information from additional research. Prior to DSM-5, these disorders were diagnosed on a separate axis, theoretically to ensure their consideration for treatment instead of otherwise being overlooked, and yet they are underdiagnosed. Explanations for this include practitioners feeling that the separate axis diagnostic system is unwieldy, a negative stigma is associated with personality disorder, the separate diagnosis does not improve treatment plans, and the diagnoses lack clarity. For example, based on different combinations of criteria, there are 256 different ways one could be diagnosed with borderline personality disorder (BOPD). Anecdotally, many practitioners also avoid diagnosing them because treatment is not usually reimbursed under some payment structures. The result is that personality disorders are often diagnosed as something else, such as BPD. One study of hospital admissions for BPD indicated that nearly 25% more accurately met criteria for BOPD; another study found that a positive score on a commonly used screening questionnaire for BPD was more consistent with BOPD nearly 30% of the time.

There are other challenges with the personality disorder diagnostic concept. It is argued that they represent a range of traits of varying severity, rather than truly discrete, separate conditions (half of the current personality disorders are strongly loaded for the same trait of neuroticism, for example). They also have only moderate short-term diagnostic consistency between initial and later assessments (as low as 50%, perhaps expectable given that personality can change over time, but problematic in that the personality disorders are defined as stable and enduring). There are often numerous comorbid diagnoses, as noted, implicating a lack of precision in identifying them; by current criteria a diagnosis of more than one personality disorder can be made at a time. This is challenging logic as a person presumably has just one basic personality.

An area of particular clinical interest is the diagnosis of a personality disorder in adolescence, possibly pertaining to JD's case. One of the criteria for a personality disorder is that it be present by adolescence or early adulthood. Most personality disorders theoretically can be diagnosed in adolescence as young as age 14 and can be fairly prevalent in this age group, although most clinicians are reluctant to do so. This may be due to the perceived stigma and other concerns. There may also be therapeutic hope that with further personality development (in association with continued brain maturation into the early to mid-twenties) that the diagnostic criteria will no longer be met or that they will resolve as the youth live independently of a possibly exacerbating family situation. For ASPD, this has been the case in particular, such that antisocial behavior in youth is typically diagnosed as CD instead.

Despite the need for ongoing study, personality disorders are accepted to be legitimate clinical conditions with implications for treatment. They have had different classifications in the several editions of the DSM used for diagnoses of mental health conditions over the past few decades. Recent subcategories or clusters of personality disorder have been those of A (odd, eccentric-unusual), B (dramatic, emotional, erratic-externalizing), and C (anxious, fearful-internalizing). Several types, including ASPD in the cluster B group, have been consistently described in the various editions.

ASPD is the diagnosis applied to an individual when there is a persistent and pervasive pattern of disregard for and violation of the rights of others. Most of the symptoms have been described in discussing JD's diagnosis. As an alternative to the categorical approach of previous editions, DSM-5 also proposes a dimensional model that includes the goal of integrating descriptions of impaired personality functioning, with separate definitions of pathological personality traits within five broad domains (and 26 specific trait facets). Disturbances in self and interpersonal functioning constitute the core of personal psychopathology. Impairments of self-functioning for ASPD include identity (being self- and ego-centric; self-esteem mostly derived from power, pleasure, or personal gain) and self-direction (goal-setting based on personal gratification, without expression of prosocial internal standards, and law-breaking and culturally normative unethical behavior). Impairments for interpersonal functioning are related to a lack of empathy (no remorse for mistreatment, general lack of concern for the feelings or suffering of others) and intimacy (no mutually intimate relationships, being characterized by exploitation, deceit, coercion, dominance, intimidation, and infidelity). For ASPD the two prominent pathological personality trait domains are disinhibition and antagonism. Disinhibition includes specific trait facets of irresponsibility, impulsivity, and risktaking; the trait of antagonism includes facets of manipulativeness, deceitfulness, hostility, and callousness.

The features of callousness have been described with CD. This characteristic may have unique significance in its relationship to the concept of psychopathy, an emotional dysfunction including reduced guilt or empathy. It is a cognitive outlook that must be more inferred, concluded, or measured on various research checklists rather than simply observed. Although all persons with significant psychopathy would likely be diagnosed with ASPD, only about a third of ASPD individuals would meet criteria for psychopathy. It has been identified in up to 25% of adult prison inmates. Often trainees are advised to note a feeling of "the hair standing up on the back of your neck" as an intuitive reaction of being considered as possible "prey" and a potential diagnostic clue during interviews of persons with ASPD, likely related to this trait. It seems to prevent individuals with ASPD from developing depression or anxiety as a result of their actions, as can otherwise occur in ASPD. Psychopathic traits have been reported in popular media to occur at mild levels in certain professions requiring dispassionate decision making, suggesting some adaptive utility, but when found in ASPD they represent a disorder with implications for poor prognosis. JD differs from his criminal friend in that his early years are characterized by a more chaotic and abusive upbringing. His criminal friend did not have the same chaotic childhood, more consistent with a developmental history of a psychopath.

EPIDEMIOLOGY

Under recent diagnostic criteria, personality disorders are present in almost 10% of the U.S. adult population and are associated with significant disability. They are even more prevalent in persons seeking mental health treatment (up to 50%). ASPD is present in about 3% of the general population, occurring three to five times more often in males. It occurs more commonly in treatment settings (15% among males and 3% among females), and is often associated with other diagnoses with greater frequency than expected, particularly forms of anxiety (up to 5%), post-traumatic stress disorder (PTSD, 10%), and alcohol use disorders (10%). These do not seem to be present in the case of JD. Symptoms in males tend to emerge in early childhood, whereas in females they tend to emerge later in puberty. Criminal behavior is a component of the diagnosis, and up to 75% of those incarcerated such as JD meet criteria for ASPD.

DIFFERENTIAL DIAGNOSIS

As with all persons presenting for psychiatric treatment, the challenge is to consolidate various symptoms, ancillary information, and clinical findings into a meaningful diagnosis that may be amenable to intervention. JD's chief concern is his temper, which can be clinically characterized as a chronic or recurrent irritable mood, excessively expressed by recurrent aggression, leading to significant difficulties for him. He additionally has enduring antisocial, criminal behaviors and interpersonal interactions that require consideration for diagnosis.

Irritability

Anger has been described as one of the emotions appearing earliest in human development and is considered normal in some defensive situations, if appropriate and proportionate in intensity and expression to the context in which it occurs. Irritability is the tendency to react chronically with anger, reflecting an inability to use cognitive strategies (such as using selective attention or self-distraction) that are more helpful in situations in which one is frustrated or prevented from achieving desired goals. Irritability is statistically associated with specific, impulsive types of aggression, differing from other types such as those resulting from fear. Irritability is associated with the misinterpretation of emotional stimuli such as facial expressions or social cues.

Irritability in adults is a current diagnostic criterion in ASPD, other personality disorders, BPD, and PTSD. In children and adolescents, irritability is a criterion for depressive disorders and for the oppositional defiant disorder (ODD), a disruptive behavior disorder (DBD). Although not specifically diagnostic, it can also be observed in other conditions, such as substance intoxication or withdrawal. It can be observed in persons with psychosis (e.g., a reaction to threatening or judgmental auditory hallucinations) or those with obsessive compulsive disorder when one's compulsive rituals cannot be completed. It is also associated with situations of adjustment to acute or chronic stresses.

JD's irritability does not seem to have the additional symptoms associated with most of the other diagnoses in which it can occur. Given his history of physical abuse, PTSD could be a possibility, but he does not endorse the reexperiencing or frank avoidance phenomena also required for that diagnosis. Substance abuse could be a diagnosis (access not being impossible even in prison), but his self-described preference for bartering rather than using substances he obtains makes this less likely, along with his symptoms occurring outside periods of intoxication. The diagnosis of ASPD would appear to be best explanation for his irritability or "temper."

Aggression

Aggression by humans can be considered an end-action with multiple causes, leading to physical or verbal injury to oneself, others, or objects. It can be normal in certain situations, such as self-defense. Pathological, maladaptive aggression has subtypes, generally separating "cold" (pathological, antisocial, predatory, instrumental, proactive, premeditated) from "hot" (reactive, prosocial, affective, hostile, impulsive, nonpremeditated). It is also considered as being overt or covert. When chronic, it has been hypothesized as a behavioral trait of moderately stable heritability.

Clinically, it also thought of as a being associated with a number of various psychiatric disorders. These include CD, ODD, attention deficit hyperactivity disorder (ADHD), substance abuse, mood and anxiety disorders, PTSD, schizophrenia, pervasive developmental disorders (such as autism), Tourette syndrome (chronic, involuntary verbalizations and physical movements), mental health conditions due to other medical conditions (agitation in dementia or delirium, undirected aggression in states of confusion after a seizure or head injuries), intermittent explosive disorder (IED), developmental delays, and personality disorders. Aggression is not diagnostic by itself.

JD's history and lack of other specific associated symptoms and signs seem to rule out the other diagnoses possibly associated with aggression. PTSD and substance abuse seem unlikely. Academic and behavioral problems from childhood make persistent ADHD a possibility, although his symptoms seem less impulsive than deferred and planned (i.e., his delayed retaliation against the other prisoner), and ADHD by itself would not account for his ongoing planned criminal activities and anger. Without the long-term criminal history, some criteria for IED could also be considered and will be discussed further later. If other neuropsychiatric findings were present, his impulsive aggression could be related to complications of past multiple traumatic brain injuries, that is, his multiple episodes of unconsciousness after physical altercations, and possible related personality change; some of the same areas of the brain associated with ASPD symptoms and aggression have been found to be the same ones affected after traumatic brain injury. ASPD remains the best diagnostic explanation for his aggression.

Antisocial Behavior

Although not part of his own reason for being evaluated, JD's long history of criminal behavior provides the most definitive clue to his diagnosis. Chronic criminality should be differentiated from occasional criminal behavior that might be precipitated by psychosocial stress of other diagnoses or poverty (in an inner-city population of low socioeconomic status, 35% of residents are reported to have committed a crime at some time, but only a 6% minority of this group commits over half of the crimes in that setting). Other personality disorders could also be considered, particularly narcissistic personality disorder, which is believed to have similar psychopathology in regard to self-centeredness. However, individuals with ASPD are described as "aggressive" or "malignant" narcissists violating societal norms beyond gratification of the ego-centrism of narcissistic personality disorder. The absence of other diagnostic symptoms seems to rule out other causes of antisocial behavior.

The overlap in symptoms and other findings among various psychiatric diagnoses suggests continuities (also suggested by recent genetic analysis) beyond their differences. Reviewing the diagnoses of IED and CD may help conceptualize ASPD.

Intermittent Explosive Disorder (IED)

IED is associated with pathological, intermittent, nonpremeditated impulsive aggression. The aggression occurs in discrete episodes resulting in serious assaults to other persons or destruction of property; the degree of aggression is out of proportion to psychosocial stressors. When diagnosed, it is not believed to result from another condition or the effects of a medication or substance.

Similarities between IED and ASPD include that they can be diagnosed together about 60% of the time. Adults with IED also describe the onset of the difficulties as occurring in adolescence. The differential diagnosis of IED is similar to that of (and includes) ASPD. Both diagnoses are associated with a history of learning disabilities and low educational achievement. Psychologically, both are associated with immature defense (coping) mechanisms.

Social histories of both disorders often include a history of childhood trauma. However, IED is more associated with being a crime victim, as opposed to persons with ASPD being perpetrators of crime. While 12–25% of U.S. adults have engaged in a physical fight in their lifetime, IED has a lifetime prevalence among adults somewhat greater than that of ASPD, approximately 6%; there is a lower male-to-female ratio of about 1–2:1. Approximately 45% of adults with IED have a childhood history of a DBD, in contrast to the current requirement of a history of CD for the diagnosis of ASPD. Aggression in IED usually has a rapid onset, and is followed by the person assuming responsibility and expressing genuine remorse for the acts, distinct from the more planned, delayed, predatory, and remorseless aggression of ASPD.

Abnormalities in biological and psychological activity are believed to be associated with the aggression in general and in IED. This includes abnormal functioning of various neurotransmitters or other substances such as serotonin, the enzyme monoamine oxidase-A involved with its metabolism and that of several other neurotransmitters including dopamine and norepinephrine; vasopressin (related to the "social hormone" oxytocin), brain-derived neurotropic factor (involved in neuron growth), endorphins, and testosterone. Similar to irritability, neuropsychological assessments indicate abnormalities in areas involving information processing and decision making, hostile attribution bias, negative responses to ambiguous social cues, and mood lability and intensity. Imaging techniques have also identified abnormalities in the structure and functioning of areas of the brain associated with these psychological processes and in areas identified in association with ASPD.

IED is described in youth at about the same rate as in adults. Isolated anger episodes (63.3%), acts of violence destroying property (31.6%), verbal threats (57.9%), or actual physical violence (39.3%) are fairly common in young people. It is reported to be the most reliably diagnosable disorder of impulse control in adolescent psychiatric inpatients. The average age of onset is about 12 years if diagnosed in adolescence, suggesting overlap with CD.

Conduct Disorder (CD)

A history of CD is a required criterion for the diagnosis of ASPD. There are other continuities between the two disorders, suggesting they are manifestations of the same psychopathology expressed at different developmental stages. In contrast to ASPD, in which a lack of remorse or empathy has to be inferred or elicited, the diagnosis of CD is based primarily on observable symptoms and behaviors. These include a pattern of violation of rules or cultural norms of behavior expected for age over a period of time, rising above a level of threshold of symptoms (3 of 18 possible), with the antisocial acts involving other people (e.g., aggression, deceitfulness), places (e.g., truancy), or property (e.g., theft, destructiveness) and is also associated with definable impairment. It is classified as having its onset either in childhood (before the age of 10 years, a more severe variant), adolescence, or unspecified age. Severity is classified as mild, moderate, or severe. A person with chronic antisocial behavior under the age of 18 usually is diagnosed with CD, although theoretically could be diagnosed if over 18 if full ASPD criteria are not met.

Similarly to a subgroup of ASPD patients having higher levels of psychopathy (as will be discussed), statistical factor analysis has identified callous-unemotional (CU) traits separate from the other components of CD, with a CU subtype having been proposed. CU traits are characterized by a poverty of emotions, with a shallow or deficient expression of feeling, which seems to be able to be turned on or off voluntarily. They are associated with a lack of guilt, empathy, or concerns about one's performance. They indicate a more severe, violent, and chronic pattern of antisocial behavior predictive of more aggressive behavior, including the premeditated and instrumental type. Persons with this trait are less sensitive to punishment cues, have poorer reversal learning from mistakes, and exhibit lower cognitive processing of negative emotional stimuli. They also have relative deficits in responding to signs of fear or distress in others and have more positive outcome expectancies in aggressive situations. However, they are less likely to have the verbal deficits otherwise associated with CD. They are more fearless and thrill-seeking, but have more trait anxiety and neuroticism. It occurs at higher levels in association with childhood- versus adolescent-onset type of CD.

CD is identified in about 5% of the general population. It is more common in males, especially the early onset type (about 10/1 over females) compared to adolescent onset (about 1.5/1). Symptoms vary with age. Aggression is more frequent earlier in childhood, but more severe in adolescence; impulsive aggression precedes the development of the more planned type by two years.

CD may occur with other diagnoses, particularly the childhood-onset type. Although not diagnosed at the same time as CD, an identified headstrong-hurtful component of ODD (as distinct from an angry/irritable component) is associated with the later development of delinquency. If ADHD is present, CD symptoms usually occur earlier and are more severe. Comorbid substance abuse is usually preceded by or coincides with the onset of the CD symptoms. CD often evolves later into MDD; a DBD diagnosis (including CD) also usually precedes a later diagnosis of BPD. Anxiety disorders are also often present. There may also be associated diagnoses of learning disorders (especially in reading or language) or general intellectual disability. There may also be an associated medical history with disability from a medical illness being associated with a threefold risk of later CD (five times more likely if the illness includes central nervous system involvement).

Family histories often include other members having diagnoses of ASPD and substance abuse. Lower IQ scores in parents have predicted the development of CD in their children. They often (particularly childhood-onset) come from large families in which there is a single parent who provides parenting that is inconsistent or neglectful, harsh, involves rejection, or is characterized by a lack of involvement (especially by fathers). In the home there is often a history of marital discord, domestic violence, parental criminality, and other parental mental illness.

Social histories frequently include victimization from abuse. A history of physical abuse is particularly associated with later physical aggression (such a history being present in 20–25% of cases of childhood aggression alone). Having been sexually abused increases the risk of developing CD up to 12 times. Exposure to violence outside the family, such as in the neighborhood or media, has been correlated with CD. There are often more problems in school, with poor achievement or failing grades. Violence exposure is associated with a generally adverse environment, such as communities of increased poverty, low overall socioeconomic status, high crime rates, or social disorganization. The effects of poverty or low community socioeconomic status on antisocial behavior are highly significant, being observed as early as age 5, with an estimated magnitude as strong as that of gender. Exposure to as little as a 1% variation in regional unemployment during infancy was associated with up to 20% increased odds of arrest, gang involvement, petty and major theft, and certain forms of substance abuse in adolescence. CD youth tend to associate with peers who engage in socially deviant behaviors.

Psychological evaluations of persons with CD have shown more attention problems, lower IQs, and impaired verbal ability. They tend to have poor social cognition with frequent misattribution of the other's intentions, and they have been associated with a negative or overreactive temperament. The diagnosis of CD can be a challenge due to difficulty in establishing rapport with the youth to gain accurate information. Often multiple sources of information are required, although such youth may be truthful in the reporting of their symptoms (often boasting of or justifying their behavior) unless they anticipate punishment. A history of aggression may also raise concern for physical safety of the evaluator, often limiting the interview to less confidential settings.

When evaluating CD behaviors, one must differentiate them from other diagnoses that may be present. Normative risk taking is isolated and not recurrent;

stressor-related adjustment problems are time-limited and associated with an identifiable external precipitant. The presence of rule-breaking behaviors and lack of other symptoms typically rule out other primary diagnoses.

As with ASPD, it is believed to result from an interaction of genetics and environment with multiple risk factors (including heredity) likely being additive and cumulative, depending on stage of development. For example, parental antisocial traits predict the later development of CD, more so if an adverse home environment is also present. Maltreatment increases the rate of later CD in five- to seven-year-olds only by 2% with a low genetic risk but by 24% in those with a high genetic risk of parental ASPD, suggesting that genes influence behavior disorders more through susceptibility or resistance to later adverse or stressful environmental experiences instead of directly. CD is thought to be moderately heritable, although early temperament and behavioral tendencies are modifiable by family counseling and later social experience.

Biological causes are suggested by gender differences in prevalence, and aggression being associated with high testosterone levels. A specific genetic/gender interaction was found in that abused boys with a variant of a gene coding for lower levels of monoamine oxidase-A activity were twice as likely to develop CD, or other mental health problems. Abnormalities in sympathetic nervous system arousal (i.e., the "fight or flight" system activated by stress or threat manifested by changes in heart rate, cortisol levels, and perspiration reactions) have also been implicated as biological causes of CD, later criminal behavior, and eventual ASPD. These findings are debatable because there is uncertainty if these effects result from genetics or are long-lasting stress responses from environmental adversity. Abnormalities of various neurotransmitters as discussed for IED have also been associated with CD.

External biological factors may also increase risk for CD. It has been associated with early exposure to lead and opioids. Maternal prenatal cigarette smoking has been associated with early antisocial behavior and CD (and later ASPD and criminality), but the later effects are now believed to be more due to subsequent suboptimal caregiving in childhood.

ETIOLOGY AND PATHOGENESIS

Personality can be considered as an individual's pattern of behavior or interactions with the environment and others that result in him or her being recognized as unique. It is considered moderately stable and recognizable early in life, although subject to considerable change. Personalities with different traits have been described or portrayed over the centuries in literature, drama, and philosophy. Attempts to more objectively classify and explain different personality types extend into antiquity. An example is that of the ancient Greek description of melancholic (pessimistic), sanguine (optimistic), choleric (irritable), and phlegmatic (apathetic) temperaments, related to the four body humors of black bile, blood, yellow bile, and phlegm.

More scientific approaches to address personality development, particularly problematic personalities, have arisen over the last century or so, beginning most extensively with psychoanalytic "case" or "depth" approaches. Vastly over-simplifying years of subsequent investigation, early psychoanalysts proposed that personality traits, particularly pathological ones ("neuroses"), occur when there are arrests or fixations in different developmental stages related to certain biological drives (oral, anal, and phallic), associated with ongoing (mostly uncon-scious) conflicts in the interaction between the internal psychological domains of the id (containing drives or wishes to be gratified), superego (regulating mor-als or principles), and ego (having practical and problem-solving abilities). Other theories were also developed, such as object relations, in which interactions between parents (particularly mothers) and their children (particularly infants) are thought to be the foundation of personality. A later attempt sought to cor-relate different personality traits such as harm avoidance, novelty seeking, and reward dependence with influences of different neurotransmitters (serotonin, dopamine, and norepinephrine, respectively). Using broad statistical analytic techniques (factor analysis), a five-factor model is more recently supported, in which personality is believed to derive from a combination of a number of traits in factor categories of openness, conscientiousness, extroversion, agreeableness, and neuroticism (the acronym OCEAN). There is as yet limited evidence that this model accurately predicts personality disorders, although a high level of traits of neuroticism (negative emotional response to frustration, threat, or loss) has been associated with an increase in some per capita mental health treatment costs compared to mental health diagnoses themselves.

Adult personality disorders have been predicted from certain characteristics and disorders earlier in life, with the hypothesis that lack of treatment for the earlier diagnoses allows the associated symptoms to become integrated into one's basic personality structure. Personality disorders are primarily associated with a history of childhood DBDs in about 40% of cases; there is a history of mood, anxiety, or other disorders in about 12% of cases, so that most personality disorders apparently are diagnostically separate and develop independently. If present, DBDs predict cluster B and C personality disorders more directly for females, although ASPD in particular is better predicted for males (likely related to the requirement for prior CD). It is unclear whether these gender differences are due to biological, sociocultural, or diagnostic assessment effects. Develop-mental language disorders are associated with approximately twice the risk for the development of an adult personality disorder. General intellectual ability is usually in the low to normal range for adult personality disorder. On psychologi-cal testing, persons with personality disorder often exhibit poor verbal, spatial, and memory function. Psychopathy in particular has been associated with poorer attention control, reversal learning from mistakes, and linguistic processing.

Families of persons with ASPD have histories of inconsistent or limited par-enting (particularly by the mother, combined with low involvement by the father). Sometimes poor attachment is the cause and not the effect of inadequate parenting. Parents often have used abusive child-rearing techniques, and actual physical abuse is more common. A history of physical or sexual abuse has been identified as risk factor for several personality disorders, especially cluster B and ASPD.

ASPD is associated with less mature coping strategies (defense mechanisms). These include acting out thoughts and feelings directly, instead of selectively suppressing and expressing them in more positive ways. The historical psychoanalytic perspective of ASPD suggests that that the individual's id is not controlled by the superego. As such individuals with ASPD (especially psychopaths) have been characterized as having "superego lacunae"—holes in their consciences—or a form of "moral insanity."

The cause of personality disorders is likely similar to that of CD, an interaction between an individual's biological or genetic makeup and personal (particularly childhood) experiences. Environmental factors are those primarily related to family (in addition to community ones as noted for CD). Specific contributions of each component remain under investigation and are not yet definitive. Initial enthusiasm for the risk associated with specific genes has been muted more recently with limited replication of some of the earlier findings and methodological problems in the genetic research.

Genetic studies include those looking at an individual's family history for patterns of inheritance. There is usually a strong family history (at least for criminal behavior) of ASPD traits and substance abuse. Male incarcerated felons have rates of ASPD of 20% and of alcohol dependence of 33% in their first-degree relatives; rates are even higher for females at 33% and 50%, respectively. ASPD shows a concordance between monozygotic compared to dizygotic twins of 36% compared to 12%, illustrating some clear but not complete genetic risk. Other studies of twins have attempted to clarify the role of genetics using the OCEAN personality factors; there seems to be no particular genetic risk for each personality disorder cluster, but some for general personality disorder pathology (particularly the associated trait of neuroticism) and traits of high impulsiveness and low agreeableness. More genetic risk was identified for susceptibility to specific environmental influences on later personality disorder types, highlighting the gene–environment interaction.

Genetic factors also may be manifested by behavioral tendencies in infants or young children, presumably before environmental influences can greatly affect them. These tendencies can potentially extend later into life: temperamental reactivity of infants at age four months has been associated with identifiable structural differences on brain imaging at age 18. More recently, emotional states of mothers during pregnancy have been shown to affect later behaviors of their infants and children, illustrating potential interactions of genetics with even the intrauterine environment. Insecure or disorganized attachment (the identification of an infant's or toddler's reaction to the return and attempted interaction by a parent, typically a mother, during various separation and reunification scenarios in a research protocol) has been associated with the later development of behavioral and emotional problems in children and adolescents. Enthusiasm for the predictive utility of this classification has been tempered more recently, with suggested limitations that these attachment patterns were more specific to the particular research population and age in which it was investigated. It also reflects more the quality of parent–child interaction and any prediction emanating more from that than from infant characteristics alone. These interactions have been demonstrated as modifiable through therapeutic interventions. However, research continues into attachment types and expectations that may manifest differently at other stages of life, and how qualities of those attachments may affect other clinical diagnoses or may be modified by intervention.

ASPD and specific associated features, including psychopathy, aggression, and violent offenses, have been associated with structural (volume and thickness changes) and functional (oxygen or glucose utilization) abnormalities in the brain. These abnormalities mostly have been identified in interconnection between different regions of the cerebral cortex gray matter (frontal lobe, anterior cingulate cortex, and others) and the amygdala that are associated with decision making based on moral judgment, language cues, response planning and inhibition, impulsiveness, social cognition, attention, learning, reward systems, emotional information management, and reactions. Although it is intuitive that diagnostic clinical characteristics would correlate with abnormalities in central nervous system locations associated with abilities related to those symptoms, it is hoped that identifying signature brain patterns eventually will help clarify specific diagnoses. However, the limited resolution of current imaging procedures and their lack of diagnostic specificity restrict their use to that of investigation at present.

Various neurotransmitters have been implicated in the etiology of ASPD and its associated symptoms, such as aggression. Additionally, a variant of a gene related to the production of serotonin has been associated with the trait of neuroticism. A variant of another gene associated with dopamine has been associated with the trait of novelty seeking hypothesized in the previous factor theory of personality development. Other neurotransmitters have been associated with specific symptoms associated with ASPD but are not clearly direct as to causality.

JD seems to have many of the known risks of developing ASPD. His family history suggests that his father had ASPD or at least related traits, providing a basic susceptibility to the disorder. The inconsistent parenting and harsh physical discipline he received while growing up, and later associations with socioeconomic deprivation, suboptimal educational history, and other criminal influences, would seem to provide the sufficient components for eventually developing ASPD.

NATURAL COURSE WITHOUT TREATMENT

Developmentally, persons with ASPD such as JD stereotypically have poor parental attachments and interactions early in childhood. They manifest CD symptoms early in life that increase in frequency and severity throughout adolescence and young adulthood, resulting in eventual criminal activity and involvement with the legal system, particularly if left untreated.

Individuals with personality disorders are more likely to be unemployed with frequent job disruption, in lower socioeconomic strata, and more often on disability. They are more often unmarried, including never married, separated, widowed, and divorced. They have increased frequency of later criminal conviction (75%, with the trait of psychopathy being associated with increased rates of violent crime and recidivism) alcohol dependence (65%), and substance abuse or dependence (80%), particularly ASPD. They have an increased use of but less satisfaction with mental health services; their presence in association with other mental health conditions typically leads to a more problematic and poorer outcome of treatment. Personality disorders (including ASPD) are associated with suicidal ideation and behavior.

Persons with ASPD in particular typically have poor job performance and work histories, because work is often "too dull" to maintain, or due to their interpersonal conflicts or criminal activities. Social relationships generally are opportunistic and do not endure. They often marry young if they do marry and are more often involved in teenage pregnancies. Like JD, they often have injuries from fights and have increased rates of early death.

If a personality disorder has been diagnosed in adolescence, adult anxiety, disruptive mood, and substance disorders are twice as common. Elevated psychopathy trait scores in adolescence (demonstrated as being stable between the ages of 7 and 17 years of age) predict later delinquent behavior, conduct disorder, and the cluster B disorders.

Personality disorders are believed more recently to show some therapeutic improvement and resolution over time, with about half no longer meeting diagnostic criteria after 2 years, and up to about 90% for some disorders resolving after 10 years. This occurs with some persistence of personality traits and impairment. This seems to be associated with "burnout" as they reach the age of 30 or 40 years for ASPD, when their high-risk lifestyle becomes less sustainable and enjoyable, as it seems to be for JD.

Early irritability (as identified in ODD separate from other symptoms) predicts the later development of MDD and generalized anxiety disorder. When present in early adolescence, it associated with the later development additional diagnoses such as CD, ODD, simple and social phobia, ADHD, and BPD, as much as 20 years later.

Aggressive behavior in young children persists in approximately 50% of cases. This is particularly noted with a family history of aggression, early onset, and if it is interpersonal and frequent. Aggressive behavior is associated with later antisocial and criminal acts, physical aggression being one of the most important predictors of later general diversified offending. Associated antisocial behavior occurs progressively, beginning with early oppositionality, followed by minor delinquent acts, then escalating to physical aggression.

CD symptoms persist in 65% of cases over three to four years, and 40% of those go on to later develop ASPD (especially in the childhood-onset type). The remaining 60% continue to have some impairment. They are also at risk for developing other mental health diagnoses, although somewhat less so if the CD symptoms remit. Associated low self-esteem (in contrast to narcissism) has been related to the later development of aggression, ASPD, and delinquency. Youths who are bullies often have later problems with depression and suicidal behavior to a greater extent than their victims.

Callous unemotional traits in CD are associated with an increased risk of adult psychopathy. When high levels of this occurring in prepubertal children are followed, persistence in males appears to be more related to genetic susceptibility, whereas in females it is maintained more by environmental factors.

EVIDENCE-BASED TREATMENT OPTIONS

It is important to establish the specific presumed causal diagnosis (which theoretically drives the treatment), potential comorbid conditions contributing to the symptoms, and potential risk and capacity for treatment as well. Evaluation of overall individual strengths and abilities, such as verbal skills (related to insight, judgment, problem solving, and ability to communicate), cognitive flexibility, capacity for empathy, and hostile attribution bias may affect the ability to engage in and respond to treatment. It is important to identify areas of ability and support, as related to family or religious involvements, social connections, and occupational and educational strengths.

The treatment of personality disorders historically has been associated with a therapeutic nihilism in that no treatment has been thought effective. This has been associated with the limited insight that individuals with personality disorders have, consequently limiting the potential benefit of more traditional psychoanalytic or psychodynamic treatments. ASPD in particular has been thought of as being very difficult to treat, because such persons often do not seek treatment without external pressure. Treatments can be classified as psychological, biological, or social. Despite challenges in treating ASPD and its symptoms, more recent guidelines have suggested areas of potential intervention with more optimistic outcomes.

Psychoanalytic or psychodynamic therapies historically have been used to treat chronic personality conditions (e.g., neurosis). For ASPD, particular caution has been advised in using traditional psychotherapy. Given related manipulative, cruel, and aggressive symptoms, a therapist may be at risk of not only possible exploitation but actual physical harm. It has been suggested that treatment be undertaken only in the context of some external behavioral control, such as the legal restraints of probation or actual environmental control when incarcerated, as in JD's case. However, individual psychotherapies are not likely to be effective if the treatment itself is specifically tied to particular incentives, such as favorable therapist reports or recommendations being linked to outcomes such as a reduction in sentence, a factor to be considered in any planned treatment for JD.

More recently, certain psychodynamic and evidence-based treatments (interpersonal therapy, cognitive behavioral therapy, and even supportive therapy) have been shown to accelerate the temporal improvement associated with personality disorders. They are more beneficial when implemented at a younger age and over a longer period of time. The improvement is particularly notable for any associated substance abuse.

For personality disorders, addressing particular associated target symptoms or comorbid diagnoses that are responsive to medications have been proposed. For ASPD itself, no specific pharmacologic interventions are known to be effective.

The category of social treatment has been primarily recommended for ASPD, given that such persons often have no motivation or desire to change outside of external incentives. As with all behavioral programs, more success is likely to be gained with rewards (incentives) and developing skills (rehabilitation, remediation) instead of punishment (incarceration) alone. One might use JD's expressed interest in obtaining more privileges as an opportunity to assist him to change in other ways, such as finding ways to anticipate and plan alternatives for when he might lose control of his temper, as well as developing skills for improved functioning in other areas.

CLINICAL COURSE WITH MANAGEMENT AND TREATMENT

In addition to a lack of insight and internal motivation, therapeutic progress may be limited by the lack of family support. Partners often have a complementary personality type that may enable the behavior of a person with ASPD (e.g., a partner may have a dependent personality disorder passively participating in or not providing any objection to antisocial behavior). JD is limited in that he has no family or social support to help reinforce any progress in treatment. Despite his incarceration, it is appropriate for JD to provide full informed consent for any planned treatment. This would include a full discussion at his intellectual and educational level regarding indications, benefits, risks, alternatives, and side effects of any treatment, as well as the option of declining treatment outside of those that are legally mandated.

When attempting to engage JD in treatment, a clinician may experience countertransference (conscious or unconscious thoughts or feelings about the patient that could potentially interfere with treatment). The inmate has a very different moral standard, which can often cause the clinician to be repulsed or angered (for example, the person's way of making a living by stealing or the frank violation of the rights of others). The clinician might have had an experience of being a victim of crime with recurrent memories of this during the course of therapy.

ASPD individuals historically do not respond well to psychodynamic psychotherapy alone, tending to resist any perceived authority they believe the therapist to have. The interpretations and confrontations of maladaptive thought processes often required in therapy may be perceived as critical due to an ASPD person's narcissism, therefore eliciting resistance or antagonism to treatment. Such a person likely will do better with the incorporation of behavioral modification principles, with immediate concrete rewards for successful completion of tasks of increasing levels of responsibility and leadership. JD could be assisted in exploring productive ways to improve his living situation. The prison provides an external limit, which imposes a firm but clear behavioral structure, allowing the therapist to align with the patient in finding ways for him to succeed in the system. In addition, carefully focusing on the therapeutic relationship potentially might help JD develop a sense of success in meeting the expectations of others instead of only his own.

For CD in particular, training in social skills and problem-solving has been shown to lead to improvement. Addressing comorbid diagnoses may be of benefit; improvement in symptoms of MDD has been associated with a decrease in CD symptoms. Theoretically, for ASPD reduction in associated anxiety or depression through treatment may be countertherapeutic, in that once unpleasant feelings are resolved, there may be less incentive to improve, with a return to the preexisting manipulative and dangerous behavior. For aggression, psychological interventions included cognitive behavioral therapy (CBT, found to decrease state aggression up to 70%) to address attention biases. Techniques include imaginal exposure, relaxation training, cognitive restructuring, and increasing coping skills. Forms of CBT have been show to be helpful in ASPD as well.

For JD, individual therapy involving practical, day-to-day problem solving of difficult situations likely would be of most benefit. The ideal program would be very structured, with concretely defined initial short-term goals and organized plans for achieving them, and a high level of psychoeducation. The therapeutic focus would ideally be on his own interpersonal functioning, with practical analysis of social situations and the development of additional skills and alternative responses to provocation real or perceived. Given JD's educational level, as well as the presence of possible language impairments, effective communication will need to be at an appropriate level. Learning disabilities such as a developmental reading disorder could be addressed while he is incarcerated. A brief screening performed by the clinician during the initial interview (asking that JD read John 3 from the provided Bible) demonstrated considerable difficulty in reading fluency and comprehension.

For target symptoms or for associated diagnoses, medications have been proposed or used for personality disorders, ASPD, and CD. Recommendations for aggression include using first-line treatments for any primary or comorbid disorder, using psychosocial or behavioral treatments initially, and preferentially using single medications if possible. For aggression, selective serotonin reuptake inhibitor (SSRI) antidepressants (fluoxetine) have been shown to decrease state aggression in up to 65% of patients, with a full remission of aggression in 29%. Other controlled trials have shown improvements in aggression with various diagnoses for other medications: these include tricyclic and monoamine oxidase inhibitor antidepressants; older neuroleptics such as chlorpromazine or haloperidol; newer atypical neuroleptics such as risperidone; lithium carbonate; and anticonvulsants such as carbamezapine, valproic acid, oxcarbazepine, and the older diphenylhydantoin. Antihypertensives such as beta blockers (e.g., propranolol) and alpha-agonists (clonidine, guanfacine, now approved for ADHD) have also been shown to be of benefit in smaller trials, possibly due to the suppression of adrenaline surges. Combination treatments such as valproic acid in combination with stimulants has been shown to decrease aggression in youth in with comorbid ADHD with a response of 58% compared to that of placebo of 15%.

Treatment with SSRIs for depression has been shown to improve personality traits related to neuroticism and extroversion beyond the improvement in mood. For psychotic-like symptoms (high levels of suspiciousness or paranoia, reality distortion), antipsychotic medications have been suggested. Anxiety has been recommended as a target given its frequent comorbidity with ASPD, although the use of sedative-hypnotics such as benzodiazepines is associated with disinhibition if used outside acute situations. Other medications could include stimulants or other medications for ADHD, or those specifically for depressive or bipolar disorders.

JD does not meet full criteria for the most common comorbid diagnoses. However, irritability and aggression can respond to biological treatments. For any prescribed medication, a fully informed consent regarding possible medications for target symptoms would be appropriate, with a plan for monitoring response and potential side effects, and alternatives discussed in advance. His history of an apparent response to lithium might be a good starting point for consideration.

Social and family interventions have the strongest evidence of benefit for treating CD and ASPD. However, "tough love" or "scared straight" programs for youth have been shown to actually increase rather than reduce antisocial behavior. The effect of being raised in a susceptible community has been reduced by instructing families in supportive, reward-based parenting practices, and attempting to overcome barriers (culture, cost, etc.) in their implementation, although family treatment programs still have a high dropout rate. Other effective interventions include increasing prosocial activities and community involvement (such as multisystemic therapy), combined with efforts to provide a less adverse home environment if needed (multidimensional treatment foster care). Three to six months are generally needed to see benefits from these programs. For ASPD, programs ordered and monitored by a court, focusing on rehabilitation and remediation rather than punishment (such as drug courts with mandated treatment instead of incarceration), have also shown beneficial results for reducing criminal behavior, as well as for associated aggression. For those with an interest in this area of human experience, encouraging participation in preferred spiritual or religious activities may provide guidance toward more positive interactions and behavior.

For JD, working with the institution to establish a more reward-based program, particularly with more frequent opportunities to demonstrate progress, might improve his motivation and compliance. In addition, occupational and educational programs (with testing for any learning or language disabilities) might help him find potential avenues for success that are more socially and legally acceptable and increase his motivation to find new ways to manage his anger and aggression.

SYSTEMS-BASED PRACTICE ISSUES

Although a majority of the prison population can be diagnosed with ASPD, there has been recent interest in looking at other mental health problems that occur in this setting. In one survey, nearly 70% of the inmates had a mental health diagnosis, including mood and anxiety disorders, and PTSD (28.6%); only 4.2% had a diagnosis of ASPD with no other diagnosis. Centers for Disease Control and Prevention information indicates that inmate populations have a history of traumatic brain injury or head injury (associated with increased substance abuse and violence) in 25–87% of cases, compared to a history in only 8% of the general population. In juvenile detention centers, up to 70% of residents have a mental health diagnosis amenable to treatment, including a rate of psychosis 10 times that expected in the general population. Identification and treatment of those incarcerated with such conditions, in addition to reducing suffering, may help improve functioning, reduce recidivism, and respond to social ethical imperatives.

LEGAL, ETHICAL, AND CULTURAL CHALLENGES

Prevention may be the most important area of treatment, given the role early inadequate parenting, maltreatment, and other social adversities have with the development of antisocial traits and behaviors. Home nurse visitations have been shown to decrease physical abuse within high-risk families and have a protective effect against the later development of CD symptoms. Programs such as Head Start have been associated with a decrease in later teenage delinquency.

Early parent training can modify self-control and callous unemotional traits up to 12 months later in three- to five-year-olds with conduct problems. A genetic risk study of twins suggests that overworked social service protection agencies possibly could prioritize for intervention those cases with a known parental history of antisocial behavior (such parents have a greater likelihood of physically abusing their children and exacerbating the already greater genetic risk). Specific targeting of and intervention for specific behaviors (e.g., bullying) may also be associated with improved later personal functioning and interpersonal interactions. Certain factors have been associated with resiliency from the effects of early adverse circumstances in youth. Ones potentially modifiable by intervention include a positive relationship with at least one parent, competence outside of school, good academic skills, and planning skills. Enhancing these areas (e.g., skills development) could facilitate more prosocial development.

TERMS

There is considerable overlap and interchange in the use of the terms *psychopathy* and *sociopathy* when discussing ASPD. In general, *psychopathy* refers to the cognitive and emotional trait of callous lack of empathy toward others in interpersonal interactions. The term *sociopathy* tends to be used more in describing a general predisposition to violate society's rules and laws. FBI reviews have attempted to categorize the relatively rare serial (as opposed to mass or "spree") murderers beyond the stereotype of the highly intellectual, "genius" psychopath who is able indefinitely to avoid being caught through their cunning and guile. However, such perpetrators have varied motivations, such as anger, financial gain, concealing criminal activity, sexual fulfillment, power, or ideology. Other than being predominantly male, they do not seem to have any specific generic profile and have varying amounts of psychopathic traits. Public fascination with and popular media publicity regarding those cases with more "pure" psychopathy would seem to derive from a common, seemingly inherent human fear of this trait in its more extreme expression. In interviewing many persons with ASPD, one is more often struck by their lack of education, limited resources, and tragic childhoods than intellect or charisma.

REFERENCES AND RESOURCES

Coccaro EF. Intermittent explosive disorder as a disorder of impulsive aggression in DSM-5. *Am J Psychiatr* 2012;169:577–88.

Duncan LE, Keller MC.A critical review of the first 10 years of candidate gene-by-environment interaction research in psychiatry. *Am J Psychiatr* 2011;168:1041–49.

Helgeland MI, Kjelsberg MD, Torgersen S. Continuities between emotional and disruptive behavior disorders in adolescence and personality disorders in adulthood. *Am J Psychiatr* 2005;162:1941–47.

Jaffee SR, et al. Nature X nurture: genetic vulnerabilities interact with physical maltreatment to promote conduct problems. *Dev Psychopathol* 2005;17(1):67–84.

Kendler KS, et al. The structure of genetic and environmental risk factors for DSM-IV personality disorders: a multivariate twin study. *Arch Gen Psychiatr* 2008;65(12):1438–46.

Maxmen JS, War NG, Kilgus MD. Intermittent explosive disorder (pp. 542–43), Antisocial personality disorder (pp. 562–65), and Conduct disorder (pp. 610–14), in *Essential Psychopathology and Its Treatment*. New York: W.W. Norton & Company, 2009.

Rodrigo C, Rajapakse S, Jayananda G. The "antisocial" person: an insight in to biology, classification and current evidence on treatment. *Ann Gen Psychiatr* 2010;9:31; published online July 6, 2010.

Westen D, Shedler J, Bradley B, DeFife JA. An empirically derived taxonomy for personality diagnosis: bridging science and practice in conceptualizing personality. *Am J Psychiatr* 2012;169:273–84.

National Institute for Clinical Excellence in the United Kingdom, www.nice.org.uk. In the publication section of this website is an article titled "Antisocial Personality Disorder: Treatment, Management, and Prevention." It summarizes more recent evidence-based interventions for evaluation and treatment of this disorder.

The Iceman (2001). A documentary about organized crime hitman Richard Kuklinski is a somewhat extreme example, but it illustrates many of the characteristics and personal history in someone who also presumably would be diagnosable as having ASPD.

Internal Affairs (1990) A crime thriller about the Los Angeles police department's Internal Affairs division. The film stars Richard Gere as Dennis Peck, a suave womanizer, clever manipulator, and crooked cop who uses his fellow officers as pawns for his own purposes.

No Country for Old Men (2007), based on a book by Cormac McCarthy, is an Oscar-winning movie with a hitman character who would seem to be psychopathic in killing with no apparent emotion or remorse.

Index